WHY PUNISH? HOW MUCH?

WHY PUNISH?
HOW MUCH?

A READER ON PUNISHMENT

Edited by

MICHAEL TONRY

OXFORD
UNIVERSITY PRESS
2011

OXFORD
UNIVERSITY PRESS

Oxford University Press, Inc., publishes works that further
Oxford University's objective of excellence
in research, scholarship, and education.

Oxford New York
Auckland Cape Town Dar es Salaam Hong Kong Karachi
Kuala Lumpur Madrid Melbourne Mexico City Nairobi
New Delhi Shanghai Taipei Toronto

With offices in
Argentina Austria Brazil Chile Czech Republic France Greece
Guatemala Hungary Italy Japan Poland Portugal Singapore
South Korea Switzerland Thailand Turkey Ukraine Vietnam

Published by Oxford University Press, Inc.
198 Madison Avenue, New York, New York 10016

www.oup.com

Oxford is a registered trademark of Oxford University Press

Library of Congress Cataloging-in-Publication Data
Why punish? How much?: a reader on punishment / [edited by] Michael Tonry.
p. cm.
Includes bibliographical references and index.
ISBN 978-0-19-532885-1; 978-0-19-532886-8 (pbk.)
1. Punishment. 2. Corrections. I. Tonry, Michael H.
HV8665.T66 2010
364.6—dc22   2009046812

1 3 5 7 9 8 6 4 2
Printed in the United States of America
on acid-free paper

PREFACE

Punishment theories address questions about what happens to people convicted of crimes. Some are timeless. Why may, must, or does the state punish wrongdoers? Whom may the state justly punish? How much? What considerations may be taken into account in answering the last two questions, and what considerations may not?

Some questions are as topical as today's newspaper. Can harsh sentencing laws—mandatory minimums, three-strikes, life-without-the-possibility-of-parole—be justified in normative terms? May offenders be compelled to participate in programs meant to change them? May offenders be confined indefinitely because they are "dangerous?" Can new approaches to responding to crime—restorative justice, community justice, therapeutic jurisprudence—be reconciled with traditional notions of justice? Should the law take account of recent research findings that suggest that retributive impulses in human beings are products of natural selection, that intuitions about deserved punishments are widely held, and that the belief that human beings have free will is false?

Aristotle, Plato, and others of the ancients wrote about punishment, but a systematic literature began to accumulate only in the eighteenth and early nineteenth centuries, when Immanuel Kant and Georg Wilhelm Friedrich Hegel laid foundations for subsequent retributive analyses and Cesar Beccaria and Jeremy Bentham did the same for utilitarian approaches. Interest in punishment theory has waxed and waned since then, but the opposing retributive and utilitarian ways of thinking held almost exclusive sway until the 1970s. Since then, ideas about restorative justice, community justice, and therapeutic jurisprudence have emerged and to varying degrees taken root.

Selection of the materials in this book was not easy. Punishment is a complex human institution. It has normative, political, social, psychological, and legal dimensions, and ways of thinking about each of them change over time. Courses taught in law schools and philosophy departments attend mostly to normative issues, and secondarily to legal ones. That is understandable but seems to me too narrow. As a result, in addition to classical and contemporary works on normative theories by philosophers and penal theorists (a term often used to describe lawyers and others who write about issues more applied than those philosophers typically address), I included writings on restorative justice, on how people think about punishment, and on social theories about the functions punishment performs in human societies.

A few paragraphs about what this book contains are in order. Its contents are premised on three propositions about punishment theories and ideas. The first is that, as with all else in life, ideas go in and out of fashion. The second is that a major shift away from utilitarian and toward retributive ideas took place in the 1960s and 1970s. The third is that retributive ideas did not manage to become hegemonic, as utilitarian ideas had been for a century. By the 1990s, retributive ideas began to lose influence. In the early decades of the twenty-first century, things are in flux. There is renewed interest in rehabilitation among theorists and policy makers, programs operating under restorative justice banners are proliferating around the globe, and new ideas—dominion, community justice, therapeutic jurisprudence—are fermenting. Only people who live so long will know what ideas will predominate in 2020.

There are six parts. The first part on "classical" writings sets the stage for the late twentieth–century shift toward retributivism. I have included longer excerpts from Kant, Hegel, and Bentham than punishment readers usually provide. This is partly because their writings are considerably more nuanced and practical than is sometimes recognized; they provide a good baseline from which readers can consider the merits and novelty of subsequent writings. This part also contains a full-throated argument for individualized utilitarian sentencing and critiques of utilitarianism in principle and practice. I do not include critiques of retributivism; these are discussed in many of the writings in other parts.

The second part contains a set of influential writings from the 1970s through the 1990s offering explanations and justifications of various retributive theories. This is where the principal theoretical action was from 1970 to the 1990s. These writings mostly discuss definitions and overriding justifications of punishment and give comparatively less attention to practical policies or to how punishments might be imposed in individual cases.

The third part concerns "mixed" theories which combine retributive with utilitarian or consequentialist elements in various ways (the term "utilitarianism" has fallen out of fashion and replaced with consequentialism). Mixed theories are often characterized as being in competition with retributive theories. They are typically attentive to practical questions of application and typically focus as much or more attention on issues relating to individual cases as to more general issues of justification of punishment as a legal or social institution. Another way to think about differences between Parts II and III is disciplinary. Most of the writers represented in this part are lawyers; those in part II are philosophers.

The fourth part concerns implications of recent developments in the behavioral and medical sciences for thinking about punishment. Recent works by evolutionary biologists and psychologists suggest that human beings may be hard-wired for moral judgment and retributive impulse because those characteristics were useful adaptations that enhanced reproductive success for thinking social animals. Work by social and other psychologists suggests that human beings in many countries share intuitions—whether biologically based or products of social learning—that wrongdoing warrants punishment and about the comparative seriousness of major forms of wrongdoing. Neurological and other brain and central nervous system research suggests that a belief in free will is unwarranted. It is too soon to know how these recent characterizations of humankind will influence punishment thinking and policy, but their implications warrant careful consideration.

The fifth part deals with restorative justice. Implementation of restorative justice and related programs is broad, but not deep. The vast majority of programs concern offenses by juveniles or minor offenses by adults. A breakthrough into adoption as the modal, or even a common, approach for handling serious crimes by adults has yet to happen. There is a large literature on roles, effects, and effectiveness of restorative justice. Among the major issues are whether restorative programs should complement or replace the official criminal justice system, and whether outcomes must be consonant with those the official system produces.

The sixth and final part concerns theories about latent functions punishment performs. A Marxist might argue that law and its institutions, including punishment, operate to further the interests of dominant economic or social classes. Emile Durkheim wrote that the criminal law and punishment are important means to preserve and reinforce basic social norms of a society, what he called the collective conscience, and that their utilitarian effects are probably small and in any case are not important. Michel Foucault proposed that the prison and punishment generally serve to shape individuals for roles they must perform in the contemporary world's mass institutions and bureaucratized existence. Loïc Wacquant and others argue that the modern American criminal justice system operates to maintain a system of racial hierarchy in which whites dominate blacks, as the late twentieth-century urban ghetto, Jim Crow laws and conventions, and slavery did in earlier times.

These are not normative accounts of how punishment ought to operate, or what goals it ought to accomplish. They are empirically-informed efforts to explain what punishment does. Readers may find any one of them more or less or not at all persuasive, but insofar as any part of them rings true...It makes you think, and it ought to make practitioners and policy makers think. What they ought to think is not clear, but a judge or legislator who worries that more is going on in the criminal courts than is consciously or widely recognized or intended may do his job in different and more self-conscious ways. I hope so.

Were space unlimited, I would have included materials on therapeutic jurisprudence and community justice, on emerging consequentialist approaches, and on political science scholarship. Therapeutic jurisprudence and community justice have had significant real-world influence. Many supporters of drug courts and other problem-solving courts, for example, say that they are applying therapeutic jurisprudence ideas. The influence of community justice ideas is harder to pin down except as an element of restorative justice, but proponents of community court and prosecution programs commonly invoke the term. The community justice and therapeutic jurisprudence literatures, however, tend not to be theoretical. The former typically explains why community considerations are important and discusses how community justice might be implemented. Prominent writers on therapeutic jurisprudence including David Wexler and Bruce Winick, the pioneers, typically deny that it is a normative theory at all but refer to it as a diagnostic tool or a methodology for identifying destructive and constructive effects of legal rules, processes, and institutions.

"Consequentialism" came into fashion as a term to describe alternatives to retributivism in classifications of normative theory. Retributivists argue that imposition of deserved punishments is a Good Thing, irrespective of the effects of doing so. Consequentialists argue that the acceptability of punishment policies or practices depends on whether they maximize particular outcomes. Bentham often wrote of happiness and satisfaction as measures of the acceptability of a rule or practice. These terms are difficult to quantify or systematize. Economists use economic efficiency as a measure. Contemporary non-retributivists have devised others. John Braithwaite and Philip Pettit argue that policies and practices should maximize dominion, an individual's capacity to participate in and enjoy the benefits of living in a community. Nicola Lacey argues that effects on the nature and sense of community are important. All of these ideas are provocative and useful. Economic theories are by definition non-normative, however, and ideas about dominion and community well-being have been little developed except by their creators. In the end I decided to stick with Bentham and the system of indeterminate sentencing which for a century in many ways embodied his approach.

Political science literatures have undeniable real world relevance. Practitioners make punishment decisions in individual cases and elected officials set the policies that guide them (or that they sometimes ignore or evade). A rich empirical literature on courtroom work groups and local legal cultures instructs that a wide range of influences—personalities, personal self-interest, political considerations, social pressures, institutional priorities, needs to allocate scarce resources—in addition to the facts of cases and the relevant laws influence decisions. Literatures on legislative policy-making and executive action also have obvious relevance.

Normative considerations inevitably influence practitioners' decisions and the policies officials set. It seems likely that they are the same kinds of normative considerations that theorists puzzle over. Their influence, however, is contingent and often they must co-exist or compete with larger political agendas, interests, and ideologies. Taking on those complexities seemed unrealistic for a reader on punishment theory.

Preparation, production, and publication of any book require work by many people. Su Smallen did indispensable bibliographical and organizational work. Adepeju Solarin, and Joe Jackson and Eileen Patten of Oxford University Press, arranged permissions to republish copyrighted work. 'Peju kept the trains on the track and on time. Michael Abts, Reece Almond, Colleen Chambers, and Eric Taubel performed the wearying and eye-blearying task of proofing retyped writings against the originals. The following friends and colleagues offered useful critiques of successive drafts of the table of contents and the introduction: Brian Bix, Susanna Blumental, Antony Duff, Barry Feld, Richard Frase, Marc Miller, Kevin Reitz, and Julian Roberts. I am grateful to them all.

This is the first book I've edited that consists mostly of previously published writings, so effusive thanks to the writers for their long-suffering and good-spirited cooperation seems not in order. Gratitude to the writers nonetheless is warranted. Isaac Newton, a giant and not by reputation a modest man, in explaining his not inconsiderable accomplishments, said that he had stood on the shoulders of giants. Some of the people whose writings appear in this book are giants and all (I except my own entry) offer original and thought-provoking insights. Standing on their shoulders, we all can learn.

M.T.
Deer Isle, Maine
June 2009

CONTENTS

PART II. RETRIBUTIVE THEORIES

PART III. MIXED THEORIES

PART IV. EMOTION, INTUITION, AND DETERMINISM

PART V. RESTORATIVE THEORIES

PART VI. SOCIAL THEORIES

CREDITS

"A Paternalistic Theory of Punishment" by Herbert Morris. Reproduced with permission of the *American Philosophical Quarterly*.

"Punishment and the Rule of Law" by T.M. Scanlon from *The Difficulty of Tolerance: Essays in Political Philosophy*. © T.M. Scanlon 2003. Reprinted with the permission of Cambridge University Press.

"Penance, Punishment, and the Limits of Community" by R.A. Duff from *Punishment & Society* 5(3): 295–312. Reprinted with the Permission of SAGE.

"Prolegomenon to the Principles of Punishment" by H.L.A. Hart from *Punishment and Responsibility: Essays in the Philosophy of Law*. Oxford University Press, 1968.

"Proportionate Sentences: A Desert Perspective": Andrew von Hirsch, as appeared in *Principled Sentencing: Readings on Theory and Policy*, edited by Andrew von Hirsch and Andrew Ashworth, 2nd ed. Reprinted with the permission of Hart Publishing Limited.

"Proportionality, Parsimony, and Interchangeability of Punishments" by Michael Tonry from *Penal Theory and Practice: Tradition and Innovation in Criminal Justice*, edited by R.A. Duff et al. Manchester University Press, 1994.

"Sentencing and Punishment in Finland: The Decline of the Repressive Ideal" by Tapio Lappi-Seppälä from *Sentencing and Sanctions in Western Countries*, edited by Michael Tonry and Richard S. Frase. Oxford University Press, 2001.

"Limiting Retributivism" by Richard Frase from *The Future of Imprisonment*, edited by Michael Tonry. Oxford University Press, 2004.

"Limiting Excessive Prison Sentencing" by Richard S. Frase from the *University of Pennsylvania Journal of Constitutional Law* 11(1):40–46. 2009. Reprinted with the permission of the *University of Pennsylvania Journal of Constitutional Law* and the author.

"Morality and the Retributive Emotions" by J.L. Mackie, as appeared in *Criminal Justice Ethics*, Volume 1, Issue 1, (Winter/Spring 1982) pp. 3–10, and *Edward Westermarck: Essays on His Life and Work*, Acta Philosophica Fennica Fasc. XXXIV (1982), Timothy Stroup. Reprinted with the permission of The Institute for Criminal Justice Ethics, 555 West 57th Street, Suite 607, New York, NY, 10019-1029, and the Philosophical Society of Finland.

"The Role of Moral Philosophers in the Competition between Deontological and Empirical Desert" by Paul H. Robinson from *William and Mary Law Review* 48:1831–43, 2007.

"For the Law, Neuroscience Changes Nothing and Everything" by Joshua Greene and Jonathan Cohen from *Philosophical Transactions of the Royal Society* 359:1775–85. Reprinted with the permission of the Royal Society.

"Restoration in Youth Justice" by Lode Walgrave from *Youth Crime and Youth Justice: Comparative and Cross-national Perspectives*, edited by Michael Tonry and Anthony N. Doob. Volume 31 of *Crime and Justice: A Review of Research*, edited by Michael Tonry. University of Chicago Press, 2004.

"In Search of Restorative Jurisprudence" by John Braithwaite from *Restorative Justice and the Law*, edited by Lode Walgrave, Willan Publishing. Reprinted with the permission of Willan Publishing.

"The Virtues of Restorative Processes, the Vices of 'Restorative Justice'" by Paul H. Robinson, originally published in the *Utah Law Review*, 2003 UTAH L. REV. 375.

Why Punish? How Much?

Introduction

Thinking about Punishment

Michael Tonry

People have been thinking about punishment for a long time. Plato pondered it. So did Aristotle and St. Thomas Aquinas. Thinking about it in our time, however, dates from the eighteenth and early nineteenth centuries when Kant and Hegel laid the foundations for modern retributivist analyses. Bentham did the same for utilitarian approaches. For most of the two centuries that followed, the Kantian and Benthamite frameworks sufficed.

The principal arguments until recently were between rather than within the frameworks. Utilitarians disparaged retributivism as vindictiveness disguised in pretty words and retributivists disparaged utilitarians as amoral, insensitive to human rights and prepared if need be to punish innocents to prevent crime. Utilitarians, however, won the hearts and minds of practitioners and policy makers in the English-speaking countries (it was a different story in continental Europe). The modern criminal justice system was invented in the nineteenth century, and most of the major institutions rested on utilitarian foundations. When the century opened, imprisonment was just beginning to take its place as the modal punishment for mid-level and serious crimes, and the penitentiary, the training school, the reformatory, the juvenile court, the probation officer, and the parole board had not yet been invented. By the end of the nineteenth century, they were all in place and all were based on the idea that decisions in individual cases should be individualized to account for the offender's rehabilitative prospects or need for incapacitation or, occasionally, to address deterrent concerns (Rothman 1971, 1980).

As a whole, sentencing and corrections institutions and processes were referred to as indeterminate, or occasionally individualized, sentencing. That is because the lengths of prison sentences could generally not be known, "determined," until in a particular case the judge, the parole board, and often prison officials had made a series of individualized decisions. There were few laws or rules governing those decisions, and there were few, usually no mechanisms for offenders to use to object to decisions they did not like. Broad discretion was the norm. In the extreme forms of indeterminate sentencing, in California and Washington, the judge decided whether to send an offender to state prison, but had no influence over how long he stayed. All prison sentences by law were for a period between one year and the statutory maximum for the offense of conviction. A parole board decided whether and when prisoners were released. The details varied from state to state (and more in other English-speaking countries), but the broad pattern was the same in every American state.

Utilitarian or, as they are now described, consequentialist ways of thinking went hand-in-hand with indeterminate sentencing, and were overwhelmingly influential through the 1960s. The *Model Penal Code* (American Law Institute 1962), the most celebrated and influential American criminal law project of the twentieth century, was unreservedly consequentialist and committed not to questioning but to perfecting indeterminate sentencing. Judges were authorized to impose probation in any case, including after murder convictions, parole boards could release most prisoners after one year no matter how long the maximum sentence, and prison officials could shorten maximum and minimum sentences by as much as half through awards of time off for good behavior (or they could effectively lengthen sentences by withdrawing previously accrued "good time" credits). The transcripts of twelve years' deliberations contain only occasional and faint allusions to retributive considerations (Tonry 2004, chap. 7).

The *Code* mentions retributive ideas only three times. Section 1.02(2)(c) identifies "safeguarding offenders against excessive, disproportionate, or arbitrary punishment" as one of the purposes of the sentencing and treatment provisions. Sections 7.01(1) and 305.9(1)(b) establish presumptions against imposition of prison sentences and in favor of parole release; one indicated basis for rebutting the presumptions is that the punishment would "depreciate the seriousness of the offense." The latter provisions were added as afterthoughts only in 1961.

Like flies in amber, the *Code*'s punishment provisions and the consequentialist ways of thinking that underlay them were vestiges of an earlier era. Although some of the *Code*'s other provisions proved highly influential, the punishment provisions did not. Even before the *Code* was finally approved, moral analysts (Lewis 1949), philosophers (Rawls 1955), legal scholars (Allen 1959), and novelists (Burgess 1962) challenged its consequentialist premises. Within a decade afterward, indeterminate sentencing came under attack from practitioners and academics for procedural unfairness and lack of transparency (Davis 1969), for unwarranted disparities between cases (Frankel 1972), and for facilitating decisions based on racist beliefs and stereotypes (American Friends Service Committee 1971). A few years later, an influential critique of rehabilitative programs raised widespread doubts about their effectiveness (Martinson 1974).

The bottom had fallen out. Maine abolished its parole board and with it indeterminate sentencing in 1975. California did likewise in 1976 and other states spanning the continent—Arizona, Illinois, Indiana, Minnesota, Pennsylvania, North Carolina, Washington—quickly followed suit. Determinate sentencing, sentencing guidelines, mandatory minimum sentences, truth-in-sentencing laws, parole guidelines, and prosecution guidelines quickly appeared throughout the United States (Blumstein et al. 1983). Changes were fewer and slower in coming, and less punitive, in other English-speaking countries, but many were proposed (Australian Law Reform Commission 1980; Canadian Sentencing Commission 1987: Home Office 1991 [England]); and some were adopted (Freiberg 2001 [Australia]; Pratt 2006 [New Zealand]; Newburn 2007 [England]; Webster and Doob 2007 [Canada]).

Consequentialist—especially rehabilitative—punishment theories fell out of favor with indeterminate sentencing. Philosophers began to espouse retributive punishment theories (e.g., Herbert Morris 1968; Kleinig 1973; Murphy 1973). So did legal scholars (e.g., Norval Morris 1974; von Hirsch 1976; Fletcher 1978).

The consequentialist door closed. The retributivist door opened. Retributivist theories take diverse forms but all explicitly or implicitly call for proportionality, for scaling the severity of punishments to the seriousness of crimes. Such schemes tidily address most of the indictments of indeterminate sentencing: rules or principles calling for proportionate punishments simultaneously address overbroad discretions, lack of procedural fairness, lack of transparency, unwarranted disparities, opportunities for racial bias, and unjustified confidence in rehabilitative programs.

Indeterminate sentencing and the predominance of consequentialist ways of thinking about punishment lasted for a century or more. It is not clear that retributivist ways of thinking subsequently ever became predominant except possibly in philosophy departments and law schools, and even there only for a few decades.

At the end of the first decade of the twenty-first century, there was no dominant sentencing paradigm in the United States or in other English-speaking countries. Two-thirds of U.S. states retained parole boards, the quintessential element of indeterminate sentencing, but often co-existing with highly determinate mandatory minimum, three-strikes-and-you're-out, and truth-in-sentencing laws.[1] Every state had mandatory minimum sentence laws, a third had sentencing guidelines, more than half had three-strikes laws. Many, however, had created new treatment programs for drug, sexual, and other offenders. Highly individualized treatment programs like drug and other problem-solving courts and prisoner re-entry programs existed in most states. Restorative justice programs existed in most states and community justice programs in many.

The stories in other English-speaking countries were broadly the same. Australia, Canada, England, and New Zealand retained parole release but narrowed its scope, and also adopted mandatory sentencing laws, experimented with restorative justice initiatives, and invested in new treatment programs. However, nothing resembling California's three-strikes law, frequent use of life-without-possibility-of-parole (LWOP) sentences, or the federal hundred-to-one mandatory minimum sentence law for crack cocaine sentencing was adopted elsewhere.

Criminal justice policies are of course not the same thing as punishment theories and philosophies, but they are not unrelated. During the most self-confident period

---

[1] Mandatory minimum laws require that every person convicted of a particular offense receive a prison sentence of at least a designated number of years. Three-strikes laws require that people convicted of a third felony receive specified minimum sentences, often twenty-five years and sometimes life. Truth-in-sentencing laws require that people convicted of specified sentences serve at least 85 percent of the designated term in prison.

of indeterminate sentencing from 1870 to 1950, many, probably most, writers on punishment theory would have described themselves as utilitarians and have argued that retributive ideas were at least obsolete if not pernicious. The first English-language text on sentencing, *The Principles of Punishment* (1877) by English judge Edward Cox, "preached a Benthamite version of utilitarianism," Nigel Walker observed, but "most remarkable, was the absence of any attention to retribution, let alone 'just deserts'" (Walker 1999, p. xi). Oliver Wendell Holmes, Jr. in *The Common Law* described retribution as only "vengeance in disguise" (1881, p. 45). Herbert Wechsler, the twentieth century's leading American criminal law scholar, and his mentor Jerome Michael, noted that retribution may represent "the unstudied belief of most men" but concluded that "no legal provision can be justified merely because it calls for the punishment of the morally guilty by penalties proportioned to their guilt, or criticized merely because it fails to do so" (Michael and Wechsler 1940, pp. 7, 11).

By 1980, after indeterminate sentencing's implosion, utilitarian punishment theorists were hard to find.[2] The virtue and value of retributive ideas seemed self-evident, as evidenced by the writings of the philosophers and penal theorists that I mentioned earlier. Most writing on punishment philosophy and theory had a pronounced retributive slant. University of Chicago law professor Albert Alschuler, writer of a major biography of Holmes (Alschuler 2000), bewilderedly described the sea change in attitudes and beliefs: "That I and many other academics adhered in large part to this reformative viewpoint only a decade or so ago seems almost incredible to most of us today" (Alschuler 1978, p. 552).

I begin this introduction to a reader on punishment philosophy and theory with a nearly two-century overview of American and other countries' punishment systems and theorizing to make three points. First, ways of thinking about punishment are as much affected by fashion as anything else. Many of the same analytical points are made in different eras but their persuasive power varies substantially. Moral claims are made but few people are listening. Holmes and Wechsler knew and had read Kant and Hegel; they just weren't persuaded. Many writers in more recent decades were predisposed to be persuaded about the importance of moral culpability and desert, even if their detailed analyses differed, and to be skeptical about consequentialist analyses of punishment.

Second, we are in a transitional period. Retributive analytical frameworks do not rest comfortably with contemporary ideas about restorative justice, community justice, therapeutic jurisprudence, and rehabilitation of offenders. In different ways they all imply that considerations other than moral culpability are importantly germane to what happens to offenders, and none of them makes retributive proportionality a major consideration. Retributive ideas also do not sit comfortably with proportionality-defying policy developments such as three-strikes laws, lengthy mandatory minimum sentences, LWOPs, and preventive detention for "dangerous" offenders.

Third, punishment philosophy and theory raise fundamentally important questions whose answers matter. Although the answers vary across space and time, they should

---

[2] Most were offered by people whose intellectual formation occurred during the era of utilitarian predominance (e.g., Walker 1969, 1991; Honderich 2005). Other major figures began their careers working within the utilitarian tradition but became proponents of "mixed" theories (e.g., Rawls 1955; Hart 1968; Morris 1974).

be the best and most affirming that people living in a particular era can devise. Criminal punishment is the paradigm instance of conflict between the individual and the state—in pursuit of collective interests, individuals are deprived of their property, their liberty, and their lives. Each generation should understand and be able to explain why and when those awesome powers may be used, and under what conditions. Especially in a transitional era such as ours, people need to struggle for the best possible answers.

I. PUNISHMENT AS FASHION

Ways of thinking go in and out of fashion—sexual freedom versus prudery, political liberalism versus conservativism, classicism in the arts versus romanticism—but generally do not disappear (Gilmore 1974 [the arts]; Boswell 1980 [homosexuality]; Musto 1987 [drug use]). That's as true of punishment theories as anything else. The fundamental contrast between the ideas that punishment is morally justified because people have behaved wrongly and that punishment is morally justified only when it has good consequences has long existed and most likely always will. When one view is predominant, some contrary souls continue to espouse the other. During periods when one is ascendant, however, relatively few people seem committed to the other.

Three periods can be identified. In the first, between 1780 and 1860, Kant and Hegel and their supporters, and Bentham and his, were in open disagreement and ideas were in flux. The preceding era, of rudimentary criminal justice systems and severe punishments, was ending in the late eighteenth century and modern criminal justice systems premised largely on utilitarian ideas were beginning to take shape. In the second, between 1860 and 1960, utilitarian ideas were ascendant. Indeterminate sentencing systems consolidated and for the final fifty years reigned. Retributive ideas did not disappear but were resisted or disparaged. In the third period, from 1960 to the present, the intellectual rationales for indeterminate sentencing collapsed, utilitarian ideas—especially those related to rehabilitation—went out of fashion, and for a short time retributive ideas seemed to predominate. It was not clear in the 1970s and 1980s whether there had been a paradigm shift from utilitarian to retributive ways of thinking, or whether those years signaled another period of transition. It is clear now that they were the beginning of a transition that is still underway en route to a future that cannot be predicted.

A. THE FIRST TRANSITIONAL PERIOD, 1780–1860

The transition away from the *ancien regime*, a period of relatively infrequent but condign punishment, is usually dated from the publication in 1764 of Cesare Beccaria's *Dei delitti e delle pene* (*On Crimes and Punishments*). Quickly translated into French and English, Beccaria's book decried the cruelty, inconsistency, and excessive severity of criminal punishments, and argued that the purpose of punishment should be to create a better society, not to inflict revenge on wrong-doers. Punishments should be scaled to the seriousness of the crime, he wrote, and should be used to deter others and to prevent the criminal from repeating the crime. Of the three elements of deterrence—certainty, severity, and celerity (speed)—certainty and celerity were the most important. The two main ideas, that punishment should be scaled to the seriousness of crime, and that punishment must be justified in terms of its consequences, laid foundations on which Kant and Bentham built.

1. EARLY RETRIBUTIVISM

Kant's views are well-known albeit not free from ambiguity.

Punishment is a "categorical imperative," which means that its imposition, irrespective of good or bad effects, is a moral requirement derivable from first principles. Three passages are especially well-known and frequently quoted. The first is often interpreted to forbid consequential considerations:

> Judicial punishment can never be used merely as a means to promote some other good for the criminal himself or for civil society, but instead it must in all cases be imposed on him only on the ground that he has committed a crime; for a human being can never be manipulated merely as a means to the purposes of someone else.... (Kant 1965 [1798], p. 100)

The second is often understood to require that punishments be strictly apportioned to the seriousness of the crime:

> What kind and what degree of punishment does public legal justice adopt as its principle and standard? None other than the principle of equality....Accordingly, any undeserved evil that you afflict on someone else among the people is one that you do to yourself. If you vilify him, you vilify yourself. If you steal from him, you steal from yourself. If you kill him, you kill yourself. Only the Law of retribution (*jus talionis*) can determine exactly the kind and degree of punishment.... (Kant 1965 [1798], p. 101)

Out of context Kant's allusion to the "principle of equality" can be misinterpreted, and has been, as requiring that punishments perfectly correspond to crimes, as in a sense execution can to murder.[3] However, Kant gives examples of punishments that do not literally "equal" the offense. For "verbal injuries," for example, a fine might

---

[3] The *jus talionis* "is obviously not capable of being extended. Crime and punishment are different things. Can they really be equated? What penalty equals the crime of forgery, perjury or kidnapping? For the state to exercise the same amount of fraud or brutality on the criminal that the criminal exercised on his victim would be demoralizing to any community" (Cohen 1940, p. 1010).

ordinarily suffice but not for a wealthy person: the "humiliation' of a public apology and kissing the hand of a lower social status victim would be better. When a high-status person assaults a social inferior, he must apologize but might also be condemned to "solitary and painful confinement, because by this means, in addition to the discomfort suffered, the pride of the offender will be painfully affected" (pp. 101–102).

The third is often understood to make clear that the effects of punishment are immaterial and that the state's legal duty to enforce the categorical imperative of deserved punishment is unqualified:

> Even if a civil society were to dissolve itself by common agreement of all its members (for example, if the people inhabiting an island decided to separate and disperse themselves around the world), the last murderer remaining in prison must first be executed, so that everyone will duly receive what his actions were worth and so that the bloodguilt thereof will not be fixed on the people because they failed to insist on carrying out the punishment; for if they fail to do so, they may be regarded as accomplices in this public violation of legal justice. (Kant 1965 [1798], p. 102)

Much in those passages is obscure.[4] Nonetheless, taken together, especially in the context of surrounding passages, they seem clearly to argue that punishment not only may but must be imposed on people who commit crimes (and who are duly convicted), and that the punishments imposed must be proportioned in a meaningful way to the seriousness of the crimes committed (and in the extreme case, murderers must be executed).

Hegel's analysis of punishment is based on a more complex metaphysic, but shares two elements with Kant's: the idea that respect for the moral autonomy of the criminal, his capacity for making moral choices, requires that he be punished, and the idea that punishments must be apportioned to the seriousness of crimes. Explaining why offenders should be punished, he wrote

> [T]he *action* of the criminal involves not only the *concept* of crime...but also the formal rationality of the *individual's volition*. In so far as the punishment which this entails is seen as embodying *the criminal's own right*, the criminal is *honoured* as a rational being. He is denied this honour if the concept and criterion of his punishment are not derived from his own act; and he is also denied it if he is regarded simply as a harmful animal which must be rendered harmless, or punished with a view to deterring him or reforming him. (Hegel 1991, p. 127; italic in original)

---

[4] In the first passage, for example, the two uses of the word "merely" might be argued to imply that a criminal may be used as a means to some good end if (but only if) he has "committed a crime." Similarly, the meaning of the proposition in the second passage that "undeserved evil that you afflict on someone else...is one that you do to yourself" is not transparently obvious.

In explaining how decisions are to be made about punishments for specific crimes (except murder, for which he also indicates that execution is inexorably appropriate[5]), Hegel offers a strikingly modern formulation:

> [T]he universal feeling of peoples and individuals towards crime is, and always has been, that it *deserves* to be punished, and that *what the criminal has done should be done to him*. . . . But the determination of *equality* has brought a major difficulty into the idea of retribution. . . . [I]t is very easy to portray the retributive aspect of punishment as an absurdity (theft as retribution for theft, robbery for robbery, an eye for an eye, and a tooth for a tooth, so that one can even imagine the miscreant as one-eyed or toothless); but the concept has nothing to do with this absurdity. . . . [E]quality remains merely the basic measure of the criminal's *essential* deserts, but not of the specific external shape which the retribution should take. . . . It is then, as already remarked, a matter for the understanding to seek an <u>approximate</u> equivalence. . . . [R]etribution cannot aim to achieve specific equality. . . . (Hegel 1991, pp. 128–29; italic in original; underscoring mine)[6]

Taken together, these passages from Kant and Hegel describe a theory of punishment not very different from those of many modern writers. People who have chosen to commit criminal offenses deserve to be punished; punishments should be proportioned to the seriousness of crimes in such a way that relative punishments can be said in a meaningful way to be equivalent to the crimes for which they are imposed. Although Kant's and Hegel's explanations for why people deserve to be punished are different from those of most modern writers, the punishment system they describe is not very different from those generated by Andrew von Hirsch's theory of commensurate desert (1998; von Hirsch and Ashworth 2005) or Paul Robinson's stricter desert theory (Robinson 1987) .

The principle criticism of retributivism is that at base it is no more than an expression of vindictiveness or vengeance.[7] Karl Menninger provides a typical if polemical example: "The reasons usually given to justify punishment do not explain why it exists. They serve only to conceal the truth, that the scheme of punishment is a barbaric system by which society tries to 'get even' with the criminal" (Menninger 1946, p. 448). Most retributivists insist otherwise.

Retributivist writers, across the centuries, share the idea that individual rights matter, that punishment is an intrusion into the lives of individuals, and that it must be justified in relation to them and actions for which they are morally responsible. This

---

[5] "For since life is the entire compass of existence, the punishment cannot consist in a value—since none is equivalent of life—but only in the taking of another life" (Hegel 1991, pp. 129–30).

[6] Hegel makes his rejection of mechanistic or absolute punishment equivalence even clearer in another passage: "Thought cannot specify how each crime should be punished; positive determinations are necessary for this purpose. With the progress of education, however, attitudes toward crime become more lenient, and punishments today are not nearly so harsh as they were a hundred years ago. It is not the crimes or punishments themselves which change, but the relation between the two" (Hegel 1991, p. 123).

[7] James Fitzjames Stephen, in his *History of the Criminal Law of England* does not evade the allegation. The criminal law "proceeds upon the principle that it is morally right to hate criminals, and it confirms and justifies that sentiment by inflicting upon criminals punishments that express it" (1883, p. 82).

remains a mainstream view in our time. It was stronger in the 1970s than it is early in the twenty-first century. Ronald Dworkin's notion (1977) that individual rights operate as "trumps" against state action and John Rawls's notion (1958, 1971) of "justice as fairness" express the 1970s ethos.

2. EARLY UTILITARIANISM

Jeremy Bentham was dead by 1860, but his ideas shaped prevailing ways of thinking about the criminal justice system in English-speaking countries then and for the following century.[8] The object of the criminal law for Bentham was to "augment the total happiness of the community" and "to exclude as far as may be, everything that tends to subtract from that happiness: in other words, to exclude mischief" (Bentham 1970, p. 158). The goal is sometimes expressed as achieving the "greatest good for the greatest number."

Critically, however, everyone's happiness—including that of offenders—counts: "But all punishment is mischief: all punishment is evil. Upon the principle of utility, if it is at all to be admitted, it ought only to be admitted in as far as it promises to exclude some greater evil" (Bentham 1970, p. 158).

Unlike Kant and Hegel, Bentham insisted that utilitarian theory had nothing to do with ideas about individual rights or respect for the moral autonomy of individuals. Commenting on the French Revolution, and the Declaration of the Rights of Man to which it gave rise, he acerbically observed that the idea of "natural rights is simple nonsense: natural and imprescriptible rights, rhetorical nonsense, nonsense upon stilts" (quoted in Harrison 1995).

Kant and Hegel fired back. Kant stressed the difference between his ideas and Bentham's: "The law concerning punishment is a categorical imperative, and woe to him who rummages around in the winding paths of a theory of happiness looking for some advantage to be gained by releasing the criminal from punishment or by reducing the amount of it" (Kant 1965 [1798], p. 100).

Hegel was as adamant: "This superficial [characterization of crime] as an *evil* is the primary assumption in the various theories of punishment as prevention, as a deterrent, a corrective, etc., and conversely what is supposed to result from it is just as superficially defined as a good....As a result of these superficial points of view, however, the objective consideration of *justice*, which is the primary and substantial point of view in relation to crime, is set aside" (Hegel 1991, p. 125; italic in original).

---

[8] Bentham's views were not exceptional; his exhaustive development of them was. William Blackstone, in his *Commentaries on the Laws of England*, wrote that the end of punishment is not "atonement or expiation" but "a precaution against future offenses of the same kind. This is effected three ways: either by the amendment of the offender himself;...or by deterring others...; or, lastly, by depriving the party injuring of the power to do future mischief [by execution, permanent confinement, slavery or exile]" (Blackstone 1979 [1769], p. 13). William Paley, in a treatise that went through fifteen editions in his lifetime, wrote, "The proper end of legal punishment is not the satisfaction of justice, but the prevention of crimes...This end, whatever it may do in the plans of infinite wisdom, does not in the designation of temporal penalties, always coincide with the proportionate punishment of guilt" (Paley 1788, pp. 273–74).

Bentham lived through the earliest phases of the development of modern criminal justice systems, most notably the penitentiary, and he proposed a model prison. His "panopticon" was a pentagonal building of tiered cell blocks with inward-facing, open-fronted, barred cells, and an open center containing a tower from which warders could observe prisoners at all times.[9]

Although ideas about moral reformation of criminals (through penitent reflection; hence the "penitentiary") were in circulation in the early nineteenth century, rehabilitative ideas were less well-developed. The primarily rehabilitative institutions (probation, parole, the reformatory, the training school, the juvenile court) came into being after his death.

Bentham's primary means of crime prevention accordingly were based mostly on deterrent ideas he shared with Beccaria, combined with a model of human rationality engaged in calculation of costs and benefits. He developed his analysis in excruciating detail in several works (Bentham 1970, 2008 [1830]).

Penalties should be set so that the expected burden of punishment is greater than the benefits of crime. Punishments should be severer for more serious crimes than for less serious ones to provide incentives to commit the less serious. They should be adjusted to take account of each element of a crime so that the offender has incentive not to take each successive step.[10] Anticipating modern economists' writings on deterrence, Bentham argued that punishments should be increased in severity in inverse relation to the likelihood that the offender would be apprehended and convicted.[11] If, for example, the appropriate happiness-maximizing punishment in a given case was two years, it should be increased to eight years if the certainty of punishment was only 25 percent. Punishments should likewise be increased to take account of delays in their imposition (Bentham 1970, pp. 165–74).

The offender's situation, however, had to be considered. First, punishment should be parsimonious: "The punishment should in no case be more than is necessary to bring it into conformity with the rules here given" (Bentham 1970, p. 169). Second, the offender's "sensibilities" must be taken into account. That is, the punishment must take account of how it would affect that particular individual offender. People have different sensitivities and are affected in different ways by the same experience, including experiences of punishment. Accordingly, "That the quantity actually inflicted on an individual offender may correspond to the quantity intended for similar offenders in general, the several circumstances influencing sensibility ought always to be taken into account" (Bentham 1970, p. 169).

---

[9] It was meant to be economically efficient, allowing a small number of guards to observe and manage a large number of prisoners. Several were built, including Stateville Prison in Illinois, which remains in operation. The panopticon was a central metaphor in Foucault's *Discipline and Punish*, a history of the prison in which he developed his ideas about a surveillant society (Foucault 1977). The French title *Surveillir et Punir* more clearly invokes the panopticon as a governing metaphor.

[10] The propositions mentioned so far are clear. An example of this one is the law of attempts where, typically, punishments are less for attempted than for completed crimes in order to give offenders an incentive to reconsider and abandon their nefarious plans.

[11] For example Posner (2007, p. 226): "Another example of the general point—that the lower the probability of punishment, the more severe the punishment must be to achieve deterrence—is the hanging of horse thieves in the nineteenth century American West."

Looked at in the abstract from two centuries later, there are some formidable practical difficulties in Bentham's scheme. Penalties are meant to be harsher for more serious crimes compared with less serious, but they are to be increased to take account of the probability that any punishment will be imposed for a particular kind of crime and of delays in imposition, and are further to be adjusted to take account of the offender's unique sensibilities. Much simpler calculations—whether a particular offender will re-offend, or what level of punishment will assure a sought-after deterrent effect—have since been shown to be enormously difficult or impossible to complete with acceptable accuracy. The requirement that the punishment be adjusted to take account of the offender's sensibilities introduces almost impossible questions of knowledge.[12]

Despite his jousting with Kant about the value of ideas about human rights, Bentham opposed punishing people who were not morally responsible for their acts. The most striking example was an injunction against punishing people who were insane. That, he argued, would be "inefficacious;" insane people by definition are beyond the reach of deterrent messages. Hart (1968, p. 19) referred to this as a "spectacular *non-sequitur*" since, if the primary means of prevention is deterrence, the broader community will not know whether an offender was sane or insane but only that he killed someone and was duly executed. Whether people like this person would be deterred is not a central question. We cannot know why Bentham made particular arguments, but it is not impossible that, without recognizing it, he shared and acted upon the widely-held intuition that people who are not morally responsible do not deserve to be punished as criminals.[13]

One principled objection frequently raised to Bentham's scheme, and to utilitarian schemes generally, is that they should sometimes result in punishment of innocent people.[14] Under some circumstances, the harms that might be avoided by punishing an innocent person, who was generally believed to be guilty, might be so great that the utilitarian calculation would justify punishment. McCloskey (1968) offered a much-discussed hypothetical of the rape of a white woman by a black man in the American south during the Jim Crow period. The sheriff believes that by framing an innocent black man seen near the scene of the crime, who will be accepted by the community as the guilty party, he can prevent racial violence in which many people will be injured or killed. Critics argue that utilitarians must approve of the framing and punishment of the innocent man.

There are two standard replies. One is that knowingly punishing an innocent person is by definition not "punishment" (Quinton 1969). This, however, is mere sleight-of-hand, using what Hart called a "definitional stop" (Hart 1968, p. 5). Anything done

---

[12] Later generations of utilitarian writers solved this by throwing up their hands and deciding that analyses should consider average effects and not take account of "interpersonal comparisons of utility" (Robbins 1938). Modern retributivist writers likewise would base punishments primarily on the offense of conviction, without adjustment to take account of subjective effects on individual offenders (Kolber 2009).

[13] He likewise argued that it would be inefficacious to punish people who were not aware that their behavior was unlawful; Anglo-American common law refers to this as "ignorance of law" and typically does not excuse it. As with his position on insanity, this position is hard to square with the notion that Bentham was unconcerned about fairness to individuals and cared only about the utilitarian calculus.

[14] Edmund Pincoffs makes the converse charge, that utilitarianism might sometimes require that the guilty be rewarded. If the best way to prevent some crimes were to give offenders forty acres, a tractor, and training in their use, at day's end some offenders might achieve greater happiness than their victims, because of their crime: "The conclusion is that to show that a policy is justified on utilitarian grounds is not to show that it is morally justifiable" (1966, pp. 36–37).

to McCloskey's innocent defendant on the putative basis that he is a rapist will feel like punishment to him, and will be regarded as punishment by onlookers. If it looks like a duck, and walks like a duck....

The second is that in life the situation described in the hypothetical is impossible.[15] The truth inevitably would become known and when it did the law's legitimacy would be undermined. People would become fearful that they too might become innocent victims of the utilitarian calculus. The resulting long-term sense of increased insecurity would, it is said, offset any short-term gains from punishing an innocent person (Hart 1968, pp. 20–24).

Huge amounts of ink have been devoted to making, refuting, and examining this charge against utilitarianism (e.g., Smart 1973; Ten 1987, chap. 10; Primoratz 1989), but as a practical matter it is not terribly important.[16] Any real-life punishment system based on utilitarian principles could and almost undoubtedly would establish a side-constraint forbidding the punishment of innocent people no matter how much might be gained by doing so. On analogy to his discussion of crimes by the insane, even Bentham should: if punishment of the insane is inefficacious because they are by presupposition unaffected by deterrent threats, the same must be true of innocent people.

B. Utilitarianism Ascendant, 1860–1960

Indeterminate sentencing systems in any case were not premised primarily on deterrent calculations but on rehabilitative and incapacitative ones. The principal criminal justice institutions took shape during the Progressive Era, and reformers commonly portrayed crime as the product of social and economic conditions or of remediable human deficiencies. A typical statement is contained in the Declaration of Principles adopted at the founding meeting of the National Prison (now American Correctional) Association in Cincinnati in 1870:

> The treatment of criminals by society is for the protection of society. But since such treatment is directed to the criminal rather than the crime, its great object should be his moral regeneration. The state has not discharged its whole duty to the criminal when it has punished him, nor even when it has reformed him. Having raised him up, it has further duty to aid in holding him up. In vain

---

[15] Sometimes there is a third reply: that while hypotheticals can be contrived in which the truth might never come out, they are so elaborate as to be fantastic and therefore are irrelevant to everyday moral arguments in the real world (Ten 1987, pp. 18–32).

[16] It is a bit odd that the issue has received so much attention when Anglo-American criminal law doctrines explicitly contemplate the conviction and punishment of morally innocent people. Statutory rape and bigamy strict liability doctrines, for example, long required (and some places still do) the conviction of people who innocently and after taking reasonable efforts to be careful had intercourse with underage women or married people they could not have known were already (or still) legally married. Self-defense doctrines usually disallow benefit of the defense to people who honestly but unreasonably believed themselves threatened. The former doctrines were predicated on deterrent rationales. The latter is based on concerns that proving a person did not make an unreasonable mistake would be difficult and might produce too many wrongful acquittals or induce villains to kill when they knew it was not necessary in the belief that they would get off.

shall we have given the convict an improved mind and heart, in vain shall we have imparted to him the capacity for industrial labor and the desire to advance himself by worthy means, if, on his discharge, he finds the world in arms against him, with none to trust him, none to meet him kindly, none to give him the opportunity of earning honest bread. (Wines 1871)

Historian David Rothman provided the leading accounts of the development of modern punishment institutions. His first book, *The Discovery of the Asylum* (1971), traced the origins and development in the nineteenth century of the prison, the reformatory, and the asylum and emphasized, amidst other inevitable political, idiosyncratic, and self-interested considerations, the centrality of the Progressive belief in social progress and the malleability of human nature, even if reformers' aspirations usually exceeded their accomplishments.

The title of his second book, *Conscience and Convenience* (1980), expresses its main argument. Reformers, policy makers, and practitioners were often motivated by conscience, by a belief that better, more caring, and better-resourced institutions could improve peoples' lives and reduce their criminality. Indeterminate sentencing also was convenient in the sense that it made officials' day-to-day work lives easier. As Lord Acton's axiom relates, however, power corrupts and absolute power corrupts absolutely. Free from meaningful possibilities of review from courts or other outsiders, judges and correctional officials had almost unlimited power over their charges. Under the infrequent best circumstances of adequate resources and facilities, officials had almost plenary discretion over offenders' lives; hubris, self-interest, or psychological eccentricity inevitably often led to abuse. In less auspicious circumstances, racism, xenophobia, grossly inadequate resources, and political patronage led to horrible abuses. These in turn weakened the system's credibility and legitimacy and contributed to its remarkably quick collapse.

Beginning in the 1950s, Americans became increasingly concerned about procedural fairness, racial bias and disparities, and official accountability. The civil rights and prisoners' rights movements focused spotlights on the punishment system, and what they showed was not pretty. When the dam that held the system in place broke, much of it washed away, and few people objected.

But for nearly a century before that happened, indeterminate sentencing and its utilitarian/rehabilitationist normative rationales reigned securely. As Rothman made clear, there were always critics—often police officials, prosecutors, and conservative politicians—who objected to the system's "leniency" and its tendency sometimes to release people from prison much sooner than critics thought appropriate. However, until the 1960s, theirs was distinctly a minority view.

From an early twenty-first century perspective, the utilitarian consensus is remarkable. Most of the few philosophers who wrote systematically about punishment subscribed to utilitarian views (e.g., Ewing 1929; Michael and Adler 1933).[17] Among penal

---

[17] Writing in the mid-sixties, Edmund Pincoffs, in the first major modern book on punishment philosophy, explained that "modern readers have much more difficulty understanding (not merely agreeing with) the retributive view than the utilitarian one" (1966, p. 2) because "in our time, there are few defenders of retributivism, the position is most often referred to by writers who are opposed to it" (p. 25, n. 1). He noted (as embodied in his own book) a recent upsurge in interest.

theorists, support for utilitarianism was almost monolithic (e.g., Michael and Wechsler 1937; Hall and Glueck 1940; Glueck 1952 [1927–28]).

Crime, Law, and Social Science (1933), by Columbia University law professor Jerome Michael and University of Chicago philosophy professor Mortimer Adler, encapsulates prevailing ways of thought and anticipates ideas that shaped the *Model Penal Code* three decades later. Michael and Adler's commitment to consequentialist values is made clear at the outset: the "criminal law provides for the official treatment of criminals.... [T]he consequences [of crime] take the form of sentences to the various modes of treatment" (pp. 334–35). "Treatment," not "punishment," is what happens to convicted offenders.

They explain that there are two incompatible theories of punishment: the "punitive" (retributive) and the "non-punitive" (consequentialist) and that "it can be shown that the punitive theory is a fallacious analysis and that the non-punitive theory is correct" (1933, p. 341). That conclusion is inexorable, they say, once one recognizes that the purpose of the criminal law is "to preserve and increase the welfare of the state, which has variously been called the common good or the political good" (p. 340). Retributivism aims to mete out deserved punishment, not to serve the common good, and accordingly is inherently unpersuasive.

Michael and Adler devote much more attention to refuting Kant and Hegel than to justifying Bentham, but the implications of their analysis are nearly pure Benthamism:

> Treatment which consists in the infliction of pain upon the criminal is justified to whatever extent such treatment achieves the ends of deterrence and reformation which, in turn, are means for the protection of society against conduct which it deems contrary to its interests. The infliction of pain is never justified merely on the ground that it visits retributive punishment upon the offender. Punitive retribution is never justifiable in itself.... (Michael and Adler 1933, p. 344)

In retrospect this is crude and mechanistic. The argument in some ways is based on a definitional stop similar to the one sometimes used by utilitarians as a defense against the punishment of the innocent critique. For Michael and Adler, a theory of punishment is persuasive only to the extent it reconciles with the criminal law aim of "the common good." Retributivism doesn't, so it isn't.

These, however, were intelligent, well-educated, and sophisticated people who reflected the ethos of their time. They were far from alone.

In 1937, Jerome Michael and his then young colleague Herbert Wechsler published a landmark article, *The Rationale of the Law of Homicide*. Concerning normative analysis of punishment, three things stand out. First, they explain at the outset that there are "two competing normative hypotheses which merit serious attention" (p. 1262). One might expect them to be retributivism and utilitarianism. Instead, they are "(1) the so-called classical hypothesis...that the dominant purpose of treatment should be the deterrence of potential offenders; (2) the positivist hypothesis which dominates contemporary criminological thought, that incapacitation and reformation should be the dominant treatment ends" (ibid). Second, they relegate retributivism to a footnote and discuss it then only to defend Bentham and others against the "improper" and inaccurate allegation that, like Kant and Hegel, they believed that punishment "*should be* retributive." When discussing what should or may happen to convicted murderers, they primarily discuss "treatment," not "punishment."[18]

A few years later, Michael and Wechsler's criminal law casebook, *Criminal Law and Its Administration* (1940), appeared. It has been described as "the template for all contemporary criminal law casebooks and perhaps the modern casebook more generally" (Simon 2003, p. 248). By this time, their views on punishment had hardened: "Since punishment consists in the infliction of pain it is, apart from its consequences, an evil; Consequently, it is good and, therefore, just only if and to the degree it serves the common good" (Michael and Wechsler 1940, p. 9). Anyone looking up "punishment" in the index finds this: "see Treatment."

Michael and Wechsler, though important, were not the only influential American law school professors or case-book editors. Harvard law professors Livingston Hall and Sheldon Glueck in their *Cases and Materials on Criminal Law* (1940) argue that "Official social institutions should not be predicated upon the destructive emotion of vengeance, which is not only the expression of an infantile way of solving a problem, but unjust and destructive of the purpose of protecting society" (1940, p. 20). In a later edition, they observe that "the *corrective theory*, based upon a conception of multiple causation and curative-rehabilitative treatment, should clearly predominate in legislation and in judicial and administrative practices" (1951, p. 14).

Of course, sentiment was not monolithic. John Barker Waite in his 1947 volume described retributivism as a "vindictive philosophy, consistent with the biblical eye for an eye and tooth for a tooth, paraphrased by the childish, 'Tit for tat; tit for tat; kill my dog, I'll kill your cat'" (pp. 3–4). Albert Harno (1933) did not express his own views in four editions of a casebook over a quarter century, but began each with a long excerpt from Saleilles' *The Individualization of Punishment* (1911). Orvill Snyder, by contrast, in his 1953 volume observed—tentatively—that the purpose of punishment, "it is said...is to satisfy the community's outraged feelings...If the feelings are considered to be merely human anger and resentment, this view in reality sets forth the satisfaction of public demand as the purpose of punishment, for which, historically, and in democratic society, there is something to be said" (p. 22).

Sheldon Glueck (1952 [1927–28]) took the next step. For serious crimes, he proposed, sentencing authority should be taken from judges and given to a Socio-Penal Commission composed of experts (including sociologists, psychologists, and psychiatrists). If sentences are meant primarily to be rehabilitative and incapacitative, judges were not qualified to set them. Expert and scientific knowledge was required. For lesser crimes, the judge could impose probation or jail sentences up to a year. For serious crimes, sentencing would be entirely indeterminate. The commission would set, oversee, and if need be modify a treatment plan for each offender. A treatment plan would be set for each. Glueck makes his case and sets out and addresses major objections.

---

[18] The relevant major section of the article is entitled "The Treatment of Persons who Commit Criminal Homicides."

Glueck was convinced. So was the Committee of United States Judges appointed by U.S. Supreme Court Chief Justice Harlan Fiske Stone in 1940. The committee observed that judges lack sufficient knowledge of defendants and also lack expertise in criminology, and that they cannot know how imprisonment will affect a prisoner. The committee proposed in all cases in which a year or more imprisonment might be ordered that the case be sent for three months to a classification center where "doctors, psychiatrists, sociologists, ministers, and criminologists" would prepare a recommendation for the judge (Laws 1955, pp. 444–45).

Michael and Wechsler were open to the suggestion: "[I]t is desirable that the problems of treatment be left for the most part to some permanent agency, experienced in deciding such questions. The crucial question is whether that agency should be [a court], or some body, a dispositional body of some sort, specially constituted for the purpose. There is much to be said for either course" (1937, p. 1311).

Glueck's "socio-penal commission" probably marks the high water mark of concrete policy proposals predicated on consequentialist thinking, but other mainstream figures proposed to go further. Barbara Wootton, a famous British social worker and magistrate, observed that the extension of strict liability in the criminal law would be "a sensible and indeed inevitable measure of adaptation to requirements of the modern world" (Wootton 1963, p. 57). The question of whether the offender had a guilty mind was "in the first instance irrelevant." Later, she wrote, "after what is now known as a conviction, the presence or absence of a guilty intention is all-important for its effect on the appropriate measures to be taken to prevent a recurrence of the forbidden act" (Wootton 1963, pp. 52–53). Karl Menninger, director of what was then America's most famous psychiatric clinic, was also prepared to do away with existing criminal justice institutions and atavistic ideas about punishment. They should be replaced, he wrote, with a system based on "a comprehensive, constructive social attitude—therapeutic in some instances, restraining in some instances, but preventive in its social impact" (Menninger 1966, p. 280).

The slightly less ambitious views represented by Michael, Adler, Wechsler, Glueck, and Hall were predominant.[19] In due course, Wechsler became the Reporter for the *Model Penal Code.* In 1949, when work began, Wechsler's ideas were mainstream, and they continued to be in 1962. In retrospect, they were already under assault.

C. The Modern Transitional Period, 1960–2010

It is customary to describe the shift away from indeterminate sentencing policies and consequentialist ideas as something that happened in the mid-1970s. The abolition

---

[19] Even people usually seen as critics of the rehabilitative/utilitarian approach shared most of its policy preferences. Harvard Law School professor Henry M. Hart, in a famous 1958 article, argued that the criminal law and punishment have multiple purposes—treatment, incapacitation, deterrence, retribution—and that they must all be taken into account. However, showing the persuasive force of the prevailing ethos, he supported many of what are now seen as radical features of indeterminate sentencing: a presumption against imposition of prison sentences; no limits on minimum sentences including probation in cases of murder, and "in an ideal system" a parole board that had complete control over release dates (Hart 1958, p. 440).

of parole in Maine and California heralded the change, and seminal books on policy (Frankel 1972) and principle (Kleinig 1973; Norval Morris 1974; von Hirsch 1976) date from that period. Ideas about punishment, however, were already in flux.

Change was in the air. The first people on whose antennae it registered were literary figures. Anthony Burgess's dystopian, graphically violent, novel *A Clockwork Orange*, published in 1962, and made by Stanley Kubrick into a celebrated 1971 film, is an example. It tells the story of Alex, a sociopathic fifteen-year-old who with his mates delights in recreational rape and mayhem. In prison for murder, Alex kills a cellmate. Rather than face a second trial, he agrees to participate in the "Ludovico treatment," a program of drug-assisted aversive conditioning that makes him physically sick whenever he thinks of sex or violence. No longer dangerous, Alex is released. Eventually, having become a political symbol of authoritarian excess, he is reconditioned and restored to his version of normalcy, to age out of violent adolescence into conformity or to continue his depredations, depending on which of two versions of the book one reads.[20]

Burgess regarded *A Clockwork Orange* as one of his lesser novels, but it was and is his best-known. Writing a quarter century later, he admitted that it would be "priggish or Pollyannaish to deny that my intention...was to titillate the nastier propensities of readers...But the book does have a moral lesson, and it is the weary traditional one of the fundamental importance of moral choice. It is because this lesson tends to stick out like a sore thumb that I tend to disparage *A Clockwork Orange* as a work too didactic to be artistic" (1986, p. ix–x).

More than a decade earlier, C.S. Lewis, in our time best-known as author of *The Chronicles of Narnia*, but in his as a British public intellectual and Christian apologist, had developed the same themes. In 1949, in an obscure Australian journal,[21] he decried the "humanitarian theory of punishment" and urged a return to the "traditional or Retributive theory." He argued that "humanitarian" rationales removed the concepts of moral culpability and proportionality from punishment; treated offenders as if they were children, imbeciles, or animals rather than morally autonomous adults; risked injustices predicated on both well-meaning and tyrannical motives; and necessarily authorized the punishment of the innocent.

Lewis and Burgess identified most of the critical themes that others later developed, but they were not alone in being ahead of their time. Philosophers also sensed the change in the direction of the penal winds, and tried in various ways to move beyond the centuries-old retributive/utilitarian stand-off. In a famous essay, John Rawls attempted to demonstrate that utilitarian theories of punishment are reconcilable with ideas of individual justice (Rawls 1955). He argued that a systematic program of punishment of innocents, which he called "telishment," would be bound to fail and generate unacceptable levels of insecurity, and so was not inherently allowed by utilitarianism.

---

[20] The American version ends with Alex, thinking of delicious depredations, ominously intoning, "I was cured all right." The English version has an additional chapter in which Alex, tired of violence, reflects on the human condition and the possible joys of fatherhood.

[21] Why? He explained, "You may ask why I send this to an Australian periodical. The reason is simple and perhaps worth recording: I can get no hearing for it in England" (1970 [1949], p. 294).

He attempted to resolve the more general utilitarian/retributive stand-off by arguing that legislators should be governed by utilitarian aims of aggregate public good and that judges should base their decisions on ideas about deserved punishment.

Edmund Pincoffs, Rawls's student, published his Ph.D. thesis, *The Rationale of Legal Punishment* in 1966. It was the first major modern American book on the philosophy of punishment and systematically considered, and generally endorsed, Rawls's argument that retribution and utilitarianism may only apparently be irreconcilable because different normative logics may apply to different institutions of government.

In England, Oxford jurisprudence professor Herbert Hart in 1959 gave a presidential address to the Aristotelian Society entitled "Prolegomenon to the Principle of Punishment" which attempted to show that seemingly irreconcilable retributive and utilitarian theories can be reconciled. Punishment involves a series of key questions, Hart argued, including its overriding aim, who may be punished, and how much. A persuasive punishment theory could coherently address different issues in different ways. For Hart's "mixed theory," the prevention of crime was the aim of punishment but retributive issues of moral responsibility and desert were pertinent to the questions of who may be punished and how much.

Practical and policy problems with indeterminate sentencing were also being raised well before the mid-1970s. University of Chicago law professor Francis A. Allen (1964), for example, wrote a series of articles in the 1950s and 1960s that developed critiques of indeterminate and individualized sentencing. In a 1959 article, he argued that confidence in rehabilitative sentencing might be misplaced because of insufficient knowledge and dangers of abuse of the broad powers given to judges, parole boards, and others. Like C. S. Lewis, he worried about the moral appropriateness of attempting to coerce changes in human beings.

A few years later, Kenneth Culp Davis (1969), the leading American academic specialist in administrative law, began paying attention to the criminal justice system. He noted that there was no administrative law of criminal justice. No one could appeal a decision by a prosecutor, to a court or to a prosecutor's superior, and the same thing was true of parole boards (and as a practical matter of sentencing judges). Separation of powers notions made the prosecutor immune from judicial review, and the logic of individualized sentencing supported the autonomy of judges and parole boards. Davis insisted that the rule of law should apply to the criminal justice agencies and that a variety of administrative devices should be developed to structure, guide, and check discretionary decision-making.

Two years later, in a 1971 speech at the University of Cincinnati Law School, federal district court judge Marvin Frankel proposed that the rule of law be extended to judges also. Decrying what he called judicial lawlessness, by which he meant that judges were subject to no rules or standards in setting sentences, Frankel's argument was expressed in the title of his book: *Criminal Sentences: Law without Order* (1972). Unless there were rules for sentences, he reasoned, there could be no appeals of sentences (appellate judges would lack criteria for identifying unjust sentences), and without appeals there was no way to bring the rule of law to sentencing. He proposed that guidelines for sentencing be created.

University of Chicago law professor Norval Morris, in his *The Future of Imprisonment* (1974), proposed a theory of "limited retributivism" that combined retributive and utilitarian elements. Culpability would set upper and lower bounds of justifiable sentences. Bentham's parsimony principle required that the lowest just sentence be imposed unless there was a very good reason to intrude more deeply into the offender's life. Accepting C. S. Lewis's argument that respect for human autonomy forbade attempting to change people against their will, and acknowledging emerging skepticism about the effectiveness of rehabilitative programs, Morris insisted that offenders not be coerced into treatment. A few years later, Andrew von Hirsch's *Doing Justice* (1976) appeared and put "just deserts" into the criminal justice lexicon, and with it the idea, harking back to Beccaria, Kant, and Hegel, that punishments should be proportioned to the severity of the crime.

No one should have been surprised when the sentencing reform movement took hold, though the changes it presaged seemed radical at the time. And many of them repudiated indeterminate and individualized sentencing and their normative premises. In the 1970s and 1980s, parole and sentencing guidelines proliferated, together with prosecutorial guidelines in a few places. New sentencing statutes, including many mandatory minimum sentence laws, were enacted. Parole release was eliminated in a third of the states and the federal system. In the 1980s, truth-in-sentencing laws requiring that prisoners serve 85 percent of the announced sentence were enacted in half of the states, and in the 1990s half of the states enacted three-strikes laws and many enacted LWOP laws.[22]

In the 1940s it would not have been unreasonable to say that there was a prevailing view of punishment: most people may have retributive instincts, but they are unworthy; offenders can be rehabilitated; punishments should be individualized; imposition of punishments not related to rehabilitation, incapacitation, or deterrence is unjust.

In the late 1970s and for a short time thereafter, a prevailing view can be described: punishments should be proportioned to the seriousness of crimes; fairness requires that standards or guidelines for sentencing should be established; punishments, particularly prison sentences, should not be based on rehabilitative considerations; offenders should not be coerced into participation in treatment programs. Members of state and federal sentencing commissions debated whether they should adopt "just deserts" or "modified just deserts" guidelines as an official governing principle. States amended their criminal laws to specify that punishment is the primary purpose of sentencing (von Hirsch, Knapp, and Tonry 1986).

In retrospect, there either was no prevailing view after the collapse of indeterminate sentencing, or there was one but it broke down within two decades. Most of the major sentencing law changes through the mid-1980s were at least broadly consistent with retributive ideas whether in their stricter "just deserts" or their looser limiting retributivist formulations. Afterward they were not.

---

[22] Detailed summaries of these developments can be found—through their publication dates—in Blumstein et al. (1983), Tonry (1986), and Tonry (1996). There have been comparatively few major changes since the mid-1990s. A few states have tweaked mandatory minimum laws to narrow their reach or make them slightly less rigid and most states with sentencing guidelines have tinkered with them. The period of wholesale enactment of severe sentencing laws seems over, at least for now, but no movement for their repeal has taken shape.

Proportionality is a central idea in retributive thinking. On the law-and-order side of the political spectrum, many of the most famous initiatives from the mid-1980s through the mid-1990s were flatly incompatible with retributivist ideas. Mandatory minimum sentence laws for drug trafficking required imposition of ten-, twenty-, and thirty-year minimum sentences, even though many people convicted of serious violent crimes received much less harsh sentences. Three-strikes laws called for comparably long prison sentences, or longer, for people convicted for the third time of a felony; sometimes as in California, the third strike could be a trivial offense.

On the opposite end of the political spectrum, beginning in the 1990s and reaching critical mass in the 1980s and 1990s, new paradigms of punishment were proposed. Advocates of therapeutic jurisprudence proposed that all legal processes and rules be assessed in terms of whether they were therapeutic, and changed when they were not (Wexler 1995, 2008; Winick 1997). Advocates of restorative justice proposed that punishment be made reintegrative rather than destructive, that crimes be reconceptualized as conflicts, and that the aim of punishment or punishment-like processes should be to rebuild relationships among offenders, victims, their personal support networks, and their communities (Braithwaite 2001). Advocates of community or communitarian justice emphasized that human beings cannot exist outside of social communities and in various ways called for increased emphasis on the community in analyses of crime and punishment (e.g., Lacey 1988; Clear and Karp 2001). None of these new punishment paradigms give a central place to ideas about proportionate punishment.

II. Punishment in Principle

Kant believed that the capacity to make moral choices is what makes human beings human. Respect for the moral autonomy of human beings, he believed, requires that they be punished in a way that is commensurate with the seriousness of their crimes, even if nothing (else, he would say) of value would be accomplished. Bentham believed that respect for offenders' capacity for happiness required that they be punished as much as could be justified by the avoidance of unhappiness to others, but no more. An offender's happiness counts as much as anyone else's. If punishment produces no practical benefits, it cannot be justified at all. Kant, in his hypothetical about the dissolution of an island society, insisted that the last murderer be executed. Bentham would have said there was no point and that the execution was not justifiable.

Both Kant and Bentham cannot, in some absolute sense, be correct. Or, put differently, although some reasonable men and women may believe that Kant is correct in an absolute sense, other equally reasonable men and women do not. Ditto Bentham. That gap probably cannot be bridged, however much proponents of mixed theories may try.

Both frameworks, however, provide coherent, articulable bases for assessing whether particular punishment policies, practices, or decisions are just. So, perhaps with less clarity, do many other normative frameworks. Proponents of limiting retributivism, Scandinavian asymmetric proportionality theory, and modern commensurate desert theories have bases for saying that some punishments are unjust. To limiting retributivists, punishment above the upper bound is undeserved and thus unjust, as are punishments above the lower bound unless a good consequentialist reason is given (Morris 1974; Frase 2004). Scandinavian asymmetric proportionality focuses mostly on the upper bound (Lappi-Seppälä 2001). Commensurate desert theorists are more concerned with proportionality than with absolute severity of punishment, but allow for consequentialist considerations to influence the overall severity of the punishment system (von Hirsch and Ashworth 2005). Proponents of "empirical desert" insist on ordinal proportionality, but argue that punishment must be largely consistent with widely held intuitions if law is to be morally persuasive and seen as legitimate (Robinson 2008). For any offense, adherents of all four views would agree that some punishments are unjust because they are more severe than is permitted by the upper bound of what is deserved relative to the seriousness of an offender's offense. Some proponents of restorative justice likewise have bases for identifying unjust punishment: those that do nothing to rebuild relationships among offenders, victims, and communities (e.g., Walgrave 2004) and those that unnecessarily stigmatize and shame the offender (e.g., Braithwaite and Pettit 1990, 2001; Braithwaite 2002).

Moral clarity about punishment has largely been absent in recent decades from the United States and England. Policies have been adopted, and people punished under them, that cannot be justified under any of the normative frameworks developed in the past two centuries. California's three-strikes law provides stark examples. One recent U.S. Supreme Court decision, *Ewing v. California*, 583 U.S. 11 (2003), for example held that a twenty-five years to life sentence for a third strike consisting of theft of three golf clubs did not violate the U.S. Constitution's prohibition against cruel and unusual punishments. For Kant, that sentence would be unjust because it is grossly disproportionate to the severity of the offense.

For Bentham, that punishment would be unjust because it was excessive under either of two utilitarian proportionality doctrines (Frase 2009). The ends-benefits test could not be met, because it could not be demonstrated that preventing subsequent thefts by a not-very-prolific offender would prevent more unhappiness than the offender's spending the rest of his life behind bars would cause. The alternative-means test could not be met, because it could not be shown that some other approach would not prevent an equal amount of unhappiness at less cost to offenders.

Ewing's punishment could not be justified under the three mixed theories or restorative justice principles. For limiting retributivists and proponents of asymmetric proportionality, it exceeds the upper bound of punishments allowable for an offense of that severity. For desert theory, it violates proportionality limits: it is harsher than punishments imposed for more serious crimes. For proponents of restorative justice, the law's rigidity and the punishment's severity neither respects the offender's dominion nor allows for more nuanced and socially constructive outcomes.

Many modern American and English laws fall prey to similar analyses. Examples include many mandatory minimum sentence laws, LWOP laws, and laws allowing indefinite confinement of "dangerous" offenders. It is hard to make a principled moral case, for example, for laws that punish sellers of a few grams of crack much more severely than people who commit serious violent or sexual assaults.

I give these examples not only to show that the laws and punishments just described are unjust under most traditional conceptions of just punishment, whether retributive, consequential, mixed, or restorative, but to demonstrate why it is regrettable that contemporary conceptions of just punishment are at best muddled and morally incoherent and at worst non-existent. The justifications given for such laws and punishments, including explicitly by the U.S. Supreme Court in *Ewing*, are usually expressed not in moral terms but in democratic ones. The people's elected representatives enacted them and it is not the courts' business, the Supreme Court says, to second guess the public will. That many such laws are enacted for emotional, political, or ideological reasons (e.g., Beckett 1997), and that the public is vastly misinformed about the criminal justice system and the punishments it imposes (e,g., Roberts et al. 2002), are seen as immaterial. Justice by plebiscite, however, is not a normative conception of justice.

We need better ways to talk and think about what may justly be done to and with offenders. Conceivably, though I doubt it, principled cases can be made for some or all of the laws and punishments described in the last few paragraphs. Someone, however, needs to do the work required to make those cases in normative terms. The works reprinted in this book embody many serious efforts by serious people to devise different ways to talk about and understand punishment. Philosophers and other theorists do not write laws and never will, and they will never agree among themselves. They can, however, help people who make laws and apply them to think more clearly and consistently and modestly about what they do, and at what costs to other human beings. That would be a good thing.

REFERENCES

Allen, Francis A. 1959. "Legal Values and the Rehabilitative Ideal." *Journal of Criminal Law, Criminology, and Police Science* 50:226–32.

———. 1964. "Legal Values and the Rehabilitative Ideal." *The Borderland of Criminal Justice: Essays in Law and Criminology*. Chicago: University of Chicago Press.

Alschuler, Albert W. 1978. "Sentencing Reform and Prosecutorial power." *University of Pennsylvania Law Review* 126:550–77.

———. 2000. *Law without Values: The Life, Work, and Legacy of Justice Holmes*. Chicago:University of Chicago Press.

American Friends Service Committee. 1971. *Struggle for Justice: A Report on Crime and Punishment in America*. New York: Hill & Wang.

American Law Institute. 1962. *Model Penal Code*. Proposed Official Draft. Philadelphia: American Law Institute.

Australian Law Reform Commission. 1980. *Sentencing of Criminal Offenders*. Cranberra: Australian Government Publishing Service.

Beccaria, Cesare. 1764. *Dei delitti e delle pene (On Crimes and Punishments)* translated by Aaron Thomas and Jeremy Parzen. Toronto: University of Toronto Press.

Beckett, Katherine. 1997. *Making Crime Pay: Law and Order in Contemporary American Politics*. New York, Oxford University Press.

Bentham, Jeremy. 1970. "The Utilitarian Theory of Punishment." In Jeremy Bentham, J.H. Burns, and H.L.A. Hart, *An Introduction to Principles of Morals and Legislation*. London: Athlone.

―――. 2008 [1830]. *The Rationale of Punishment*. Amherst, N.Y.: Kessinger.

Blackstone, William. 1979 [1769]. *Commentaries on the Laws of England*. Volume 4. Chicago: University of Chicago Press.

Blumstein, Alfred, Jacqueline Cohen, Susan Martin, and Michael Tonry, eds. 1983. *Research on Sentencing: The Search for Reform*. Washington, D. C.: National Academy Press.

Boswell, John. 1980. *Christianity, Social Tolerance, and Homosexuality*. Chicago: University Press.

Braithwaite, John. 2001. *Restorative Justice and Responsive Regulation*. New York: Oxford University Press.

―――. 2002. "In Search of Restorative Jurisprudence." In *Restorative Justice and the Law*, edited by Lode Walgrave. Cullompton, Devon: Willan.

Braithwaite, John, and Philip Pettit. 1990. *Not Just Deserts : A Republican Theory of Criminal Justice*. New York: Oxford University Press.

―――2001. "Republicanism and Restorative Justice: An Explanatory and Normative Connection." In *Restorative Justice: Philosophy to Practice*, edited by John Braithwaite and Heather Strang. Burlington, Vermont: Ashgate.

Burgess, Anthony. 1962. *A Clockwork Orange*. London: Heinemann.

Burgess, Anthony. 1986. "Introduction: A Clockwork Orange Resucked." *A Clockwork Orange*. New York: W.W. Norton.

Canadian Sentencing Commission. 1987. *Sentencing Reform: A Canadian Approach*. Ottawa: Canadian Government Publishing Centre.

Clear, Todd R., and David E. Karp. 2001. *The Community Justice Ideal: Preventing Crime and Achieving Justice*. Boulder, Colorado: Westview.

Cohen, Morris R. 1940. "Moral Aspects of the Criminal Law." *Yale Law Journal* 49: 987–1026.

Cox, Edward. 1877. *The Principles of Punishment*. London: Law Times Office.

Davis, Kenneth Culp. 1969. *Discretionary Justice: A Preliminary Inquiry*. Baton Rouge: Louisiana State University Press.

Duff, Antony. 2001. *Punishment, Communication, and Community*. New York: Oxford University Press.

Dworkin, Ronald. 1977. *Taking Rights Seriously*. Cambridge: Harvard University Press.

Ewing, A.C. 1929. *The Morality of Punishment*. London: Kegan Paul, Trench, Trubner.

Fletcher, George. 1978. *Rethinking Criminal Law*. Boston: Little Brown.

Foucault, Michel. 1977. *Discipline and Punish: The Birth of the Prison*. New York: Pantheon.

Frankel, Marvel. 1972. *Criminal Sentences—Law without Order*. New York: Hill & Wang.

Frase, Richard. 2004. "Limiting Retributivism." In *The Future of Imprisonment*, edited by Michael Tonry. New York: Oxford University Press.

―――. 2009. "Limiting Excessive Prison Sentencing." *University of Pennsylvania Journal of Constitutional Law* 11(1): 39–72.

Freiberg, Arie. 2001. "Three Strikes and You're Out—It's Not Cricket: Colonization and Resistance in Australian Sentencing." In *Sentencing and Sanctions in Western Countries*, edited by Michael Tonry and Richard S. Frase. New York: Oxford University Press.

Gilmore, Grant. 1974. *The Death of Contract*. Columbus: Ohio State University Press.

Glueck, Sheldon. 1952 [1927–28]. "Principles of a Rational Penal Code." *Crime and Correction: Selected Papers*. Boston: Addison-Wesley.

Hall, Livingston, with Sheldon Glueck. 1940. *Cases and Materials on Criminal Law*. St. Paul, MN: West.

Hall, Livingston, and Sheldon Glueck. 1951. *Cases on Criminal Law and its Enorcement.* St. Paul, MN: West.

Hrrison, Ross. 1995. "Jeremy Bentham." In *The Oxford Companion to Philosophy,* edited by Ted Honderich. Oxford: Oxford University Press.

Harno, Albert J. 1933. *Cases and Materials on Criminal Law and Procedure.* Chicago: Callaghan.

Hart, Henry M. 1958. "The Aims of the Criminal Law." *Law and Contemporary Problems* 23:401–42.

Hart, H.L.A. 1959. "Prolegomenon to the Principles of Punishment." *Proceedings of the Aristotelian Society,* New Series 60:1–26.

———. 1968. *Punishment and Responsibility: Essays in the Philosophy of Law.* Oxford: Oxford University Press

Hegel, G.W.F. 1991. "Wrong [Das Unrecht]." *Elements of the Philosophy of Right,* edited by Allen W. Wood, translated by H.B. Nisbet. Cambridge: Cambridge University Press.

Holmes, Olive Wendell. 1881. *The Common Law.* Boston: Little Brown.

Home Office. 1991. *Crime, Justice and Protecting the Public.* Cm 965. London: Her Majesty's Printing Office.

———. 2001. *Making Punishments Work: Report of a Review of the Sentencing Framework for England and Wales.* London: Home Office Communication Directorate.

Honderich, Ted. 2005. *Punishment: The Supposed Justifications Revisited.* Revised edition. Ann Arbor: Pluto Press.

Kant, Immanuel. 1965 [1798] "The Penal Law and the Law of Pardon." *The Metaphysical Elements of Justice,* translated by John Ladd. Indianapolis: Bobbs-Merrill.

Kleinig, John. 1973. *Punishment and Desert.* New York: Springer.

Kolber, Adam. 2009. "The Subjective Experience of Punishment." *Columbia Law Review* 109:182–236.

Lacey, Nicola. 1988. *State Punishment: Political Principles and Community Values.* New York: Routledge.

Lappi-Seppälä, Tapio. 2001. "Sentencing and Punishment in Finland: The Decline of the Repressive Ideal." In *Sentencing and Sanctions in Western Countries,* edited by Michael Tonry and Richard S. Frase. New York: Oxford University Press.

Laws, Bolitha J. 1955. "It is the Sentence of the Court…" *Collier's,* October 14, 1955, pp. 40–45.

Lewis, C. S. 1949. "The Humanitarian Theory of Punishment." *20th Century: An Australian Quarterly Review.* 3(3):5–12 (reprinted in *God in the Dock: Essays on Theology and Ethics (1970),* edited by Walter Hooper. Grand Rapids MI: Eerdmans).

Martinson, Robert L. 1974. "What Works?—Questions and Answers about Prison Reform." *Public Interest* 35(2):22–54.

McCloskey, H.J. 1968. "A Non-utilitarian Approach to Punishment." In *Contemporary Utilitarianism,* edited by Michael D. Bayles. New York: Doubleday.

Menninger, Karl. 1946. *The Human Mind.* 3d ed. New York: Alfred Knopf.

———. 1966. *The Crime of Punishment.* New York: Viking.

Michael, Jerome, and Mortimer Adler. 1933. *Crime, Law, and Social Science.* New York: Harcourt Press.

Michael, Jerome, and Herbert Wechsler. 1937. "A Rationale of the Law of Homicide." *Columbia Law Review* 37: 701–61 (Part I), 1261–1335 (Part II).

————. 1940. *Criminal Law and Its Administration*. Chicago: Foundation Press.

Morris, Herbert. 1968. "Persons and Punishment." *Monist* 52:475–501.

Morris, Norval. 1974. *The Future of Imprisonment*. Chicago: University of Chicago Press.

Murphy, Jeffrey. 1973. "Marxism and Retribution." *Philosophy and Public Affairs* 2: 217–43.

Musto, David. 1987. *The American Disease: Origins of Narcotic Control*. Revised edition (originally published 1973). New Haven: Yale University Press.

Newburn, Tim. 2007. " 'Tough on Crime': Penal Policy in England and Wales." In *Crime, Punishment, and Politics in Comparative Perspective*, edited by Michael Tonry. Volume 36 of *Crime and Justice: A Review of Research*, edited by Michael Tonry. Chicago: University of Chicago Press.

Paley, William. 1788. *The Principles of Moral and Political Philosophy*. 6th ed. London: Printed by J. Davis for R. Faulder.

Pincoffs, Edmund. 1966. *The Rationale of Legal Punishment*. Atlantic Highlands, N.J.: Humanities Press.

Posner, Richard A. 2007. *Economic Analysis of Law*, 7th ed. New York: Aspen.

Pratt, John. 2006. "The Dark Side of Paradise: Explaining New Zealand's History of High Imprisonment." *British Journal of Criminology* 46(4):541–60.

Primoratz, Igor. 1989. *Justifying Legal Punishment*. Atlantic Highlands, NJ: Humanities Press.

Quinton, Anthony M. 1969. "On Punishment." In *The Philosophy of Punishment*, edited by H.B. Acton. London: St Martin's Press.

Rawls, John. 1955. "Two Concepts of Rules." *The Philosophical Review* 44:3–13.

————. 1958. "Justice as Fairness." *The Philosophical Review* 67(2):164–94.

————. 1971. *A Theory of Justice*. Cambridge: Harvard University Press.

Robbins, Lionel. 1938. "Interpersonal Comparisons of Utility: A Consensus." *The Economic Journal* XLVIII:635–41.

Roberts, Julian V., Loretta J. Stalans, David Indermaur, and Mike Hough. 2002. *Penal Populism and Public Opinion*. New York: Oxford University Press.

Robinson, Paul. 1987. "Hybrid Principles for the Distribution of Criminal Sanctions." *Northwestern Law Review* 82: 19–42.

Robinson, Paul. 2008. *Distuributive Principles of Criminal Law*. New York: Oxford University Press.

Rothman, David J. 1971. *The Discovery of the Asylum: Social Order and Disorder in the New Republic*. Boston: Little Brown.

————. 1980. *Conscience and Convenience*. Boston: Little Brown.

Saleilles, Raymond. 1911. *The Individualization of Punishment*. Boston: Little Brown.

Simon, Jonathan. 2003. "Wechsler's Century and Ours: Reforming Criminal Law in a Time of Shifting Rationalities of Government." *Buffalo Criminal Law Review* 7:247–74.

Smart, J.J.C. 1973. "An Outline of a System of Utilitarian Ethics." In *Utilitarianism— For and Against*, by J.J.C. Smart and Bernard Williams. Cambridge: Cambridge University Press.

Snyder, Orvill C. 1953. *An Introduction to Criminal Justice and its Enforcement*. Englewood Cliffs, N.J.: Prentice-Hall.

Stephen, James Fitzjames. 1883. *A History of the Criminal Law of England*. Volume 2. London: Macmillan.

Ten, C.L. 1987. *Crime, Guilt, and Punishment*. Oxford: Oxford University Press.

Tonry, Michael. 1986. *Sentencing Reform Impacts*. Washington, D.C.: U.S. Government Printing Office.

Tonry, Michael. 2004. *Thinking about Crime: Sense and Sensibility in American Penal Culture.* New York: Oxford University Press.

Tonry, Michael. 1996. *Sentencing Matters.* New York: Oxford University Press.

von Hirsch, Andrew. 1976. *Doing Justice.* New York: Hill & Wang.

von Hirsch, Andrew. 1998. "Proportionate Sentences: A Desert Perspective." In *Principled Sentencing: Readings on Theory and Policy,* edited by Andrew von Hirsch and Andrew Ashworth, 2d ed. Oxford: Hart.

von Hirsch, Andrew, and Andrew Ashworth. 2005. *Proportionate Sentencing: Exploring the Principles.* Oxford: Oxford University Press.

von Hirsch, Andrew, Kay Knapp, and Michael Tonry. 1986. *The Sentencing Commission and its Guidelines.* Boston: Northeastern University Press.

Waite, John Barker. 1947. *The Criminal Law and its Enforcement.* 3d ed. Chicago: Foundation.

Walgrave, Lode. 2004. "Restoration in Youth Justice." In *Youth Crime and Youth Justice: Comparative and Cross-national Perspectives,* edited by Michael Tonry and Anthony N. Doob. Volume 31 of *Crime and Justice: A Review of Research,* edited by Michael Tonry. Chicago: University of Chicago Press.

Walker, Nigel. 1969. *Sentencing in a Rational Society.* London: Allen Lane.

Walker, Nigel. 1991. *Why Punish?* Oxford: Oxford University Press.

Walker, Nigel. 1999. *Aggravation, Mitigation, and Mercy in English Criminal Law.* London: Blackwell.

Webster, Cheryl Marie, and Anthony N. Doob. 2007. "Punitive Trends and Stable Imprisonment Rates in Canada." In *Crime, Punishment, and Politics in Comparative Perspective,* edited by Michael Tonry. Volume 36 of *Crime and Justice: A Review of Research,* edited by Michael Tonry. Chicago: University of Chicago Press.

Wexler, David. 1995. "Reflections on the Scope of Therapeutic Jurisprudence." *Psychology, Public Policy, and Law* 1(1): 230–36.

Wexler, David. 2008. *Rehabilitating Lawyers: Principles of Therapeutic Jurisprudence for Criminal Law Practice.* Durham, N.C.: Carolina Academic Press.

Winick, Bruce J. 1997. "The Jurisprudence of Therapeutic Jurisprudence." *Psychology, Public Policy, and Law* 3(1): 184–206.

Wines, E.C., ed. 1871. *Transactions of the National Congress on Penitentiary and Reformatory Discipline.* Albany: Weed, Parsons and Company. (Reprinted in 1970 by the American Correctional Association, Boulder, Colorado).

Wootton, Barbara. 1963. *Crime and the Criminal Law.* London: Stevens.

I

CLASSICAL THEORIES

For two centuries, retributive and consequentialist ways of thinking about punishment were generally discussed as if they are irreconcilable. There seemed to be only three positions: one of those two, or a muddled view that everything—retribution, deterrence, incapacitation, rehabilitation, moral education—was pertinent, and that relative emphases could be sorted out only case-by-case. In principle, consequentialists had the upper hand until the mid-1970s. In practice, muddlers had it. Retributivists were on the sidelines.

The writings in this part include selections from foundational works by Kant (chapter 1 in this volume), Hegel (chapter 2), and Bentham (chapter 3). They are not easy, but they reward careful reading. All three tried to think broadly about the justification of punishment and to work out practical implications of their ideas.

This often does not come through in contemporary writings about them. They are often represented by short excerpts that suggest that Kant is committed to a remarkably rigid conception of punishment, that Hegel is impenetrable, and that Bentham's exquisite and intricate proposals are slightly mad. All three to the contrary discuss practical issues that are as timely now as when they wrote, and that in some ways remain ahead of our times.

For all three, proportionality in punishment was essential in a just system of punishment. Kant and Hegel famously insisted that punishments be apportioned to the degree of the offender's wrongdoing. Bentham's insistence on proportionality is less well known. His proportionality principles, based on the premise that no more punishment should be imposed than is absolutely necessary—Richard Frase (2009 [chapter 17 in this volume]) calls them "ends-benefits" and "alternative-means" proportionality—have largely disappeared from view. A punishment could be disproportionately severe because it would cause more harm than it would prevent (ends-benefits) or because the end being sought could be achieved in some other way that caused less harm to offenders (alternative means). For Bentham, disproportionate punishments in either sense were "evil" (his term) because they inflicted unnecessary pain on offenders.

Supreme Court Justice Antonin Scalia, in his opinion in *Ewing v. California*, 583 U.S. 11 (2003), upholding the constitutionality of a 25-years-to-life sentence for theft of three golf clubs, observed that proportionality is a retributive concept. Since legislatures have not enacted retribution as the governing principle for punishment, he acerbically noted, the disproportionality of Ewing's sentence did not make it a cruel and unusual punishment under the Eighth Amendment of the U.S. Constitution. Scalia, however, was wrong. Bentham would have disapproved Ewing's sentence every bit as much as Kant and Hegel would, but for different reasons.

Kant and Bentham, despite the stark differences between the retributive and utilitarian premises on which their theories were based, insisted that decisions about punishments in individual cases must take account of their effects on the offender, subjectively considered. A series of hypothetical cases Kant discusses makes it clear that to him the effect of a punishment on an individual offender is a morally necessary part of the calculus of just punishment. The notion that offenders' "sensibilities" must be taken into account in fashioning a punishment was a major element of Bentham's view.

To proponents of indeterminate and individualized sentencing in the United States, fashioning the punishment to fit the offender's subjective circumstances was the goal of the enterprise. Most modern retributivists disagree and propose sentencing systems in which punishment is based primarily on the objective criteria of the offender's crime, and to a lesser extent (if at all) his or her prior convictions. Much opposition by judges and prosecutors to modern sentencing laws, by contrast, derives from their belief that they are too rigid and do not allow meaningful differences between offenders and their circumstances to be taken into account.

The other three articles in this part represent the high water mark of indeterminate sentencing based on utilitarian or consequentialist ideas, and the major critiques that brought it down. Sheldon Glueck's article (1952 [chapter 4 in this volume]), originally published in 1928, proposed that sentencing be taken away from judges and put in the hands of an expert commission; judges, he said, lack the time, the information, and the necessary specialized expertise to individualize sentences optimally. That proposal, almost unthinkable now and politically unimaginable, was mainstream when first offered and for thirty years thereafter. C. S. Lewis (1949 [chapter 5]) and Francis Allen (1959 [chapter 6]) raised moral and practical objections to punishment systems based on rehabilitative and utilitarian premises. Between them, they offered most of the criticisms that undermined indeterminate sentencing in the 1970s.

References. Bibliographic details concerning works mentioned that are not reprinted in this volume can be found in the reference list to the introduction.

1

THE PENAL LAW AND THE LAW OF PARDON

Immanuel Kant

I THE RIGHT TO PUNISH

The right to punish contained in the penal law [*das Strafrecht*] is the right that the magistrate has to inflict pain on a subject in consequence of his having committed a crime. It follows that the suzerain of the state cannot himself be punished; we can only remove ourselves from his jurisdiction. A transgression of the public law that makes him who commits it unfit to be a citizen is called either simply a crime (*crimen*) or a public crime (*crimen publicum*). [If, however, we call it a public crime, then we can use the term "crime" generically to include both private and public crimes.][11] The first (a private crime) is brought before a civil court, and the second (a public crime), before a criminal court. Embezzlement, that is, misappropriation of money or wares entrusted in commerce, and fraud in buying and selling, if perpetrated before the eyes of the party who suffers, are private crimes. On the other hand, counterfeiting money or bills of exchange, theft, robbery, and similar acts are public crimes, because through them the commonwealth and not just a single individual is exposed to danger. These crimes may be divided into those of a base character (*indolis abjectae*) and those of a violent character (*indolis violentae*).

Judicial punishment (*poena forensis*) is entirely distinct from natural punishment (*poena naturalis*). In natural punishment, vice punishes itself, and this fact is not taken into consideration by the legislator. Judicial punishment can never be used merely as a means to promote some other good for the criminal himself or for civil society, but

---

[11] [Natorp and Cassirer agree that there is something wrong with the sentence following this one. Either a sentence has been omitted or the sentence in question has been misplaced. Kant's meaning is, however, perfectly clear, and I have inserted a sentence to provide the transition.]

instead it must in all cases be imposed on him only on the ground that he has committed a crime; for a human being can never be manipulated merely as a means to the purposes of someone else and can never be confused with the objects of the Law of things [*Sachenrecht*]. His innate personality [that is, his right as a person] protects him against such treatment, even though he may indeed be condemned to lose his civil personality. He must first be found to be deserving of punishment before any consideration is given to the utility of this punishment for himself or for his fellow citizens. The law concerning punishment is a categorical imperative, and woe to him who rummages around in the winding paths of a theory of happiness looking for some advantage to be gained by releasing the criminal from punishment or by reducing the amount of it—in keeping with the Pharisaic motto: "It is better that one man should die than that the whole people should perish." If legal justice perishes, then it is no longer worth while for men to remain alive on this earth. If this is so, what should one think of the proposal to permit a criminal who has been condemned to death to remain alive, if, after consenting to allow dangerous experiments to be made on him, he happily survives such experiments and if doctors thereby obtain new information that benefits the community? Any court of justice would repudiate such a proposal with scorn if it were suggested by a medical college, for [legal] justice ceases to be justice if it can be bought for a price.

What kind and what degree of punishment does public legal justice adopt as its principle and standard? None other than the principle of equality (illustrated by the pointer on the scales of justice), that is, the principle of not treating one side more favorably than the other. Accordingly, any undeserved evil that you inflict on someone else among the people is one that you do to yourself. If you vilify him, you vilify yourself; if you steal from him, you steal from yourself; if you kill him, you kill yourself. Only the Law of retribution (*jus talionis*) can determine exactly the kind and degree of punishment; it must be well understood, however, that this determination [must be made] in the chambers of a court of justice (and not in your private judgment). All other standards fluctuate back and forth and, because extraneous considerations are mixed with them, they cannot be compatible with the principle of pure and strict legal justice.

Now, it might seem that the existence of class distinctions would not allow for the [application of the] retributive principle of returning like for like. Nevertheless, even though these class distinctions may not make it possible to apply this principle to the letter, it can still always remain applicable in its effects if regard is had to the special sensibilities of the higher classes. Thus, for example, the imposition of a fine for a verbal injury has no proportionality to the original injury, for someone who has a good deal of money can easily afford to make insults whenever he wishes. On the other hand, the humiliation of the pride of such an offender comes much closer to equaling an injury done to the honor of the person offended; thus the judgment and Law might require the offender, not only to make a public apology to the offended person, but also at the same time to kiss his hand, even though he be socially inferior. Similarly, if a man of a higher class has violently attacked an innocent citizen who is socially inferior to him, he may be condemned, not only to apologize, but to undergo solitary and painful confinement, because by this means, in addition to the discomfort suffered, the pride of the offender will be painfully affected, and thus his humiliation will compensate for the offense as like for like.

But what is meant by the statement: "If you steal from him, you steal from yourself"? Inasmuch as someone steals, he makes the ownership of everyone else insecure, and hence he robs himself (in accordance with the Law of retribution) of the security of any possible ownership. He has nothing and can also acquire nothing, but he still wants to live, and this is not possible unless others provide him with nourishment. But, because the state will not support him gratis, he must let the state have his labor at any kind of work it may wish to use him for (convict labor), and so he becomes a slave, either for a certain period of time or indefinitely, as the case may be.

If, however, he has committed a murder, he must die. In this case, there is no substitute that will satisfy the requirements of legal justice. There is no sameness of kind between death and remaining alive even under the most miserable conditions, and consequently there is also no equality between the crime and the retribution unless the criminal is judicially condemned and put to death. But the death of the criminal must be kept entirely free of any maltreatment that would make an abomination of the humanity residing in the person suffering it. Even if a civil society were to dissolve itself by common agreement of all its members (for example, if the people inhabiting an island decided to separate and disperse themselves around the world), the last murderer remaining in prison must first be executed, so that everyone will duly receive what his actions are worth and so that the bloodguilt thereof will not be fixed on the people because they failed to insist on carrying out the punishment; for if they fail to do so, they may be regarded as accomplices in this public violation of legal justice.

Furthermore, it is possible for punishment to be equal in accordance with the strict Law of retribution only if the judge pronounces the death sentence. This is clear because only in this way will the death sentence be pronounced on all criminals in proportion to their inner viciousness (even if the crime involved is not murder, but some other crime against the state that can be expiated only by death). To illustrate this point, let us consider a situation, like the last Scottish rebellion, in which the participants are motivated by varying purposes, just as in that rebellion some believed that they were only fulfilling their obligations to the house of Stuart (like Balmerino and others),[12] and others, in contrast, were pursuing their own private interests. Suppose that the highest court were to pronounce as follows: Each person shall have the freedom to choose between death and penal servitude. I say that a man of honor would choose death and that the knave would choose servitude. This is implied by the nature of human character, because the first recognizes something that he prizes more highly than life itself, namely, honor, whereas the second thinks that a life covered with disgrace is still better than not being alive at all (*animam praeferre pudori*).[13] The first is without doubt less

---

[12] [Arthur Elphinstone, Sixth Baron Balmerino (1688–1746), participated in the Jacobite rebellion that attempted to put Prince Charles Edward Stuart on the British throne. He was captured, tried, found guilty, and beheaded. He is said to have acted throughout with great constancy and courage.]

[13] ["To prefer life to honor"—Juvenal, *Satire* 8. 83. The complete text, lines 79–84, is quoted by Kant in the *Critique of Practical Reason*, Part II: "Be a stout soldier, a faithful guardian, and an incorruptible judge; if summoned to bear witness in some dubious and uncertain cause, though Phalaris himself should command you to tell lies and bring up his bull and dictate to you a perjury, count it the greatest of all sins

deserving of punishment than the other, and so, if they are both condemned to die, they will be punished exactly in proportion [to their inner viciousness]; the first will be punished mildly in terms of his kind of sensibility, and the second will be punished severely in terms of his kind of sensibility. On the other hand, if both were condemned to penal servitude, the first would be punished too severely and the second too mildly for their baseness. Thus, even in sentences imposed on a number of criminals united in a plot, the best equalizer before the bar of public legal justice is death.

It may also be pointed out that no one has ever heard of anyone condemned to death on account of murder who complained that he was getting too much [punishment] and therefore was being treated unjustly; everyone would laugh in his face if he were to make such a statement. Indeed, otherwise we would have to assume that, although the treatment accorded the criminal is not unjust according to the law, the legislative authority still is not authorized to decree this kind of punishment and that, if it does so, it comes into contradiction with itself.

Anyone who is a murderer—that is, has committed a murder, commanded one, or taken part in one—must suffer death. This is what [legal] justice as the Idea of the judicial authority wills in accordance with universal laws that are grounded a priori. The number of accomplices (*correi*) in such a deed might, however, be so large that the state would soon approach the condition of having no more subjects if it were to rid itself of these criminals, and this would lead to its dissolution and a return to the state of nature, which is much worse, because it would be a state of affairs without any external legal justice whatsoever. Since a sovereign will want to avoid such consequences and, above all, will want to avoid adversely affecting the feelings of the people by the spectacle of such butchery, he must have it within his power in case of necessity (*casus necessitatis*) to assume the role of judge and to pronounce a judgment that, instead of imposing the death penalty on the criminals, assigns some other punishment that will make the preservation of the mass of the people possible, such as, for example, deportation. Such a course of action would not come under a public law, but would be an executive decree [*Machtspruch*], that is, an act based on the right of majesty, which, as an act of reprieve, can be exercised only in individual cases.

In opposition to this view, the Marquis of Beccaria,[14] moved by sympathetic sentimentality and an affectation of humanitarianism, has asserted that all capital punishment is illegitimate. He argues that it could not be contained in the original civil contract, inasmuch as this would imply that every one of the people has agreed to forfeit his life if he murders another (of the people); but such an agreement would be impossible, for no one can dispose of his own life.

No one suffers punishment because he has willed the punishment, but because he has willed a punishable action. If what happens to someone is also willed by him,

---

to prefer life to honour, and to lose, for the sake of living, all that makes life worth having." Trans. G. G. Ramsey, "Loeb Classical Library." (Phalaris, tyrant of Agrigentum, had criminals burned to death in a brass ox.)]

[14] [Cesare Bonesana, Marquis di Beccaria (1738–1794), Italian publicist. His *Dei delitti e delle pene* (1764) (*On Crimes and Punishments*, trans. Henry Paolucci, "The Library of Liberal Arts," No. 107 [New York: The Liberal Arts Press, 1963]) was widely read and had great influence on the reform of the penal codes of various European states.]

it cannot be a punishment. Accordingly, it is impossible to will to be punished. To say, "I will to be punished if I murder someone," can mean nothing more than, "I submit myself along with everyone else to those laws which, if there are any criminals among the people, will naturally include penal laws." In my role as colegislator making the penal law, I cannot be the same person who, as subject, is punished by the law; for, as a subject who is also a criminal, I cannot have a voice in legislation. (The legislator is holy.) When, therefore, I enact a penal law against myself as a criminal it is the pure juridical legislative reason (*homo noumenon*) in me that submits myself to the penal law as a person capable of committing a crime, that is, as another person (*homo phaenomenon*) along with all the others in the civil union who submit themselves to this law. In other words, it is not the people (considered as individuals) who dictate the death penalty, but the court (public legal justice); that is, someone other than the criminal. The social contract does not include the promise to permit oneself to be punished and thus to dispose of oneself and of one's life, because, if the only ground that authorizes the punishment of an evildoer were a promise that expresses his willingness to be punished, then it would have to be left up to him to find himself liable to punishment, and the criminal would be his own judge. The chief error contained in this sophistry (πρωτονψευδος) consists in the confusion of the criminal's own judgment (which one must necessarily attribute to his reason) that he must forfeit his life with a resolution of the Will to take his own life. The result is that the execution of the Law and the adjudication thereof are represented as united in the same person.

There remain, however, two crimes deserving of death with regard to which it still remains doubtful whether legislation is authorized to impose the death penalty. In both cases, the crimes are due to the sense of honor. One involves the honor of womanhood; the other, military honor. Both kinds of honor are genuine, and duty requires that they be sought after by every individual in each of these two classes. The first crime is infanticide at the hands of the mother (*infanticidium maternale*); the other is the murder of a fellow soldier (*commilitonicidium*) in a duel.

Now, legislation cannot take away the disgrace of an illegitimate child, nor can it wipe away the stain of suspicion of cowardice from a junior officer who fails to react to a humiliating affront with action that would show that he has the strength to overcome the fear of death. Accordingly, it seems that, in such circumstances, the individuals concerned find themselves in a state of nature, in which killing another (*homicidium*) can never be called murder (*homicidium dolosum*); in both cases, they are indeed deserving of punishment, but they cannot be punished with death by the supreme power. A child born into the world outside marriage is outside the law (for this is [implied by the concept of] marriage), and consequently it is also outside the protection of the law. The child has crept surreptitiously into the commonwealth (much like prohibited wares), so that its existence as well as its destruction can be ignored (because by right it ought not to have come into existence in this way); and the mother's disgrace if the illegitimate birth becomes known cannot be wiped out by any official decree.

Similarly, a military man who has been commissioned a junior officer may suffer an insult and as a result feel obliged by the opinions of his comrades in arms to seek satisfaction and to punish the person who insulted him, not by appealing to the law and taking him to court, but instead, as would be done in a state of nature, by challenging him to a duel; for, even though in doing so he will be risking his life, he will thereby be able to demonstrate his military valor, on which the honor of his profession rests. If, under such circumstances, his opponent should be killed, this cannot properly be called a murder (*homicidium dolosum*), inasmuch as it takes place in a combat openly fought with the consent of both parties, even though they may have participated in it only reluctantly.

What, then, is the actual Law of the land with regard to these two cases (which come under criminal justice)? This question presents penal justice with a dilemma: either it must declare that the concept of honor (which is no delusion in these cases) is null and void in the eyes of the law and that these acts should be punished by death or it must abstain from imposing the death penalty for these crimes, which merit it; thus it must be either too cruel or too lenient. The solution to this dilemma is as follows: the categorical imperative involved in the legal justice of punishment remains valid (that is, the unlawful killing of another person must be punished by death), but legislation itself (including also the civil constitution), as long as it remains barbaric and undeveloped, is responsible for the fact that incentives of honor among the people do not accord (subjectively) with the standards that are (objectively) appropriate to their purpose, with the result that public legal justice as administered by the state is injustice from the point of view of the people.[15]

---

[15] [See Appendix, § 5. In the *Critique of Pure Reason*, trans. Kemp Smith, B 373, Kant writes: "The more legislation and government are brought into harmony with the...idea...(of a constitution allowing *the greatest possible human freedom* in accordance with laws by which *the freedom of each is made to be consistent with that of all others*)...the rarer would punishments become, and it is therefore quite rational to maintain, as Plato does, that in a perfect state no punishments whatsoever would be required." The order of the sentence has been changed.]

2

WRONG [*DAS UNRECHT*]

G. W. F. Hegel

§ 82

In contract, right *in itself* is present as something *posited*, and its inner universality is present as a *common factor* in the arbitrariness and particular wills of those concerned. This *appearance* of right, in which right itself and its essential *existence* [*Dasein*], the particular will, coincide immediately – i.e. in a contingent manner – goes on, in the case of *wrong*, to become a *semblance* – an opposition between right in itself and the particular will as that in which right becomes a *particular right*. But the truth of this semblance is that it is null and void, and that right re-establishes itself by negating this negation of itself.[1] Through this process of mediation whereby right returns to itself from its negation, it determines itself as *actual* and *valid*, whereas it was at first only *in itself* and something *immediate*.

Addition (H). Right in itself, the universal will, is essentially determined by the particular will, and thus stands in relation [*Beziehung*] to something inessential. This is the relationship [*Verhältnis*] of the essence to its appearance. Even if the appearance is in conformity with the essence, it is not in conformity with it from another point of view, for appearance is the stage of contingency, or essence in relation [*Beziehung*] to the inessential. But in the case of wrong, appearance goes on to become a semblance. A semblance is existence inappropriate to the essence, the empty detachment and positedness of the essence, so that in both [semblance and essence], their distinctness is [mere] difference. Semblance is therefore the untruth which disappears because it seeks to exist for itself, and in this disappearance, essence has shown itself as essence, that is, as the power

---

[1] See § 57, note 2.

over semblance. The essence has negated its own negation, and is thereby confirmed. Wrong is a semblance of this kind, and through its disappearance, right acquires the determination of something fixed and valid. What we have just referred to as essence is right in itself, in contrast to which the particular will is superseded [*sich aufhebt*] as untrue. Whereas right previously had only an immediate being, it now becomes *actual* as it returns out of its negation; for actuality is that which is effective[a] and sustains itself in its otherness, whereas the immediate still remains liable to negation.

§ 83

Right, as something *particular* and therefore complex in contrast to the universality and simplicity of its being *in itself*, acquires the form of a *semblance*. It is this semblance either *in itself* or immediately, or it is posited by *the subject as semblance*, or it is posited by *the subject as completely null and void* – that is, it becomes *unintentional or civil wrong, deception*, or *crime*.

Addition (H). Wrong is thus the semblance of essence which posits itself as self-sufficient. If the semblance is present only in itself and not also for itself – that is, if the wrong is in my opinion right – the wrong is unintentional. Here, the semblance exists from the point of view of right, but not from my point of view. The second [kind of] wrong is deception. In this case, the wrong is not a semblance from the point of view of right in itself; instead, what happens is that I create a semblance in order to deceive another person. When I deceive someone, right is for me a semblance. In the first case, wrong was a semblance from the point of view of right. In the second case, right is only a semblance from my point of view, i.e. from the point of view of wrong. Finally, the third [kind of] wrong is crime. This is wrong both in itself and for me. But in this case, I will the wrong and do not employ even the semblance of right. The other person against whom the crime is committed is not expected to regard the wrong, which has being in and for itself, as right. The difference between crime and deception is that in the latter, a recognition of right is still present in the form of the action, and this is correspondingly absent in the case of crime.

[A. Unintentional wrong and B. Deception omitted]

C. COERCION AND CRIME

§ 90

When I own property, my will is embodied in an *external thing* [*Sache*]. This means that my will, to the extent that it is reflected in the external thing, is also caught up in it and subjected to necessity. In this situation, it may either experience *force* in general, or it

---

[a] *Translator's note:* Hegel defines the term *Wirklichkeit* ('actuality') by exploiting its relationship with the verb *wirken* ('to be effective').

may be forced to sacrifice or do something as a condition of retaining some possession or positive being, thereby suffering *coercion*.

Addition (H). Wrong in the proper sense is crime, where neither right in itself nor [right] as it appears to me is respected – that is, where both sides, objective and subjective, are infringed.

§ 91

As a living being, the human being can certainly be *dominated* [*bezwungen*] – i.e. his physical side and other external attributes may be brought under the power of others. But the free will in and for itself cannot be *coerced* [*gezwungen*] (see § 5), except in so far as *it fails to withdraw itself from the external dimension* in which it is caught up, or from its idea [*Vorstellung*] of the latter (see § 7). Only he who *wills* to be *coerced* can be coerced into anything.[1]

§ 92

The will is Idea or actually free only in so far as it has existence [*Dasein*], and the existence in which it has embodied itself is the being of freedom. Consequently, force or coercion immediately destroys itself in its concept, since it is the expression of a will which cancels [*aufhebt*] the expression or existence of a will. Force or coercion, taken in the abstract, is therefore *contrary to right*.

§ 93

Because coercion destroys itself in its concept, it has its real expression [*Darstellung*] in the fact *that coercion is cancelled* [*aufgehoben*] *by coercion*; it is therefore not only conditionally right but necessary – namely as a *second* coercion which cancels an initial coercion.

> The violation of a contract through failure to perform what it stipulates or to fulfil rightful duties towards the family or state, whether by action or by default, is an initial coercion, or at least force, in so far as I withhold or withdraw from another person a property which belongs to him or a service which is due to him. – Pedagogical coercion, or coercion directed against savagery and barbarism [*Wildheit und Rohheit*], admittedly looks like a primary coercion rather than one which comes after a primary coercion which has already occurred. But the merely natural will is *in itself* a force directed against the Idea of freedom as that which has being in itself, which must be protected against this uncivilized [*ungebildeten*] will and given

---

[1] Cf. NR 476–480/88–92.

recognition within it. Either an ethical existence [*Dasein*] has already been posited in the family or state, in which case the natural condition referred to above is an act of violence against it, or there is nothing other than a state of nature, a state governed entirely by force, in which case the Idea sets up a *right of heroes*[1] against it.

Addition (H). Within the state, heroes are no longer possible: they occur only in the absence of civilization. The end they pursue is rightful, necessary, and political,[a] and they put it into effect as a cause [*Sache*] of their own. The heroes who founded states and introduced marriage and agriculture admittedly did not do this as their recognized right, and these actions still appear as [a product of] their particular will. But as the higher right of the Idea against the state of nature, this coercion employed by heroes is a rightful coercion, for goodness alone can have little effect when confronted with the force of nature.

§ 94

Abstract right is a *coercive right*, because a wrong committed against it is a force directed against the *existence* [*Dasein*] of my freedom in an *external* thing [*Sache*]. Consequently, the protection of this existence against such a force will itself appear as an external action and as a force which supersedes the original one.

> To define abstract right – or right in the strict sense – from the start as a *right* which justifies the use of coercion[1] is to interpret [*auffassen*] it in the light of a consequence which arises only indirectly by way of wrong.

Addition (H). Special attention must be paid here to the distinction between right and morality. In the moral sphere – that is, when I am reflected into myself – there is also a duality, for the good is my end and the Idea by which I should determine myself. The existence of the good is my decision, and I actualize it within myself; but this existence is wholly inward, so that coercion cannot be applied to it. Thus, the laws of the state cannot claim to extend to a person's disposition, for in the moral sphere, I exist [only] for myself, and force is meaningless in this context.

§ 95

The initial use of coercion, as force employed by a free agent in such a way as to infringe the existence [*Dasein*] of freedom in its *concrete* sense – i.e. to infringe right as right – is

---

[1] Cf. VG 100–105/83–89.
[a] *Translator's note:* Instead of *staatlich* ('political'), the equivalent adjective in Hotho's notes (VPR III, 295), on which Gans based this Addition, is *sittlich* ('ethical').
[1] An allusion to Kant's equation of 'right' with 'warrant to use coercion' (RL 232/37).

crime. This constitutes a *negatively infinite judgement* in its complete sense (see my [*Science of*] *Logic*, Vol. II, p. 99)[1] whereby not only the particular – i.e. the subsumption of a thing [*Sache*] under my will (see § 85) – is negated, but also the universal and infinite element in the predicate 'mine' – i.e. my *capacity for rights*. This does not involve the mediation of my opinion (as it does in deception; see § 88), but runs counter to it. This is the sphere of *penal law*.

Right, whose infringement is crime, has admittedly appeared up till now only in those shapes which we have considered; hence crime likewise, for the moment, has only the more specific meaning associated with these determinations. But the substantial element within these forms is the universal, which remains the same in its further development and in the further shapes it assumes; thus its infringement, i.e. crime, also remains the same, in conformity with its concept. Hence the determination which will be considered in the following paragraph also applies to the particular and further determined content [of crime], e.g. in perjury, treason, counterfeiting, forgery, etc.

§ 96

It is only the *existent* will which can be infringed. But in its existence [*Dasein*], the will enters the sphere of quantitative extension and qualitative determinations, and therefore varies accordingly. Thus, it likewise makes a difference to the objective side of crime whether the will's existence and determinacy in general is infringed throughout its entire extent, and hence in that infinity which corresponds to its concept (as in murder, slavery, religious coercion, etc.) or only in one part, and if so, in which of its qualitative determinations.

The Stoic view that there is only *one* virtue and *one* vice,[1] the laws of Draco[2] which punish every crime with death, and the barbarous code of formal honour which

---

[1] WL VI, 324–326/641–643; cf. § 88, note 1.

[1] There seems little foundation for the claim that the Stoics believed there is only one virtue and one vice. They apparently did hold (with Plato) that the virtues are inseparable from one another:

Zeno [founder of the Stoic school] admits several virtues, as Plato does, namely prudence, courage, moderation and justice, on the grounds that although inseparable they are distinct and different from one another...[The Stoics] say that the virtues are inter-entailing, not only because he who has one has them all but also because he who does any action in accordance with one does so in accordance with them all.

(Plutarch, *On Stoic Self-Contradictions* 1034C–F, in A. A. Long and D. N. Sedley, *The Hellenistic Philosophers* 1 (Cambridge University Press, 1987), pp. 378–379)

If Hegel is alluding to a Stoic doctrine which might be compared with the notion that all crimes are of equal gravity, then he may be thinking of the Stoic rejection of Aristotle's view that virtue and vice admit of degrees: 'It is their [the Stoics'] doctrine that nothing is in between virtue and vice, though the Peripatetics say that progress is in between these. For as, they say, a stick must be either straight or crooked, so a man must be either just or unjust but not either more just or more unjust, and likewise with the other virtues' (Diogenes Laertius 7.127, in *The Hellenistic Philosophers* 1, p. 380).

[2] Draco recodified Athenian laws in 621 B.C., with the aim of replacing private vengeance with public justice. The proverbial rigidity and severity of his punishments is probably exaggerated in most accounts,

regards every infringement as an offence against the infinite personality, all have this in common: they go no further than the abstract thought of the free will and personality, and do not consider the latter in the concrete and determinate existence which it must have as Idea. – The distinction between *robbery* and *theft* is a qualitative one,[3] for in the case of robbery, [my] 'I' is also infringed as present consciousness and hence as *this subjective* infinity, and force is used against my person. – Various qualitative determinations [of crime], such as *danger to public security*, have their basis in more precisely determined circumstances, but they are often apprehended only indirectly in the light of other consequences rather than in terms of the concept of the thing [*Sache*]. Thus, the crime which is more dangerous in itself [*für sich*], in its immediate character, is a more serious infringement in its extent or quality. – The subjective, *moral* quality [of a crime] relates to the higher distinction regarding the extent to which an event or deed is in any sense an action, and concerns the latter's subjective nature itself (which will be discussed later).

Addition (H). Thought cannot specify how each crime should be punished; positive determinations are necessary for this purpose. With the progress of education, however, attitudes toward crime become more lenient, and punishments today are not nearly so harsh as they were a hundred years ago. It is not the crimes or punishments themselves which change, but the relation between the two.

§ 97

When an infringement of right as right occurs, it does have a *positive* external *existence* [*Existenz*], but this existence *within itself* is null and void. The *manifestation* of its nullity is that the nullification of the infringement likewise comes into existence; this is the actuality of right, as its necessity which mediates itself with itself through the cancellation [*Aufhebung*] of its infringement.

Addition (H). Through a crime, something is altered, and the thing [*Sache*] exists in this alteration; but this existence is the opposite of the thing itself, and is to that extent within itself [*in sich*] null and void. The nullity is [the presumption] that right as right has been cancelled [*aufgehoben*]. For right, as an absolute, cannot be cancelled, so that the expression of crime is within itself null and void, and this nullity is the essence of the effect of crime. But whatever is null and void must manifest itself as such – that is,

---

such as Plutarch's description of Solon's reforms of them in 594 B.C.: 'Being once asked why he made death the punishment of most offences, [Draco] replied, "Small ones deserve that, and I have no higher for the greater crimes"' (Plutarch, *Life of Solon* in *Plutarch's Lives*, tr. John Dryden (New York: Random House, 1960), p. 107; cf. Aristotle, *Politics* 2.12.1274b).

[3] Roman law distinguishes 'theft' (*furtum*) from 'robbery' (*rapina, vi bona rapta*) which involves the taking of a thing by force (Justinian, *Institutes* 4.1–2). *Furtum*, however, has a much broader meaning than the English 'theft', and includes embezzlement and conversion (*Institutes* 4.1.6), the application of a borrowed item to a use not intended by the lender (*Institutes* 4.1.7) and even the use of one's own property if it has been pledged to another (*Institutes* 4.1.10).

it must itself appear as vulnerable. The criminal act is not an initial positive occurrence followed by the punishment as its negation, but is itself negative, so that the punishment is merely the negation of the negation. Actual right is thus the cancellation [*Aufhebung*] of this infringement, and it is in this very circumstance that it demonstrates its validity and proves itself as a necessary and mediated existence [*Dasein*].

§ 98

An infringement which affects only external existence [*Dasein*] or possessions is an evil [*Übel*] or *damage* done to some kind of property or resources; the cancellation [*Aufhebung*] of the infringement, where the latter has caused damage, is civil satisfaction in the form of *compensation* (in so far as any compensation is possible).

With regard to this satisfaction, the *universal* character of the damage, as *value*, must in any case take the place of its specific qualitative character where the damage amounts to destruction and is altogether irreparable.

§ 99

But an injury [*Verletzung*] suffered by the will which has being *in itself* (and hence also by the will of the injuring party as well as by the injured and everyone else) has no *positive existence* [*Existenz*] in this will as such, no more than it has in the mere product [of the injury]. *For itself*, this will which has being in itself (i.e. right or law in itself) is rather something which has no external existence and is to that extent invulnerable. In the same way, the injury is a purely negative thing for the particular will of the injured party and of others. The *positive existence of the injury* consists solely in the *particular will of the criminal*. Thus, an injury to the latter as an existent will is the cancellation [*Aufheben*] of the crime, *which would otherwise be regarded as valid*, and the restoration of right.

The theory of punishment is one of the topics which have come off worst in the positive jurisprudence [*Rechtswissenschaft*] of recent times; for in this theory, the understanding is inadequate, and the essential factor is the concept. – If the crime and its cancellation [*Aufhebung*], which is further determined as punishment, are regarded only as *evils* [*Übel*] in general, one may well consider it unreasonable to will an evil merely *because another evil is already present* (see Klein's *Elements of Penal Law* [*Grundsätze des peinlichen Rechts*], §§ 9f.).[1] This

---

[1] Hegel may be alluding to the following passage: 'By punishment in the most universal sense is understood an evil [*Übel*] which follows upon an illegal action as such. In so far as such an evil is used for the effecting of future lawful actions or omissions, a punishment in the usual signification is present. A genuine punishment in the usual signification presupposes that the evil is voluntarily [*willkürlich*] combined with the unallowed action toward the end specified' (Ernst Ferdinand Klein (1744–1810), *Grundsätze des*

superficial character of an *evil* is the primary assumption in the various theories of punishment as prevention, as a deterrent, a threat, a corrective, etc.; and conversely, what is supposed to result from it is just as superficially defined [*bestimmt*] as a *good*. But it is neither a question merely of an evil nor of this or that good; on the contrary, it is definitely [*bestimmt*] a matter of *wrong* and of *justice*. As a result of these superficial points of view, however, the objective consideration of *justice*, which is the primary and substantial point of view in relation to crime, is set aside; it automatically follows that the essential consideration is now the moral point of view, i.e. the subjective aspect of crime, intermixed with trivial psychological ideas [*Vorstellungen*] of stimuli and the strength of sensuous motives [*Triebfedern*] as opposed to reason, of psychological coercion and of psychological influences on representational thought [*die Vorstellung*] (as if such influences were not themselves reduced by freedom to something purely contingent). The various considerations which are relevant to punishment as a phenomenon [*Erscheinung*] and to its relation [*Beziehung*] to the particular consciousness, and which concern its effect on representational thought (as a deterrent, corrective, etc.), are of essential significance in their proper context, though primarily only in connection with the *modality* of punishment. But they take it for granted that punishment in and for itself is *just*. In the present discussion, we are solely concerned with the need to cancel [*aufzuheben*] crime – not as a source of *evil*, but as an infringement of right as right – and also with the kind of *existence* which crime possesses, which must also be cancelled. This existence is the true evil which must be removed, and the essential point is [to discover] where it lies. So long as the concepts relating to this have not been definitely [*bestimmt*] recognized, confusion must prevail in our views on punishment.

Addition (H). Feuerbach's theory[2] bases punishment on threat and maintains that, if anyone commits a crime in spite of the threat, the punishment must follow because the criminal knew about it in advance. But to what extent is the threat compatible with right? The threat presupposes that human beings are not free, and seeks to coerce

---

gemeinen deutschen und preußischen peinlichen Rechts (*Principles of Common German and Prussian Penal Law*) (Halle: Hemmende & Schmetzke, 1799), p. 6). Klein was one of the co-authors of the *Prussian General Legal Code* of 1794. Hegel thinks that it is an error to build consequentialist considerations into the very concept of punishment, as Klein suggests here. Instead, Hegel insists that the concept of punishment involves retributive considerations ('wrong and justice'), even if punishment is also used to achieve desirable consequences (such as preventing future violations of law).

   [2] Paul Johann Anselm Ritter von Feuerbach (1775–1833), father of the Young Hegelian philosopher Ludwig Feuerbach (1804–1872), was author of the influential *Lehrbuch des gemeinen in Deutschland gültigen peinlichen Rechts* (*Textbook of the Penal Law Commonly Valid in Germany*) (1801). He was a proponent of penal reform, best known for successfully implementing the rule *nullum crimen, nulla poena sine lege* ('no crime, no punishment without law') – which restricted the power of courts to administer punishment unless there was a crime and a corresponding punishment for it provided by legal statute. He was also author of the *Bavarian Penal Code* (1813) which, along with the Napoleonic Code, formed the basis of continental penal legislation throughout most of the nineteenth century. His philosophical theory of punishment, based on the idea of a threat published in advance, is found in his *Textbook*: Book 1 ('Philosophical or Universal Part of Penal Law') (5th ed., Giessen: G.F. Heyer, 1812), pp. 13–18.

them through the representation [*Vorstellung*] of an evil. But right and justice must have their seat in freedom and the will, and not in that lack of freedom at which the threat is directed. To justify punishment in this way is like raising one's stick at a dog; it means treating a human being like a dog instead of respecting his honour and freedom. But a threat, which may ultimately provoke someone into demonstrating his freedom in defiance of it, sets justice aside completely. Psychological coercion can refer only to qualitative and quantitative differences within crime, not to the nature of crime itself, and any legal codes which may have originated in this doctrine consequently have no proper foundation.

§ 100

The injury [*Verletzung*] which is inflicted on the criminal is not only just *in itself* (and since it is just, it is at the same time his will as it is *in itself*, an existence [*Dasein*] of his freedom, *his* right); it is also a *right for the criminal himself*, that is, a right *posited* in his *existent* will, in his action. For it is implicit in his action, as that of a *rational* being, that it is universal in character, and that, by performing it, he has set up a law which he has recognized for himself in his action, and under which he may therefore be subsumed as under *his* right.

> It is well known that Beccaria[1] questioned the right of the state to impose capital punishment, on the grounds that it could not be presumed that the social contract included the consent of individuals [*Individuen*] to allow themselves to be killed, and that we ought rather to assume the contrary. But the state is by no means a contract (see § 75), and its substantial essence does not consist unconditionally in the *protection* and *safeguarding* of the lives and property of individuals as such. The state is rather that higher instance which may even itself lay claim to the lives and property of individuals and require their sacrifice. – Furthermore, the *action* of the criminal involves not only the *concept* of crime, its rationality *in and for itself* which the state must enforce *with* or *without* the consent of individuals [*der Einzelnen*], but also the formal rationality of the *individual's* [*des Einzelnen*] volition. In so far as the punishment which this entails is seen as embodying *the criminal's own right*, the criminal is *honoured*

---

[1] Cesare Beccaria (1738–1794), often considered the father of modern criminology, is the most important theorist of penal reform in the eighteenth century. His influence is based almost entirely on his *Dei delitti e delle pene* (*On Crimes and Punishments*) (1764), which was best known in the French translation of the Abbé Morellet (1766). It influenced enlightened sovereigns throughout Europe, including the Grand Duke Leopold of Tuscany, Frederick the Great of Prussia, Catherine the Great of Russia (who invited Beccaria to reside at her court), and Maria Theresa and Joseph II of Austria. Jeremy Bentham and John Adams were among Beccaria's admirers. Beccaria opposed capital punishment, both on the contractarian ground that citizens cannot be understood to have alienated to the state their right not to be killed, and on the consequentialist ground that life imprisonment is a more effective deterrent than the death penalty. See Beccaria, *On Crimes and Punishments*, tr. Henry Paolucci (Indianapolis: Bobbs-Merrill, 1963), pp. 10–14, 45–53, 62–64.

as a rational being. – He is denied this honour if the concept and criterion of his punishment are not derived from his own act; and he is also denied it if he is regarded simply as a harmful animal which must be rendered harmless, or punished with a view to deterring or reforming him. – Besides, so far as the mode of existence [*Existenz*] of justice is concerned, the form which it has within the state, namely that of *punishment*, is not its only form, and the state is not a necessary condition of justice in itself.

Addition (H,G). Beccaria is quite right to demand that human beings should give their consent to being punished, but the criminal gives this consent by his very act. Both the nature of crime and the criminal's own will require that the infringement for which he is responsible should be cancelled [*aufgehoben*]. Nevertheless, Beccaria's efforts to have capital punishment abolished [*aufheben zu lassen*] have had advantageous effects. Even if neither Joseph II nor the French have ever managed to secure its complete abolition,[2] people have begun to appreciate which crimes deserve the death penalty and which do not. The death penalty has consequently become less frequent, as indeed this ultimate form of punishment deserves to be.[3]

§ 101

The cancellation [*Aufheben*] of crime is *retribution* in so far as the latter, by its concept, is an infringement of an infringement, and in so far as crime, by its existence [*Dasein*], has a determinate qualitative and quantitative magnitude, so that its negation, as existent, also has a determinate magnitude. But this identity [of crime and retribution], which is based on the concept, is not an *equality* in the specific character of the infringement, but in its character *in itself* – i.e. in terms of its *value*.

It is usual in science for a determination – in this case, that of punishment – to be defined in terms of the *universal representations* [*Vorstellung*] of conscious psychological experience. In the present case, this experience would indicate that the universal feeling of peoples and individuals towards crime is, and always has been, that it *deserves* to be punished, and that *what the criminal has done should also happen to him*. It is incomprehensible how those sciences which derive their determinations from universal representations [*Vorstellung*] should on other occasions accept propositions which contradict such so-called universal *facts* of consciousness. – But the determination of *equality* has brought a major difficulty into the idea [*Vorstellung*] of retribution, although the justice (in terms

---

[2] The Emperor Joseph II of Austria (reigned 1765–1790) promulgated a new penal law in 1787 which substituted life imprisonment for the death penalty, but the death penalty was reinstituted in 1795. The death penalty was retained in the French Penal Code of 1791, but only with restrictions and after a long and searching debate.

[3] Hegel criticizes the English practice of using the death penalty to punish theft (VPR III, 304–305).

of their qualitative and quantitative character) of whatever punishments are
determined is in any case a matter which arises later than the substance of the
thing [*Sache*] itself. Even if, for this later determination of punishments, we had
to look around for principles other than those which apply to the universal aspect
of punishment, this universal aspect remains what it is. Yet the concept itself
must always contain the basic principle, even for the particular instance. This
determination of the concept, however, is precisely that necessary connection
[which dictates] that crime, as the will which is null and void in itself, accordingly
contains within itself its own nullification, and this appears in the form of
punishment. It is this inner *identity* which, for the understanding, is reflected in
external existence [*Dasein*] as *equality*. The qualitative and quantitative character
of crime and its cancellation [*seines Aufhebens*] thus falls into the sphere of
externality, in which no absolute determination is in any case possible
(cf. § 49). *In the realm of finite things*, the absolute determination remains only a
requirement, on which the understanding must impose increasing restrictions –
and this is of the utmost importance – but which continues *ad infinitum* and
admits in perpetuity of only an *approximate* fulfilment. – If we not only overlook
this nature of the finite realm but also proceed no further than abstract and
specific equality, an insuperable difficulty arises when we come to determine
punishments (especially if psychology also invokes the strength of sensuous
motives [*Triebfedern*] and, as a corollary, either the *correspondingly greater strength*
of the evil will or – *if we prefer* – the *correspondingly lesser strength* and freedom
of the will in general). Furthermore, it is very easy to portray the retributive
aspect of punishment as an absurdity (theft as retribution for theft, robbery
for robbery, an eye for an eye, and a tooth for a tooth,[1] so that one can even
imagine the miscreant as one-eyed or toothless); but the concept has nothing
to do with this absurdity, for which the introduction of that [idea of] *specific
equality* is alone to blame. *Value*, as the *inner equality* of things [*Sachen*] which,
in their existence [*Existenz*], are specifically quite different, is a determination
which has already arisen in connection with contracts (see [§ 77] above) and
with civil suits against crimes (see § 98),[a] and which raises our representation
[*Vorstellung*] of a thing above its *immediate* character to the universal. In the
case of crime, whose basic determination is the *infinite* aspect of the deed, that
aspect which is only externally specific disappears all the more readily, and
equality remains merely the basic measure of the criminal's *essential* deserts,
but not of the specific external shape which the retribution should take. It is
only in terms of this specific shape that theft and robbery [on the one hand] and
fines and imprisonment etc. [on the other] are completely unequal, whereas
in terms of their value, i.e. their universal character as injuries [*Verletzungen*],
they are *comparable*. It is then, as already remarked, a matter [*Sache*] for the

---

[1] 'Eye for eye, tooth for tooth, hand for hand, foot for foot, burning for burning, wound for wound, stripe for stripe' (Exodus 21:24).

[a] *Translator's note*: The reference in all editions of Hegel's text is to § 95, which appears to be an error. I follow T. M. Knox in substituting § 98 as more appropriate.

understanding to seek an approximate equivalence in this common value. If we do not grasp either the connection, as it is in itself, between crime and its nullification, or the thought of *value* and the comparability of crime and punishment in terms of value, we may reach the point (see Klein's *Elements of Penal Law*, § 9)[2] of regarding a proper punishment as a purely *arbitrary* association of an evil [*eines Übels*] *with an illicit action*.

Addition (H). Retribution is the inner connection and the identity of two determinations which are different in appearance and also have a different external existence [*Existenz*] in relation to one another. When the criminal meets with retribution, this has the appearance of an alien destiny [*Bestimmung*] which does not belong to him; yet as we have seen, the punishment is merely a manifestation of the crime, i.e. it is one half which is necessarily presupposed by the other. What is at first sight objectionable about retribution is that it looks like something immoral, like revenge, and may thus be interpreted as a personal matter. Yet it is not the personal element, but the concept itself which carries out retribution. 'Vengeance is mine' is the word of God in the Bible,[3] and if the word *retribution* should evoke the idea [*Vorstellung*] of a particular caprice of the subjective will, it must be replied that it signifies merely the shape of the crime turned round against itself. The Eumenides[4] sleep, but crime awakens them; thus the deed brings its own retribution with it. But although retribution cannot aim to achieve specific equality, this is not the case with murder, which necessarily incurs the death penalty. For since life is the entire compass of existence [*Dasein*], the punishment [for murder] cannot consist [*bestehen*] in a *value* – since none is equivalent to life – but only in the taking of another life.

§ 102

In this sphere of the immediacy of right, the cancellation [*Aufheben*] of crime is primarily *revenge*, and its *content* is just so far as it constitutes retribution. But in its *form*, it is the action of a *subjective* will which can place *its infinity* in any infringement [of right] which occurs, and whose justice is therefore altogether contingent, just as it exists *for the other party* only as a *particular* will. Thus revenge, as the positive action of a *particular* will, becomes *a new infringement*; because of this contradiction, it becomes part of an infinite progression and is inherited indefinitely from generation to generation.

[2] See above § 99, note 1.

[3] 'Dearly beloved, avenge not yourselves, but rather give place unto wrath: for it is written, "Vengeance is mine; I will repay", saith the Lord' (Romans 12:19); cf. 'To me belongeth vengeance, and recompense' (Deuteronomy 32:35).

[4] According to Hesiod, the Erinyes (the Furies) were primeval beings, born from the blood of Uranus, who was mutilated by his son Zeus. Their office it was to avenge crime, especially crimes against ties of kinship. ('Eumenides' is a propitiatory name for them, meaning 'the kindly ones'.) They are represented as three winged women, sometimes with snakes about them. Their vengeance against the matricide of Orestes, and their appeasement at the court of Athens through the intercession of Apollo on Orestes' behalf and the final verdict of acquittal by Athena, are the focus of Aeschylus' tragedy *The Eumenides*.

Where the crimes are prosecuted and punished not as *crimina publica* but as *crimina privata* (as with theft and robbery among the Jews and Romans, and even today with certain offences in England, etc.) the punishment still has at least an element of revenge about it.[1] Private revenge is distinct from the revenge of heroes, knightly adventurers, etc., which belongs to the period when states first arose.

Addition (H). In a social condition in which there are neither magistrates nor laws, punishment always takes the form of revenge; this remains inadequate inasmuch as it is the action of a subjective will, and thus out of keeping with the content. It is true that the members of a tribunal are also persons, but their will is the universal will of the law, and they do not seek to include in the punishment anything but what is naturally present in the matter [*Sache*] in hand. On the other hand, the injured party does not perceive wrong in its quantitative and qualitative limitation [*Begrenzung*], but simply as wrong without qualification, and he may go too far in his retaliation, which will in turn lead to further wrong. Among uncivilized [*ungebildeten*] peoples, revenge is undying, as with the Arabs, where it can be suppressed only by superior force or by the impossibility of putting it into effect. There is still a residue of revenge in several legal codes in use today, as in those cases where it is left to individuals to decide whether they wish to bring an offence [*Verletzung*] to court or not.

§ 103

To require that this contradiction, which in the present case is to be found in the manner in which wrong is cancelled [*der Art und Weise des Aufhebens*], should be resolved in the same way as contradictions in other kinds of wrong (see §§ 86 and 89), is to require a justice freed from subjective interest and subjective shape and from the contingency of power – that is, a *punitive* rather than an *avenging justice*. *Primarily*, this constitutes a requirement for a will which, as a particular and *subjective* will, also wills the universal as such. But this concept of *morality* is not just a requirement; it has emerged in the course of this movement itself.

---

[1] In Roman law, both theft (*furta*) and robbery (*rapina*) are classed as *crimina privata*, as distinct from *crimina publica* or crimes against the state (Gaius, *Institutes* 3.182). A civil action for damages could be brought against a thief (Justinian, *Institutes* 4.1.11–15, 4.2, cf. *Digest* 44.7.4, Gaius, *Institutes* 3.182, 4.8). In Jewish law, thefts are punishable by restoration to the victim of more than was stolen; the victim of a theft is permitted to wound or even kill the thief, if the theft occurs at night (if such a killing occurs during the day, it is murder and punishable by death) (Exodus 22:1–4). Blackstone also draws the distinction between private and public crimes (*Commentaries on the Laws of England* III (Chicago: University of Chicago Press, 1979) p. 2).

3

AN INTRODUCTION TO THE PRINCIPLES OF MORALS AND LEGISLATION

Jeremy Bentham

CHAPTER I

OF THE PRINCIPLE OF UTILITY

I. Nature has placed mankind under the governance of two sovereign masters, *pain* and *pleasure*. It is for them alone to point out what we ought to do, as well as to determine what we shall do. On the one hand the standard of right and wrong, on the other the chain of causes and effects, are fastened to their throne. They govern us in all we do, in all we say, in all we think: every effort we can make to throw off our subjection, will serve but to demonstrate and confirm it. In words a man may pretend to abjure their empire: but in reality he will remain subject to it all the while. The *principle of utility*[a] recognises this subjection, and assumes it for the foundation of that system, the object of which is to rear the fabric of felicity by the hands of reason and of law. Systems

---

[a] Note by the Author, July 1822.

To this denomination has of late been added, or substituted, the *greatest happiness* or *greatest felicity* principle: this for shortness, instead of saying at length *that principle* which states the greatest happiness of all those whose interest is in question, as being the right and proper, and only right and proper and universally desirable, end of human action: of human action in every situation, and in particular in that of a functionary or set of functionaries exercising the powers of Government. The word *utility* does not so clearly point to the ideas of *pleasure* and *pain* as the words *happiness* and *felicity* do: nor does it lead us to the consideration of the *number*, of the interests affected; to the *number*, as being the circumstance, which contributes, in the largest proportion, to the formation of the standard here in question; the *standard of right and wrong*, by which alone the propriety of human conduct, in every situation, can with propriety be tried. This want of a sufficiently manifest connexion between the ideas of *happiness* and *pleasure* on the one hand, and the idea of *utility* on the other, I have every now and then found operating, and with but too much efficiency, as a bar to the acceptance, that might otherwise have been given, to this principle.

which attempt to question it, deal in sounds instead of sense, in caprice instead of reason, in darkness instead of light.

But enough of metaphor and declamation: it is not by such means that moral science is to be improved.

II. The principle of utility is the foundation of the present work: it will be proper therefore at the outset to give an explicit and determinate account of what is meant by it. By the principle[b] of utility is meant that principle which approves or disapproves of every action whatsoever, according to the tendency which it appears to have to augment or diminish the happiness of the party whose interest is in question: or, what is the same thing in other words, to promote or to oppose that happiness. I say of every action whatsoever; and therefore not only of every action of a private individual, but of every measure of government.

III. By utility is meant that property in any object, whereby it tends to produce benefit, advantage, pleasure, good, or happiness, (all this in the present case comes to the same thing) or (what comes again to the same thing) to prevent the happening of mischief, pain, evil, or unhappiness to the party whose interest is considered: if that party be the community in general, then the happiness of the community: if a particular individual, then the happiness of that individual.

IV. The interest of the community is one of the most general expressions that can occur in the phraseology of morals: no wonder that the meaning of it is often lost. When it has a meaning, it is this. The community is a fictitious *body*, composed of the individual persons who are considered as constituting as it were its *members*. The interest of the community then is, what?—the sum of the interests of the several members who compose it.

V. It is in vain to talk of the interest of the community, without understanding what is the interest of the individual.[c] A thing is said to promote the interest, or to be *for* the interest, of an individual, when it tends to add to the sum total of his pleasures: or, what comes to the same thing, to diminish the sum total of his pains.

VI. An action then may be said to be conformable to the principle of utility, or, for shortness sake, to utility, (meaning with respect to the community at large) when the tendency it has to augment the happiness of the community is greater than any it has to diminish it.

VII. A measure of government (which is but a particular kind of action, performed by a particular person or persons) may be said to be conformable to or dictated by the principle of utility, when in like manner the tendency which it has to augment the happiness of the community is greater than any which it has to diminish it.

---

[b] (Principle) The word principle is derived from the Latin *principium*: which seems to be compounded of the two words *primus*, first, or chief, and *cipium*, a termination which seems to be derived from *capio*, to take, as in *mancipium, municipium*; to which are analogous *auceps, forceps*, and others. It is a term of very vague and very extensive signification: it is applied to any thing which is conceived to serve as a foundation or beginning to any series of operations: in some cases, of physical operations; but of mental operations in the present case.

The principle here in question may be taken for an act of the mind; a sentiment; a sentiment of approbation; a sentiment which, when applied to an action, approves of its utility, as that quality of it by which the measure of approbation or disapprobation bestowed upon it ought to be governed.

[c] (Interest, &c.) Interest is one of those words, which not having any superior *genus*, cannot in the ordinary way be defined.

VIII. When an action, or in particular a measure of government, is supposed by a man to be conformable to the principle of utility, it may be convenient, for the purposes of discourse, to imagine a kind of law or dictate, called a law or dictate of utility: and to speak of the action in question, as being conformable to such law or dictate.

IX. A man may be said to be a partisan of the principle of utility, when the approbation or disapprobation he annexes to any action, or to any measure, is determined by, and proportioned to the tendency which he conceives it to have to augment or to diminish the happiness of the community: or in other words, to its conformity or unconformity to the laws or dictates of utility.

X. Of an action that is conformable to the principle of utility, one may always say either that it is one that ought to be done, or at least that it is not one that ought not to be done. One may say also, that it is right it should be done; at least that it is not wrong it should be done: that it is a right action; at least that it is not a wrong action. When thus interpreted, the words *ought*, and *right* and *wrong*, and others of that stamp, have a meaning: when otherwise, they have none.

XI. Has the rectitude of this principle been ever formally contested? It should seem that it had, by those who have not known what they have been meaning. Is it susceptible of any direct proof? it should seem not: for that which is used to prove every thing else, cannot itself be proved: a chain of proofs must have their commencement somewhere. To give such proof is as impossible as it is needless.

XII. Not that there is or ever has been that human creature breathing, however stupid or perverse, who has not on many, perhaps on most occasions of his life, deferred to it. By the natural constitution of the human frame, on most occasions of their lives men in general embrace this principle, without thinking of it: if not for the ordering of their own actions, yet for the trying of their own actions, as well as of those of other men. There have been, at the same time, not many, perhaps, even of the most intelligent, who have been disposed to embrace it purely and without reserve. There are even few who have not taken some occasion or other to quarrel with it, either on account of their not understanding always how to apply it, or on account of some prejudice or other which they were afraid to examine into, or could not bear to part with. For such is the stuff that man is made of: in principle and in practice, in a right track and in a wrong one, the rarest of all human qualities is consistency.

CHAPTER VII

OF HUMAN ACTIONS IN GENERAL

I. The business of government is to promote the happiness of the society, by punishing and rewarding. That part of its business which consists in punishing, is more particularly the subject of penal law. In proportion as an act tends to disturb that happiness, in proportion as the tendency of it is pernicious, will be the demand it creates for punishment. What happiness consists of we have already seen: enjoyment of pleasures, security from pains.

II. The general tendency of an act is more or less pernicious, according to the sum total of its consequences: that is, according to the difference between the sum of such as are good, and the sum of such as are evil.

III. It is to be observed, that here, as well as henceforward, where-ever consequences are spoken of, such only are meant as are *material*. Of the consequences of any act, the multitude and variety must needs be infinite: but such of them only as are material are worth regarding. Now among the consequences of an act, be they what they may, such only, by one who views them in the capacity of a legislator, can be said to be material,* as either consist of pain or pleasure, or have an influence in the production of pain or pleasure.[a]

IV. It is also to be observed, that into the account of the consequences of the act, are to be taken not such only as might have ensued, were intention out of the question, but such also as depend upon the connection there may be between these first-mentioned consequences and the intention. The connection there is between the intention and certain consequences is, as we shall see hereafter, a means of producing other consequences. In this lies the difference between rational agency and irrational.

V. Now the intention, with regard to the consequences of an act, will depend upon two things: 1. The state of the will or intention, with respect to the act itself. And, 2. The state of the understanding, or perceptive faculties, with regard to the circumstances which it is, or may appear to be, accompanied with. Now with respect to these circumstances, the perceptive faculty is susceptible of three states: consciousness, unconsciousness, and false consciousness. Consciousness, when the party believes precisely those circumstances, and no others, to subsist, which really do subsist: unconsciousness, when he fails of perceiving certain circumstances to subsist, which, however, do subsist: false consciousness, when he believes or imagines certain circumstances to subsist, which in truth do not subsist.

VI. In every transaction, therefore, which is examined with a view to punishment, there are four articles to be considered: 1. The *act* itself, which is done. 2. The *circumstances* in which it is done. 3. The *intentionality* that may have accompanied it. 4. The *consciousness*, unconsciousness, or false consciousness, that may have accompanied it.

What regards the act and the circumstances will be the subject of the present chapter: what regards intention and consciousness, that of the two succeeding.

VII. There are also two other articles on which the general tendency of an act depends: and on that, as well as on other accounts, the demand which it creates for punishment. These are, 1. The particular *motive* or motives which gave birth to it. 2.

---

* Or *of importance*.

[a] In certain cases the consequences of an act may be material by serving as evidences indicating the existence of some other material fact, which is even *antecedent* to the act of which they are the consequences: but even here, they are material only because, in virtue of such their evidentiary quality, they have an influence, at a subsequent period of time, in the production of pain and pleasure: for example, by serving as grounds for conviction, and thence for punishment. See tit. [Simple Falsehoods] *verbo* [material.]

The general *disposition* which it indicates. These articles will be the subject of two other chapters.

VIII. Acts may be distinguished in several ways, for several purposes.

They may be distinguished, in the first place, into *positive* and *negative*. By positive are meant such as consist in motion or exertion: by negative, such as consist in keeping at rest; that is, in forbearing to move or exert one's self in such and such circumstances. Thus, to strike is a positive act: not to strike on a certain occasion, a negative one. Positive acts are stiled also acts of commission; negative, acts of omission or forbearance.[b]

IX. Such acts, again, as are negative, may either be *absolutely* so, or *relatively*: absolutely, when they import the negation of all positive agency whatsoever; for instance, not to strike at all: relatively, when they import the negation of such or such a particular mode of agency; for instance, not to strike such a person or such a thing, or in such a direction.

X. It is to be observed, that the nature of the act, whether positive or negative, is not to be determined immediately by the form of the discourse made use of to express it. An act which is positive in its nature may be characterized by a negative expression: thus, not to be at rest, is as much as to say to move. So also an act, which is negative in its nature, may be characterized by a positive expression: thus, to forbear or omit to bring food to a person in certain circumstances, is signified by the single and positive term *to starve*.

XI. In the second place, acts may be distinguished into *external* and *internal*. By external, are meant corporal acts; acts of the body: by internal, mental acts; acts of the mind. Thus, to strike is an external or exterior[c] act: to intend to strike, an internal or interior one.

XII. Acts of *discourse* are a sort of mixture of the two: external acts, which are no ways material, nor attended with any consequences, any farther than as they serve to express the existence of internal ones. To speak to another to strike, to write to him to strike, to make signs to him to strike, are all so many acts of discourse.

XIII. Thirdly, acts that are external may be distinguished into *transitive* and *intransitive*. Acts may be called transitive, when the motion is communicated from the person of the agent to some foreign body: that is, to such a foreign body on which the effects of it are considered as being *material*; as where a man runs against you, or throws water in your face. Acts may be called intransitive, when the motion is communicated to no

---

[b] The distinction between positive and negative acts runs through the whole system of offences, and sometimes makes a material difference with regard to their consequences. To reconcile us the better to the extensive, and, as it may appear on some occasions, the inconsistent signification here given to the word *act*, it may be considered, 1. That in many cases, where no exterior or overt act is exercised, the state which the mind is in at the time when the supposed act is said to happen, is as truly and directly the result of the will, as any exterior act, how plain and conspicuous soever. The not revealing a conspiracy, for instance, may be as perfectly the act of the will, as the joining in it. In the next place, that even though the mind should never have had the incident in question in contemplation (insomuch that the event of its not happening should not have been so much as obliquely intentional) still the state the person's mind was in at the time when, if he *had* so willed, the incident might have happened, is in many cases productive of as material consequences, and not only as likely, but as fit to call for the interposition of other agents, as the opposite one. Thus, when a tax is imposed, your not paying it is an act which at any rate must be punished in a certain manner, whether you happened to think of paying it or not.

[c] (Exterior.) An exterior act is also called by lawyers *overt*.

other body, on which the effects of it are regarded as material, than some part of the same person in whom it originated: as where a man runs, or washes himself.

*   *   *

XXI. So much with regard to acts considered in themselves: we come now to speak of the *circumstances* with which they may have been accompanied. These must necessarily be taken into the account before any thing can be determined relative to the consequences. What the consequences of an act may be upon the whole can never otherwise be ascertained: it can never be known whether it is beneficial, or indifferent, or mischievous. In some circumstances even to kill a man may be a beneficial act: in others, to set food before him may be a pernicious one.

XXII. Now the circumstances of an act, are, what? Any objects* whatsoever. Take any act whatsoever, there is nothing in the nature of things that excludes any imaginable object from being a circumstance to it. Any given object may be a circumstance to any other.[h]

XXIII. We have already had occasion to make mention for a moment of the *consequences* of an act: these were distinguished into material and immaterial. In like manner may the circumstances of it be distinguished. Now *materiality* is a relative term: applied to the consequences of an act, it bore relation to pain and pleasure: applied to the circumstances, it bears relation to the consequences. A circumstance may be said to be material, when it bears a visible relation in point of causality to the consequences: immaterial, when it bears no such visible relation.

XXIV. The consequences of an act are events.[†] A circumstance may be related to an event in point of causality in any one of four ways: 1. In the way of causation or production. 2. In the way of derivation. 3. In the way of collateral connection. 4. In the way of conjunct influence. It may be said to be related to the event in the way of causation, when it is of the number of those that contribute to the production of such event: in the way of derivation, when it is of the number of the events to the production of which that in question has been contributory: in the way of collateral connection, where the circumstance in question, and the event in question, without being either of them instrumental in the production of the other, are related, each of them, to some common object, which has been concerned in the production of them both: in the way of conjunct influence, when, whether related in any other way or not, they have both of them concurred in the production of some common consequence.

*   *   *

XXVI. These several relations do not all of them attach upon an event with equal certainty. In the first place, it is plain, indeed, that every event must have some circum-

---

* Or entities. See B. II. tit. (Evidence). § (Facts).

[h] The etymology of the word circumstance is perfectly characteristic of its import: *circum stantia*, things standing round: objects standing round a given object. I forget what mathematician it was that defined God to be a circle, of which the center is every where, but the circumference no where.[1] In like manner the field of circumstances, belonging to any act, may be defined a circle, of which the circumference is no where, but of which the act in question is the center. Now then, as any act may, for the purpose of discourse, be considered as a centre, any other act or object whatsoever may be considered as of the number of those that are standing round it.

[†] See B. II. tit. (Evidence). § (Facts).

stance or other, and in truth, an indefinite multitude of circumstances, related to it in the way of production: it must of course have a still greater multitude of circumstances related to it in the way of collateral connection. But it does not appear necessary that every event should have circumstances related to it in the way of derivation: nor therefore that it should have any related to it in the way of conjunct influence. But of the circumstances of all kinds which actually do attach upon an event, it is only a very small number that can be discovered by the utmost exertion of the human faculties: it is a still smaller number that ever actually do attract our notice: when occasion happens, more or fewer of them will be discovered by a man in proportion to the strength, partly of his intellectual powers, partly of his inclination.[k] It appears therefore that the multitude and description of such of the circumstances belonging to an act, as may appear to be material, will be determined by two considerations: 1. By the nature of things themselves. 2. By the strength or weakness of the faculties of those who happen to consider them.

CHAPTER XIII
CASES UNMEET FOR PUNISHMENT

§ 1. GENERAL VIEW OF CASES UNMEET FOR PUNISHMENT

I. The general object which all laws have, or ought to have, in common, is to augment the total happiness of the community; and therefore, in the first place, to exclude, as far as may be, every thing that tends to subtract from that happiness: in other words, to exclude mischief.

II. But all punishment is mischief: all punishment in itself is evil. Upon the principle of utility, if it ought at all to be admitted, it ought only to be admitted in as far as it promises to exclude some greater evil.[a]

---

[k] The more remote a connection of this sort is, of course the more obscure. It will often happen that a connection, the idea of which would at first sight appear extravagant and absurd, shall be rendered highly probable, and indeed indisputable, merely by the suggestion of a few intermediate circumstances.

At Rome, 390 years before the Christian œra, a goose sets up a cackling: two thousand years afterwards a king of France is murdered. To consider these two events, and nothing more, what can appear more extravagant than the notion that the former of them should have had any influence on the production of the latter? Fill up the gap, bring to mind a few intermediate circumstances, and nothing can appear more probable. It was the cackling of a parcel of geese, at the time the Gauls had surprised the Capitol, that saved the Roman commonwealth: had it not been for the ascendancy that commonwealth acquired afterwards over most of the nations of Europe, amongst others over France, the Christian religion, humanly speaking, could not have established itself in the manner it did in that country. Grant then, that such a man as Henry IV would have existed, no man, however, would have had those motives, by which Ravaillac, misled by a mischievous notion concerning the dictates of that religion, was prompted to assassinate him.

[a] What follows, relative to the subject of punishment ought regularly to be preceded by a distinct chapter on the ends of punishment. But having little to say on that particular branch of the subject, which has not been said before, it seemed better, in a work, which will at any rate be but too voluminous, to omit this title, reserving it for another hereafter to be published, intituled *The Theory of Punishment*. To the same work I must refer the analysis of the several possible modes of punishment, a particular and minute examination of the nature of each, and of its advantages and disadvantages, and various other disquisitions, which did not seem absolutely necessary to be inserted here. A very few words, however, concerning the *ends* of punishment, can scarcely be dispensed with.

The immediate principal end of punishment is to control action. This action is either that of the offender, or of others: that of the offender it controls by its influence, either on his will, in which case it

III. It is plain, therefore, that in the following cases punishment ought not to be inflicted.

1. Where it is *groundless*; where there is no mischief for it to prevent; the act not being mischievous upon the whole.

2. Where it must be *inefficacious*: where it cannot act so as to prevent the mischief.

3. Where it is *unprofitable*, or too *expensive*; where the mischief it would produce would be greater than what it prevented.

4. Where it is *needless*: where the mischief may be prevented, or cease of itself, without it: that is, at a chcapcr ratc.

§ 2. CASES IN WHICH PUNISHMENT IS GROUNDLESS

These are,

IV. 1. Where there has never been any mischief: where no mischief has been produced to any body by the act in question. Of this number are those in which the act was such as might, on some occasions, be mischievous or disagreeable, but the person whose interest it concerns gave his *consent* to the performance of it.[†] This consent, provided it be free, and fairly obtained,[b] is the best proof that can be produced, that, to the person who gives it, no mischief, at least no immediate mischief, upon the whole, is done. For no man can be so good a judge as the man himself, what it is gives him pleasure or displeasure.

V. 2. Where the mischief was *outweighed*: although a mischief was produced by that act, yet the same act was necessary to the production of a benefit which was of greater value[*] than the mischief. This may be the case with any thing that is done in the way of precaution against instant calamity, as also with any thing that is done in the exercise of the several sorts of powers necessary to be established in every community, to wit, domestic, judicial, military, and supreme.[‡]

---

is said to operate in the way of *reformation*; or on his physical power, in which case it is said to operate by *disablement*: that of others it can influence no otherwise than by its influence over their wills; in which case it is said to operate in the way of *example*. A kind of collateral end, which it has a natural tendency to answer, is that of affording a pleasure or satisfaction to the party injured, where there is one, and, in general, to parties whose ill-will, whether on a self-regarding account, or on the account of sympathy or antipathy, has been excited by the offence. This purpose, as far as it can be answered *gratis*, is a beneficial one. But no punishment ought to be allotted merely to this purpose, because (setting aside its effects in the way of controul) no such pleasure is ever produced by punishment as can be equivalent to the pain. The punishment, however, which is allotted to the other purpose, ought, as far as it can be done without expence, to be accommodated to this. Satisfaction thus administered to a party injured, in the shape of a dissocial pleasure, may be stiled a vindictive satisfaction or compensation: as a compensation, administered in the shape of a self-regarding profit, or stock of pleasure, may be stiled a lucrative one. See B. I. tit. vi (Compensation). Example is the most important end of all, in proportion as the *number* of the persons under temptation to offend is to *one*.

[†] See Ch. x (Motives).
[b] See B. I. tit. (Justifications).
[*] See supra, Ch. iv (Value).
[‡] See Book I. tit. (Justifications).

VI. 3. Where there is a certainty of an adequate compensation: and that in all cases where the offence can be committed. This supposes two things: 1. That the offence is such as admits of an adequate compensation: **2.** That such a compensation is sure to be forthcoming. Of these suppositions, the latter will be found to be a merely ideal one: a supposition that cannot, in the universality here given to it, be verified by fact. It cannot, therefore, in practice, be numbered amongst the grounds for absolute impunity. It may, however, be admitted as a ground for an abatement of that punishment, which other considerations, standing by themselves, would seem to dictate.[b]

§ 3. CASES IN WHICH PUNISHMENT MUST BE INEFFICACIOUS
These are,

VII. 1. Where the penal provision is *not established* until after the act is done. Such are the cases, 1. Of an *ex-post-facto* law; where the legislator himself appoints not a punishment till after the act is done. **2.** Of a sentence beyond the law; where the judge, of his own authority, appoints a punishment which the legislator had not appointed.

VIII. 2. Where the penal provision, though established, is *not conveyed* to the notice of the person on whom it seems intended that it should operate. Such is the case where the law has omitted to employ any of the expedients which are necessary, to make sure that every person whatsoever, who is within the reach of the law, be apprized of all the cases whatsoever, in which (being in the station of life he is in) he can be subjected to the penalties of the law.[*]

IX. 3. Where the penal provision, though it were conveyed to a man's notice, *could produce no effect* on him, with respect to the preventing him from engaging in any act of the *sort* in question. Such is the case, 1. In extreme *infancy*; where a man has not yet attained that state or disposition of mind in which the prospect of evils so distant as those which are held forth by the law, has the effect of influencing his conduct. 2. In *insanity*; where the person, if he has attained to that disposition, has since been deprived of it through the influence of some permanent though unseen cause. 3. In *intoxication*; where he has been deprived of it by the transient influence of a visible cause: such as the use of wine, or opium, or other drugs, that act in this manner on the nervous system: which condition is indeed neither more nor less than a temporary insanity produced by an assignable cause.[c]

---

[b] This, for example, seems to have been one ground, at least, of the favour shewn by perhaps all systems of laws, to such offenders as stand upon a footing of responsibility: shewn, not directly indeed to the persons themselves; but to such offences as none but responsible persons are likely to have the opportunity of engaging in. In particular, this seems to be the reason why embezzlement, in certain cases, has not commonly been punished upon the footing of theft: nor mercantile frauds upon that of common sharping.[‡]

[‡] See tit. (Simple merc. Defraudment).

[*] See B. II. Appendix. tit. III (Promulgation).

[c] Notwithstanding what is here said, the cases of infancy and intoxication (as we shall see hereafter) cannot be looked upon in practice as affording sufficient grounds for absolute impunity. But this exception in point of practice is no objection to the propriety of the rule in point of theory. The ground of the exception is neither more nor less than the difficulty there is of ascertaining the matter of fact: viz. whether at the requisite point of time the party was actually in the state in question; that is, whether a given case comes really under the rule. Suppose the matter of fact capable of being perfectly ascertained, without danger or mistake, the impropriety of punishment would be as indubitable in these cases as in any other.[‡]

The reason that is commonly assigned for the establishing an exemption from punishment in favour of infants, insane persons, and persons under intoxication, is either false in fact, or confusedly expressed.

X. 4. Where the penal provision (although, being conveyed to the party's notice, it might very well prevent his engaging in acts of the sort in question, provided he knew that it related to those acts) could not have this effect, with regard to the *individual* act he is about to engage in: to wit, because he knows not that it is of the number of those to which the penal provision relates. This may happen, 1. In the case of *unintentionality*; where he intends not to engage, and thereby knows not that he is about to engage, in the *act* in which eventually he is about to engage.[†] 2. In the case of *unconsciousness*; where, although he may know that he is about to engage in the *act* itself, yet, from not knowing all the material *circumstances* attending it, he knows not of the *tendency* it has to produce that mischief, in contemplation of which it has been made penal in most instances. 3. In the case of *mis-supposal*; where, although he may know of the tendency the act has to produce that degree of mischief, he supposes it, though mistakenly, to be attended with some circumstance, or set of circumstances, which, if it had been attended with, it would either not have been productive of that mischief, or have been productive of such a greater degree of good, as has determined the legislator in such a case not to make it penal.[‡]

XI. 5. Where, though the penal clause might exercise a full and prevailing influence, were it to act alone, yet by the *predominant* influence of some opposite cause upon the will, it must necessarily be ineffectual; because the evil which he sees himself about to undergo, in the case of his *not* engaging in the act, is so great, that the evil denounced by the penal clause, in case of his engaging in it, cannot appear greater. This may happen, 1. In the case of *physical danger*; where the evil is such as appears likely to be brought about by the unassisted powers of *nature*. 2. In the case of a *threatened mischief*; where it is such as appears likely to be brought about through the intentional and conscious agency of *man*.[d]

XII. 6. Where (though the penal clause may exert a full and prevailing influence over the *will* of the party) yet his *physical faculties* (owing to the predominant influence of some physical cause) are not in a condition to follow the determination of the will insomuch that the act is absolutely *involuntary*. Such is the case of physical *compulsion* or *restraint*, by whatever means brought about; where the man's hand, for instance, is pushed against some object which his will disposes him *not* to touch; or tied down from touching some object which his will disposes him to touch.

The phrase is, that the will of these persons concurs not with the act; that they have no vicious will; or, that they have not the free use of their will. But suppose all this to be true? What is it to the purpose? Nothing: except in as far as it implies the reason given in the text.

   ‡ See B. I. tit. iv (Exemptions) and tit. vii (Extenuations).

   † See Ch. VIII (Intentionality).

   ‡ See Ch. IX (Consciousness).

   d The influences of the *moral* and *religious* sanctions, or, in other words, of the motives of *love of reputation* and *religion*, are other causes, the force of which may, upon particular occasions, come to be greater than that of any punishment which the legislator is *able*, or at least which he will *think proper*, to apply. These, therefore, it will be proper for him to have his eye upon. But the force of these influences is variable and different in different times and places: the force of the foregoing influences is constant and the same, at all times and every where. These, therefore, it can never be proper to look upon as safe grounds for establishing absolute impunity: owing (as in the above-mentioned cases of infancy and intoxication) to the impracticability of ascertaining the matter of fact.

§ 4. CASES WHERE PUNISHMENT IS UNPROFITABLE

These are,

XIII. 1. Where, on the one hand, the nature of the offence, on the other hand, that of the punishment, are, *in the ordinary state of things*, such, that when compared together, the evil of the latter will turn out to be greater than that of the former.

XIV. Now the evil of the punishment divides itself into four branches, by which so many different sets of persons are affected. 1. The evil of *coercion* or *restraint*: or the pain which it gives a man not to be able to do the act, whatever it be, which by the apprehension of the punishment he is deterred from doing. This is felt by those by whom the law is *observed*. 2. The evil of *apprehension*: or the pain which a man, who has exposed himself to punishment, feels at the thoughts of undergoing it. This is felt by those by whom the law has been *broken*, and who feel themselves in *danger* of its being executed upon them. 3. The evil of *sufferance*[†]: or the pain which a man feels, in virtue of the punishment itself, from the time when he begins to undergo it. This is felt by those by whom the law is broken, and upon whom it comes actually to be executed. 4. The pain of sympathy, and the other *derivative* evils resulting to the persons who are in *connection* with the several classes of original sufferers just mentioned.[*] Now of these four lots of evil, the first will be greater or less, according to the nature of the act from which the party is restrained: the second and third according to the nature of the punishment which stands annexed to that offence.

XV. On the other hand, as to the evil of the offence, this will also, of course, be greater or less, according to the nature of each offence. The proportion between the one evil and the other will therefore be different in the case of each particular offence. The cases, therefore, where punishment is unprofitable on this ground, can by no other means be discovered, than by an examination of each particular offence; which is what will be the business of the body of the work.

XIV. 2. Where, although in the *ordinary state* of things, the evil resulting from the punishment is not greater than the benefit which is likely to result from the force with which it operates, during the same space of time, towards the excluding the evil of the offence, yet it may have been rendered so by the influence of some *occasional circumstances*. In the number of these circumstances may be, 1. The multitude of delinquents at a particular juncture; being such as would increase, beyond the ordinary measure, the *quantum* of the second and third lots, and thereby also of a part of the fourth lot, in the evil of the punishment. 2. The extraordinary value of the services of some one delinquent; in the case where the effect of the punishment would be to deprive the community of the benefit of those services. 3. The displeasure of the *people*; that is, of an indefinite number of the members of the *same* community, in cases where (owing to the influence of some occasional incident) they happen to conceive, that the offence or the offender ought not to be punished at all, or at least ought not to be punished in the way in question. 4. The displeasure of *foreign powers*; that is, of the governing body, or a considerable number of the members of some *foreign* community or communities, with which the community in question, is connected.

[†] See Ch. v (Pleasures and Pains).
[*] See Ch. xii (Consequences) iv.

§ 5. CASES WHERE PUNISHMENT IS NEEDLESS

These are,

XVII. 1. Where the purpose of putting an end to the practice may be attained as effectually at a cheaper rate: by instruction, for instance, as well as by terror: by informing the understanding, as well as by exercising an immediate influence on the will. This seems to be the case with respect to all those offences which consist in the disseminating pernicious principles in matters of *duty*; of whatever kind the duty be; whether political, or moral, or religious. And this, whether such principles be disseminated *under*, or even *without*, a sincere persuasion of their being beneficial. I say, even *without*: for though in such a case it is not instruction that can prevent the writer from endeavouring to inculcate his principles, yet it may the readers from adopting them: without which, his endeavouring to inculcate them will do no harm. In such a case, the sovereign will commonly have little need to take an active part: if it be the interest of *one* individual to inculcate principles that are pernicious, it will as surely be the interest of *other* individuals to expose them. But if the sovereign must needs take a part in the controversy, the pen is the proper weapon to combat error with, not the sword.

CHAPTER XIV

OF THE PROPORTION BETWEEN PUNISHMENTS AND OFFENCES

I. We have seen that the general object of all laws is to prevent mischief; that is to say, when it is worth while; but that, where there are no other means of doing this than punishment, there are four cases in which it is *not* worth while.

II. When it *is* worth while, there are four subordinate designs or objects, which, in the course of his endeavours to compass, as far as may be, that one general object, a legislator, whose views are governed by the principle of utility, comes naturally to propose to himself.

III. 1. His first, most extensive, and most eligible object, is to prevent, in as far as it is possible, and worth while, all sorts of offences whatsoever[a]: in other words, so to manage, that no offence whatsoever may be committed.

IV. 2. But if a man must needs commit an offence of some kind or other, the next object is to induce him to commit an offence *less* mischievous, *rather* than one *more* mischievous: in other words, to choose always the *least* mischievous, of two offences that will either of them suit his purpose.

V. 3. When a man has resolved upon a particular offence, the next object is to dispose him to do *no more* mischief than is *necessary* to his purpose: in other words, to do as little mischief as is consistent with the benefit he has in view.

---

[a] By *offences* I mean, at present, acts which appear to him to have a tendency to produce mischief.

VI. 4. The last object is, whatever the mischief be, which it is proposed to prevent, to prevent it at as *cheap* a rate as possible.

VII. Subservient to these four objects, or purposes, must be the rules or canons by which the proportion of punishments[b] to offences is to be governed.

Rule 1

VIII. The first object, it has been seen, is to prevent, in as far as it is worth while, all sorts of offences; therefore,

The value of the punishment must not be less in any case than what is sufficient to out-weigh that of the profit[c] of the offence.[*]

If it be, the offence (unless some other considerations, independent of the punishment, should intervene and operate efficaciously in the character of tutelary motives[**]) will be sure to be committed notwithstanding[d]: the whole lot of punishment will be thrown away: it will be altogether *inefficacious.*

IX. The above rule has been often objected to, on account of its seeming harshness: but this can only have happened for want of its being properly understood. The strength of the temptation, *cœteris paribus*, is as the profit of the offence: the quantum of the punishment must rise with the profit of the offence: *cœteris paribus*, it must therefore rise with the strength of the temptation. This there is no disputing. True it is, that the stron-

---

[b] (Punishments). The same rules (it is to be observed) may be applied, with little variation, to rewards as well as punishment: in short, to motives in general, which, according as they are of the pleasurable or painful kind, are of the nature of *reward* or *punishment*: and, according as the act they are applied to produce is of the positive or negative kind, are stiled impelling or restraining. See Ch. x (Motives) xliii.

[c] (Profit). By the profit of an offence, is to be understood, not merely the pecuniary profit, but the pleasure or advantage, of whatever kind it be, which a man reaps, or expects to reap, from the gratification of the desire which prompted him to engage in the offence.[‡]

It is the profit (that is, the expectation of the profit) of the offence that constitutes the *impelling* motive, or, where there are several, the sum of the impelling motives, by which a man is prompted to engage in the offence. It is the punishment, that is, the expectation of the punishment, that constitutes the *restraining* motive, which, either by itself, or in conjunction with others, is to act upon him in a *contrary* direction, so as to induce him to abstain from engaging in the offence. Accidental circumstances apart, the strength of the temptation is as the force of the seducing, that is, of the impelling motive or motives. To say then, as authors of great merit and great name have said that the punishment ought not to increase with the strength of the temptation, is as much as to say in mechanics, that the moving force or *momentum* of the *power* need not increase in proportion to the momentum of the *burthen*.

[‡] See Ch. x (Motives) § 1.

[*] Beccaria, dei delitti, § 6. id. trad. par Morellet, § 23.

[**] See Ch. xi (Dispositions) xxix.

[d] It is a well-known adage, though it is to be hoped not a true one, that every man has his price. It is commonly meant of a man's virtue. This saying, though in a very different sense, was strictly verified by some of the Anglo-saxon laws: by which a fixed price was set, not upon a man's virtue indeed, but upon his life: that of the sovereign himself among the rest. For 200 shillings you might have killed a peasant: for six times as much, a nobleman: for six-and-thirty times as much you might have killed the king.[†] A king in those days was worth exactly 7,200 shillings. If then the heir to the throne, for example, grew weary of waiting for it, he had a secure and legal way of gratifying his impatience: he had but to kill the king with one hand, and pay himself with the other, and all was right. An earl Godwin, or a duke Streon, could have bought the lives of a whole dynasty. It is plain, that if ever a king in those days died in his bed, he must have had something else, besides this law, to thank for it. This being the production of a remote and barbarous age, the absurdity of it is presently recognized: but, upon examination, it would be found, that the freshest laws of the most civilized nations are continually falling into the same error. This, in short, is the case wheresoever the punishment is fixed while the profit of delinquency is indefinite: or, to speak more precisely, where the punishment is limited to such a mark, that the profit of delinquency may reach beyond it.

[†] Wilkin's Leg. Anglo-sax. p. 71, 72. See Hume, vol. i. append. i. p. 219.

ger the temptation, the less conclusive is the indication which the act of delinquency affords of the depravity of the offender's disposition.|| So far then as the absence of any aggravation, arising from extraordinary depravity of disposition, may operate, or at the utmost, so far as the presence of a ground of extenuation, resulting from the innocence or beneficence of the offender's disposition, can operate, the strength of the temptation may operate in abatement of the demand for punishment. But it can never operate so far as to indicate the propriety of making the punishment ineffectual, which it is sure to be when brought below the level of the apparent profit of the offence.

The partial benevolence which should prevail for the reduction of it below this level, would counteract as well those purposes which such a motive would actually have in view, as those more extensive purposes which benevolence ought to have in view: it would be cruelty not only to the public, but to the very persons in whose behalf it pleads: in its effects, I mean, however opposite in its intention. Cruelty to the public, that is cruelty to the innocent, by suffering them, for want of an adequate protection, to lie exposed to the mischief of the offence: cruelty even to the offender himself, by punishing him to no purpose, and without the chance of compassing that beneficial end, by which alone the introduction of the evil of punishment is to be justified.

RULE 2

X. But whether a given offence shall be prevented in a given degree by a given quantity of punishment, is never any thing better than a chance; for the purchasing of which, whatever punishment is employed, is so much expended in advance. However, for the sake of giving it the better chance of outweighing the profit of the offence,

The greater the mischief of the offence, the greater is the expence, which it may be worth while to be at, in the way of punishment.[c]

RULE 3

XI. The next object is, to induce a man to choose always the least mischievous of two offences; therefore

Where two offences come in competition, the punishment for the greater offence must be sufficient to induce a man to prefer the less.[*]

RULE 4

XII. When a man has resolved upon a particular offence, the next object is, to induce him to do no more mischief than what is necessary for his purpose: therefore

The punishment should be adjusted in such manner to each particular offence, that for every part of the mischief there may be a motive to restrain the offender from giving birth to it.[f]

|| See Ch. xi; (Dispositions) xlii.

[c] For example, if it can ever be worth while to be at the expence of so horrible a punishment as that of burning alive, it will be more so in the view of preventing such a crime as that of murder or incendiarism, than in the view of preventing the uttering of a piece of bad money. See B. I. tit. (Defraudment touching the Coin) and (Incendiarism).

[*] Espr. des Loix, L. vi. c. 16.[1]

[f] If any one have any doubt of this, let him conceive the offence to be divided into as many separate offences as there are distinguishable parcels of mischief that result from it. Let it consist for example, in a man's giving you ten blows, or stealing from you ten shillings. If then, for giving you ten blows, he is

RULE 5

XIII. The last object is, whatever mischief is guarded against, to guard against it at as cheap a rate as possible: therefore

The punishment ought in no case to be more than what is necessary to bring it into conformity with the rules here given.

RULE 6

XIV. It is further to be observed, that owing to the different manners and degrees in which persons under different circumstances are affected by the same exciting cause, a punishment which is the same in name will not always either really produce, or even so much as appear to others to produce, in two different persons the same degree of pain: therefore,

That the quantity actually inflicted on each individual offender may correspond to the quantity intended for similar offenders in general, the several circumstances influencing sensibility ought always to be taken into account.*

XV. Of the above rules of proportion, the four first, we may perceive, serve to mark out the limits on the side of diminution; the limits *below* which a punishment ought not to be *diminished*: the fifth, the limits on the side of increase; the limits *above* which it ought not to be *increased*. The five first are calculated to serve as guides to the legislator: the sixth is calculated, in some measure, indeed, for the same purpose; but principally for guiding the judge in his endeavours to conform, on both sides, to the intentions of the legislator.

XVI. Let us look back a little. The first rule, in order to render it more conveniently applicable to practice, may need perhaps to be a little more particularly unfolded. It is to be observed, then, that for the sake of accuracy, it was necessary, instead of the word *quantity* to make use of the less perspicuous term *value*. For the word *quantity* will not properly include the circumstances either of certainty or proximity: circumstances which, in estimating the value of a lot of pain or pleasure, must always be taken into the account.† Now, on the one hand, a lot of punishment is a lot of pain; on the other hand, the profit of an offence is a lot of pleasure, or what is equivalent to it. But the profit of the offence *is* commonly more *certain* than the punishment, or, what comes to the same thing, *appears* so at least to the offender. It is at any rate commonly more *immediate*. It follows, therefore, that, in order to maintain its superiority over the profit of the offence, the punishment must have its value made up in some other way, in proportion to that whereby it falls short in

---

punished no more than for giving you five, the giving you five of these ten blows is an offence for which there is no punishment at all: which being understood, as often as a man gives you five blows, he will be sure to give you five more, since he may have the pleasure of giving you these five for nothing. In like manner, if for stealing from you ten shillings, he is punished no more than for stealing five, the stealing of the remaining five of those ten shillings is an offence for which there is no punishment at all. This rule is violated in almost every page of every body of laws I have ever seen.

The profit, it is to be observed, though frequently, is not constantly, proportioned to the mischief: for example, where a thief, along with the things he covets, steals others which are of no use to him. This may happen through wantonness, indolence, precipitation, ‡c. ‡c.

* See ch. vi (Sensibility).

† See ch. iv (Value).

the two points of *certainty* and *proximity*. Now there is no other way in which it can receive any addition to its *value*, but by receiving an addition in point of *magnitude*. Wherever then the value of the punishment falls short, either in point of *certainty*, or of *proximity*, of that of the profit of the offence, it must receive a proportionable addition in point of *magnitude*.[g]

XVII. Yet farther. To make sure of giving the value of the punishment the superiority over that of the offence, it may be necessary, in some cases, to take into the account the profit not only of the *individual* offence to which the punishment is to be annexed, but also of such *other* offences of the *same sort* as the offender is likely to have already committed without detection. This random mode of calculation, severe as it is, it will be impossible to avoid having recourse to, in certain cases: in such, to wit, in which the profit is pecuniary, the chance of detection very small, and the obnoxious act of such a nature as indicates a habit: for example, in the case of frauds against the coin. If it be *not* recurred to, the practice of committing the offence will be sure to be, upon the balance of the account, a gainful practice. That being the case, the legislator will be absolutely sure of *not* being able to suppress it, and the whole punishment that is bestowed upon it will be thrown away. In a word (to keep to the same expressions we set out with) that whole quantity of punishment will be *inefficacious*.

Rule 7

XVIII. These things being considered, the three following rules may be laid down by way of supplement and explanation to Rule **1**.

To enable the value of the punishment to outweigh that of the profit of the offence, it must be encreased, in point of magnitude, in proportion as it falls short in point of certainty.

Rule 8

XIX. *Punishment must be further encreased in point of magnitude, in proportion as it falls short in point of proximity.*

Rule 9

XX. *Where the act is conclusively indicative of a habit, such an encrease must be given to the punishment as may enable it to outweigh the profit not only of the individual offence, but of such other like offences as are likely to have been committed with impunity by the same offender.*

XXI. There may be a few other circumstances or considerations which may influence, in some small degree, the demand for punishment: but as the propriety of these is either not so demonstrable, or not so constant, or the application of them not so determinate, as that of the foregoing, it may be doubted whether they be worth putting on a level with the others.

---

[g] It is for this reason, for example, that simple compensation is never looked upon as sufficient punishment for theft or robbery.

RULE 10

XXII. *When a punishment, which in point of quality is particularly well calculated to answer its intention, cannot exist in less than a certain quantity, it may sometimes be of use, for the sake of employing it, to stretch a little beyond that quantity which, on other accounts, would be strictly necessary.*

RULE 11

XXIII. *In particular, this may sometimes be the case, where the punishment proposed is of such a nature as to be particularly well calculated to answer the purpose of a moral lesson.*[h]

RULE 12

XXIV. The tendency of the above considerations is to dictate an augmentation in the punishment: the following rule operates in the way of diminution. There are certain cases (it has been seen[*]) in which, by the influence of accidental circumstances, punishment may be rendered unprofitable in the whole: in the same cases it may chance to be rendered unprofitable as to a part only. Accordingly,

In adjusting the quantum of punishment, the circumstances, by which all punishment may be rendered unprofitable, ought to be attended to.

RULE 13

XXV. It is to be observed, that the more various and minute any set of provisions are, the greater the chance is that any given article in them will not be borne in mind: without which, no benefit can ensue from it. Distinctions, which are more complex than what the conceptions of those whose conduct it is designed to influence can take in, will even be worse than useless. The whole system will present a confused appearance: and thus the effect, not only of the proportions established by the articles in question, but of whatever is connected with them, will be destroyed.[†] To draw a precise line of direction in such case seems impossible. However, by way of memento, it may be of some use to subjoin the following rule.

Among provisions designed to perfect the proportion between punishments and offences, if any occur, which, by their own particular good effects, would not make up for the harm they would do by adding to the intricacy of the Code, they should be omitted.[i]

---

[h] A punishment may be said to be calculated to answer the purpose of a moral lesson, when, by reason of the ignomy it stamps upon the offence, it is calculated to inspire the public with sentiments of aversion towards those pernicious habits and dispositions with which the offence appears to be connected; and thereby to inculcate the opposite beneficial habits and dispositions.

It is this, for example, if anything, that must justify the application of so severe a punishment as the infamy of a public exhibition, hereinafter proposed, for him who lifts up his hand against a woman, or against his father. See B. I. tit. [Simp. corporal injuries].

It is partly on this principle, I suppose, that military legislators have justified to themselves the inflicting death on the soldier who lifts up his hand against his superior officer.

[*] See ch. xiii (Cases unmeet), § iv.

[†] See B. II. tit. (Purposes). Append. tit. (Composition).[1]

[i] Notwithstanding this rule, my fear is, that in the ensuing model, I may be thought to have carried my endeavours at proportionality too far. Hitherto scarce any attention has been paid to it. Montesquieu seems to have been almost the first who has had the least idea of any such thing. In such a matter, therefore, excess seemed more eligible than defect. The difficulty is to invent; that done, if any thing seems superfluous, it is easy to rétrench.

XXVI. It may be remembered, that the political sanction, being that to which the sort of punishment belongs, which in this chapter is all along in view, is but one of four sanctions, which may all of them contribute their share towards producing the same effects. It may be expected, therefore, that in adjusting the quantity of political punishment, allowance should be made for the assistance it may meet with from those other controuling powers. True it is, that from each of these several sources a very powerful assistance may sometimes be derived. But the case is, that (setting aside the moral sanction, in the case where the force of it is expressly adopted into and modified by the political*) the force of those other powers is never determinate enough to be depended upon. It can never be reduced, like political punishment, into exact lots, nor meted out in number, quantity, and value. The legislator is therefore obliged to provide the full complement of punishment, as if he were sure of not receiving any assistance whatever from any of those quarters. If he does, so much the better: but least he should not, it is necessary he should, at all events, make that provision which depends upon himself.

XXVII. It may be of use, in this place, to recapitulate the several circumstances, which, in establishing the proportion betwixt punishments and offences, are to be attended to. These seem to be as follows:

I. *On the part of the offence:*

1. The profit of the offence;
2. The mischief of the offence;
3. The profit and mischief of other greater or lesser offences, of different sorts, which the offender may have to choose out of;
4. The profit and mischief of other offences, of the same sort, which the same offender may probably have been guilty of already.

II. *On the part of the punishment:*

5. The magnitude of the punishment: composed of its intensity and duration;
6. The deficiency of the punishment in point of certainty;
7. The deficiency of the punishment in point of proximity;
8. The quality of the punishment;
9. The accidental advantage in point of quality of a punishment, not strictly needed in point of quantity;

---

* See, B. I. tit. (Punishments).

10. The use of a punishment of a particular quality, in the character of a moral lesson.

III. *On the part of the offender:*

11. The responsibility of the class of persons in a way to offend;
12. The sensibility of each particular offender;
13. The particular merits or useful qualities of any particular offender, in case of punishment which might deprive the community of the benefit of them;
14. The multitude of offenders on any particular occasion.

IV. *On the part of the public*, at any particular conjuncture:

15. The inclinations of the people, for or against any quantity or mode of punishment;
16. The inclinations of foreign powers.

V. *On the part of the law*: that is, of the public for a continuance:

17. The necessity of making small sacrifices, in point of proportionality, for the sake of simplicity.

XXVIII. There are some, perhaps, who, at first sight, may look upon the nicety employed in the adjustment of such rules, as so much labour lost: for gross ignorance, they will say, never troubles itself about laws, and passion does not calculate. But the evil of ignorance admits of cure[*]: and as to the proposition that passion does not calculate, this like most of these very general and oracular propositions, is not true. When matters of such importance as pain and pleasure are at stake, and these in the highest degree (the only matters, in short, that can be of importance) who is there that does not calculate? Men calculate, some with less exactness, indeed, some with more: but all men calculate. I would not say, that even a madman does not calculate.[k] Passion calculates, more or less, in every man: in different men, according to the warmth or coolness of their dispositions: according to the firmness or irritability of their minds: according to

---

[*] See Append. tit. (Promulgation).
[k] There are few madmen but what are observed to be afraid of the strait waistcoat.

the nature of the motives by which they are acted upon. Happily, of all passions, that is the most given to calculation, from the excesses of which, by reason of its strength, constancy, and universality, society has most to apprehend[†]: I mean that which corresponds to the motive of pecuniary interest: so that these niceties, if such they are to be called, have the best chance of being efficacious, where efficacy is of the most importance.

[†] See ch. XII (Consequences) xxxiii.

4

PRINCIPLES OF A RATIONAL PENAL CODE

Sheldon Glueck

THE recent widespread interest on the part of individuals, institutions of learning and of less learning, research foundations and governmental organizations in the problem of criminality is the outcome of an alleged collapse of the administration of criminal justice in the American city. Thus far, effort has taken the form of popular articles, crime surveys, commissions, conferences. But in all of the survey reports thus far published, and in the work of commissions and conferences, no serious attempt seems to have been made at a basic analysis of the presuppositions and prejudices crystallized in the substantive and procedural criminal law. And no suggestions of principles for fundamental revision of the existing régime seem to have been made. Not even the standard-setting Cleveland survey, which remains unique in the thoroughness of its execution and scholarliness of its interpretation, made any attempt to suggest the prolegomena to a criminal procedure more scientific than that under which society now is so ineffectively waging the struggle against crime.[1]

One need hardly defend the thesis that what is required in this field is a fundamental reëxamination[2] of the foundations of criminal law and procedure in the light of what is known today of psychiatry, psychology, and social case work — that rapidly growing trinity

---

[1] Dean Pound's summary of the Cleveland survey findings, and his philosophical interpretation of the inherent and acquired difficulties of the situation in which the administration of American criminal justice now finds itself, is, however, of the utmost value in an understanding of the principal reasons for the inefficiencies and conflicting aims of the present régime.

[2] The Italian penal code commission headed by Professor Enrico Ferri, appointed September 14, 1919, was faced at the outset with the choice of making "a simple revision and technical correction of the statutes now in force," or propounding "a new and autonomous systematization of legislative norms in accord with the advance of scientific doctrines." The president of the commission said that the reason why it chose the latter alternative was "to avoid the inconveniences already experienced in Italy and abroad from attempting reforms that are fragmentary and often contradictory," and insisted that the reforms proposed "ought to

of the yet to be developed master-discipline, the "science of human nature." Such a reëx-amination, however, must go more deeply than the drafting of logically-articulated but wrongly-premised penal codes. It can certainly not be limited to "getting a law passed." It cannot be satisfied by "speeding up justice," when nobody has any clear notion of what justice is, and just why, and at what link in a complicated procedural chain speed is desirable. Finally, it cannot be made by persons whose only qualification, profound as that may be, is learning in "dogmatic law," and whose minds move logically, but provincially, within the ambit of "legal reasoning." The most creative legal treatises and judicial opinions have come from scholars whose disciplined learning in the law has not blinded them to the possibilities of infusion therein of wisdom from other arts and sciences. The twentieth century sociological school of jurisprudence expresses the movement to interrelate the social sciences, of which the law is but one. Law is no longer regarded as a self-sufficient, cabalistic discipline, isolated from the general stream of culture. We are realizing more and more that methods and attitudes from outside the realm of the formal law must be imported into the legal order as powerful catalyzers to creativity. We can no longer be content with the use of exclusively legal materials in the critique of the law.[3]

It is not easy, however, to find the means of this creative cross-fertilization, especially with regard to the penal régime. Deep-rooted fears and prejudices are embalmed in our penal law. For the purpose of focussing thought upon this problem, we set down some tentative principles for a penal code that, in the light of modern ethical, psycho-logical-psychiatric, and sociological views give some promise of being more rational and just than the procedure under which we are ineffectively laboring.

UNDERLYING SOCIAL-ETHICAL PRINCIPLE OF PENAL CODE

The basic social-ethical principle of any system of penal law should express the *raison d'être* of that system. Too often in the past has the basic principle of penal codes been implied, rather than expressed and defended, with the result that our penal statutes are

---

respond to one general direction and one organic system." 1 Ferri, Relazione sul Progetto Preliminare di Codice Penale Italiano (1921) 3–4, 180–81. This volume will hereinafter be referred to as the Italian Project. For an able discussion of this code project, see Collin, Enrico Ferri et l'avant-projet de Code Pénal Italien de 1921 (1925).

The London Times for November 23, 1927, reports that the draft of the Fascist penal code, prepared largely by Signor Rocco, the Fascist Minister of Justice, affirms as a basic principle the criterion which Ferri's code abandoned as unsatisfactory because unscientific. As a preliminary to enunciation of the penal philosophy of the positive school of criminology (Lombroso, Garofalo, Ferri), Professor Ferri many years ago pulled the foundation from the classical theory which bases criminal responsibility on freedom of will, substituting "social accountability" therefor. The new code, however, which appears to have every chance of adoption, is supported by Signor Rocco's statement that "there must be no modification of the principle of responsibility, which has rested for centuries on the basis of the individual capacity of understanding and will, and of consciousness and volition in human action." London Times, *supra*. For the text of the Rocco code, see Progetto Preliminare di un Nuovo Codice Penale (1927). See also Ferri, *Il Progetto Rocco di Codice Penale* (1927) 7 Scuola Positiva (n. s.) no. 11–12.

[3] See Ogburn and Goldenweiser, The Social Sciences and their Interrelations (1927), for abundant evidences of the recognition of the need for an assault upon the more or less artificial barriers between the sciences. A few colleges of political science and one or two law schools are beginning to recognize the possible value of systematic collaboration among the social scientists.

full of confusions and inconsistencies, containing statutory and case-law accretions of many epochs and philosophies. We submit the following basic principle: *Society should utilize every scientific instrumentality for self-protection against destructive elements in its midst, with as little interference with the free life of its members as is consistent with such social self-protection.* This proposition is basic to any discussion of social problems. If one denies that a society should protect itself, he not only denies to it the fundamental right of self-preservation, but jeopardizes his own security. Only by repelling criminal attacks against itself or its members can organized society offer the peace, security, and traditional expectancy of orderliness which are indispensable to the pursuit of the affairs of life by itself and its members. One who denies this indirectly advocates his own destruction.

In this basic work of self-protection, society should utilize every available scientific instrumentality. This is dictated both by the principle of justice and that of economy. While society has a primary interest in maintaining the general security, it also has an interest in the welfare of the individual life, and a duty to use every reasonable instrumentality for the rehabilitation of its antisocial members. Even a socially harmful criminal has a right, in justice, to be treated with those instrumentalities that give him the greatest promise of self-improvement and rehabilitation.

Justice demands also that, in its work of self-protection, society interfere as little as possible with the free life of its members. If one conceives of society as a necessary instrument for the harmonious integration of the more or less conflicting desires of human beings with the demands of the general welfare, one must acknowledge that social interference should cease at the point where such integration cannot be brought about by interference. A law or procedure, which, in the general opinion, unnecessarily or arbitrarily overemphasizes the social interest in the general security to the undue interference with the social and individual interests in the life and well-being of each person, is unjust, for it unnecessarily enslaves human beings.[4]

Not only justice but economy dictates the employment of scientific devices in the work of social self-protection. It is wasteful for society to be satisfied with a continuance of the present judicial and peno-correctional régimes, because the large figures of recidivism[5] are an indication that the present methods are not preventing criminals from repeating their anti-social behavior.

---

[4] It is much easier to formulate this general principle than to apply it in any specific instance. It cannot be denied, however, that a society which interferes substantially more with the liberty of its members than is dictated by a scientific conception of the general welfare is to that degree unjust.

[5] Almost every prison census and work on criminology refers to the problem of recidivism. See Bernard Glueck, *A Study of 608 Admissions to Sing Sing Prison* (1918) 2 MENTAL HYGIENE 177. On the basis of his Sing Sing studies, Glueck found that 66.8% of 608 consecutive admissions to Sing Sing Prison were recidivists, *i.e.*, persons who had been previously sentenced to penal institutions. FIRST ANNUAL REPORT OF THE PSYCHIATRIC CLINIC IN COLLABORATION WITH SING SING PRISON (1917) 11, 16. In a relatively recent examination by the National Committee for Mental Hygiene, of 1288 unselected prisoners of 34 county jails and penitentiaries in New York State (exclusive of New York City) it was found that 66% were repeated offenders. This figure for petty offenders (drunkards, vagrants, prostitutes, and those who have committed petty larceny) is strangely about the same as that for the more serious offenders of Sing Sing prison. "This is but in keeping with similar studies in penal and correctional institutions throughout the country, and means that we are in a large measure dealing with the same material over and over again — locking up and turning out the same individuals, and failing adequately to protect society from their depredations." A PLAN FOR THE CUSTODY AND TRAINING OF PRISONERS SERVING SENTENCES IN THE COUNTY JAILS IN NEW YORK STATE (1924) 16.

Rationale of punishment: Retributive-expiative theory. The chief means which society has long relied upon to maintain the general security is punishment either on a retributive-expiative theory, or for the pragmatic purposes discussed below. The old argument was that punishment was necessary as a "just retribution" or requital of wickedness. No thoughtful person today seriously holds this theory of sublimated social vengeance, nor that "expiative theory" which is the reverse of the shield of retribution. Official social institutions should not be predicated upon the destructive emotion of vengeance, which is not only the expression of an infantile way of solving a problem, but unjust and destructive of the purpose of protecting society. The official social institutions of criminal law and penal treatment should not be occupied with the criminal's expiation of his sins; that is properly the domain of religion. Society's legal institutions are concerned with the utilitarian possibilities of a punishment régime, possibilities which are founded upon the social purpose of the machinery of justice, namely, the maintenance of the general security with as little interference with the individual's rights as a human being and citizen as is necessary for the achievement of that social purpose.

It is sometimes argued that it is "natural" and thus "right and proper" that we "hate the criminal" and show our hatred. But (aside from the question whether everything that is "natural" is necessarily right) much of our hate-reaction toward criminals has been conditioned by education. Men used to hate the insane, and punished them accordingly. To hate acts that are socially harmful may be proper; but to base a policy of social protection upon the hatred of those who commit such acts is both uneconomical and unjust. It is uneconomical because, far from the vengeful attitude having produced socially desirable results, it has failed throughout to stem the tide of recidivism.[6] It is unjust because every human being has the right to be considered as such, with his hereditary and acquired weaknesses, as well as his strengths. This is to some extent feasible with modern scientific instrumentalities; but no device yet invented can dive into the heart and mind of an individual and come up with that exact apportionment of blame and blamelessness which even a rationalized vengeance called "solemn justice" demands as a prerequisite to castigation.

The attitude we are discussing may also be conceived of as a "rationalization" of something which is psychologically more profound. To one unfamiliar with the data of psychoanalytic psychology the following analyses of this attitude will doubtless be a surprise; but upon mature and honest reflection such a reader will gradually become convinced that there is more than "a grain of truth" in these suggestions. Says Dr. William A. White, dean of American psychiatrists:

> "The criminal thus becomes the handy scapegoat upon which he [the ordinary
> citizen] can transfer his feeling of his own tendency to sinfulness and thus
> by punishing the criminal he deludes himself into a feeling of righteous

---

[6] It is a well known fact that when punishment becomes so severe as to suggest the revenge motif rather than the idea of social protection, juries are loath to convict.

indignation, thus bolstering up his own self-respect and serving in this roundabout way, both to restrain himself from like indulgences and to keep himself upon the path of cultural progress. The legal punishment of the criminal today is, in its psychology, a dramatic tragic action by which society pushes off its criminal impulses upon a substitute. The principle is the same as that by which an emotion such as anger is discharged upon an inoffensive lifeless object."[7]

Discussing Spinoza's views on determinism and psychology, Dr. M. Hamblin Smith, gives a similar analysis of the "righteous indignation" rationalization of man's fear and anger responses and its social crystallization into a program of punishment *qua* punishment:

"It is often said that determinism leaves practical questions exactly as they were before. Generally speaking this statement is true. But it is not true in one important particular. All ground for blame, in the ordinary sense of that word, has been removed. This deprives the ordinary man of what he finds a great comfort.... We may point out that man always wants to blame others for what he finds in himself. The matter goes much deeper than the influence of the primitive instinct of vengeance. Man is always trying to get rid of something that makes him unhappy. If this something happens to be wrong, according to the ethical standards of the herd, he attempts to escape his personal responsibility for it. In punishing an offender, man is trying to get rid of a wrong which he feels is resident in himself. Hence the offender becomes a convenient scapegoat."[8]

Turning now to the utilitarian justifications of punishment, much confusion in the discussion of this subject can be avoided by referring to the influence of the *threat* of arrest, imprisonment, or execution, as the *deterrent* effect of punishment, and the influence of the memory of past punishment upon the individual punished as the *preventive* effect of punishment. The first is the psychological effect of a continuous appeal to the fear emotion in the form of a threat of enforced suffering in making "the rest of us" behave in conformity with the law; the second, the psychological effect of the recollection of past punishment in influencing the future conduct of an ex-prisoner to bring it within legal bounds.

Punishment as a deterrent. As to the first influence, knowledge of psychology must convince one that much of conduct can be and in fact is influenced by the threat of punishment. Fear plays an important rôle in deterring most persons from the commission of legally prohibited acts, although other motives are, of course, also operative. Since the threat of arrest and punishment is an appeal to fear, which for most persons

---

[7] White, Insanity and the Criminal Law (1923) 13–14.
[8] Cited by Root, A Psychological and Educational Survey of 1916 Prisoners in the Western Penitentiary of Pennsylvania (1927) 11–12.

is probably the strongest motive, it doubtlessly has a deterrent value. It is fallacious to argue, as many do, that because the volume of crime in proportion to the population has not diminished, or is rising (if such be the case), such a condition proves that the threat of punishment is no deterrent. No one can say how much *more* crime there would be on the part of the law-abiding public were the restraint of the threat of punishment removed. During the Boston police strike, for example, not all of the increased crime was due to "imported criminals," or local habitual criminals. Some of it was probably brought about by persons on the brink of criminality who needed just that removal of the threat of apprehension and punishment to push them over into the criminal ranks. The same phenomenon is observable after every great public catastrophe when among those who steal from the bodies of dead and wounded there are a number of people who formerly were law-abiding but who commit crimes, upon the removal of organized restraint in the post-catastrophic confusion.

But though the threat of punishment has some deterrent value, it must be pointed out that a scientific system of penal law taking the point of view of modern psychiatry would not, in any real sense, deprive society of whatever deterrent effect such threat might have. The modern psychiatric school of criminology does not ask that we pass by, unnoticed, the acts of criminal aggression committed by individuals, and thus break down the defensive breastworks of the threat of punishment. Under the régime proposed herein,[9] for example, anti-social persons would still be deprived of their liberty. Nay more, it may justly be claimed that the proposed procedure of scientific individualization would have a greater deterrent effect than does the present mechanized and bargaining procedure. Under the existing system, prospective criminals know in advance the chances of probation, and, essentially, the length of imprisonment as related to contemplated crimes; and they know that with the mechanically applied rules as to "time off for good behavior," parole as an automatic "reward" after the minimum limit of a sentence euphoniously designated "indeterminate" has been reached, and similar unscientific devices, they will be given their freedom *regardless of their improvement or further deterioration*. This is so because the present system bases penal treatment on a single or a few isolated acts of a person rather than upon knowledge of the personality and motivations of the offender and his social background.

With the emphasis shifted, as is proposed, from the isolated criminal act to the personality of the offender — his potentialities for good and evil, his response to treatment and so on — and his social setting, a prospective wrongdoer will not be able to estimate in advance the length of his incarceration, on the basis of the seriousness of the contemplated offense as set down in the statute books or the mechanized treatment of judges and parole boards. For an offense relatively venial in itself, it is conceivable that a socially-dangerous *personality* may remain incarcerated for life; and for one relatively serious it is likewise conceivable that a person who has profited by institutional or extra-mural treatment and gives reasonable scientific promise of permanent rehabilitation, will be given his liberty after a comparatively short period. The vital element of the possibility of lifelong incarceration if the individual is shown by scientific investigation

---

[9] See p. 475, *infra*.

to require it, may reasonably be expected to reinforce the natural deterrent effect of the threat of punishment.[10]

Punishment as a preventive. Considering now the second question, the prevention of further wrongdoing by the recollection of the punishment for the last, here again we cannot go along with most of the modern radicals in criminology. It cannot be seriously denied that the fear of the repetition of a painful experience of the past plays an important rôle in the guidance of conduct. Such anticipation of a painful reaction to a certain form of behavior (founded upon the psychological phenomenon of memory or whatever its neurological correlate may be) acts as a powerful influencer of conduct. The rôle of punishment and reward as determinants of behavior is clear in the laboratory when one deals experimentally with animals. Punishment is recognized also as an instrument for influencing the conduct of children and adults. It is daily used in the affairs of life and in penal institutions to influence conduct.

It is submitted, however, that punishment is an instrumentality that should not be used blindly, but by trained scientists, and only where "indicated," as the physicians would say. Moreover, punishment is but one of numerous "medicines" or devices that are more and more being put at the disposal of trained experts. It, as well as these other instrumentalities, should be utilized only after careful examination of the individual criminal has demonstrated his peculiar needs. It is the conviction of psychologists and psychiatrists that the emotion of fear is not the only motive of conduct, lawful or unlawful. It is certainly not the highest motive to appeal to, and not necessarily the most effective. It may well be that in the excitement of a criminal act the memory of the former suffering is beclouded; that in particular individuals (whether they are mentally "abnormal" or not) such former punishment has had little, if any, lasting effect; that the appeal to other motives promises to "build in" a more lasting change of character and habit than the appeal to fear alone or primarily; that in certain individuals, emphasis of the appeal to fear is the worst possible method of treatment, resulting, as it so often does with juvenile delinquents, in the building up of strong defensive or compensatory bulwarks of defiance, distrust, grudgefulness, or "low cunning," which in turn lead to further misconduct.

Our discussion indicates, then, that to continue in operation a penal system grounded largely upon the appeal to fear is unjust and uneconomical; but that a rational approach to the problems of crime and its treatment would not ignore the possible utility of punishment either as a deterrent or a preventive. It seeks merely to evaluate

---

[10] Another advantage of a change in basic principle of the penal system along the lines proposed herein is suggested by the following words of Professor Ferri: "Since [under the present régime] the judges have before them a man and not an objective fact, a contrast often arises in their consciences and in their sentences between the law and the human reality, and their judgments do not carry public approval because deemed too rigorous or too inadequate." ITALIAN PROJECT, 183–84. This public attitude is founded on the old notion that the sentence is the payment to society of an amount of suffering precisely proportionate to the amount of harmfulness of the crime, something in itself impossible of measurement.

The principle of penocorrectional treatment of the offending personality rather than of punishment supposedly commensurate to the precise gravity of an act will gradually become prevalent. Indeed, the widespread use of probation and the juvenile court is already transforming the public attitude toward the entire problem. We may expect the gradual replacement of the bargaining attitude by one in which length of deprivation of liberty will be recognized to depend upon the response of the offender to treatment.

it according to its true worth, and to control it in accordance with a well-rounded, preventive-therapeutic program. Moreover, such a view of the rôle of the appeal to the emotion of fear promises not only to retain whatever present effectiveness there may be in punishment, as a preventive or deterrent, but to increase it.

Individualization, with the Aid of Appropriate Sciences, as the Means of Enforcement

The need, and the technical instruments, of individualization. As long as the legal order confined itself to a reliance upon fear as the principal instrument for the protection of society against criminal aggression, there was not much need for scientific individualization of peno-correctional treatment. The criminal law defined the crimes, the penal statutes set down for each offense the precise dosage of punishment fatuously believed to "fit the crime," and the judge mechanically sentenced convicted persons on the basis of this schedule of punishments. But with the recognition of the futility of that system because of the complex mental and social factors which enter into the commission or failure to commit crimes, individualization of treatment must be recognized as indispensable. Effective individualization must be based upon as complete an understanding of each offender as modern science will permit. Hence psychiatry, psychology, and social case work — not to mention those disciplines more remotely concerned with the problems of human motivation and behavior — must be drawn into the program for administering criminal justice. And this is true not alone in those cases in which a definite mental disorder is present, but in the general run of cases. For only by recognition of the motives behind and the social setting of criminal conduct can the treatment prescribed by the judge be intelligently calculated to protect society, through the rehabilitation of those who respond to treatment and the permanent isolation of those who do not so react.

Only through the systematic assistance of psychiatrists, psychologists, and social investigators can even the existing individualizing instrumentalities — probation, the indeterminate sentence, parole, the juvenile court — be effectively utilized. Thus, "probation" in some jurisdictions means the evil practice of releasing almost every first offender and many a dangerous repeater "to give him another chance." The hoped-for rehabilitation is ostensibly to be brought about by some miracle. For in such jurisdictions no effort whatsoever is made, either in the way of examination into the social-psychiatric conditions of the offender to determine his fitness for probation, or in the way of constructive supervision during the probation period. Thus an instrumentality, the very creation of which was due to recognition of the importance of individualization, is used mechanically, perfunctorily, and in some cases even corruptly. Probation in a few jurisdictions,[11] however, is based on careful, individualized examination and

---

[11] As indicative of what probation ought to be and of its tremendous importance in the protection of society through rehabilitation of promising offenders, the reader should consult Cooley, Probation and Delinquency (1927). Notice particularly the sub-title — The Study and Treatment of the Individual Delinquent. See also Van Waters, Youth in Conflict (1925).

treatment, in which psychiatrists, psychologists, and social workers are the interpretive agencies, while the judge represents the tempering wisdom of the legally-experienced magistrate. The same distinctions could be made between so-called "indeterminate sentences," "parole," and "juvenile courts," and the genuine devices whose titles have thus been wrongly preempted. In a word, individualization is necessary on the part of the court and other institutions dealing with the offender; and effective individualization is not based on guesswork, mechanical routine, "hunches," political considerations, or even (as so many judges seem to think) on past criminal record alone. It must rest on a scientific recognition and evaluation of those mental and social factors involved in the criminal situation which make each crime a unique event and each criminal a unique personality.

Objection to utilization of scientific instrumentalities in administration of criminal justice. The objection has been made against the consistent use of psychiatry, psychology, and social case work in the administration of criminal justice, that these instrumentalities are still in a highly experimental and formative state and that experts representing these disciplines frequently disagree when asked to give opinions. The principle is self-evident that in a wise legal order we should proceed cautiously in absorbing methods or attitudes from outside of the law. But it must be said that the disagreement between experts has been "greatly exaggerated." On fundamental symptomatology of the various mental and behavior disorders most psychiatrists are agreed. On basic mental "mechanisms"[12] many of them are coming more and more to agree. True, there are some real differences of opinion on questions of *theory*, on attempts to account for the phenomena observed. But this is a healthy sign of a growing discipline; it is not absent in the law itself. There is also disagreement as to the effectiveness of various methods of therapy, which is likewise a sign of vitality. Again, in the realm of psychology, standardized intelligence tests of various kinds are admittedly far from perfect and are undergoing continuous improvement on the basis of experimentation. Yet their use is becoming more and more widespread if also more critical. Further, a complete, perfectly logical set of principles of social case work has not yet been developed; but a body of wisdom, based on experience, is gradually crystallizing, and scientific method is little by little being infused into social case work.[13] The imperfection in social service technique did not prevent the rapid spread of the movement to substitute "constructive social work" for indiscriminate, mass-treating, wasteful, pauperizing "charity." Though the instruments for "constructive social work" are still far from ideally suitable to the purpose, nobody would seriously propose the return to the old methods of almsgiving. In the field of criminal justice, society has experimented for many years with mass-treatment, unscientific methods. Is it not time to make a serious effort at experimentation with the more promising techniques? Any system of diagnosis and treatment of

---

[12] See White, Mechanisms of Character Formation (1918), Hart, Psychology of Insanity (1920), and Barrett, *Mental Disorders in Medicolegal Relations* in 1 Peterson, Haines and Webster, Legal Medicine and Toxicology (1923).

[13] See, *e.g.*, Richmond, Social Diagnosis (1917), and What is Social Case Work? (1922). Consult Cooley, *op. cit. supra* note 11, for striking illustrations of the possibilities of constructive social case work methods in the service of the court.

the individual delinquent, based on a responsible application of such scientific instru-mentalities as exist, few and imperfect as these may be, is superior to a practice which treats human acts *in vacuo*, and human beings mechanically, perfunctorily, and in the mass, on the basis of impossible rules set down by the legislature in advance of the events to which they are to be applied by perplexed judges.

Types and stages of existing individualization. Assuming the necessity of individual-ization, at what stage in the procedure of criminal justice shall it be made and by what legal agency? The work of individualization of one kind or another may, of course, be attempted at various stages and by differing means. The district attorney may crudely "individualize" as to types of cases he is going to stress in prosecution out of a mass of cases. Again, definitions in the substantive criminal law itself, such as the historical distinction between murder and manslaughter,[14] distinctions between voluntary and involuntary manslaughter, or between burglary and larceny, represent crude judicial and legislative categorizations of types of somewhat analogous criminal acts, on the ground that the individual acts differ in degree of seriousness. So also, the breaking up of crimes into rather detailed "degrees," which was so common a phenomenon in American codes and statutes in the nineteenth century and which is still a characteris-tic, represents a later and less crude process of legislative individualization in the trial and punishment of varieties of a similar type of criminal act rather than of classes of criminal.[15] Such code or statutory provisions are customarily accompanied by stipula-tions as to fixed length and type of punishment, leaving the trial judge, or (in states where the jury has anything to do with fixing the punishment) the jury, relatively little discretion as to penal treatment. These are very crude individualizations of various classes of offenses by the legislature. Within such crime categories, however, there is no distinction made between individual delinquents; all offenders committing the same crime are punishable equally.

The "indeterminate sentence" movement which began late in the nineteenth cen-tury as a recognition of the need of individualization of punishment has in practice had but little effect upon these fixed provisions regarding punishment or upon the attitude which inspired them. For, in the first place, not all states have indeterminate sentences; secondly, indeterminate sentence provisions apply in most jurisdictions only to speci-fied types of crime or to persons within specified age limits; and thirdly, the aims of the proponents of the indeterminate sentence have frequently been defeated on the one hand by judges imposing sentences which practically make the minimum limit identi-cal with the maximum (as a sentence, say, of from twenty-four years and six months to twenty-five years), and, on the other, by parole boards automatically releasing prisoners

---

[14] See authorities collected in Sayre, Cases on Criminal Law (1927) 767 *et seq.*

[15] Such, *e.g.*, are the distinctions in varieties of arson found in the N. Y. Penal Law §§ 221–23, dividing the crime into three degrees dependent largely on the type of structure burned and whether the burning was by day or night; the familiar practice of breaking up burglary into degrees, depending upon whether or not the entry is accompanied by one or more of the common law requisites of burglary or not; the division of murder and manslaughter into degrees based on such mental and other accompaniments of the homicide as whether or not the act was done with "deliberately premeditated malice aforethought" (Mass. Gen. Laws (1921) c. 265, § 1), whether or not it was committed in the perpetration or attempted perpetration of specified other crimes, such as rape, arson, robbery or burglary, whether the means were poison (Pa. Act of April 22, 1794, § 2), or interference with railroad tracks (N. Y. Penal Law § 1044).

after the minimum limit of the sentence has been served. We may fairly say then that although crude attempts have been made at individualization of penal treatment on the basis of type of crime, and by use of the so-called "indeterminate sentence," the mass-treatment method of dealing with offenders, founded on legislative prescription in advance of detailed rules for the guidance of the judiciary is, by and large, still in vogue in the American criminal court.

The provision for pleas in mitigation or aggravation of punishment after conviction but prior to sentence represents another stage and method of individualization of penal treatment. This is, however, also a crude and unreliable instrument, the appeal to judicial discretion consisting, as it frequently does, of one-sided emotional or irrelevant pleas to the judge rather than unbiased reports founded on scientific examination. Then there is the crude, mechanical, unimaginative individualization of the judge who has made up his mind in advance to impose heavy sentences on offenders against certain laws, or on second offenders, or to place only offenders against certain legislation on probation, and that regardless of how often they have already failed under such extramural treatment in the past, and of how promising of redemption offenders against other laws might be.

As to all these methods of "separating the sheep from the goats," one may safely say that they do not constitute efficient instruments of that scientific individualization which we found to be the *sine qua non* to economical as well as just administration of criminal law. Legislative prescription in advance of detailed degrees of offenses is individualization of acts and not of human beings, and is, therefore, bound to be inefficient. Judicial "individualization," without adequate scientific facilities in aid of the court, is bound to deteriorate into a mechanical process of application of certain rules of thumb or of implied or expressed prejudices.

Essence of Professor Ferri's scheme of individualization. It is along the lines of an even more detailed legislative prescription of rules to be applied by trial courts in individualizing punishment of future criminals than exists in America today that Professor Enrico Ferri's penal code commission has drafted its basic provision. American experience, however, both with the detailed definitions of the pre-indeterminate-sentence era, and with the indeterminate sentence as applied by judges, would suggest that this setting down of detailed rules of individualization by the legislature in advance, for the guidance of the bench in the imposition of sentence, is not the best road out of the jungle of the present inefficient judicio-penal practice.

Ferri's commission recommends that a schedule of "conditions of dangerousness" and "conditions of less dangerousness" be adopted for the guidance of judges in individualizing punishment. The basic criterion of his scholarly project for an Italian Penal Code, is "the principle of the dangerousness of the offender."[16] The penal code and the penal and correctional institutions take this principle as their point of departure. This must be admitted to be a great stride in advance, when one compares it with the basis of our criminal law as expounded by Dean Pound:

---

[16] Italian Project, 7, 49 *et seq.*, 153, 183 *et seq.*, 229 *et seq.*, 342.

"Historically, our substantive criminal law is based upon a theory of punishing the vicious will. It postulates a free agent confronted with a choice between doing right and doing wrong and choosing freely to do wrong. It assumes that the social interest in the general security and the social interest in the general morals are to be maintained by imposing upon him a penalty corresponding exactly to the gravity of his offense."[17]

This existing criminal law stresses but one act of the offender, without going into the causes of that act or considering other acts or the personality of the actor. Since it thus treats *a symptom* instead of regarding the entire symptom complex and its causes, it is bound to be almost as ineffective as a medical régime which prescribes for a single symptom, not troubling with its relation to other symptoms nor with the causes of the symptoms.

But in the light of what was said above, it must be obvious that to found a new penal code on the sole principle of the dangerousness of the offender[18] which condition is to be arrived at by judicial application of a legislative schedule of "conditions of dangerousness" and those of "less dangerousness" is open to objections. First, it emphasizes a single feature (although it improves upon existing practice in that that feature is a more or less lasting *condition* rather than an individual act), and, secondly, it employs in the work of individualization an instrument that has already been shown to be inadequate.

As to the first point — which is incidental to the main discussion at this stage — if the offender is "dangerous," is not that but one feature of his personality make-up? To look only at his dangerousness is both unjust and unscientific. In overemphasizing the social interest in the general security to the underemphasis of the social interest in the individual life, it is unjust. The easiest way to dispose of criminals, when one stresses their social dangerousness, is to execute them all. But such a principle, standing alone, does not recognize the social justice of construc- tive rehabilitative work with delinquents on the basis of individual case-study and need. It is uneconomical, for it does not recognize that the most efficient way of cop- ing with the problem, in the long run, is this same constructive rehabilitative effort with the individual delinquent, on the basis of scientific understanding. For while executed criminals do not destroy, neither do they build; and this latter possibility is certainly not to be ignored merely because the traditional, mechanical, punitive régime has failed to reform many criminals. Besides, if we are ever going to learn anything about criminal motivation, it is short-sighted to destroy our "laboratory material" without study.

It is true that, as to the penal organization, Ferri agrees with the soundest Ameri- can thought on the problem, when he says: "In place of the traditional system of prison penalties for a fixed period, there must be substituted segregation for a period rela- tively or absolutely unlimited, while the necessary guarantees for individual rights are

---

[17] Introduction to Sayre, *op. cit. supra* note 14, at xxxvi-xxxvii.
[18] The other principle Ferri employs, "social defense," while broader is still subject to the above criticism, when used as Ferri proposes.

secured."[19] Nevertheless, by stressing the dangerousness of the offender, Ferri unduly underemphasizes the rehabilitative possibilities of the offender.

Basic criterion of penal system. We would therefore substitute for Ferri's basic criterion the following: *The legal and institutional provisions for the protection of society must be based not so much upon the gravity of the particular act for which an offender happens to be tried, as upon his personality, that is, upon his dangerousness,*[20] *his personal assets, and his responsiveness to peno-correctional treatment.*

This criterion takes account of the well known fact that a relatively innocuous act may happen to be, and not infrequently is, committed by one who fundamentally is socially dangerous, while a relatively serious offense (even murder)[21] may be committed by one who fundamentally is no longer socially dangerous. But it also takes account of the fact that when we speak of "personality," rather than "crime" or "act," we are dealing with a developing, dynamic phenomenon rather than a static fact, a complex phenomenon of which dangerousness at the time of conviction is but one symptom.

The second point of criticism of Ferri's system is more serious. It is doubtful whether any scheme of individualization based on a schedule of minute rules set down by the legislature to govern judges in future cases can be successful. This can no more be done by the legislature as to a person's character than it can (as at present attempted) as to single acts. The legislature cannot possibly conceive in advance the subtle *nuances* that distinguish different offenders from each other, nor the types or lengths of treatment required by various individuals. What the legislature can do is to set down certain broad penological standards and leave to trained judges, psychiatrists, and psychologists, forming a quasi-judicial treatment body, the application of those standards in the individual case.

An examination of the details of Ferri's scheme will indicate that this criticism is sound. In accordance with his policy of emphasizing the dangerousness of the offender and at the same time providing for "necessary guarantees" of individual rights, Ferri furnishes an elaborate, narrowly-defined schedule of "conditions of dangerousness" and "conditions of less dangerousness," to be prescribed by the code in advance and to be applied by judges as a basis for computation of the type and length of the individual convict's incarceration. At the same time, he stresses the necessity of "segregation for a period relatively or absolutely unlimited." The "degree of dangerousness" is to "be

---

[19] ITALIAN PROJECT, 15, 192.

[20] It is quite true, as Ferri points out, that the emphasis of the dangerousness of the offender becomes of vital significance in treating of the law of attempts. It is conceivable, for example, that one who attempts a crime but does not for some reason bring about its completion may be a much more dangerous person than another whose attempt has ripened into a completed act. Both would ordinarily be guilty of some offense at present, but the former would be punishable far less, *i.e.*, only for an attempt, the latter for the more serious, completed crime. But the question is, shall dangerousness be the sole criterion, and provided for in the substantive law, or by its inclusion among the "conditions of dangerousness," or shall its recognition, together with the many other factors disclosed by scientific examination of the individual case, be by a "treatment board" with wide administrative discretion? See p. 475, *infra*.

[21] Mrs. Jessie D. Hodder, one of the foremost prison administrators in the country, has on several occasions said that the inmates of her institution (The Massachusetts Reformatory for Women) who make the least trouble and who are the most trustworthy are those who have committed certain types of homicides.

determined according to the gravity and modalities of the offense, the determining motives and the personality of the offender."

From a perusal of the items quoted in the footnote, it must be admitted that Professor Ferri and his colleagues have evidenced an enviable ingenuity in analyzing and defining the conditions of "dangerousness" and "less dangerousness" to be used as a schedule of individualization by judges. It will be noticed, however, that practically all of the "circumstances" listed are those mental and physical accompaniments of the criminal act itself which today are taken into account in definitions distinguishing degrees of crimes in American penal statutes, or as conditions in aggravation or mitigation of sentence, or by some judges in determining fitness for probation, by some prison officials in dealing with prisoners within the institution, by some parole boards in considering their release on parole; and it is a serious question whether more is not lost than gained by removing the application of such criteria from the discretion of the last-named agencies and putting the criteria into the code to be applied by judges. For example, to the extent that it substitutes the application of criteria of dangerousness and less dangerousness *at the time of original sentence* for application of similar criteria at a later stage, the procedure provided for is inferior to that of the better parole boards. How can a judge possibly know in advance how long it will take to rehabilitate a person or even what type of institutional or extra-mural régime is required, without a provision for observation of the progress of treatment, and for the trial and error method of continuous modification of treatment in the light of results? In Ferri's scheme not only are the criteria solely those of "dangerousness," but the prisoner is permanently labeled in advance of treatment.

Such detailed legislative prescription of criteria to be judicially applied to individual cases constitutes a peculiarly unsatisfactory and confusing solution of the dilemma of which judicial discretion is one horn and detailed legislative prescription the other. Subsequent articles of the Code only increase the confusion. They provide for the judicial application of the "sanctions" in a manner that would transform the judge into a computer of his own sum of discretion in different types of cases.

The details given in the footnotes abundantly indicate the mechanical nature of the individualization provided for. They are quite on a parity with the traditional practice in the criminal law which Dean Pound has criticized as based on an erroneous assumption.[27] While ostensibly reforming this situation, what does Ferri's scheme propose but the substitution of minute rules, mechanically to be applied by judges, the difference being that now, instead of the legislature measuring the exact gravity of the *offense* in advance, it is provided that it measure the exact dangerousness of every type of *offender* in advance. The practice is so mechanical and complicated in its conception that one has a picture of a judge checking up whether, say, "circumstances of greater dangerousness," numbered 1, 3, 7 and 14, and "circumstances of less dangerousness," numbered 5, 9 and 11 are applicable to a defendant before him,

[27] See *supra* p. 468.

ascertaining which of the numerous "sanctions" or combinations thereof are pertinent, then using a computing machine to figure out just how much incarceration the so-called "unlimited" sentence really calls for. Both in making such provisions to be used at the time of sentence in a judicial computation of the length of incarceration[28] and in setting down a schedule of periods of time before which prisoners may not apply for conditional release, the purpose of individualized treatment is largely defeated.

Machinery of individualization. This discussion brings us to the conviction that instead of the penal code setting down in advance, and in great detail, rules of "dangerousness" and "less dangerousness," numerous "sanctions," and mathematical formulae for figuring out sentences and determining the length of incarceration and time for release from custody on the basis of such rules — all this practice to be resorted to by a trial judge — we must seek some instrumentality which will retain the essence as well as the name of individualization. But this does not mean that to provide for true individualization the treatment of the offender must be left to judges or other officials wholly without guidance and without control as to the length or nature of that treatment. A more promising method out of the dilemma than the Italian must probably be based upon four principles which should underlie individualizing criminal procedure:

(1) The treatment (sentence-imposing) feature of the proceedings must be sharply differentiated from the guilt-finding phase. (2) The decision as to treatment must be made by a board or tribunal specially qualified in the interpretation and evaluation of psychiatric, psychological, and sociologic data. (3) The treatment must be modifiable in the light of scientific reports of progress. (4) The rights of the individual must be safeguarded against possible arbitrariness or other unlawful action on the part of the treatment tribunal.

As to the first point, although it has long been urged by psychiatrists, it was not until the Ninth International Prison Congress of London, in 1925, that the following resolution was adopted:

> "The trial ought to be divided into two parts: In the first the examination and decision as to...guilt should take place; in the second one the punishment should be discussed and fixed. From this part the public and the injured party should be excluded."[29]

This resolution expresses the general recognition that while the public may be concerned with the trial proceedings, the inquiries pertaining to treatment should be of a scientific, non-sensational nature not deliberately accommodated, as so many modern trials are, to the greedy appetites of "yellow journalism."

---

[28] The determination, in advance, of how long the anti-social patient will be confined in the peno-correctional hospital!

[29] PRISON ASS'N OF NEW YORK, EIGHTY-FIRST ANNUAL REPORT (1926) 74.

The second principle has abundant reason to support it. While a legally trained judge can act as an impartial referee during a technical trial, ruling upon the exclusion or inclusion of evidence, giving a legally unimpeachable charge to the jury, and performing similar functions, his education and habit of mind have not qualified him for the more difficult task of determining the type of treatment best suited to the individual delinquent on the basis of reports of scientific investigations. It would therefore seem that the work of the ordinary criminal court should cease with the finding of guilt or innocence. Recognition of the illogical and unscientific present procedure led us to propose the establishment of a "Socio-Penal Commission,"[30] or treatment board to be composed, say, of a psychiatrist or psychologist, a sociologist and a lawyer. Such a tribunal would begin to function beyond the point where the substantive and procedural criminal law has prepared the case for the imposition of sentence. The primary duty of such a board would be to determine the psychiatric, social, or peno-correctional treatment appropriate to the individual delinquent, as well as its duration. But such treatment and its duration would, in accordance with the general essence of the treatment board idea, have to be extremely flexible. This treatment tribunal would perform its functions on the basis of psychiatric, psychological and social reports of the investigations of each delinquent.

The third principle of wise individualization — modifiability of the length and type of treatment in the light of progress thereunder — is dictated by the logic of the foregoing. For a treatment tribunal to carry out its functions more intelligently than do the present criminal courts it is not only necessary that it be an independent, specially qualified body, but that it evolve methods for the observation of the individual delinquent's progress under the treatment originally ordered, so that, if necessary, such treatment may be modified, much as the physician modifies treatment, in the light of progress.[31] Probably periodic reports upon, and review of cases as a routine procedure of the treatment board would have to be provided for.

The fourth proposition raises the greatest technical difficulties. Here one must look to the fertile field of administrative law for devices which with appropriate modification can be adapted to criminal procedure. Indeed it must already be evident that the problem in its essence is analogous to those of various types of administrative instrumentalities. At least that phase of criminal law and procedure which begins with the sentencing function has or should have some of the earmarks of what is commonly called "administrative law." First, it is "public law"; that is, it involves the relationship

---

[30] "The jury could still pass upon the mental element of the crime — the *mens rea*; — but the work of scientific determination of the *peno-correctional consequences of conviction* by a jury, would be lodged in a skilled, administrative board specially qualified for such a task." GLUECK, MENTAL DISORDER AND THE CRIMINAL LAW (1925) 486. So practical a statesman as Governor Smith of New York has recently urged the adoption of a treatment board device as a fundamental reform of existing practice. See N. Y. Times, Dec. 8, 1927 (address before New York Crime Commission); *ibid.*, Jan. 5, 1928 (Annual Message).

[31] We do not by this mean to suggest that all criminals are "sick people"; but that the same common sense that dictates observation of the results of treatment of various types in medicine is necessary (perhaps even more so) in the case of peno-correctional treatment of the individual offender. In brief, we are in a realm where the trial and error method will have to be resorted to. What must at all events be avoided is the present practice of slapping a man into prison and then forgetting him until he is again brought into court.

of the individual to the state, or the social interest in the general welfare (security), instead of private litigation. Secondly, it contains an element of "preventive justice," in that, for effectiveness, it requires continuity of effort with an aim to prevention of recidivism. The present procedure discharges criminals from penal institutions automatically, without much regard to whether or not further crime might be prevented by their continued incarceration. As long as the end of criminal procedure was punishment for the sake of punishment or even for the sake of prevention and deterrence as ordinarily conceived, the notion of continuity of treatment did not enter the minds of legal scholars; and indeed few students of criminal law seem even today to be aware of the vital significance of this point. The sentence disposed of the convict until the end of the precise term prescribed in advance by a legislature which fatuously measured the length of punishment to make it just enough to restore the imaginary "balance" of the disturbed "jural order." In the meantime the convict was forgotten until his next appearance in court; and even then his past misconduct was frequently unknown to the trial judge. Nobody concerned himself with the response of the prisoner to the dosage of punishment prescribed him by this judicial medicine man. Unfortunately the use of the past tense in this criticism is not precisely justified; many legislatures still prescribe the length of punishment in advance, and many trial judges still mechanically apply this treatment without ever going near the penal institutions to which they daily sentence criminals. A third evidence of the administrative law essence of the problem is that criminal procedure, beginning with the stage of sentence, if it is to be at all effective, requires technical experts learned in matters outside of the ken of the law — psychiatrists, psychologists, social workers, penologists.

Finally, when once we recognize that punishment *qua* punishment does not bring about the desired result of protection of society, and that constructive individualized treatment of offenders against the law is more likely to achieve it, we are met with the basic problem in administrative law — the need and the methods of safeguarding individual rights against the possible arbitrary action of a technically skilled, yet "all too human," administrative board.

In the light of these evidences of the administrative essence of penal procedure, it is surprising that Continental criminologists, such as Ferri, have resorted to the clumsy device described above — legislative prescription of detailed rules of individualization — as a way out of the dilemma of free judicial discretion versus protection of individual liberty. The field of administrative law would have suggested the much more simple and effective device of a treatment board. Discussion of the scope of such a tribunal's jurisdiction, its manner of functioning, its relation to existing services (parole, probation, peno-correctional régimes), and, above all, the legal means for safeguarding individual rights against possible arbitrariness on the part of the treatment body is beyond the scope of this paper.[32] The idea raises many vexing problems of policy and law, and much thorough-going study will be required to sketch in the vital details.

---

[32] Without discussing possible means of "judicialization of the administrative act" of determination of appropriate treatment for every "individual delinquent," it may be said that in general the solution of this problem probably involves, first, the definition of broad legal categories of a social-psychiatric nature within

To make the work of such a treatment body effective, a temporary detention institution or "clearing house" manned by able psychiatrists, psychologists and social investigators would have to form an integral part of the board's equipment.[33] Careful records of examinations and field investigations of each offender would have to be maintained. Above all, however, the actual work of peno-correctional treatment — probation, institutional régimes, parole — would have to be greatly improved, and new devices experimented with. The possibilities of various types of the newer psychotherapy in the treatment of offenders, for example, have thus far been practically ignored by those who deal with the problems of penology. Nor have different schemes of inmate self-government been sufficiently experimented with.

The substantive law. The system briefly sketched above would not necessarily involve changes in the substantive law; but no doubt modifications would gradually be suggested on the basis of carefully accumulated, scientific experience with treatment. Modifications in substantive law have not infrequently followed in the wake of procedural changes. Perhaps, eventually, the basic mode of analysis of crimes into act and intent, which Dean Pound has pointed out to be faulty,[34] will be radically modified. One can conceive, for example, that the effective operation of the type of board described will have its influence on the "tests" of the irresponsibility of the insane; if might even render them superfluous. It would probably also have its effect on the reduction of the number and variety of "degrees" in the definition of homicide, robbery, rape, larceny, and so on. It might, further, influence the substantive law of attempts. The minute splitting up of offenses into degrees and the distinguishing of attempts from completed criminal acts, with the meticulous setting down of supposedly appropriate dosages of punishment, belongs to an era when punishment based upon degrees of "vicious will" as reflected in types of crime was thought to be the only or best means of coping with anti-social behavior.

---

which the treatment board will classify individual delinquents; secondly, the safeguarding of individual rights by permitting the defendant to have counsel and witnesses (of fact and opinion), and to examine psychiatric and social reports filed with the tribunal, while at the same time avoiding a technical, litigious procedure, hidebound by strict rules of evidence; thirdly, provision for judicial review of the administrative action of the treatment tribunal when it is alleged to have acted "arbitrarily" or otherwise unlawfully. I am indebted to Prof. Felix Frankfurter's course in Administrative Law for valuable clues as to the intricacies of this general problem and hints as to the direction which its solution will probably take.

COLLIN, *op. cit. supra* note 2, at 189, rightly points out that since, under Ferri's system of minute legislative prescriptions, judges will not be called upon to "interpret the will of the legislator" but to investigate the nature of the individual delinquent, the course of judicial decision ("*la jurisprudence*") "will have to adapt itself constantly to the evolution of scientific doctrines," presenting the dangerous alternative that, either the course of decision will have to follow step by step the development of science, "which would give rise to the most conflicting and perhaps most erroneous decisions," or judges will have to continue to apply the ideas of the framers of the project, "at the risk of maintaining, in the courts of justice, a scientific system abandoned by the majority of scholars." The system proposed herein will avoid at least the latter difficulty; since the *content* of the social-psychiatric categories could change with the advance of science, which advance it is presumed would be reflected in the techniques of the experts attached to the treatment tribunals. The former difficulty could be minimized by providing for a specialized appellate tribunal which would tend to unify the findings of the different treatment boards of a state, and for frequent conferences of the officials and associated scientists of the boards, for exchange of ideas on policy and treatment.

[33] The training of this personnel is a *sine qua non* to the success of the entire project. Present training facilities and prejudices are not suitable.

[34] "We know that the old analysis of act and intent can stand only as an artificial legal analysis and that the mental element in crime presents a series of difficult problems." POUND, CRIMINAL JUSTICE IN CLEVELAND (1922) 586.

Indeterminate sentence. The system under consideration should logically have as a basic provision a wholly and truly indeterminate sentence.[35] The present "indeterminate sentence" is indeterminate only within maximum-minimum limits or embraces variations of this principle. The so-called indeterminate sentence of Ferri is, as was indicated, even less satisfactory. But even if concessions will have to be made to public opinion in such matters as murder and rape (that is, even if, as to certain serious offenses, *minimum* limits of an indeterminate sentence will have to be retained), the system ought to work more effectively than the present order. Similarly, if concessions will have to be made to public opinion in regard to such crimes as larceny (that is, even if, as to certain less serious offenses, *maximum* limits of an indeterminate sentence will have to be retained) the machinery ought to operate more satisfactorily than the present régime. It should constitute a promising as well as interesting social experiment.

Summary

The underlying principles of a rational penal code are:

1. Society should utilize every scientific instrumentality for self-protection against destructive elements in its midst, with as little interference with the free life of its members as is consistent with such an aim.
2. To put this principle into practice, scientific individualization of peno-correctional diagnosis and treatment is necessary.
3. Professor Ferri's scheme of judicial individualization on the basis of a detailed legislative schedule of "conditions of dangerousness" and "conditions of less dangerousness" and a penal calculus is unsatisfactory. Individualization should be effected by a scientifically qualified treatment board, to begin to function after the individual offender has been found (or has pleaded) guilty in the existing criminal court. In addition to the original disposition of cases, the treatment tribunal should periodically review the progress of offenders under treatment, modifying the original

---

[35] One of the most important resolutions adopted by the Ninth International Prison Congress in 1925 was "that the indeterminate sentence is the necessary consequence of the individualization of punishment and one of the most efficacious means of social defence." Prison Ass'n of New York, Eighty-first Annual Report (1926) 73.

Joseph F. Scott, formerly superintendent of reformatories for New York, in discussing the origin of the first American indeterminate sentence law in New York, says that Mr. Brockway's original draft of the bill in 1877 "embodied an indeterminate sentence without limitation, which was approved by the board of managers and incorporated in their report to the legislature. But, previous to its introduction in the legislature, fearing that the bill in this form might not pass, the draft was altered, limiting the sentence to 'the maximum term provided by law for the crime for which the prisoner was convicted and sentenced.'" This has been the model for all subsequent legislation on the subject. Superintendent Scott was of the conviction, in 1910, that, "Undoubtedly, had the section containing the indeterminate sentence clause as originally drafted been left in the bill, it would have become law, as drafted, and would have given to us the purely indeterminate sentence which we have not been able to obtain up to the present time." Scott, *American Reformatories for Male Adults* in Henderson, Penal and Reformatory Institutions (1910) 89, 94.

prescription ("sentence") if found necessary. The board should utilize existing scientific facilities (psychiatry, psychology, social work) in individualization.

4. Provision is necessary for protecting individual rights against possible arbitrariness or other unlawful conduct of the treatment board.

5. Certain modifications in substantive law may be expected to result from this basic change in procedure, and these, together with a truly indeterminate sentence provision and improvements in peno-correctional practice, would facilitate the work of the treatment body.

5

The Humanitarian Theory of Punishment

C. S. Lewis

IN ENGLAND WE HAVE LATELY HAD A CONTROVERSY ABOUT Capital Punishment. I do not know whether a murderer is more likely to repent and make a good end on the gallows a few weeks after his trial or in the prison infirmary thirty years later. I do not know whether the fear of death is an indispensable deterrent. I need not, for the purpose of this article, decide whether it is a morally permissible deterrent. Those are questions which I propose to leave untouched. My subject is not Capital Punishment in particular, but that theory of punishment in general which the controversy showed to be almost universal among my fellow-countrymen. It may be called the Humanitarian theory. Those who hold it think that it is mild and merciful. In this I believe that they are seriously mistaken. I believe that the 'Humanity' which it claims is a dangerous illusion and disguises the possibility of cruelty and injustice without end. I urge a return to the traditional or Retributive theory not solely, not even primarily, in the interests of society, but in the interests of the criminal.

According to the Humanitarian theory, to punish a man because he deserves it, and as much as he deserves, is mere revenge, and, therefore, barbarous and immoral. It is maintained that the only legitimate motives for punishing are the desire to deter others by example or to mend the criminal. When this theory is combined, as frequently happens, with the belief that all crime is more or less pathological, the idea of mending tails off into that of healing or curing and punishment becomes *therapeutic*. Thus it appears at first sight that we have passed from the harsh and self-righteous notion of giving the wicked their deserts to the charitable and enlightened one of tending the psychologically sick. What could be more amiable? One little point which is taken for granted in this theory needs, however, to be made explicit. The things done to the criminal, even if they are called cures, will be just as compulsory as they were in the old days when we called them punishments. If a tendency to steal can be cured by psychotherapy, the thief will no doubt be forced to undergo the treatment. Otherwise, society cannot continue.

My contention is that this doctrine, merciful though it appears, really means that each one of us, from the moment he breaks the law, is deprived of the rights of a human being.

The reason is this. The Humanitarian theory removes from Punishment the concept of Desert. But the concept of Desert is the only connecting link between punishment and justice. It is only as deserved or undeserved that a sentence can be just or unjust. I do not here contend that the question 'Is it deserved?' is the only one we can reasonably ask about a punishment. We may very properly ask whether it is likely to deter others and to reform the criminal. But neither of these two last questions is a question about justice. There is no sense in talking about a 'just deterrent' or a 'just cure'. We demand of a deterrent not whether it is just but whether it will deter. We demand of a cure not whether it is just but whether it succeeds. Thus when we cease to consider what the criminal deserves and consider only what will cure him or deter others, we have tacitly removed him from the sphere of justice altogether; instead of a person, a subject of rights, we now have a mere object, a patient, a 'case'.

The distinction will become clearer if we ask who will be qualified to determine sentences when sentences are no longer held to derive their propriety from the criminal's deservings. On the old view the problem of fixing the right sentence was a moral problem. Accordingly, the judge who did it was a person trained in jurisprudence; trained, that is, in a science which deals with rights and duties, and which, in origin at least, was consciously accepting guidance from the Law of Nature, and from Scripture. We must admit that in the actual penal code of most countries at most times these high originals were so much modified by local custom, class interests, and utilitarian concessions, as to be very imperfectly recognizable. But the code was never in principle, and not always in fact, beyond the control of the conscience of the society. And when (say, in eighteenth-century England) actual punishments conflicted too violently with the moral sense of the community, juries refused to convict and reform was finally brought about. This was possible because, so long as we are thinking in terms of Desert, the propriety of the penal code, being a moral question, is a question on which every man has the right to an opinion, not because he follows this or that profession, but because he is simply a man, a rational animal enjoying the Natural Light. But all this is changed when we drop the concept of Desert. The only two questions we may now ask about a punishment are whether it deters and whether it cures. But these are not questions on which anyone is entitled to have an opinion simply because he is a man. He is not entitled to an opinion even if, in addition to being a man, he should happen also to be a jurist, a Christian, and a moral theologian. For they are not questions about principle but about matter of fact; and for such *cuiquam in sua arte credendum.*[1] Only the expert 'penologist' (let barbarous things have barbarous names), in the light

---

[1] 'We must believe the expert in his own field.'

of previous experiment, can tell us what is likely to deter: only the psychotherapist can tell us what is likely to cure. It will be in vain for the rest of us, speaking simply as men, to say, 'but this punishment is hideously unjust, hideously disproportionate to the criminal's deserts'. The experts with perfect logic will reply, 'but nobody was talking about deserts. No one was talking about *punishment* in your archaic vindictive sense of the word. Here are the statistics proving that this treatment deters. Here are the statistics proving that this other treatment cures. What is your trouble?'

The Humanitarian theory, then, removes sentences from the hands of jurists whom the public conscience is entitled to criticize and places them in the hands of technical experts whose special sciences do not even employ such categories as rights or justice. It might be argued that since this transference results from an abandonment of the old idea of punishment, and, therefore, of all vindictive motives, it will be safe to leave our criminals in such hands. I will not pause to comment on the simple-minded view of fallen human nature which such a belief implies. Let us rather remember that the 'cure' of criminals is to be compulsory; and let us then watch how the theory actually works in the mind of the Humanitarian. The immediate starting point of this article was a letter I read in one of our Leftist weeklies. The author was pleading that a certain sin, now treated by our laws as a crime, should henceforward be treated as a disease. And he complained that under the present system the offender, after a term in gaol, was simply let out to return to his original environment where he would probably relapse. What he complained of was not the shutting up but the letting out. On his remedial view of punishment the offender should, of course, be detained until he was cured. And of course the official straighteners are the only people who can say when that is. The first result of the Humanitarian theory is, therefore, to substitute for a definite sentence (reflecting to some extent the community's moral judgment on the degree of ill-desert involved) an indefinite sentence terminable only by the word of those experts — and they are not experts in moral theology nor even in the Law of Nature — who inflict it. Which of us, if he stood in the dock, would not prefer to be tried by the old system?

It may be said that by the continued use of the word punishment and the use of the verb 'inflict' I am misrepresenting Humanitarians. They are not punishing, not inflicting, only healing. But do not let us be deceived by a name. To be taken without consent from my home and friends; to lose my liberty; to undergo all those assaults on my personality which modern psychotherapy knows how to deliver; to be re-made after some pattern of 'normality' hatched in a Viennese laboratory to which I never professed allegiance; to know that this process will never end until either my captors have succeeded or I grown wise enough to cheat them with apparent success — who cares whether this is called Punishment or not? That it includes most of the elements for which any punishment is feared — shame, exile, bondage, and years eaten by the locust — is obvious. Only enormous ill-desert could justify it; but ill-desert is the very conception which the Humanitarian theory has thrown overboard.

If we turn from the curative to the deterrent justification of punishment we shall find the new theory even more alarming. When you punish a man *in terrorem*,[2] make

---

[2] 'to cause terror'.

of him an 'example' to others, you are admittedly using him as a means to an end; someone else's end. This, in itself, would be a very wicked thing to do. On the classical theory of Punishment it was of course justified on the ground that the man deserved it. That was assumed to be established before any question of 'making him an example' arose. You then, as the saying is, killed two birds with one stone; in the process of giving him what he deserved you set an example to others. But take away desert and the whole morality of the punishment disappears. Why, in Heaven's name, am I to be sacrificed to the good of society in this way? — unless, of course, I deserve it.

But that is not the worst. If the justification of exemplary punishment is not to be based on desert but solely on its efficacy as a deterrent, it is not absolutely necessary that the man we punish should even have committed the crime. The deterrent effect demands that the public should draw the moral, 'If we do such an act we shall suffer like that man.' The punishment of a man actually guilty whom the public think innocent will not have the desired effect; the punishment of a man actually innocent will, provided the public think him guilty. But every modern State has powers which make it easy to fake a trial. When a victim is urgently needed for exemplary purposes and a guilty victim cannot be found, all the purposes of deterrence will be equally served by the punishment (call it 'cure' if you prefer) of an innocent victim, provided that the public can be cheated into thinking him guilty. It is no use to ask me why I assume that our rulers will be so wicked. The punishment of an innocent, that is, an undeserving, man is wicked only if we grant the traditional view that righteous punishment means deserved punishment. Once we have abandoned that criterion, all punishments have to be justified, if at all, on other grounds that have nothing to do with desert. Where the punishment of the innocent can be justified on those grounds (and it could in some cases be justified as a deterrent) it will be no less moral than any other punishment. Any distaste for it on the part of a Humanitarian will be merely a hang-over from the Retributive theory.

It is, indeed, important to notice that my argument so far supposes no evil intentions on the part of the Humanitarian and considers only what is involved in the logic of his position. My contention is that good men (not bad men) consistently acting upon that position would act as cruelly and unjustly as the greatest tyrants. They might in some respects act even worse. Of all tyrannies a tyranny sincerely exercised for the good of its victims may be the most oppressive. It may be better to live under robber barons than under omnipotent moral busybodies. The robber baron's cruelty may sometimes sleep, his cupidity may at some point be satiated; but those who torment us for our own good will torment us without end for they do so with the approval of their own conscience. They may be more likely to go to Heaven yet at the same time likelier to make a Hell of earth. Their very kindness stings with intolerable insult. To be 'cured' against one's will and cured of states which we may not regard as disease is to be put on a level with those who have not yet reached the age of reason or those who never will; to be classed with infants, imbeciles, and domestic animals. But to be punished, however severely, because we have deserved it, because we 'ought to have known better', is to be treated as a human person made in God's image.

In reality, however, we must face the possibility of bad rulers armed with a Humanitarian theory of punishment. A great many popular blue prints for a Christian society are merely what the Elizabethans called 'eggs in moonshine' because they assume that the whole society is Christian or that the Christians are in control. This is not so in most contemporary States. Even if it were, our rulers would still be fallen men, and, therefore, neither very wise nor very good. As it is, they will usually be unbelievers. And since wisdom and virtue are not the only or the commonest qualifications for a place in the government, they will not often be even the best unbelievers.

The practical problem of Christian politics is not that of drawing up schemes for a Christian society, but that of living as innocently as we can with unbelieving fellow-subjects under unbelieving rulers who will never be perfectly wise and good and who will sometimes be very wicked and very foolish. And when they are wicked the Humanitarian theory of punishment will put in their hands a finer instrument of tyranny than wickedness ever had before. For if crime and disease are to be regarded as the same thing, it follows that any state of mind which our masters choose to call 'disease' can be treated as crime; and compulsorily cured. It will be vain to plead that states of mind which displease government need not always involve moral turpitude and do not therefore always deserve forfeiture of liberty. For our masters will not be using the concepts of Desert and Punishment but those of disease and cure. We know that one school of psychology already regards religion as a neurosis. When this particular neurosis becomes inconvenient to government, what is to hinder government from proceeding to 'cure' it? Such 'cure' will, of course, be compulsory; but under the Humanitarian theory it will not be called by the shocking name of Persecution. No one will blame us for being Christians, no one will hate us, no one will revile us. The new Nero will approach us with the silky manners of a doctor, and though all will be in fact as compulsory as the *tunica molesta* or Smithfield or Tyburn, all will go on within the unemotional therapeutic sphere where words like 'right' and 'wrong' or 'freedom' and 'slavery' are never heard. And thus when the command is given, every prominent Christian in the land may vanish overnight into Institutions for the Treatment of the Ideologically Unsound, and it will rest with the expert gaolers to say when (if ever) they are to re-emerge. But it will not be persecution. Even if the treatment is painful, even if it is life-long, even if it is fatal, that will be only a regrettable accident; the intention was purely therapeutic. In ordinary medicine there were painful operations and fatal operations; so in this. But because they are 'treatment', not punishment, they can be criticized only by fellow-experts and on technical grounds, never by men as men and on grounds of justice.

This is why I think it essential to oppose the Humanitarian theory of punishment, root and branch, wherever we encounter it. It carries on its front a semblance of mercy which is wholly false. That is how it can deceive men of good will. The error began, perhaps, with Shelley's statement that the distinction between mercy and justice was invented in the courts of tyrants. It sounds noble, and was indeed the error of a noble mind. But the distinction is essential. The older view was that mercy 'tempered' justice, or (on the highest level of all) that mercy and justice had met and kissed. The essential act of mercy was to pardon; and pardon in its very essence involves the recognition of guilt and ill-desert in the recipient. If crime is only a disease which needs cure, not sin which deserves punishment, it cannot be pardoned. How can you pardon a man for having a gumboil or a club foot? But the Humanitarian theory wants simply to abolish Justice and substitute Mercy for it. This means that you start being 'kind' to people before you have considered their rights, and then force upon them supposed kindnesses which no one but you will recognize as kindnesses and which the recipient will feel as abominable cruelties. You have overshot the mark. Mercy, detached from Justice, grows unmerciful. That is the important paradox. As there are plants which will flourish only in mountain soil, so it appears that Mercy will flower only when it grows in the crannies of the rock of Justice: transplanted to the marshlands of mere Humanitarianism, it becomes a man-eating weed, all the more dangerous because it is still called by the same name as the mountain variety. But we ought long ago to have learned our lesson. We should be too old now to be deceived by those humane pretensions which have served to usher in every cruelty of the revolutionary period in which we live. These are the 'precious balms' which will 'break our heads'.[3]

There is a fine sentence in Bunyan: 'It came burning hot into my mind, whatever he said, and however he flattered, when he got me home to his House, he would sell me for a Slave.'[4] There is a fine couplet, too, in John Ball:

Be war or ye be wo;
Knoweth your frend from your foo.[5]

---

[3] Psalm cxli. 6.

[4] *The Pilgrim's Progress*, ed. James Blanton Wharey, second edition revised by Roger Sharrock, Oxford English Texts (Oxford, 1960), Part I, p. 70.

[5] 'John Ball's Letter to the Peasants of Essex, 1381', lines 11-12, found in *Fourteenth Century Verse and Prose*, ed. Kenneth Sisam (Oxford, 1921), p. 161.

6

LEGAL VALUES AND THE REHABILITATIVE IDEAL

Francis Allen

Although one is sometimes inclined to despair of any constructive changes in the administration of criminal justice, a glance at the history of the past half-century reveals a succession of the most significant developments. Thus, the last fifty years have seen the widespread acceptance of three legal inventions of great importance: the juvenile court, systems of probation, and systems of parole. During the same period, under the inspiration of Continental research and writing, scientific criminology has become an established field of instruction and inquiry in American universities and in other research agencies. At the same time, psychiatry has made its remarkable contributions to the theory of human behavior and, more specifically, to that form of human behavior described as criminal. These developments have been accompanied by nothing less than a revolution in public conceptions of the nature of crime and the criminal and in public attitudes toward the proper treatment of the convicted offender.

This history with its complex developments of thought, institutional behavior, and public attitudes must be approached gingerly; for in dealing with it we are in peril of committing the sin of oversimplification. Nevertheless, despite the presence of contradictions and paradox, it seems possible to detect one common element in much of this thought and activity which goes far to characterize the history we are considering. This common element or theme I shall describe, for want of a better phrase, as the rise of the rehabilitative ideal.

The rehabilitative ideal is itself a complex of ideas which, perhaps, defies an exact definition. The essential points, however, can be identified. It is assumed, first, that human behavior is the product of antecedent causes. These causes can be identified as part of the

First delivered as a lecture at the Institute for Juvenile Research, Chicago, Illinois, on March 17, 1959, and printed in 50 J. Crim. L., C. & P.S. 226–32 (1959). Reprinted by permission.

physical universe, and it is the obligation of the scientist to discover and to describe them with all possible exactitude. Knowledge of the antecedents of human behavior makes possible an approach to the scientific control of human behavior. Finally, and of primary significance for the purposes at hand, it is assumed that measures employed to treat the convicted offender should serve a therapeutic function; that such measures should be designed to effect changes in the behavior of the convicted person in the interests of his own happiness, health, and satisfactions and in the interest of social defense.

Although these ideas are capable of quite simple statement, they have provoked some of the modern world's most acrimonious controversies. And the disagreements among those who adhere in general to these propositions have been hardly less intense than those prompted by the dissenters. This is true, in part, because these ideas possess a delusive simplicity. No idea is more pervaded with ambiguity than the notion of reform or rehabilitation. Assuming, for example, that we have the techniques to accomplish our ends of rehabilitation, are we striving to produce in the convicted offender something called "adjustment" to his social environment or is our objective something different from or more than this? By what scale of values do we determine the ends of therapy?[1]

These are intriguing questions, well worth extended consideration. But it is not my purpose to pursue them here. Rather, I am concerned with describing some of the dilemmas and conflicts of values that have resulted from efforts to impose the rehabilitative ideal on the system of criminal justice. There is no area in which a more effective demonstration can be made of the necessity for greater mutual understanding between the law and the behavioral disciplines.

There is, of course, nothing new in the notion of reform or rehabilitation of the offender as being one objective of the penal process. This idea is given important emphasis, for example, in the thought of the medieval churchmen. The church's position, as described by Sir Francis Palgrave, was that punishment was not to be "thundered in vengeance for the satisfaction of the state, but imposed for the good of the offender: in order to afford the means of amendment and to lead the transgressor to repentance, and to mercy."[2] Even Jeremy Bentham, whose views modern criminologists have often scorned and more often ignored, is found saying: "It is a great merit in a punishment to contribute to the *reformation of the offender*, not only through fear of being punished again, but by a change in his character and habits."[3] But this is far from saying that the modern expression of the rehabilitative ideal is not to be sharply distinguished from earlier expressions. The most important differences, I believe, are two. First, the modern statement of the rehabilitative ideal is accompanied by, and largely

---

[1] "We see that it is not easy to determine what we consider to be the sickness and what we consider to be the cure." FROMM, PSYCHO-ANALYSIS AND RELIGION 73 (1950). See also the author's development of these points at 67–77.

[2] Quoted in DALZELL, BENEFIT OF CLERGY AND RELATED MATTERS 13 (1955).

[3] BENTHAM, THE THEORY OF LEGISLATION 338–39 (Ogden ed. 1931). (Italics in the original.) But Bentham added: "But when [the writers] come to speak about the means of preventing offenses, of rendering men better, of perfecting morals, their imagination grows warm, their hopes excited; one would suppose they were about to produce the great secret, and that the human race was going to receive a new form. It is because we have a more magnificent idea of objects in proportion as they are less familiar, and because the imagination has a loftier flight amid vague projects which have never been subjected to the limits of analysis." *Id.* at 359.

stems from, the development of scientific disciplines concerned with human behavior, a development not remotely approximated in earlier periods when notions of reform of the offender were advanced. Second, and of equal importance for the purposes at hand, in no other period has the rehabilitative ideal so completely dominated theoretical and scholarly inquiry, to such an extent that in some quarters it is almost assumed that matters of treatment and reform of the offender are the only questions worthy of serious attention in the whole field of criminal justice and corrections.

THE NARROWING OF SCIENTIFIC INTERESTS

This narrowing of interests prompted by the rise of the rehabilitative ideal during the past half-century should put us on our guard. No social institutions as complex as those involved in the administration of criminal justice serve a single function or purpose. Social institutions are multivalued and multipurposed. Values and purposes are likely on occasion to prove inconsistent and to produce internal conflict and tension. A theoretical orientation that evinces concern for only one or a limited number of the purposes served by the institution must inevitably prove partial and unsatisfactory. In certain situations it may prove positively dangerous. This stress on the unfortunate consequences of the rise of the rehabilitative ideal need not involve failure to recognize the substantial benefits that have also accompanied its emergence. Its emphasis on the fundamental problems of human behavior, its numerous contributions to the decency of the criminal-law processes are of vital importance. But the limitations and dangers of modern trends of thought need to be clearly identified in the interest, among others, of the rehabilitative ideal itself.

My first proposition is that the rise of the rehabilitative ideal has dictated what questions are to be investigated, with the result that many matters of equal or even greater importance have been ignored or insufficiently examined. This tendency can be abundantly illustrated. Thus, the concentration of interest on the nature and needs of the criminal has resulted in a remarkable absence of interest in the nature of crime. This is, indeed, surprising, for on reflection it must be apparent that the question of what is a crime is logically the prior issue: how crime is defined determines in large measure who the criminal is who becomes eligible for treatment and therapy.[4] A related observation was made some years ago by the late Karl Llewellyn: "When I was younger I used to hear smuggish assertions among my sociological friends, such as: 'I take the sociological, *not* the legal, approach to crime'; and I suspect an inquiring reporter could still hear much the same (perhaps with 'psychiatric' often substituted for 'sociological')—though it is surely somewhat obvious that when you take 'the legal' out, you also take out 'crime.'"[5] This disinterest in the definition of criminal behavior has afflicted the lawyers quite as much as the behavioral scientists. Even the criminal law scholar has tended, until recently, to assume that problems of procedure and

---

[4] *Cf.* Hart, *The Aims of the Criminal Law*, 23 LAW & CONTEMP. PROB. 401 (1958).
[5] *Law and the Social Sciences—Especially Sociology*, 62 HARV. L. REV. 1286, 1287 (1949).

treatment are the things that "really matter." Only the issue of criminal responsibility as affected by mental disorder has attracted the consistent attention of the non-lawyer, and the literature reflecting this interest is not remarkable for its cogency or its wisdom. In general, the behavioral sciences have left other issues relevant to crime definition largely in default. There are a few exceptions. Dr. Hermann Mannheim, of the London School of Economics, has manifested intelligent interest in these matters.[6] The late Professor Edwin Sutherland's studies of "white-collar crime" may also be mentioned, although, in my judgment, Professor Sutherland's efforts in this field are among the least perceptive and satisfactory of his many valuable contributions.[7]

The absence of widespread interest in these areas is not to be explained by any lack of challenging questions. Thus, what may be said of the relationships between legislative efforts to subject certain sorts of human behavior to penal regulation and the persistence of police corruption and abuse of power?[8] Studies of public attitudes toward other sorts of criminal legislation might provide valuable clues as to whether given regulatory objectives are more likely to be attained by the provision of criminal penalties or by other kinds of legal sanctions. It ought to be re-emphasized that the question, What sorts of behavior should be declared criminal? is one to which the behavioral sciences might contribute vital insights. This they have largely failed to do, and we are the poorer for it.

Another example of the narrowing of interests that has accompanied the rise of the rehabilitative ideal is the lack of concern with the idea of deterrence—indeed many modern criminologists are hostile toward it.[9] This, again, is a most surprising development. It must surely be apparent that the criminal law has a general preventive function to perform in the interests of public order and of security of life, limb, and possessions. Indeed, there is reason to assert that the influence of criminal sanctions on the millions who never engage in serious criminality is of greater social importance than their impact on the hundreds of thousands who do. Certainly, the assumptions of those who make our laws is that the denouncing of certain kinds of conduct as criminal and providing the means for the enforcement of legislative prohibitions will generally prevent or minimize such behavior. Just what the precise mechanisms of deterrence are is not well understood. Perhaps it results, on occasion, from the naked threat of punishment. Perhaps, more frequently, it derives from a more subtle process wherein the mores and moral sense of the community are recruited to advance the attainment of the criminal law's objectives. The point is that we know very little about these vital matters, and the resources of the behavioral sciences have rarely been employed to contribute knowledge and insight in their investigation. Not only have the criminologists displayed little interest in these matters, some have suggested that the whole idea of general prevention is invalid or worse. Thus, speaking of the deterrent theory of

---

[6] See, especially, his CRIMINAL JUSTICE AND SOCIAL RECONSTRUCTION (1946).

[7] WHITE-COLLAR CRIME (1949). See also CLINARD, THE BLACK MARKET (1952). *Cf.* Caldwell, *A Re-examination of the Concept of White-Collar Crime*, 22 Fed. Prob. 30 (1958).

[8] An interesting question of this kind has recently been debated in England centering on the proposals for enhanced penalties for prostitution offenses made in the recently-issued Wolfenden Report. See Fairfield, *Notes on Prostitution*, 9 BRIT. J. DELIN. 164, 173 (1959).

[9] But see Andenaes, *General Prevention—Illusion or Reality?* 43 J. CRIM. L., C. & P.S. 176 (1952).

punishment, the authors of a leading textbook in criminology assert: "This is simply a derived rationalization of revenge. Though social revenge is the actual psychological basis of punishment today, the apologists for the punitive regime are likely to bring forward in their defense the more sophisticated, but equally futile, contention that punishment deters from [*sic*] crime."[10] We are thus confronted by a situation in which the dominance of the rehabilitative ideal not only diverts attention from many serious issues but leads to a denial that these issues even exist.

DEBASEMENT OF THE REHABILITATIVE IDEAL

I now turn to another kind of difficulty that has accompanied the rise of the rehabilitative ideal in the areas of corrections and criminal justice. It is a familiar observation that an idea once propagated and introduced into the active affairs of life undergoes change. The real significance of an idea as it evolves in actual practice may be quite different from that intended by those who conceived it and gave it initial support. An idea tends to lead a life of its own; and modern history is full of the unintended consequences of seminal ideas. The application of the rehabilitative ideal to the institutions of criminal justice presents a striking example of such a development. My second proposition, then, is that the rehabilitative ideal has been debased in practice and that the consequences resulting from this debasement are serious and, at times, dangerous.

This proposition may be supported, first, by the observation that, under the dominance of the rehabilitative ideal, the language of therapy is frequently employed, wittingly or unwittingly, to disguise the true state of affairs that prevails in our custodial institutions and at other points in the correctional process. Certain measures, like the sexual psychopath laws, have been advanced and supported as therapeutic in nature when, in fact, such a characterization seems highly dubious.[11] Too often the vocabulary of therapy has been exploited to serve a public-relations function. Recently, I visited an institution devoted to the diagnosis and treatment of disturbed children. The institution had been established with high hopes and, for once, with the enthusiastic support of the state legislature. Nevertheless, fifty minutes of an hour's lecture, delivered by a supervising psychiatrist before we toured the building, were devoted to custodial problems. This fixation on problems of custody was reflected in the institutional arrangements which included, under a properly euphemistic label, a cell for solitary confinement.[12] Even more disturbing was the tendency of the staff to justify these custodial measures in therapeutic terms. Perhaps on occasion the requirements of institutional security and treatment coincide. But the inducements to self-deception in such situations are strong and all too apparent. In short, the language of therapy

---

[10] BARNES & TEETERS, NEW HORIZONS IN CRIMINOLOGY 337 (2d ed. 1954). The context in which these statements appear also deserves attention.

[11] See discussion pp. 14–15 *supra*.

[12] As I recall, it was referred to as the "quiet room." In another institution the boy was required to stand before a wall while a seventy pound fire hose was played on his back. This procedure went under name of "hydrotherapy."

has frequently provided a formidable obstacle to a realistic analysis of the conditions that confront us. And realism in considering these problems is the one quality that we require above all others.[13]

There is a second kind of unintended consequence that results from the application of the rehabilitative ideal to the practical administration of criminal justice. Surprisingly enough, the rehabilitative ideal has often led to increased severity of penal measures. This tendency may be seen in the operation of the juvenile court. Although frequently condemned by the popular press as a device for leniency, the juvenile court is authorized to intervene punitively in many situations in which the conduct, were it committed by an adult, would be wholly ignored by the law or would subject the adult to the mildest of sanctions. The tendency of proposals for wholly indeterminate sentences, a clearly identifiable fruit of the rehabilitative ideal, is unmistakably in the direction of lengthened periods of imprisonment.[14] A large variety of statutes authorizing what is called "civil" commitment of persons, but which, except for the reduced protections afforded the parties proceeded against, are essentially criminal in nature, provide for absolutely indeterminate periods of confinement. Experience has demonstrated that, in practice, there is a strong tendency for the rehabilitative ideal to serve purposes that are essentially incapacitative rather than therapeutic in character.[15]

THE REHABILITATIVE IDEAL AND INDIVIDUAL LIBERTY

This reference to the tendency of the rehabilitative ideal to encourage increasingly long periods of incarceration brings me to my final proposition. It is that the rise of the rehabilitative ideal has often been accompanied by attitudes and measures that conflict, sometimes seriously, with the values of individual liberty and volition. As I have already observed, the role of the behavioral sciences in the administration of criminal justice and in the areas of public policy lying on the borderland of the criminal law is one of obvious importance. But I suggest that, if the function of criminal justice is considered in its proper dimensions, it will be discovered that the most fundamental problems in these areas are not those of psychiatry, sociology, social case work, or social psychology. On the contrary, the most fundamental problems are those of political philosophy and political science. The administration of the criminal law presents to any community the most extreme issues of the proper relations of the individual citizen to state power. We are concerned here with the perennial issue of political authority: Under what circumstances is the state justified in bringing its force to bear on the individual human being? These issues, of course, are not confined to the criminal law, but it is in the area of penal regulation that they are most dramatically manifested. The criminal law, then,

---

[13] *Cf.* Wechsler, *Law, Morals, and Psychiatry*, 18 COLUM. L. SCHOOL NEWS 2, 4 (1959): "The danger rather is that coercive regimes we would not sanction in the name of punishment or of correction will be sanctified in the name of therapy without providing the resources for a therapeutic operation."

[14] *Cf.* Tappan, *Sentencing under the Model Penal Code*, 23 LAW & CONTEMP. PROB. 528, 530 (1958).

[15] *Cf.* HALL, GENERAL PRINCIPLES OF CRIMINAL LAW 551 (1947). And see SELLIN, THE PROTECTIVE CODE: A SWEDISH PROPOSAL 9 (1957).

is located somewhere near the center of the political problem, as the history of the twentieth century abundantly reveals. It is no accident, after all, that the agencies of criminal justice and law enforcement are those first seized by an emerging totalitarian regime.[16] In short, a study of criminal justice is fundamentally a study in the exercise of political power. No such study can properly avoid the problem of the abuse of power.

The obligation of containing power within the limits suggested by a community's political values has been considerably complicated by the rise of the rehabilitative ideal. For the problem today is one of regulating the exercise of power by men of good will, whose motivations are to help not to injure, and whose ambitions are quite different from those of the political adventurer so familiar to history. There is a tendency for such persons to claim immunity from the usual forms of restraint and to insist that professionalism and a devotion to science provide sufficient protection against unwarranted invasion of individual rights. This attitude is subjected to mordant criticism by Aldous Huxley in his book, *Brave New World Revisited*. Mr. Huxley observes: "There seems to be a touching belief among certain Ph.D's in sociology that Ph.D's in sociology will never be corrupted by power. Like Sir Galahad's, their strength is the strength of ten because their heart is pure—and their heart is pure because they are scientists and have taken six thousand hours of social studies."[17] I suspect that Mr. Huxley would have been willing to extend his point to include professional groups other than the sociologists. There is one proposition which, if generally understood, would contribute more to clear thinking on these matters than any other. It is not a new insight. Garofalo, asserted: "The mere deprivation of liberty, however benign the administration of the place of confinement, is undeniably punishment."[18] This proposition may be rephrased as follows: Measures which subject individuals to the substantial and involuntary deprivation of their liberty contain an inescapable punitive element, and this reality is not altered by the facts that the motivations that prompt incarceration are to provide therapy or otherwise contribute to the person's well-being or reform. As such, these measures must be closely scrutinized to insure that power is being applied consistently with those values of the community that justify interference with liberty for only the most clear and compelling reasons.

But the point I am making requires more specific and concrete application to be entirely meaningful. It should be pointed out, first, that the values of individual liberty may be imperiled by claims to knowledge and therapeutic technique that we, in fact, do not possess and by our failure to concede candidly what we do not know. At times, practitioners of the behavioral sciences have been guilty of these faults. At other times, such errors have supplied the assumptions on which legislators, lawyers, and lay people generally have proceeded. An illustration of these dangers is provided by the sexual psychopath laws, to which I return, for they epitomize admirably some of the worst tendencies of modern practice.[19] Doubts almost as serious can be raised as to a whole range of other measures. The laws providing for the commitment of persons displaying the classic symp-

---

[16] This development in the case of Germany may be gleaned from Crankshaw, Gestapo (1956).
[17] Huxley, Brave New World Revisited 34–35 (1958).
[18] Garofalo, Criminology 241–42 (Millar transl. 1914).
[19] See discussion pp. 14–15 *supra*.

toms of psychosis and advanced mental disorder have proved a seductive analogy for other proposals. But does our knowledge of human behavior really justify the extension of these measures to provide for the indefinite commitment of persons otherwise afflicted?

There are other ways in which the modern tendencies of thought accompanying the rise of the rehabilitative ideal have imperiled basic political values. The most important of these is the encouragement of procedural laxness and irregularity. It is my impression that there is a greater awareness of these dangers today than at some other times in the past. Nevertheless, in our courts of so-called socialized justice one may still observe, on occasion, a tendency to assume that, since the purpose of the proceeding is to "help" rather than to "punish," some lack of concern in establishing the charges against the person before the court may be justified. Thus, in some courts the judge is supplied with a report on the offender by the psychiatric clinic before the judgment of guilt or acquittal is announced. Such reports, while they may be relevant to the defendant's need for therapy or confinement, are ordinarily wholly irrelevant to the issue of his guilt of the particular offense charged. Yet it asks too much of human nature to assume that the judge is never influenced on the issue of guilt or innocence by a strongly adverse psychiatric report.

Let me give one final illustration of the problems that have accompanied the rise of the rehabilitative ideal. Some time ago we encountered a man in his eighties incarcerated in a state institution. He had been confined for some thirty years under a statute calling for the automatic commitment of defendants acquitted on grounds of insanity in criminal trials. It was generally agreed by the institution's personnel that he was not then psychotic and probably had never been psychotic. The fact seemed to be that he had killed his wife while drunk. An elderly sister of the old man was able and willing to provide him with a home, and he was understandably eager to leave the institution. When we asked the director of the institution why the old man was not released, he gave two significant answers. In the first place, he said, the statute requires me to find that this inmate is no longer a danger to the community; this I cannot do, for he may kill again. And of course the director was right. However unlikely commission of homicide by such a man in his eighties might appear, the director could not be certain. But, as far as that goes, he could not be certain also about himself or about you or me. The second answer was equally interesting. The old man, he said, is better off here. To understand the full significance of this reply it is necessary to know something about the place of confinement. Although called a hospital, it was in fact a prison, and not at all a progressive prison. Nothing worthy of the name of therapy was provided and very little even by way of recreational facilities.

This case points several morals. It illustrates, first, a failure of the law to deal adequately with the new requirements which are being placed upon it. The statute, as a condition of the release of the inmate, required the director of the institution virtually to warrant the future good behavior of the inmate, and, in so doing, made unrealistic and impossible demands on expert judgment. This might be remedied by the formulation of release criteria more consonant with actuality. Provisions for conditional release to test the inmate's reaction to the free community would considerably reduce the strain on administrative decision-making. But there is more here. Perhaps the case reflects that arrogance and insensitivity to human values to which men who have no reason to doubt their own motives appear peculiarly susceptible.[20]

I have attempted to describe some of the continuing problems and difficulties associated with, what I have called, the rise of the rehabilitative ideal. In so doing, I have not sought to cast doubt on the substantial benefits associated with that movement. It has exposed some of the most intractable problems of our time to the solvent properties of human intelligence. Moreover, the devotion to the ideal of empirical investigation provides the movement with a self-correcting mechanism of great importance and justifies hopes for constructive future development.

Nevertheless, no intellectual movement produces only unmixed blessings. I have suggested that the ascendency of the rehabilitative ideal has, as one of its unfortunate consequences, diverted attention from other questions of great criminological importance. This has operated unfavorably to the full development of criminological science. Not only is this true, but the failure of many students and practitioners in the relevant areas to concern themselves with the full context of criminal justice has produced measures dangerous to basic political values and has, on occasion, encouraged the debasement of the rehabilitative ideal to produce results which are unsupportable whether measured by the objectives of therapy or of correction. The worst manifestations of these tendencies are undoubtedly deplored as sincerely by competent therapists as by others. But the occurrences are neither so infrequent nor so trivial that they can be safely ignored.

[20] Another remarkable example is provided by the case, In re Maddox, 351 Mich. 358, 88 N.W.2d 470 (1958). Professor Wechsler, *op. cit. supra* note 13, at 4, describes the facts and holding as follows: "Only the other day, the Supreme Court of Michigan ordered the release of a prisoner in their State prison at Jackson, who had been transferred from the Ionia State Hospital to which he was committed as a psychopath. The ground of transfer, which was defended seriously by a State psychiatrist, was that the prisoner was 'adamant' in refusing to admit sexual deviation that was the basis of his commitment; and thus, in the psychiatrist's view, resistant to therapy. The Court's answer was, of course, that he had not been tried for an offense."

II

RETRIBUTIVE THEORIES

In 1975, consequentialist ideas had been predominant in the English-speaking countries for at least a century. Officials in the United States were given broad discretion to individualize sentences to take account of individual offenders' circumstances. Judges could usually impose any sentence, ranging from unsupervised probation to the statutory maximum prison sentence. Prison officials could shorten prisoners' sentences to take account of good behavior, participation in treatment, programs, and work. Parole boards could release any prisoner who was eligible.

In the early 1970s, indeterminate sentencing fell out of favor. Many people began to be concerned about the dangers of arbitrary and idiosyncratic decisions by officials accorded such broad discretion (e.g., Davis 1969). The civil rights and prisoners' rights movements focused attention on the disproportionate number of black people in prison and the likelihood that indeterminate sentencing facilitated biased decisions (e.g., American Friends Service Committee 1971). The U.S. Supreme Court in the 1960s and 1970s issued a number of decisions—most notably *Goldberg v. Kelly*, 397 U.S. 254 (1970)—extending procedural rights to citizens in a wide range of their interactions with the state. This had obvious relevance to a sentencing process that provided no guidance to judges about their decisions, produced unwarranted disparities, and afforded defendants no meaningful opportunities to appeal their sentences (e.g., Frankel 1972). Finally, researchers evaluating the effectiveness of rehabilitative programs concluded that few if any could be shown to reduce re-offending (e.g., Martinson 1974).

The primacy of consequentialist ideas had already begun to wane decades earlier, however, as the readings in Part I by C. S. Lewis and Francis Allen demonstrate. There was renewed interest in the philosophy of punishment. A few percipient works attempted to reconcile retributive and utilitarian theories. John Rawls (1955) and

Edmond Pincoffs (1966) offered analyses that assigned different kinds of theories to different realms. Utilitarian considerations were said to pertain to legislative decisions about criminal law doctrine and statutory frameworks for sentencing. Retributive considerations were said to be germane to judges' decisions about punishment in individual cases. For a variety of reasons, that analysis persuaded few people.

Two literatures developed. Philosophers developed various kinds of retributive theories that mostly discussed how systems of punishment can be justified. A second group of "penal theorists," mostly lawyers, focused more on practical questions about sentencing policy and on what judges should do in individual cases. To some extent in recent years, disciplinary insularity has been breaking down and the two literatures have begun to merge. The line between them is necessarily artificial. Part II contains writings by philosophers. Part III on mixed theories contains writings mostly by lawyers.

Retributive theorizing by philosophers blossomed (e.g., Pincoffs 1966; Hart 1968; Morris 1968; Kleinig 1973; Murphy 1973). Few modern writers, however, were satisfied with Kant's notion that imposition of punishments proportioned to wrongdoing is a categorical imperative, derivable from elusive moral first principles, and predicated on respect for the individual's autonomy as a moral agent. So they tried to develop other analyses. This part contains influential examples of some of the different approaches.

It is in the nature of things that philosophers offer subtle and nuanced analyses. This makes it difficult to say how many different kinds of retributive or quasi-retributive theories there are. Various catalogues offer various counts. J. G. Cottingham (1979) discussed nine. Nigel Walker (1999) rehearsed those nine and offered more.[1] I think a plausible case can be made for five. The lines between them are blurry and reasonable people will disagree with my partitioning. Their common property is that they explicitly or implicitly call for apportioning punishments to the moral gravity of offenders' wrongdoing.

1. *Benefits and burdens* theories, sometimes referred to as *unfair advantage, equilibrium,* or *social contract* theories, attracted considerable support in the 1960s (e.g., Morris 1968) through the mid-1970s (e.g., Murphy 1973 [chapter 8 in this volume]; von Hirsch 1976), though many early proponents later repudiated them (e.g., Morris 1981; von Hirsch 1986; Murphy and Hampton 1988). The theories start from the premise that organized society enables citizens to plan their own lives and pursue their own goals. For that to happen, citizens must respect legitimate interests of others and honor basic behavioral rules. Criminals are free-riders who benefit from others' law-abidingness but do not reciprocate. Punishment

---

[1] Cottingham (1979), Mackie (1982 [reprinted in this volume, chapter 18]), Walker (1991), Walker (1999), and Honderich (2005) discuss various typologies of retributive theories and conclude that all are either incoherent or are utilitarian theories in disguise. Each came of intellectual age during the period when consequentialist theories reigned.

is a process for forcing offenders to disgorge their unfair benefit and bring social relations back into balance. These theories lost support for a number of reasons. The most important was recognition that gaining an unfair advantage is not an adequate or even plausible characterization of the wrongfulness of many offenses. Rape is a compelling example. Scanlon (2003 [chapter 10 in this volume]) offers a contemporary version of a contract theory.

2. *"Expressive"* (e.g., Feinberg 1970 [chapter 7 in this volume]), or *"moral education"* (Hampton 1984) theories focus on punishment as an authoritative declaration that what the offender did is criminally wrongful. Feinberg illustrates this by distinguishing between civil and administrative fines and punishments, and argues that what distinguishes them is that punishments express condemnation and not merely noncompliance with rules. Hampton emphasizes that punishment demonstrates that what the offender did was wrong and publicly acknowledges the wrong done to the victim.

3. The line between expressive and *"communicative"* theories is not a bright one, since both characterize punishment's message as its core feature. Herbert Morris's paternalistic theory (1981 [chapter 9 in this volume]), however, stresses that the communication is with the offender and has as its aim helping the offender understand why what he or she did was wrong and thereby help reattach him or her to right values. Antony Duff's penitence theory (2001, 2003 [chapter 11 in this volume]) also aims at the offender's ultimate well-being through helping him or her understand why the offense was wrong, to expiate it through penance, and to reestablish his or her connections with the community.

4. *"Intuitionist"* theorists (of which no example is included in this volume) argue that the justification for punishment is the widely shared intuition that people who commit very serious crimes deserve to be punished and that most people would accept that they themselves would also deserve punishment if they committed such acts (e.g., Moore 1993). Their principal limitations are that even if such claims are true about the most serious crimes, it is less obvious that they are true about less serious ones, and that such analyses have been offered only in relation to punishment's general justification and not in relation to imposition of punishment in individual cases.

5. In *"blaming"* or *"censure"* theories, the gravamen of punishment is its authoritative declaration to the offender that he or she has done something for which he or she is morally culpable (von Hirsch 1993, 1998 [chapter 13 in this volume], and punishments should be closely attuned to the degree of wrongfulness. They are the closest descendants of Kantian theories and exemplify *positive* retributive theories in which offenders *must* (as opposed to *may*) be punished as much as they deserve.

In principle, the lines between retributivist and consequentialist theories are easy to state. In practice, they are difficult to draw. In benefits and burdens theories, the calculus centers on the offender's unfair advantage, but the implicit contextual consideration is that society will not long survive if free-riders are free to continue unconstrained down their nefarious paths. In expressive theories, the message is predicated on the offender's wrongdoing, but the audience is the general community, including the victim. In communicative theories, the intended recipient of the message is the offender, and the sender's motivation is the offender's moral well-being, but the general community is watching and being influenced. The most influential blaming theories explicitly justify imposition of pain on offenders ("*hard treatment*") as an element of punishment over and above communication of blame in order to provide "prudential" reasons to obey the law (e.g., von Hirsch and Ashworth 2005).

REFERENCES

Bibliographic details concerning works that are mentioned but are not reprinted in this volume can be found in the reference list to the introduction except for the following:

Cottingham, J. G. 1979. "Varieties of Retributivism." *Philosophical Quarterly* 29:238–46.

Hampton, Jean. 1984. "The Moral Education Theory of Punishment." *Philosophy and Public Affairs* 13(3):208–38.

Moore, Michael. 1993. "Justifying Retributivism." *Israel Law Review* 24:15–49.

Murphy, Jeffrie G., and Jean Hampton. 1988. *Forgiveness and Mercy.* Cambridge: Cambridge University Press.

von Hirsch, Andrew. 1986. *Past and Future Crimes: Deservedness and Dangerousness in the Sentencing of Criminals.* New Brunswick, N.J.: Rutgers University Press.

———. 1993. *Censure and Sanctions.* Oxford: Oxford University Press.

7

The Expressive Function
of Punishment

Joel Feinberg

It might well appear to a moral philosopher absorbed in the classical literature of his discipline, or to a moralist sensitive to injustice and suffering, that recent philosophical discussions of the problem of punishment have somehow missed the point of his interest. Recent influential articles[1] have quite sensibly distinguished between questions of definition and justification, between justifying general rules and particular decisions, between moral and legal guilt. So much is all to the good. When these articles go on to *define* "punishment," however, it seems to many that they leave out of their ken altogether the very element that makes punishment theoretically puzzling and morally disquieting. *Punishment is defined in effect as the infliction of hard treatment by an authority on a person for his prior failing in some respect (usually an infraction of a rule or command).*[2] There may be a very general sense of the word "punishment" which is well expressed by this definition; but even if that is so, we can distinguish a narrower, more emphatic sense that slips through its meshes. Imprisonment at hard labor for committing a felony is a clear case of punishment in the emphatic sense. But I think we would be less willing to apply that term to parking tickets, offside penalties, sackings, flunkings, and disqualifications. Examples of the latter sort *I propose to call penalties* (merely),

---

[1] See esp. the following: A.G.N. Flew, "The Justification of Punishment," *Philosophy*, 29 (1954), 291–307; S. I. Benn, "An Approach to the Problems of Punishment," *Philosophy*, 33 (1958), 325–341; and H.L.A. Hart, "Prolegomenon to the Principles of Punishment," *Proceedings of the Aristotelian Society*, 60 (1959/60), 1–26.

[2] Hart and Benn both borrow Flew's definition. In Hart's paraphrase (*op.cit.*, 4), punishment "(i)...must involve pain or other consequences normally considered unpleasant. (ii) It must be for an offense against legal rules. (iii) It must be of an actual or supposed offender for his offense. (iv) It must be intentionally administered by human beings other than the offender. (v) It must be imposed and administered by an authority constituted by a legal system against which the offense is committed."

so that I may inquire further what distinguishes punishment, in the strict and narrow sense that interests the moralist, from other kinds of penalties.[3]

One method of answering this question is to focus one's attention on the class of nonpunitive penalties in an effort to discover some clearly identifiable characteristic common to them all, and absent from all punishments, on which the distinction between the two might be grounded. The hypotheses yielded by this approach, however, are not likely to survive close scrutiny. One might conclude, for example, that mere penalties are less severe than punishments, but although this is generally true, it is not necessarily and universally so. Again, we might be tempted to interpret penalties as mere "pricetags" attached to certain types of behavior that are generally undesirable, so that only those with especially strong motivation will be willing to pay the price.[4] In this way deliberate efforts on the part of some Western states to keep roads from urban centers to wilderness areas few in number and poor in quality would be viewed as essentially no different from various parking fines and football penalties. In each case a certain kind of conduct is discouraged without being absolutely prohibited: anyone who desires strongly enough to get to the wilderness (or park overtime, or interfere with a pass) may do so provided he is willing to pay the penalty (price). On this view, *penalties are in effect licensing fees*, different from other purchased permits in that the price is often paid afterward rather than in advance. Since a similar interpretation of punishments seems implausible, it might be alleged that this is the basis of the distinction between penalties and punishments. However, even though a great number of penalties can no doubt plausibly be treated as retroactive licensing fees, it is hardly possible to view all of them as such. It is certainly not true, for example, of most demotions, firings, and flunkings that they are "prices" paid for some already consumed benefit; and even parking fines are sanctions for rules "meant to be taken seriously as...standard[s] of behavior"[5] and thus are more than mere public parking fees.

Rather than look for a characteristic common and peculiar to the penalties on which to ground the distinction between penalties and punishments, we would be

---

[3] The distinction between punishments and penalties was first called to my attention by Dr. Anita Fritz of the University of Connecticut. Similar distinctions in different terminologies have been made by many. Sir Frederick Pollock and Frederic Maitland speak of "true afflictive punishments" as opposed to outlawry, private vengeance, fine, and emendation. *The History of English Law Before the Time of Edward I*, 2nd edn. (Cambridge: At the University Press, 1968), II, 451ff. The phrase "afflictive punishment" was invented by Bentham: "These [corporal] punishments are almost always attended with a portion of ignominy, and this does not always increase with the organic pain, but principally depends upon the condition [social class] of the offender." *The Rationale of Punishment* (London: Heward, 1830), 83. Sir James Stephen says of legal punishment that it "should always connote...moral infamy." *A History of the Criminal Law of England*, 3 vols. (London: Macmillan & Co., 1883), II, 171. Lasswell and Donnelly distinguish "condemnation sanctions" and "other deprivations." "The Continuing Debate over Responsibility: An Introduction to Isolating the Condemnation Sanction," *Yale Law Journal*, 68 (1959). The traditional common law distinction is between "infamous" and "non-infamous" crimes and punishments. Conviction of an "infamous crime" rendered a person liable to such postpunitive civil disabilities as incompetence to be a witness.

[4] That even punishments proper are to be interpreted as taxes on certain kinds of conduct is a view often associated with O. W. Holmes, Jr. For an excellent discussion of Holmes's fluctuations of this question, see Mark De Wolfe Howe, *Justice Holmes, The Proving Years* (Cambridge: *Harvard University Press*, 1963), 74–80. See also Lon Fuller, *The Morality of Law* (New Haven: Yale University Press, 1964), Ch. 2, Part 7, and H.L.A. Hart, *The Concept of Law* (Oxford: Clarendon Press, 1961), 39, for illuminating comparisons and contrasts of punishment and taxation.

[5] H.L.A. Hart, *loc. cit.*

better advised, I think, to turn our attention to the examples of punishments. Both penalties and punishments are authoritative deprivations for failures; but, apart from these common features, penalties have a miscellaneous character, whereas punishments have an important additional characteristic in common. That characteristic, or specific difference, I shall argue, is a certain expressive function: *punishment is a conventional device for the expression of attitudes of resentment and indignation*, and of judgments of disapproval and reprobation, on the part either of the punishing authority himself or of those "in whose name" the punishment is inflicted. Punishment, in short, has a *symbolic significance* largely missing from other kinds of penalties.

The reprobative symbolism of punishment and its character as "hard treatment," though never separate in reality, must be carefully distinguished for purposes of analysis. Reprobation is itself painful, whether or not it is accompanied by further "hard treatment," and hard treatment, such as fine or imprisonment, because of its conventional symbolism, can itself be reprobatory. Still, we can conceive of ritualistic condemnation unaccompanied by any *further* hard treatment, and of inflictions and deprivations which, because of different symbolic conventions, have no reprobative force.

It will be my thesis in this essay that (1) both the "hard treatment" aspect of punishment and its reprobative function must be part of the *definition* of legal punishment, and that (2) each of these aspects raises its own kind of question about the *justification* of legal punishment as a general practice. I shall argue that some of the jobs punishment does, and some of the conceptual problems it raises, cannot be intelligibly described unless (1) is true, and that the incoherence of a familiar form of the retributive theory results from failure to appreciate the force of (2).

I

That the expression of the community's condemnation is an essential ingredient in legal punishment is widely acknowledged by legal writers. Henry M. Hart, for example, gives eloquent emphasis to the point:

What distinguishes a criminal from a civil sanction and all that distinguishes it, it is ventured, is the judgment of community condemnation which accompanies ... its imposition. As Professor Gardner wrote not long ago, in a distinct but cognate connection:

"The essence of punishment for moral delinquency lies in the criminal conviction itself. One may lose more money on the stock market than in a court-room; a prisoner of war camp may well provide a harsher environment than a state prison; death on the field of battle has the same physical characteristics as death by sentence of law. It is the expression of the community's hatred, fear, or contempt for the convict which alone characterizes physical hardship as punishment."

If this is what a "criminal" penalty is, then we can say readily enough what a "crime" is. ... It is conduct which, if duly shown to have taken place, *will incur a formal and solemn pronouncement of the moral condemnation of the community*. ... Indeed the condemnation plus the added [unpleasant physical] consequences may well be considered, compendiously, as constituting the punishment.[6]

Professor Hart's compendious definition needs qualification in one respect. The moral condemnation and the "unpleasant consequences" that he rightly identifies as essential elements of punishment are not as distinct and separate as he suggests. It does not always happen that the convicted prisoner is first solemnly condemned and then subjected to unpleasant physical treatment. It would be more accurate in many cases to say that *the unpleasant treatment itself expresses the condemnation*, and that this expressive aspect of his incarceration is precisely the element by reason of which it is properly characterized as punishment and not mere penalty. The administrator who regretfully suspends the license of a conscientious but accident-prone driver can inflict a deprivation without any scolding, express or implied; but the reckless motorist who is sent to prison for six months is thereby inevitably subject to shame and ignominy—the very walls of his cell condemn him, and his record becomes a stigma.

To say that the very physical treatment itself expresses condemnation is to say simply that certain forms of hard treatment have become the conventional symbols of public reprobation. This is neither more nor less paradoxical than to say that certain words have become conventional vehicles in our language for the expression of certain attitudes, or that champagne is the alcoholic beverage traditionally used in celebration of great events, or that black is the color of mourning. Moreover, particular kinds of punishment are often used to express quite specific attitudes (loosely speaking, this is part of their "meaning"); note the differences, for example, between beheading a nobleman and hanging a yeoman, burning a heretic and hanging a traitor, hanging an enemy soldier and executing him by firing squad.

It is much easier to show that punishment has a symbolic significance than to state exactly what it is that punishment expresses. At its best, in civilized and democratic countries, *punishment surely expresses the community's strong disapproval of what the criminal did*. Indeed, it can be said that *punishment expresses the judgment* (as distinct from any emotion) *of the community that what the criminal did was wrong*. I think it is fair to say of our community, however, that punishment generally expresses more than judgments of disapproval; it is also a symbolic way of getting back at the criminal, of expressing a kind of vindictive resentment. To any reader who has in fact spent time in a prison, I venture to say, even Professor Gardner's strong terms—"hatred, fear, or contempt for the convict"—will not seem too strong an account of what imprisonment is universally taken to express. Not only does the criminal feel the naked hostility of his guards and the outside world—that would be fierce enough—but that hostility is self-righteous as well. His punishment bears the aspect of legitimized vengefulness. Hence there is much truth in J. F. Stephen's celebrated remark that "The criminal law stands to the passion of revenge in much the same relation as marriage to the sexual appetite."[7]

If we reserve the less dramatic term "resentment" for the various vengeful attitudes and the term "reprobation" for the stern judgment of disapproval, then perhaps

---

[6] Henry M. Hart, "The Aims of the Criminal Law," *Law and Contemporary Problems*, 23 (1958), II, A, 4.
[7] *General View of the Criminal Law of England* (London: Macmillan & Co., 1863), 99.

we can characterize *condemnation* (or denunciation) as a kind of fusing of resentment and reprobation. That these two elements are generally to be found in legal punishment was well understood by the authors of the *Report of the Royal Commission on Capital Punishment*:

> Discussion of the principle of *retribution* is apt to be confused because the word is not always used in the same sense. Sometimes it is intended to mean vengeance, sometimes reprobation. In the first sense the idea is that of satisfaction by the State of a wronged individual's desire to be avenged; in the second it is that of the State's *marking its disapproval* of the breaking of its laws by a punishment proportionate to the gravity of the offense.[8]

II

The relation of the expressive function of punishment to its various central purposes is not always easy to trace. Symbolic public condemnation added to deprivation may help or hinder deterrence, reform, and rehabilitation—the evidence is not clear. On the other hand, there are other functions of punishment, often lost sight of in the preoccupation with deterrence and reform, that presuppose the expressive function and would be difficult or impossible without it.

Authoritative disavowal. Consider the standard international practice of demanding that a nation whose agent has unlawfully violated the complaining nation's rights should punish the offending agent. For example, suppose that an airplane of nation *A* fires on an airplane of nation *B* while the latter is flying over international waters. Very likely high authorities in nation *B* will send a note of protest to their counterparts in nation *A* demanding, among other things, that the transgressive pilot be punished. Punishing the pilot is an emphatic, dramatic, and well-understood way of *condemning* and thereby *disavowing* his act. It tells the world that the pilot had no right to do what he did, that he was on his own in doing it, that his government does not condone that sort of thing. It testifies thereby to government *A*'s recognition of the violated rights of government *B* in the affected area and, therefore, to the wrongfulness of the pilot's act. Failure to punish the pilot tells the world that government *A* does not consider him to have been personally at fault. That in turn is to claim responsibility for the act, which in effect labels that act as an "instrument of deliberate national policy" and hence an act of war. In that case either formal hostilities or humiliating loss of face by one side or the other almost certainly will follow. None of this scenario makes any sense without the clearly understood reprobative symbolism of punishment. In quite parallel ways punishment enables employers to disavow the acts of their employees (though not civil liability for those acts), and fathers the destructive acts of their sons.

---

[8] (London, 1953), 17–18. *My italics.*

Symbolic nonacquiescence: "Speaking in the name of the people." The symbolic function of punishment also explains why even those sophisticated persons who abjure resentment of criminals and look with small favor generally on the penal law are likely to demand that certain kinds of conduct be punished when or if the law lets them go by. In the state of Texas, so-called paramour killings were regarded by the law as not merely mitigated, but completely justifiable.[9] Many humanitarians, I believe, will feel quite spontaneously that a great injustice is done when such killings are left unpunished. The sense of violated justice, moreover, might be distinct and unaccompanied by any frustrated *Schadenfreude* toward the killer, lust for blood or vengeance, or metaphysical concern lest the universe stay "out of joint." The demand for punishment in cases of this sort may instead represent the feeling that paramour killings deserve to be *condemned*, that the law in condoning, even approving of them, speaks for all citizens in expressing a wholly inappropriate attitude toward them. For in effect the law expresses the judgment of the "people of Texas," in whose name it speaks, that the vindictive satisfaction in the mind of a cuckolded husband is a thing of greater value than the very life of his wife's lover. The demand that paramour killings be punished may simply be the demand that this lopsided value judgment be withdrawn and that the state *go on record* against paramour killings and the law *testify to the recognition* that such killings are wrongful. Punishment no doubt would also help deter killers. This too is a desideratum and a closely related one, but it is not to be identified with reprobation; for deterrence might be achieved by a dozen other techniques, from simple penalties and forfeitures to exhortation and propaganda; but effective public denunciation and, through it, symbolic non-acquiescence in the crime seem virtually to require punishment.

This symbolic function of punishment was given great emphasis by Kant, who, characteristically, proceeded to exaggerate its importance. Even if a desert island community were to disband, Kant argued, its members should first execute the last murderer left in its jails, "for otherwise they might all be regarded as participators in the [unpunished] murder...."[10] This Kantian idea that in failing to punish wicked acts society endorses them and thus be comes *particeps criminis* does seem to reflect, however dimly, something embedded in common sense. A similar notion underlies whatever is intelligible in the widespread notion that all citizens share the responsibility for political atrocities. Insofar as there is a coherent argument behind the extravagant distributions of guilt made by existentialists and other literary figures, it can be reconstructed in some such way as this: to whatever extent a political act is done "in one's name," to that extent one is responsible for it; a citizen can avoid responsibility in advance by explicitly disowning the government as his spokesman, or after the fact through open protest, resistance, and so on; otherwise, by "acquiescing" in what is done in one's

---

[9] The Texas Penal Code (Art. 1220) until recently stated: "Homicide is justifiable when committed by the husband upon one taken in the act of adultery with the wife, provided the killing takes place before the parties to the act have separated. Such circumstances cannot justify a homicide when it appears that there has been on the part of the husband, any connivance in or assent to the adulterous connection." New Mexico and Utah have similar statutes. For some striking descriptions of perfectly legal paramour killings in Texas, see John Bainbridge, *The Super-Americans* (Garden City: Doubleday, 1961), 238ff.

[10] *The Philosophy of Law*, tr. W. Hastie (Edinburgh: T. & T. Clark, 1887), 198.

name, one incurs the responsibility for it. The root notion here is a kind of "power of attorney" a government has for its citizens.

Vindication of the law. Sometimes the state goes on record through its statutes, in a way that might well please a conscientious citizen in whose name it speaks, but then owing to official evasion and unreliable enforcement gives rise to doubts that the law really means what it says. It is murder in Mississippi, as elsewhere, for a white man intentionally to kill a Negro; but if grand juries refuse to issue indictments or if trial juries refuse to convict, and this fact is clearly recognized by most citizens, then it is in a purely formal and empty sense indeed that killings of Negroes by whites are illegal in Mississippi. Yet the law stays on the books, to give ever less convincing lip service to a noble moral judgment. A statute honored mainly in the breach begins to lose its character as law, unless, as we say, it is *vindicated* (emphatically reaffirmed); and clearly the way to do this (indeed the only way) is to punish those who violate it.

Similarly, *punitive damages*, so called, are sometimes awarded the plaintiff in a civil action, as a supplement to compensation for his injuries. What more dramatic way of vindicating his violated right can be imagined than to have a court thus forcibly condemn its violation through the symbolic machinery of punishment?

Absolution of others. When something scandalous has occurred and it is clear that the wrongdoer must be one of a small number of suspects, then the state, by punishing one of these parties, thereby relieves the others of suspicion and informally absolves them of blame. Moreover, quite often the absolution of an accuser hangs as much in the balance at a criminal trial as the inculpation of the accused. A good example of this point can be found in James Gould Cozzens's novel *By Love Possessed*. A young girl, after an evening of illicit sexual activity with her boy friend, is found out by her bullying mother, who then insists that she clear her name by bringing criminal charges against the boy. He used physical force, the girl charges; she freely consented, he replies. If the jury finds him guilty of rape, it will by the same token absolve her from (moral) guilt; and her reputation as well as his rides on the outcome. Could not the state do this job without punishment? Perhaps, *but when it speaks by punishing, its message is loud and sure of getting across.*

III

A philosophical theory of punishment that, through inadequate definition, leaves out the condemnatory function not only will disappoint the moralist and the traditional moral philosopher; it will seem offensively irrelevant as well to the constitutional lawyer, whose vital concern with punishment is both conceptual, and therefore genuinely philosophical, as well as practically urgent. The distinction between punishment and mere penalties is a familiar one in the criminal law, where theorists have long engaged in what Jerome Hall calls "dubious dogmatics distinguishing 'civil penalties' from punitive sanctions, and 'public wrongs' from crimes."[11] Our courts now regard it as true (by

---

[11] *General Principles of Criminal Law*, 2nd edn. (Indianapolis: The Bobbs-Merrill Co., 1960), 328.

definition) that all criminal statutes are punitive (merely labeling an act a crime does not make it one unless sanctions are specified); but to the converse question whether all statutes specifying sanctions are *criminal* statutes, the courts are reluctant to give an affirmative reply. There are now a great number of statutes that permit "unpleasant consequences" to be inflicted on persons and yet surely cannot be regarded as criminal statutes—tax bills, for example, are aimed at regulating, not forbidding, certain types of activity. How to classify borderline cases as either "regulative" or "punitive" is not merely an idle conceptual riddle; it very quickly draws the courts into questions of great constitutional import. There are elaborate constitutional safeguards for persons faced with the prospect of punishment; but these do not, or need not, apply when the threatened hard treatment merely "regulates an activity."

The 1960 Supreme Court case of *Flemming* v. *Nestor*[12] is a dramatic (and shocking) example of how a man's fate can depend on whether a government-inflicted deprivation is interpreted as a "regulative" or "punitive" sanction. Nestor had immigrated to the United States from Bulgaria in 1913 and became eligible in 1955 for old-age benefits under the Social Security Act. In 1956, however, he was deported in accordance with the Immigration and Nationality Act for having been a member of the Communist Party from 1933 to 1939. This was a harsh fate for a man who had been in America for forty-three years and who was no longer a Communist; but at least he would have his social security benefits to support him in his exiled old age—or so he thought. Section 202 of the amended Social Security Act, however, "provides for the termination of old-age, survivor, and disability insurance benefits payable to...an alien individual who, after September 1, 1954 (the date of enactment of the section) is deported under the Immigration and Nationality Act on any one of certain specified grounds, including past membership in the Communist Party."[13] Accordingly, Nestor was informed that his benefits would cease.

Nestor then brought suit in a district court for a reversal of the administrative decision. The court found in his favor and held Section 202 of the Social Security Act unconstitutional, on the grounds that "termination of [Nestor's] benefits amounts to punishing him without a judicial trial, that [it] constitutes the imposition of punishment by legislative act rendering §202 a bill of attainder; and that the punishment exacted is imposed for past conduct not unlawful when engaged in, thereby violating the constitutional prohibition on *ex post facto* laws."[14] The Secretary of Health, Education, and Welfare, Mr. Flemming, then appealed this decision to the Supreme Court.

It was essential to the argument of the district court that the termination of old-age benefits under Section 202 was in fact punishment, for if it were properly classified as non-punitive deprivation, then none of the cited constitutional guarantees was relevant. The Constitution, for example, does not forbid all retroactive laws, but only those providing punishment. (Retroactive tax laws may also be harsh and unfair, but they are not unconstitutional.) The question before the Supreme Court, then, was whether the

---

[12] *Flemming* v. *Nestor*, 80 S. Ct. 1367 (1960).
[13] *Ibid.*, 1370.
[14] *Ibid.*, 1374 (interspersed citations omitted).

hardship imposed by Section 202 was punishment. Did this not bring the Court face to face with the properly philosophical question "What is punishment?" and is it not clear that, under the usual definition that fails to distinguish punishment from mere penalties, this particular judicial problem could not even arise?

The fate of the appellee Nestor can be recounted briefly. The five-man majority of the Court held that he had not been punished—this despite Mr. Justice Brennan's eloquent characterization of him in a dissenting opinion as "an aging man deprived of the means with which to live after being separated from his family and exiled to live among strangers in a land he quit forty-seven years ago."[15] Mr. Justice Harlan, writing for the majority, argued that the termination of benefits, like the deportation itself, was the exercise of the plenary power of Congress incident to the regulation of an activity.

> Similarly, the setting by a State of qualifications for the practice of medicine, and their modification from time to time, is an incident of the State's power to protect the health and safety of its citizens, and its decision to bar from practice persons who commit or have committed a felony is taken as evidencing an intent to exercise that regulatory power, and not a purpose to add to the punishment of ex-felons.[16]

Mr. Justice Brennan, on the other hand, contended that it is impossible to think of any purpose the provision in question could possibly serve except to "strike" at "aliens deported for conduct displeasing to the lawmakers."[17]

Surely, Justice Brennan seems right in finding in the sanction the expression of Congressional reprobation and, therefore, "punitive intent"; but the sanction itself (in Justice Harlan's words, "the mere denial of a noncontractual governmental benefit"[18]) was not a conventional vehicle for the expression of censure, being wholly outside the apparatus of the criminal law. It therefore lacked the reprobative symbolism essential to punishment generally and was thus, in its hybrid character, able to generate confusion and judicial disagreement. It was as if Congress had "condemned" a certain class of persons privately in stage whispers, rather than by pinning the infamous label of criminal on them and letting that symbol do the condemning in an open and public way. Congress without question "intended" to punish a certain class of aliens and did indeed select sanctions of appropriate severity for that purpose; but the deprivation they chose was not of an appropriate kind to perform the function of public condemnation. A father who "punishes" his son for a displeasing act the father had not thought to forbid in advance, by sneaking up on him from behind and then throwing him bodily across the room against the wall, would be in much the same position as the legislators of the amended Social Security Act, especially if he then denied to the son that his physical

---

[15] *Ibid.*, 1385.
[16] *Ibid.*, 1375–76.
[17] *Ibid.*, 1387.
[18] *Ibid.*, 1376.

assault on him had had any "punitive intent," asserting that it was a mere exercise of his paternal prerogative to rearrange the household furnishings and other objects in his own living room. To act in such a fashion would be to tarnish the paternal authority and infect all later genuine punishments with hollow hypocrisy. The same effect is produced when legislators go outside the criminal law to do the criminal law's job.

In 1961 the New York State legislature passed the so-called Subversive Drivers Act requiring "suspension and revocation of the driver's license of anyone who has been convicted, under the Smith Act, of advocating the overthrow of the Federal government," *The Reporter* magazine[19] quoted the sponsor of the bill as admitting that it was aimed primarily at one person, Communist Benjamin Davis, who had only recently won a court fight to regain his driver's license after his five-year term in prison. *The Reporter* estimated that at most a "few dozen" people would be kept from driving by the new legislation. Was this punishment? Not at all, said the bill's sponsor, Assemblyman Paul Taylor. The legislature was simply exercising its right to regulate automobile traffic in the interest of public safety:

> Driving licenses, Assemblyman Taylor explained...are not a "right" but a "valuable privilege." The Smith Act Communists, after all, were convicted of advocating the overthrow of the government by force, violence, or assassination. ("They always leave out the assassination," he remarked. "I like to put it in.") Anyone who was convicted under such an act had to be "a person pretty well dedicated to a certain point of view," the assemblyman continued, and anyone with that particular point of view "can't be concerned about the rights of others." Being concerned about the rights of others, he concluded, "is a prerequisite of being a good driver."[20]

This example shows how transparent can be the effort to mask punitive intent. The Smith Act ex-convicts were treated with such severity and in such circumstances that no nonpunitive legislative purpose could *plausibly* be maintained; yet that *kind* of treatment (quite apart from its severity) lacks the reprobative symbolism essential to clear public denunciation. After all, aged, crippled, and blind persons are also deprived of their licenses, so it is not *necessarily* the case that reprobation attaches to that kind of sanction. And so victims of a cruel law understandably claim that they have been punished, and retroactively at that. Yet, strictly speaking, they have not been *punished*; they have been treated much worse.

IV

The distinction between punishments and mere penalties, and the essentially reprobative function of the former, can also help clarify the controversy among writers on

---

[19] *The Reporter* (May 11, 1961), 14.
[20] *Loc.cit.*

the criminal law about the propriety of so-called strict liability offenses—offenses for the conviction of which there need be no proof of "fault" or "culpability" on the part of the accused. If it can be shown that he committed an act proscribed by statute, then he is guilty irrespective of whether he had any justification or excuse for what he did. Perhaps the most familiar examples come from the traffic laws: leaving a car parked beyond the permitted time in a restricted zone is automatically to violate the law, and penalties will be imposed however good the excuse. Many strict liability statutes do not even require an overt act; these proscribe not certain conduct, but certain *results*. Some make mere unconscious possession of contraband, firearms, or narcotics a crime, others the sale of misbranded articles or impure foods. The liability for so-called public welfare offenses may seem especially severe:

> ...with rare exceptions, it became definitely established that *mens rea* is not essential in the public welfare offenses, indeed that even a very high degree of care is irrelevant. Thus a seller of cattle feed was convicted of violating a statute forbidding misrepresentation of the percentage of oil in the product, despite the fact that he had employed a reputable chemist to make the analysis and had even understated the chemist's findings.[21]

The rationale of strict liability in public welfare statutes is that violation of the public interest is more likely to be prevented by unconditional liability than by liability that can be defeated by some kind of excuse; that, even though liability without "fault" is severe, it is one of the known risks incurred by businessmen; and that, besides, the sanctions are *only fines*, hence not really "punitive" in character. On the other hand, strict liability to *imprisonment* (or "punishment proper") "has been held by many to be incompatible with the basic requirements of our Anglo-American, and indeed, any civilized jurisprudence."[22] What accounts for this difference in attitude? In both kinds of case, defendants may have sanctions inflicted upon them even though they are acknowledged to be without fault; and the difference cannot be merely that imprisonment is always and necessarily a greater harm than a fine, for this is not always so. Rather, the reason why strict liability to imprisonment (punishment) is so much more repugnant to our sense of justice than is strict liability to fine (penalty) is simply that imprisonment in modern times has taken on the symbolism of public reprobation. In the words of Justice Brandeis, "It is...imprisonment in a penitentiary, which now renders a crime infamous."[23] We are familiar with the practice of penalizing persons for "offenses" they could not help. It happens every day in football games, business firms, traffic courts, and the like. But there is something very odd and offensive in *punishing* people for admittedly faultless conduct; for not only is it arbitrary and cruel to *condemn* someone for something he did (admittedly) without fault, it is also self-defeating and irrational.

---

[21] Hall, *op.cit.*, 329.
[22] Richard A Wasserstrom, "Strict Liability in the Criminal Law," *Stanford Law Review*, 12 (1960), 730.
[23] *United States* v. *Moreland*, 258 U.S. 433, 447–448 (1922). Quoted in Hall, *op.cit.*, 327.

Although their abundant proliferation[24] is a relatively recent phenomenon, statutory offenses with nonpunitive sanctions have long been familiar to legal commentators, and long a source of uneasiness to them. This discomfort is "indicated by the persistent search for an appropriate label, such as 'public torts,' 'public welfare offenses,' 'prohibitory laws,' 'prohibited acts,' 'regulatory offenses,' 'police regulations,' 'administrative misdemeanors,' 'quasi-crimes,' or 'civil offenses.'"[25] These represent alternatives to the unacceptable categorization of traffic infractions, inadvertent violations of commercial regulations, and the like, as *crimes*, their perpetrators as *criminals*, and their penalties as *punishments*. The drafters of the new Model Penal Code have defined a class of infractions of penal law forming no part of the substantive criminal law. These they call "violations," and their sanctions "civil penalties."

Section 1.04. Classes of Crimes: Violations

(1) An offense defined by this code or by any other statute of this State, for which a sentence of [death or of] imprisonment is authorized, constitutes a crime. Crimes are classified as felonies, misdemeanors, or petty misdemeanors.

[(2), (3), (4) define felonies, misdemeanors, and petty misdemeanors.]

(5) An offense defined by this Code or by any other statute of this State constitutes a violation if it is so designated in this Code or in the law defining the offense or if no other sentence than a fine, or fine and forfeiture or other civil penalty is authorized upon conviction or if it is defined by a statute other than this Code which now provides that the offense shall not constitute a crime. A violation does not constitute a crime and conviction of a violation shall not give rise to any disability or legal disadvantage based on conviction of a criminal offense.[26]

Since violations, unlike crimes, carry no social stigma, it is often argued that there is no serious injustice if, in the interest of quick and effective law enforcement, violators are held unconditionally liable. This line of argument is persuasive when we consider only parking and minor traffic violations, illegal sales of various kinds, and violations of health and safety codes, where the penalties serve as warnings and the fines are light. But the argument loses all cogency when the "civil penalties" are severe—heavy fines, forfeitures of property, removal from office, suspension of a license, withholding of an important "benefit," and the like. The condemnation of the faultless may be the most flagrant injustice, but the good-natured, noncondemnatory infliction of severe hardship on the innocent is little better. It is useful to distinguish violations and civil penalties from crimes and punishments; yet it does not follow that the safeguards of culpability requirements and due process which justice demands for the latter are always irrelevant encumbrances to the former. Two things are morally wrong: (1) to condemn a faultless man while inflicting pain or deprivation on him however slight

---

[24] "A depth study of Wisconsin statutes in 1956 revealed that of 1113 statutes creating criminal offenses [punishable by fine, imprisonment, or both] which were in force in 1953, no less than 660 used language in the definitions of the offenses which omitted all reference to a mental element, and which therefore, under the canons of construction which have come to govern these matters, left it open to the courts to impose strict liability if they saw fit." Colin Howard, "Not Proven," *Adelaide Law Review*, 1 (1962), 274. The study cited is: Remington, Robinson, and Zick, "Liability Without Fault Criminal Statutes," *Wisconsin Law Review* (1956), 625, 636.

[25] Rollin M. Perkins, *Criminal Law* (Brooklyn: The Foundation Press, 1957), 701–702.

[26] American Law Institute, *Model Penal Code, Proposed Official Draft* (Philadelphia, 1962).

(unjust punishment); and (2) to inflict unnecessary and severe suffering on a faultless man even in the absence of condemnation (unjust civil penalty). To exact a two-dollar fine from a hapless violator for overtime parking, however, even though he could not possibly have avoided it, is to do neither of these things.

V

Public condemnation, whether avowed through the stigmatizing symbolism of punishment or unavowed but clearly discernible (mere "punitive intent"), can greatly magnify the suffering caused by its attendant mode of hard treatment. Samuel Butler keenly appreciated the difference between reprobative hard treatment (punishment) and the same treatment without reprobation:

> ...we should hate a single flogging given in the way of mere punishment more than the amputation of a limb, if it were kindly and courteously performed from a wish to help us out of our difficulty, and with the full consciousness on the part of the doctor that it was only by an accident of constitution that he was not in the like plight himself. So the Erewhonians take a flogging once a week, and a diet of bread and water for two or three months together, whenever their straightener recommends it.[27]

Even floggings and imposed fastings do not constitute punishments, then, where social conventions are such that they do not express public censure (what Butler called "scouting"); and as therapeutic treatments simply, rather than punishments, they are easier to take.

Yet floggings and fastings do hurt, and far more than is justified by their Erewhonian (therapeutic) objectives. The same is true of our own state mental hospitals where criminal psychopaths are often sent for "rehabilitation": solitary confinement may not hurt *quite* so much when called "the quiet room," or the forced support of heavy fire extinguishers when called "hydrotherapy";[28] but their infliction on patients can be so cruel (whether or not their quasi-medical names mask punitive intent) as to demand justification.

Hard treatment and symbolic condemnation, then, are not only both necessary to an adequate definition of "punishment"; each also poses a special problem for the justification of punishment. The reprobative symbolism of punishment is subject to attack not only as an independent source of suffering but as the vehicle of undeserved responsive attitudes and unfair judgments of blame. One kind of skeptic, granting that penalties are needed if legal rules are to be enforced, and also that society would be impossible without general and predictable obedience to such rules, might nevertheless

---

[27] *Erewhon*, new and rev. edn. (London: Grant Richards, 1901), Ch. 10.

[28] These two examples are cited by Francis A. Allen in "Criminal Justice, Legal Values and the Rehabilitative Ideal," *Journal of Criminal Law, Criminology and Police Science*, 50 (1959), 229.

question the need to add condemnation to the penalizing of violators. Hard treatment of violators, he might grant, is an unhappy necessity, but reprobation of the offender is offensively self-righteous and cruel; adding gratuitous insult to necessary injury can serve no useful purpose. A partial answer to this kind of skeptic has already been given. The condemnatory aspect of punishment does serve a socially useful purpose: it is precisely the element in punishment that makes possible the performance of such symbolic functions as disavowal, nonacquiescence, vindication, and absolution.

Another kind of skeptic might readily concede that the reprobative symbolism of punishment is necessary to, and justified by, these various derivative functions. Indeed, he may even add deterrence to the list, for condemnation is likely to make it clear, where it would not otherwise be so, that a penalty is not a mere price tag. Granting that point, however, this kind of skeptic would have us consider whether the ends that justify public condemnation of criminal conduct might not be achieved equally well by means of less painful symbolic machinery. There was a time, after all, when the gallows and the rack were the leading clear symbols of shame and ignominy. Now we condemn felons to penal servitude as the way of rendering their crimes infamous. Could not the job be done still more economically? Isn't there a way to stigmatize without inflicting any further (pointless) pain to the body, to family, to creative capacity?

One can imagine an elaborate public ritual, exploiting the most trustworthy devices of religion and mystery, music and drama, to express in the most solemn way the community's condemnation of a criminal for his dastardly deed. Such a ritual might condemn so very emphatically that there could be no doubt of its genuineness, thus rendering symbolically superfluous any further hard physical treatment. Such a device would preserve the condemnatory function of punishment while dispensing with its usual physical media—incarceration and corporal mistreatment. Perhaps this is only idle fantasy; or perhaps there is more to it. The question is surely open. The only point I wish to make here is one about the nature of the question. The problem of justifying punishment, when it takes this form, may really be that of justifying our particular symbols of infamy.

Whatever the form of skeptical challenge to the institution of punishment, however, there is one traditional answer to it that seems to me to be incoherent. I refer to that version of the retributive theory which mentions neither condemnation nor vengeance but insists instead that the ultimate justifying purpose of punishment is to match off moral gravity and pain, to give each offender exactly that amount of pain the evil of his offense calls for, on the alleged principle of justice that the wicked should suffer pain in exact proportion to their turpitude.

I shall only mention in passing the familiar and potent objections to this view.[29] The innocent presumably deserve *not* to suffer, just as the guilty are supposed to deserve to suffer; yet it is impossible to hurt an evil man without imposing suffering on those who love or depend on him. Deciding the right amount of suffering to inflict in a given case would require an assessment of the character of the offender as manifested

---

[29] For more convincing statements of these arguments, see *iter alia*: W. D. Ross, *The Right and the Good* (Oxford: Clarendon Press, 1930), 56–65; J. D. Mabbott, "Punishment," *Mind*, 49 (1939); A. C. Ewing, *The Morality of Punishment* (London: Kegan Paul, Trench, Trubner & Co., 1929), Ch. 1; and F. Dostoevski, *The House of the Dead*, tr. H. Sutherland Edwards (New York: E. P. Dutton, 1912).

throughout his whole life and also his total lifelong balance of pleasure and pain—an obvious impossibility. Moreover, justice would probably demand the abandonment of general rules in the interests of individuation of punishment since there will inevitably be inequalities of moral guilt in the commission of the same crime and inequalities of suffering from the same punishment. If not dispensed with, however, general rules must list all crimes in the order of their moral gravity, all punishments in the order of their severity, and the matchings between the two scales. But the moral gravity scale would have to list as well motives and purposes, not simply types of overt acts, for a given crime can be committed in any kind of "mental state," and its "moral gravity" in a given case surely must depend in part on its accompanying motive. Condign punishment, then, would have to match suffering to motive (desire, belief, or whatever), not to dangerousness or to amount of harm done. Hence some petty larcenies would be punished more severely than some murders. It is not likely that we should wish to give power to judges and juries to make such difficult moral judgments. Worse yet, the judgments required are not merely "difficult"; they are in principle impossible to make. It may seem "self-evident" to some moralists that the passionate impulsive killer, for example, deserves less suffering for his wickedness than the scheming deliberate killer; but if the question of comparative *dangerousness* is left out of mind, reasonable men not only can but will disagree in their appraisals of comparative blameworthiness, and there appears to be no rational way of resolving the issue.[30] Certainly, there is no rational way of demonstrating that one criminal deserves exactly twice or three-eighths or twelve-ninths as much suffering as another; yet, according to at least some forms of this theory, the amounts of suffering inflicted for any two crimes should stand in exact proportion to the "amounts" of wickedness in the criminals.

For all that, however, the pain-fitting-wickedness version of the retributive theory does erect its edifice of moral superstition on a foundation in moral common sense, for justice *does* require that in some (other) sense "the punishment fit the crime." What justice demands is that the *condemnatory aspect* of the punishment suit the crime, that the crime be of a kind that is truly worthy of reprobation. Further, the degree of disapproval expressed by the punishment should "fit" the crime only in the unproblematic sense that the more serious crimes should receive stronger disapproval than the less serious ones, the seriousness of the crime being determined by the amount of harm it generally causes and the degree to which people are disposed to commit it. That is quite another thing than requiring that the "hard treatment" component, considered apart from its symbolic function, should "fit" the moral quality of a specific criminal act, assessed quite independently of its relation to social harm. Given our conventions, of course, condemnation is expressed by hard treatment, and the degree of harshness of the latter expresses the degree of reprobation of the former. Still, this should not blind us to the fact that it is social disapproval and its appropriate expression that should fit the crime, and not hard treatment (pain) as such. Pain should match guilt only insofar as its infliction is the symbolic vehicle of public condemnation.

[30] Cf. Jerome Michael and Herbert Wechsler, *Criminal Law and Its Administration* (Chicago: The Foundation Press, 1940), "Note on Deliberation and Character," 170–172.

8

MARXISM AND RETRIBUTION
Jeffrie G. Murphy

Punishment in general has been defended as a means either of ameliorating or of intimidating. Now what right have you to punish me for the amelioration or intimidation of others? And besides there is history—there is such a thing as statistics—which prove with the most complete evidence that since Cain the world has been neither intimidated nor ameliorated by punishment. Quite the contrary. From the point of view of abstract right, there is only one theory of punishment which recognizes human dignity in the abstract, and that is the theory of Kant, especially in the more rigid formula given to it by Hegel. Hegel says: "Punishment is the right of the criminal. It is an act of his own will. The violation of right has been proclaimed by the criminal as his own right. His crime is the negation of right. Punishment is the negation of this negation, and consequently an affirmation of right, solicited and forced upon the criminal by himself."

There is no doubt something specious in this formula, inasmuch as Hegel, instead of looking upon the criminal as the mere object, the slave of justice, elevates him to the position of a free and self-determined being. Looking, however, more closely into the matter, we discover that German idealism here, as in most other instances, has but given a transcendental sanction to the rules of existing society. Is it not a delusion to substitute for the individual with his real motives, with multifarious social circumstances pressing upon him, the abstraction of "free will"—one among the many qualities of man for man himself?... Is there not a necessity for

An earlier version of this essay was delivered to the Third Annual Colloquium in Philosophy ("The Philosophy of Punishment") at the University of Dayton in October, 1972. I am grateful to the Department of Philosophy at the University of Dayton for inviting me to participate and to a number of persons at the Colloquium for the useful discussion on my paper at the time. I am also grateful to Anthony D. Woozley of the University of Virginia and to two of my colleagues, Robert M. Harnish and Francis V. Raab, for helping me to clarify the expression of my views.

deeply reflecting upon an alteration of the system that breeds these crimes, instead of glorifying
the hangman who executes a lot of criminals to make room only for the supply of new ones?

Karl Marx, "Capital Punishment,"
New York Daily Tribune, *18 February 1853*[1]

Philosophers have written at great length about the moral problems involved in punishing the innocent—particularly as these problems raise obstacles to an acceptance of the moral theory of Utilitarianism. Punishment of an innocent man in order to bring about good social consequences is, at the very least, not always clearly wrong on utilitarian principles. This being so, utilitarian principles are then to be condemned by any morality that may be called Kantian in character. For punishing an innocent man, in Kantian language, involves using that man as a mere means or instrument to some social good and is thus not to treat him as an end in himself, in accord with his dignity or worth as a person.

The Kantian position on the issue of punishing the innocent, and the many ways in which the utilitarian might try to accommodate that position, constitute extremely well-worn ground in contemporary moral and legal philosophy.[2] I do not propose to wear the ground further by adding additional comments on the issue here. What I do want to point out, however, is something which seems to me quite obvious but which philosophical commentators on punishment have almost universally failed to see—namely, that problems of the very same kind and seriousness arise for the utilitarian theory with respect to the punishment of the guilty. For a utilitarian theory of punishment (Bentham's is a paradigm) must involve justifying punishment in terms of its social results—e.g., deterrence, incapacitation, and rehabilitation. And thus even a guilty man is, on this theory, being punished because of the instrumental value the action of punishment will have in the future. He is being used as a means to some future good—e.g., the deterrence of others. Thus those of a Kantian persuasion, who see the importance of worrying about the treatment of persons as mere means, must, it would seem, object just as strenuously to the punishment of the guilty on utilitarian grounds as to the punishment of the innocent. Indeed the former worry, in some respects, seems more serious. For a utilitarian can perhaps refine his theory in such a way that it does not commit him to the punishment of the innocent. However, if he is to approve of punishment at

---

[1] In a sense, my paper may be viewed as an elaborate commentary on this one passage, excerpted from a discussion generally concerned with the efficacy of capital punishment in eliminating crime. For in this passage, Marx (to the surprise of many I should think) expresses a certain admiration for the classical retributive theory of punishment. Also (again surprisingly) he expresses this admiration in a kind of language he normally avoids—i.e., the moral language of rights and justice. He then, of course, goes on to reject the applicability of that theory. But the question that initially perplexed me is the following: what is the explanation of Marx's ambivalence concerning the retributive theory; why is he both attracted and repelled by it? (This ambivalence is not shared, for example, by utilitarians—who feel nothing but repulsion when the retributive theory is even mentioned.) Now except for some very brief passages in *The Holy Family*, Marx himself has nothing more to say on the topic of punishment beyond what is contained in this brief *Daily Tribune* article. Thus my essay is in no sense an exercise in textual scholarship (there are not enough texts) but is rather an attempt to construct an assessment of punishment, Marxist at least in spirit, that might account for the ambivalence found in the quoted passage. My main outside help comes, not from Marx himself, but from the writings of the Marxist criminologist Willem Bonger.

[2] Many of the leading articles on this topic have been reprinted in *The Philosophy of Punishment*, ed. H. B. Acton (London, 1969). Those papers not included are cited in Acton's excellent bibliography.

all, he must approve of punishing the guilty in at least some cases. This makes the worry about punishing the guilty formidable indeed, and it is odd that this has gone generally unnoticed.[3] It has generally been assumed that if the utilitarian theory can just avoid entailing the permissibility of punishing the innocent, then all objections of a Kantian character to the theory will have been met. This seems to me simply not to be the case.

What the utilitarian theory really cannot capture, I would suggest, is the notion of persons having rights. And it is just this notion that is central to any Kantian outlook on morality. Any Kantian can certainly agree that punishing persons (guilty or innocent) may have either good or bad or indifferent consequences and that insofar as the consequences (whether in a particular case or for an institution) are good, this is something in favor of punishment. But the Kantian will maintain that this consequential outlook, important as it may be, leaves out of consideration entirely that which is most morally crucial—namely, the question of rights. Even if punishment of a person would have good consequences, what gives us (i.e., society) the moral right to inflict it? If we have such a right, what is its origin or derivation? What social circumstances must be present for it to be applicable? What does this right to punish tell us about the status of the person to be punished—e.g., how are we to analyze his rights, the sense in which he must deserve to be punished, his obligations in the matter? It is this family of questions which any Kantian must regard as morally central and which the utilitarian cannot easily accommodate into his theory. And it is surely this aspect of Kant's and Hegel's retributivism, this seeing of rights as basic, which appeals to Marx in the quoted passage. As Marx himself puts it: "What right have you to punish me for the amelioration or intimidation of others?" And he further praises Hegel for seeing that punishment, if justified, must involve respecting the rights of the person to be punished.[4] Thus Marx, like Kant, seems prepared to draw the important distinction between (a) what it would be good to do on grounds of utility and (b) what we have a right to do. Since we do not always have the right to do what it would be good to do, this distinction is of the greatest moral importance; and missing the distinction is the Achilles heel of all forms of Utilitarianism. For consider the following example: A Jehovah's Witness needs a blood transfusion in order to live; but, because of his (we can agree absurd) religious belief that such transfusions are against God's commands, he instructs his doctor not to give him one. Here is a case where it would seem to be good or for the best to give the transfusion and yet, at the very least, it is highly doubtful that the doctor has a right to give it. This kind of distinction is elementary, and any theory which misses it is morally degenerate.[5]

To move specifically to the topic of punishment: How exactly does retributivism (of a Kantian or Hegelian variety) respect the rights of persons? Is Marx really correct

---

[3] One writer who has noticed this is Richard Wasserstrom. See his "Why Punish the Guilty?" *Princeton University Magazine* 20 (1964), pp. 14–19.

[4] Marx normally avoids the language of rights and justice because he regards such language to be corrupted by bourgeois ideology. However, if we think very broadly of what an appeal to rights involves—namely, a protest against unjustified coercion—there is no reason why Marx may not legitimately avail himself on occasion of this way of speaking. For there is surely at least some moral overlap between Marx's protests against exploitation and the evils of a division of labor, for example, and the claims that people have a right not to be used solely for the benefit of others and a right to self-determination.

[5] I do not mean to suggest that under no conceivable circumstances would the doctor be justified in giving the transfusion even though, in one clear sense, he had no right to do it. If, for example, the Jehovah's Witness was a key man whose survival was necessary to prevent the outbreak of a destructive war, we might

on this? I believe that he is. I believe that retributivism can be formulated in such a way that it is the only morally defensible theory of punishment. I also believe that arguments, which may be regarded as Marxist at least in spirit, can be formulated which show that social conditions as they obtain in most societies make this form of retributivism largely inapplicable within those societies. As Marx says, in those societies retributivism functions merely to provide a "transcendental sanction" for the status quo. If this is so, then the only morally defensible theory of punishment is largely inapplicable in modern societies. The consequence: modern societies largely lack the moral right to punish.[6] The upshot is that a Kantian moral theory (which in general seems to me correct) and a Marxist analysis of society (which, if properly qualified, also seems to me correct) produces a radical and not merely reformist attack not merely on the scope and manner of punishment in our society but on the institution of punishment itself. Institutions of punishment constitute what Bernard Harrison has called structural injustices[7] and are, in the absence of a major social change, to be resisted by all who take human rights to be morally serious—i.e., regard them as genuine action guides and not merely as rhetorical devices which allow people to morally sanctify institutions which in fact can only be defended on grounds of social expediency.

Stating all of this is one thing and proving it, of course, is another. Whether I can ever do this is doubtful. That I cannot do it in one brief article is certain. I cannot, for example, here defend in detail my belief that a generally Kantian outlook on moral matters is correct.[8] Thus I shall content myself for the present with attempting to render at least plausible two major claims involved in the view that I have outlined thus far: (1) that a retributive theory, in spite of the bad press that it has received, is a morally credible theory of punishment—that it can be, H. L. A. Hart to the contrary,[9] a reasonable general justifying aim of punishment; and (2) that a Marxist analysis of a society can undercut the practical applicability of that theory.

THE RIGHT OF THE STATE TO PUNISH

It is strong evidence of the influence of a utilitarian outlook in moral and legal matters that discussions of punishment no longer involve a consideration of the right of anyone to inflict it. Yet in the eighteenth and nineteenth centuries, this tended to be regarded

---

well regard the transfusion as on the whole justified. However, even in such a case, a morally sensitive man would have to regretfully realize that he was sacrificing an important principle. Such a realization would be impossible (because inconsistent) for a utilitarian, for his theory admits only one principle—namely, do that which on the whole maximizes utility. An occupational disease of utilitarians is a blindness to the possibility of genuine moral dilemmas—i.e., a blindness to the possibility that important moral principles can conflict in ways that are not obviously resolvable by a rational decision procedure.

[6] I qualify my thesis by the word "largely" to show at this point my realization, explored in more detail later, that no single theory can account for all criminal behavior.

[7] Bernard Harrison, "Violence and the Rule of Law," in *Violence*, ed. Jerome A. Shaffer (New York, 1971), pp. 139–176.

[8] I have made a start toward such a defense in my "The Killing of the Innocent," forthcoming in *The Monist* 57, no. 4 (October 1973).

[9] H. L. A. Hart, "Prolegomenon to the Principles of Punishment," from *Punishment and Responsibility* (Oxford, 1968), pp. 1–27.

as the central aspect of the problem meriting philosophical consideration. Kant, Hegel, Bosanquet, Green—all tended to entitle their chapters on punishment along the lines explicitly used by Green: "The Right of the State to Punish."[10] This is not just a matter of terminology but reflects, I think, something of deeper philosophical substance. These theorists, unlike the utilitarian, did not view man as primarily a maximizer of personal satisfactions—a maximizer of individual utilities. They were inclined, in various ways, to adopt a different model of man—man as a free or spontaneous creator, man as autonomous. (Marx, it may be noted, is much more in line with this tradition than with the utilitarian outlook.)[11] This being so, these theorists were inclined to view punishment (a certain kind of coercion by the state) as not merely a causal contributor to pain and suffering, but rather as presenting at least a prima facie challenge to the values of autonomy and personal dignity and self-realization—the very values which, in their view, the state existed to nurture. The problem as they saw it, therefore, was that of reconciling punishment as state coercion with the value of individual autonomy. (This is an instance of the more general problem which Robert Paul Wolff has called the central problem of political philosophy—namely, how is individual moral autonomy to be reconciled with legitimate political authority?)[12] This kind of problem, which I am inclined to agree is quite basic, cannot even be formulated intelligibly from a utilitarian perspective. Thus the utilitarian cannot even see the relevance of Marx's charge: Even if punishment has wonderful social consequences, what gives anyone the right to inflict it on me?

Now one fairly typical way in which others acquire rights over us is by our own consent. If a neighbor locks up my liquor cabinet to protect me against my tendencies to drink too heavily, I might well regard this as a presumptuous interference with my own freedom, no matter how good the result intended or accomplished. He had no right to do it and indeed violated my rights in doing it. If, on the other hand, I had asked him to do this or had given my free consent to his suggestion that he do it, the same sort of objection on my part would be quite out of order. I had given him the right to do it, and he had the right to do it. In doing it, he violated no rights of mine— even if, at the time of his doing it, I did not desire or want the action to be performed. Here then we seem to have a case where my autonomy may be regarded as intact even though a desire of mine is thwarted. For there is a sense in which the thwarting of the desire can be imputed to me (my choice or decision) and not to the arbitrary intervention of another.

How does this apply to our problem? The answer, I think, is obvious. What is needed, in order to reconcile my undesired suffering of punishment at the hands of the state with my autonomy (and thus with the state's right to punish me), is a political theory which makes the state's decision to punish me in some sense my own decision. If I have willed my own punishment (consented to it, agreed to it) then—even if at the time I happen not to desire it—it can be said that my autonomy and dignity

---

[10] Thomas Hill Green, *Lectures on the Principles of Political Obligation* (1885), (Ann Arbor, 1967), pp. 180–205.

[11] For an elaboration of this point, see Steven Lukes, "Alienation and Anomie," in *Philosophy, Politics and Society* (Third Series), ed. Peter Laslett and W. G. Runciman (Oxford, 1967), pp. 134–156.

[12] Robert Paul Wolff, *In Defense of Anarchism* (New York, 1970).

remain intact. Theories of the General Will and Social Contract theories are two such theories which attempt this reconciliation of autonomy with legitimate state authority (including the right or authority of the state to punish). Since Kant's theory happens to incorporate elements of both, it will be useful to take it for our sample.

Moral Rights and the Retributive Theory of Punishment

To justify government or the state is necessarily to justify at least some coercion.[13] This poses a problem for someone, like Kant, who maintains that human freedom is the ultimate or most sacred moral value. Kant's own attempt to justify the state, expressed in his doctrine of the *moral title* (*Befugnis*),[14] involves an argument that coercion is justified only in so far as it is used to prevent invasions against freedom. Freedom itself is the only value which can be used to limit freedom, for the appeal to any other value (e.g., utility) would undermine the ultimate status of the value of freedom. Thus Kant attempts to establish the claim that some forms of coercion (as opposed to violence) are morally permissible because, contrary to appearance, they are really consistent with rational freedom. The argument, in broad outline, goes in the following way. Coercion may keep people from doing what they desire or want to do on a particular occasion and is thus prima facie wrong. However, such coercion can be shown to be morally justified (and thus not absolutely wrong) if it can be established that the coercion is such that it could have been rationally willed even by the person whose desire is interfered with:

> Accordingly, when it is said that a creditor has a right to demand from his debtor the payment of a debt, this does not mean that he can *persuade* the debtor that his own reason itself obligates him to this performance; on the contrary, to say that he has such a right means only that the use of coercion to make anyone do this is entirely compatible with everyone's freedom, *including the freedom of the debtor*, in accordance with universal laws.[15]

Like Rousseau, Kant thinks that it is only in a context governed by social practice (particularly civil government and its Rule of Law) that this can make sense. Laws may

---

[13] In this section, I have adapted some of my previously published material: *Kant: The Philosophy of Right* (London, 1970), pp. 109–112 and 140–144; "Three Mistakes About Retributivism," *Analysis* (April 1971): 166–169; and "Kant's Theory of Criminal Punishment," in *Proceedings of the Third International Kant Congress*, ed. Lewis White Beck (Dordrecht, 1972), pp. 434–441. I am perfectly aware that Kant's views on the issues to be considered here are often obscure and inconsistent—e.g., the analysis of "willing one's own punishment" which I shall later quote from Kant occurs in a passage the primary purpose of which is to argue that the idea of "willing one's own punishment" makes no sense! My present objective, however, is not to attempt accurate Kant scholarship. My goal is rather to build upon some remarks of Kant's which I find philosophically suggestive.

[14] Immanuel Kant, *The Metaphysical Elements of Justice* (1797), trans. John Ladd (Indianapolis, 1965), pp. 35ff.

[15] *Ibid.*, p. 37.

require of a person some action that he does not desire to perform. This is not a violent invasion of his freedom, however, if it can be shown that in some antecedent position of choice (what John Rawls calls "the original position"),[16] he would have been rational to adopt a Rule of Law (and thus run the risk of having some of his desires thwarted) rather than some other alternative arrangement like the classical State of Nature. This is, indeed, the only sense that Kant is able to make of classical Social Contract theories. Such theories are to be viewed, not as historical fantasies, but as ideal models of rational decision. For what these theories actually claim is that the only coercive institutions that are morally justified are those which a group of rational beings could agree to adopt in a position of having to pick social institutions to govern their relations:

> The contract, which is called *contractus originarius*, or *pactum sociale*...need not be assumed to be a fact, indeed it is not [even possible as such. To suppose that would be like insisting] that before anyone would be bound to respect such a civic constitution, it be proved first of all from history that a people, whose rights and obligations we have entered into as their descendants, had *once upon a time* executed such an act and had left a reliable document or instrument, either orally or in writing, concerning this contract. Instead, this contract is a *mere idea* of reason which has undoubted practical reality; namely, to oblige every legislator to give us laws in such a manner that the laws *could* have originated from the united will of the entire people and to regard every subject in so far as he is a citizen as though he had consented to such [an expression of the general] will. This is the testing stone of the rightness of every publicly-known law, for if a law were such that it was impossible for an entire people to give consent to it (as for example a law that a certain class of subjects, by inheritance, should have the privilege of the *status of lords*), then such a law is unjust. On the other hand, if there is a mere *possibility* that a people might consent to a (certain) law, then it is a duty to consider that the law is just even though at the moment the people might be in such a position or have a point of view that would result in their refusing to give their consent to it if asked.[17]

The problem of organizing a state, however hard it may seem, can be solved even for a race of devils, if only they are intelligent. The problem is: "Given a multiple of rational beings requiring universal laws for their preservation, but each of whom is secretly inclined to exempt himself from them, to establish a constitution in such a way that, although their private intentions conflict, they check each other, with the result that their public conduct is the same as if they had no such intentions."[18]

---

[16] John Rawls, "Justice as Fairness," *The Philosophical Review* 67 (1958): 164–194; and *A Theory of Justice* (Cambridge, Mass., 1971), especially pp. 17–22.

[17] Immanuel Kant, "Concerning the Common Saying: This May be True in Theory but Does Not Apply in Practice (1793)," in *The Philosophy of Kant*, ed. and trans. Carl J. Friedrich (New York, 1949), pp. 421–422.

[18] Immanuel Kant, *Perpetual Peace* (1795), trans. Lewis White Beck in the Kant anthology *On History* (Indianapolis 1963), p. 112.

Though Kant's doctrine is superficially similar to Mill's later self-protection principle, the substance is really quite different. For though Kant in some general sense argues that coercion is justified only to prevent harm to others, he understands by "harm" only certain invasions of freedom and not simply disutility. Also, his defense of the principle is not grounded, as is Mill's, on its utility. Rather it is to be regarded as a principle of justice, by which Kant means a principle that rational beings could adopt in a situation of mutual choice:

> The concept [of justice] applies only to the relationship of a will to another person's will, not to his wishes or desires (or even just his needs) which are the concern of acts of benevolence and charity.... In applying the concept of justice we take into consideration only the form of the relationship between the wills insofar as they are regarded as free, and whether the action of one of them can be conjoined with the freedom of the other in accordance with universal law. Justice is therefore the aggregate of those conditions under which the will of one person can be conjoined with the will of another in accordance with a universal law of freedom.[19]

How does this bear specifically on punishment? Kant, as everyone knows, defends a strong form of a retributive theory of punishment. He holds that guilt merits, and is a sufficient condition for, the infliction of punishment. And this claim has been universally condemned—particularly by utilitarians—as primitive, unenlightened and barbaric.

But why is it so condemned? Typically, the charge is that infliction of punishment on such grounds is nothing but pointless vengeance. But what is meant by the claim that the infliction is "pointless"? If "pointless" is tacitly being analyzed as "disutilitarian," then the whole question is simply being begged. You cannot refute a retributive theory merely by noting that it is a retributive theory and not a utilitarian theory. This is to confuse redescription with refutation and involves an argument whose circularity is not even complicated enough to be interesting.

Why, then, might someone claim that guilt merits punishment? Such a claim might be made for either of two very different reasons. (1) Someone (e.g., a Moral Sense theorist) might maintain that the claim is a primitive and unanalyzable proposition that is morally ultimate—that we can just intuit the "fittingness" of guilt and punishment. (2) It might be maintained that the retributivist claim is demanded by a general theory of political obligation which is more plausible than any alternative theory. Such a theory will typically provide a technical analysis of such concepts as crime and punishment and will thus not regard the retributivist claim as an indisputable primitive. It will be argued for as a kind of theorem within the system.

Kant's theory is of the second sort. He does not opt for retributivism as a bit of intuitive moral knowledge. Rather he offers a theory of punishment that is based on

---

[19] Immanuel Kant, *The Metaphysical Elements of Justice*, p. 34.

his general view that political obligation is to be analyzed, quasi-contractually, in terms of reciprocity. If the law is to remain just, it is important to guarantee that those who disobey it will not gain an unfair advantage over those who do obey voluntarily. It is important that no man profit from his own criminal wrongdoing, and a certain kind of "profit" (i.e., not bearing the burden of self-restraint) is intrinsic to criminal wrongdoing. Criminal punishment, then, has as its object the restoration of a proper balance between benefit and obedience. The criminal himself has no complaint, because he has rationally consented to or willed his own punishment. That is, those very rules which he has broken work, when they are obeyed by others, to his own advantage as a citizen. He would have chosen such rules for himself and others in the original position of choice. And, since he derives and voluntarily accepts benefits from their operation, he owes his own obedience as a debt to his fellow-citizens for their sacrifices in maintaining them. If he chooses not to sacrifice by exercising self-restraint and obedience, this is tantamount to his choosing to sacrifice in another way—namely, by paying the prescribed penalty:

> A transgression of the public law that makes him who commits it unfit to be a citizen is called...a crime....
>
> What kind and what degree of punishment does public legal justice adopt as its principle and standard? None other than the principle of equality (illustrated by the pointer of the scales of justice), that is, the principle of not treating one side more favorably than the other. Accordingly, any undeserved evil that you inflict on someone else among the people is one you do to yourself. If you vilify him, you vilify yourself; if you steal from him, you steal from yourself; if you kill him, you kill yourself....
>
> To say, "I will to be punished if I murder someone" can mean nothing more than, "I submit myself along with everyone else to those laws which, if there are any criminals among the people, will naturally include penal laws."[20]

This analysis of punishment regards it as a debt owed to the law-abiding members of one's community; and, once paid, it allows reentry into the community of good citizens on equal status.

Now some of the foregoing no doubt sounds implausible or even obscurantist. Since criminals typically desire not to be punished, what can it really mean to say that they have, as rational men, really willed their own punishment? Or that, as Hegel says, they have a right to it? Perhaps a comparison of the traditional retributivist views with those of a contemporary Kantian—John Rawls—will help to make the points clearer.[21]

---

[20] *Ibid.*, pp. 99, 101, and 105, in the order quoted.

[21] In addition to the works on justice by Rawls previously cited, the reader should consult the following for Rawls's application of his general theory to the problem of political obligation: John Rawls, "Legal Obligation and the Duty of Fair Play," in *Law and Philosophy*, ed. Sidney Hook (New York, 1964), pp. 3–18. This has been reprinted in my anthology *Civil Disobedience and Violence* (Belmont, Cal., 1971), pp. 39–52. For a direct application of a similar theory to the problem of punishment, see Herbert Morris, "Persons and Punishment," *The Monist* 52, no. 4 (October 1968): 475–501.

Rawls (like Kant) does not regard the idea of the social contract as an historical fact. It is rather a model of rational decision. Respecting a man's autonomy, at least on one view, is not respecting what he now happens, however uncritically, to desire; rather it is to respect what he desires (or would desire) as a rational man. (On Rawls's view, for example, rational men are said to be unmoved by feelings of envy; and thus it is not regarded as unjust to a person or a violation of his rights, if he is placed in a situation where he will envy another's advantage or position. A rational man would object, and thus would never consent to, a practice where another might derive a benefit from a position at his expense. He would not, however, envy the position *simpliciter*, would not regard the position as itself a benefit.) Now on Kant's (and also, I think, on Rawls's) view, a man is genuinely free or autonomous only in so far as he is rational. Thus it is man's rational will that is to be respected.

Now this idea of treating people, not as they in fact say that they want to be treated, but rather in terms of how you think they would, if rational, will to be treated, has obviously dangerous (indeed Fascistic) implications. Surely we want to avoid cramming indignities down the throats of people with the offhand observation that, no matter how much they scream, they are really rationally willing every bit of it. It would be particularly ironic for such arbitrary repression to come under the mask of respecting autonomy. And yet, most of us would agree, the general principle (though subject to abuse) also has important applications—for example, preventing the suicide of a person who, in a state of psychotic depression, wants to kill himself. What we need, then, to make the general view work, is a check on its arbitrary application; and a start toward providing such a check would be in the formulation of a public, objective theory of rationality and rational willing. It is just this, according to both Kant and Rawls, which the social contract theory can provide. On this theory, a man may be said to rationally will X if, and only if, X is called for by a rule that the man would necessarily have adopted in the original position of choice—i.e., in a position of coming together with others to pick rules for the regulation of their mutual affairs. This avoids arbitrariness because, according to Kant and Rawls at any rate, the question of whether such a rule would be picked in such a position is objectively determinable given certain (in their view) noncontroversial assumptions about human nature and rational calculation. Thus I can be said to will my own punishment if, in an antecedent position of choice, I and my fellows would have chosen institutions of punishment as the most rational means of dealing with those who might break the other generally beneficial social rules that had been adopted.

Let us take an analogous example: I may not, in our actual society, desire to treat a certain person fairly—e.g., I may not desire to honor a contract I have made with him because so doing would adversely affect my own self-interest. However, if I am forced to honor the contract by the state, I cannot charge (1) that the state has no right to do this, or (2) that my rights or dignity are being violated by my being coerced into doing it. Indeed, it can be said that I rationally will it since, in the original position, I would have chosen rules of justice (rather than rules of utility) and the principle, "contracts are to be honored," follows from the rules of justice.

Coercion and autonomy are thus reconciled, at least apparently. To use Marx's language, we may say (as Marx did in the quoted passage) that one virtue of the retributive theory, at least as expounded by Kant and Hegel on lines of the General Will and Social Contract theory, is that it manifests at least a formal or abstract respect for rights, dignity, and autonomy. For it at least recognizes the importance of attempting to construe state coercion in such a way that it is a product of each man's rational will. Utilitarian deterrence theory does not even satisfy this formal demand.

The question of primary interest to Marx, of course, is whether this formal respect also involves a material respect; i.e., does the theory have application in concrete fact in the actual social world in which we live? Marx is confident that it does not, and it is to this sort of consideration that I shall now pass.

ALIENATION AND PUNISHMENT

What can the philosopher learn from Marx? This question is a part of a more general question: What can philosophy learn from social science? Philosophers, it may be thought, are concerned to offer a priori theories, theories about how certain concepts are to be analyzed and their application justified. And what can the mundane facts that are the object of behavioral science have to do with exalted theories of this sort?

The answer, I think, is that philosophical theories, though not themselves empirical, often have such a character that their intelligibility depends upon certain empirical presuppositions. For example, our moral language presupposes, as Hart has argued,[22] that we are vulnerable creatures—creatures who can harm and be harmed by each other. Also, as I have argued elsewhere,[23] our moral language presupposes that we all share certain psychological characteristics—e.g., sympathy, a sense of justice, and the capacity to feel guilt, shame, regret, and remorse. If these facts were radically different (if, as Hart imagines for example, we all developed crustaceanlike exoskeletons and thus could not harm each other), the old moral language, and the moral theories which employ it, would lack application to the world in which we live. To use a crude example, moral prohibitions against killing presuppose that it is in fact possible for us to kill each other.

Now one of Marx's most important contributions to social philosophy, in my judgment, is simply his insight that philosophical theories are in peril if they are constructed in disregard of the nature of the empirical world to which they are supposed to apply.[24] A theory may be formally correct (i.e., coherent, or true for some possible world) but materially incorrect (i.e., inapplicable to the actual world in which we live). This insight, then, establishes the relevance of empirical research to philosophical theory and is a part, I think, of what Marx meant by "the union of theory and practice." Specifically relevant to the argument I want to develop are the following two related points:

---

[22] H. L. A. Hart, *The Concept of Law* (Oxford, 1961), pp. 189–195.

[23] Jeffrie G. Murphy, "Moral Death: A Kantian Essay on Psychopathy," *Ethics* 82, no. 4 (July 1972): 284–298.

[24] Banal as this point may seem, it could be persuasively argued that all Enlightenment political theory (e.g., that of Hobbes, Locke and Kant) is built upon ignoring it. For example, once we have substantial empirical evidence concerning how democracies really work in fact, how sympathetic can we really be to classical theories for the justification of democracy? For more on this, see C. B. Macpherson, "The Maximization of Democracy," in *Philosophy, Politics and Society* (Third Series), ed. Peter Laslett and W. G. Runciman (Oxford, 1967), pp. 83–103. This article is also relevant to the point raised in note 11 above.

(1) The theories of moral, social, political and legal philosophy presuppose certain empirical propositions about man and society. If these propositions are false, then the theory (even if coherent or formally correct) is materially defective and practically inapplicable. (For example, if persons tempted to engage in criminal conduct do not in fact tend to calculate carefully the consequences of their actions, this renders much of deterrence theory suspect.)

(2) Philosophical theories may put forth as a necessary truth that which is in fact merely an historically conditioned contingency. (For example, Hobbes argued that all men are necessarily selfish and competitive. It is possible, as many Marxists have argued, that Hobbes was really doing nothing more than elevating to the status of a necessary truth the contingent fact that the people around him in the capitalistic society in which he lived were in fact selfish and competitive.)[25]

In outline, then, I want to argue the following: that when Marx challenges the material adequacy of the retributive theory of punishment, he is suggesting (a) that it presupposes a certain view of man and society that is false and (b) that key concepts involved in the support of the theory (e.g., the concept of "rationality" in Social Contract theory) are given analyses which, though they purport to be necessary truths, are in fact mere reflections of certain historical circumstances.

In trying to develop this case, I shall draw primarily upon Willem Bonger's *Criminality and Economic Conditions* (1916), one of the few sustained Marxist analyses of crime and punishment.[26] Though I shall not have time here to qualify my support of Bonger in certain necessary ways, let me make clear that I am perfectly aware that his analysis is not the whole story. (No monolithic theory of anything so diverse as criminal behavior could be the whole story.) However, I am convinced that he has discovered part of the story. And my point is simply that insofar as Bonger's Marxist analysis is correct, then to that same degree is the retributive theory of punishment inapplicable in modern societies. (Let me emphasize again exactly how this objection to retributivism differs from those traditionally offered. Traditionally, retributivism has been rejected because it conflicts with the moral theory of its opponent, usually a utilitarian. This is not the kind of objection I want to develop. Indeed, with Marx, I have argued that the retributive theory of punishment grows out of the moral theory—Kantianism—which seems to me generally correct. The objection I want to pursue concerns the empirical

---

[25] This point is well developed in C. B. Macpherson, *The Political Theory of Possessive Individualism* (Oxford, 1962). In a sense, this point affects even the formal correctness of a theory. For it demonstrates an empirical source of corruption in the analyses of the very concepts in the theory.

[26] The writings of Willem Adriaan Bonger (1876–1940), a Dutch criminologist, have fallen into totally unjustified neglect in recent years. Anticipating contemporary sociological theories of crime, he was insisting that criminal behavior is in the province of normal psychology (though abnormal society) at a time when most other writers were viewing criminality as a symptom of psychopathology. His major works are: *Criminality and Economic Conditions* (Boston, 1916); *An Introduction to Criminology* (London, 1936); and *Race and Crime* (New York, 1943).

falsity of the factual presuppositions of the theory. If the empirical presuppositions of the theory are false, this does indeed render its application immoral. But the immorality consists, not in a conflict with some other moral theory, but immorality in terms of a moral theory that is at least close in spirit to the very moral theory which generates retributivism itself—i.e., a theory of justice.)[27]

To return to Bonger. Put bluntly, his theory is as follows. Criminality has two primary sources: (1) need and deprivation on the part of disadvantaged members of society, and (2) motives of greed and selfishness that are generated and reinforced in competitive capitalistic societies. Thus criminality is economically based—either directly in the case of crimes from need, or indirectly in the case of crimes growing out of motives or psychological states that are encouraged and developed in capitalistic society. In Marx's own language, such an economic system alienates men from themselves and from each other. It alienates men from themselves by creating motives and needs that are not "truly human." It alienates men from their fellows by encouraging a kind of competitiveness that forms an obstacle to the development of genuine communities to replace mere social aggregates.[28] And in Bonger's thought, the concept of community is central. He argues that moral relations and moral restraint are possible only in genuine communities characterized by bonds of sympathetic identification and mutual aid resting upon a perception of common humanity. All this he includes under the general rubric of reciprocity.[29] In the absence of reciprocity in this rich sense, moral relations among men will break down and criminality will increase.[30] Within bourgeois society, then, crimes are to be regarded as normal, and not psychopathological, acts. That is, they grow out of need, greed, indifference to others, and sometimes even a sense of indignation—all, alas, perfectly typical human motives.

To appreciate the force of Bonger's analysis, it is necessary to read his books and grasp the richness and detail of the evidence he provides for his claims. Here I can but quote a few passages at random to give the reader a tantalizing sample in the hope that he will be encouraged to read further into Bonger's own text:

[27] I say "at least in spirit" to avoid begging the controversial question of whether Marx can be said to embrace a theory of justice. Though (as I suggested in note 4) much of Marx's own evaluative rhetoric seems to overlap more traditional appeals to rights and justice (and a total lack of sympathy with anything like Utilitarianism), it must be admitted that he also frequently ridicules at least the terms "rights" and "justice" because of their apparent entrenchment in bourgeois ethics. For an interesting discussion of this issue, see Allen W. Wood, "The Marxian Critique of Justice," *Philosophy & Public Affairs* 1, no. 3 (Spring 1972): 244–282.

[28] The importance of community is also, I think, recognized in Gabriel de Tarde's notion of "social similarity" as a condition of criminal responsibility. See his *Penal Philosophy* (Boston, 1912). I have drawn on de Tarde's general account in my "Moral Death: A Kantian Essay on Psychopathy."

[29] By "reciprocity" Bonger intends something which includes, but is much richer than, a notion of "fair trading or bargaining" that might initially be read into the term. He also has in mind such things as sympathetic identification with others and tendencies to provide mutual aid. Thus, for Bonger, reciprocity and egoism have a strong tendency to conflict. I mention this lest Bonger's notion of reciprocity be too quickly identified with the more restricted notion found in, for example, Kant and Rawls.

[30] It is interesting how greatly Bonger's analysis differs from classical deterrence theory—e.g., that of Bentham. Bentham, who views men as machines driven by desires to attain pleasure and avoid pain, tends to regard terror as the primary restraint against crime. Bonger believes that, at least in a healthy society, moral motives would function as a major restraint against crime. When an environment that destroys moral motivation is created, even terror (as statistics tend to confirm) will not eradicate crime.

The abnormal element in crime is a social, not a biological, element. With the exception of a few special cases, crime lies within the boundaries of normal psychology and physiology....

We clearly see that [the egoistic tendencies of the present economic system and of its consequences] are very strong. Because of these tendencies the social instinct of man is not greatly developed; they have weakened the moral force in man which combats the inclination towards egoistic acts, and hence toward the crimes which are one form of these acts.... Compassion for the misfortunes of others inevitably becomes blunted, and a great part of morality consequently disappears....

As a consequence of the present environment, man has become very egoistic and hence more *capable of crime*, than if the environment had developed the germs of altruism....

There can be no doubt that one of the factors of criminality among the bourgeoisie is bad [moral] education.... The children—speaking of course in a general way—are brought up with the idea that they must succeed, no matter how; the aim of life is presented to them as getting money and shining in the world....

Poverty (taken in the sense of absolute want) kills the social sentiments in man, destroys in fact all relations between men. He who is abandoned by all can no longer have any feeling for those who have left him to his fate....

[Upon perception that the system tends to legalize the egoistic actions of the bourgeoisie and to penalize those of the proletariat], the oppressed resort to means which they would otherwise scorn. As we have seen above, the basis of the social feeling is reciprocity. As soon as this is trodden under foot by the ruling class the social sentiments of the oppressed become weak towards them....[31]

The essence of this theory has been summed up by Austin J. Turk. "Criminal behavior," he says, "is almost entirely attributable to the combination of egoism and an environment in which opportunities are not equitably distributed."[32]

No doubt this claim will strike many as extreme and intemperate—a sample of the old-fashioned Marxist rhetoric that sophisticated intellectuals have outgrown. Those who are inclined to react in this way might consider just one sobering fact: of the 1.3 million criminal offenders handled each day by some agency of the United States correctional system, the vast majority (80 percent on some estimates) are members of the lowest 15-percent income level—that percent which is below the

---

[31] *Introduction to Criminology*, pp. 75–76, and *Criminality and Economic Conditions*, pp. 532, 402, 483–484, 436, and 407, in the order quoted. Bonger explicitly attacks Hobbes: "The adherents of [Hobbes's theory] have studied principally men who live under capitalism, or under civilization; their correct conclusion has been that egoism is the predominant characteristic of these men, and they have adopted the simplest explanation of the phenomenon and say that this trait is inborn." If Hobbists can cite Freud for modern support, Bonger can cite Darwin. For, as Darwin had argued in the *Descent of Man*, men would not have survived as a species if they had not initially had considerably greater social sentiments than Hobbes allows them.

[32] Austin J. Turk, in the Introduction to his abridged edition of Bonger's *Criminality and Economic Conditions* (Bloomington, 1969), p. 14.

"poverty level" as defined by the Social Security Administration.[33] Unless one wants to embrace the belief that all these people are poor because they are bad, it might be well to reconsider Bonger's suggestion that many of them are "bad" because they are poor.[34] At any rate, let us suppose for purposes of discussion that Bonger's picture of the relation between crime and economic conditions is generally accurate. At what points will this challenge the credentials of the contractarian retributive theory as outlined above? I should like to organize my answer to this question around three basic topics:

1. *Rational Choice.* The model of rational choice found in Social Contract theory is egoistic—rational institutions are those that would be agreed to by calculating egoists ("devils" in Kant's more colorful terminology). The obvious question that would be raised by any Marxist is: Why give egoism this special status such that it is built, a priori, into the analysis of the concept of rationality? Is this not simply to regard as necessary that which may be only contingently found in the society around us? Starting from such an analysis, a certain result is inevitable—namely, a transcendental sanction for the status quo. Start with a bourgeois model of rationality and you will, of course, wind up defending a bourgeois theory of consent, a bourgeois theory of justice, and a bourgeois theory of punishment.

Though I cannot explore the point in detail here, it seems to me that this Marxist claim may cause some serious problems for Rawls's well-known theory of justice, a theory which I have already used to unpack some of the evaluative support for the retributive theory of punishment. One cannot help suspecting that there is a certain sterility in Rawls's entire project of providing a rational proof for the preferability of a certain conception of justice over all possible alternative evaluative principles, for the description which he gives of the rational contractors in the original position is such as to guarantee that they will come up with his two principles. This would be acceptable if the analysis of rationality presupposed were intuitively obvious or argued for on independent grounds. But it is not. Why, to take just one example, is a desire for

---

[33] Statistical data on characteristics of offenders in America are drawn primarily from surveys by the Bureau of Census and the National Council on Crime and Delinquency. While there is of course wide disagreement on how such data are to be interpreted, there is no serious disagreement concerning at least the general accuracy of statistics like the one I have cited. Even government publications openly acknowledge a high correlation between crime and socioeconomic disadvantages: "From arrest records, probation reports, and prison statistics a 'portrait' of the offender emerges that progressively highlights the disadvantaged character of his life. The offender at the end of the road in prison is likely to be a member of the lowest social and economic groups in the country, poorly educated and perhaps unemployed....Material failure, then, in a culture firmly oriented toward material success, is the most common denominator of offenders" (*The Challenge of Crime in a Free Society, A Report by the President's Commission on Law Enforcement and Administration of Justice*, U. S. Government Printing Office, Washington, D.C., 1967, pp. 44 and 160). The Marxist implications of this admission have not gone unnoticed by prisoners. See Samuel Jorden, "Prison Reform: In Whose Interest?" *Criminal Law Bulletin* 7, no. 9 (November 1971): 779–787.

[34] There are, of course, other factors which enter into an explanation of this statistic. One of them is the fact that economically disadvantaged guilty persons are more likely to wind up arrested or in prison (and thus be reflected in this statistic) than are economically advantaged guilty persons. Thus economic conditions enter into the explanation, not just of criminal behavior, but of society's response to criminal behavior. For a general discussion on the many ways in which crime and poverty are related, see Patricia M. Wald, "Poverty and Criminal Justice," *Task Force Report: The Courts*, U.S. Government Printing Office, Washington, D.C., 1967, pp. 139–151.

wealth a rational trait whereas envy is not? One cannot help feeling that the desired result dictates the premises.[35]

2. *Justice, Benefits, and Community.* The retributive theory claims to be grounded on justice; but is it just to punish people who act out of those very motives that society encourages and reinforces? If Bonger is correct, much criminality is motivated by greed, selfishness, and indifference to one's fellows; but does not the whole society encourage motives of greed and selfishness ("making it," "getting ahead"), and does not the competitive nature of the society alienate men from each other and thereby encourage indifference—even, perhaps, what psychiatrists call psychopathy? The moral problem here is similar to one that arises with respect to some war crimes. When you have trained a man to believe that the enemy is not a genuine human person (but only a gook, or a chink), it does not seem quite fair to punish the man if, in a war situation, he kills indiscriminately. For the psychological trait you have conditioned him to have, like greed, is not one that invites fine moral and legal distinctions. There is something perverse in applying principles that presuppose a sense of community in a society which is structured to destroy genuine community.[36]

Related to this is the whole allocation of benefits in contemporary society. The retributive theory really presupposes what might be called a "gentlemen's club" picture of the relation between man and society—i.e., men are viewed as being part of a community of shared values and rules. The rules benefit all concerned and, as a kind of debt for the benefits derived, each man owes obedience to the rules. In the absence of such obedience, he deserves punishment in the sense that he owes payment for the benefits. For, as rational man, he can see that the rules benefit everyone (himself included) and that he would have selected them in the original position of choice.

Now this may not be too far off for certain kinds of criminals—e.g., business executives guilty of tax fraud. (Though even here we might regard their motives of greed to be a function of societal reinforcement.) But to think that it applies to the typical criminal, from the poorer classes, is to live in a world of social and political

---

[35] The idea that the principles of justice could be proved as a kind of theorem (Rawls's claim in "Justice as Fairness") seems to be absent, if I understand the work correctly, in Rawls's recent *A Theory of Justice*. In this book, Rawls seems to be content with something less than a decision procedure. He is no longer trying to pull his theory of justice up by its own bootstraps, but now seems concerned simply with a certain elaborate conception of justice in the belief that it will do a good job of systematizing and ordering most of our considered and reflective intuitions about moral matters. To this, of course, the Marxist will want to say something like the following: "The considered and reflective intuitions current in our society are a product of bourgeois culture, and thus any theory based upon them begs the question against us and in favor of the status quo." I am not sure that this charge cannot be answered, but I am sure that it deserves an answer. Someday Rawls may be remembered, to paraphrase Georg Lukács's description of Thomas Mann, as the last and greatest philosopher of bourgeois liberalism. The virtue of this description is that it perceives the limitations of his outlook in a way consistent with acknowledging his indisputable genius. (None of my remarks here, I should point out, are to be interpreted as denying that our civilization derived major moral benefits from the tradition of bourgeois liberalism. Just because the freedoms and procedures we associate with bourgeois liberalism—speech, press, assembly, due process of law, etc.—are not the only important freedoms and procedures, we are not to conclude with some witless radicals that these freedoms are not terribly important and that the victories of bourgeois revolutions are not worth preserving. My point is much more modest and noncontroversial—namely, that even bourgeois liberalism requires a critique. It is not self-justifying and, in certain very important respects, is not justified at all.)

[36] Kant has some doubts about punishing bastard infanticide and dueling on similar grounds. Given the stigma that Kant's society attached to illegitimacy and the halo that the same society placed around military honor, it did not seem totally fair to punish those whose criminality in part grew out of such approved motives. See *Metaphysical Elements of Justice*, pp. 106–107.

fantasy. Criminals typically are not members of a shared community of values with their jailers; they suffer from what Marx calls alienation. And they certainly would be hard-pressed to name the benefits for which they are supposed to owe obedience. If justice, as both Kant and Rawls suggest, is based on reciprocity, it is hard to see what these persons are supposed to reciprocate for. Bonger addresses this point in a passage quoted earlier (p. 236): "The oppressed resort to means which they would otherwise scorn....The basis of social feelings is reciprocity. As soon as this is trodden under foot by the ruling class, the social sentiments of the oppressed become weak towards them."

3. *Voluntary Acceptance.* Central to the Social Contract idea is the claim that we owe allegiance to the law because the benefits we have derived have been voluntarily accepted. This is one place where our autonomy is supposed to come in. That is, having benefited from the Rule of Law when it was possible to leave, I have in a sense consented to it and to its consequences—even my own punishment if I violate the rules. To see how silly the factual presuppositions of this account are, we can do no better than quote a famous passage from David Hume's essay "Of the Original Contract":

> Can we seriously say that a poor peasant or artisan has a free choice to leave his country—when he knows no foreign language or manners, and lives from day to day by the small wages which he acquires? We may as well assert that a man, by remaining in a vessel, freely consents to the dominion of the master, though he was carried on board while asleep, and must leap into the ocean and perish the moment he leaves her.

A banal empirical observation, one may say. But it is through ignoring such banalities that philosophers generate theories which allow them to spread iniquity in the ignorant belief that they are spreading righteousness.

It does, then, seem as if there may be some truth in Marx's claim that the retributive theory, though formally correct, is materially inadequate. At root, the retributive theory fails to acknowledge that criminality is, to a large extent, a phenomenon of economic class. To acknowledge this is to challenge the empirical presupposition of the retributive theory—the presupposition that all men, including criminals, are voluntary participants in a reciprocal system of benefits and that the justice of this arrangement can be derived from some eternal and ahistorical concept of rationality.

THE upshot of all this seems rather upsetting, as indeed it is. How can it be the case that everything we are ordinarily inclined to say about punishment (in terms of utility and retribution) can be quite beside the point? To anyone with ordinary language sympathies (one who is inclined to maintain that what is correct to say is a function of what we do say), this will seem madness. Marx will agree that there is madness, all right, but in his view the madness will lie in what we do say—what we say only because of our massive (and often self-deceiving and self-serving) factual ignorance or indifference to the circumstances of the social world in which we live. Just as our whole way of talking about mental phenomena hardened before we knew any neurophysiology—and this leads us astray, so Marx would argue that our whole way of talking about moral and political phenomena hardened before we knew any of the relevant empirical facts about man and society—and this, too, leads us astray. We all suffer from what might be called the *embourgeoisment* of language, and thus part of any revolution will be a linguistic or conceptual revolution. We have grown accustomed to modifying our language or conceptual structures under the impact of empirical discoveries in physics. There is no reason why discoveries in sociology, economics, or psychology could not and should not have the same effect on entrenched patterns of thought and speech. It is important to remember, as Russell remarked, that our language sometimes enshrines the metaphysics of the Stone Age.

Consider one example: a man has been convicted of armed robbery. On investigation, we learn that he is an impoverished black whose whole life has been one of frustrating alienation from the prevailing socio-economic structure—no job, no transportation if he could get a job, substandard education for his children, terrible housing and inadequate health care for his whole family, condescending-tardy-inadequate welfare payments, harassment by the police but no real protection by them against the dangers in his community, and near total exclusion from the political process. Learning all this, would we still want to talk—as many do—of his suffering punishment under the rubric of "paying a debt to society"? Surely not. Debt for what? I do not, of course, pretend that all criminals can be so described. But I do think that this is a closer picture of the typical criminal than the picture that is presupposed in the retributive theory—i.e., the picture of an evil person who, of his own free will, intentionally acts against those just rules of society which he knows, as a rational man, benefit everyone including himself.

But what practical help does all this offer, one may ask. How should we design our punitive practices in the society in which we now live? This is the question we want to ask, and it does not seem to help simply to say that our society is built on deception and inequity. How can Marx help us with our real practical problem? The answer, I think, is that he cannot and obviously does not desire to do so. For Marx would say that we have not focused (as all piecemeal reform fails to focus) on what is truly the real problem. And this is changing the basic social relations. Marx is the last person from whom we can expect advice on how to make our intellectual and moral peace with bourgeois society. And this is surely his attraction and his value.

What does Bonger offer? He suggests, near the end of his book, that in a properly designed society all criminality would be a problem "for the physician rather than the judge." But this surely will not do. The therapeutic state, where prisons are called hospitals and jailers are called psychiatrists, simply raises again all the old problems about the justification of coercion and its reconciliation with autonomy that we faced in worrying about punishment. The only difference is that our coercive practices are now surrounded with a benevolent rhetoric which makes it even harder to raise the important issues. Thus the move to therapy, in my judgment, is only an illusory solution—alienation remains and the problem of reconciling coercion with autonomy remains unsolved. Indeed, if the alternative is having our personalities involuntarily restructured by some state psychiatrist, we might well want to claim the "right to be punished" that Hegel spoke of.[37]

Perhaps, then, we may really be forced seriously to consider a radical proposal. If we think that institutions of punishment are necessary and desirable, and if we are morally sensitive enough to want to be sure that we have the moral right to punish before we inflict it, then we had better first make sure that we have restructured society in such a way that criminals genuinely do correspond to the only model that will render punishment permissible—i.e., make sure that they are autonomous and that they do benefit in the requisite sense. Of course, if we did this then—if Marx and Bonger are right—crime itself and the need to punish would radically decrease if not disappear entirely.

---

[37] This point is pursued in Herbert Morris, "Persons and Punishment." Bonger did not appreciate that "mental illness," like criminality, may also be a phenomenon of social class. On this, see August B. Hollingshead and Frederick C. Redlich, *Social Class and Mental Illness* (New York, 1958). On the general issue of punishment versus therapy, see my *Punishment and Rehabilitation* (Belmont, Cal., forthcoming 1973).

9

A PATERNALISTIC THEORY OF PUNISHMENT

Herbert Morris

I

NOTHING is more necessary to human life, and fortunately nothing more common, than parents' concern for their children. The infant's relatively lengthy period of help-lessness requires that others nourish and protect it. And the child's existence as a vital being with an interest in the world, a capacity for eagerness and trust, and a sense of its own worth, all depend upon its receiving loving care, understanding, and attention. With time the normally developing child relinquishes its almost total dependence; it acquires the capacity to conceive of itself as an agent, to set out on its own, and to live in a world less dominated by its bodily needs and by its parents. Inevitably, this growth in competence and strength brings greater potential for self-harm, for the child's fan-tasies of its power and knowledge stand in marked contrast to the reality of its relative ignorance and vulnerability. In the ordinary course of events, the more powerful and knowledgeable parent often interferes with the child's choices in order to prevent harm and to bring about good and the reason for this is frequently, if the appropriate degree of parental selflessness is present, the child's own best interests, not primarily the interests of the parents or others.

Concern for the child often, of course, is manifested in allowing and encourag-ing experimentation just as it sometimes is in forceful intrusion. The child's develop-ing individuality and sense of personal responsibility require that others encourage in it a sense of its own power and competence, support its venturing out, and exercise judgment in forbearing from intrusion, permitting it to err and to learn some pain-ful truths from painful consequences suffered. God commanded Adam and Eve but left them free to disobey, thereby providing evidence both of his love and respect. The

Devil, preferring for humans a state of permanent infantalism, would, no doubt, have acted differently as Dostoevsky's *Grand Inquisitor* nicely illustrates.[1]

The rational love of parents for their children then guides the parents' conduct so that their children may one day be fortunate enough to say with St. Paul, "…when I became a man, I put away childish things." A central drama of many lives is a result of imbalance in the relations between parents and children in this area—of being left too much on one's own or too little, of counting on one's parents too much, or of not being able to count upon them enough, of parental conduct that fosters too great dependence or conduct that imposes upon the child too great a personal responsibility, creating in the child not self-confidence but a sense of being alone and insecure in a threatening world.

Paternalism as a social phenomenon is prefigured in this elemental and universal situation of solicitous parental conduct that has its roots in our common humanity. But paternalism is of philosophic interest, not because of the way parents legitimately relate to their children—indeed there is oddity in describing this conduct as "paternalistic"—but rather because something like this practice is introduced into relations among adults. If our responses to adults mirror intrusive and solicitous parental responses to children we behave paternalistically.

Contemporary discussions of paternalism, understood in this way, proceed by focusing primarily on specific laws, laws that either prohibit or require certain conduct and that, arguably, have as their principal or sole reason for existence the good of those individuals to whom they are addressed. My focus in this paper is entirely different, for I consider paternalism, its meaning and its possible legitimacy, not in the context of specific laws prohibiting or requiring conduct, but rather with regard to the existence of a system of punitive responses for the violation of any law. I shall consider several issues and make a number of proposals. First, I define my particular version of a paternalistic theory of punishment. Second, I argue for, and consider a variety of objections to, this paternalistic theory. Third, I argue that the paternalistic theory I have constructed implies, in a more natural way than other common justifications for punishment, certain restrictions on the imposition of punishment.

II

Let us turn to the first topic. My aim here is to describe the paternalistic theory of punishment I later defend. I set out a variety of moral paternalism, for the good that is sought is a specific moral good.

First, then, in order to punish paternalistically we must be punishing. I assume that the human institution of punishment presupposes, of course among other things, that certain conduct has been determined to be wrongful, that what are generally recognized as deprivations are imposed in the event of such conduct, that these deprivations are imposed upon the wrongdoer by someone in a position of authority, that

---

[1] What is gained and what is lost by allowing a choice to disobey is also brought out in C. S. Lewis' engaging replay of the Adam and Eve myth in his novel *Pelandra*.

wrongdoers are generally made aware that the deprivation is imposed because of the wrongdoing, and that the context makes evident that the deprivation is not a tax on a course of conduct or in some way a compensation to injured individuals but rather a response to the doing of what one was not entitled to do.

I have placed a logical constraint on the concept of punishment that is not customarily explicitly associated with it. I have claimed that in order for a person to be punished there must be an intention—one normally simply taken for granted—to convey to the wrongdoer, and where it is punishment for breach of a community's requirement, to others as well, that the deprivation is imposed because of wrongdoing. A communicative component is a defining characteristic of punishment and in part distinguishes it from mere retaliation or acting out of revenge where the goal of bringing about evil for another may achieve all that one desires. The paternalistic theory I present relies essentially on the idea of punishment as a complex communicative act—the components of which I hope will become clear as I proceed.[2]

A central theme in paternalism is to justify one's conduct out of a concern for the good of another. And so a paternalistic theory of punishment will naturally claim that a principal justification for punishment and a principal justification for restrictions upon it are that the system furthers the good of potential and actual wrongdoers. This contrasts with views—though many of the practices supported may be the same—that it is justice that requires that guilty persons be punished or that it is the utility to society that requires punishment. The theory I put forward emphasizes what retributivist and utilitarian theories largely, if not entirely, ignore, that a principal justification for punishment is the potential and actual wrongdoer's good. The theory should not, however, be confused with "reform" or "rehabilitative" theories. First, these theories may be based, not on consideration of what promotes the good of actual and potential wrongdoers, but on what promotes value for society generally. A reform theory, further, may countenance responses ruled out under the paternalistic theory proposed in these pages. And, finally, reform theories usually fail to address the issue of how instituting a practice of punishment, meaning by this both the threat of punishment and its actual infliction, may promote a specific moral good and this is a central feature of the theory I propose.[3]

I also assume that paternalistic measures characteristically involve disregard of, indeed conflict with, a person's desires. Giving a person what they want and being motivated to do so for that person's good is benevolence not paternalism. And so, if a longing for punishment were characteristically the way in which people responded to the prospect of its imposition, there would, I think, be no role for a paternalistic theory regarding the practice, for it would simply be a practice that generally supplied people with what

---

[2] See generally Walter Moberly's splendid *The Ethics of Punishment* (London: Faber and Faber, 1968), particularly pp. 201 ff.

[3] The reform theories discussed by H. L. A. Hart and found to be unacceptable as answers to the question what could be "the general justifying aim of punishment" differ, then, from the theory developed in these pages. Hart's change of mind in the notes to his collection of essays is occasioned by consideration of theories that still differ markedly from the one I propose. See *Punishment and Responsibility* (New York and Oxford: Oxford University Press, 1968), pp. 24–27, 240–41.

they acknowledged wanting. We may speak meaningfully of a paternalistic theory of punishment for two reasons: first, punishment by its nature characteristically involves a deprivation that individuals seek to avoid, with the implication that there is some conflict between what people want and what they get; second, the practice is such that the desires of a person at the time of the deprivation are not determinative of what they receive. Thus, while there are obviously persons guilty of wrongdoing who desire punishment, this fact will not affect either its being punishment that is meted out to such a person or the punishment being possibly based on paternalistic consideration, for what is customarily viewed as a deprivation is being imposed independently of the individual's desires.

Most importantly, the theory I am proposing requires that the practice of punishment promote a particular kind of good for potential and actual wrongdoers. The good is a moral one, and it is, arguably, one upon which all morality is grounded.

What is the character of this good? It has a number of component parts but it is essentially one's identity as a morally autonomous person attached to the good. This statement obviously needs explanation. First, it is a part of this good that one comes to appreciate the nature of the evil involved for others and for oneself in one's doing wrong. This requires empathy, a putting oneself in another's position; it also requires the imaginative capacity to take in the implications for one's future self of the evil one has done; it further requires an attachment to being a person of a certain kind. The claim is that it is good for the person, and essential to one's status as a moral person, that the evil underlying wrongdoing and the evil radiating from it be comprehended, comprehended not merely, if at all, in the sense of one's being able to articulate what one has done, but rather comprehended in the way remorse implies comprehension of evil caused. A person's blindness about such matters—this view assumes—is that person's loss. The Devil's splendid isolation is his hell.

Of course, this element of the good makes it apparent that for this theory, as with other moral justifications for punishment, that the rules defining wrongdoing, the rules whose violation occasions punishment, themselves meet certain minimal moral conditions. I assume, and do not argue for the view, that attachment to the values underlying these rules partly defines one's identity as a moral being and as a member of a moral community, that it gives one a sense of who one is and provides some meaning to one's life, and that the price paid for unconcern is some rupture in relationships, a separation from others, a feeling ill at ease with oneself, and some inevitable loss of emotional sustenance and sense of identity. I further assume that attachment to these values is a natural by-product of certain early forms of caring, understanding and respect and that the practice of punishment applies to those with such an attachment and not to those who because of some early disasters in primary relationships might value nothing or possess values we might attribute to the Devil.

Second, it is a part of the good that one feel guilt over the wrongdoing, that is, that one be pained at having done wrong, that one be distressed with oneself, that one be disposed to restore what has been damaged, and that one accept the appropriateness of some deprivation, and the making of amends. Not to experience any of this would be to evidence an indifference to separation from others that could only, given the assumptions I have made, diminish one as a person.

Third, it is also part of the good that one reject the disposition to do what is wrong and commit oneself to forbearance in the future. I assume that this makes possible, indeed that it is inextricably bound up with, one's forgiving oneself, one's relinquishing one's guilt, and one's having the capacity fully to enter into life.

Finally, it is part of the good that one possess and vividly retain a conception of oneself as an individual worthy of respect, a conception of oneself as a responsible person, responsible for having done wrong and responsible, through one's own efforts at understanding and reflection, at more clearly coming to see things as they are with a deepened attachment to what is good. This conception of oneself is further nourished by freely accepting the moral conditions placed upon restoring relationships with others and oneself that one has damaged.

It is a moral good, then, that one feel contrite, that one feel the guilt that is appropriate to one's wrongdoing, that one be repentant, that one be self-forgiving and that one have reinforced one's conception of oneself as a responsible being. Ultimately, then, the moral good aimed at by the paternalism I propose is an autonomous individual freely attached to that which is good, those relationships with others that sustain and give meaning to a life.

The theory I propose claims that the potential of punishment to further the realization of this moral good is one principal justification for its existence. From the perspective of this form of paternalism there must be full respect in the design of the practice of punishment for the individual's moral and intellectual capacities. The good places logical and moral constraints on the means that it is permissible to employ to realize it. This is the principal reason that I earlier emphasized the communicative aspect of punishment, for on this theory we seek to achieve a good entirely through the mediation of the wrongdoer's efforts to understand the full significance of the wrongful conduct, the significance of the punishment being imposed, and the significance of acceptance of that punishment. Thus, unacceptable to this theory would be any response that sought the good of a wrongdoer in a manner that bypassed the human capacity for reflection, understanding, and revision of attitude that may result from such efforts. Any punitive response to a fully responsible being, then, and it might be no more than the giving of an evil-tasting pill or some form of conditioning, that directly in some causal way, with or without the agent's consent, sought to bring about a good, say, instantaneous truth or aversion to acting violently, would be incompatible with this constraint. There is, then, a good to be achieved but one cannot, logically or morally, be compelled to obtain it. Throughout there must be complete respect for the moral personality of the wrongdoer; it is a respect also, as I later argue, that must be given despite the wrongdoer's consent to be treated otherwise.

It is evident that this paternalistic goal is not to make people feel less burdened or more content. Once the good is achieved, these may be likely results; they are not, however, what is sought. It is important, too, to recognize that this good differs markedly from those particular goods associated with specific paternalistic legislation. It is not one's health; it is not even one's moral health with respect to any particular matter that is sought to be achieved; it is one's general character as a morally autonomous individual attached to the good.

III

What might be said in favor of such a theory and what might be objections to it? Two major issues will be considered. First, can a plausible case be presented that punishment is connected with the good as I have defined it? Second, is there anything morally offensive or otherwise objectionable, as there often is with particular legislation, in having as one's goal in limiting freedom, the person's own good?

Let us direct attention again to the relationship between parent and child with which I commenced this essay and in which paternalistic-like elements seem clearly and appropriately present. The range of situations here is very great. Sometimes parents coercively interfere to protect the child from hurting itself, sometimes to assure its continued healthy growth, sometimes so that the child will learn to move about comfortably in a world of social conventions. But sometimes, of course, coercion enters in with respect to matters that are moral; certain modes of conduct are required if valued relationships among individuals within the family and outside the family are to come into existence and be maintained.

Slowly such values as obedience, respect, loyalty, and a sense of personal responsibility are integrated into the young person's life. This results to a considerable degree—of course not entirely and in differing degrees in different stages of development—from the child's conduct sometimes meeting with unpleasant responses. Written vividly upon children are lessons associated with some loss or some pain visited upon them by those to whom they are attached. It is important for my purposes that a difference in the significance of the painful responses be noted. The pain experienced by the child subjected to a parent's anger or disapproval only has the significance of punishment if the parent deliberately visits upon the child some pain because of the perceived wrongdoing. The parent's spontaneous anger or disapproval or blame cause the child distress. They may motivate future compliant conduct. They may arouse in the child guilt. They are not, however, by themselves requital for wrongdoing and by themselves do not relieve guilt. My view is that punishment has some special and logical relationship to wrongdoing and to the possibility of a child's acquiring the concept. Because of this relationship, punishment is connected with the good that I have described in a way that blame or disapproval by themselves are not.

First, because of punishment children come to acquire an understanding of the meaning of a limit on conduct. Logically connected with the concept of wrongdoing is the concept of a painful response that another is entitled to inflict because of the wrongful conduct.[4] Second, a punitive response conveys to children the depth of parental attachment to the values underlying the limit. Just as children know from experience that they are disposed to strike out when they or what they care for are injured, so they come to appreciate the seriousness of their parents' attachment to the limit and to the values supported by its existence by the parents' visiting some pain upon them. The degree of punishment, then, conveys to the child the importance

---

[4] Fingarette, "Punishment and Suffering," *Proceedings of the American Philosophical Association*, Vol. 51 (1977).

parents attach to their child's responding to the limit and promotes in children, not just an appreciation that something is wrong, but how seriously wrong it is. It conveys, too, the significance of different degrees of fault in the doing of what is wrong. Further, particular punishments that are chosen often communicate to children the peculiar character of the evil caused by their disregard of the limit, the evil to others and the evil to themselves. Thus, even young children will find it particularly fitting to penalize a cheater by not permitting, for a time at least, further play, for such punishment conveys the central importance of honesty in the playing of the game and one's placing oneself outside the community of players by dishonesty. "If you will not abide by what makes this segment of our lives together possible, suffer the consequence of not being here a part of our lives."

Finally, punishment "rights the wrong." It has, in contrast to blame and disapproval, the character of closure, of matters returning to where they were before, of relationships being restored. Just as a limit being placed upon conduct serves to provide a bounded, manageable, world for the child, so the punitive response to a breach defines a limit to separation that is occasioned by wrongdoing. The debt is paid, life can go on.

The young hero in Styron's SOPHIE'S CHOICE gives into a desire for an exciting ride with a friend and forgets his agreeing to tend the fire before which his invalided mother sits for heat in the freezing weather. The young man is guilty and remorseful. Why, we may wonder, was he grateful to his father for placing him for a period of time in a shed without heat? The answer seems clear. It diminished the young boy's guilt, diminished it in a way that it would not have been were the father merely to have said, "You did something dreadful; I know you feel bad; don't let it happen again!" The young boy's guilt and remorse were painful; but because they were not deprivations imposed because of wrongdoing, they could not serve to reestablish what had been upset in the relations between parents and child.

What I have described is familiar. What needs emphasizing is that this parental practice of punishing is a complex communication to the child. It aids the child in learning what as a moral person it must know, that some things are not permitted, that some wrongs are more serious than others, that it is sometimes responsible for doing wrong and sometimes not, and that its degree of blameworthiness is not always the same. Further, the child's response to wrongdoing by feeling guilt, its willingness to accept some deprivation, and its commitment to acting differently in the future, all play an indispensable role in its restoring relationships it has damaged, relationships with others and with itself. The claim, then, is that this practice is, in fact, a significant contributing factor in one's development as a moral person.

Now, what more acceptably motivates a parent when it punishes its child than the desire to achieve a goal such as I have described? It would be perverse if the parent were generally to punish primarily from motives of retributive justice or optimal utility for the family. These ends are secondary to, though with retributive ends, to some extent essential to, the child's acquiring the characteristics of a moral person. This much may seem plausible but also quite beside the point. The topic is, after all, punishment in the adult world and there are significant differences between adults and children that may carry fatal implications for a paternalistic theory. I do not believe this is so, but before moving on I want to note a phenomenon that may cast doubt upon the legitimacy of the parental practice itself.

Parents sometimes, when imposing some deprivation upon their children, say, "I'm only doing this for your own good!" There is, I think, something offensive about this. Does it affect the legitimacy of parental concern primarily for the child's moral development in inflicting punishment?

The answer I think is clearly "no," for the offensiveness of those words is not limited to situations in which punishment is imposed. Giving some unpleasant medicine or compelling the child to eat some distasteful but allegedly nourishing food, if accompanied by a statement that it is for the child's own good, is equally offensive. The words are customarily uttered in response to some sign of resistance, of some anger, and what they neglect to address is the child's unhappiness. They rather defend the parents before the child, making the child feel guilty because of its failure to be grateful for the good done it. And so imposed upon the child is the burden of getting what it does not want, the burden of checking its understandable anger because of this, and, finally, the burden of having to be grateful for getting what it does not want and, if not grateful, then guilty. It is not the motive of promoting the child's good that is suspect in these cases; it is communicating to the child what one's motive is, with its distressing consequences for the child, and with the still more serious problem, perhaps, that the parent's own guilt is unconsciously sought to be transferred to the child.

IV

One can acknowledge the place of punishment in the moral development of children and acknowledge, too, that it must to some degree be imposed to further this development and wonder what all this has to do with legal punishment of adults. For the law as a means of social control presupposes that the individuals to whom it applies are already responsible persons, responsible both in the sense of having the capacity to govern their actions through an understanding of the meaning of the norms addressed to them and responsible in the sense that they possess a knowledge of and an attachment to the values embodied in the society's laws. There is, nevertheless, a place for punishment in society analogous to its role in the family. I shall briefly sketch what this is.

Through promulgation of laws, through provision of sanctions for their violation, and through the general imposition of sanctions in the event of violation, each citizen learns what is regarded as impermissible by society, the degree of seriousness to be attached to wrongdoing of different kinds, and the particular significance—especially when the punishment is in its severity and character linked to the offense—of the evil underlying offenses. Punishment is a forceful reminder of the evil that is done to others and oneself. Were it not present, or were it imposed in circumstances markedly at odds with criteria for its imposition during the process of moral development, only confusion would result. Brandeis, in a quite different context, observed: "Our government is the potent, the omnipresent teacher. For good or for ill, it teaches the whole people by its example." My point is that law plays an indispensable role in our knowing what for society is good and evil. Failure to punish serious wrongdoing, punishment of wrongdoing in circumstances where fault is absent, would serve only to baffle our moral understanding and threaten what is so often already precarious.

Further, our punitive responses guide the moral passions as they come into play with respect to interests protected by the law. Punishment, among other things, permits purgation of guilt and ideally restoration of damaged relationships. Punishment, then, communicates what is wrong and in being imposed both rights the wrong and serves, as well, as a reminder of the evil done to others and to oneself in the doing of what is wrong.

Now in addition to making out that punishment may reasonably be thought to play its part, even with adults, in promoting the good of one's moral personality, the paternalist has to have some argument for this as a morally permissible way of proceeding. The paternalist is, I believe, on firm ground here. The guilty wrongdoer is not viewed as damned by his wrongful conduct to a life forever divorced from others. He is viewed as a responsible being, responsible for having done wrong and possessing the capacity for recognizing the wrongfulness of his conduct. Further, the evil—as Socrates long ago pointed out—that he has done himself by his wrongdoing is a moral evil greater than he has done others. His soul is in jeopardy as his victim's is not. What could possibly justify an unconcern with this evil if the person is one of us and, if we sense, rightly I believe, that there but for the grace of God go we? In considering, for example, why we might wish to have a society of laws, of laws associated with sanctions for their violation, of laws that are in fact enforced against others and ourselves, it would be rational, indeed it would be, I think, among the most persuasive of considerations for establishing such a social practice, that it would promote our own good as moral persons. Thinking of ourselves as potential, and thinking of ourselves as actual wrongdoers, and appreciating the connection of punishment with one's attachment to the good, to one's status as a moral person, and to the possibility it provides of closure and resumption of relationships, would we not select such a system, if for no other reason, than that it would promote our own good?

V

We have now to consider certain objections to the theory. First, does it fail to respect one as an autonomous being? The answer is that it does not. One's choices are throughout respected, and it is one's status as a moral person that is sought to be affirmed. But is there not something offensively demeaning in instituting punishment for such a reason? More demeaning, one might ask, than addressing the wrongdoer's sense of fear to which others appeal in their theories of punishment? More demeaning than an indifference to the moral status of the person but totally committed to retributive justice? I am not convinced that this is so either. On the theory I propose one is throughout responded to as a moral person.

But does not a paternalistic theory lead to two unacceptable extremes with respect to punishment, the first that we should always warn before punishing, and wait to see the effects of our warning, the other that we should continue punishing until we achieve the desired effects? The answers here can be brief. First, the announcement of the norm and the provision for punishment in the event of its violation is itself the warning and to allow a person to disobey and threaten that next time there will be punishment is to issue not one but two warnings. Second, the practice of punishment, given the paternalistic goals I have described, cannot permit open-ended punishments, repeated punishments or punishments that are excessively severe. For, first, the goal is not repentance at all costs, if that has meaning, but repentance freely arrived at and not merely a disposition toward conformity with the norms; secondly, the punishment provided for wrongdoing must reflect judgments of the seriousness of the wrong done; such punishment cannot focus on some end state of the person and disregard the potential for moral confusion that would arise from repeated or excessive punishment.

Another criticism might go as follows: "You have ruled out conditioning a person, even with their consent, so that they might not be disposed to do evil in the future. But surely, while perhaps an unjustifiable practice without consent, it is acceptable with it, for it provides a person what they freely choose and delivers them from an affliction that promotes evil." Two points need to be made here. First, the theory would not preclude freely chosen forms of conditioning, surgery and the like in those circumstances in which it is acknowledged that the person is not, with respect to the conduct involved, an autonomous agent. There is nothing wrong, for example, in a person choosing surgery to remove a tumor that is causally related to outbursts of violence over which the person has no control. The class of person, then, whose choice would be accorded respect is made up of those we should be disposed to excuse from criminal liability. Second, the theory would regard as morally unacceptable a response, conditioning or otherwise, that had as its goal, not just aversion to doing wrong, but obliteration of one's capacity to choose to do so. What must be aimed at is that the afflicted become autonomous not automatons. There must be freedom to disobey, for the moral price is too high that is paid in purchasing immunity from temptation and guaranteed conformity.

The most troubling objections to the theory are, I think, these: First, it cannot account for the accepted disposition to punish those who are already, as it were, awakened and repentant. And, second, even more seriously, it cannot account for the disposition to punish those who know what the values of society are but who are indifferent to or opposed to them. Someone, for example, may feel inclined to say: "Look—most serious crimes—and your theory surely most neatly fits such crimes not petty offenses—are committed by individuals who are perfectly aware of what they are doing and perfectly aware that society's values are being flouted. These individuals are not going to be instructed about evil or brought to any moral realization about themselves by punishment. Surely, you can't be serious about repentance when considering them, and they certainly do not care a jot about paying off any debt because they do not feel any guilt over what they have done. Your theory fails so to match reality as to be just one more tedious example of a philosopher spinning out fantastic yarns without any genuine relevance to reality." What can be said in response to these points?

As to the first, I would claim that the guilty and repentant wrongdoers are naturally disposed to accept the appropriateness of the punishment provided, both because this will evidence to them and to others the genuineness of their feelings and because the punishment rights the wrong, brings about closure and restores relationships that have been damaged. The experience of guilt and remorse, the avowal of repentance do not by themselves achieve this.[5] A general practice of pardoning persons who claimed that they were repentant would destroy the principal means of reestablishing one's membership in the community.

Now for the second major objection. A response here requires that attention be paid to certain general features of the theory that has been put forward. The theory is, of course, not intended as a description of any actual practice of legal punishment or even as realistically workable in a society such as ours. Things are in such a state that it is not. What is proposed is a moral theory of punishment and, as such, it includes at least two conditions that may be only marginally congruent with our social world. The first is that the norms addressed to persons are generally just and that the society is to some substantial extent one in which those who are liable to punishment have roughly equal opportunitites to conform to those just norms. The second condition is equally important. The theory presupposes that there is a general commitment among persons to whom the norms apply to the values underlying them. If these two conditions are not met, we do not have what I understand as a practice of punishment for which any moral justification can be forthcoming.

At this point it may be thought, "fair enough, but then what is the point of the whole exercise?" My response is this: First, the theory is not without applicability to significant segments of our society. Second, it has value, for it provides an important perspective upon actual practices; it throws into relief our society's failures to realize the conditions I have stipulated. And, finally, it assists us in sensitive and intelligent forbearance from putting our moral imprimatur upon practices which the paternalistic model would find unacceptable. Excessively lengthy prison terms and the inhumane conditions under which they are served, for example, can be effectively criticized with a clear conception of the good defined by the paternalistic theory. The theory may serve as a guide in our attempts to adjust present practices so that they more closely accord with moral dictates, to work for precisely that society in which the paternalistic conception provides not just the ring of moral truth but descriptive truth as well.

VI

I want now to shift attention to the issue of restrictions on punishment. The proposed paternalistic theory limits punishment, I believe, in a way that accords more closely with our moral intuitions than a number of alternative theories. First, it follows from the theory that any class of persons incapable of appreciating the significance of the norms addressed to them cannot justifiably be punished. Absence of a free and knowing departure from the norm makes pointless imposition of punishment. Second, it

---

[5] On the connections of guilt and suffering, see Morris, *On Guilt and Innocence* (Berkeley and Los Angeles: University of California Press, 1976), pp. 89–110.

also follows that excuses must be recognized and that mitigating factors be taken into account, including as an excuse, of course, reasonable ignorance or mistake of law.

Perhaps most significantly, a paternalistic orientation implies a position that matches our moral intuitions more closely than other theories on the issue of what kinds of punishment may be inflicted. Punishments that are aimed at degrading or brutalizing a person are not conducive to moral awakening but only to bitterness and resentment. But there is also, I believe, another paternalistic route to limitations upon certain modes of punishment, a limitation that follows from the conception of the moral good.

The wrongdoer has, as we all do, a basic right to be free. How, we may wonder, are we able to justify our imposing our will upon him and limiting his freedom? One answer is that by wrongful conduct he has forfeited his right to freedom. The wrongdoer is in no position to complain if he meets with a response that is similar to what has been visited by him upon another. Such a theory of forfeiture places great weight upon an individual's choice. It holds that rights are forfeitable, waivable and relinquishable—just so long as the choice involved is informed and free. A person might forfeit his right to life by murdering; a person might relinquish his right to be free by selling himself into slavery. The paternalistic position that I have proposed holds otherwise. It implies that there is a non-waivable, non-forfeitable, non-relinquishable right—the right to one's status as a moral being, a right that is implied in one's being a possessor of any rights at all.

Such a view, when punishment is at issue, makes morally impermissible any response to a person, despite what that person has done, that would be inconsistent with this fundamental right, even though the person were unattached to it, indifferent to its moral value and eager to forfeit it. A retributivist might respond in kind to any wrong done. A social utilitarian might calculate the effects on people and society in doing so. A paternalist, attached to the good of the wrongdoer, would reject retributive justice and utility as the sole determinative criteria, and would propose a good to be realized that is independent of these values. Punishment will not be permitted that destroys in some substantial way one's character as an autonomous creature. Certain cruel punishments, then, may be ruled out, not merely because they are conducive to hardening the heart but, more importantly, because they destroy a good that can never rightly be destroyed. As I see it, this precludes, on moral grounds, punishment that may be like for like but which nevertheless violates one's humanity by either destroying one's life or destroying one's capacity for rejecting what is evil and again attaching oneself to the good.

Let me be more specific. Suppose that a sadist has cruelly destroyed another human being's capacity for thought while leaving the person alive. Is there a retributivist argument that would bar a like treatment for the sadist? I do not know of it. Certainly, the lex talionis would seem to sanction it. Is our inclination to forbear from treating the sadist in a manner that he has treated his victim derived exclusively, then, from social evils that we foresee might flow from such punishment? I do not find this persuasive. Our moral repugnance precedes such calculation and findings inconsistent with this repugnance would be rejected. Is it simply revulsion at the thought of oneself or one's agents deliberately perpetrating such acts? Is it a concern for our own good that motivates us? No doubt, this may play a role, but my conviction is that something else is involved. It is the ingredient to which the moral paternalist draws attention. The wrongdoer possesses something destroyed in another. The wrongdoer may desire to destroy it in himself as well, but that is not his moral prerogative. It is immune from moral transformations brought about by free choice.

VII

I would like, in conclusion, to make somewhat clearer what I am and am not claiming for the theory proposed in these pages and, further, to draw attention to two ironies connected with it.

I have claimed that to have as one's aim in punishing the good of the wrongdoer counts strongly in favor of the moral legitimacy of punishing. I do not claim, of course, that this is the sole justification for punishment, though I do believe that what it seeks to promote is among the most important, if not the most important, of human goods. The practice of punishment is complex and any justification proposed as an exclusive one must, in my judgment, be met with skepticism, if not scorn. There is, too, as I earlier briefly noted, a significant logical overlapping of this theory with retributivism, though at a certain point, when one considers types of punishment, they diverge. A paternalistic theory, given the good as defined, would support principles that are familiar dictates of retributivism—that only the guilty may be punished, that the guilty must be, and that the punishment inflicted reflect the degree of guilt. Failure to comply with the demands of retributivism would preclude realization of the paternalist's goal. I have also, however, suggested that retributivism needs supplementing if it is to meet our intuitions of what is morally permissible punishment. But, of course, this overlapping of justifications for punishment includes as well some form of utilitarianism, for if our goal is as I have defined it, and punishments are threatened and imposed, deterrent values are also furthered. I do not question the rich over-determination of goods promoted by the practice of punishment. I do urge that weight be given, and on the issue of restrictions on punishment, determinative weight, to paternalistic ends.

There are, finally, two ironies to which I wish to draw attention. The first is this. I have selected as the good to be realized by this paternalistic theory of punishment the very good to which philosophers often make appeal in their principled objections to paternalism with regard to specific prohibitions and requirements. Secondly, I have proposed a theory that justifies forceful intrusion into the lives of people. But it is also an atypical paternalistic theory, for it prohibits certain types of intrusion. I reach this conclusion because the good sought does not allow weight to be given to an individual's free choice when the issue is relinquishment of one's status as a moral being. The paternalistic aspect in this derives from the fact that there is a good for the person to which we are attached, though the person might not be, and which we continue to respect in disregard of the usual consequences of a person's free choice. I would guess that something like these thoughts underlies the view that we possess some goods as gifts from God and that it is not within our moral prerogative to dispose of them. It is easy to suppose, but a mistake nevertheless, that because we may be favored by the gods that we are one of them.

10

Punishment and the Rule of Law

T. M. Scanlon

This essay will consider how some central issues that Carlos Nino discussed in his writings on the philosophical theory of punishment are relevant to the difficult empirical and political problem of building a legal order that preserves the rule of law and provides remedies for victims of past human rights abuses. Carlos Nino was remarkable in combining philosophical scholarship with important and courageous contributions to this difficult political problem. My first contact with him came when he submitted his article "A Consensual Theory of Punishment" to the journal *Philosophy and Public Affairs*, of which I was then an associate editor. This article attempts to provide a justification for criminal penalties that avoids retributivism but also explains why a system of penalties cannot be justified solely on the basis of its deterrent effects. It was, for me, an exciting paper to read. I very much agreed with the main line of Nino's theory, although I thought that there were certain rather subtle ways in which it went astray. We had a brief but stimulating correspondence about these issues. In retrospect it is striking – indeed, to someone like me who has spent his adult life in the sheltered academy it is truly amazing – that the seemingly academic issues discussed in Nino's article, including the rather subtle point on which we disagreed, turned out later to be of very considerable practical importance.

Philosophical reflection on the problem of punishment has focused on two general questions: the justification for punishment and the limits on its legitimate application. Theoretical reflection of this kind bears on the practical problems we are discussing in at least four ways:

1. It bears on the grounds and interpretation of the prohibition against retroactive punishment.

2. It bears more generally on the state of mind required in an offender as a precondition of legal guilt.

3. It bears on the permissibility of selective punishment. Nino stated, for example, in his response to Diane Orentlicher in the *Yale Law Journal* that only a retributivist theory of punishment requires punishing *all* of those believed guilty of a given offense.[1] All other views, he argued, leave open the possibility that even where punishment is merited, it may be omitted for other reasons, including reasons of political necessity.

4. Finally, theoretical reflection on the problem of punishment bears on the interpretation and legitimacy of the demands of victims for legal response to the wrongs done them.

Let me begin my consideration of philosophical theories by distinguishing four moral ideas that are often cited in arguments about punishment. We will need to bear in mind the degree to which each of them figures in a rationale for having a *system* of punishment or in a rationale for carrying out punishment in an individual case.

The first idea is *retribution*. I will identify retributivism as an account of the rationale for legal punishment, with the view that, first, it is a good thing morally that those who have committed certain moral wrongs should themselves suffer some loss as a result and, second, that bringing about this coincidence between welfare and desert is a central part of the justification for legal institutions of punishment. On such a view there are good moral reasons to bring about losses to those who are guilty of wrongdoing, and the force of these reasons is sufficient to justify not only the suffering of the guilty parties but also the costs to others involved in bringing this about. Both the guilt in question here and the reason for repaying it with loss are to be understood in an extra-institutional (that is to say a moral, not a legal) sense. So understood, retributivism is to be distinguished from the view that because the institution of the criminal law is justified on other grounds, there is reason that those who are *legally* guilty should suffer the penalties that are *legally* prescribed.

Nino was firm in rejecting retributivism as a justification for punishment, and in this he was in agreement with the majority of contemporary philosophical and legal thought. The reason for this widespread rejection is not skepticism about the ideas of moral guilt or moral justification but one or both of two further ideas. The first is rejection of the notion of moral desert, at least in the form of the thesis that it is a good thing, morally, that those who are guilty of moral wrongs should suffer. The second is the idea that even if this thesis is accepted it is not a proper basis for the justification of a political institution. An institutional practice of depriving some citizens of their rights and inflicting other losses on them cannot be justified simply on the ground that this brings their fate more nearly in line with moral desert. I myself accept both

---

[1] Nino, "The Duty to Punish Past Abuses of Human Rights Put into Context," *Yale Law Journal* 100 (1991), 2619–40, p. 2620, replying to Diane Orentlicher, "Settling Accounts: The Duty to Prosecute Human Rights Violations of a Prior Regime," *Yale Law Journal* 100 (1991), 2537–615.

of these ideas, and therefore agree with Nino in rejecting retributivism.[2] The central thesis of retributivism struck both of us as, in Herbert Hart's words, "a mysterious piece of moral alchemy, in which the two evils of moral wickedness and suffering are transmuted into good."[3]

But something *like* retributivism is not so easy to avoid. In the Argentine context, retributivism was appealing to many because it seemed to support what they thought of as the correct answers to the four questions I listed: it explained why retroactive punishment was justified; it identified what it was about the torturers and kidnappers that called for punishment: the evil of their actions; it provided a basis for insisting that all such criminals must be punished; and it thereby accounted for the legitimacy of the demands of the victims' families for a response to what had been done to them and their loved ones.

The main alternative to retributivism as a rationale for punishment has, of course, been *deterrence*. This is in the first instance a rationale for having a *system* of punishment, and it provides a rationale for punishing in individual cases only indirectly: punishment should be carried out in an individual case because that is required by an institution that is (in light of its deterrence effects and perhaps other considerations) justified.[4] Thus, while punishment is addressed to a past crime, its rationale is addressed to future possible crimes which, one hopes, may not occur. So, in cases of the kind I am concerned with in this essay, the deterrence account appeals to the need, first, for a general practice of punishing human rights offenders even if their actions were allowed by the legal and political order in place at the time they were committed, and then, second, to the justifiability of punishment in particular cases as something that must be required by any such system.

This future orientation makes pure deterrence theory seem deficient from the perspective of another moral idea, which I will call *affirmation* of the victims' sense of having been wronged. This idea is not often discussed in philosophical theories of punishment, but nonetheless plays an important part in our thinking about the subject.[5] It is, I am afraid, a rather vague idea. I will try to clarify it as I go along, but part of my point is simply to call attention to the importance of examining the various ways in which this idea might be understood and incorporated into a larger theory of punishment.

This importance is particularly clear in the Argentine case, in which one crucial political element was the pressure of victims' groups such as the Madres de la Plaza de Mayo, who demanded retribution. In fact, as Carlos Nino points out in *Radical Evil on Trial*, insistence on a retributivist view of punishment was something that the Madres and the members of the juntas had in common, although they of course used

---

[2] This rejection, on grounds close to those just mentioned, is spelled out in chapter 4 of Carlos Nino, *Radical Evil on Trial* (New Haven: Yale University Press, 1996).

[3] H. L. A. Hart, *Punishment and Responsibility* (New York: Oxford University Press, 1968), pp. 234–5.

[4] Deterrence theorists may disagree as to whether the need for deterrence can be taken into account in adjusting the penalty in an individual case, some holding, perhaps, that this is required in any efficient system, while others see it as introducing an unacceptable form of arbitrary inequality.

[5] It is recognized by Joel Feinberg in "The Expressive Function of Punishment," in his collection of essays, *Doing and Deserving* (Princeton: Princeton University Press, 1970).

it to draw opposite conclusions.[6] The Madres argued that everyone who took part in the dirty war was guilty and therefore must be punished; the generals maintained that none of them should be punished, since what they had done was morally justified. This agreement between opposites is not surprising. Both are drawn to retributivism because each is looking for a standard safely beyond law: in the case of the generals, in order to argue that whatever the law may be now, their acts were *morally* justifiable and hence unpunishable; in the case of the Madres, in order to argue that whatever the law may have been *then*, these acts were morally evil and hence deserve punishment. This common strategy suggests that in its emphasis on an extralegal standard, the rationale of retributive theory is in some tension with the idea of the rule of law.

Despite this tension, if retributivism is the only theory of punishment that adequately incorporates the idea of affirmation, this may seem to count in favor of its claim to moral adequacy. Even more likely, this will give retributivism real political force, especially in a dramatic context like that of Argentina in the 1980s but also in the somewhat cooler debates about crime in the United States.

So it is worth asking whether demands like those of the Madres de la Plaza de Mayo might be recognized as legitimate (but in a more tractable form) outside of a retributive theory. This illustrates a more general suggestion that philosophical theory can contribute to actual politics by helping to distinguish various ways in which popular demands can be understood.

Another intuition that is sometimes cited as supporting retributivism is the widespread sense that there is something seriously amiss when those who have committed terrible crimes are allowed to go on living as normal citizens as if nothing had happened. In the Argentine case, for example, many expressed outrage that the officers who had ordered and carried out the kidnapping, torture, and murder of thousands of citizens should be allowed to go on living as respected members of Argentine society. I share this intuition, but I do not believe that what it supports is properly called retributivism. It is important that terrible wrongs be recognized by an appropriate response, and the victims of such wrongs are demeaned when the victimizers are treated as respected citizens with no mention of their crimes. But what makes it appropriate to recognize these wrongs is not that this involves suffering or loss on the part of the wrongdoers. It is rather that the absence of such recognition reflects indifference on the part of society toward the wrongs and those who suffered them. What is crucial is recognition, not suffering. Ideally, of course, one wants the perpetrators themselves to acknowledge these wrongs and express contrition for them. This will be painful, but it is not the pain that makes it desirable.

Like retribution, affirmation is an aim that responds to the past and is addressed in the first instance to each particular case. But it also provides a reason for having a system in which particular claims to be wronged can be recognized and given a form in which they can be publicly expressed and responded to.[7] Having such a system is also relevant to the aim of deterrence, understood in a general sense of discouraging

---

[6] Nino, *Radical Evil on Trial*, ch. 4.

[7] The idea that one of the crucial functions of a system of criminal law is to give definite form to the sense of being wronged was emphasized by Nietzsche. See *The Genealogy of Morals*, second essay, sections 10–15.

future crime, rather than the narrower sense of doing this by threatening retaliation.[8] People whose sense of being wronged is not recognized and affirmed by the law have less respect for and less investment in it. Lack of affirmation, then, supports what Nino calls anomie, the cynical lack of respect for law which he identified as a main problem of Argentine society. The right response to the demand for affirmation may undermine this dangerous tendency, thereby building the rule of law. As Nino emphasized in his writings on deliberative democracy, the public character of the proceedings within a trial, and the public discussion surrounding it, can play a crucial positive role of this kind. One can hope that occasions like the dramatic trials of the members of the juntas in the Federal Court of Buenos Aires will lead to greater public commitment to the rule of law. Surely they are one of our best hopes.

I have mentioned affirmation as a value and suggested that it is something citizens may reasonably demand of a system of law. It does not seem likely that a system of law that fails, in general, to respond to such demands is likely to survive. I am not suggesting, however, that victims have a right that those who have wronged them be punished. A defensible legal order must, in general, define and defend citizens' rights, but this does not require that every offender be punished. In the case of the crimes of the dirty war, for example, prosecution of those in decision-making positions, and those who went beyond orders to commit private wrongs (i.e. those in Alfonsín's first two categories)[9] could be held to represent adequate recognition of every sufferer's wrong, even though not every wrongdoer was called to account. There is also the possibility, which I will not be able to explore here, that legitimate demands for affirmation of wrongs may be met through means other than punishment – for example, through some form of public authoritative recognition and declaration.[10]

Finally, let me mention a fourth value, or category of values, which I will label *fairness*. Considerations of fairness do not provide a justification for having a system of criminal punishment, but constitute a class of reasons for insisting that this system be of a certain kind. In principle, fairness might provide a reason for insisting on punishment in a particular case insofar as refraining from punishment is seen as unfair or arbitrary, in view of the fact that others were punished for similar crimes.

In this respect, fairness may seem to be allied with retributivism, and perhaps even to presuppose some form of it. It may seem to presuppose retributivism insofar as the idea of fairness appealed to is that punishment should go equally to those who are equally *deserving* of it. But this need not be retributivist in the hard sense I am discussing, since fairness need not appeal to a pre-institutional sense of moral desert as the relevant standard. Still, fairness may seem allied with retributivism in the answer it implies to my third question, about the permissibility of punishing some offenders but not others, for political reasons.

---

[8] Nino calls this more general view "preventionism." See *Radical Evil on Trial*, ch 4.

[9] Nino describes these categories, which he says were first outlined by Alfonsín in a lecture at the Argentine Federation of Lawyers' Colleges in August 1983, as follows: "(a) those who planned the repression and gave the accompanying orders; (b) those who acted beyond orders, moved by cruelty, perversity, or greed; (c) those who strictly complied with the orders." *Radical Evil on Trial*, p. 63.

[10] As argued, with reference to the case of Chile, by Jorge Correa Sutil, in "Dealing with Past Human Rights Violations," *Notre Dame Law Review* 67 (1993), 1455–94.

Carlos Nino believed that selective punishment could be defended as a political necessity. As I have mentioned, he said that only a retributivist theory of punishment would require punishing *all* of those believed guilty of a given offense. All other views, he argued, leave open the possibility that even where punishment is merited, it may be omitted for other reasons, such as political necessity. Against this, it might be claimed that considerations of fairness, which need not have a retributivist basis, at least *normally* speak against selective punishment. There is room for argument, however, that unequal punishment for reasons of political necessity would not be unfair (even though differential penalties for political reasons of other sorts would be). I will not pursue this argument here. My point is just that this is another case where a consideration whose moral significance might seem to rest on (and hence to support) retributivism can in fact be explained on other grounds.

I have suggested in passing that one important step in building respect for the rule of law lies in ensuring that people have the right sense of what they can demand from a legal system and that they see the legal order as valuable because it provides these benefits. Looking at the various possible rationales for punishment from this point of view, we can ask what answers they suggest to the question, what can citizens reasonably demand from a system of criminal law?

I have suggested that it is not appropriate for them to demand retribution. What they can demand of a system of law is:

1. That it be effective in deterring private wrongdoers.
2. That it affirm their rights and provide a hearing for their sense of having been wronged.
3. That it be fair.
4. That it be safe.

The creation of a coercive apparatus of punishment to enforce the criminal law is the creation of a potentially dangerous instrument of force and violence. Even though this may be necessary as a protection against private wrong, law-abiding citizens can reasonably demand assurance that it will not attack them as well.

This question of safety brings me to the second side of the philosophical theory of punishment: from the justification for punishment to the limits on its application. The safety just mentioned was that of law-abiding citizens, but the theoretical question is why the safety of law-breakers should be any less important. Why is it permissible to inflict losses on those who break the law, in order to deter future crime, when it is not permissible to "use" others in this way? The aim of deterrence itself provides no answer, since sweeping a wider net that inflicts losses on guilty and innocent alike may have an even greater deterrent effect, and may be claimed to make everyone safer in the end. Justifications of this kind were actually offered for the "dirty war against subversion," and they are a chilling reminder that this argument is not just a stale academic warhorse. This point was particularly important for the Alfonsín administration: because one of the things they most wanted to overcome was the crude expediency of the juntas' justification of their policies, they needed a principled basis for deciding who could be punished for the crimes of that period. Merely to appeal to the importance of deterring such acts in future would just be more expediency.

Retributivists have an answer to this question: it is all right to punish law-breakers insofar as they are morally guilty and hence deserve to suffer. And retributivists might go on to add that the problem I am now addressing is just the natural result of replacing retribution, the proper moral aim of punishment, with the mere expediency of deterrence.

Nonetheless, Nino and many others (myself included) reject retributivism, so we need some other answer. Nino's answer is provided by his consensual theory of punishment. According to this theory, those who commit crimes thereby consent to the normative consequences of their actions. This consent provides the crucial element in "licensing" punishment, even though it does not justify or require it. I want to examine this theory in more detail.

Following Herbert Hart, Nino pointed out that there is a wide range of cases, not restricted to punishment, in which acts implying consent have a licensing effect – that is, they make permissible other actions to which there would otherwise be serious objections.[11] He mentions in particular two such cases. The first is that of legal contracts, in which the consent implied by entering into a contract licenses the state in enforcing it, thereby depriving the party of a liberty he or she would have otherwise enjoyed. The second example is the assumption of risk in tort cases, in which the fact that a person voluntarily undertook some risky behavior licenses the denial of a remedy when injury results. In order for an act to "imply consent" in a way that has this licensing effect, Nino says, an act must be voluntary and the agent must know what the legal consequences of his or her action are – know, for example, that he or she is giving up certain legal claims or immunities.[12]

The idea of consent (or of an action implying consent) fits the case of contract much better than it does cases of assumption of risk. The condition of knowledge that Nino mentions seems out of place in the latter context: surely a person need not be aware of tort law in order to "assume a risk" in a legally significant way. Even in the case of contracts, the requirement that an agent know the legal consequences of his or her act may seem too strong when understood literally. But it does seem that a party to a contract must intend, and hence believe, that he or she is laying down some legal right (whether or not he or she must know exactly what that right is). This makes it appropriate to speak of consent. In the case of assumed risk, however, it is a stretch to speak even of implied consent to a *legal* consequence. In both cases we may say that some right is laid down, or some possible future claim stopped, but in saying this are we merely reiterating the *legal* consequence or saying something more?

If these examples are to point toward an answer to the question that puzzled us in the case of punishment, rather than merely being further examples which raise that

---

[11] Carlos Nino, "A Consensual Theory of Punishment," *Philosophy and Public Affairs* 12 (1983), 295–6. See the essays in Hart's *Punishment and Responsibility*, especially "Prolegomenon to the Principles of Punishment" and "Legal Responsibility and Excuses."

[12] Nino, "A Consensual Theory," p. 296.

same question, they must suggest some explanation of why defensible legal institutions must take a particular form – why they must, for example, make the loss of certain legal immunities dependent on actions that imply consent (or something like it). To provide this explanation we need to appeal to some extra-institutional value, like the extra-institutional idea of desert on which retributivism is founded. To what value, should we appeal?

One possibility is the idea that, *morally speaking*, consent has a licensing effect. This may be what Nino had in mind. He wrote, "Another way of describing the situation is to say that the consent to certain *legal* normative consequences involves *moral* normative consequences. The individual who, for instance, consents to undertake some legal obligation is, in principle, morally obligated to do the act which is the object of that obligation."[13] What is appealed to here is not an idea of desert, but a deontological idea about how people's actions affect what they are (morally) entitled to, hence what they can (morally speaking) demand of their legal institutions. But insofar as this idea involves a full-bodied notion of consent it is, as I have said, more clearly applicable to the case of contracts than to torts or punishment.

An alternative would be to appeal not to deontological ideas of consent and entitlement but rather to the value that people reasonably place on having certain forms of control over what happens to them. Because we have reason to value these forms of control, they are factors that must be taken into account in assessing legal institutions. Such factors play somewhat different roles in the two cases Nino mentions.

In the case of contracts, the value of control figures both positively and negatively. Positively, it is a central aim of the law of contracts to give effect to the wills of the parties. In order to do this, it must make the legal normative consequences of an act dependent on the beliefs and intentions of the agent. Negatively, this dependence greatly weakens the case of a person who complains about the enforcement of a contract knowingly and voluntarily undertaken: if he or she wished not to be bound, he or she could simply have refrained from consenting. In offering this way out, the law gives us a crucial form of protection against unwanted obligations.

The law of torts has a different aim: compensating people for loss and injury. The positive part of the case just made thus has no application in the case of torts, but an analogue of the negative part still applies. The law of torts is supposed to protect us against injury and loss, but there are limits to the protection we can demand. By having the opportunity to avoid loss simply by avoiding behavior that can be seen to be very risky, we already have an important form of protection against that loss. Indeed, it can be argued that this is as much protection as can reasonably be asked.

This account explains why Nino's strong requirement of knowledge of the legal normative consequences of one's action makes more sense in the case of contracts than in that of assumed risk. In the first case, creating legal normative consequences that reflect the parties' intentions is a central aim of the law. (This was the "positive" appeal to the value of control.) So knowledge, or something like it, has a natural

[13] Ibid.

relevance.[14] Where only the negative value of control is at issue, however, an agent's state of mind is less relevant. Since the question is whether the person had the protection provided by an opportunity to avoid the loss, what is relevant is not what the person knew about the normative consequences of his or her act but what he or she could have known, by exercising a reasonable level of care, about its likely consequences, and about the availability of alternative courses of action.

With all this as background, then, let me turn to the case of punishment. In Nino's view, the consent-implying character of a criminal's act licenses punishment but does not justify it. That is to say, the inclusion in a system of law of the requirement that punishment can be inflicted only on those who have voluntarily (and perhaps knowingly) violated it is a necessary but not sufficient condition for that system's being morally justifiable, and the occurrence of a consent-implying act is a necessary but not necessarily sufficient condition for punishment to be justifiably applied in a particular case. The idea of consent thus fills the "gap" discussed above in the justification of punishment. The fuller account of that justification is summarized by Nino as follows:

> If the punishment is attached to a justifiable obligation, if the authorities involved are legitimate, if the punishment deprives the individual of goods he can alienate, and if it is a necessary and effective means of protecting the community against greater harms, then the fact that the individual has freely consented to make himself liable to that punishment (by performing a voluntary act with the knowledge that the relinquishment of his immunity is a necessary consequence of it) provides a prima facie moral justification for exercising the correlative legal power of punishing him.
>
> The principle of distribution, which that moral justification presupposes, is the same as that which justifies the distribution of advantages and burdens ensuing from contracts and the distribution achieved in the law of torts when the burdens that follow from a tort are placed on the consenting injured party. This justification of course presupposes that several conditions have been satisfied. First, the person punished must have been capable of preventing the act to which the liability is attached (this excludes the rare case of punishing an innocent person that pure social protection might allow). Second, the individual must have performed the act with knowledge of its relevant factual properties. Third, he must have known that the undertaking of a liability to suffer punishment was a necessary consequence of such an act. This obviously implies that one must have knowledge of the law, and it also proscribes the imposition of retroactive criminal laws.[15]

There is much in this account that I agree with. In particular, the idea of using something *like* consent to fill the logical gap left by the removal of desert is very

---

[14] Even here, it may be too strong a requirement, but I will not go into the details. As I have said, it does seem that the party to a contract must at least intend and believe that he or she is performing an act with normative legal consequences.

[15] Nino, "A Consensual Theory," p. 299.

appealing. I want, however, to raise two related questions. The first is whether the knowledge requirement entailed by Nino's notion of consent is too strong. The second is whether the underlying moral idea, which explains, among other things, the permissibility of retroactive criminal laws, is best understood in terms of consent or in some other way.

The question of knowledge is well raised by the problems faced by successor governments in punishing human rights violations under prior regimes. A coup d'état, we may suppose, is a heady affair. Might not those who carry it out be convinced by the rhetoric of their own decrees and believe that previous law had been swept away giving them full legal power to do what they thought necessary to put the society in order? If they did believe this, and hence did not *know* that their acts had the normative consequence of leaving them legally liable to punishment, would this provide a defense against later charges?

I am not in a position to say what the facts were in this regard in the cases of the members of the Argentine juntas. They sounded as if they were convinced that what they did was *morally* justifiable. Perhaps they also thought it was legally permitted; perhaps not. Perhaps they simply did not give much thought to matters of legality, at least not until the end when thoughts about what the next government might do led them to enact the "self-amnesty" law. The question I am concerned with, however, is whether their liability to punishment depended on this question about their state of mind.

Whatever the facts may have been in that case, this general question remains, and is raised by more humdrum examples. Consider, for example, the overconfident law graduate who is firmly convinced that he or she has found a way, without being guilty of murder or even manslaughter, to do away with the now burdensome spouse, who worked at a dull job to pay the law school fees. This state of mind does not seem to constitute a defense.

What is relevant in all these cases is not what the agent knew about the legal normative consequences of his or her action, but rather what the agent could, through the exercise of due care, have reasonable grounds for believing about these consequences. This suggests that the underlying value in these cases is not the deontological licensing power of consent but rather the value of having a fair opportunity to avoid falling afoul of the law – analogous to the "negative" appeal to the value of control which I discussed above. Both the overconfident law graduate and the members of real and imaginary juntas have this opportunity.[16]

What I would like to do, then, is to follow Carlos Nino's strategy for filling the "gap" in a nonretributivist account of punishment, but to de-emphasize his literal appeal to *consent*.[17] This strategy runs the risk of minimizing, in an implausible way, the difference between civil and criminal law. The moral idea of consent, as Nino

---

[16] One way to make it particularly clear that violations of human rights incur legal liability would be to eliminate constitutional provisions licensing suspension of basic liberties by declaration of a "state of siege." This suggestion may be thought unrealistic, but such provisions (in addition to offering an air of legality to acts that do not merit it) invite a kind of cynicism by suggesting that even the law itself recognizes that civil liberties are something that can be enjoyed only in "good times."

[17] I have presented a view of this kind in "The Significance of Choice," in S. McMurrin, ed., *The Tanner Lectures on Human Values*, vol. 8 (Salt Lake City: University of Utah Press, 1988), pp. 151–216.

invoked it, was not an idea of desert. Nonetheless, insofar as it was a matter of the actual state of mind of the agent, it retained a link with that aspect of the criminal to which the criminal law and punishment are appropriately addressed: a state of mind that separates the criminal from the law-abiding citizen. In moving from consent to fair opportunity to avoid a sanction, we move away from the agent's state of mind to a mere benefit that the criminal has enjoyed, by virtue of which he cannot object to being punished. The result may seem a passionless and rather apologetic account of the mental element in criminal law, the sort of thing that is taken in some quarters to give "liberals" like me a bad name.

Newspaper editorialists and talk-show hosts would say that this view of punishment is so concerned with the rights of criminals that it pays no attention to the claims of victims. I can give this objection a more theoretical form by repeating that, as I said earlier, one thing citizens may reasonably demand of a system of law is that it affirm their rights and, in particular, their sense of having been wronged. To this I would add that a system that affirms a victim's sense of being wronged must condemn the agent who inflicted the wrong, and the mental element that makes this appropriate must go beyond merely having had the opportunity to avoid this sanction.

Here it is important to bear in mind the diverse elements that must go together to make punishment justified in Nino's view or mine, and to recognize the different contributions that these elements make to that justification.

The idea that justifiable punishment must be for something that is properly condemned figures in a theory of punishment in at least two ways. First, a defensible criminal law must defend something that the victim is entitled to have defended *and that the perpetrator cannot object to being excluded from.* (Otherwise that law would be an unacceptable deprivation of liberty.) Second, the fact that actions of a certain type are in this sense unjustifiable intrusions against their victims is a necessary condition for making these actions the object of a law with condemnatory force. A "mental element," in the form of specific intent or reckless disregard for the likely consequences of one's actions is important here: harms do not constitute unjustifiable intrusions if they were unavoidable.

The fact that an action is an unjustifiable intrusion (in the sense just described) is a necessary condition for condemning it, and usually also a sufficient condition for doing so. But it is not (on a nonretributive view) a sufficient condition for depriving the agent of liberty or inflicting other forms of harsh treatment on him. For such harsh treatment, some further justification is required beyond the desirability of expressing our judgments. This is where we must appeal to the utility of deterrence as a way of providing a kind of protection that we need and are entitled to, and to the fact that everyone will have a fair opportunity to avoid liability to the penalties involved.

This account enables us to put what I have been calling "affirmation" in its proper place. I said above that this notion has seemed puzzling because the expression of condemnation seems to be importantly connected with justifiable punishment, yet does not seem weighty enough to provide that justification. The central function of criminal law is to protect rights whose violation makes condemnation appropriate. So punishment will not be justifiable except where condemnation, and hence the affirmation of victims' rights, is appropriate, and just punishment will constitute such affirmation. In addition, as I pointed out in the case of Argentina, authoritative condemnation of certain acts as criminal can play an important role in building respect for the rule of law, and hence in a strategy of deterrence broadly understood.

The "mental element" in the definition of a crime plays two roles in the account I have just given. It occurs once as part of what makes an action an unjustifiable intrusion, which is justifiably condemned. It occurs again, in the form of "fair opportunity to avoid," as part of the account of why it is permissible not only to condemn certain actions but also to attach severe penalties to them as a mechanism of deterrence.

The mistake (as I see it) of retributive theories is that they lump together these two roles for the "mental element" in criminal punishment: its role as a condition for the appropriateness of condemnation and its role as a condition for the permissibility of inflicting loss. The weakness of non-retributive theories is that they may seem unsatisfactory because they separate these elements too widely and concentrate too much on the second (the permissibility of inflicting loss on the criminal) because the question it raises is seen as theoretically more challenging.

What philosophers do, of course, is to work hard at identifying the differences between theories of this kind and then try to decide which of them offers the most satisfactory account of "our" settled convictions. Reaching agreement about such matters is not easy, even when the "we" in question is just the group of people around a seminar table, or even when it is the single person in front of the computer screen.

The real-world political problems to which this inquiry is addressed involve building at least a partial consensus among a large and varied group of people on such issues as what the rule of law is, why it is to be valued, and what the preconditions are for just punishment. Some of us may think, after years of philosophical reflection, that we have answers to these questions. It would be hopeless to think that others will take our word for these conclusions, or even that everyone will agree with them. What we can do, however, is to try to call the alternatives we have distinguished to the attention of our fellow citizens, so that they can decide, for example, whether their view of punishment is actually retributivist or just seemed to be so because they had not noticed what the alternatives were.

Even imagining this role for philosophy in public discourse may seem optimistic, particularly given the abysmal level of recent debates in the United States. But this is the hopeful model that Carlos Nino's idea of deliberative democracy seems to suggest. More remarkably, it is the model he put into practice in his life, in ways which made him an inspiration to us all.

11

PENANCE, PUNISHMENT, AND THE LIMITS OF COMMUNITY

R. A. Duff

ABSTRACT

The thought that religious ideas could have any place in a normative theory of criminal punishment will be anathema to many liberals. I argue, however, that we can understand criminal punishment as a species of secular penance, as part of a communicative enterprise in which the polity seeks to involve its citizens. After explaining what a penance amounts to in this context, I meet the liberal objection that punishment as thus conceived would be an oppressive and illegitimate intrusion into the realm of moral character and conscience which is not the state's, or the law's, business. Finally, I raise (without offering any confident answer to) the question of whether there are any kinds of crime that are so destructive of the very possibility of political community that punishment as communicative penance is no longer morally possible, and focus in particular on the version of this question that is raised by terrorist crimes.

LIBERALISM, THE STATE AND THE CRIMINAL LAW

The question for this conference was: 'what legitimate role, if any, may be played in the criminal law and its mechanism of punishment by religious reasons and by values often associated with religion – e.g. duties to God, love (agape), atonement, repentance, forgiveness, mercy and self-perfection and moral goodness?'. In his article (Murphy, this issue), Jeff Murphy asks how a religious believer's beliefs should influence her ideas about criminal law and punishment; in this article, I will pursue the question of whether and how a non-believer's secular ideas about criminal law and punishment might properly be influenced by ideas which find at least their historical origins in religious doctrines and practices.

A striking feature of contemporary legal philosophy, especially for those of us who were introduced to the subject in the 1960s, is that this issue is seen, even by firmly secular theorists, as one that merits serious discussion: for by the 1960s something like a liberal consensus seemed to have emerged, which united many legal and political theorists in the view that religious ideas and values had *no* proper role in the criminal law – and that any who denied this thereby showed themselves to be reactionary figures who had not embraced the key liberal values of individual autonomy and privacy. The belief was not just that the state should not give religious doctrines the authoritative stamp of the law; that it should remain neutral on such matters. It was also that the values most closely associated with religion, such as those mentioned above, were taken to belong firmly in the 'private' realm of our individual lives and relationships, not in the 'public' realm that concerned the criminal law. To put it crudely, those values have to do with the soul, with our inner spiritual or moral condition: but a liberal state has no proper interest in the state of its citizens' souls.

This liberal attitude, characterized by an emphasis on individual autonomy and privacy, and on the neutrality of the state in relation to conceptions (whether moral or religious) of 'the good', generated a familiar account of the proper scope of the criminal law: this account was grounded in Mill's 'Harm Principle' (perhaps supplemented by an 'Offense Principle' that allowed the law to penalize conduct which, while not strictly harmful, was seriously offensive), and drew a firm distinction between moral or religious ideas of sin and the conception of wrongdoing that was appropriate to the criminal law (see Wolfenden, 1957; Hart, 1963; Feinberg, 1984, 1985).

(It will be evident that the 'liberal account' sketched here is a crude construct from a range of different sources, and many who call themselves liberals might reject it. I hope, however, that it is not so crude as to be an utter caricature – that it captures one recognizable liberal stance.)

Two aspects of this account are worth distinguishing. First, while sins might be committed in one's heart, or in conduct that causes no harm to others, crimes must involve conduct that has or threatens to have some harmful (or offensive) impact on the external world; they must cause or threaten some identifiable harm (or offense) to others. Second, while the mere causation of harm (or risk) is not sufficient for criminal liability, since 'fault' is also required, the question of fault is simply the question of whether the harmful or dangerous conduct can be attributed to this agent as something for which she was responsible (see Fletcher, 1978: 141–6); and responsibility can be explained in terms of choice and control – I am responsible for what I choose to do or to bring about, or for that which lies within my control (see Hart, 1968; Ashworth, 1987). Priests and moralists are properly interested in those deeper dimensions of motives, attitudes and feelings, of character or the soul, that lie behind external conduct and constitute the essence of sin or vice; the criminal law's proper interest is limited to conduct and the austerely specified conditions of responsibility for conduct.

This account reflects a particular conception of the 'private' realm, into which the criminal law should not intrude. The proper function of the criminal law is to prevent

kinds of harm that are caused by human conduct and that seriously set back the interests of others – and thus to help maintain the structures of conduct and expectations
within which individuals can safely pursue their own conceptions of the good. Our
conduct, insofar as it impinges on the significant interests of others, and our responsibility for such conduct, are thus 'public' matters that properly concern the criminal
law: it can demand that we refrain from harmful conduct, and it can inquire into our
responsibility for such conduct if we do engage in it. Other kinds of conduct, however,
belong in the 'private' realm that is not the law's concern; and so too do our deeper
motives, attitudes and feelings – our conceptions of the good, our moral or spiritual
characters.

This conception of the proper scope of the criminal law also underpinned the two
dominant conceptions of criminal punishment in the 1960s and 1970s.

Among consequentialists who thought that punishment must be justified by its
beneficial effects, deterrence came to seem a more plausible aim than reform or rehabilitation: both because it seemed empirically more promising, given the apparent failure of more ambitious reformative or rehabilitative penal enterprises to achieve their
avowed ends, and because it seemed morally more acceptable. For would-be reformative interventions threatened to deny the offender's status as a responsible moral
agent: they sought to mold him into conformity with the polity's values, rather than
leaving him free to determine his own values; they sought to intrude into his moral
personality in a way that denied his freedom and privacy. By contrast, deterrent punishments address potential offenders as rational agents, offering them prudential reasons to obey the law which should appeal to rationally self-interested beings; nor do
they 'impinge upon the inner citadels of [the offender's] soul' (Lucas, 1968: 215) in the
way that reformative or therapeutic punishments aim to impinge (see generally Duff,
2000: 3–14, 82–8).

Consequentialist conceptions of punishment came under pressure from a revived
'positive' retributivism which sought the justification of punishment in its relationship
to the past offense for which it was imposed; what is relevant here is the form that that
retributivism took. For it connected punishment not to ideas of wickedness or sin, as
older accounts might have done, but to the abstract idea of the unfair advantage that
offenders supposedly gained in committing their crimes, and that punishment was to
remove (e.g. H. Morris, 1968; Murphy, 1973). Again, the focus was not on the offender's
motives or attitudes, on the state of his soul or moral character, but on the abstractly
conceived 'profit' that his crime involved; and his punishment, without attempting to
impinge on the citadels of his soul, simply burdened him as a way of removing that
profit.

The last two decades, however, have seen some striking developments in legal theory: these can be connected to the developing critiques of orthodox (individualist and
neutralist) liberalism from self-styled communitarians (see Mulhall and Swift, 1992)
and from perfectionist liberals (see Raz, 1986; George, 1993), as well as to the revival of
interest in virtue theory in ethics (see Crisp and Slote, 1997). One line of development,
which I cannot discuss here, has been in the normative understanding of criminal culpability: there has been a revival in 'character'-based conceptions, in preference to the

model of choice and control (Bayles, 1982; Arenella, 1990; Finklestein, 1995), and an even more striking revival in virtue-based theories which analyze criminal culpability in terms of certain kinds of vice (Huigens, 1995; Kahan and Nussbaum, 1996). These kinds of account require the criminal law to take an interest not merely in our conduct and our responsibility for it, but in those deeper attitudes and dispositions from which conduct and choice flow – in aspects of our moral character and condition that were, on the more orthodox liberal conception, simply not the law's business. (They also, of course, bring the criminal law back into a closer relationship with our ordinary moral understandings of human wrongdoing.)

Other lines of development have been in penal theory. There has been, as part of a larger attempt to reconnect the emotions with the criminal law (see Kahan and Nussbaum, 1996; Bandes, 1999), a revival of the idea that punishment could, at least in principle, be properly motivated by and expressive of certain emotions that crime appropriately arouses (Murphy and Hampton, 1988: chs 1, 3; but see Pillsbury, 1989; Murphy, 1999); this implies a richer conception of punishment and its meaning than that allowed by deterrent theories or by the 'unfair advantage' version of retributivism. There has been a revival of the idea that punishment should constitute a mode of moral education (H. Morris, 1981; Hampton, 1984) – which implies that the state should take a strenuous interest in the moral condition of its citizens' souls, and should seek not merely to bring their conduct into conformity with the law's demands, but to make them morally better people. And there has been a revival of interest in the idea that punishment should involve such elements as repentance and atonement (see Duff, 1986, 2000; Garvey, 1999; Tudor, 2001) – which again implies an attempt to impinge upon the inner citadels of offenders' souls that seems utterly alien to the kind of liberalism which informed deterrent or 'unfair advantage' conceptions of punishment.[1]

This last trend will provide the focus of this article: partly because it is the one that connects most obviously with religious ideas and practices, and partly because I still believe that it offers a fruitful way of understanding criminal punishment – not punishment as it is actually inflicted under our existing systems of criminal law, but punishment as it should (ideally) be. I will also argue that one merit of this kind of view is that it offers us a powerful *critical* tool for the identification of the major defects that vitiate our existing penal systems; and I will finish by asking whether there are kinds of crime with which such an account cannot deal.

PENANCES RELIGIOUS AND SECULAR

We can begin by considering what punishment might amount to in a religious context – within a religious community defined and united by its shared commitment to a

---

[1] We can also note the growth of the 'restorative justice' movement (see Braithwaite, 1999): though its advocates generally portray restorative justice as an *alternative* to punishment, they also think that our responses to crime should take a kind of interest in the offender's relationships with others, and in her attitudes and feelings, that goes well beyond the limits set by an orthodox liberal conception of law.

particular theology. There are of course many diverse kinds of penal practice not only among different religions, but even within Christianity: but I hope that what follows is a recognizable sketch of one familiar kind of religious penality, which draws on some familiar Christian values.

A member of the community has sinned. That sin might have involved some overt conduct impinging materially on the interests of other people: but essential to its character as a sin is its 'inner' dimension of motives and attitudes – its character as a betrayal of the values by which the community defines itself, as a failure in spiritual orientation and concern, and as a breach in the sinner's relationship to God and to her fellows. The sinner would be expected to confess her sin – if not wholly spontaneously, at least when suitably prompted. That confession might be made in private prayer, or through the mediation of a confessor, or in public to the whole community:[2] but what matters is that it express her sincere and thus necessarily repentant recognition of the wrong she has done. For confession is more than a bare statement that I did the deed in question: to confess is to admit to having done what I recognize – and must thus repent – as a wrong. Such an admission must also, in this context, involve a certain baring of the soul: what the sinner must confess is the sin that she committed; and that sin consisted in essential part in some defect in her motives, her attitudes, her spiritual concerns.

Confession is closely related to apology. A confession, if made to those whom I wronged, or betrayed, or let down, might indeed *constitute* an apology to them; and the recognition of one's sin that is intrinsic to confession is also a recognition of the need to apologize for that sin. Both confession and apology own the sin as mine, as something for which I am culpably responsible; both also disown it, as something that I now repudiate and am committed to avoiding in future; both thus seek forgiveness from, and reconciliation with, those whom I wronged. Sin damages or threatens the sinner's relationships – with God, with those whom she directly wronged, with her religious community as a whole: for it implicitly denies, by flouting, the values by which those relationships are defined. That damage is repaired by confession and apology (and forgiveness), which constitute a reaffirmation of the sinner's commitment to those values and relationships.

However, confession and apology are liable not to be the end of the matter: the sinner might also have to undertake a penance – whether spontaneously, or because this is required of her.

A penance is something necessarily painful or burdensome that is required of or undertaken by the sinner because of her sin – it is, in other words, a punishment for that sin. To say that it is necessarily painful or burdensome is to say that this is part of its point or meaning: a would-be penance that was not painful or burdensome would for just that reason be defective as a penance. (It is not to say, however, that a penance must be undergone unwillingly – that it must be against the sinner's will: a repentant sinner might welcome or seek out an appropriate penance, but what she welcomes or

---

[2] How far confession (or apology – see below) is a private matter between the sinner and God, or also a public matter between her and the whole religious community, will depend on just how sin is understood: primarily as an offense against God and God's will, or also as an offense against the Church and its members.

seeks must be something painful or burdensome.) Penances can take different forms (I leave aside those that involve degradation, or physical injury or mutilation): they might consist in the performance of a suitable ritual – the saying of 'Hail Mary's; or the deprivation of some ordinary good – refraining from some enjoyable activity; or undertaking some task for the benefit of others.

Penance serves several related purposes. It aims to induce (in a sinner who is not yet fully repentant), or to deepen and strengthen (in sinners who are repentant), an adequately repentant understanding of the sin: for it provides a structure that can keep the sinner's attention focused on his sin and its implications – a focus that it is all too easy to lose without some such help. It thus aims to assist the sinner's self-reform: for to repent my sin is also to recognize the need so to reform myself that I can avoid such sins in future. It also serves to communicate the sinner's repentance to those whom he wronged – to God, to his fellows: by undertaking this burdensome task he gives more forceful expression to his apology, to his recognition of his sin, as something that really matters to him. The point here is not just an evidential one – that undertaking penance gives others stronger evidence of sincere repentance than merely verbal confession and apology could give (after all, God does not need *evidence* of our sincerity). It is rather that undertaking a penance, giving this outward and materially burdensome expression to the painfully burdensome recognition of one's own wrongdoing, is a way of taking the matter seriously; it part *constitutes* the repentant sinner's earnest repentance. In a similar way giving a gift to express gratitude, or engaging in the overt rituals of grief, are not just ways of evidencing feelings that were already fully formed; they are ways of adding depth and structure to those feelings themselves. Finally, insofar as penance is prescribed for the sinner by others, or undertaken within a formal structure, its prescription and administration serve to communicate to the sinner the seriousness with which others take his sin.[3]

Penance thus looks both backward, to the sin for which it is undertaken, and forward, to the restoration of the sinner's relationships with those whom she wronged, and to the renewal of her commitment to the values which define those relationships. It is also intrinsically *inclusionary*, not exclusionary: it is required of and undertaken by the sinner as a member of the community – as someone who violated values that are her values as a member of the community, and whose relationships with the community can be repaired in this way. That is why excommunication, if permanent, is not a penance, since it constitutes an irrevocable exclusion from the community (compare Garvey, 1999: 1855). Temporary excommunication can, however, constitute a penance: its imposition communicates the judgment that the wrong was so serious as to be incompatible with membership of the community, unless it is adequately repented; by undergoing the period of excommunication the sinner can display his repentant recognition of his sin, and reconcile himself with the community from which that sin threatened to exclude him.

---

[3] Contrast Garvey (1999: 1819–23), for a rather different explanation of the meaning and purpose of penance, as expiating the sin by annulling the false message conveyed by the sin, and vindicating the victim's moral worth. I am not convinced, however, either that sin (or criminal wrongdoing, which is his main focus) always convey that kind of false message, or that the (self-) imposition of a burdensome penance is necessary to annul it.

I have argued elsewhere that we should understand criminal punishment as, ideally, a kind of secular penance (Duff, 2000). The culpable commission of a crime involves wrongdoing that violates the central values of the political community, as expressed in its criminal law; the crime thus damages or threatens the offender's normative relationships not only with the direct victim, but also with her fellow citizens. To see how the offender's punishment can constitute a penance, we should focus initially not on imprisonment (which, although it is one of the more dramatically oppressive and exclusionary modes of punishment, is also one of the less frequently used even in the United States),[4] but on non-custodial punishment. Consider, for instance, Community Service Orders (see N. Morris and Tonry, 1990: ch. 6; Ashworth, 1995: 277–81). The imposition of such a punishment, the requirement that – because of the offense for which she has been convicted – the offender undertake these hours of burdensome work, itself communicates to the offender the community's formal judgment that she has committed a serious wrong for which she must make this reparation. The punishment itself, the hours of burdensome work that she must do because of her crime, provides a structure which can focus her attention on her crime and its implications (especially, but not only, when the nature of the work is related to the character of the crime), and can thus help to induce or to strengthen a repentant understanding of the crime as a wrong against her community. And this burdensome work can also be seen as a material and forceful expression of the apology that she owes to those whom she wronged – to the direct victim of her crime, if there was one, and to the wider community whose values she flouted. The point of the Community Service Order is not to make material reparation for the material harm – if any – that the crime caused (although it could sometimes include such material reparation). It is rather to make *moral* reparation for the *wrong* that was done; and such reparation is made not by a merely verbal apology, but by a burdensome penance which can do justice to the seriousness of the wrong.

Punishment, on this account, should be a communicative process between the offender and the polity: it aims to communicate to the offender the censure that his crime deserves; to bring him to recognize and repent that crime as a wrong for which he must make moral reparation; to bring him to make that reparation by undertaking or undergoing a burdensome penalty which constitutes and communicates a forceful apology to those he has wronged; and thus to reconcile him with the community whose values he flouted. Punishment is also a reformative enterprise: the offender who is brought to repent his crime is thus brought to recognize the need to reform his future conduct; and his punishment should, when appropriate, assist him in this process – as probation aims to do, for instance.

I cannot explain this account in more detail here; what I do want to do is to note and respond to some objections that liberals may bring against any such portrayal of criminal punishment in a secular state. They might agree that penances can make moral sense, and are morally acceptable, within an appropriate religious context: but they are likely to argue strenuously that they can play no proper role in a system of state punishment.

---

[4] Imprisonment would still have a role, but a very limited role, within the kind of penal system that my account favors: see Duff (2000: 148–52).

Penances, and penitential punishments as I have portrayed them, address not just offenders' conduct, but their moral attitudes, dispositions and feelings. They seek not just to dissuade, or to condemn, criminal conduct, but to bring the offender to repent it; and what he must repent is, it seems, not just the conduct itself, but the motives, attitudes and moral dispositions from which it flowed.[5] They are also meant to constitute modes of moral reparation – expressions of an attitude of remorseful apology, and of a desire for forgiveness and reconciliation. In these ways, penance and penitential punishment precisely seek to 'impinge upon the inner citadels of [the offender's] soul' (Lucas, 1968: 215) – to address and improve his moral character, to exact repentance and apology.

This might, from a familiar liberal perspective, be acceptable within a religious community, membership of which is voluntary or consensual – or indeed within other kinds of community or relationship that are likewise voluntary or consensual. Several aspects of this requirement are worth distinguishing. First, even those who were born into the religious community, rather than choosing to join it, must have the option of leaving: not, perhaps, the option of abandoning their religious beliefs, but at least the option of separating themselves from the institutional structures that require them to undertake penances. Second, the sins for which penances are required are identified and judged as sins in the light of values to which the sinner herself is committed, as a (voluntary) member of the community. Third, penance presupposes a confession that is itself voluntary in the sense that, even if others urge the sinner to confess, no one forces her to do so. Fourth, although a penance might be required or demanded of the sinner, perhaps under threat of excommunication if she refuses, it is still left up to her to agree or to refuse to undertake it; if she refuses to undertake it, no one will forcibly inflict it on her.

(I do not suggest that the penances undergone within religious communities always have this voluntary character, they clearly do not. But just to the extent that penances are imposed on those who do not consent to them, just to the extent that the demands of the community are imposed on those who wish to leave it, liberals will have moral qualms about their legitimacy.)

Individuals might find their own good within communities or relationships of which penance is an integral part; within communities or relationships in which participants take a close interest in each other's moral or spiritual condition, and in which confession, repentance, sincere apology and moral reparation play an important role. Indeed, liberals might agree that a life that involved *no* such intimate relationships would be lacking in an important dimension of human good. But, they are likely to insist, the state cannot legitimately *impose* membership of such communities or participation in such relationships on its citizens: a proper respect for the autonomy and privacy of individual citizens requires it to leave them free to determine such matters for themselves. The state can legitimately demand that we refrain from certain kinds of wrongfully harmful conduct; it can legitimately condemn us if we commit such wrongs, and seek to dissuade their commission by a system of deterrent punishments:

---

[5] Contrast von Hirsch (1993) for an account of punishment as communicating censure, without aiming to induce repentance.

but it does not have the right to induce us, by the coercive mechanisms of criminal punishment, to accept the values in the light of which our conduct may be condemned, or to repent or apologize for our wrongdoing.

That is, however, just what the state would be doing if it used criminal punishment as a kind of secular penance. First, despite various contractualist efforts to portray membership of political communities as (quasi-) voluntary, it is clear that such membership, and the obligations it brings with it, are not voluntary (see generally Horton, 1992; Simmons, 1996): citizens cannot simply separate themselves from a state that they find uncongenial. Second, even if we can claim that they *should* all accept the values by which their conduct is judged, it is clear that not all actually do so. Third, punishment is not and could not be conditional on voluntary confession; and the privilege against self-incrimination, which reflects an important liberal constraint on what states can demand from their citizens, forbids not merely coerced confessions but also a requirement to confess. Fourth, punishment is not and could not be optional: even if it is initially required of the offender, rather than simply being inflicted on her, it is not in the end up to her whether she is punished or not; it will be imposed on the offender regardless of her will.

This is not to say that punishment itself is illegitimate: liberals can argue that the enterprise of criminal law and punishment, insofar as it is necessary to protect the freedom and autonomy of all citizens, and is subject to suitable side-constraints, can be consistent with a due respect for the citizens as rational moral agents. But it is to say that criminal punishment, as an exercise of the state's coercive power, should not aim to impinge on offenders' souls – on their moral values or attitudes, on their conception of or responses to their own wrongdoing: for those are matters of private conscience and feeling, which must be left for individuals to determine for themselves; they are not the state's proper concern.[6]

The answer to this objection comes in three parts. First, while penitential punishment does indeed address offenders as moral agents, and seeks to engage their moral attitudes and feelings, it does not (it should not) seek to *coerce* those attitudes and feelings. It is coercive in that it is, if necessary, imposed on offenders against their will: but it aims to persuade, rather than to coerce, their moral understanding. It is an exercise in forceful moral communication, which we hope will persuade them to recognize and repent their wrongdoing, and to accept their punishment as an appropriate penance, through which they can make appropriate reparation for their crimes. But – as with any mode of communication with a rational moral agent – it must be left to them to be persuaded, or not, by the rational moral force of their punishment; it must, in particular, be left open to them to remain unpersuaded and defiant. We can try to force them to hear the message that their punishment aims to convey: but we must not try to force them to accept it – or even to listen to it or to take it seriously.

Second, criminal punishment need not and should not be as ambitious as religious penance; it should not try to engage the offender's innermost spiritual concerns

---

[6] See generally Lipkin (1988); Baker (1992); von Hirsch (1999). Murphy's comments on 'character retributivism' are also relevant here; see Murphy (1994, 1999); also Murphy (1985).

or moral character, or to impinge on the innermost 'citadels' of his soul. He has committed a kind of wrong that properly counts as public – it properly concerns the whole polity; he must be censured for that wrong, and should recognize and repent it as a wrong: but what must be censured, what he should repent, as a wrong need not be identified in a way that involves the deeper aspects of his soul or character. Criminal wrongfulness cannot, of course, be analyzed purely in terms of overt behavior. Perhaps it cannot be adequately analyzed in terms of choice and control either: it can be plausibly argued that there is more to the wrongfulness of murder, or theft, or assault than the choice to engage in conduct that constitutes the *actus reus* of such a crime; that what must be censured, and repented, is also the kind of attitude or (lack of) concern manifested in such conduct (see Duff, 1996: ch. 7). But the identification of such wrongs as wrongs – by others in censuring them, or by the offender in repenting them – need not take us as deeply into the offender's soul as does the identification and repentance of religious sins. This is not just because the criminal law will cover a narrower range of wrongs than does a religious notion of sin, although that is an important point about any liberal system of criminal law; it is also because, although criminal law and criminal punishment must look beyond overt behavior and choice, they need not look as far as the offender's deepest moral or spiritual attitudes and concerns. Perhaps we would hope that, at least with very serious crimes, the offender would be led to a profound re-examination and re-orientation of his entire being: but criminal punishment, as an exercise in penitential communication, need not be *that* ambitious; it need not aspire to the kind of 'deep character retributivism' against which Murphy rightly warns us (Murphy, 1994, 1999). It focuses on the wrongfulness of the criminal deed, on the wrongful attitudes or concerns directly manifested in that deed; but it should not try to focus on the offender's whole moral being.

Third, a state that is to show its citizens the respect due to them as responsible moral agents must address them in the kind of moral language that is central to this account of punishment. The criminal law should not simply prohibit certain kinds of conduct, on pain of sanctions: for sanction-backed prohibitions address those on whom they are imposed as mere subjects, whereas the law should address those whom it claims to bind as citizens who share in the values that it embodies. The criminal law should, rather, aim to define as public wrongs kinds of action that the citizens can recognize as wrongs, in terms of the values that the law claims to embody and protect; and the reasons it offers citizens for refraining from such actions should be those reasons that justify it in declaring such actions to be criminal – their wrongfulness. So too, a state that is to respect its citizens as responsible agents must be ready to censure their public wrongdoing and to try to persuade them to recognize and repent it: simply to ignore such wrongdoing, or merely to deter them from it by the threat of sanctions, would be to cease to respect or address them as moral agents. A communicative system of punishment, I would claim, is what we are *owed* – as citizens who can do wrong, and whose public wrongdoings should be censured, but who can also repair those wrongs by suitable kinds of apology and moral reparation.

A further question is whether this kind of view of criminal law and punishment can count as a 'liberal' view; or whether it must be grounded in some species of 'communitarianism'. This is not a question I can pursue here – nor, given the variety of theories that could count as 'liberal', and the increasing fuzziness of the distinction between 'liberalism' and 'communitarianism' (see Mulhall and Swift, 1992), is it a question whose meaning is very clear. I think myself that such a view of criminal law and punishment fits most happily within a (liberal) communitarian account of the state, which emphasizes the offender's membership of the political community whose law she has broken and whose values she has flouted, and to which she can be reconciled through her punishment: but it might also be possible within a perfectionist liberal perspective (see Garvey, 1999: 1856–8 – though the notion of community also plays a large part in his account).

IDEAL THEORY AND ACTUAL PRACTICE

It will be obvious that criminal punishment as I portray it, as a species of moral communication with offenders that respects them as responsible agents and that seeks to reconcile them with the community whose shared values they have violated, is a very long way from punishment as it is actually practiced in our existing systems of criminal justice. Although there are penal practices – some forms of probation, for instance – that could be seen in this light, it would be a callously bad joke to suggest that much of what is inflicted under the name of 'punishment' in our existing systems is or even seriously aspires to be this kind of respectful moral communication. But what I have sketched here as an account of punishment is not meant to provide either a description or a justification of our existing practices. It is, rather, a normative account of what punishment *ought* to be – of what punishment must be if it is to be adequately justified; it offers not a justification for current practice, but an ideal standard against which actual practice can be judged – and be shown, no doubt, to be seriously wanting.

I take this to be a feature of any normative theory of punishment, and of normative theories in general: they aim to show us or to help us see what we *should* do, how we *should* live; and we can expect to find a significant gap between any plausible normative account of how we should live and any plausible descriptive account of how we actually live. It is, however, worth noticing three more particular points about the relation between such a normative account of punishment and actual penal practice.

First, insofar as our existing penal institutions and practices are not just imperfect (that much will be true of any human practice), but radically unjust, oppressive, or morally corrupt (which I fear is true of too much of what passes for punishment both in Britain and in the United States), they put all of us in a morally problematic position. For criminal punishment is imposed in our name, by courts that claim to be acting on our collective behalf; and most of us rely implicitly on the criminal law and its penal institutions for protection against crime, and look to the police and the criminal courts for protection and satisfaction if we are victimized by crime. We are therefore all complicit in these practices, and in the injustices and the oppression that they perpetrate.

Second, the task of so reforming our current practices that they can become, if not perfect, at least close enough to the ideal to be justified, is not just the task of reforming our penal practices and institutions themselves – massive though that task is. For there are preconditions which must be satisfied before a penal system can be justified: conditions having to do not with the nature or operations of the system itself, but with the larger political, social and legal context within which it is set (see further Duff, 2000: ch. 5.2). If we are to be collectively justified in calling a person to answer a charge of wrongdoing at a criminal trial, or in punishing her for it, we must be sure that she is indeed bound, morally as well as legally, by the law; that we have the moral standing thus to call her to account for her conduct; and that there is a genuine political community with which punishment can reconcile her. We must be sure, that is, that she is and has been treated as a full member of the normative political community whose laws she is charged with breaking, that she is answerable to that community and its members for her wrongdoing and that they are ready to be reconciled with her. It could be plausibly argued that these preconditions are not satisfied for too many of those who appear before our criminal courts and suffer our criminal punishments: but in that case the legitimacy of their punishment is fatally undermined.

Third, punishment as I have portrayed it makes arduous moral demands – not just on those who are punished, but on those who administer punishment and on all members of the political community. It is, in moral terms, easy enough to administer a system of deterrent punishments, or a system of retributive punishments that aims simply to impose a suitably onerous burden on offenders: it is a very much harder task to administer communicative punishments which are to address offenders as responsible moral agents, and to persuade them to repent their crimes and to reform themselves – and to administer them in such a way and with such a spirit that they do not become either empty rituals or oppressive attempts at moral bullying. It is easy for those who are not directly involved in the penal system to leave the administration of punishments, whether as deterrent or as retribution, to the system's officials: it is much harder to treat offenders who have been punished as fellow citizens with whom we must be reconciled – but that is what punishment as I have portrayed it demands of us.

This point leads me into my final topic. Can we, or should we, believe that reconciliation is always both possible and morally necessary; or are there kinds of wrongdoing which make such reconciliation, reconciliation through punishment, not just psychologically or socially difficult, but morally impossible?

THE LIMITS OF COMMUNITY?

Punishment, on the account offered here, is an essentially inclusionary activity. The offender is called to account, at a criminal trial, for his alleged violation of values that are supposedly his as a member of the political community – he is called to answer to his fellow citizens through the court. He is censured for that violation, if it is proved, by his fellow citizens; and his punishment, as a secular penance, is supposed to constitute a mode of moral reparation through which he is to be reconciled with those he has wronged – through which the bonds of political community are to be repaired and strengthened. Punishment, that is, treats and addresses offenders as members of the political community: as fellow citizens to whom we owe respect and concern.

Now it seems to me an advantage of this account that it has this inclusionary character, and a defect in some other accounts that they portray punishment in exclusionary terms – as something that 'we' must do to an alien 'them' with whom we recognize no such community.[7] But this does raise a difficult question: whether there are any crimes whose character is such that we need not, or should not, or cannot maintain such community with the offender – crimes such that complete and irrevocable exclusion is a legitimate, appropriate or even necessary response.

Features of our existing practices imply that this is quite often the case. Capital punishment excludes the executed offender from any continued life and community; its message is that his crime has made any restoration of human community impossible.[8] Some versions of the 'three strikes and you're out' policy, and indeed any provision for life imprisonment without prospect of parole, imply that those subject to them are to be permanently and irrevocably expelled from ordinary community with their fellow citizens – from citizenship; that, after all, is what 'out' must mean in this context. We should also notice the extent to which offenders, even after their formal punishment has been completed, often suffer some degree of 'civil death', the permanent loss of many of the ordinary rights or benefits of citizenship (see Garvey, 1999: 1852–3); and the way that a metaphorical 'war' on crime, or on a particular type of crime, can too easily become a not-so-metaphorical war on criminals who are seen as the enemy, rather than as fellow citizens (compare Hulsman, 1986).

I certainly do not want to justify these features of our existing practices; they should indeed be rejected, just because they display a failure to take seriously enough, or an excessive readiness to give up on, the bonds of citizenship and community. With at least the vast majority of crimes and criminals, we should continue to see and to treat them as fellow members of the normative community who must be punished, but whose moral standing as members is not to be denied or qualified; this remains true even if we are confident, on good empirical grounds, that punishment will not bring or has not brought an offender to repent her crime or to make any sincere apology for it. The question is, however, whether there are limits to such community – whether there can come a point at which we need not, or should not, or cannot continue to treat the offender as a full member of the normative political community.

Three kinds of example might seem to raise this question quite sharply. First, could there be individual crimes so horrible in their cruelty and inhumanity that they make any continuation or restoration of human community with the criminal impossible? Second, could there be criminal *careers*, involving the persistent commission of dangerous and violent crimes, which display in the end such an incorrigible rejection of the community's central values that the criminal should be excluded, be taken to

---

[7] See, for example, Goldman (1982); C.W. Morris (1991) (criminals forfeit their rights of citizenship, or their moral standing): for further discussion see Dubber (1998); Duff (2000: 14–16, 77–9).

[8] More precisely, one could imagine capital punishment, as accepted by a repentant murderer, reconciling him with his fellows: but it would still do so only by marking their shared recognition that he must be excluded, or must exclude himself, from continued life with them. See further Duff (2000: 152–5).

have excluded himself, from that community? Third, do terrorist attacks such as, most terribly, those committed on New York and Washington in September 2001, leave any room to see their perpetrators as offenders who should be punished – as members of a polity whose values they have flouted, but of which they must still be treated as full members?

I am *fairly* confident that the answer to the first of these questions should be 'No': no single deed, however terrible, should put a person beyond civic redemption. With many horrific crimes, there might be room for serious doubt about the perpetrator's status as a responsible agent: but if he is a responsible agent, we must treat him as such – as someone who could, and who should be given the chance to, repent his crime and redeem himself.

I would like to be able to answer the second question, about persistent dangerous offenders, with an equally confident 'No', but find it hard to do so. I can confidently say that no individual criminal career, however persistently dangerous, could warrant irrevocable exclusion – detention without prospect of parole, for instance: the offender must still be left with the chance to redeem and restore himself. But could there not come a point at which the need to protect other potential victims against the offender could warrant his presumptively permanent detention – detention for life unless and until he shows that he can be safely restored to ordinary community? I would like to be able to say 'No' even to this, as many liberals would say. To say this, however, one must be able to believe that the bonds of community, and the status of citizenship, are unconditional and absolute – that nothing, not even a person's own persistent demonstration that he utterly rejects the demands of citizenship and community, can destroy them (this is something that liberals who reject any species of preventive detention do not always recognize); and I am not sure whether I should, or honestly can, believe that (see further Duff, 2000: 170–4). An analogous belief does make morally impressive sense within a religious context: although some Christian ideas of Hell imply the possibility of permanent and irrevocable exclusion from God's love, other strands in Christian thought portray God's love as unconditional, and encourage us to aspire to a similarly unconditional concern for our fellows – whatever they have done, and however persistently and seriously they sin. But can we really extend this religious ideal to the secular context of a modern state: can we really believe (and tell a persistent criminal's victims that they should believe) that the bonds of civic community are similarly unconditional and unbreakable?

The third question, about terrorism, raises further issues about war and punishment. It is also complicated by the distinction between domestic and international terrorism – between terrorism committed by people who are, in the law's eyes if not in their own, citizens of or visitors to the policy against which their actions are directed, who are therefore bound by and answerable to its laws; and terrorism committed against a foreign state or its institutions by people who are not its citizens. I cannot discuss the implications of this distinction here: but it leads to questions about the proper role of international criminal courts and about the idea of crimes against humanity – crimes that flout the bonds not of citizenship of a particular polity, but of humanity itself; crimes whose perpetrators must be called to account, and punished, by the international community. I do want to say something, however, about war and punishment.[9]

Suppose we have collectively been victims of a major terrorist attack, and investigators have a good idea of who the perpetrators are; they have evidence which, while not sufficient to ensure a conviction in a criminal court, would certainly be sufficient to justify arresting and charging the suspects. Assuming that we then embark on the pursuit of those suspects, should we treat this as an attempt to arrest suspected criminals, with a view to their prosecution and (if duly convicted) punishment; or as a defensive war to be prosecuted against an alien enemy?[10]

We must of course recognize some moral constraints – such as those embodied in 'Just War' theory – on our engagement in warfare. We might say too that we must still recognize *some* bond of community with the enemy we are fighting: that we must still recognize them as fellow human beings – a recognition which constrains what we can properly do to them.[11] But the aims even of a just war and the moral constraints on its conduct clearly differ from the aims and constraints of a system of communicative punishments. War aims not at reconciliation with the enemy (which might at best be a post-war endeavor) but at victory – successful defense against their aggression. Its conduct does not involve attempts at moral communication with the enemy, but the attempt to kill or incapacitate them. While in war we must aim our violence only against 'combatants', we need not have made sure that each of them is individually engaged in the aggression that justifies the war.[12] And even if we take enemy combatants prisoner, that imprisonment is not punishment: its aim is not to bring them to repentance or reconciliation, but simply to incapacitate them. (A further, more general point that underpins some of these differences is that in war we deal with a collective enemy, and with individuals only as members of that collectivity; whereas in pursuing and punishing criminals we are usually, though not always, dealing with them as individuals.)

The terrorists themselves will be likely to see their activities in this way: they see themselves as engaged not (merely) in attacking specific individuals, but in a war against this regime or this state; and, if captured and imprisoned, they might see themselves as prisoners of war, rather than as offenders who are being punished. The question is, though: should *we* take this view?

I do not, I confess, have anything like a clear answer to this question – perhaps because it is set as an either/or question, when any normatively plausible account of the situation would need to be much more complex and nuanced than such a simple 'either/or' allows. In favor of seeing this genuinely as a war against terrorists, as well as against terrorism, is the fact that is how *they* see it: so perhaps we should accept their self-definition, rather than insisting on treating them as members of a polity which they

---

[9] I should of course also say more about what I mean by 'terrorism', given the controversial and morally laden character of that concept: but that is something else that I cannot embark on here.

[10] I have learned from Murphy's discussion of this question in his (as yet) unpublished paper 'September 11: Some philosophical reflections'.

[11] See Gaita (1991: especially chs 1, 3), for an insightful development of this idea.

[12] And – though this is one of the more morally problematic features at least of contemporary warfare – the moral constraints on knowingly harming innocents as a side-effect of military action are notoriously weaker than the analogous constraints on police or penal activities; that we are engaged in a war makes it easier (which is not to say that it *should* make it easier) to tolerate 'collateral damage'.

have so violently rejected (so long as we still treat them with the respect and concern due to them as fellow human beings); indeed, we might wonder whether it is possible to see them not just as fellow human beings (which might be hard enough) but as fellow citizens (this argument will, I suspect, seem especially forceful insofar as the terrorists belong to an identifiable community of their own). On the other hand, we should surely be very reluctant to abandon the moral constraints that belong with the enterprise of criminal justice, in favor of the rather weaker constraints that apply to the conduct of war – especially, though I think not only, if we bear in mind that those who will suffer from the abandonment of such constraints will include not only terrorists themselves, but also those who are suspected of terrorism or of contacts with terrorists; and (perhaps especially when we are dealing with terrorists who do not belong to any identifiable alternative community of their own, membership of which they can still retain), we should also be very reluctant to exclude the perpetrator from any prospect of community with us.

There is of course a third, even more disturbing possibility – that we should see and treat the terrorists neither as criminal wrongdoers subject to the demands and entitled to the protections of our criminal laws; nor as enemy soldiers subject to the demands and entitled to the protections of the laws and conventions of war; but as 'unlawful combatants' who have no such moral claims on our respect or concern, and whom we may treat in anyway that seems necessary to ensure our own safety and to 'defeat terrorism'. Now it is easy for liberal outsiders to say, as many do, that this third perspective must simply be rejected as morally intolerable: to insist that, whatever they have done, we must strive to recognize them as fellow human beings whose humanity sets strict limits on the ways in which we can treat them – even if they recognized no such limits in their treatment of those whom they attacked. Here again, however, we confront a very difficult moral question – a question that moral *theory* cannot answer for us: can we find, within a secular world view, the resources not just to understand, but to make our own, such an *unconditional* respect for the humanity of any and every other human being, whatever they have done? From within a religious perspective (of the appropriate kind), such an attitude can at least be seen as an ideal of perfection towards which we should aspire. (By contrast, from within the kind of contractualist moral perspective that some theorists still favor in explaining the rational foundations of morality as well as of the state, it is hard to see such an attitude as rational: contracts involve some idea of reciprocity, and cannot be sustained in its absence.) The question is: could purely secular moral beings come to see such unconditional concern as an ideal towards which they should aspire?

On which unhappily and uneasily uncertain note, I must end. I am fairly confident about the merits of the account of punishment sketched in section 2 (Penances religious and secular); I am, as is evident, far less confident about the range or extent of its application, even as a matter of ideal theory.

ACKNOWLEDGEMENTS

I'm grateful to Jeff Murphy and to Arizona State University for inviting me to the conference at which this article was first given; and to Claire Finklestein for her comments on that occasion.

REFERENCES

Arenella, P. (1990) 'Character, choice, and moral agency', *Social Philosophy and Policy* 7: 59–83.

Ashworth, A.J. (1987) 'Belief, intent and criminal liability', in J. Eekelaar and J. Bell (eds) *Oxford essays in jurisprudence*, 3rd series (pp. 1–31). Oxford: Oxford University Press.

———. (1995) *Sentencing and criminal justice*, 2nd edn. London: Butterworths.

Baker, B.M. (1992) 'Penance as a model for punishment', *Social Theory and Practice* 18: 311–31.

Bandes, S., ed. (1999) *The passions of law*. New York: New York University Press.

Bayles, M. (1982) 'Character, purpose, and criminal responsibility', *Law and Philosophy* 1: 5–20.

Braithwaite, J. (1999) 'Restorative justice: Assessing optimistic and pessimistic accounts', in M. Tonry (ed.) *Crime and justice: A review of research*, vol. 23 (pp. 241–367). Chicago, IL: University of Chicago Press.

Crisp, R. and M. Slote, eds (1997) *Virtue ethics*. Oxford: Oxford University Press.

Dubber, M. (1998) 'The right to be punished: Autonomy and its demise in modern penal thought', *Law and History Review* 16: 113–62.

Duff, R.A. (1986) *Trials and punishments*. Cambridge: Cambridge University Press.

———. (1996) *Criminal attempts*. Oxford: Oxford University Press.

———. (2000) *Punishment, communication, and community*. New York: Oxford University Press.

Feinberg, J. (1984) *Harm to others*. New York: Oxford University Press.

———. (1985) *Offense to others*. New York: Oxford University Press.

Finklestein, C. (1995) 'Duress: A philosophical account of the defense in law', *Arizona Law Review* 37: 251–83.

Fletcher, G. (1978) *Rethinking criminal law*. Boston, MA: Little Brown.

Gaita, R. (1991) *Good and evil: An absolute conception*. London: Macmillan.

Garvey, S.P. (1999) 'Punishment as atonement', *UCLA Law Review* 46: 1801–58.

George, R.P. (1993) *Making men moral: Civil liberties and public morality*. Oxford: Oxford University Press.

Goldman, A.H. (1982) 'Toward a new theory of punishment', *Law and Philosophy* 1: 57–76.

Hampton, J. (1984) 'The moral education theory of punishment', *Philosophy and Public Affairs* 13: 208–38.

Hart, H.L.A. (1963) *Law, liberty and morality*. New York: Random House.

———. (1968) *Punishment and responsibility*. Oxford: Oxford University Press.

Horton, J. (1992) *Political obligation*. London: Macmillan.

Huigens, K. (1995) 'Virtue and inculpation', *Harvard Law Review* 108: 1423–80.

Hulsman, L. (1986) 'Critical criminology and the concept of crime', *Contemporary Crises* 10: 63–80.

Kahan, D. and M. Nussbaum (1996) 'Two conceptions of emotion in criminal law', *Columbia Law Review* 96: 269–374.

Lipkin, R.J. (1988) 'Punishment, penance and respect for autonomy', *Social Theory and Practice* 14: 87–104.

Lucas, J.R. (1968) 'Or else', *Proceedings of the Aristotelian Society* 69: 207–22.

Morris, C.W. (1991) 'Punishment and loss of moral standing', *Canadian Journal of Philosophy* 21: 53–79.

Morris, H. (1968) 'Persons and punishment', *The Monist* 52: 475–501.

———. (1981) 'A paternalistic theory of punishment', *American Philosophical Quarterly* 18: 263–71.

Morris, N. and M. Tonry (1990) *Between prison and probation: Intermediate punishments in a rational sentencing system.* New York: Oxford University Press.

Mulhall, S. and A. Swift (1992) *Liberals and communitarians.* Oxford: Blackwell.

Murphy, J.G. (1973) 'Marxism and retribution', *Philosophy and Public Affairs* 2: 217–43.

———. (1985) 'Retributivism, moral education and the liberal state', *Criminal Justice Ethics* 4: 3–11.

———. (1994) 'Cognitive and moral obstacles to imputation', *Jahrbuch für Recht und Ethik* 2: 67–79.

———. (1999) 'Moral epistemology, the retributive emotions, and the "clumsy moral philosophy" of Jesus Christ', in S. Bandes (ed.) *The passions of law*, pp. 149–67. New York: New York University Press.

———. and J. Hampton (1988) *Forgiveness and mercy.* Cambridge: Cambridge University Press.

Pillsbury, S. (1989) 'Emotional justice: Moralizing the passions of criminal punishment', *Cornell Law Review* 74: 655–710.

Raz, J. (1986) *The morality of freedom.* Oxford: Oxford University Press.

Simmons, A.J. (1996) 'Associative political obligations', *Ethics* 106: 247–73.

Tudor, S. (2001) 'Accepting one's punishment as meaningful suffering', *Law and Philosophy* 20: 581–604.

Von Hirsch, A. (1993) *Censure and sanctions.* Oxford: Oxford University Press.

———. (1999) 'Punishment, penance and the state', in M. Matravers (ed.) *Punishment and political theory*, pp. 69–82. Oxford: Hart Publishing.

Wolfenden, J. (1957) *Report of the Committee on homosexual offences and prostitution.* London: HMSO.

III

MIXED THEORIES

John Rawls (1955), Edmond Pincoffs (1966), and H. L. A. Hart (1959, 1968) offered the first modern mixed theories that combined retributive and consequentialist elements. After that, though, many philosophers writing about punishment continued primarily to discuss questions of justification of the institution of punishment (e.g., Moore 1993) or of the state's moral authority to punish (Matravers 2000; Boonin 2008).

A breakthrough occurred in H. L. A. Hart's *Punishment and Responsibility* (1968 [chapter 12 in this volume]). Hart argued that the conflict between utilitarians and retributivists is misconceived because it is based on the assumption that punishment raises a single fundamental question: "How is punishment to be justified?" To the contrary, Hart argued, there are several separate important questions. How is the existence of punishment as a state institution or practice to be justified? Who may be punished? How much?

Hart argued that a comprehensive theory of punishment might coherently provide different answers to those questions. His own, which he called a "middle way," was that crime prevention, a consequentialist idea, is the general justifying aim of punishment, that—possibly with some exceptions[1]—punishment should be imposed only on morally culpable offenders, for offenses, and that both retributive and consequentialist considerations are relevant to determining the amount of punishment.

For some kinds of theories, Hart's three questions changed nothing. For a Kantian theorist who believed that respect for moral autonomy requires that offenders

---

[1] Relating to administrative and regulatory offenses for which violators are strictly liable. The phrase "culpable offenders" in the next phrase refers to the traditional mens rea requirements that convicted offenders have been proven to be acting purposely, knowingly, recklessly, or negligently.

be punished, the same answer would be given to all three questions. What is the general justifying aim of punishment? The imposition of morally deserved punishments. Who should be punished? Offenders, for offenses. How much? As much as is deserved.

For other theories, however, things did change. A consequentialist could neatly side-step the punishment-of-the-innocent challenge. Crime prevention, utility, happiness, or economic efficiency could be the justifying aim, and decisions about the amount of punishment could be predicated on maximizing it. Liability to punishment, however, could be based on culpability criteria.

Most people writing about mixed theories have been lawyers. This is probably because lawyers tend to be interested in the practical application of theoretical ideas. Many have tried to tease out the implications of punishment theories for formulation of sentencing policy and sentencing of individual offenders. Two broad approaches have been dominant. *Desert* theories proposed that punishments be linked systematically to scales of offense severity and that little latitude be accorded judges to take account of consequentialist concerns in individual cases. Desert theory is a *positive retributivist* theory (punishments must be imposed, as opposed to may be). The critical issue is proportionality. Scales that tie severity of punishment to the seriousness of crimes are essential, but once the scales are in place they can be stretched or squeezed like an accordion to take account of consequentialist considerations. The leading figures have long been Andrew von Hirsch (1976, 1986, 1993, 1998 [chapter 13 in this volume], 2005 [with Ashworth]) and Paul Robinson (2007 [chapter 19 in this volume], 2008).

The second approach, *limiting retributivism,* is most famously associated with Norval Morris (1974, 1990 [with Tonry]; see also Tonry 1994 [chapter 14 in this volume] and Frase 2004 [chapter 16 in this volume]). Limiting retributivist theories posit that no absolute judgments are possible about precisely how much punishment any particular offender deserves, but that broad agreements can be reached that some punishments are too severe and for the most serious crimes that some are too lenient. Within that range, and assuming other criteria are satisfied, judges may take consequentialist considerations into account. A similar perspective, *asymmetric proportionality,* is influential in Scandinavian countries (e.g., Lappi-Seppälä 2001 [chapter 15 in this volume]): proportionality concerns set the upper limit of allowable punishments, but not a lower limit. These are *negative retributivist* theories in which offenders may be punished as much as they deserve (but not more), but need not be. Morris and his followers adopted Bentham's notion of *parsimony:* the infliction of pain on anyone, including offenders, is a bad thing to do, and should not be done more than is necessary to achieve valid preventive purposes.

In the 1980s, desert theories were highly influential and government bodies as diverse as the Australian Law Reform Commission (1980), the Canadian Sentencing Commission (1987), and the Home Office of England and Wales (1991) explicitly adopted desert theory as their guiding normative rationale. More recently, limiting retributivist theories have become more influential as evidenced by their adoption by the American Law Institute (2007) in the second edition of the *Model Penal Code,* and by a major English sentencing reform body (Home Office 2001) as guiding rationales.

REFERENCES

Bibliographic details concerning works that are mentioned but are not reprinted in this volume can be found in the reference list to the introduction except for the following:

American Law Institute. 2007. *Model Penal Code: Sentencing.* Tentative Draft no. 1 (April 9, 2007). Philadelphia: American Law Institute.

Boonin, David. 2008. *The Problem of Punishment.* Cambridge: Cambridge University Press.

Matravers, Matt. 2000. *Punishment and Political Theory.* Oxford University Press.

Morris, Norval, and Michael Tonry. 1990. *Between Prison and Probation: Intermediate Punishments in a Rational Sentencing System.* Chicago: University of Chicago Press.

von Hirsch, Andrew. 1986. *Past and Future Crimes: Deservedness and Dangerousness in the Sentencing of Criminals.* New Brunswick, N.J.: Rutgers University Press.

———. 1993. *Censure and Sanctions.* Oxford: Oxford University Press.

12

PROLEGOMENON TO THE PRINCIPLES OF PUNISHMENT

H. L. A. Hart

1. INTRODUCTORY

The main object of this paper is to provide a framework for the discussion of the mounting perplexities which now surround the institution of criminal punishment, and to show that any morally tolerable account of this institution must exhibit it as a compromise between distinct and partly conflicting principles.

General interest in the topic of punishment has never been greater than it is at present and I doubt if the public discussion of it has ever been more confused. The interest and the confusion are both in part due to relatively modern scepticism about two elements which have figured as essential parts of the traditionally opposed 'theories' of punishment. On the one hand, the old Benthamite confidence in fear of the penalties threatened by the law as a powerful deterrent, has waned with the growing realization that the part played by calculation of any sort in anti-social behaviour has been exaggerated. On the other hand a cloud of doubt has settled over the keystone of 'retributive' theory. Its advocates can no longer speak with the old confidence that statements of the form 'This man who has broken the law could have kept it' had a univocal or agreed meaning; or where scepticism does not attach to the *meaning* of this form of statement, it has shaken the confidence that we are generally able to distinguish the cases where a statement of this form is true from those where it is not.[1]

Yet quite apart from the uncertainty engendered by these fundamental doubts, which seem to call in question the accounts given of the efficacy, and the morality of punishment by all the old competing theories, the public utterances of those who

[1] See Barbara Wootton, *Social Science and Social Pathology* (1959), for a comprehensive modern statement of these doubts.

conceive themselves to be expounding, as plain men for other plain men, orthodox or common-sense principles (untouched by modern psychological doubts) are uneasy. Their words often sound as if the authors had not fully grasped their meaning or did not intend the words to be taken quite literally. A glance at the parliamentary debates or the *Report of the Royal Commission on Capital Punishment*[2] shows that many are now troubled by the suspicion that the view that there is just one supreme value or objective (e.g. Deterrence, Retribution, or Reform) in terms of which *all* questions about the justification of punishment are to be answered, is somehow wrong; yet, from what is said on such occasions no clear account of what the different values or objectives are, or how they fit together in the justification of punishment, can be extracted.[3]

No one expects judges or statesmen occupied in the business of sending people to the gallows or prison, or in making (or unmaking) laws which enable this to be done, to have much time for philosophical discussion of the principles which make it morally tolerable to do these things. A judicial bench is not and should not be a professorial chair. Yet what is said in public debates about punishment by those specially concerned with it as judges or legislators is important. Few are likely to be more circumspect, and if what they say seems, as it often does, unclear, one-sided and easily refutable by pointing to some aspect of things which they have overlooked, it is likely that in our inherited ways of talking or thinking about punishment there is some persistent drive towards an over-simplification of multiple issues which require separate consideration. To counter this drive what is most needed is *not* the simple admission that instead of a single value or aim (Deterrence, Retribution, Reform, or any other) a plurality of different values and aims should be given as a conjunctive answer to some *single* question concerning the justification of punishment. What is needed is the realization that different principles (each of which may in a sense be called a 'justification') are relevant at different points in any morally acceptable account of punishment. What we should look for are answers to a number of different questions such as: What justifies the general practice of punishment? To whom may punishment be applied? How severely may we punish? In dealing with these and other questions concerning punishment we should bear in mind that in this, as in most other social institutions, the pursuit of one aim may be qualified by or provide an opportunity, not to be missed, for the pursuit of others. Till we have developed this sense of the complexity of punishment (and this prolegomenon aims only to do this) we shall be in no fit state to assess the extent to which the whole institution has been eroded by, or needs to be adapted to, new beliefs about the human mind.

---

[2] (1953) Cmd. 8932.

[3] In the Lords' debate in July 1956 the Lord Chancellor agreed with Lord Denning that 'the ultimate justification of any punishment is not that it is a deterrent but that it is the emphatic denunciation by the community of a crime' yet also said that 'the real crux' of the question at issue is whether capital punishment is a uniquely effective deterrent. See 198 *H. L. Deb* 576, 577, 596 (1956). In his article, 'An Approach to the Problems of Punishment', *Philosophy* 33 (1958), Mr. S. I. Benn rightly observes of Lord Denning's view that denunciation does not imply the deliberate imposition of suffering which is the feature needing justification (p. 328, n.1).

2. JUSTIFYING AIMS AND PRINCIPLES OF DISTRIBUTION

There is, I think, an analogy worth considering between the concept of punishment and that of property. In both cases we have to do with a social institution of which the centrally important form is a structure of *legal* rules, even if it would be dogmatic to deny the names of punishment or property to the similar though more rudimentary rule-regulated practices within groups such as a family, or a school, or in customary societies whose customs may lack some of the standard or salient features of law (e.g. legislation, organized sanctions, courts). In both cases we are confronted by a complex institution presenting different inter-related features calling for separate explanation; or, if the morality of the institution is challenged, for separate justification. In both cases failure to distinguish separate questions or attempting to answer them all by reference to a single principle ends in confusion. Thus in the case of property we should distinguish between the question of the *definition* of property, the question why and in what circumstance it is a *good* institution to maintain, and the questions in what ways individuals may become *entitled* to acquire property and *how much* they should be allowed to acquire. These we may call questions of *Definition, General Justifying Aim,* and *Distribution* with the last subdivided into questions of *Title* and *Amount*. It is salutary to take some classical exposition of the idea of property, say Locke's chapter 'Of Property' in the *Second Treatise*,[4] and to observe how much darkness is spread by the use of a single notion (in this case 'the labour of (a man's) body and the work of his hands') to answer all these different questions which press upon us when we reflect on the institution of property. In the case of punishment the beginning of wisdom (though by no means its end) is to distinguish similar questions and confront them separately.

(A) DEFINITION

Here I shall simply draw upon the recent admirable work scattered through English philosophical[5] journals and add to it only an admonition of my own against the abuse of definition in the philosophical discussion of punishment. So with Mr. Benn and Professor Flew I shall define the standard or central case of 'punishment' in terms of five elements:

    (i) It must involve pain or other consequences normally considered unpleasant.

    (ii) It must be for an offence against legal rules.

    (iii) It must be of an actual or supposed offender for his offence.

    (iv) It must be intentionally administered by human beings other than the offender.

---

[4] Chapter V.

[5] K. Baier, 'Is Punishment Retributive?', *Analysis* 16 (1955), p. 25; A. Flew, 'The Justification of Punishment', *Philosophy* 29 (1954), p. 291; S. I. Benn, op. cit., pp. 325–6.

(v) It must be imposed and administered by an authority constituted by a
legal system against which the offence is committed.

In calling this the standard or central case of punishment I shall relegate to the
position of sub-standard or secondary cases the following among many other possibilities:

(a) Punishments for breaches of legal rules imposed or administered
otherwise than by officials (decentralized sanctions).

(b) Punishments for breaches of non-legal rules or orders (punishments in a
family or school).

(c) Vicarious or collective punishment of some member of a social
group for actions done by others without the former's authorization,
encouragement, control, or permission.

(d) Punishment of persons (otherwise than under (c)) who neither are in
fact nor supposed to be offenders.

The chief importance of listing these sub-standard cases is to prevent the use of
what I shall call the 'definitional stop' in discussions of punishment. This is an abuse
of definition especially tempting when use is made of conditions (ii) and (iii) of the
standard case in arguing against the utilitarian claim that the practice of punishment
is justified by the beneficial consequences resulting from the observance of the laws
which it secures. Here the stock 'retributive' argument[6] is: If *this* is the justification of
punishment, why not apply it, when it pays to do so, to those innocent of any crime,
chosen at random, or to the wife and children of the offender? And here the wrong
reply is: *That*, by definition, would not be 'punishment' and it is the justification of
punishment which is in issue.[7] Not only will this definitional stop fail to satisfy the
advocate of 'Retribution', it would prevent us from investigating the very thing which
modern scepticism most calls in question: namely the rational and moral status of
our preference for a system of punishment under which measures painful to individuals are to be taken against them only when they have committed an offence. Why
do we prefer this to other forms of social hygiene which we might employ to prevent
anti-social behaviour and which we do employ in special circumstances, sometimes
with reluctance? No account of punishment can afford to dismiss this question with
a definition.

[6] A. C. Ewing, *The Morality of Punishment* (1929); D. J. B. Hawkins, 'Punishment and Moral
Responsibility', (1944) 7 *M.L.R.* 205; J. D. Mabbott, 'Punishment', *Mind* 48 (1939), p. 152.

[7] Mr. Benn seemed to succumb at times to the temptation to give 'The short answer to the critics of
utilitarian theories of punishment—that they are theories of *punishment* not of any sort of technique
involving suffering' (op. cit., p. 332). He has since told me that he does not now rely on the definitional
stop.

(B) THE NATURE OF AN OFFENCE

Before we reach any question of justification we must identify a preliminary question to which the answer is so simple that the question may not appear worth asking; yet it is clear that some curious 'theories' of punishment gain their only plausibility from ignoring it, and others from confusing it with other questions. This question is: Why are certain kinds of action forbidden by law and so made crimes or offences? The answer is: To announce to society that these actions are not to be done and to secure that fewer of them are done. These are the common immediate aims of making any conduct a criminal offence and until we have laws made with these primary aims we shall lack the notion of a 'crime' and so of a 'criminal'. Without recourse to the simple idea that the criminal law sets up, in its rules, standards of behaviour to encourage certain types of conduct and discourage others we cannot distinguish a punishment in the form of a fine from a tax on a course of conduct.[8] This indeed is one grave objection to those theories of law which in the interests of simplicity or uniformity obscure the distinction between primary laws setting standards for behaviour and secondary laws specifying what officials must or may do when they are broken. Such theories insist that all legal rules are 'really' directions to officials to exact 'sanctions' under certain conditions, e.g. if people kill.[9] Yet only if we keep alive the distinction (which such theories thus obscure) between the primary objective of the law in encouraging or discouraging certain kinds of behaviour, and its merely ancillary sanction or remedial steps, can we give sense to the notion of a crime or offence.

It is important however to stress the fact that in thus identifying the immediate aims of the criminal law we have not reached the stage of justification. There are indeed many forms of undesirable behaviour which it would be foolish (because ineffective or too costly) to attempt to inhibit by use of the law and some of these may be better left to educators, trades unions, churches, marriage guidance councils, or other non-legal agencies. Conversely there are some forms of conduct which we believe cannot be effectively inhibited without use of the law. But it is only too plain that in fact the law may make activities criminal which it is morally important to promote and the suppression of these may be quite unjustifiable. Yet confusion between the simple immediate aim of any criminal legislation and the justification of punishment seems to be the most charitable explanation of the claim that punishment is *justified* as an 'emphatic denunciation by the community of a crime'. Lord Denning's dictum that this is the ultimate justification of punishment[10] can be saved from Mr. Benn's criticism, noted above, only if it is treated as a blurred statement of the truth that the aim not of punishment, but of criminal legislation is indeed to denounce certain types of conduct

---

[8] This generally clear distinction may be blurred. Taxes may be imposed to discourage the activities taxed though the law does not announce this as it does when it makes them criminal. Conversely fines payable for some criminal offences because of a depreciation of currency become so small that they are cheerfully paid and offences are frequent. They are then felt to be mere taxes because the sense is lost that the rule is meant to be taken seriously as a standard of behaviour.

[9] cf. Kelsen, *General Theory of Law and State* (1945), pp. 30–3, 33–4, 143–4. 'Law is the primary norm, which stipulates the sanction.' (ibid. 61).

[10] In evidence to the Royal Commission on Capital Punishment, Cmd. 8932. para. 53 (1953). *Supra*, p. 2, n. 3.

as something not to be practised. Conversely the immediate aim of criminal legislation cannot be any of the things which are usually mentioned as justifying punishment: for until it is settled what conduct is to be legally denounced and discouraged we have not settled from what we are to *deter* people, or who are to be considered *criminals* from whom we are to exact *retribution*, or on whom we are to wreak *vengeance*, or whom we are to *reform*.

Even those who look upon human law as a mere instrument for enforcing 'morality as such' (itself conceived as the law of God or Nature) and who at the stage of justifying punishment wish to appeal not to socially beneficial consequences but simply to the intrinsic value of inflicting suffering on wrongdoers who have disturbed by their offence the moral order, would not deny that the aim of criminal legislation is to set up types of behaviour (in this case conformity with a pre-existing moral law) as legal standards of behaviour and to secure conformity with them. No doubt in all communities certain moral offences, e.g. killing, will always be selected for suppression as crimes and it is conceivable that this may be done not to protect human beings from being killed but to save the potential murderer from sin; but it would be paradoxical to look upon the law as designed not to discourage murder at all (even conceived as sin rather than harm) but simply to extract the penalty from the murderer.

(C) GENERAL JUSTIFYING AIM

I shall not here criticize the intelligibility or consistency or adequacy of those theories that are united in denying that the practice of a system of punishment is justified by its beneficial consequences and claim instead that the main justification of the practice lies in the fact that when breach of the law involves moral guilt the application to the offender of the pain of punishment is itself a thing of value. A great variety of claims of this character, designating 'Retribution' or 'Expiation' or 'Reprobation' as the justifying aim, fall in spite of differences under this rough general description. Though in fact I agree with Mr. Benn[11] in thinking that these all either avoid the question of justification altogether or are in spite of their protestations disguised forms of Utilitarianism, I shall assume that Retribution, defined simply as the application of the pains of punishment to an offender who is morally guilty, may figure among the conceivable justifying aims of a system of punishment. Here I shall merely insist that it is one thing to use the word Retribution *at this point* in an account of the principle of punishment in order to designate the General Justifying Aim of the system, and quite another to use it to secure that to the question 'To whom may punishment be applied?' (the question of Distribution), the answer given is 'Only to an offender for an offence'. Failure to distinguish Retribution as a General Justifying Aim from retribution as the simple insistence that only those who have broken the law—and voluntarily broken it—may be punished, may be traced in many writers: even perhaps in

[11] Op. cit., pp. 326–35.

Mr. J. D. Mabbott's[12] otherwise most illuminating essay. We shall distinguish the latter from Retribution in General Aim as 'retribution in Distribution'. Much confusing shadow-fighting between utilitarians and their opponents may be avoided if it is recognized that it is perfectly consistent to assert *both* that the General Justifying Aim of the practice of punishment is its beneficial consequences *and* that the pursuit of this General Aim should be qualified or restricted out of deference to principles of Distribution which require that punishment should be only of an offender for an offence. Conversely it does not in the least follow from the admission of the latter principle of retribution in Distribution that the General Justifying Aim of punishment is Retribution though of course Retribution in General Aim entails retribution in Distribution.

We shall consider later the principles of justice lying at the root of retribution in Distribution. Meanwhile it is worth observing that both the old fashioned Retributionist (in General Aim) and the most modern sceptic often make the same (and, I think, wholly mistaken) assumption that sense can only be made of the restrictive principle that punishment be applied only to an offender for an offence if the General Justifying Aim of the practice of punishment is Retribution. The sceptic consequently imputes to all systems of punishment (when they are restricted by the principle of retribution in Distribution) all the irrationality he finds in the idea of Retribution as a General Justifying Aim; conversely the advocates of the latter think the admission of retribution in Distribution is a refutation of the utilitarian claim that the social consequences of punishment are its Justifying Aim.

The most general lesson to be learnt from this extends beyond the topic of punishment. It is, that in relation to any social institution, after stating what general aim or value its maintenance fosters we should enquire whether there are any and if so what principles limiting the unqualified pursuit of that aim or value. Just because the pursuit of any single social aim always has its restrictive qualifier, our main social institutions always possess a plurality of features which can only be understood as a compromise between partly discrepant principles. This is true even of relatively minor legal institutions like that of a contract. In general this is designed to enable individuals to give effect to their wishes to create structures of legal rights and duties, and so to change, in certain ways, their legal position. Yet at the same time there is need to protect those who, in good faith, understand a verbal offer made to them to mean what it would ordinarily mean, accept it, and then act on the footing that a valid contract has been concluded. As against them, it would be unfair to allow the other party to say that the words he used in his verbal offer or the interpretation put on them did not express his real wishes or intention. Hence principles of 'estoppel' or doctrines of the 'objective sense' of a contract are introduced to prevent this and to qualify the principle that the law enforces contracts in order to give effect to the joint wishes of the contracting parties.

---

[12] Op. cit. *supra* p. 5, n. 6. It is not always quite clear what he considers a 'retributive' theory to be.

(D) Distribution

This as in the case of property has two aspects (i) Liability (Who may be punished?) and (ii) Amount. In this section I shall chiefly be concerned with the first of these.[13]

From the foregoing discussions two things emerge. First, though we may be clear as to what value the practice of punishment is to promote, we have still to answer as a question of Distribution 'Who may be punished?' Secondly, if in answer to this question we say 'only an offender for an offence' this admission of retribution in Distribution is not a principle from which anything follows as to the severity or amount of punishment; in particular it neither licenses nor requires, as Retribution in General Aim does, more severe punishments than deterrence or other utilitarian criteria would require.

The root question to be considered is, however, why we attach the moral importance which we do to retribution in Distribution. Here I shall consider the efforts made to show that restriction of punishment to offenders is a simple consequence of whatever principles (Retributive or Utilitarian) constitute the Justifying Aim of punishment.

The standard example used by philosophers to bring out the importance of retribution in Distribution is that of a wholly innocent person who has not even unintentionally done anything which the law punishes if done intentionally. It is supposed that in order to avert some social catastrophe officials of the system fabricate evidence on which he is charged, tried, convicted, and sent to prison or death. Or it is supposed that without resort to any fraud more persons may be deterred from crime if wives and children of offenders were punished vicariously for their crimes. In some forms this kind of thing may be ruled out by a consistent sufficiently comprehensive utilitarianism.[14] Certainly expedients involving fraud or faked charges might be very difficult to justify on utilitarian grounds. We can of course imagine that a negro might be sent to prison or executed on a false charge of rape in order to avoid widespread lynching of many others; but a *system* which openly empowered authorities to do this kind of thing, even if it succeeded in averting specific evils like lynching, would awaken such apprehension and insecurity that any gain from the exercise of these powers would by any utilitarian calculation be offset by the misery caused by their existence. But official resort to this kind of fraud on a particular occasion in breach of the rules and the subsequent indemnification of the officials responsible might save many lives and so be thought to yield a clear surplus of value. Certainly vicarious punishment of an offender's family might do so and legal systems have occasionally though exceptionally resorted to this. An example of it is the Roman *Lex Quisquis* providing for the punishment of the children of those guilty of *majestas*.[15] In extreme cases many might still think it right to resort to these expedients but we should do so with the sense of sacrificing an important principle. We should be conscious of choosing the lesser of two evils, and this would be inexplicable if the principle sacrificed to utility were itself only a requirement of utility.

---

[13] Amount is considered below in Section III (in connexion with Mitigation) and Section V.
[14] See J. Rawls, 'Two Concepts of Rules', *Philosophical Review* 64 (1955), pp. 4–13.
[15] Constitution of emperors Arcadius and Honorius (A.D. 397).

Similarly the moral importance of the restriction of punishment to the offender cannot be explained as merely a consequence of the principle that, the General Justifying Aim is Retribution for immorality involved in breaking the law. Retribution in the Distribution of punishment has a value quite independent of Retribution as Justifying Aim. This is shown by the fact that we attach importance to the restrictive principle that only offenders may be punished, even where breach of this law might not be thought immoral. Indeed even where the laws themselves are hideously immoral as in Nazi Germany, e.g. forbidding activities (helping the sick or destitute of some racial group) which might be thought morally obligatory, the absence of the principle restricting punishment to the offender would be a further *special* iniquity; whereas admission of this principle would represent some residual respect for justice shown in the administration of morally bad laws.

5. REFORM AND THE INDIVIDUALIZATION OF PUNISHMENT

The idea of Mitigation incorporates the conviction that though the amount or severity of punishment is primarily to be determined by reference to the General Aim, yet Justice requires that those who have special difficulties to face in keeping the law which they have broken should be punished less. Principles of Justice however are also widely taken to bear on the amount of punishment in at least two further ways. The first is the somewhat hazy requirement that 'like cases be treated alike'. This is certainly felt to be infringed at least when the ground for different punishment for those guilty of the same crime is neither some personal characteristic of the offender connected with the commission of the crime nor the effect of punishment on him. If a certain offence is specially prevalent at a given time and a judge passes heavier sentences than on previous offenders ('as a warning') some sacrifice of justice to the safety of society is involved though it is often acceptable to many as the lesser of two evils.

The further principle that different kinds of offence of different gravity (however that is assessed) should not be punished with equal severity is one which like other principles of Distribution may qualify the pursuit of our General Aim and is not deducible from it. Long sentences of imprisonment might effectually stamp out car parking offences, yet we think it wrong to employ them; *not* because there is for each crime a penalty 'naturally' fitted to its degree of iniquity (as some Retributionists in General Aim might think); not because we are convinced that the misery caused by such sentences (which might indeed be slight because they would rarely need to be applied) would be greater than that caused by the offences unchecked (as a Utilitarian might argue). The guiding principle is that of a proportion within a system of penalties between those imposed for different offences where these have a distinct place in a commonsense scale of gravity. This scale itself no doubt consists of very broad judgements both of relative moral iniquity and harmfulness of different types of offence: it draws rough distinctions like that between parking offences and homicide, or between 'mercy killing' and murder for gain, but cannot cope with any precise assessment of an individual's wickedness in committing a crime (Who can?) Yet maintenance of proportion of this kind may be important: for where the legal gradation of crimes expressed in the relative severity of penalties diverges sharply from this rough scale, there is a risk of either confusing common morality or flouting it and bringing the law into contempt.

The ideals of Reform and Individualization of punishment (e.g. corrective training, preventive detention) which have been increasingly accepted in English penal practice since 1900 plainly run counter to the second if not to both of these principles of Justice or proportion. Some fear, and others hope, that the further intrusion of these ideals will end with the substitution of 'treatment' by experts for judicial punishment. It is, however, important to see precisely what the relation of Reform to punishment is because its advocates too often misstate it. 'Reform' as an objective is no doubt very vague; it now embraces any strengthening of the offender's disposition and capacity to keep within the law, which is intentionally brought about by human effort otherwise than through fear of punishment. Reforming methods include the inducement of states of repentance, or recognition of moral guilt, or greater awareness of the character and demands of society, the provision of education in a broad sense, vocational training, and psychological treatment. Many seeing the futility and indeed harmful character of much traditional punishment speak as if Reform could and should be the General Aim of the whole practice of punishment or the dominant objective of the criminal law:

The *corrective theory* based upon a conception of multiple causation and curative-rehabilitative treatment, should clearly predominate in legislation and in judicial and administrative practices.[26]

Of course this is a possible ideal but is not an ideal for punishment. Reform can only have a place within a system of punishment as an exploitation of the opportunities presented by the conviction or compulsory detention of offenders. It is not an alternative General Justifying Aim of the practice of punishment but something the pursuit of which within a system of punishment qualifies or displaces altogether recourse to principles of justice or proportion in determining the amount of punishment. This is where both Reform and individualized punishment have run counter to the customary morality of punishment.

There is indeed a paradox in asserting that Reform should 'predominate' in a system of Criminal Law, as if the main purpose of providing punishment for murder was to reform the murderer not to prevent murder; and the paradox is greater where the legal offence is not a serious moral one: e.g. infringing a state monopoly of transport. The objection to assigning to Reform this place in punishment is not merely that punishment entails suffering and Reform does not; but that Reform is essentially a remedial step for which *ex hypothesi* there is an opportunity only at the point where the criminal law has failed in its primary task of securing society from the evil which breach of the law involves. Society is divisible at any moment into two classes (i) those who have actually broken a given law and (ii) those who have not yet broken it but may. To take Reform as the dominant objective would be to forgo the hope of influencing

---

[26] Hall and Glueck, *Cases on Criminal Law and its Enforcement* (1951) p. 14.

the second and—in relation to the more serious offences—numerically much greater class. We should thus subordinate the prevention of first offences to the prevention of recidivism.

Consideration of what conditions or beliefs would make this appear a reasonable policy brings us to the topic to which this paper is a mere prolegomenon: modern sceptical doubt about the whole institution of punishment. If we believed that nothing was achieved by announcing penalties or by the example of their infliction, either because those who do not commit crimes would not commit them in any event or because the penalties announced or inflicted on others are not among the factors which influence them in keeping the law, then some dramatic change concentrating wholly on actual offenders, would be necessary. Just because at present we do not entirely believe this, we have a dilemma and an uneasy compromise. Penalties which we believe are required as a threat to maintain conformity to law at its maximum may convert the offender to whom they are applied into a hardened enemy of society; while the use of measures of Reform may lower the efficacy and example of punishment on others. At present we compromise on this relatively new aspect of punishment as we do over its main elements. What makes this compromise seem tolerable is the belief that the influence which the threat and example of punishment extracts is often independent of the severity of the punishment, and is due more to the disgrace attached to conviction for crime or to the deprivation of freedom which many reforming measures at present used in any case involve.

13

PROPORTIONATE SENTENCES:
A DESERT PERSPECTIVE

Andrew von Hirsch

Criminologists' interest in desert dates from the mid-1970s, with the publication of a number of works arguing that this notion should be seen as the central requirement of justice in sentencing. Once broached, the idea of desert quickly became influential. A number of American states' sentencing-guidelines systems (most notably, those of Minnesota and Oregon) have explicitly relied on it; some European sentencing-reform efforts (particularly those of Finland, Sweden and more recently, England) have done likewise, although these latter schemes make use of statutory statements of guiding principle, rather than specific, numerical guidelines.[1]

The groundwork for this revival of interest in desert was laid already in the post-Second World War literature of analytical moral philosophy. These writings supplied a principled critique of purely instrumental ways thinking about social and penal issues, suggesting how such reckonings were capable of sacrificing individual rights to serve majority interests. The philosophical literature also began exploring the conception of desert, suggesting how it constitutes an integral part of everyday moral judgements.[2]

The movement toward a proportionality-based sentencing theory began, perhaps, in 1971 with the publication of the Quaker-sponsored American Friends Service Committee report, *Struggle for Justice* (1971). The report recommended moderate, proportionate punishments, and opposed deciding sentence severity on predictive or rehabilitative grounds. The Friends Committee report did not rely explicitly on the idea of

---

[1] For an analysis of the Oregon and Minnesota Guidelines, see von Hirsch (1994) and von Hirsch, Knapp and Tonry (1987), ch. 5; for the Swedish sentencing scheme, see Jareborg 1994; for the English system after the Criminal Justice Act 1991, see Ashworth (1995). For guidelines and statutory sentencing principles generally, see Chapter 5 below.

[2] For a critique of utilitarianism, see Williams (1973); for writings on the idea of desert, see Armstrong (1961); H. Morris (1968).

desert as the basis for its proposals; that was left to subsequent writings, including the Australian philosopher John Kleinig's *Punishment and Desert* (1973), my own *Doing Justice* (1976), and the British philosopher R.A. Duff's *Trials and Punishments* (1986). A number of influential British and Scandinavian penologists have also contributed to this literature, including A.E. Bottoms, Andrew Ashworth, Martin Wasik, and Nils Jareborg.[3] The present essay is designed to summarize recent writing in this area, including subsequent work of Duff's and mine (Duff (1996); von Hirsch (1993)).

Desert theories for sentencing have had the attraction that they purport to be about *just* outcomes: the emphasis is on what the offender should fairly receive for his crime, rather than on how his punishment might affect his future behaviour or that of others. It also seems capable of providing more guidance: the sentencer, instead of having to address elusive empirical questions of the crime-preventative effect of the sentence, can address matters more within his or her ken, concerning the seriousness of the criminal offence—how harmful the conduct typically is, how culpable the offender was in committing it (see Selection 4.6 below).

CENSURE AND PENAL DESERT

There have been a variety of retributive or desert-based accounts of punishment, ranging from intuitionist theories (see Selection 4.1 above), to talionic notions of requiting evil for evil, to conceptions that see punishment as taking away the "unjust advantage" over others which the offender obtains by choosing to offend (see Finnis (1980), pp. 263–4).[4] The desert-based conception examined in this essay, however, relies on a different account: one emphasizing the communicative features of punishment.

The criminal sanction censures: punishing consists of doing something unpleasant to someone, because he purportedly has committed a wrong, under circumstances and in a manner that conveys disapprobation of the person for his wrong. Treating the offender as a wrongdoer, Richard Wasserstrom (1980) has pointed out, is central to the idea of punishment. The difference between a tax and a fine, for example, does not rest in the material deprivation imposed—which is money in both cases. It consists, rather, in the fact that with the fine, money is taken in a manner that conveys disapproval or censure; whereas with a tax, no disapproval is implied.

A sanction that treats the conduct as wrong—that is, not a "neutral" sanction—has two important moral functions that are not reducible to crime prevention. One is to recognize the importance of the rights that have been infringed. The censure in punishment conveys to victims and potential victims the acknowledgment that they are wronged by criminal conduct, that rights to which they properly are entitled have been infringed. The other (and perhaps, still more important) role of censure is that of addressing the offender as a moral agent, by appealing to his or her sense of right and wrong. This is not just a crime-prevention strategy, however, for otherwise there would

---

[3] See Suggestions for Further Reading, this chapter, for references.
[4] For a critique of the "unjust advantage" theory, see von Hirsch (1986) pp. 57–9; Duff (1986), ch. 8.

be no point in censuring actors who are repentant already (since they need no blame to make them regret their actions and to try to desist in future) or who seemingly are incorrigible (since they will not change despite the censure). Any human actor, this communicative perspective suggests, should be treated as a moral agent, having the capacity (unless clearly incompetent) of evaluating others' assessment of their conduct. A response to criminal wrongdoing that conveys blame gives the individual the opportunity to respond in ways that are typically those of an agent capable of moral deliberation: to recognize the wrongfulness of the action; feel remorse; to make efforts to desist in future—or to try to give reasons why the conduct was not actually wrong. What a purely "neutral" sanction not embodying blame would deny, even if no less effective in preventing crime, is precisely this recognition of the person's status as a moral agent. A neutral sanction would treat offenders and potential offenders much as beasts in a circus—as beings which must be restrained, intimidated, or conditioned into submission because they are incapable of understanding that predatory conduct is wrong (von Hirsch (1993), ch. 2; Narayan (1993))

Relying on this idea of censure helps remove some of the seeming mysteriousness of penal desert judgements: censure or blaming involves everyday moral judgments used in a wide variety of social contexts, of which punishment is just one. This account also helps address another objection traditionally raised against retributive penal theories, namely, their seeming harshness—their apparent insistence on an eye for an eye. Once the paying back of evil for evil is not seen as the underlying idea, penal desert does not demand visitation of suffering equal to the harm done. What is called for instead is punishments that are *proportionate* to the seriousness of the criminal conduct. Proportionate punishments—even if not involving harm-for-harm equivalence—would suffice to convey blame for various crimes according to their degree of reprehensibleness. Indeed, several advocates of the desert perspective (including myself) have advocated substantial reductions of penalty levels.[5]

Can the institution of punishment be explained purely in terms of censure? Punishment does convey blame, but does so in a special way—through visitation of deprivation ("hard treatment") on the offender. That deprivation is, of course, the vehicle through which the blame is expressed. But why use this vehicle, rather than simply expressing blame in symbolic fashion? Some adherents of the communicative view of desert, most notably R.A. Duff, hold that the hard-treatment component of the penal sanction can itself be explained in desert terms: Duff treats the deprivations involved in punishment as providing a kind of secular penance (see Selection 4.3 above).[6] I have my doubts, however. The reason for having the institution of punishment (that is, for expressing disapproval through hard treatment, instead of merely censuring) seems to have to do with keeping predatory behaviour within tolerable limits. Had the criminal sanction no usefulness in preventing crime, there should be no need to visit material deprivation on those who offend. True, we might still wish to devise another way of issuing

---

[5] See, e.g., Singer (1979); Ashworth (1995), ch. 9; Duff (1986); Jareborg (1995); von Hirsch (1993).

[6] On Duff's view, the hard treatment in punishment should serve to bring the criminal to understand, and repent of his wrongdoing—and also to provide a vehicle which will enable him to work through and express his penitent understanding.

authoritative judgements of blaming, for such predatory behaviour as occurs. But those judgements, in the interest of keeping state-inflicted suffering to a minimum, would no longer be linked to purposive infliction of suffering (von Hirsch 1993, 14).

If the criminal sanction thus serves to prevent crime as well as censure, how is this consistent with treating offenders and potential offenders as moral agents? The hard-treatment in punishment, on my view, serves a prudential reason for obedience to those insufficiently motivated by the penal censure's moral appeal. But this should *supplement* rather than replace the normative reasons for desisting from crime conveyed by penal censure—that is, it provides an *additional* reason for compliance to those who are capable of recognizing the law's moral demands, but who arc also tempted to disobey them. The law thus addresses *ourselves*, not a distinct "criminal" class of those considered incapable of grasping moral appeals. And it addresses us neither as perfectly moral agents (we are not like angels), nor as beasts which only can be coerced through threats; but rather, as moral but fallible agents who need some prudential supplement to help us resist criminal temptation (von Hirsch (1993) pp. 12–14; see also Narayan (1993)). However, this account (as will be discussed further below) calls for moderation in the overall severity in punishment levels. The harsher the penalty system is, the less plausible it becomes to see it as embodying chiefly a moral appeal rather than a system of bare threats.

THE RATIONALE FOR PROPORTIONALITY

In a minimal sense, proportionality always had a role in sentencing policy: penalties that were grossly excessive in relation to the gravity of the offence were perceived as unfair. Statutory maximum sentences reflected that understanding, and it also had a constitutional dimension: some jurisdictions adopted a constitutional bar against grossly excessive punishments.[7] This, however, gave the notion of proportionality only the outer, constraining role of barring draconian sanctions for lesser offences. Short of these (rather high) maximum limits, proportionality had small weight in theories about how sanctions should be determined, with consequentialist concerns (about rehabilitation, incapacitation, and deterrence) counting chiefly instead.

What is distinctive about contemporary desert theory is it moves notions of proportionality from this merely peripheral to a central role in deciding sanctions. The primary basis for deciding quanta of punishments, under this theory, is the principle of proportionality or "commensurate deserts", requiring the severity of the penalty to be proportionate to the gravity of the defendant's criminal conduct. The criterion for deciding the quantum of punishment is thus retrospective rather than consequentialist: the seriousness of the offence for which the defendant stands convicted.

---

[7] The U.S. Supreme Court has formerly held that grossly excessive punishments violated the Constitutional ban on cruel and unusual punishments (see *Weems v. U.S.* [(1910) 217 U.S. 349]), but the Court later overruled that doctrine (see *Rummel v. Estelle* (1980) 445 U.S. 263).The German Constitutional Court has adopted doctrines barring gross disproportionality of sentence in relation to the seriousness of the crime.

What is the basis for this principle? The censure account, just discussed, provides the explanation. If punishment embodies blame, then how much one punishes will convey how much the conduct is condemned. If crime X is punished more severely than crime Y, this connotes the greater disapprobation of crime X. Punishments, consequently, should be allocated consistently with their blaming implications. When penalties are arrayed in severity according to the gravity of offences, the disapprobation thereby conveyed will reflect the degree of reprehensibleness of the conduct. When punishments are arrayed otherwise, this is not merely inefficient (who knows?—it might sometimes "work"), but unfair; offenders are being visited with more or less censure than the comparative blameworthiness of their conduct would warrant (von Hirsch 1993, ch. 2).

Equity is sacrificed when the proportionality principle is disregarded, even when this is done for the sake of crime prevention. Suppose that offenders A and B commit and are convicted of criminal conduct of approximately the same degree of seriousness. Suppose B is deemed more likely to re-offend, and therefore is given a longer sentence. Notwithstanding the possible preventative utility of that sentence, the objection remains that B, through his more severe punishment, is being treated as more to blame than A, though their conduct has the same degree of blameworthiness.

A possible objection (see Dolinko (1992)) to this argument might run as follows: if the component of "hard treatment" in the criminal sanction serves a crime-preventative as well as a purely censuring function (as argued earlier in this essay), then why cannot one allocate the relative severities of punishment in part on preventative grounds rather than purely on the basis of offence seriousness? The reply is that punishment's deprivations and its reprobative connotations are inextricably intermixed: it is the threatened penal deprivation that expresses the degree of censure. If the deprivations visited on a given type of crime are increased, even for preventative reasons, this (necessarily) increases the severity of the punishment. But changing the severity, relative to other penalties, alters the implicit censure—which would not be justified if the seriousness of the conduct is itself unchanged (von Hirsch 1993, pp. 16–17).

DESERT AS "DETERMINING" OR "LIMITING"?

If the principle of proportionality is so important, is it a "determining" or merely a "limiting" principle? While our sense of justice tells us that criminals should be punished as they deserve, there do not seem to be definite quanta of severity associated with our desert-judgements. Armed robbers have committed a serious offence, deserving of substantial punishment, but it is not apparent whether that should consist of two years' confinement, three years, or some shorter or longer period.

One response to this problem has been Norval Morris's: to say that desert is merely a limiting principle (see Selection 4.5 below). It tells us, he asserts, not how much robbers deserve, but only some broad limits beyond which their punishments would be *un*deserved. Within such limits, the sentence can be decided on other (for example, predictive) grounds. This view, however, would mean that persons who commit similar crimes could receive quite different amounts of punishment. If punishment embodies blame as a central characteristic, it becomes morally problematic to visit such different degrees of severity, and hence of implicit blame, on comparably blameworthy transgressions.

A conceivable opposite response, but scarcely a plausible one, would be the heroic intuitionist stance: that if we only ponder hard enough we will perceive deserved quanta of punishments: that robbers ordinarily deserve so-and-so many months or years of confinement, and so forth. Our intuitions, however, fail to provide such answers.

The way out of this apparent dilemma is to recognize the crucial difference between the comparative ranking of punishments on one hand, and the overall magnitude and anchoring of the penalty scale on the other. With respect to comparative rankings, *ordinal* proportionality provides considerable guidance: persons convicted of similar crimes should receive punishments of comparable severity (save in special aggravating or mitigating circumstances altering the harm or culpability of the conduct in the particular circumstances); and persons convicted of crimes of differing gravity should suffer punishments correspondingly graded in onerousness. These ordinal-proportionality requirements are no mere limits, and they are infringed when equally reprehensible conduct is punished markedly unequally in the manner that Morris suggests (von Hirsch 1986, ch. 4).

Desert provides less constraint, however, on the penalty scale's overall dimensions and anchoring points. This is because the censure expressed through penal deprivations is, to a considerable degree, a convention. When a penalty scale reflects the comparative gravity of crimes, making *pro rata* decreases or increases in the prescribed sanctions constitutes a change in that convention.

This distinction helps resolve the dilemma just mentioned. The leeway which desert allows in fixing the scale's overall degree of onerousness explains why we cannot perceive a single right or fitting penalty for a crime. Whether X months, Y months, or somewhere in between is the appropriate penalty for robbery depends on how the scale has been anchored and what punishments are prescribed for other crimes. Once those anchoring points are decided, however, the more restrictive requirements of ordinal proportionality apply. This explains why it would be inappropriate to give short prison terms to some robbers and long ones to other robbers, on the basis (say) of predictive factors not reflecting the degree of seriousness of the criminal conduct.

Does this purported solution still leave the anchoring of the scale too wide open? Could it not permit a very severe penalty scale, as long it is not *so* harsh as to impose drastic penalties on manifestly trivial crimes? My suggested answer to this question has been that high overall severity levels are inconsistent with the moral functions of penal censure. Through punishments' censuring features, the criminal sanction offers a normative reason for desisting to human beings seen as moral agents: that doing certain acts is wrong and hence should be refrained from. Punishments' material deprivations can then be viewed (as noted earlier) as providing a supplemental disincentive—as providing humans (given human fallibility and the temptations of offending) an additional prudential reason for complying with the law. The higher penalty levels rise, however, the less the normative reasons for desisting supplied by penal censure will count, and the more the system becomes in effect a bare system of threats (in Hegel's apt words, a stick that might be raised to a dog). To the extent this argument is accepted, it points toward keeping penalties at moderate levels (von Hirsch 1993, ch. 5).[8]

INCLUSION OF CRIME-CONTROL AIMS?

Desert theory sets priorities among sentencing aims: it assumes that it is more important to have proportionately ordered sanctions than to seek other objectives—say, incapacitating those deemed higher risks. This understandably evokes discomfort: why cannot one seek proportionality *and* pursue other desired ends, whether they be treatment, incapacitation or something else?

To some extent, a desert model permits consideration of other aims: namely, to the degree this is consistent with the proportionate ordering of penalties. Thus when there is a choice between two non-custodial sanctions of approximately equivalent severity (say, a unit-fine of so many days' earnings and intensive probation for a specified duration), proportionality constraints are not offended when one of these is chosen over the other on (say) treatment grounds. Desert theorists thus have come forward with schemes for scaling intermediate, non-custodial penalties; these sanctions would be ranked in severity according to the gravity of the crime, but penalties of roughly equivalent onerousness could be substituted for one another when treatment or feasiblity concerns so indicate (see more fully, Selection 6.4 below). Nevertheless, a pure desert model remains a constraining one: ulterior aims may be relied upon only where these do not substantially alter the comparative severity of penalties. Giving substantial extra prison time to persons deemed high risks would thus breach the model's requirements. Why not, then, relax the model's constraints to allow greater scope to such other aspirations?

A possibility—sometimes referred to as a "modified" desert model—would be to relax the constraints to a limited degree. Proportionality would ordinarily determine comparative punishment levels, but deviations would be permitted in case of the gravest risks of crime (see Robinson (1987); von Hirsch (1993) pp. 48–53). Here, the idea is that avoiding extraordinary harms is so important a goal as to warrant some sacrifice of fairness. This position differs from ordinary penal consequentialism, however, in that departures from desert requirements could be invoked only exceptionally, to deal with threats of an extraordinary nature (von Hirsch 1993, pp. 48–53).[9] Alternatively, deviations could more regularly be permitted, but these would be restricted ones: say, a deviation of no more than 10 or 15 per cent from the deserved sentence. While departures from proportionality involve a sacrifice of equity, the extent of that sacrifice depends on the degree of the deviation from desert constraints. Limited deviations, it might be

---

[8] There exists a conceptually separate further reason for keeping penalty levels low—namely, the idea of "parsimony"—of keeping state-inflicted suffering to a minimum; see von Hirsch (1993), p. 111.

[9] For another defence of such a position, see Bottoms and Brownsword (Selection 3.4 above). Unlike those authors, however, I do not see the issue as one involving conflict of rights—for reasons set forth in von Hirsch (1993), p. 51.

argued, would permit the pursuit of ulterior objectives without "too much" unfairness (von Hirsch 1993, pp. 54–56).

These mixed approaches still make desert the primary determinant for the ordering of penalties, but give some extra scope for ulterior purposes. Even such schemes remain constraining, however: especially dangerous offenders might be given substantial extra prison time, but not the ordinary potential recidivist; some extra leeway might be granted to suit a non-custodial penalty to the offender's apparent treatment needs, but not a great deal.

Could still more scope be given to non-desert considerations? In a hybrid rationale, either desert will predominate or something else will. If—in the ordinary case— the seriousness of the crime is the penalty's primary determinant, the system remains desert-dominated. If other (say, crime-preventive) aims are given the greater emphasis, however, that creates a system dominated by those aims. That will re-introduce the familiar problems of consequentialist sentencing schemes—for example, those relating to equity among offenders, and those of insufficient systematic knowledge of preventive effects (see Chapters 1 to 3 above).

In assessing these alternatives, it needs to be borne in mind that even a "purely" desert-based sentencing scale is likely to have collateral crime-prevention benefits— in such deterrence as its penalties achieve, and in the possible incapacitative effects of the prison sentences it prescribes for serious crimes. Departing from proportionality for the sake of crime prevention, then, will call not just for a showing that preventative effects might be achieved (for a desert-based system may achieve these too); instead, it would call for a showing that the departures are likely to yield *enhanced* preventative effects—which is no easy matter to establish. And here, one is likely to confront a fairness/effectiveness trade-off: because crime rates tend to be rather insensitive to small variations in punishment, modest departures from proportionality are likely to have relatively little impact; large departures might possibly work better, but these precisely are the ones that are most troublesome on moral grounds (see Selection 3.7 above).

OTHER ISSUES: SEVERITY AND SOCIAL DEPRIVATION

Must desert lead to harsh penalties? As the theory emerged and became influential at a time when penalty levels rose in many jurisdictions, some critics have argued that the theory must in part be responsible for such increases (Hudson 1987). However, desert theory itself does not require a severe sentencing policy—indeed, as noted earlier, it permits (indeed, arguably points toward) considerable penalty reductions. Moreover, the sentence-reform schemes which rely explicitly on notions of desert tend not to be severe ones: the Minnesota and Oregon sentencing guidelines, for example, call for relatively modest penalties by American standards; European desert-oriented sentencing standards, such as those of Finland and Sweden, are likewise associated with penal moderation (von Hirsch 1993, ch. 10). Measures which most clearly call for tougher sanctions tend to utilize criteria inconsistent with proportionality: mandatory sentences, for example, select particular offence categories for harsh treatment, without regard to the gravity of the offence involved, or the penalties imposed for other offences (see Chapter 9 below).

Another issue is that concerning just punishment and social deprivation (see Murphy 1973). Many offenders live in grim social environments that restrict their opportunities for living tolerable and law-abiding lives. Should such persons be punished differently? The penal law is a poor instrument for rectifying social ills: it is social policy, rather than criminal policy, that is the appropriate instrument for addressing problems of social deprivation. But the question remains disturbing, nevertheless. If social policy fails to alleviate poverty and deprivation, how should the deprived offender be sentenced?

It has been pointed out that desert theory at least does not *add* to the punishment imposed on deprived persons—whereas penal consequentialism would do so, to the extent that social deprivation is a sign (say) of greater dangerousness (von Hirsch 1976, ch. 17). But the question remains whether such persons deserve *reduced* punishments. Arguably, reductions could be warranted on grounds of reduced culpability—in view of the greater obstacles such persons face in leading law-abiding lives (see Selection 4.9 below).[10] Granting such mitigation would, however, create a host of practical and political difficulties—so that the perplexity remains.

REFERENCES

American Friends Service Committee (1971) *Struggle for Justice* (New York: Hill & Wang).

Armstrong, K. G. (1961) "The Retributivist Hits Back" 70 *Mind* 471.

Ashworth, A., *Sentencing and Criminal Jsutice* (2nd edn., 1995).

Dolinko, D. (1992) "Three Mistakes of Retributivism", 39 *UCLA Law Review* 39.

Duff, R. A. (1986) *Trials and Punishments* (Cambridge: Cambridge University Press).

——(1996) "Penal Communications", in M. Tonry (ed.), *Crime and Justice: A Review of Research*, Vol. 20, p. 1.

Dworkin, R. (1977) *Taking Rights Seriously* (Cambridge, Mass.: Harvard University Press).

Finnis, J. (1980) *Natural Law and Natural Rights* (Oxford: Oxford University Press).

Hudson, B. (1987) *Justice Through Punishment* (London: St. Martin's Press).

Jareborg, N. (1995) "The Swedish Sentencing Reform", in C. M. V. Clarkson and R. Morgan (eds.), *The Politics of Sentencing Reform* (Oxford: Oxford University Press).

Kleinig, J. (1973) *Punishment and Desert* (The Hague: Martinus Nijhoff).

Morris, H. (1968) "Persons and Punishment" 52 *The Monist* 475.

Murphy, J. G. (1973), "Marxism & Retribution", 2 *Philosophy and Public Affairs* 217.

Narayan, U. (1993) "Adequate Responses and Preventive Benefits" 13 *Oxford Journal of Legal Studies* 13.

Robinson, P. (1987) "Hybrid Principles for the Distribution of Criminal Sanctions" 82 *Northwestern Law Review* 19.

Singer, R. (1979) *Just Deserts* (Cambridge, Mass.: Ballinger Publishing Co.).

von Hirsch, A. (1994) "Proportionality and Parsimony in American Sentencing

---

[10] For the pros and cons of granting such mitigation, see von Hirsch (1993), pp. 106–8.

Guidelines", in C. M. V. Clarkson and R. Morgan (eds.), *The Politics of Sentencing Reform* (Oxford: Oxford University Press).

———(1993) *Censure and Sanctions* (Oxford: Oxford University Press).

———(1986) *Past or Future Crimes* (Manchester: Manchester University Press).

———(1976) *Doing Justice* (New York: Hill and Wang).

von Hirsch, A., Knapp, K., and Tonry, M. (1987) *The Sentencing Commission and Its Guidelines* (Boston, Mass.: Northeastern University Press).

Wasserstrom, R. (1980) "Punishment", in R. Wasserstrom, *Philosophy and Social Issues: Five Studies* (Notre Dame, Ind.: University of Notre Dame Press).

Williams, B. (1973) "A Critique of Utilitarianism" in J. S. C. Smart and B. Williams, *Utilitarianism: For and Against* (Cambridge Univeristy Press).

14

PROPORTIONALITY, PARSIMONY, AND INTERCHANGEABILITY OF PUNISHMENTS

Michael Tonry

If intermediate punishments are to be used more widely, procedures and principles governing their use must be developed. Although new intermediate punishments are often conceived in large part for use in lieu of incarceration, experience on three continents shows that many judges prefer to impose such penalties on offenders who would not otherwise be bound for prison. Working out procedures governing intermediate punishments will be hard enough. Working out principles governing imposition of penalties in individual cases may be harder and will require consideration of finer-grained issues than writing on the philosophy of punishment traditionally addresses. Most philosophical writing on punishment deals with broad issues of justification. Insofar as questions of distribution are considered, attention focuses on prison sentences. Because prison sentences can be expressed in seemingly objective units of months or years, and since 'disparity' in prison terms looks prima facie to be a bad thing, recent writing on the distribution of punishment celebrates what Andrew von Hirsch (1992) calls 'the principle of proportionality.'

The theses of this essay are that strong proportionality constraints in the distribution of punishments generally are likely to cause more injustice than they prevent, and that application of strong proportionality constraints to intermediate sanctions will stifle their development, circumscribe their use, and produce avoidable injustices.

There are three fundamental problems with a strong proportionality principle. First, by celebrating equality in suffering for 'like-situated' offenders, it often requires imposition of more severe and intrusive punishments than are required by prevailing social norms and political values. Second, it misleadingly objectifies punishment, by allocating punishments in terms of 'like-situated offenders' and generic penalties. Third, it ignores the problem of 'just deserts in an unjust society'. Most offenders committing common law crimes come from disadvantaged backgrounds, and disproportionately they come from minority groups. Arguments for a highly proportional system of deserved punishments evade the question of whether offenders from deeply deprived backgrounds deserve the same penalties as do other, less deprived, offenders.

A punishment system permitting interchangeability of roughly equivalent penalties is likely, overall, to be more just, less harsh, and more sensitive to problems of social injustice than a punishment system predicated on desert-based proportionality. 'Like-situated offenders' convicted of comparable crimes can justly receive quite different sentences including financial penalties for some, incarceration for others, and community-based sanctions for still others.

This essay attempts to demonstrate and defend the preceding observations. Part I describes policy developments that make consideration of the applied philosophy of intermediate sanctions timely. Part II reviews philosophical writings on punishment and argues that principles of proportionality and parsimony are in stark conflict in general and in many specific cases. Part III examines in some detail Andrew von Hirsch's arguments for a strong principle of proportionality and his proposals for devising a punishment scheme premised on proportionality concerns. Part IV offers a critique of von Hirsch's proposals and Part V sketches a counter-proposal that reconciles concerns for proportionality and parsimony.

WHY INTERMEDIATE PUNISHMENTS?

Policy makers in the United Kingdom and the United States are considering how to incorporate intermediate punishments into comprehensive sentencing policies.[1] Passage in the UK of the Criminal Justice Act 1991 with its increased emphasis on non-custodial penalties has drawn attention to the subject.

In the United States, historically high and growing prison populations, severe pressures on public budgets, and the evolution of the American sentencing reform movement have combined to focus interest on non-custodial (or partly custodial) penalties, and on the integration of non-custodial penalties into comprehensive systems of sentencing guidelines.

American incarceration rates have risen steadily since 1970 but startlingly since 1980, when the number of sentenced offenders held in state prisons (that is, disregarding those in county jails serving sentences of one year or less) stood at 330,000. By 30 June 1992, that number had increased to 856,000. The combined prison and jail incarceration rate in 1990 was 455 per 100,000 population, a level five to ten times that of most developed countries. On 31 December 1991, state prisons were on average operating at 131 per cent of rated capacity and federal prisons at 146 per cent.

Competition for scarce public funds, coupled with a continuing federal commitment to a 'war on drugs' and an ever-toughening crime control strategy, produced great interest in the 1980s in a wide range of intermediate punishments, including house

---

[1] Citations of sources for empirical assertions in this section can be found in Morris and Tonry (1990).

arrest, intensive (sometimes fifteen to twenty-five contacts per month) probation, day-reporting centers, restitution, community service, electronic monitoring, residential drug treatment, day fines, and boot camps.

Many intermediate punishment programs have failed to achieve their objectives. Initiated in hopes of reducing prison crowding (by diverting less serious offenders from prison), reducing recidivism (by enhancing surveillance and some services), and reducing costs (by shifting offenders from more-expensive prisons to less-expensive community programs), in many programs none of these goals are being realised. When tested, these programs generally achieve no worse, but no better, recidivism rates than do prisons when comparable groups of offenders are compared. Many judges order intermediate punishments for offenders who otherwise would receive probation. This increases costs. Moreover, because intermediate sanctions are more intensive and structured than probation, more condition violations and new offenses are observed and acted upon; in many programs 40 to 50 per cent of offenders are ejected for misconduct and sent to prison or jail as punishment. Since many of these offenders would in past years have received probation, they are in effect shifted twice upwards, first to an intermediate sanction and then to prison. This also increases costs. If intermediate punishments are to achieve their goals, it has become clear that standards are needed both for assigning offenders to particular penalties and for setting 'back-up' penalties for violations of program conditions.

A few states have taken tentative steps toward standards for use of intermediate sanctions. Washington allows for modest interchangeability of punishments (e.g., day-for-day substitution of community service days for up to thirty days confinement). Oregon, in addition to setting presumptive sentencing ranges in months, specifies 'punishment units' for each cell in its guidelines grid, to provide a generic coin to permit (an as yet uncompleted task) convertibility of sanctions. Pennsylvania includes the words 'intermediate punishments' in the lower levels of its guidelines, although no other guidance is offered. Many Minnesota counties, and some individual judges across the country, use local guidelines for non-custodial penalties.

There are, however, no well-established models for devising comprehensive systems of structured sentencing discretion that incorporate intermediate punishments. Both mechanics and normative rationales need development. Unusually, policy makers are interested in learning what theorists and philosophers can tell them, and if the advice makes sense, policy makers are likely to pay attention.

Two broad, albeit not fully developed, approaches have been proposed. One, associated with Andrew von Hirsch, Martin Wasik, and Andrew Ashworth, among others, calls for stacking of punishments: prison terms scaled to offense severity for the most serious crimes, restrictive community sanctions for the next-most-serious, large financial penalties for the next-most-serious, and so on, allowing relatively little latitude for imposition of different kinds of punishment on like-situated offenders (Wasik and von Hirsch, 1988; Ashworth, 1992). A second, proposed by Norval Morris and me, allows for much greater substitution and interchangeability of punishments and proportions maximum penal vulnerability to offense severity but allows substantial discretion to impose less severe sentences (Morris and Tonry, 1990).

Increased interest in intermediate sanctions has sharply posed the conflict between principles of proportionality and parsimony. Concern for proportionality calls for like treatment of like-situated offenders. Concern for parsimony, a Hippocratic criminal justice prescription to do least harm, calls for imposing the least severe punishment that meets legitimate social purposes.

The tension between proportionality and parsimony has always existed below the surface in indeterminate sentencing systems, and is likely to survive silently in recent Swedish and English schemes that rely on principles rather than numbers for guidance to judges. Without guidelines, judges can balance concerns for deserved punishments and parsimony in individual cases. Lip service can be paid to concern for horizontal equity, avoiding disparity, and treating like cases alike. Without concrete criteria of proportionate sentencing, individual sentences cannot easily be assessed for their consistency with proportionality principles.

The tension between proportionality and parsimony, however, became apparent when American jurisdictions began to develop sentencing guidelines for prison sentences and it became acute when policy makers began to work on standards for non-custodial penalties. American sentencing guidelines to date mostly set standards for prison sentences calibrated to measures of current and past criminality. Proportionality is a prominent feature. Guidelines derive in part from concern to alleviate sentencing disparities; once offenses are scaled for severity, some proportionality between penalties for different offenses inexorably follows. In effect, sentencing guidelines for prison sentences prefer proportionality over parsimony. If some sentences are harsher than judges believe appropriate, the harshness is said to be justifiable because the punishment is no more or less severe than that suffered by 'like-situated' offenders.

Jurisdiction and Distribution

The tension between proportionality and parsimony and the problem of just deserts in an unjust world are the fundamental problems facing an applied philosophy of punishment concerning intermediate sanctions. This section attempts to frame these issues by considering how Bentham and Kant might address proportionality in distribution and then looking at how modern writers have addressed it.

Proportionality based on justification

Neither classical utilitarian punishment theories in principle nor classical retributive theories in practice provide convincing explanations of why punishment should (or can) observe strict proportionality conditions.

Proportionality is presumably a value for utilitarians only to the extent that its non-observance produces net dissatisfaction. For utilitarians, invoking Bentham, punishment itself is an evil and should be used as sparingly as possible: 'upon the principle of utility, if [punishment] ought at all to be admitted, it ought only to be admitted in as far as it promises to exclude some greater evil' (Bentham, 1948 [1789], p. 281, quoted in Pincoffs, 1966, p. 20).

No doubt utilitarian concerns require some observance of proportionality in punishment. Punishments completely divorced from community notions of fairness – in our time, perhaps, to refuse to punish child abusers, or to sentence two of three equally culpable participants in a crime to five years imprisonment and the third to a $50 fine – would produce unacceptable levels of dissatisfaction and indicate, on utility grounds, that some greater acknowledgement of the importance of violated community values is required; however, that imposes at most only a weak proportionality condition, relating punishment not to notions of desert but to notions of social consequences.

Thoroughgoing retributivists, for whom a retributive justification of punishment entails retribution in distribution, might prefer a system of perfectly proportioned punishments, but in practice such a system is unrealizable. Kant's principle of equality, the Right of Retaliation, 'the mode and measure of punishment which public justice takes as its principle and standard', has practical limits. It may be that 'the principle of equality...may be rendered by saying that the undeserved evil which anyone commits on another is to be regarded as perpetrated on himself' (Kant, 1887 [1797], pp. 195–7), but it is far from clear what that means. Capital punishment for murder, a $500 penalty for a $500 theft, perhaps (squeamishly) a beating for an assault; these crimes and punishments satisfy the test. But how to punish an attempted murder, a rape, emotional abuse of the elderly, securities fraud, environmental crimes? No doubt systems of scaled punishment can be devised, but only with formidable working out of details. Does Kant's principle of equality require punishment scaled to the offender's culpability, to the offender's benefit, to the victim's harm? What of villainous attempts that serendipitously produce no harm? What of venial crimes that unforeseeably produce great harm? Is the offender's evil-doing to be assessed as the Recording Angel would, taking account of his weaknesses, the pressures to which he was subject, his motives, or primarily as measured by the objective evil his offense embodies?

PROPORTIONALITY IN DISTRIBUTION

The normative conflict concerning proportionality in distribution is between those (e.g., Ashworth, 1992; von Hirsch, 1992) who believe that equality and proportion in distribution are overridingly important and those (Hart, 1968; Honderich, 1989, pp. 237–41; Morris and Tonry, 1990, ch. 4; Walker, 1991, ch. 15) who do not.

There are at least three major categories of writers on punishment who argue for weak proportionality conditions. First, writing in a utilitarian framework, and positing that punishment has principally preventive purposes, H. L. A. Hart writes of 'the somewhat hazy requirement that 'like cases be treated alike'' (1968, p. 24). Hart's argument for this modest recognition of proportionality is, however, not retributively premised but derives from concern for the adverse social effects of divorcing punishment too greatly from common morality: 'for where the legal gradation of crime expressed in the relative severity of penalties diverges sharply from this rough scale, there is a risk of confusing common morality or flouting it and bringing the law into contempt' (p. 25).

Second, proponents of hybrid theories, including Morris (1974) and Honderich (1989), argue that principled systems of punishment must take account of both preventive and retributive considerations. Honderich (1989), for example, argues that retribution, in James Fitzjames Stephens' sense of revenge and satisfaction of grievance, and deterrence, each have roles to play (1989, pp. 233–7). Morris (1974) argues for a system of limiting retributivism in which punishment's primary purposes are preventive but subject to the desert constraint that punishments be 'not undeserved' and, within the range of not undeserved punishments, the parsimonious constraint that no punishment be imposed that is more severe than is necessary to achieve legitimate social purposes.

Third, proponents of a variety of ideal punishment theories reject their policy implications on 'just deserts in an unjust world' grounds but presumably would allow room for distributive echoes of their ideal rationales. R. A. Duff, for example, rejects his own retributive/expressive ideal theory in favor of deterrent approaches for social injustice reasons. This is my own view as well: in the abstract I have some sympathy for a retributive scheme with strong proportionality conditions; in practice, observing that the vast preponderance of common law offenders are poor, ill-educated, often mentally subnormal, and often from minority groups, I believe that punishment strongly committed to proportionality will exacerbate social injustice and further disadvantage the already disadvantaged.

THE PRINCIPLE OF PROPORTIONALITY

Andrew von Hirsch has, over the last fifteen years (e.g., 1976, 1985, 1992), shown how a punishment system can be devised and justified that has equality and proportionality as central elements. For many people, there is strong intuitive appeal in a punishment system that attaches high value to equality and proportionality. Public opinion surveys have repeatedly demonstrated strong public support for the maxim 'treat like cases alike and different cases differently' (e.g., Doble, Immerwahr, and Richardson, 1991).

Von Hirsch acknowledges both the limits of Kant's 'principle of equality' and human incapacity to specify the single ideally appropriate punishment for any individual offender who has committed a particular offense, but nonetheless offers a comprehensive scheme for assuring proportionality. He distinguishes between ordinal and cardinal magnitudes of punishments (1985, ch. 4). The cardinal magnitude is the unknowable, single deserved penalty. Ordinal magnitude indicates a crime's seriousness relative to other crimes. In von Hirsch's scheme, cardinal magnitudes can be approximated or negotiated for use in setting the 'anchoring points' of a punishment scale, the most and (possibly) the least severe punishments that can appropriately be imposed on offenders. Within these anchoring points, punishments can be scaled in terms of relative severity of offenses. Assuming, for example, that crimes were divided into fifteen severity categories, level 8 offenses should, all else being equal, be punished more severely than level 7 offenses and less severely than level 9 offenses. Thus, the combination of cardinal anchors with ordinal rankings celebrates equality (all level 8 offenses receive similar punishments) and proportionality (less serious offenses receive less severe punishments, more serious offenses receive more severe punishments). Some subsidiary issues remain a bit vague, including specification of anchoring points, the step problem (how many severity categories), and the interval problem (are the severity differences between offense levels the same throughout the scale, or may it be that, for example, level 10 offenses are only 10 per cent more serious than level 9 offenses while level 5 offenses are twice as serious as those at level 4?). In a work in progress, von Hirsch is addressing these and other questions.

RATIONALE

The overall premise of von Hirsch's argument is that punishment is an exercise in blaming, and proportionality is a necessary implication. Persons committing relatively more severe offenses are relatively more blameworthy and deserve relatively more severe punishments.

PRIOR RECORD

Von Hirsch's punishment scheme is based principally on *offenses*, with only minor adjustments to take account of prior criminality. Some writers on just deserts (Fletcher, 1978; Singer, 1979) argue that prior criminality should have no effect on punishment for a new crime; prior penalties have 'paid for' prior crimes.

Von Hirsch allows some increases of penalty for past crimes on the rationale that penalties for a first offense should be somewhat less than is deserved. Because a first offense may be out of character and result from extenuating situational conditions, first offenders may be less blameworthy than it appears and should be given the benefit of the doubt. For some number of subsequent offenses, a gradually disappearing discount may be appropriate. Thereafter each offense should receive its full, deserved, proportionate punishment.

MEASURE OF OFFENSE

Although von Hirsch has written about concepts of scaling crime severity, his proportionality analysis takes criminal codes more or less as given. Thus, answers to classical, substantive law harm-versus-culpability arguments – whether attempts should be punished as seriously as completed crimes, whether fortuitous harm (the picked pocket containing the unexpected thousand-dollar coin, the assault that unforeseeably results in death) is relevant to punishment, whether there should be a general defense of necessity – do not shape the scale.

Measure of culpability

Von Hirsch's scheme is premised on legal, rather than moral, assessments of blame-worthiness (although the rationale for leniency for first offenders shades into character assessment). The offender is to be blamed for the *offense*, not for the moral culpability it expresses. If Jean Valjean and Leona Helmsley are both convicted of stealing bread, they are to be blamed for stealing bread and identically punished accordingly. Although von Hirsch coined the phrase 'just deserts in an unjust society' in *Doing Justice* (1976), he argues that, on balance, disadvantaged offenders will be better served under a desert scheme than under a utilitarian scheme: they will be punished no more severely than others for a given offense (as they might under predictive [more likely to reoffend] or deterrent [more likely to be tempted] systems). And if they are stigmatised by conviction and punishment, at least the resulting 'disabilities are the consequence of the person's own actions in having violated the law' (1976, p. 148).

Standard punishments

Just as offenses are considered generically for purposes of scaling and punishment, punishments are designed to deal with 'standard cases' and the 'characteristic oner-ousness of various sanctions' (von Hirsch, 1990, p. 10). One contrary view, as with the contrary view of offender culpability, would be to consider the subjective impact of the sanction on the offender. Another would be to take account of the objective conditions of different kinds of institutions, different probation regimes, and so on.

Von Hirsch notes these possibilities but responds in three ways. First, the 'law generally works with standard cases', and why not here? Second, in special (limited) circumstances, such as illness or advanced age, there might be deviations from the standard case. Third, although sanction severity depends in part on subjective painful-ness, it also depends on 'the moral importance of the rights taken away' (1990, p. 10) and prison deprives crucial liberty rights of free movement and association.

Von Hirsch's scheme could provide a comprehensive desert-based system of punishment. The question is whether such a system offers a just and practicable system for punishing convicted offenders.

Critique of Principle of Proportionality

Efforts to apply philosophers' distinctions to policy-makers' decisions necessarily raise different concerns than do disagreements among philosophers. Current initiatives to increase use of 'non-custodial' penalties in the United Kingdom and 'intermediate' sanctions in the United States necessarily require translation of theorists' distinctions into practitioners' realities.

It is at this point of translation that the case for strong proportionality conditions breaks down. There are at least five major difficulties. First, strong proportionality conditions require objectification of categories of offenders and offenses that are over-simplified and overinclusive. Second, proportionality arguments are often premised on objective legal measures of desert, typically current and past crimes, rather than on the subjective degree of moral culpability expressed by the offender, under particular circumstances and conditions. Third, strong proportionality conditions run head-on into 'just deserts in an unjust society'. Fourth, strong proportionality conditions violate notions of parsimony by requiring imposition of unnecessarily severe punishments in individual cases in order to assure formal equivalence of suffering. Fifth, strong proportionality conditions presuppose that imposition of offenders' deserved punishments is an overriding moral imperative rather than one of several competing ethical considerations.

THE ILLUSION OF 'LIKE-SITUATED OFFENDERS'

If recent efforts in the United Kingdom and the United States to increase use of intermediate sanctions are to succeed, the appropriateness of different punishments for 'like-situated offenders' must be recognised.

'Like-situated offender' is nested in quotation marks to express the artificiality of notions of like-situated offenders, comparable crimes, and generic punishments. A strong proportionality-in-punishment argument insists on equal treatment of like-situated offenders and proportionately different treatment of differently situated offenders. A fundamental difficulty is that this assumes that offenders can conveniently and justly be placed into a manageable number of more-or-less desert categories and that standard punishments can be prescribed for each category. Unfortunately, neither side of the desert-punishment equation lends itself to standardization.

Neither offenders nor punishments come in standard cases. The practice of dividing offenders and punishments into generic categories produces much unnecessary suffering and provides only illusory proportionality. A look at Minnesota's sentencing guidelines shows why.

Figure 14.1 sets out the original 1980 Minnesota sentencing guidelines grid, which was expressly premised on 'modified just deserts'.[2] Offenses are divided on the vertical axis into ten categories and on the horizontal axis into seven categories of criminal history. An offender's presumptive sentence is determined by consulting the cell at which the row containing his conviction offense meets the column expressing his criminal history. Cases falling in cells below the bold black line are presumed bound for state prison for a term of months within the narrow range specified. Cases falling above the line are presumed not bound for prison (the number in the above-the-line cells represents the prison sentence to be imposed if the offender fails satisfactorily to complete a nonprison sentence).

---

[2] Since the guidelines took effect in 1980, law-and-order political pressures have influenced statutory changes and policy decisions by the commission that have selectively but substantially increased penalties for controversial crimes and made the system's claims for principled scaling and proportionality weaker (Frase, 1991).

Because the guidelines attach high value to proportionality, 'departures' are discouraged. Either party may appeal a departure which, to be upheld, must be found to have been based on 'substantial and compelling' reasons. Rules set out illustrative bases for departures and forbid some. For example, the original rules prohibited departures based on offenders' educational, vocational, family, or marital circumstances and also forbade departures based on predictions of dangerousness or 'amenability' to treatment.[3] The reasons behind these prohibitions are not unattractive – to prevent judges from favoring more advantaged, often white, offenders over more disadvantaged, often black or Indian, offenders, to prevent imposition or prolongation of prison sentences on rehabilitative or incapacitative grounds, and to prevent judges from departing from presumptive prison sentences for middle-class offenders because they are especially amenable to non-incarcerative sentences.

Minnesota's tidy system, whatever its abstract merits, overaggregates offenders in at least four ways. First, consider Table 14.1, which shows the offenses that fall within offense severity levels five and six, and Table 14.2, which shows the rudiments of the scheme for calculating criminal histories. Persons convicted of solicitation of some

Severity levels of conviction offense		Criminal history score						
		0	1	2	3	4	5	6
Unauthorised use of motor vehicle Possession of Marijuana	I	12*	12*	12*	15	18	21	24
Theft-related crimes ($150–2,500) Sale of marijuana	II	12*	12*	14	17	20	23	27 25–29
Theft crimes ($150–2,500)	III	12*	13	16	19	22 21–23	27 25–29	32 30–34
Burglary–felony intent Receiving stolen goods ($150–2,500)	IV	12*	15	18	21	25 24–26	32 30–34	41 37–45
Simple robbery	V	18	23	27	30 29–31	38 36–40	46 43–49	54 50–58
Assault, 2nd degree	VI	21	26	30	34 33–35	44 42–46	54 50–58	65 60–70
Aggravated robbery	VII	24 23–25	32 30–34	41 38–44	49 45–53	65 60–70	81 75–87	97 90–104
Assault, 1st degree Criminal sexual conduct, 1st degree	VIII	43 41–45	54 50–58	65 60–70	76 71–81	95 89–101	113 106–120	132 124–140
Murder, 3rd degree	IX	97 94–100	119 116–122	127 124–130	149 143–155	176 168–184	205 195–215	230 218–242
Murder, 2nd degree	X	116 111–121	140 133–147	162 153–171	203 192–214	243 231–255	284 270–298	324 309–339

FIGURE 3.1 Minnesota sentencing guidelines grid (in months)
Notes: *One year and one day
Italicized numbers within the grid denote the range within which a judge may sentence without the sentence being deemed a departure.
Source: Minnesota Sentencing Guidelines Commission (1980)

[3] Appellate decisions have since recognised limited 'amenability to probation' and 'non-amenability to prison' criteria for departures (see Frase, 1991).

TABLE 14.1 Offense levels V and VI, Minnesota Sentencing Guidelines (1 January 1980 Version)

Level V
Vehicular homicide
Criminal sexual conduct (3rd degree) – statutory rape, offender more than 2 years older
Manslaughter (2nd degree)
Perjury–in felony trial or firearms permit application
Possession of incendiary device
Robbery
Solicitation of prostitution
Tampering with a witness

Level VI
Arson (2nd degree) – with over $2,500 loss
Assault (2nd degree) – with a deadly weapon
Burglary of a dwelling while armed
Crimial sexual conduct (2nd degree) – statutory rape
Criminal sexual conduct (4th degree) – forcible rape or incompetent victim
Escape – with violence or threat
Kidnapping – victim released unharmed
Receipt of stolen goods – over $2,500
Sale of hallucinogens
Sale of heroin
Sale of other narcotics

Source: Minnesota Sentencing Guidelines Commission (1980).

TABLE 14.2 Criminal history score, Minnesota sentencing guidelines (1 January 1980 version)

Each previous felony conviction	1 point
Current offense committed while on probation or parole, in jail or prison, or released pending sentencing for prior crime	1 point
Four prior misdemeanor convictions	1 point
Two prior gross misdemeanor convictions	1 point

Source: Minnesota Sentencing Guidelines Commission (1980).

forms of prostitution are considered equally as culpable as people convicted of robbery or second degree manslaughter, and persons convicted of four minor property misdemeanors are considered as culpable as people convicted of a violent felony. A person convicted of solicitation with four prior misdemeanor convictions is thus, for Minnesota sentencing purposes, like-situated to a person convicted of manslaughter or robbery with a prior robbery conviction. Similarly, a person convicted of sale of marijuana with four misdemeanor convictions is like-situated to a person convicted of forcible rape with a prior rape conviction. There are plausible arguments for why offenders were grouped and criminal history scores calibrated as they were. The Minnesota commission was serious and idealistic in making these decisions. Nonetheless, at day's end, offenders classified by Minnesota as like-situated will in many peoples' eyes look very unlike indeed.

Second, Minnesota's guidelines are based on *conviction offenses*,[4] which are at best imperfect and inconsistent measures of culpability. Because of ubiquitous plea

---

[4] The US Sentencing Commission, to avoid problems described in this paragraph, based its guidelines on 'relevant conduct', by which it refers to the defendant's actual behavior and its consequences. In practice, prosecutors manipulate the federal guidelines extensively but use more ingenious subterfuges (Federal Courts Study Committee, 1990).

bargaining in the United States, one of two equal participants in a robbery may be convicted of robbery and the other of aggravated robbery. Similarly, one may plead guilty to the reduced charge of robbery while the other is convicted at trial of aggravated robbery. Of two otherwise comparable robbers, one might be charged in a rural county where prosecutorial policy requires guilty pleas to the full offense (aggravated robbery), whilst another is allowed to plead to robbery in an urban county where aggravated robberies are common and office policy routinely permits acceptance of pleas to lesser offenses. For reasons of local prosecution priorities, or limited manpower, or concern with evidentiary problems, one offender may be convicted of a greatly reduced offense while another comparable offender not affected by those considerations will be convicted of the full offense. The point is not to challenge the legitimacy of the considerations that lead to convictions of particular crimes in particular cases, but to point out that offenders convicted of the same offense may have committed very different acts reflecting very different culpability and, conversely, that offenders convicted of different crimes may have committed comparable acts with similar culpability.

Third, looking behind the grid, Minnesota allows little play for non-criminal-record factors to influence penalties. Consider a minority offender who grew up in a single-parent, welfare-supported household, who has several siblings in prison and who was formerly drug-dependent but who has been living in a common-law marriage for five years, has two children whom he supports, and has worked steadily for three years at a service station – first as an attendant, then an assistant mechanic, and now a mechanic. In Minnesota, none of these personal characteristics are supposed to influence the sentencing decision, and certainly not to justify imposition of a non-custodial sentence on a presumed prison-bound offender. For people who believe in individualised sentences, on either utilitarian or retributive grounds, Minnesota's refusal to consider my hypothetical offender's promising features will seem regrettable. For people concerned by the gross over-representation in courts, jails, and prisons of deeply disadvantaged people, Minnesota's refusal to consider evidence that my hypothetical offender is overcoming the odds will seem deeply regrettable.

Fourth, Minnesota attaches no significance to the collateral effects of a prison sentence on the offender, or on the offender's family or children, what Nigel Walker (1991, pp. 106–08) calls incidental (on the offender) and obiter (on the offender's dependents and associates) effects of punishment. Incarceration for a drug crime for a woman raising children by herself may result in the break-up of her family and placement of her children in foster homes or institutions, or in homes of relatives who will not be responsible care-providers. Incarceration of an employed father and husband may mean loss of the family's home and car, perhaps the break-up of a marriage, perhaps the creation of welfare dependency by the wife and children. To ignore that incidental and obiter effects of punishments vary widely among seemingly like-situated offenders is to ignore things that most people find important.

Thus, for a wide diversity of reasons, offenders whom Minnesota's sentencing guidelines treat as like-situated often are not. A similar analysis could be offered of the punishment side of the crime and punishment equation. Objectively, punishments valued in the generic coin of imprisonment can be very different. In most American jurisdictions, a prison sentence means 'placed in the custody of the department of corrections', which in turn can mean anything from placement in a fear-ridden, gang-dominated maximum security prison under lock-up twenty-three hours a day, through placement in a minimum security camp or campus, to home confinement. Objectively, a sentence to twenty-four months probation can mean anything from living normally and mailing a bi-monthly postcard to the probation office to being contacted ten to twenty-five times a month, reporting to the probation office three times a week, observing a curfew, and being subject to frequent unannounced urinalyses.

Subjectively, three years' imprisonment may mean very different things to a twenty-three-year-old gang member, for whom it is a rite of passage; a forty-year-old employed husband and father, for whom it will likely destroy the material conditions of his and his family's lives; a frightened, effeminate twenty-year-old middle-class student, for whom it may result in sexual victimization; or a seventy-year-old, for whom it may be life imprisonment.

Problems of objectification of crimes, offenders, and punishments are especially stark in a numerical guidelines system. In systems that feature written policy guidelines, they lurk beneath the surface. The Minnesota illustration is generally relevant to analysis of proportionality in punishment, however, because it makes real world implications of strong proportionality conditions starkly apparent. If proportionality is an, or the, overriding principle in the distribution of punishment in practice, then the imperfections of objectification that I describe are presumably regrettable but acceptable costs to be paid for a principled punishment system. If they appear unacceptable, the problem may be that the principle of proportionality offers less helpful guidance than its proponents urge.

OBJECTIVE MEASURES OF RESPONSIBILITY

Von Hirsch's proportionality argument relies on objective measures of penal deservedness. This is curious. Desert theories, especially blaming theories, are premised on notions of individual blameworthiness, which seem inexorably linked to particularised judgments about moral responsibility. Objective measures of harm are seldom sufficient for conviction in the criminal law: that is why doctrines of competency, *mens rea*, and affirmative defense exist and why doctrines like strict liability and felony-murder are disfavored. If individualised moral judgments are germane to conviction, it is not obvious why they are not also germane to punishment.

If punishment is principally about blaming, surely it is relevant whether the offender was mentally impaired, socially disadvantaged, a reluctant participant, or moved by humane motives. Surely it is morally relevant, whatever the path to conviction, what the offender did, with what *mens rea*, and under what circumstances. Surely it is morally relevant whether a particular punishment will be more intensely experienced by one person than by another. In other words, the three subjective considerations that Minnesota's guidelines ignore – what did he really do, what will the conditions of his sanction really be, will he suffer more intensely than others – are relevant to moral judgments of blameworthiness and proportionate punishments. Nigel Walker expresses this when he observes: 'Retributive reasoning would lead instead to a 'personal price list' which would take into account not only gradations of harm but offenders' culpability and sensibility' (1991, p. 103).[5]

The failure of von Hirsch's arguments to take account of individualised differences in culpability and individual effects of punishment looks strange when we recall that von Hirsch's is a retributive theory. Utilitarian theories reject interpersonal comparisons of utility, as Lionel Robbins' classic essay (1938) explains, either on measurement grounds (variable intensity of satisfactions, utility monsters, and so on), or on normative grounds (no individual's satisfactions *should* count for more). However, utilitarian theories are concerned with general policies and aggregate social measures and not with fine-tuned moral judgments.

AN UNJUST SOCIETY

Punishment schemes that attach high value to proportionality necessarily ignore the differing material conditions of life, including poverty, social disadvantage, and bias, in which human personalities and characters take form. The substantive criminal law rejects motive for intention and in the English-speaking countries allows no formal excusing or mitigating defense of social disadvantage. Yet in both the United Kingdom and the United States, most common law offenders are products of disadvantaged and deprived backgrounds and in both countries vastly disproportionate numbers of alleged, convicted, and imprisoned offenders are members of racial and ethnic minorities. The likelihood, for example, that a black American male is in prison today is eight times greater than that a white American male is in prison.

The problem of 'just deserts in an unjust world' is a fundamental problem for a strong proportionality constraint. Whether retributive theories are rationalised in terms of benefits and burdens, or equilibrium, or blaming, or condemnation, or penance, they must presume equal opportunities for all to participate in society. When some are disabled from full participation by discrimination, disability, or exclusion, by denial of access to public goods, by the burdens of social and economic disadvantage, it is difficult to claim that they enjoy the benefits of autonomy that produce obligation. To take just one example, proponents of benefits and burdens theories are hard pressed to explain how a person who is denied society's benefits deserves to be burdened by social obligation.

Many writers on the philosophy of punishment from both retributive and utilitarian premises recognise this problem. R. A. Duff, after developing an ideal theory of expressive punishment based on social condemnation and individual penance, rejects his own proposals in favor of a deterrence-premised system because: 'punishment is not justifiable within our present legal system; it will not be justifiable unless and until

---

[5] Walker defines 'sensibility': 'the intensity of the suffering, hardship, or inconvenience which a given penalty will inflict depends on the individual: on sex, age, social position, and so on' (Walker, 1991, p. 99).

we have brought about deep and far-reaching social, political, legal, and moral changes in ourselves and our society' (1986, p. 294).

Jeffrey Murphy, after developing an ideal punishment theory deriving from a Rawlsian original-position analysis of benefits and burdens, rejects it on grounds that it will not serve justice until 'we have restructured society in such a way that criminals genuinely do correspond to the only model that will render punishment permissible – i.e., make sure that they are autonomous and that they do benefit in the requisite sense' (1973, p. 110).

Even Andrew von Hirsch, arguing that a desert-based system of distribution will achieve less additional disadvantage to the disadvantaged than a utilitarian system, concludes nonetheless: 'as long as a substantial segment of the population is denied adequate opportunities for a livelihood, any scheme for punishing must be morally flawed' (1986, p. 149).

Not surprisingly, proponents of utilitarian and mixed punishment theories acknowledge the same problem. H. L. A. Hart, for example, in explaining the role of excuses in the substantive criminal law, notes in respect of deeply disadvantaged people, 'The admission that the excusing condition may be of no value to those who are below a minimum level of economic prosperity may mean, of course, that we should incorporate as a further excusing condition the pressure of gross forms of economic necessity' (1968, p. 51).

Ted Honderich, who argues for a hybrid punishment theory, observes: 'there is nothing that can be called the question of [punishment's] moral justification which is left to be considered if one puts aside the great question of the distribution of goods in society' (1989, pp. 238–9).

In the United States, giving lip service to concern for offenders from disadvantaged backgrounds, most sentencing commissions have forbidden judges to 'depart' from sentencing guidelines on grounds of offenders' personal circumstances. The putative rationale for such policies is that judges would favor middle-class offenders in mitigating sentences. This rationale is empirically misconceived and perverse; only an insignificant proportion of common law offenders are from middle- and upper-class backgrounds. The normal range of socioeconomic backgrounds of common law offenders ranges from the deeply disadvantaged to the merely deprived. The chimerical middle-class offender is conspicuous by his absence. The perversity of such policies is that they forbid special treatment of offenders from deprived backgrounds who have achieved some personal successes. The minority offender from a broken home and a devastated neighborhood who has nonetheless managed a reasonably stable domestic life, achieved some educational success, and found secure employment is as unentitled to a mitigated sentence as a middle-class offender. Thus, policies designed to prevent unfair treatment of disadvantaged offenders as a class have the likely effect of unfair treatment of disadvantaged offenders as individuals.

A proponent of proportionality might respond by noting that loosening proportionality conditions to permit mitigation of sentences for 'deserving' disadvantaged offenders also permits aggravation of sentences for the 'undeserving,' especially those who appear likeliest to offend again. This is a different problem and one that can be addressed by placing strict proportionate limits on maximum sentences and by establishing stringent standards to guide decisions to aggravate punishments.

PARSIMONY

Proponents of strong proportionality conditions necessarily prefer equality over minimization of suffering. For nearly two decades in the United States, Andrew von Hirsch and Norval Morris have been disagreeing over the role of parsimony in punishment. Von Hirsch (1985) has argued for strong desert limits on punishment and high priority to pursuit of equality and proportionality in punishment. Morris (1974) has argued that desert is a limiting, not a defining, principle of punishment and that policy should prescribe imposition of the least severe 'not undeserved' sanction that meets legitimate policy ends. Within these outer bounds of 'not undeserved' punishments Morris has consistently argued for observance of a principle of parsimony.

To some extent Morris and von Hirsch have argued past each other. Morris argues that a desert approach is unnecessarily harsh and von Hirsch responds by noting that he personally favors relatively modest punishments and, in any case, desert schemes are not inherently more severe than other schemes. In turn, von Hirsch argues that Morris's 'not undeserved' proportionality constraints are vague, the breadth of allowable ranges of sentencing discretion is never specified, and Morris responds by noting that absolute measures of deserved punishment are unknowable and that his aim is to minimise imposition of penal suffering within bounds that any given community finds tolerable.

The problem is that they start from different major premises – von Hirsch's is the 'principle of proportionality', Morris's the 'principle of parsimony'. The difference between them can be seen by imagining a comprehensive punishment scheme, perhaps resembling Minnesota's (see Figure 3.1). Imagine that policy makers have conscientiously classified all offenders into ten categories and, using von Hirsch's ordinal/cardinal magnitude and anchoring points approach, have decided that all offenses at level VII deserve twenty-three- to twenty-five-month prison terms. Imagine further that reliable public opinion surveys have shown that 90 per cent of the general public would find a restrictive non-custodial punishment 'not unduly lenient' and a 36-month prison term 'not unduly severe' for level VII offenses.

Von Hirsch would, I presume, argue that for non-exceptional cases concern for proportionality requires that persons convicted of level VII crimes receive at least a twenty-three-month prison term, even though public opinion would support much less severe punishments. To achieve greater proportionality, von Hirsch would punish some offenders much more severely than is socially or politically required.

Morris, by contrast, would presumably argue that imposing twenty-three-month terms on all level VII cases would be unjust because it would constitute imposition of punishment that is not required by public attitudes or preventive considerations. Morris would argue that, barring exceptional circumstances, no level-VII offender should receive more than twenty-five months' incarceration but that many should receive less than twenty-three months. To achieve less aggregate suffering, Morris would punish some offenders much less severely than concern for proportionality would suggest.

The preceding hypothetical is overstated. Von Hirsch would, at least for exceptional cases, approve departures from the twenty-three to twenty-five-month range or perhaps approve a wider range (for example, eighteen to twenty-eight months). Morris would almost certainly want to establish a normal upper bound lower than thirty-six months and would want to devise some system for assuring that level VII offenders receive roughly equivalent punishments.

SORTING OUT PRINCIPLES

Disagreements about just punishments, like disagreements about the death penalty or abortion, are often in the end disagreements about powerful intuitions or deeply embedded values. It may be that differences in view between those who give primacy to proportionality and those who give primacy to parsimony cannot be bridged.

The burden of persuasion should rest, however, it seems to me on those who reject Isaiah Berlin's observations that 'not all good things are compatible, still less all the ideals of mankind' (1969, p. 167) and that 'the necessity of choosing between absolute claims is then an inescapable characteristic of the human condition' (1969, p. 169).

Punishment raises at least two important conflicts between ideals – between the principles of proportionality and parsimony, between the quests for criminal justice and social justice.

Punishment is not unique in this respect. *Justice, Equal Opportunity, and the Family* (1983) by James Fishkin shows similar irreconcilable conflicts in ideals that are posed by family policy. Even in ideal theory, he argues, values inherent in support for equal opportunity conflict with values inherent in support for family autonomy. Notions of equal opportunity, he argues, must include a 'principle of merit', that 'there should be a fair competition among individuals for unequal positions in society' (p. 19), and a 'principle of equal life chances specifying roughly equal expectations for everyone regardless of the conditions into which they are born' (p. 20). Without equal life chances, both common experience and modern sociology instruct, scarce social goods will not be distributed according to merit. As Fishkin observes, 'if I can predict the outcomes achieved by an individual merely by knowing his or her race, sex, ethnic origin, or family background, then equality of life chances has not been realised' (p. 34).

If we were single-mindedly devoted to equal opportunity, then, we should view equalization of life chances as an overriding goal of social policy. However, Fishkin argues, efforts to equalize life chances run head on into another powerful principle, that the value of autonomy in a private sphere of liberty encompasses a principle of family autonomy, of non-intrusion by the state into the family's sphere of private liberty.

In other words, equal opportunity and family autonomy conflict fundamentally. Full respect for equal opportunity would involve intrusion into the family that would widely be seen as objectionably intrusive. Full respect for family autonomy would widely be seen as cruel disregard for children's basic needs.

And so it may be with punishment. Principles of proportionality and parsimony may simply conflict, with resolutions between them necessarily partial and provisional.

RECONCILING PROPORTIONALITY AND PARSIMONY

A middle ground exists on which a punishment scheme can be built that honors both proportionality and parsimony – development of sentencing guidelines that establish presumptive sentencing ranges in which the upper bounds are set in accordance with the proportionality principle and the lower bounds are sufficiently flexible to honor the parsimony principle. This would discourage disparately severe punishments, including aggravation of sentences on predictive or rehabilitative grounds beyond what would otherwise be deemed appropriate. If von Hirsch is correct as a social psychologist of punishment when he insists that desert schemes are not necessarily more severe than other schemes, use of proportionality constraints to set upper bounds (within higher statutory maxima) should result in upper-bound penalties that are no harsher than would occur in a scheme with narrow ranges. Below those upper bounds, however, judges could set sentences not premised on 'standard cases' or 'standard punishments'.

The challenge is not to decide between proportionality and parsimony, but to balance them in ways that preserve important elements of each. This is not the place to discuss mechanics at length. A reconciliation can be sketched.[6]

USE PROPORTIONALITY TO ESTABLISH PRESUMPTIVE MAXIMUM SENTENCES

Much of von Hirsch's proportionality analysis can be used in setting maximum bounds of sentencing authority for ordinary cases. By using standardized measures of offense severity, proportionate maximum sentences can be specified, the gap between those upper bounds and statutory maxima to be reserved for extraordinary cases subject to the provision of reasons and the possibility of appellate sentence review. The Advisory Council on the Penal System (1978) proposed such a scheme, albeit not in the vocabulary of guidelines. The worst injustices in sentencing and the worst disparities are those suffered by people who receive aberrantly long or severe penalties. Presumptive guidelines for maximum sentences scaled to proportionality could both lessen the likelihood of aberrantly severe penalties and achieve proportionality among those offenders receiving the most severe presumptive sentences.

---

[6] Among the issues that might be discussed: the strengths and weaknesses of the punishment units approach; whether sentencing grids should have two, three, four or more 'bands' representing different presumptions concerning the appropriate type of sentence; at what offense severity level the normal offense is so serious that only incarceration sentences should be authorised; the widths of bands of authorised sentences for categories of cases; whether equivalences should be conceptualised in terms of suffering, intrusiveness, or some other measure. There is little literature on any of these subjects and this essay does not add to it.

PARSIMONY PRESUMPTION

Within the authorised bounds, judges should be directed to impose the least severe sentence consistent with the governing purposes *at* sentencing (e.g., Morris and Tonry, 1990, pp. 90–2). Within, for example, any category of offenses encompassed in an offense severity level in Minnesota's sentencing guidelines grid, judges should be directed to consider monetary penalties or their equivalents (e.g., community service) when retribution or deterrence is the governing purpose, stringent community controls when incapacitation is at issue, and community controls with treatment conditions when sex or drug or alcohol treatment is called for, reserving incarcerative sentences only for cases when deterrence, public attitudes, or incapacitation seem to dictate. If the parsimony presumption favored the least restrictive alternative, judges would have to devise particularised reasons for doing otherwise – including imposition of sentences for incapacitative or deterrent reasons.

ROUGH EQUIVALENCE

Efforts to devise ways to make punishments interchangeable have foundered on proportionality's shoals. If prison is used as the norm, and all other penalties must be converted to carceral coin, interchangeability soon collapses. Almost inexorably, one day in prison equals two or more days of house arrest equals two or more days of community service. Something about the process seems to force literal thinking. If sentences must be proportionate in incarceration time, the scope for use of non-custodial penalties necessarily is limited.

Thinking about equivalences becomes easier if proportionality constraints are loosened. If any prison sentence up to twenty-four months can be imposed in a given case, then the range for substitution is broadened immensely.

Thinking about equivalences also becomes easier if prison is replaced by money, say a day's net pay, as the basic unit from and to which sanctions are converted.

Thinking about equivalences becomes easier if we think about different purposes to be served *at* sentencing in a given case. If the goals are retribution and deterrence, then prison and financial penalties ought to be fully interchangeable, as might also, for the indigent, a combination of residential controls, community service, restitution, and supervision.

If, for normative reasons, sentencing guidelines and guidance are to be scaled proportionately to the severity of crime, objectively measured, and expressed in standardized units of incarceration, objectively characterised, the scope for non-custodial penalties will necessarily be slight. It is not easy to devise non-custodial penalties that are objectively equivalent to twenty-three months' incarceration.

If non-custodial penalties are to be widely adopted and used, proportionality constraints must be loosened to take account of the almost infinite variety of offender circumstances, offense contexts, and punishment dimensions. If ways can be devised to institutionalise principles both of proportionality and parsimony in punishment, we are likely to do less injustice than if we establish systems that seek an illusion of equality of suffering for offenders in whose lives equality in most other things has been conspicuously absent.

REFERENCES

Advisory Council on the Penal System (1978), *Sentences of Imprisonment – A Review of Maximum Penalties*, HMSO, London.

Ashworth, A. (1992), 'Non-custodial sentences', *Criminal Law Review*, pp. 242–51.

Bentham, J. (1948) [1789], *Introduction to the Principles of Morals and Legislation*, edited by W. Harrison, Oxford University Press, Oxford.

Berlin, I. (1969), *Four Essays on Liberty*, Oxford University Press, Oxford.

Doble, J., Immerwahr, S., and Richardson, A. (1991), *Punishing Criminals – The People of Delaware Consider the Options*, The Public Agenda Foundation, New York.

Duff, R. A. (1986), *Trials and Punishments*, Cambridge University Press, Cambridge.

Federal Courts Study Committee (1990), *Report*, Administrative Office of the US Courts, Washington, DC.

Fishkin, J. S. (1983), *Justice, Equal Opportunity, and the Family*, Yale University Press, New Haven.

Fletcher, G. (1978), *Rethinking Criminal Law*, Little Brown, Boston.

Frase, R. (1991), 'Sentencing reform in Minnesota: ten years after', *Minnesota Law Review*, LXXV, pp. 727–54.

Hart, H. L. A. (1968), *Punishment and Responsibility: Essays in the Philosophy of Law*, Oxford University Press, Oxford.

Honderich, T. (1989), *Punishment – The Supposed Justifications*, Polity, Cambridge.

Kant, I. (1887) [1797], *Rechtslehre*, Part Second, 49, trans. by W. Hastie, T. & T. Clark, Edinburgh.

Minnesota Sentencing Guidelines Commission (1980), *Report to the Legislature – January 1, 1980*, Minnesota Sentencing Guidelines Commission, St. Paul, Minnesota.

Morris, N. (1974), *The Future of Imprisonment*, University of Chicago Press, Chicago.

———and Tonry, M. (1990), *Between Prison and Probation: Intermediate Punishments in a Rational Sentencing System*, Oxford University Press, New York.

Murphy, J. (1973), 'Marxism and retribution', *Philosophy and Public Affairs*, II, pp. 217–43.

Pincoffs, E. L. (1966), *The Rationale of Legal Punishment*, Humanities Press, New York.

Robbins, L. (1938), 'Interpersonal comparisons of utility: a comment', *The Economic Journal*, XLVIII, pp. 635–41.

Singer, R. G. (1979), *Just Deserts: Sentencing Based on Equality and Desert*, Ballinger, Cambridge, MA.

von Hirsch, A. (1976), *Doing Justice – The Choice of Punishments*, Hill and Wang, New York (rev. edn. 1986, Northeastern University Press, Boston).

———. (1985), *Past or Future Crimes – Deservedness and Dangerousness in the Sentencing of Criminals*, Rutgers University Press, New Brunswick, NJ.

———. (1990), 'Scaling intermediate punishments: a comparison of two models', unpublished manuscript, Rutgers University Department of Criminal Justice, Rutgers, NJ.

————. (1992), 'Proportionality in the philosophy of punishment', *Crime and Justice – A Review of Research*, XVI, edited by M. Tonry, University of Chicago Press, Chicago, pp. 55–98.

Walker, N. (1991), *Why Punish?*, Oxford University Press, Oxford.

Wasik, M., and von Hirsch, A (1988), 'Non-custodial penalties and the principles of desert', *Criminal Law Review*, pp. 555–72.

15

SENTENCING AND PUNISHMENT IN FINLAND: THE DECLINE OF THE REPRESSIVE IDEAL

Tapio Lappi-Seppälä

III. PENAL POLICY AND THE LAW OF SENTENCING

Sentences are set within minima and maxima prescribed by law. The decision of the court consists of three distinct decisions or steps. First, the court must establish the applicable sentencing ranges. The basic scale is defined in each statutory crime definition. However, in some cases the scale may be reduced. The second decision is usually the choice of the type of the sanction to be applied. For minor offenses the options are a fine and waiver of sanctions. For middle-range and more serious offenses, the additional options are conditional and unconditional imprisonment, community service, and a juvenile penalty. The third decision concerns the amount of punishment (the number of day fines and the amount of the individual day fine, the length of imprisonment, and the number of community service hours). "Sentencing" in its narrowest sense thus refers to the discretion exercised by judges within the given latitude in deciding on the amount of punishment. The widest sense would include also a choice among different types of sanctions, and the establishment of the penal range in cases where there are reasons to adjust it (in other words, to go below the prescribed minimum penalty). In the following, the term is used in the latter, widest, sense.[15]

Finnish law contains provisions on each of these subdecisions. The provisions to be taken into account in deciding on the severity of sanctions (quantity) are gathered

---

[15] This is, presumably, even narrower than the meaning of this term in the Anglo-Saxon tradition where sentencing covers almost everything from the establishment of guidelines to release on parole. In a civil law tradition, the latter type of issues (such as the types of penalties to be adopted in the criminal law) are deemed part of legislative action and the planning of criminal policy. These are dealt with in sections I and II.

together in chapter 6 of the Criminal Code. Those provisions are of fundamental importance also in the choice of sanctions in cases where the choice between different sentencing alternatives is at the same time a decision on the severity of the sentence (as it usually is).

A. Material Principles and Sentencing Criteria

The penal ideology behind the sentencing provisions in chapter 6 of the Criminal Code makes a clear choice among theories of punishment and aims of the criminal justice system. The aim of the penal system is general prevention. The assumption is that this effect is reached not through fear (deterrence) but through the moral-educative effects of punishment. According to this theory, the disapproval expressed in punishment is assumed to influence the values and moral views of individuals. As a result of this process, the norms of criminal law and the values they reflect are internalized. People refrain from illegal behavior not because it is followed by unpleasant punishment but because the behavior itself is regarded as morally blameworthy.

The general policy implications of this theory are discussed above. In general terms, this ideology emphasizes the fairness and justness of sanctions. In sentencing, proportionality, predictability, and equality are the central values. These ideas are also clearly expressed in the basic norm of sentencing (chap. 6, sec. 1 of the Criminal Code).[16]

> In measuring a punishment all the relevant grounds increasing and decreasing the punishment, as well as the uniformity of sentencing practice, shall be taken into consideration. The punishment shall be measured so that it is in just proportion to the harm and risk involved in the offense and to the culpability of the offender manifested in the offense.

The leading principle in sentencing is proportionality. The foundation of this principle is often sought in retributive notions. But beyond these notions lie the values of liberty and the classical prohibitions against misuse and arbitrariness. The principle of proportionality has its roots in the concept of the rule of law (*Rechtstaat*), legal safeguards, and the guarantees of citizens against the excessive use of force. From this point of view, it is more important to prevent overly harsh and unjustified penalties than it is to prevent overly lenient ones. The main function of the proportionality principle is, thus, to impose the upper limit that the punishment may never exceed. It is much less restrictive when considering the possibilities of imposing sentences that are less severe than the offender's act would prima facie have deserved (see Törnudd 1996, p. 85).

---

[16] The construction of the entire penal structure reflects these same aims. In order to ensure proportionality as well as consistency in sentencing, different offenses are, as a rule, graded into different degrees of seriousness with corresponding specific penalty scales for each subtype of offense. For example, the crime of theft appears in law in three degrees: petty theft (fines), ordinary theft (either a fine or imprisonment up to one year and six months), and aggravated theft (imprisonment for from four months to four years).

This ordering of priorities and the "asymmetry of the proportionality principle" has been confirmed in several provisions in the Criminal Code. The courts have a general right to go below the prescribed minimum whenever exceptional reasons call for such a deviation. Also, the grading of offenses reflects this same idea: the lists of criteria that make an offense an aggravated one are always exhaustive, while the lists of mitigating criteria are always "open-ended." If a particular feature of the offense would call for a milder assessment, then the courts have the discretionary power to consider the offense one requiring special consideration, even if none of the criteria specified in the law are at hand. Also the sentencing rules in chapter 6 of the Criminal Code embody the same principle, since the phrasing of the mitigating criteria leave somewhat more scope for judicial discretion than does the phrasing of the aggravated factors (see Anttila and Törnudd 1992, p. 15). In addition, the principles guiding the use of community service allow the courts to impose a sentence more lenient than is prima facie required. And, finally, the law recognizes a specific group of sentencing provisions that allow deviation in a more lenient direction on grounds other than those related to "just deserts."

The principle of proportionality raises three types of questions: how can one assess the seriousness and blameworthiness of offenses, how can one assess the severity of sanctions, and how can one link these two together in a manner that respects the requirement of "just proportion"? The provisions in chapter 6 deal primarily with the first issue. The remaining two are the subject of philosophical, policy, and legal theory inquries, for which the present context allows very little scope.

ASSESSING SERIOUSNESS AND BLAMEWORTHINESS

According to the general provision (chap. 6, sec. 1 of the Criminal Code) the starting points in assessing the seriousness (and blameworthiness) of offenses are, first, harm and risk, and, second, the culpability manifested in the offense. In addition, the law contains (in chap. 6, sec. 2–4 of the Criminal Code) a list of specific aggravating[17] and mitigating criteria. Some of these specify the concept of culpability, and some can be explained by other factors. The list is not, however, exhaustive, and the elaboration and more detailed development of these criteria is left partly to legal doctrine and partly to the courts.

Consequences—harm and the risk of harm. The consequences and their seriousness are determined by the extent to which the crime has in fact either harmed or endangered the interest being protected. The starting points in assessing the harm and risk created by the offense are, thus, to be found in the interpretation of the statutory crime definition and the interests that the criminal prohibition is

---

[17] Aggravating factors are listed in chapter 6, section 2 of the Criminal Code. Grounds that increase punishment are the degree of premeditation; commission of the offense as a member of a group organized for serious offenses; committing the offense for remuneration, and the previous criminality of the offender if the relation between the offenses on the basis of their similarity or for another reason shows that the offender is apparently heedless of the prohibitions and commands of the law.

supposed to protect. Additional guidance is given in the statutory grading criteria (in cases where the legislature has graded the offense into different degrees of seriousness, which is a common practice in Finnish law). Two additional principles govern this assessment. The "principle of endangerment" requires that attention be paid not only to those harms that have already resulted from the act but also to those harms that could have been anticipated before the act. The "principle of subjective coverage" requires that only those consequences that the actor foresaw (intentional crimes) or could (and should) have foreseen (crimes of negligence) may be taken into account.

Assessing the seriousness of the consequences is, in a way, an "offense-internal" matter.[18] The issue may be decided without a need to turn to outside sources or guidance. Accordingly, the Sentencing Act does not contain closer instructions in this respect. The only criteria that deal with the dimension of harm is a provision on organized crime in chapter 6, section 2(2) of the Criminal Code: "the commission of the offense as a member of a group organized for serious offenses" serves as a general ground for aggravation. The provision was motivated with reference to the threat that organized crime poses for security and social order (and, thus, to the exceptionally harmful consequences of this sort of criminality).

Culpability. Culpability focuses basically on the mental state of the actor at the time of the offense. To assess the content and the degrees of culpability, one has to dive into the theory of criminal justice and the principles of substantive criminal law. Sentencing theory makes the following distinctions.

Culpability as act-oriented guilt	The wording of chapter 6, section 1 of the Criminal Code (culpability "manifested in the offense") stresses "act-orientation." The moral evaluation of the reprehensibleness of the actor must be restricted to the concrete offense and it may not be expanded to take account, for example, of the entire personality of the offender or the moral merits and demerits of his or her way of life.
Culpability as desires and/or beliefs	Substantive criminal law theory contains several clues and distinctions regarding the degree of culpability. Direct intent and purpose reflect higher culpability than does mere foresight of consequences; on the other hand, the degree of probability with which the actor judged that his or her act would constitute an offense has an effect. Also, the firmness of the criminal decision and the decisiveness with which the perpetrator works his or her way towards the desired

---

[18] See also Jareborg 1992. Together with von Hirsch, Jareborg has developed a more general theory of offense seriousness ("living standard" analyses, see von Hirsch and Jareborg 1991 and the comments by Ashworth 1992b, sec. 90 ss).

result help define the degree of culpability. The legislature has taken this dimension into account by confirming the "degree of premeditation" as a general aggravating criterion in sentencing in chapter 6, section 2(1) of the Criminal Code.

Culpability as an ability to conform with the law

Blame presupposes that the actor could have acted (and could have been required to act) otherwise (on the "conformity principle," see esp. Jareborg 1988, p. 75). It is an essential requirement of justice that the amount of blame and punishment must be graded according to the actor's ability to conform with the law. An important part of the legislative sentencing criteria specifies the concept of culpability by describing situations in which the actor's ability to follow the demands of norms is to a greater or lesser level influenced by external or internal impulses or forces (chap. 6, sec. 3(1) and 3(2) of the Criminal Code).

Culpability as acceptable/ reprehensible motives

Motives matter. Acts that are committed for respectable and altruistic motives or with the intention to benefit other members of society (compassion, mercy, civil disobedience, social adequacy) incur lesser punishments. This idea is partly reflected in the provision in chapter 6, section 3(1) of the Criminal Code, which allows mitigation for crimes that have been committed because of "strong human compassion." Unacceptable and reprehensible motives (envy, spite, greed, egoism, revenge, racism), in contrast, easily call for harsher punishments. So far the legislature has confirmed only one type of aggravated motive, committing an offense for remuneration (chap. 6, see 2(3) of the Criminal Code). In 1999 the law reform committee was considering whether racist and xenophobic motives should also be included in the law as a general aggravating factor.[19]

---

[19] Aggravation based on xenophobic motives (the "hate-crime" concept) has been recognized in several European legal systems in various ways. Usually this has been done in the special part of the Criminal Code (for example, in the definitions of crimes of violence). In Scandinavia, only Sweden has adopted a general sentencing provision on the matter in 1994 (chapter 29, sec. 2, para. 7 the Criminal Code (1994:306)). Also the European Community has undertaken a joint action against crimes committed on racist or xenophobic motives.

RECIDIVISM AND PRIOR CONVICTIONS

The role of prior criminality in sentencing is puzzling. The principle that first-time offenders deserve more lenient treatment is generally accepted (see esp. von Hirsch 1981). Almost (but not quite) equally accepted is the principle that the number of prior convictions or previous crimes increases the penalty. The reasons for identifying an offender's prior record as an aggravating factor, however, are far from clear. Much depends on the concept of culpability adopted, general policy considerations, the overall aims in sentencing, and the underlying "crime ideology" (what is essentially "wrong" in any crime; on this, see Jareborg 1988). Use of one's prior record as an aggravating factor may be justified by pointing out that those who repeatedly break the law are likely to do so also in the future (dangerousness). It could be argued, too, that those who still continue committing crimes after having been punished show a clearer lack of respect for the provisions of the law (culpability in the sense of "evil will"). One might also refer to the need to maintain the credibility of the system of criminal justice and the urge to uphold the message that the norms on criminal law are to be taken seriously (general prevention). Since this message is given in the form of a sanction, recidivism requires increased penalties, since otherwise it would be hard to convince anyone that the legislature is seriously concerned with the protection of the interests that had been violated.

The problem is not so much in justifying the use of recidivism as an aggravating factor (there are more than enough competing justifications) but in determining how to keep it in proper limits. In fact, most of the justifying reasons suffer from serious drawbacks. It may well be that repeating an offense shows that the offender is in some way "stubborn" in the face of the norms of society, but whether this really is a result of the offender's free and unrestricted choice is another matter. The effects of imprisonment are well known; prison weakens the offender's ability to live up to the standards of society, and sometimes a relapse into crime is simply the result of lost opportunities. The argument of dangerousness hardly fits with most cases of repeated offending, since the majority of crimes committed by persistent offenders are of a petty nature. Mechanical aggravation of penalties for recidivists has had a long tradition in European criminal codes—and as with so many other traditions in the field of criminal justice, there are good reasons to take a critical look of this practice. One of the achievements of the criminal legislation passed during the twentieth century was a kind of "devaluation" of this aggravation that was accomplished by replacing old casuistic rules with more flexible models of regulation. In Finland this achievement took place with the sentencing reform in 1976. One of the main aims was to limit the significance of prior record in sentencing by replacing old mechanical provisions with a regulation that allowed aggravation only when recidivism implies increased culpability.

According to chapter 6, section 2(4) of the Criminal Code, the previous criminality of the offender may increase the penalty "if the relation between the offenses on the basis of their similarity or for another reason shows that the offender is apparently heedless of the prohibitions and commands of the law." Recidivism should increase punishment only if it indicates greater act-oriented culpability.

Casual or occasional repetition should not increase punishments. Neither should recidivism that is due more to a lack of social possibilities to conform with the law than to the offender's hostile and heedless attitudes towards the norms of criminal law. To find out whether the accused has shown "apparent heedlessness," the judge must compare the new crime with the previous ones and look at the lapse of time between crimes, the amount of premeditation, and the motivational connection between these crimes.[20]

ON MITIGATION

Mitigating factors fall technically into two subgroups: grounds that justify the use of a reduced penalty scale and grounds that are to be taken into account only within the chosen latitude.

Grounds for reduction. The Criminal Code recognizes six circumstances under which the court may choose the sentence from a reduced penalty scale: young age, diminished responsibility, excessive self-defense, nonexculpatory necessity in certain cases, attempt, and aiding. All these provisions reflect the general principles of liability that separate punishable from nonpunishable behavior. Between the area of total exemption from liability and full responsibility is the intermediate area of diminished blame. Children under the age of 15 are free from all criminal liability, but young offenders between the ages of 15 and 17 years receive a mitigated sentence. Those lacking penal capacity are not punished, and those for whom this capacity is only diminished are less blameworthy and deserve mitigation on the grounds for culpability. (This mitigation may be counter-balanced by prior convictions or evident dangerousness of the offender.) Self-defense and necessity exclude liability (either by justifying the act or by excusing the offender), while self-defense or necessity that are almost justifying or exculpatory may mitigate the sentence. The same idea applies to all defenses (and to the principles of liability, as well). In a way, most mitigating factors carry the job of the general principles and grounds for criminal liability only one step further. They remind us that those very same arguments that dictate whether the offender is to be punished usually are of relevance also after the border between nonpunishable and punishable behavior has been passed. Sentencing law is a "microcosm" not only of the principles of punishment and the aims of criminal justice but also of the principles of substantive criminal law. This sets a rather challenging task for anyone who wishes to condense the principles of sentencing into a nutshell (or into a sentencing grid).

Grounds for mitigation related to culpability. Most of the mitigating criteria in chapter 6, section 3 of the Criminal Code specify the concept of culpability by describing the situations in which the actor's ability to control his or her actions has been diminished

---

[20] Despite the reform, prior record is still perhaps the most influental factor in sentencing. It also is true that the guidance given by the legislator is somewhat "elusive" (von Hirsch 1987, p. 54). Still, there is evidence that some of the objectives have been achieved. The mere number of previous convictions is not the only criterion to be taken into account. One sign of the change is that while sentencing a multiple offender, the courts may aggravate the sentence and apply the prior record provision selectively to only some of the crimes.

by external or internal impulses or forces. According to chapter 6, section 3(1) of the Criminal Code, the punishment may be mitigated if the crime has been committed under "significant pressure, threat or other similar influence on the perpetration of the offense." Pressure may be direct or indirect, physical or psychological. Chapter 6, section 3(2) of the Criminal Code grants the benefit of mitigation when there is "strong human compassion leading to the offense or exceptional and sudden temptation or a similar factor that has been conducive to lowering noticeably the offender's ability to obey the law." Temptation may mitigate the sentence only when it has been both exceptional and sudden. Provocation may be included in a list of the "similar" factors, but self-imposed intoxication may not mitigate the sentence, even if there would be no disagreement that the offender's ability to control his actions has been substantially impaired.

Mitigation on other grounds. The provisions in chapter 6 of the Criminal Code also contain mitigating rules that fall outside the scope of culpability and seriousness of the offense. These "external" arguments are based either on pragmatic reasons of criminal political expediency or on values such as equity and mercy.

The meritorious conduct of the offender belongs primarily in the first category. According to chapter 6, section 3(3) of the Criminal Code, voluntary attempts by the offender to prevent or remove the effects of the offense or to further the clearing up of his or her offense will reduce the punishment. An offender who honestly repents the crime and shows remorse may deserve mitigation also on grounds of culpability. However, the scope of this provision is wider. The point is not so much the offender's moral evaluation but more pragmatic reasons and reasons of criminal justice policy expediency. The promised mitigation in these cases may encourage the offender to compensate the victim for the damage incurred. Also, cooperation with the police may be rewarded. However, the provision refers only to the offender's "own" offense. The law offers no reduction in cases where the offender discloses information that helps to clear up criminal offenses committed by other persons. Finnish law does not recognize the institution of "crown witness," nor does the law recognize any form of plea bargaining.

Another group of "external" factors is based on the principles of equity, mercy, and humanity. The provision concerning the cumulation of sanctions (chap. 6, sec. 4 of the Criminal Code) states: "If the offense has caused or the resultant punishment has imposed on the offender another consequence that together with the punishment imposed on the basis of the application of the grounds mentioned previously in this chapter would lead to a result that is unreasonable in comparison with the nature of the offense, such a situation is to be taken into consideration so far as is reasonable in measuring the punishment." In other words, extra hardship resulting from the consequences of the act (for example, if the offender was injured or lost his or her job) may reduce the penalty from the normal level.

These ideas are reflected also in the provisions on waiver of penal measures. According to chapter 3, section 5(2.4) of the Criminal Code, the court may waive penal measures in case "punishment is to be deemed unreasonable or lacking in purpose, with consideration to (a) reconciliation between the offender and the complainant, (b) other action taken by the offender to prevent or remove the effects of his or her offense, or to further its being cleared up, (c) his or her personal circumstances, (d) the other consequences of the offense to him or her, or (e) actions by the social security and health authorities." Essentially the same provision applies to nonprosecution as well.

ON PREVENTION AND PROPORTIONALITY

Chapter 6 contains a clear statement against aggravation of punishment for the purpose of general prevention (deterrence). In routine cases such a policy would hardly be a sensible option anyway, since the intended marginal preventive effect would remain practically nonexistent. The sentence of a certain drunken driver is of no interest to the general public, and even fewer people would be aware that the judge decided to raise the penalty by one month from the tariff of which the public has, at best, only a vague idea.

No aggravation of punishment for the purpose of general prevention. But what if the case has aroused intensive public interest? Then the cognitive requirements of marginal prevention might be met and there might rise the temptation of a general preventive aggravation in order to give warning examples for potential law-breakers. The counterarguments are well known. It would be a breach of the principles of predictability, equality, and proportionality to sacrifice someone only because his or her case has become "national news." We must first ask, of course, what has made the case so interesting, and then only if this reason has nothing to do with the seriousness and blameworthiness of the case, would aggravation be in conflict with the principle of proportionality. How to solve this conflict depends on how much we appreciate these principles, how serious the deviation would be, and what we expect to achieve by this deviation. For those who would be willing to sacrifice the principle of proportionality in these cases on consequentialist grounds, two points have to be made. First, even if the case has attracted much public interest, it is highly unlikely that the examples given would have long-lasting effects (if any). It might also be wise to stop for a moment to consider what features people really value in the legal system and how the public expects their courts to operate when they are under political and public pressure. Would it really increase public confidence and the legitimacy of the system of criminal justice if the courts every now and then made examples of people and then returned to normal routines? Would it not be more sensible to assume that a system that in such a manner disrespects the basic principles of liberty and justice will in a long run lose its respect and legitimacy and thereby also its positive effects on behavior?

The Finnish penal policy takes a definite position, not only on the relevance of deterrent considerations in routine cases but also on general preventive aggravation in the form of exemplary sentences. However, there remains a third case of general preventive aggravation, based not on examples or on routine decisions in lower courts but on the aim of changing the whole practice also in future cases. But this is another matter. Here we are dealing with "sentencing policy." The subject is not the implementation of certain policies but the content of the underlying principles and norms. The question is, who has and who should have the power to make such decisions? In the continental tradition this is in the hands of the legislature. But whether the legislature or the Supreme Court (or the sentencing commission) has this power, these decisions are of such a general social importance that there are good reasons to demand that they be made only after careful consideration and planning, on the basis of best possible knowledge, and after open discussions. Courtrooms seldom provide the proper framework for this type of planning and decision processes.

Value- and goal-rationality of the sentencing criteria. Nothing that has been said indicates that the system of criminal sanctions would lack motivational or deterrent effect, nor that the aggregate sentencing results from the courts would be irrelevant from the point of view of prevention. Of course, the general level of sanctions and the way these sanctions have been allocated in general is of some preventive significance (albeit a smaller one than the public and politicians usually tend to think). The point is that it is not the task of a single judge to decide on the general level of sanctions, nor is it the task of the judge to establish general rules on how the sanctions are allocated. It is the task of the judge to apply the law in a manner that takes into account legal safeguards and the individual rights of the parties in criminal proceedings; it is the task of the legislator to establish the norms that meet societal requirements and protect vital individual and collective interests. It is also the task of the legislator to formulate these rules in such a manner that the practices that grow out of their concrete application fulfill the utilitarian goals that are being sought in the best possible way, respecting also all the other aims and values to be taken into account while using criminal law as an instrument (among others) for promoting the "good life" and the protection of autonomy (and other goals of criminal law).

This brings us finally to the question of the relation between rational sentencing criteria and political aims involving crime prevention. In order to judge the goal rationality of a single rule or sentencing criterion, one has to draw a distinction between the decisions that concern the whole system (the total amount of available penalties) and decisions that concern the allocation of penalties within the given limits. From this point of view, there is an evident (but often overlooked) link between consequentialist aims (the protection of interests) in the legislative level and value-based argumentation in court decisions. Once we have agreed on the general level of penalties, we have to think what would be the most rational way to allocate those resources. And when we consider this, we find that the very same criteria that are typically justified with reference to the principle of proportionality turn out to be functional—once sentences are seen not as isolated decisions but as aggregated practices. For example, assuming that the preventive effect of punishments at least is grossly related to its severity, it is wise to relate the level of sanctions with the harmfulness of the offense (since it is more important to prevent more harmful offenses than less harmful ones). But it is wise also to save resources when this expenditure would not benefit anyone, for example, in cases where the actor would have been uninfluenced by any motivational threat.[21]

---

[21] In other words, the same logic applies to culpability-based reasons. A diminished ability of an individual to control his or her actions will result in a concomitant reduction in the ability to influence such actions with punishments. Under the assumption that penalty resources are not limitless, this reduction of controllability should lead in a goal-rational system to the lowering of penalties. Assuming that the total amount of penalty resources is given, an increase in any one sector means a decrease in

THE CHOICE OF SANCTION

Sentencing decisions involve not only the amount of punishment but also the type of punishment. Only in the most serious cases is unconditional imprisonment the only alternative available. In more than 95 percent of the sentencing decisions to be made the court has at least two options. Bringing in the qualitative dimension does not obliterate the basic ladder model, consisting of five levels: waiver of sentence, fines, conditional imprisonment, conditional imprisonment combined with a supplementary fine, and unconditional imprisonment (see figure 3.1).

There are no problems in the application in this model to the principles and provisions of chapter 6 of the Criminal Code: they can be applied to the extent that the different sanctions offer alternatives with different degrees of severity. Thus, both the choice between fine and imprisonment and the decision between conditional and unconditional imprisonment are based primarily on the seriousness of the offense (the harm and the risk of harm), culpability, and the previous convictions of the offender, and on other factors described in chapter 6, sections 2–4 of the Criminal Code. However, the recently adopted community sanctions (community service and the juvenile penalty) represent a partial exception to this rule. In these cases, a "third dimension" must be taken into account.

According to section 3 of the Community Service Act, "an offender who is sentenced to imprisonment shall be sentenced to community service instead of a specific, unconditional sentence of imprisonment of at most eight months, unless the unconditional sentences of imprisonment or the earlier community service sentences of the offender or other weighty reasons are to be deemed an obstacle to sentencing him or her to community service." Further prerequisites for sentencing the offender to community service are stipulated in section 4, which requires that the "offender has given his or her consent to performing community service and that it may be assumed that he or she will be able to cope with community service." Section 3 creates a clear presumption in favor of community service over unconditional imprisonment. This presumption may, however, be overturned with reference to the offender's previous criminality, and especially by his or her previous community service orders. An offender who would otherwise be eligible for community service but who has already been sentenced to this punishment several times may lose this benefit. The fundamental criteria to be taken into account in all cases are the consent of the offender and his or her suitability for community service.

---

another sector. In this instance it would not be rational to sacrifice the same amount of resources for the prevention of an equal amount of harm, if the outcome is different (see in more detail, Lappi-Seppälä 1992a). The point is not to say that all value-based arguments in sentencing may be given a goal-rational— let alone crime-preventive—explanation at the legislative (aggregate) level but to show that it usually makes a lot of (goal-rational) sense (in an aggregate level) to follow the proportionality principle in the level of judicial application. Still, the tension between the protection of preventive aims and collective interests and the protection of individual rights remains. One cannot escape this tension and the need for balanced compromises in criminal justice simply by adopting one principle or by announcing that different principles are relevant at different stages of the criminal justice system. However, the latter point, made by the analytical philosophers (first of all by H. L. A. Hart [1968]) offers a valuable conceptual key in order to clarify the questions and to organize the arguments.

According to section 3 of the Juvenile Penalty Act, this sanction, which has been introduced as an experiment in a few jurisdictions, can be imposed for an offense where a fine "in consideration of the seriousness of the offense and the circumstances that led to the offense is to be deemed an insufficient punishment and there are no weighty reasons that demand the imposition of unconditional imprisonment." In other words, if no juvenile penalty would be imposed in this case the offender would in principle be sentenced to conditional imprisonment, which in terms of severity falls between a fine and unconditional imprisonment. A supplementary provision introduced into the act in 1999 clarifies the choice between conditional imprisonment and the juvenile penalty. According to this provision, the offender shall be sentenced to a juvenile penalty rather than conditional imprisonment when "the imposition of a juvenile penalty is to be deemed justified for the prevention of new offenses and for the promotion of the social adjustment of the offender." Through the amendment, the application of the juvenile penalty has been tied more clearly than before to individual-preventive and rehabilitation-oriented goals.

The decision on the selection of the type of sanction is ultimately based on criteria other than the principle of proportionality. However, the principle of proportionality is also present. The question of the imposition of a community service order is raised only in situations where the seriousness of the offense and the culpability of the offender already have led to the selection of unconditional imprisonment. The juvenile penalty, in turn, may be applied only when it has been determined that the seriousness of the crime and the culpability of the offender require a heavier penalty than a fine (but when unconditional imprisonment is still deemed unduly harsh). In other words, community sanctions can also be placed in the ladder model. The special feature is that more than one sanction is situated on the same level of severity, and the selection between them is then based on criteria other than the principle of proportionality.[22]

SUMMARY: PROPORTIONALITY AND OTHER VALUES IN COURT DECISIONS ON PUNISHMENT

The principles for the application of sanctions and the relative position of the available sanctions are summarized in figure 3.13. The sanctions are situated on the ladder vertically from the least to the most punitive. In the horizontal dimension, three basic points of departure can be identified: the principle of proportionality, the rehabilitative grounds for applying community-based sanctions, and the general mitigation

---

[22] There is some similarity with the theory of "Interchangeability of Sanctions" by Morris and Tonry (1990). As the authors point out, all that the proportionality principle demands is a "rough equivalence" between the seriousness of the offense and the severity of the sanction. A choice can be made within these limits on other grounds without breaching the requirements of the proportionality principle. One has to admit that the equivalence between community service and imprisonment (one hour equals one day) may be "a bit more than rough." Still, the criticism against this lenient exchange rate has been quite mild. Evidently there was a kind of silent, collective agreement that the purpose was valuable enough in order to justify this slight deviation from the strict requirements of proportionality. The overall social benefits of community service (for both the offender and the society) in a way overrode the strict requirement that the intrusiveness of these sanctions should be of exactly the same level with imprisonment. It also is interesting to note that in international comparisons (based on focus-group method), the Finnish judges rely more on community service than do the judges in England and California (see Takala 1997).

of sanctions for reasons of expediency and equity (A–C). Moving from left to right within the framework of the principle of proportionality demonstrates an increase in the blameworthiness of the conduct in question. At the same time, moving from the bottom to the top one moves toward more severe sanctions (A). If there is more than one option on the same level of severity, the selection between them takes place on the basis of criteria other than blameworthiness (B). Grounds that are external to an assessment of blameworthiness that also appear are the principles of expediency and equity in general criminal policy (C). These may justify both a change in the amount of a certain sanction and the application of a lower rung on the ladder.

The principle of *ultima ratio* requires that the use of criminal law be restricted to the smallest justifiable minimum. Argument in sentencing should begin at the lowest level of the ladder. The judge must first consider the more lenient options. In borderline cases the principle of *in dubio mitius* applies; this principle advises the judge to choose the least restrictive option.[23]

Arguments of proportionality and sentence severity. In minor cases, the court may first consider the possibility of waiver of sentence, provided that the prosecutor has not employed his or her own right of non prosecution (figure 15.1, steps 1–2). At the second level, the court must decide between fines and imprisonment. This choice is based on the seriousness of the offense and the blameworthiness of the offender. If the offense may be settled by fines, the seriousness of the offense determines the number of day fines while the daily income and financial situation of the offender determine the amount of day fines (steps 2–3). If the blameworthiness of the act requires a prison sentence, the court may take a position on both the type (conditional or unconditional) and the length of the sentence.[24] The choice between conditional and unconditional imprisonment is based primarily on harm, culpability, and prior convictions. The age of the offender is also of importance (steps 3/4–5). In borderline cases the court may combine a conditional sentence with a fine (steps 4–5).

Preventive aims and community sanctions. If the court decides in favor of a conditional sentence, and the offender was under 18 at the time of the commission of the offense, the court may order a juvenile penalty. The decision is made primarily (after the 1999 reform) on rehabilitative and preventive grounds (level 3/4). If the court decides on a sentence of unconditional imprisonment that is no more than eight months long, community service may be imposed instead of imprisonment if the offender is deemed to be suitable for community service, and earlier community service orders are not a bar to this (level 5).

Mitigation based on external factors. The meritorious conduct of the offender after the commission of the act—repairing damages, taking part in mediation, or cooperating

---

[23] These legal principles have been deemed to be part of customary law and are considered part of the legal order even without the support of written law. The Swedish Criminal Code contains a provision that expresses this idea in connection with the use of imprisonment. According to chapter 30, section 4, "in choosing the sanction, the court shall especially pay heed to circumstances that suggest a less severe sanction than imprisonment."

[24] There are no formal rules governing the order of these decisions. Since only terms of imprisonment not exceeding two years may be imposed conditionally, the length of the sentence may usually be determined first. However, both decisions are based on similar types of arguments and it is equally possible that the courts consider these two issues (both the length and the type of imprisonment) at the same time in what essentially amounts to an overall assessment.

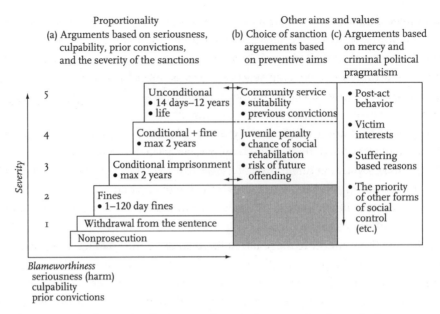

FIGURE 15.1. Principle of proportionality in sentencing and other sentencing aims and values

with the policy—may be grounds for mitigating the sentence on more or less pragmatic grounds. Mitigation on the grounds of reasonableness and equity may be relevant if the offender is of an advanced age, there has been an accumulation of sanctions, or there is another serious reason for this. These factors may justify the use of a more lenient sentence, other mitigation in the sentence, or a waiver of the sentence.[25]

This juxtaposition crystallizes the relationship between the sanctions and the leading principles in their application. However, it does not provide any guidance in concluding what acts would go on which rung of the ladder. Indeed, we need other tools to locate the concrete points of departure for sentencing. The Finnish system does not recognize numeric guidelines. However, the points of departure are provided by the concept of the "normal punishment," which was presented in connection with the drafting of chapter 6 of the Criminal Code.

REDUCING UNWARRANTED DISPARITY: THE NOTION OF NORMAL PUNISHMENTS

The Sentencing Act also contains a model, usually referred to as the "notion of normal punishments," for the structuring of the sentencing decision. Its purpose is to reduce

---

[25] Whether mitigation based, for example, on the old age or sickness of the offender really is a deviation from the principle of proportionality or "equality" depends much on the content given to these principles (and the concept of justice itself). Proportionality based on a broad (individualized) concept of justice might encompass also acts of equity and mercy under "proportionally just" sentences. Furthermore, from the point of view of the "principle of equal impact" (see Ashworth 1992a, p. 136), it would be perfectly correct to treat such a "deviation" as something that is required by the "principle of equality." A reasoned discussion of a "preferable sentencing model" would require a more careful definition (and justification) of basic concepts and principles than the present space allows.

unwarranted disparity by structuring the decision so that the courts can have a firm starting point for their decisions. This sentencing model is based on a provision in chapter 6, section 1 of the Criminal Code that requires the judge to pay special attention to "uniformity of sentencing practice." Unless special reasons are at hand, the response to the offense should be the penal sanction that is imposed most frequently in similar cases, referred to as "normal punishment."

Sentencing according to the ideology of normal punishments has been outlined as a two-stage process. First, the points of comparison are defined: the most typical cases of the offense in question (the "normal offense") and the relevant punishment (that is, the range or zone of normal punishments). During the second stage, the case at issue is compared with the typical case. The comparison is based on an interpretation of sentencing criteria and arguments.[26]

All in all, the sentencing judge needs three kinds of information. First, statistical information about the penalties (the ranges of normal punishment). What penalties are used most often, for example, in typical cases of drunken driving? Second, information about the typical cases (descriptions of normal offenses). What is the typical case of drunken driving that corresponds with the penalties used most frequently? Third, the criteria that should be taken into account when the case at hand is compared with the normal offense. What aggravating or mitigating features would justify a departure from the normal sentence? Answers to the third (normative) question above are given partly by the legislature, partly by higher court decisions, and partly by the legal doctrine. The judge may receive information concerning questions one and two from several sources. Annual court statistics contain information on the average penalties. In addition, several separate analyses have been made that give a rather detailed picture of the court practice at least in respect of the most common type of offenses. They enable the courts to see what penalties have been imposed for offenses that were committed in an approximately similar manner, in which the consequences have been on about the same level and the offenders had generally the same type of criminal record (see Lappi-Seppälä 1990, 1992b).

Of course, empirical analysis does not relieve the judge of the duty of making normative evaluations. It only provides the relevant information that is needed to give the judge a practical "starting point." The comparison between the case at hand and that described as being the "typical offense" is made by interpreting the normative sentencing criteria (the aggravating and mitigating circumstances) as given by the normal sources of sentencing law and through the accepted principles of legal argumentation. Sentencing is, and remains, an act of the normal application of law. The use of statistical information in sentencing does not turn the decision into mechanical application of statistical average penalties.

The benefit of this method is that the ranges of normal punishments help in the decision-making process by offering a concrete basis for comparisons and by anchoring the scale of crimes and the scale of punishments to each other. One could say

---

[26] The talk about "a" normal offense or punishment is, of course, a simplification. Instead of one normal offense it would be better to speak of several "typical offenses" and of the corresponding "zones of normal punishments" that have been used in these cases.

that by offering the starting points, the model solves (part of) the problem of cardinal proportionality. What remains is, of course, the comparison between the offense at hand and the "normal offense" (with the corresponding "normal punishment"). This problem of ordinal proportionality is easier to solve, because it is easier to compare entities of the same quality (internal offense seriousness, rather than offenses and sentence severity).

REFERENCES

Anttila, Inkeri, and Patrik Törnudd. 1992. "The Dynamics of the Finnish Criminal Code Reform." In *Criminal Law Theory in Transition: Finnish and Comparative Perspectives*, edited by R. Lahti and K. Nuotio. Tampere: Finnish Lawyer's Publishing Company.

Ashworth, Andrew. 1992a. *Sentencing and Criminal Justice*. London: Weidenfeld and Nicolson.

———. 1992b. "Sentencing Reform Structures." In *Crime and Justice: A Review of Research*, vol. 16, edited by Michael Tonry. Chicago: University of Chicago Press.

Hart, H. L. A. 1968. *Punishment and Responbility*. Oxford: Oxford University Press.

Jareborg, Nils. 1988. *Essays in Criminal Law*. Uppsala, Sweden: Iustus.

———. 1992. *Straffrättsideologiska Fragment*. Uppsala, Sweden: Iustus.

Lappi-Seppälä, Tapio. 1990. "Sentencing Theory in Practice: Implementing the Notion of Normal Punishments in Finland." In *Scandinavian Criminal Policy and Criminology, 1985–1990*, edited by Norman Bishop. Stockholm: Scandinavian Research Council for Criminology.

———. 1992a. "Community Service and the Neo-Classical Framework of Penal Sanctions." In *Rapport fra Kontaksteminar om Samfundstjänste*. Reykjavik, Iceland: Scandinavian Research Council for Criminology.

———. 1992b. "Penal Policy and Sentencing Theory in Finland." *The Canadian Journal of Law and Jurisprudence* 5: 95–120.

Morris, Norval and Michael Tonry. 1990. *Between Prison and Probation: Intermediate Punishments in a Rational Sentencing System*. New York: Oxford University Press.

Takala, Jukka-Pekka. 1997. "Responses in Finland to Community Sanctions." In *Penological Esperanto and Sentencing Parochialism*, edited by Malcolm Davies, Jukka-Pekka Takala, and Jane Tyrer. Aldershot, England: Dartmouth.

Törnudd, Patrik. 1996. *Facts, Values, and Visions: Essays in Criminology and Crime Policy*. Helsinki: National Research Institute of Legal Policy.

von Hirsch, Andrew. 1981. "Desert and Previous Convictions in Sentencing." *Minnesota Law Review* 65: 591–634.

———. 1987. "Numeric Grids or Guiding Principles." In *The Sentencing Commission and Its Guidelines*, edited by Andrew von Hirsch, Kay Knapp, and Michael Tonry. Boston: Northeastern University Press.

——— and Nils Jareborg. 1991. "Gauging Criminal Harm: A Living Standard Analysis." *Oxford Journal of Legal Studies* 11:1–38.

16

Limiting Retributivism

Richard S. Frase

Norval Morris's Theory of Punishment

Throughout his career, Norval Morris has been concerned with the interrelated problems of sentencing disparity and the conflicting purposes of, and at, sentencing. His earliest works also show his strong belief in the importance of relating sentencing theory to sentencing practice (Morris 1951, p. 16). Morris is an empiricist and a realist; he believes that sentencing theory should reflect the accumulated wisdom of the past and avoid imposing highly unpopular rules that will only be circumvented in practice. Morris was one of the first mainstream writers to suggest the empirical and moral defects of the "rehabilitative ideal" of coerced, prison-based treatment linked to the timing of parole release ("Penal Sanctions and Human Rights," in Morris and Howard 1964, p. 175). He explicitly linked retributive sentencing goals to the human rights of defendants and implied that such rights place firm upper limits on the severity of punishments imposed to achieve crime-control purposes (Bottoms 1995, pp. 19, 22–23). He argued strongly in favor of community-based sentencing and treatment, much broader use of fines in lieu of short custodial terms, and elimination of mandatory-minimum statutes and other arbitrary limitations on probation eligibility (Morris and Hawkins 1970, pp. 112–113, 115–124, and 141–143; see also Morris 1977a, p. 150; 1977b, pp. 279–280; Morris and Hawkins 1977, pp. 60–61; Morris 1993, p. 310).

THE EMERGENCE OF MORRIS'S LIMITING RETRIBUTIVE THEORY

A more comprehensive statement of Morris's LR theory was first presented in his 1974 book, *The Future of Imprisonment,* and was further developed in later lectures and writings. Morris's upper limits of desert are strict and explicit: "No sanction should be imposed greater than that which is 'deserved' for the last crime, or series of crimes" being sentenced (Morris 1974, pp. 60, 73–77). However, Morris strongly emphasized that courts are not obligated to impose the maximum that the offender deserves (ibid., p. 75). In later writings, Morris extended the concept of maximum desert to include the defendant's prior record of convictions (Morris 1982, pp. 151–152, 162–163, 184–186; 1992, p. 145).

In Morris's view, "desert also sometimes dictates the minimum sanction a community will tolerate" (Morris 1974, p. 78), thus, the sentence must not "depreciate the seriousness" of the current offense (ibid., p. 60). This language was taken from the Model Penal Code (see further discussion in the section "LR Concepts Recognized by Other Writers and in Model Codes and Standards"). Although Morris often refers to this as a retributive concept, he also saw it as consistent with a norm-reinforcement theory: such minimum severity limits are needed because "[t]he criminal law has general behavioral standard-setting functions; it acts as a moral teacher" (Morris 1974, p. 78). However, Morris has consistently opposed mandatory-minimum statutes.

Within the upper and lower limits of desert, Morris envisioned a range of "not undeserved" penalties. In some writings he characterizes these ranges as "overlapping and quite broad" (Morris 1982, p. 151). He also explicitly differentiated his own views from other desert-based theories by distinguishing between purposes of punishment which are "defining," those which are "limiting," and those which are only "guiding" principles (Morris 1977a, pp. 140–142; 1982, pp. 182–187). Morris suggested that deterrent purposes could precisely define the proper punishment, but only if we knew much more than we now do about the deterrent effects of punishment. As for desert, however, he argued that this concept is inherently too imprecise (and perhaps also too lacking in political and philosophical consensus, Morris and Tonry 1990, pp. 86–89) to precisely define the sentence; it can only establish rough outer limits, an allowable sentencing range, beyond which penalties would be widely seen as clearly undeserved (i.e., either excessively severe or excessively lenient) (Morris 1977a, pp. 158–159; 1982, pp. 198–199; Morris and Tonry 1990, pp. 104–105). Within those broad ranges of desert, other punishment goals, acting as "guiding principles," will interact to "fine-tune" the sentence. A guiding principle is "a general value which should be respected unless other values sufficiently strongly justify its rejection in any given case" (Morris 1977a, p. 142).

What, then, are Morris's "guiding principles" and what precise role does each play? Morris was an early critic of the rehabilitative ideal. In later writings he argued that post-prison risk cannot reliably be predicted based on in-prison behavior; that coerced in-prison treatment programs waste resources on unamenable subjects, while encouraging feigned cooperation which may actually preclude genuine reform; and that such coercive treatment would be morally wrong even if it were effective (Morris and

Hawkins 1970, ch. 5; Morris 1974, pp. 12–27; 1977a, p. 139; Morris and Hawkins 1977, ch. 6). Thus, Morris concluded that rehabilitation is not a reason either to impose or to extend a prison sentence, and that all in-prison treatment programs must be voluntary and not linked to the timing of release. However, Morris strongly advocates community-based treatment and apparently does not object to requiring a person on probation or parole to participate in an appropriate community-based treatment program closely related to the conviction offense (Morris and Hawkins 1970, pp. 112–113, 118–124; Morris 1974, pp. 34, 42–43; Morris and Tonry 1990, pp. 186–203, 206–212).

Morris's views on the goal of incapacitation were similarly in conflict with the traditional theory and practices of indeterminate sentencing—he opposed basing prison commitment, duration, and release decisions on individualized assessments of the defendant's degree of "dangerousness" (Morris 1974, pp. 62–73; 1977b, pp. 276–277). Again, Morris argued that we lack the ability to accurately predict future behavior and are very likely to err on the side of massive overprediction and overincarceration. However, he would permit parole release decisions to be based on actuarial predictions of parole success, for various offender categories (Morris 1977a, p. 148), as well as predictions based on the defendant's past behavior (Morris 1974, p. 34). In later writings, Morris—always the realist—recognized that individualized predictions of dangerousness will be made, whether they are formally permitted or not (Morris 1992, p. 139). He therefore sought to define the narrow conditions under which such predictions might be a fair and effective basis for prison commitment and duration decisions. In particular, he argued that sentencing severity may be increased (up to the retributive maximum) if "reliable actuarial data" indicates that the defendant's risk of assaultive behavior is "substantially" higher than that of other offenders with very similar prior record and current offense (Morris 1982, pp. 166–172; 1992, pp. 138–147; see also Morris and Miller 1985 and Miller and Morris 1986). However, Morris felt that these conditions would rarely be met.

Morris would also allow increased severity (up to the retributive maximum) for recidivists, when "other less restrictive sanctions have been frequently or recently applied to this offender" (Morris 1974, pp. 60, 79–80). He seemed to base such increases on retributive grounds (Morris 1974, pp. 79–80), but they can also be justified on a theory of special deterrence or incapacitation of high-risk defendants. Although Morris rejected most individual assessments of risk, he approved of parole release decisions based on actuarial predictions—"[t]he best predictor of future criminality is past criminality" (Morris 1982, pp. 162–163). He would also permit sentencing severity to be increased (up to the retributive maximum) if such an increase "is necessary to achieve socially justified [general] deterrent purposes, and the punishment of this offender is an appropriate vehicle to this end" (Morris 1974, pp. 60, 79).

In Morris's view, the goal of equality in punishment is important "but it is by no means a categorical imperative...the principle of equality—that like cases should be treated alike—is...only a guiding principle which will enjoin equality of punishment unless there are other substantial utilitarian reasons to the contrary" (Morris 1982, pp. 160, 198; see also Morris 1977a, pp. 137, 142). Morris acknowledges "the long tradition of justice as equality" (Morris 1982, p. 204) and also recognizes that equality is an especially important value in the American context (Morris 1982, p. 180). Nevertheless, he argues that, within the range of "not undeserved" penalties, punishment can be unequal—and even, in some sense, "unfair"—and yet still be "just" (Morris 1977a, pp. 151–163; 1982, pp. 187–192). He noted that numerous traditional law enforcement and sentencing practices (e.g., giving leniency to defendants who turn state's evidence; pardon and amnesty; granting of early parole release to avoid prison overcrowding) are inconsistent with a very restrictive requirement of equality. In light of such substantial (and, perhaps, inevitable) system-wide inequality, the sentencing process cannot, and should not, attempt to observe strict equality constraints (Morris 1982, pp. 206–208). This conclusion also follows from his strong belief in the concept of parsimony (discussed later on), which "overcomes the principle of equality" (Morris 1982, p. 191; 1977a, p. 154).

Parsimony is one of Morris's most important guiding principles—"[t]he least restrictive (punitive) sanction necessary to achieve defined social purposes should be imposed" (Morris 1974, p. 59). Morris found direct support for this principle in the ABA's Sentencing Standards, the Model Penal Code, and Eighth Amendment principles (see the section on "LR Concepts Recognized by Other Writers and in Model Codes and Standards"), as well as in mental health and juvenile justice dispositional standards (Morris 1974, pp. 60–62). For Morris, the principle of parsimony "is both utilitarian and humanitarian" (Morris 1974, p. 61). Parsimony in the use of custodial sentences also permits the preservation of the defendant's social ties (Morris 1974, pp. 8, 75) and the avoidance of needless suffering and expense (Morris 1977a, p. 154). In any event, Morris argued, the ability, to grant case-level mitigation of punishment, without strict desert or equality constraints, is a necessary and inevitable feature of our chronically overloaded and underfunded criminal justice system (Morris 1977a, pp 156–158; 1982, p. 190).

To summarize, Morris believed that judges should use the lower end of the range of deserved punishments as a starting point and should increase that penalty only to the extent that one or more of his other guiding factors requires increased severity. Thus, the specific sentence would be determined by whichever factor required the greatest severity. Of course, the guiding principles of equality and parsimony will often be in conflict. But if the presumption in favor of the least severe sentence is a *strong* one, and if judges thus usually sentence near the bottom of the "not-undeserved" range, then sentences will tend to be fairly uniform among offenders whose cases fall in the same range. Morris probably did expect that sentences would cluster near the bottom of the desert range—if only for lack of sufficient utilitarian justification for raising them higher; he has often argued that criminal laws and punishments have very little effect on crime rates (Morris 1977b, pp. 267–269; 1993, p. 309).

WEAK REQUIREMENTS OF PROPORTIONALITY AND UNIFORMITY

Other writers have, like Morris, viewed desert and equality principles as only loose constraints. H. L. A. Hart gave these principles a "subordinate role" (Hart 1968, p. 233); he acknowledged "the somewhat hazy requirement that 'like cases be treated alike'" (p. 24) and argued that only "broad judgments" and "rough distinctions" of moral desert can be made (p. 25). Lord Longford (1961, p. 33) would only avoid penalties "conspicuously out of proportion"; Ted Honderich (1969, p. 168) objected only to "gross" inequalities; Herbert Packer (1968, p. 140) advocated punishments that are "individualized but within limits" set by the need for general deterrence and "judgments about comparative morality"; Michael Tonry (1994) similarly prefers weak proportionality constraints.

On the other hand, even strongly utilitarian writers have recognized the importance of maintaining proportionality between offense and punishment severity, both to give offenders an incentive to "stop at the lesser" crime and to match punishment costs with crime-control benefits (Bentham (1748–1832), p. 326). Hart suggested an educative or norm-reinforcing reason to preserve at least rough proportionality; if "the relative severity of penalties diverges sharply from this rough scale, there is a risk of either confusing common morality or flouting it and bringing the law into contempt" (p. 25).

RETRIBUTIVE LIMITS ON MAXIMUM ALLOWABLE SANCTION SEVERITY

Several writers besides Morris have recognized the particular importance of placing desert limits on maximum sanction severity (Hart 1968, p. 237; Longford 1961, pp. 61–62; Honderich 1969, p. 139). This principle is also made explicit in Model Penal Section 1.02(2)(c) (no "excessive, disproportionate or arbitrary punishment"). According to the Code's revised commentary, section 1.02, in combination with other Code provisions setting "relatively modest" maximum terms and regulating extended terms, provides "a kind of retributive limit on utilitarian objectives...as a general matter, people should not be punished more severely than they deserve even if such punishment would have beneficial social consequences" (American Law Institute 1985, Pt. I, vol. 3, Introduction to Articles 6 and 7, pp. 3–4). An even stronger role for LR, based explicitly on Morris's writings, can be found in the early drafts of the revised MPC sentencing provisions (American Law Institute 2002, Section 1.02(2)(a) through (c) at p. 6, and comment at pp. 14–20).

Maximum severity LR is also explicit or implicit in the two most recent editions of the American Bar Association (ABA) sentencing standards. The second edition, adopted in 1979, explicitly stated that the sentence must never "exceed a ceiling equal to that level justly deserved by the offender for the instant offense" (ABA 1979b, Standard 18–3.2(a)(i)). The third edition dropped this limitation from the black letter, but the commentary urged legislatures to consider adopting Morris's LR theory, with emphasis on limiting maximum sanction severity (ABA 1993, Standard 18–2.1, commentary, at 13–14).

All three editions of the ABA's guilty plea standards incorporate a form of maximum severity LR (ABA 1968a, 1979a, 1997). These standards allow defendants who plead guilty to receive charge and sentence concessions for various reasons, some of which do not relate closely or at all to blame (ABA 1997, Standard 14–1.8(a)). But a defendant who refuses to plead guilty may not receive a sentence "in excess of that which would be justified by any of the protective, deterrent, or other purposes of the criminal law" (Standard 14–1.8(b)). The commentary explains that "there is an essential difference between [giving such a defendant] the greatest punishment justifiable under accepted principles of penology [while a similar defendant who pleads guilty] receives something less" (ABA 1979a, p. 21).

LOOSER REQUIREMENTS OF MINIMUM SANCTION SEVERITY

Although he rejected mandatory-minimum statutes, Morris agreed that some minimum degree of sanction severity is necessary, at least in serious cases, for retributive reasons or deterrence and norm reinforcement. The Model Penal Code drafters, like Morris, rejected mandatory minimums, and the Code's only expression of a minimum severity concept is the provision, in Section 7.01(1)(c), calling for a custody sentence when "necessary for the protection of the public" because a lesser penalty would "depreciate the seriousness" of the offense. However, the commentary makes clear that this limitation is based on crime prevention, not retributive grounds; the Institute "wholly rejected the idea" that desert might require imprisonment even if public protection did not (American Law Institute 1985, Pt. 1, vol. 3, pp. 227, 231, 233–234).

The ABA sentencing standards contain no explicit minimum severity requirements, although such a requirement is weakly implied in the second edition's appeals to equality goals (see later discussion). The ABA Guilty Plea standards, discussed earlier, which allow undeserved concessions to defendants who plead guilty, place no lower limits on sanction severity. Several writers (Tonry 1994, p. 80; Crocker 1992, *passim*) have argued explicitly that minimum severity requirements should be deemed more flexible than maximum severity limits.

Can such an asymmetrical, "softer down than up" (von Hirsch 1994, p. 45) conception of desert be justified? I believe that it can, and in any event, such asymmetry is unavoidable in practice. As a matter of principle, the upper and lower limits of desert raise different questions (a similar "bias" in favor of leniency underlies the requirement of proof beyond a reasonable doubt). Maximum allowable desert is a human rights issue; it is about fairness to the defendant and the limits of governmental power. Minimum required desert is about fairness to victims, fairness to lawabiding persons who refrained from similar conduct, and perhaps especially, fairness, to other, similarly situated defendants. If fairness in the minimum-desert context is primarily a question of uniformity (fairness to other defendants), not proportionality (fairness to victims and the lawabiding), then this focus, as well as the absence of governmental power, human rights concerns here, would help to explain why Morris viewed lower limits as less confining. In Morris's view, equality is only a guiding principle that should be followed "unless there are other substantial utilitarian reasons to the contrary" (Morris 1982, pp. 160, 198). Although Morris's later support for sentencing guidelines suggests an increased concern for uniformity, he still would require only "roughly equivalent" sanctions for comparable offenders, and a "weak version" of the equality goal (Morris and Tonry 1990, p. 89).

In any event, strict requirements of minimum sanction severity are unenforceable in practice, for the same reason that mandatory-minimum prison terms are widely evaded (Tonry 1996, ch. 5). Defendants can be counted on to object to the sentencing court and to file an appeal if necessary, whenever the sentence exceeds the maximum allowed, or even the presumptive (guidelines) maximum. But prosecutors will rarely object or appeal sentences below the minimum (and no one else has standing to raise this issue) because in many cases the prosecution will have agreed to the sentence as part of a plea bargain; even if the sentence was not agreed to, prosecutors tend to be very selective in filing appeals (Frase 1991, pp. 752–753; 1993a, pp. 316–319; MSGC 2003, p. 23).

REFERENCES

American Bar Association ["ABA"]. 1968a. *Standards Relating to the Administration of Criminal Justice: Pleas of Guilty.* Chicago: American Bar Association.

————. 1979a. *Standards Relating to the Administration of Criminal Justice: Pleas of Guilty.* 2d ed. Chicago: American Bar Association.

————. 1979b. *Standards Relating to the Administration of Criminal Justice: Sentencing Alternatives and Procedures.* 2d ed. Washington, D.C.: American Bar Association.

————. 1993. *ABA Standards for Criminal Justice: Sentencing.* 3d ed. Washington, D.C.: American Bar Association.

————. 1997. *Standards for Criminal Justice: Pleas of Guilty.* 3d ed. Chicago: American Bar Association.

American Law Institute. 1985. *Model Penal Code and Commentaries, Official Draft and Revised Comments,* Part I, vols. 1–3; Part II, vols. 1–3. Philadelphia: American Law Institute.

————. 2002. *Model Penal Code: Sentencing, Preliminary Draft No. 1.* Philadelphia: American Law Institute.

Bentham, Jeremy (1748–1832). 1931. *The Theory of Legislation,* ed. C. K. Ogden. New York: Harcourt, Brace & Co.

Bottoms, Anthony. 1995. "The Philosophy and Politics of Punishment and Sentencing." In *The Politics of Punishment and Sentencing,* ed. Chris Clarkson and Rod Morgan. Oxford. Oxford University Press.

Crocker, Lawrence. 1992. "The Upper Limits of Just Punishment." *Emory Law Journal* 41:1059–1110.

Frase, Richard S. 1991. "Sentencing Reform in Minnesota, Ten Years After: Reflections on Dale G. Parent's *Structuring Criminal Sentences: The Evolution of Minnesota's Sentencing Guidelines.*" *Minnesota Law Review* 75:727–754.

————. 1993a. "Implementing Commission-based Sentencing Guidelines: The Lessons of the First Ten Years in Minnesota." *Cornell Journal of Law and Public Policy* 2:279–337.

Hart. H. L. A. 1968. *Punishment and Responsibility: Essays in the Philosophy of Law.* New York: Oxford University Press.

Honderich, Ted. 1969. *Punishment: The Supposed Justifications.* London: Hutchinson & Co.

Longford, Frank Pakenham (Lord). 1961. *The Idea of Punishment.* London: Geoffrey Chapman.

Miller, Marc, and Norval Morris. 1986. "Predictions of Dangerousness: Ethical Concerns and Proposed Limits." *Notre Dame Journal of Law, Ethics, and Public Policy* 2:393–444.

Minnesota Sentencing Guidelines Commission ["MSGC"].

———. 2003. *Sentencing Practices: Annual Summary Statistics for Felony Offenders Sentenced in 2001.* Available: http://www.msgc.state.mn.us/.

Morris, Norval. 1951. *The Habitual Criminal.* New York: Longmans, Green.

———. 1953. "Sentencing Convicted Criminals." *Australian Law Journal* 27:186–200.

———. 1974. *The Future of Imprisonment.* Chicago: University of Chicago Press.

———. 1977a. "Punishment, Desert and Rehabilitation." In *Equal Justice under Law* (U.S. Dept. of Justice, Bicentennial Lecture Series), pp. 137–167. Washington, D.C.: U.S. Government Printing Office.

———. 1977b. "Towards Principled Sentencing." *Md. Law Review* 37:267–285.

———. 1982. *Madness and the Criminal Law.* Chicago: University of Chicago Press.

———. 1992. "Incapacitation within Limits." In *Principled Sentencing,* ed. Andrew von Hirsch and Andrew Ashworth. Boston: Northeastern University Press.

———. 1993. "The Honest Politician's Guide to Sentencing Reform." In *The Socio-economics of Crime and Justice,* ed. Brian Forst. Armonk, N.Y.: M. E. Sharpe, Inc.

———and Gordon Hawkins. 1970. *The Honest Politician's Guide to Crime Control.* Chicago: University of Chicago Press.

———. 1977. *Letter to the President on Crime Control.* Chicago: University of Chicago Press.

———and Colin Howard. 1964. *Studies in Criminal Law.* Oxford: Clarendon Press.

———and Marc Miller. 1985. "Predictions of Dangerousness." In *Crime and Justice: A Review of Research,* vol. 6, ed. Michael Tonry and Norval Morris. Chicago: University of Chicago Press.

———and Michael Tonry. 1990. *Between Prison and Probation: Intermediate Punishments in a Rational Sentencing System.* New York: Oxford University Press.

Packer, Herbert. 1968. *The Limits of the Criminal Sanction.* Stanford, Calif.: Stanford University Press.

Tonry, Michael. 1994. "Proportionality, Parsimony, and the Interchangeability of Punishments." In *Penal Theory and Penal Practice: Tradition and Innovation in Criminal Justice,* ed. Antony Duff et al. Manchester: Manchester University Press.

———. 1996. *Sentencing Matters.* New York: Oxford University Press.

von Hirsch, Andrew. 1994. "Sentencing Guidelines and Penal Aims in Minnesota." *Criminal Justice Ethics* 13:39–49.

17

EXCESSIVE RELATIVE TO WHAT? DEFINING CONSTITUTIONAL PROPORTIONALITY PRINCIPLES

Richard S. Frase

Excessiveness and disproportionality are meaningless concepts in the absence of a clearly defined and defensible normative framework. It is therefore rather surprising that courts, when called upon to determine constitutional limits on excessive punishments, have rarely stated, let alone sought to justify, any such framework. Justice Scalia has repeatedly asserted that proportionality is inherently tied to retributive theories of punishment,[3] a concept that the majority of the Court has thus far refused to expressly endorse. But in fact, there are at least two well-established non-retributive proportionality doctrines, which will be discussed after an initial clarification of the applicable retributive principles. As discussed below, each of these three proportionality principles has strong historical and academic support. And as will be shown in Part II, the same three principles are also implicit in many of the Court's Eighth Amendment decisions.

A. LIMITING RETRIBUTIVE PROPORTIONALITY

There is extensive literature on retributive (or "just deserts") punishment theories.[4] For present purposes, the most important and widely accepted principles of these theories may be summarized as follows. Unlike utilitarianism or other consequentialist

---

[3] *E.g.*, Ewing v. California, 538 U.S. 11, 31 (2003) (Scalia, J., concurring) ("Proportionality—the notion that the punishment should fit the crime—is inherently a concept tied to the penological goal of retribution."); Harmelin v. Michigan, 501 U.S. 957, 989 (1991) (opinion of Scalia, J.) (describing proportionality as a retributive concept in part of an opinion joined only by Chief Justice Rehnquist).

[4] *See, e.g.*, Joshua Dressler, Understanding Criminal Law 16–17 (4th ed. 2006) (discussing retributivism as a theory of punishment); Joel Feinberg, Doing & Deserving: Essays in the Theory of Responsibility 217–21 (1970) (explaining strong and weak retributivism).

theories, retributive theories ignore the offender's probable future conduct or the effects that the punishment might have on crime rates or otherwise. Instead, the retributive theory focuses on the actor's degree of blameworthiness for his or her past actions, and in particular, on both the nature and seriousness of the harm foreseeably caused or threatened by the crime, and the offender's degree of culpability in committing the crime—namely, his or her intent (mens rea), motive, role in the offense, possible diminished capacity to obey the law, and so forth. Some retributive scholars believe that prior convictions are irrelevant to this assessment, while other such scholars accept that prior crimes modestly increase an offender's blameworthiness.[5]

Some scholars believe desert principles should define the degree of punishment severity as precisely as possible. As elaborated by writers such as Andrew von Hirsch, this precise-desert theory permits crime-control, budgetary, or other non-retributive values to affect the choice among penalties of more or less equal severity, as well as the overall scale of punishment severity, as determined by the most and least severe penalties.[6] But within that scale, this theory requires strict "ordinal" retributive proportionality in the relative severity of penalties imposed on different offenders.[7] This version of retributive theory is clearly too narrow for constitutional purposes, since it leaves little room for the operation of non-retributive values and goals in individual cases. The Supreme Court has repeatedly held that the Eighth Amendment permits state and federal governments to pursue a variety of non-retributive sentencing goals.[8]

A more modest theory, often referred to as "limiting retributivism," allows non-retributive punishment purposes to be applied within a range defined by upper and lower desert-based limits—penalties must not be clearly too severe nor clearly too lenient, relative to the offender's just deserts.[9] One widely cited version of this theory was proposed by Norval Morris, who viewed retributive assessments as imprecise and therefore posited a range of "not undeserved" penalties.[10] Other writers have proposed

---

[5] *Compare* ANDREW VON HIRSCH, PAST OR FUTURE CRIMES: DESERVEDNESS AND DANGEROUSNESS IN THE SENTENCING OF CRIMINALS 88–91 (1985) (arguing that repeat offenders deserve somewhat greater punishment), *with* GEORGE P. FLETCHER, RETHINKING CRIMINAL LAW 460–66 (1978) (questioning whether a prior record should increase an offender's culpability to any degree). *See generally* Julian V. Roberts, *The Role of Criminal Record in the Sentencing Process, in* 22 CRIME AND JUSTICE: A REVIEW OF RESEARCH 303, 317–20 (Michael Tonry ed., 1997) (discussing the issue of criminal record in theories of punishment).

[6] *See, e.g.,* ANDREW VON HIRSCH, CENSURE AND SANCTIONS (1993).

[7] *See, e.g., id.*

[8] *See, e.g., Ewing,* 538 U.S. at 25 (opinion of O'Connor, J.) (listing permissible non-retributive sentencing goals in an opinion joined by Chief Justice Rehnquist and Justice Kennedy, who provided the necessary votes to affirm, albeit on the narrowest grounds).

[9] Limiting retributive principles also apply to issues of criminal liability, as well as the severity of punishment; only blameworthy persons may be convicted and made eligible for punishment. *See generally* SULLIVAN & FRASE, *supra* note 1, at ch. 6.

[10] NORVAL MORRIS, THE FUTURE OF IMPRISONMENT (1974). Morris's theory is elaborated in Richard S. Frase, *Limiting Retributivism, in* THE FUTURE OF IMPRISONMENT 83–119 (Michael Tonry ed., 2004). *See also* Steven Grossman, *Proportionality in Non-Capital Sentencing: The Supreme Court's Tortured Approach to Cruel and Unusual Punishment,* 84 KY. L.J. 107, 168–72 (1996) (arguing that Eighth Amendment proportionality should be construed in accordance with Morris's theory); Youngjae Lee, *The Constitutional Right Against Excessive Punishment,* 91 VA. L. REV. 677 (2005) (proposing Eighth Amendment retributive limits). Morris's limiting retributive theory has been adopted as the theoretical framework for the revised Model Penal Code sentencing provisions. *See* MODEL PENAL CODE § 1.02(2) (a) cmt. b (Tentative Draft No. 1, 2007) ("Subsection (2) (a)...borrows from the theoretical writings of Norval Morris."). *But see* Alice Ristroph, *Desert, Democracy, and Sentencing Reform,* 96 J. CRIM. L. & CRIMINOLOGY 1293 (2006) (arguing that the concept of deserved punishment is too elastic, opaque, and non-falsifiable to provide meaningful limits

flexible retributive limits on different grounds, emphasizing the special importance of avoiding unfairly severe penalties. For example, the philosopher K.G. Armstrong wrote that justice grants

> the *right* to punish offenders up to some limit, but one is not necessarily and invariably *obliged* to punish to the limit of justice.... For a variety of reasons (amongst them the hope of reforming the criminal) the appropriate authority may choose to punish a man less than it is entitled to, but it is never just to punish a man more than he deserves.[11]

As shown in the cases discussed in Part II of this Article, the Supreme Court's implicit invocations of desert principles are consistent with a limiting retributivism theory, especially one which emphasizes the prevention of excessively severe penalties. This approach finds support in the text of two of the three Eighth Amendment clauses (forbidding excessive bail and excessive fines), and is also consistent with the essential role of constitutional guarantees as protectors of human rights, and as bulwarks against unfairness and abuse of governmental power.

B. NON-RETRIBUTIVE PROPORTIONALITY

Utilitarian (or consequentialist) purposes of punishment focus on the desirable effects (mainly, future crime reduction) which punishments have on the offender being punished, or on other would-be offenders, and on the costs and undesired consequences of punishments.[12] The most widely accepted of these purposes are the following: special (or individual, or specific) deterrence, incapacitation, and rehabilitation of the offender (because he is thought likely to commit further crimes); general deterrence of other would-be violators through fear of receiving similar punishment; and a more diffuse, long-term form of deterrence (sometimes referred to as expressive or denunciation purposes) which focuses on the norm-defining and norm-reinforcing effects that penalties have on the public's views about the relative seriousness, harmfulness, or wrongness of various crimes.[13]

---

on punishment severity; however, Ristroph recognizes that crime-control sentencing goals are also rather elastic and opaque, and that such goals have often been used to justify severe penalties, notwithstanding the greater potential, in theory at least, for using empirical evidence to falsify such claims).

[11] K.G. Armstrong, *The Retributivist Hits Back, in* THE PHILOSOPHY OF PUNISHMENT: A COLLECTION OF PAPERS 138, 155 (H.B. Acton ed., 1969); *see also* H.L.A. HART, PUNISHMENT AND RESPONSIBILITY: ESSAYS IN THE PHILOSOPHY OF LAW 237 (1968) ("[M]any self-styled retributivists treat appropriateness to the crime as setting a *maximum* within which penalties [are chosen on crime-control grounds]...."). *See generally* Frase, *supra* note 10, at 92–94 (stating that numerous authors and model codes emphasize strict desert limits on maximum severity, with looser requirements of minimum sanction severity).

[12] *See generally* DRESSLER, *supra* note 4, at 14–16 (providing a general background on the utilitarian justifications behind criminal punishment); Richard S. Frase, *Punishment Purposes*, 58 STAN. L. REV. 67 (2005) (explaining how judges should consider the purpose of punishment determining sentences).

[13] *See* Kent Greenawalt, *Punishment, in* 3 ENCYCLOPEDIA OF CRIME AND JUSTICE 1282, 1286–89 (Joshua Dressier ed., 3d ed. 2002) (explaining utilitarian justifications for punishment). *See generally* Paul H. Robinson & John M. Darley, *The Utility of Desert*, 91 NW. U. L. REV. 453 (1997) (providing utilitarian arguments for punishments based on desert).

From a utilitarian perspective, a penalty can be disproportionate (or excessive) in two distinct and independent ways corresponding to the ends-benefits and alternative means proportionality principles described below: 1) the costs and burdens of the sentence (or the added costs and burdens, compared to a lesser penalty) may outweigh the likely benefits (or added benefits) produced by the sentence; or 2) the sentence may be disproportionate (that is, unnecessary and therefore excessive) when compared to other, less costly or less burdensome means of achieving the same goals. Each of these utilitarian proportionality principles has ancient roots, as discussed more fully below.

1. Ends-Benefits Proportionality

This principle has been recognized by utilitarian philosophers since the eighteenth century. Cesare Beccaria maintained that criminal penalties should be proportional to the seriousness of the offense, as measured by the social harm caused or threatened by the offense.[14] Jeremy Bentham elaborated several more specific utilitarian arguments for punishing in proportion to the seriousness of the crime.[15] First, he argued that "[t]he greater an offence is, the greater reason there is to hazard a severe punishment for the chance of preventing it"—that is, greater social harm justifies greater preventive effort and expense.[16] Second, Bentham argued that a scale of penalties proportionate to social harm would give offenders "a motive to stop at the lesser" crime.[17] Third, he argued that "the evil of the punishment [should not exceed] the evil of the offence."[18] In addition to public costs, punishments impose suffering on offenders (and also often on their families), and such suffering should not be disproportionate to the seriousness of the crime(s) which the punishment hopes to prevent.

The utilitarian ends-benefits principle and retributive proportionality both require proportionality relative to an offense's severity, but the two theories measure such severity differently. Utilitarian theory punishes in proportion to the harm caused or threatened by the offense, but only when and to the extent that such punishment will prevent future crimes by this offender or others. On the other hand, utilitarian theory considers not only the harm associated with a particular act similar to the defendant's, but also the aggregate harm caused by all such actions, and the difficulty of detecting and deterring such actions. As for the second retributive element of offense severity, offender culpability (as determined by intent, motive, etc.), utilitarians consider culpability factors only when and to the extent that they are related to the likely future benefits of punishment (for example, the dangerousness

---

[14] *See, e.g.*, Cesare Beccaria, An Essay on Crimes and Punishments 21–28 (Adolph Caso ed., Int'l Pocket Library 4th ed. 1992) (1764).

[15] *See, e.g.*, Jeremy Bentham, Theory of Legislation (R. Hildreth trans., Trübner & Co. 4th ed. 1882) (1789).

[16] *Id.* at 326 (emphasis omitted).

[17] *Id.* (emphasis omitted); *see also* Beccaria, *supra* note 14, at 28 ("If an equal punishment be ordained for two crimes that injure society in different degrees, there is nothing to deter men from committing the greater, as often as it is attended with greater advantage."); Andrew von Hirsch et al., Criminal Deterrence and Sentence Severity: An Analysis of Recent Research 41–43 (1999) (discussing the marginal deterrent benefits of penalties proportioned to harms associated with different crimes).

[18] Bentham, *supra* note 15, at 323; *see also* Hart, *supra* note 11, at 173 n.20 (describing the "simple Utilitarian ground that the law should not inflict greater suffering than it is likely to prevent").

and deterrability of this offender or others). Finally, in choosing the proper sentence for a particular offender or group of similar offenders, utilitarian theory considers not only the actual crime control or other benefits produced by sanctions, but also any undesirable consequences of the sanction. Such consequences might include perverse incentives produced by harsh penalties (such as when such penalties encourage offenders to kill potential witnesses or arresting officers). Another example would be the tendency for disproportionate penalties to undermine the public's sense of the relative gravity of different crimes, and cause a public loss of respect for, and willingness to obey and cooperate with, criminal justice authorities. As the philosopher H.L.A. Hart said, "[if] the relative severity of penalties diverges sharply from this rough scale [of proportionality], there is a risk of either confusing common morality or flouting it and bringing the law into contempt."[19]

2. ALTERNATIVE-MEANS PROPORTIONALITY

Utilitarian efficiency values require that, among equally effective means to achieve a given end, those that are less costly or burdensome should be preferred. This has sometimes been referred to as the principle of parsimony,[20] and like the ends-benefits principle discussed above, it has been recognized since the eighteenth century. Cesare Beccaria argued that all punishments should be "necessary; the least possible in the case given."[21] Jeremy Bentham similarly held that punishment itself is evil and should be used as sparingly as possible; in particular, a penalty should not be used "in cases where the same end may be obtained by means more mild."[22] In modern times, alternative-means proportionality principles have frequently been endorsed by scholars and model code drafters.[23]

---

[19] HART, *supra* note 11, at 25. *See generally* Robinson & Darley, *supra* note 13 (arguing for a criminal law system based on the community's ideas of desert); MODEL PENAL CODE § 1.02(2)(a), reporter's n.0 (Tentative Draft No. 1, 2007) (addressing the concern for moral legitimacy in sentencing).

[20] *See, e. g.,* MORRIS, *supra* note 10, at 60–61, 75, 78 (describing parsimony as the "least restrictive—least punitive—sanction necessary to achieve defined social purposes").

[21] BECCARIA, *supra* note 14, at 99.

[22] BENTHAM, *supra* note 15, at 323. Similar means proportionality principles were endorsed in the French Declaration of the Rights of Man and Citizen, Aug. 26, 1789, *reprinted in* FRANK MALOV ANDERSON, THE CONSTITUTIONS AND OTHER SELECT DOCUMENTS ILLUSTRATIVE OF THE HISTORY OF FRANCE: 1789–1901, at 15, 58–60 (1904). Article 8 of the Declaration limited punishments to those that are "strictly and obviously necessary." *Id.* at 59.

[23] *See, e.g.,* MORRIS, *supra* note 10, at 60–61 ("The principle of parsimony infuses the recommendations of the two national crime commissions of the past decade."); FRANKLIN E. ZIMRING ET AL., PUNISHMENT AND DEMOCRACY: THREE STRIKES AND YOU'RE OUT IN CALIFORNIA 189–91 (2001) (describing classes of excessive punishment claims); Margaret Jane Radin, *The Jurisprudence of Death: Evolving Standards for the Cruel and Unusual Punishments Clause,* 126 U. PA. L. REV. 989, 1043–56 (1978) (discussing dignity and excessiveness in light of utilitarian theories of punishment); Richard G. Singer, *Sending Men to Prison: Constitutional Aspects of the Burden of Proof and the Doctrine of the Least Drastic Alternative as Applied to Sentencing Determinations,* 58 CORNELL L. REV. 51, 72–89 (1972) (explaining the least drastic alternative doctrine); Michael Tonry, *Parsimony and Desert in Sentencing, in* PRINCIPLED SENTENCING: READINGS ON THEORY & POLICY 202 (Andrew von Hirsch & Andrew Ashworth eds., 2d. ed. 1998) ("[J]udges should be directed to impose the least severe sentence consistent with the governing purposes at sentencing." (emphasis omitted)). Notably, "[t]he Model Penal Code and all three editions of the [American Bar Association] sentencing standards explicitly or implicitly recognized the principle of parsimony." Frase, *supra* note 10, at 94–95. The principle is also endorsed in the proposed revisions of the Model Penal Code sentencing provisions. MODEL PENAL CODE § 1.02(2) (a) (iii) cmt. f (Tentative Draft No. 1, 2007) ("[T]he rule of parsimony states a logical truism—punishments beyond those 'necessary' are by definition gratuitous.").

IV

EMOTION, INTUITION, AND DETERMINISM

Traditional disagreements between retributivists and consequentialists are implicitly based on two assumptions. The first is that there is a choice to be made between their positions. The second is that human beings possess free will, thereby justifying the imputation of moral responsibility to offenders. Both assumptions face challenges.

Social and cognitive psychologists in recent years argue that human beings, probably as a product of natural selection, are hard-wired to be retributivists. If this is so, there is no choice to be made: we are all retributivists. A new body of writing on "empirical desert" has emerged from this finding, and other related ones on intuitions about punishment (Robinson 2008).

Neuroscientists documenting brain functioning increasingly argue that the evidence for determinism, and its correlate, the absence of free will, are becoming unarguable (Greene and Cohen 2004 [chapter 20 in this volume]). If this is so, the case for retributivism becomes impossible to make: neither an offender nor anyone else is in a moral sense responsible for their actions.

The argument that human beings are intuitively punitive has long been recognized and is easier to address (e.g., Mackie 1982 [chapter 18 in this volume]). If human beings are capable of making moral choices, we can decide that our intuitions are ignoble and disregard them. Herbert Wechsler and Jerome Michael acknowledged that retribution represents "the unstudied belief of most men" but concluded, "no legal provision can be justified merely because it calls for the punishment of the morally guilty by penalties proportioned to their guilt, or criticized merely because it fails to do so" (Michael and Wechsler 1940, pp. 7, 11). Paul Robinson (2007 [chapter 19 in this volume], 2008) responds interestingly, on consequentialist grounds, that the effectiveness of law depends on its legitimacy in the eyes of citizens, and accordingly that punishment practices should be premised on retributivist ideas in order to accord with widely held intuitions. Otherwise, they will be perceived as illegitimate.

The determinism/free will challenge may be harder to meet. There are three mainstream positions. "Libertarians"[1] believe that the evidence for determinism is unpersuasive and that human beings possess free will. For them, retributivism presents no inherent logical problem. "Hard determinists" believe the evidence is clear, and will steadily become clearer, and accordingly that the concepts of human free will and moral responsibility are meaningless. Clearer evidence will result in "rejection of common-sense conceptions of free will" and lead to "rejection of retributivism and an ensuing shift towards a consequentialist approach to punishment" (Greene and Cohen 2004, p. 1776). The third group, "compatibilists," argue that free will and determinism are compatible.

Not many writers on punishment theory have addressed the problem of determinism in light of the findings of modern neuroscience. Those who have are nearly all compatibilists (e.g., Morse 2004; Moore 2009). They argue that imputations to offenders of moral responsibility require only that people have some general capacity for rational choice, and that nothing neuroscience is likely to establish will refute that proposition.

REFERENCES

Bibliographic details concerning works that are mentioned but are not reprinted in this volume can be found in the reference list to the introduction except for the following:

Moore, Michael S. 2009. *Causation and Responsibility.* New York: Oxford University Press.

Morse, Stephen J. 2004. "New Neuroscience, Old Problems." In *Neuroscience and the Law: Brain, Mind, and the Scales of Justice,* edited by B. Garland. New York: Dana.

Paul H. Robinson. 2008. *Distributive Principles of Criminal Law: Who Should be Punished How Much.* New York: Oxford University Press.

---

[1] The term "libertarian" is used in a special sense in this literature and does not have the same meaning it does in political philosophy.

18

MORALITY AND THE RETRIBUTIVE EMOTIONS

J. L. Mackie

The Finnish philosopher Edward Westermarck, in the first two chapters of *Ethical Relativity*, argues against the supposed objectivity of moral judgments, claiming that the concepts which are used as predicates in these judgments are ultimately based on emotions. In the next two chapters he tries to substantiate this claim by identifying the special class of moral emotions on which these concepts are based, moral approval and moral disapproval or indignation. He says that these are a sub-class of what he calls retributive emotions, resentment and retributive kindly emotion (which also includes anger, revenge, and gratitude), and are marked off from their nonmoral counterparts by disinterestedness and at least apparent impartiality. He explains these differentiating features by the fact that "society is the birth-place of the moral consciousness," that "tribal custom was the earliest rule of duty."[1] Westermarck also argues that disapproval is more important than approval, and that the resentment of which it is a subspecies is likewise more important, and occurs more widely in the animal kingdom, than retributive kindly emotion. He maintains that the retributive element in punishment is uneliminable, and cannot be wholly replaced by such principles as deterrence and reformation, though he also says that there is "some connection between these ends and the retributive aim of moral resentment."[2]

These theses are all, I believe, substantially correct, but the arguments Westermarck gives for them are inconclusive. He does not really show that moral concepts

---

[1] Edward Westermarck, *Ethical Relativity* (London: Kegan Paul, Trench, Trubner & Co., Ltd., 1932), p. 109.
[2] Ibid., p. 80.

are derived from what he identifies as the moral emotions, nor that these emotions are derived from their nonmoral counterparts, nor how disinterestedness and apparent impartiality result from society and its customs. The causal claims implicit in his account are not strongly supported by the merely descriptive facts that there are resemblances between, for example, the various feelings that he classes under the heading of resentment, and while he says that "rightly understood, resentment is preventive in its nature,"[3] he does not explain this except by showing that resentment tends to be modified by the offender's repentance and that an act of moral resentment is "apt to resemble a punishment inflicted with a view to deterring from crime."[4]

But a more conclusive case can be made out for his theses. This turns upon what I shall call the paradox of retribution. This paradox, I shall argue, cannot be resolved except with the help of a hypothetical account in which all of Westermarck's main assertions take their place. The paradox is that, on the one hand, a retributive principle of punishment cannot be explained or developed within a reasonable system of moral thought, while, on the other hand, such a principle cannot be eliminated from our moral thinking. As Westermarck says, "It is one of the most interesting facts relating to the moral consciousness of the most humane type, that it in vain condemns the gratification of the very desire from which it sprang."[5]

To explain this paradox, I must first identify the crucial retributive principle and then show how all attempts fail to make moral sense of it. Within what can be broadly called a retributive theory of punishment, we should distinguish negative retributivism, the principle that one who is not guilty must not be punished, from positive retributivism, the principle that one who is guilty ought to be punished. We can, indeed, add a third principle of permissive retributivism, that one who is guilty may be punished. In these principles, "must not," "ought," and "may" are meant to express moral judgments. For completeness, we should think also of quantitative variants of each principle, that even one who is guilty must not be punished to a degree that is out of proportion to his guilt, that one who is guilty ought to be punished in proportion to his guilt, or may be punished in proportion to his guilt. Also, while it might be possible to defend such judgments, perhaps all three (or all six) of them, as derived rules within, say, a utilitarian moral system, that would not constitute a retributive theory of punishment. To yield anything worth counting as a retributive theory, such principles must be thought of as having some immediate, underived moral appeal or moral authority. Now I suggest that in moral thinking they are very widely, perhaps universally, felt to have such an immediate appeal and underived authority. This is undoubtedly true of negative retributivism, including its quantitative variant. Permissive retributivism, too, is immediately plausible. When the three principles are distinguished, many people are inclined to reject that of positive retributivism, to say that only some possible future benefit, such as deterrence or reformation, can justify punishment; yet I suspect that when we consider

[3] Ibid., p. 83.
[4] Ibid., p. 81.
[5] Ibid., p. 86.

actual or possible cases of crimes or wrongdoing of kinds that we really regard as unmitigated and inexcusable, then we do after all tend to see them as in themselves calling for the infliction of some adequate penalty. Indeed, if we did not feel that there was such a positive retributivist reason for imposing a penalty, we should not feel that even sound arguments in terms of deterrence or reformation or any similar future benefit would make it morally right to inflict suffering or deprivation on the criminal. Certainly this is Westermarck's opinion, though his discussion of the point is obscured by his failure to distinguish positive retributivism, which is the really controversial issue, from the negative and permissive views.

If these retributivist principles have such immediate appeal and apparent authority, how are we to make sense of them, to relate them to some system of moral ideas? One suggestion which we must mention, though only in order to dismiss it, is that the connection between crime or wrongdoing and punishment is analytic. An old and often-criticized move of this sort is to say that negative retributivism is not needed as a moral principle, because it is logically impossible to punish the innocent. It is very doubtful whether this is true, but even if it were true it would be trivial, it would not cover quantitative negative retributivism, and there would still be room for, and a strong call for, the moral principle that one who is not guilty must not be made to suffer in any of the ways that would ordinarily count as punishment, call them what you will. A less familiar move of the same sort is to say that we simply have not fully grasped the concept of punishment unless we integrate it with the three retributive principles: in particular it is part of that concept that punishment is called for by wrongdoing. But again, even if this is true, it merely shifts the crucial problem to another place: how are we to make moral sense of a concept which includes this requirement, which envisages suffering or deprivation as being called for by a previous wrong action? Let us run through some possible answers to this question.[6]

It would be idle in this context to refer to the satisfaction that may be felt by the surviving victims of a crime when the criminal suffers, or to the likelihood that they will have recourse to more damaging kinds of retaliation if there is no legal penalty. This would be an attempt to justify punishment by its consequences, and does not help us to make sense of an essentially retributive principle. True, it presupposes that those victims themselves have retributive sentiments, but that does nothing to explain the retributivist moral principle. Similarly the suggestion that the punishment will satisfy the outraged feelings of the public at large, or will placate a god who has been offended by the crime, is equally forward-looking or consequentialist, equally useless for making sense of the backward-looking principles of retribution. Indeed, it presupposes that a morally respectable public or a morally respectable god already accepts such principles, and therefore must assume that there is some *other* morally coherent defense and

---

[6] J. G. Cottingham, in "Varieties of Retribution," *Philosophical Quarterly* 29 (1979), lists the following nine different approaches, each of which has been called retributivist: Repayment Theory; Desert Theory; Penalty Theory; Minimalism; Satisfaction Theory; Fair Play Theory; Placation Theory; Annulment Theory; and Denunciation Theory. Of these, Minimalism is negative retributivism; Penalty Theory is the above-mentioned reference to logical necessity; and Desert Theory seems to be the bald, unexplained assertion that crime simply does deserve punishment; all the others on this list, as well as two further suggestions, are examined below.

explanation of them. The notion that punishment may impress upon the public the wrongness of the crime, and so have a useful educative effect, is also consequentialist, and it too seems to presuppose independent retributivist views: the public will take a penalty as a dramatic assertion of the wrongness of the act for which it is imposed only if it already has the concept of punishment as being called for by wrongdoing.

It is often suggested that by being punished a criminal pays a debt to society. But how can this be, unless what he suffers does some good to society? Reparation might be justified in this way, but reparations are clearly different from punishments; only the already rejected principle of satisfaction would turn punishment into a sort of reparation.

A more serious attempt to explain the retributivist principle as the retrospective principle that it is, without turning it into something that is primarily forward-looking, is the suggestion made explicitly by Hegel, but perhaps anticipated by Kant, that an appropriate penalty annuls or cancels the crime. If left unpunished, the crime would still be alive and flourishing, but punishment tramples on it and wipes it out. But this really is incoherent. The punishment may trample on the criminal, but it does not do away with the crime. It may, perhaps, by way of deterrence, reformation, and the like help to prevent future similar crimes, and it may put a temporary or a permanent stop to this particular offender's criminal career; but again all of these are only possible consequentialist justifications, yet it seems that it is merely by confusion with them that it could be thought that the punishment annuls the crime. It should be clear beyond all question that the past wrong act, just because it is past, cannot be annulled. Might a crime be like a marriage or a contract or a conviction which can be annulled in the sense of being made to be without legal effect or validity? Though the act has occurred, can it be made to be no longer a crime? Perhaps this is the notion of expiation, that the suffering of the penalty absorbs and wipes out the guilt. This would make sense if the guilt was itself seen as consisting essentially in the wrong action's calling for an appropriate penalty: that call would die out when it was satisfied. But again this line of thought presupposes and therefore cannot explain positive retributivism.

It is often suggested that by being punished a criminal pays a debt to society.

A related suggestion uses the notion of fair play. All the members of a society are seen as being engaged in some kind of competition in accordance with rules; the criminal has gained an unfair advantage by breaking the rules; fairness is restored by the imposition of a penalty that takes this advantage away from him. Now what is annulled or cancelled is not the past crime, but the present advantage that has accrued from it. This suggestion at last offers us something that is both coherent and genuinely retributive. This explanation is retrospective, nonconsequentialist, in that the justification for the penalty is complete as soon as the penalty has itself been carried out; the balance is thereby restored, irrespective of any future results. This principle has well-known and obviously reasonable exemplifications in what are literally rule-governed competitive games, such as association football. If a player commits a foul in the "penalty area," that is, wrongly obstructs an opponent or his shot in the neighborhood of his own goal, then the other side is awarded a penalty kick which gives it a good chance of scoring a goal. But the notion is that fairness has been (roughly) restored whether a goal results or not. However, this principle has little application to the punishment of most wrongdoing or crime. Above all, it would make penalties proportional not to the degree of wrongness or guilt, but to the advantages gained thereby; unsuccessful criminal attempts would not be punished at all. This is clearly so in the games where this principle is at home: a foul not near the offender's goal is penalized less, and there is an "advantage rule": the referee will not stop play to penalize an infringement if the innocent side has the advantage anyway. All this is very far from the central notion of positive retributivism, which sees punishment as having its point in somehow counterbalancing the wrongness of the previous act, not in correcting the present advantage that the wrongdoer has gained by it.

It is often argued that the retributive approach to punishment respects the dignity of the people concerned in a way that the rival utilitarian approach does not. Each person is seen as a responsible agent. He has the right not to be made to suffer as long as he commits no wrong. If he does something wrong he loses his immunity in proportion to the degree of his guilt; but only by his own choice. If he has unfairly invaded the rights of others, he cannot reasonably complain at what would otherwise be a corresponding invasion of his own rights. This line of thought does seem to make sense of negative and permissive retributivism; but it still leaves positive retributivism unexplained. It is sometimes said that this is covered by an extension of the same line of thought. The criminal has freely chosen his own punishment insofar as he, as a citizen, has shared in the making of the law in accordance with which he is punished; he endorsed this law in general and in application to others, so he cannot fairly protest against its application to himself. This is plausible, and it would yield a partly retributive justification of punishment in that if such a law had really been endorsed, explicitly or implicitly, by the criminal among others, and if such endorsement could itself be seen as reasonable, then the only further justification required for the imposition of the penalty in a particular case would be the retrospective one that an offense of the sort condemned by the law has indeed been committed. But now all the weight falls on the conditional clauses. This justification would apply only in a society whose laws were themselves fair in their incidence upon various classes of citizens and had been made by something like Rousseau's general will; those who support retributivism may be happy to accept this restriction.[7] But, further, the law imposing this penalty must be one which the free and equal citizens of such a society could reasonably make. What reason could they have for doing so? Since no other explanation of positive retributivism has stood up to criticism, this condition requires that there should be some other, forward-looking, consequentialist reason for having such a law. The general practice of punishing requires, for this approach to be coherent, a consequentialist justification, though, given this practice, reasonably endorsed by the general will, the imposing of individual penalties needs only retrospective grounds to justify it.

---

[7] For example Jeffrie G. Murphy, in "Marxism and Retribution," *Philosophy and Public Affairs* 2 (1973): 217–43, says that "there may be some truth in Marx's claim that the retributive theory, though formally correct, is materially inadequate," in that the "presupposition that all men, including criminals, are voluntary participants in a reciprocal system of benefits" is empirically false about actual societies.

This survey shows that all these attempts to make sense of the principle of positive retributivism, as an independent principle with immediate moral authority, have signally failed. And we have, I believe, covered all the main lines of thought that have been used to try to make retributivism coherent. Yet this survey has also indicated how deeply ingrained retributivist—even positive retributivist—ideas are, if only by bringing to light the circularity of many of the explanations that have been widely thought to be satisfactory, that is, the tendency of proposed accounts to build upon the supposed existence of already valid positive retributive principles. People find the proposed accounts plausible because they are so firmly wedded to retributivist ways of thinking that they find it difficult to confront the task of justifying retributivism from cold, without implicitly assuming what they are setting out to explain. We do have a concept of punishment which involves positive as well as negative and permissive retributivism, and, as Westermarck says, attempts to reconstruct that concept so as to free it from that involvement are radically unsatisfying. We are indeed faced, therefore, with the paradox of retribution.

For all that has been said so far, it might be thought that this is just a special problem about one particular concept, that of punishment. But if we analyze the concept of a morally wrong action it will be seen to have much wider significance. In the central cases, the wrongness of an action is thought of as being made up of three elements, its being harmful, its being forbidden, and its calling for a hostile response. No one of these elements, if the others are somehow denied, is sufficient to make an action wrong in the full sense. Even if we try to think of an action's having any two of these features, but not the third, we hesitate to say that it would then be wrong. In particular, if we think of an action's being both harmful and forbidden, but nevertheless try to withhold the judgment that it calls for any sort of hostile response, I suggest that we cannot then judge wholeheartedly that it is morally wrong. Moreover, all three elements involve what Westermarck calls objectivization. The wrong action is not harmful just to this or that person, it is harmful *simpliciter*, or, as Sidgwick put it, from the point of view of the universe. It is not forbidden just by this or that authority, it is somehow forbidden intrinsically, absolutely; it simply should not be done. Its moral quality includes both a generalized harmfulness and an intrinsic not-to-be-done-ness. And similarly it is not just from this or that particular person that it calls for a hostile response; rather, it is such that a hostile response *from somewhere* is needed, the situation is somehow generally unsatisfactory if the wrong action gets by without any proportional reaction.

The attempts to make sense of the principle of positive retributivism, as an independent principle with immediate moral authority, have signally failed.

To complete the analysis of this concept, we have to note that the three elements we have identified are not merely conjoined. It is not that we have moral wrongness whenever all three just happen to occur together: they are rather seen as being necessarily connected with one another. A wrong action is intrinsically forbidden because it is harmful from the point of view of the universe, and it calls for a hostile response because it is both harmful generally and intrinsically forbidden.

It might be thought that this analysis makes redundant the vain search in which we have been engaged for some way of making moral sense of positive retributivism. What need is there for any further explanation of the principle that one who has done wrong ought to be punished, if it is involved in the very concept of wrongness that a wrong action calls for a hostile response? But this is a mistake. Buried inside the complex concept of wrongness, lying behind the analytic judgment that what is wrong calls for a hostile response, is the synthetic judgment that what is harmful generally and intrinsically forbidden calls on that account for a hostile response. It is for an elucidation and justification of this synthetic judgment that we have so far sought in vain; what would come to the same thing would be a "deduction" in Kant's sense of the complex concept of moral wrongness itself.

On other occasions I have stressed the difficulties in the second of these three elements, the notion of intrinsic not-to-be-done-ness, or the supposed objective prescriptivity of moral features of which this is an instance. I have argued that our central moral concepts are prescriptive but also include a claim to objectivity for that prescriptiveness itself. I have argued, as Westermarck does, against the actual objectivity of moral qualities or moral facts, while insisting that this subjectivist conclusion cannot be established by the mere analysis of moral concepts and judgments, since, as I say, such analysis reveals this claim to objectivity. My main argument has been based on the "queerness" of this notion of objective prescriptivity, on the metaphysical and epistemological difficulties it involves; these are such that the best explanatory hypothesis to account for the phenomena of moral thinking does not include the postulate that there are any such objectively prescriptive truths; instead, it will use Westermarck's view that the belief in such truths results from moral emotions, whose distinctive features are developed by social interactions and then, through objectivization, yield the misleading appearance of objective reality.[8]

Now, however, we can reinforce this argument in another way. The central moral concept of the wrongness of an action includes, as we have seen, the synthetic judgment that what is harmful generally and intrinsically forbidden calls for a hostile response: this concept contains a very general form of the positive retributivist principle. In this general form, it applies not just to the special topic of punishment, but pervasively, wherever the central concept of moral wrongness is in force. But the apparent impossibility of making moral sense of this retributive principle must then add to the implausibility of the moral concepts' claim to objectivity. Although many, perhaps most, or even all moral thinkers have an apparent intuition in favor of this principle—a moral intuition, not merely a linguistic or conceptual one—it cannot be defended as an immediately valid and authoritative principle with the status of an objective truth. This is over and above the general metaphysical and epistemological difficulties that beset the notion of *any* objectively prescriptive truth; but, because it affects the very central concept of moral wrongness, it casts its shadow over moral thought as a whole.

---

[8] These arguments can be found in Chapter 1 of my *Ethics: Inventing Right and Wrong* (Harmondsworth: Penguin, 1977).

I have concentrated on hostile rather than on kindly retribution, on punishment rather than on gratitude and reward, on the wrong rather than on the good and the right, because gratitude and reward do not generate so acute a paradox as their hostile counterparts. Reasons for doing good are not so hard to integrate into a moral system as reasons for doing harm. Yet there is some element of paradox even here, as extreme utilitarians have seen. Why should previous good actions be in themselves a reason for doing good to these agents in particular, rather than simply seeking to maximize overall utility? But hostile retributivism is more of a problem, and, as Westermarck says, kindly retributive tendencies are less pervasive and less central in morality than hostile ones. The more forceful moral notions, of what is obligatory or of what justice requires or of rights that must not be infringed, all involve the concept of its being wrong to do something, or wrong not to do something, and the concept of wrongness, as we have seen, itself includes the principle of positive retributivism.

How, then, are we to resolve the paradox of retribution? It ceases to be puzzling when, like Westermarck, we make the Humean move of saying that moral distinctions are founded on sentiment, not on reason, and so ask not, "Why do wrong actions deserve penalties and good actions deserve rewards?" but rather, "Why do we have an ingrained tendency to see wrong actions as calling for penalties and good actions as calling for rewards?" I suggest that we can find a biological explanation for the tendency to feel nonmoral resentment of injuries and gratitude for benefits, and a sociological explanation for the development, out of these, of their moral counterparts.

Suppose that an animal, human or nonhuman, is injured by another, either of the same species or of some other, where the first is able to do some harm to the second which the second can associate with its aggression and perhaps recognize as a reaction to it. Then such retaliation will tend to benefit the retaliator, since the aggressor will be discouraged from repeating the attack. This mechanism can operate either at the psychological level, by negative reinforcement in an individual aggressor, or at a genetic level, where there will be some selective pressure against a kind of aggression that commonly proves harmful to the aggressor. For both reasons there will then be some selective pressure in favor of the tendency to retaliate. This need not be, and originally will certainly not be, the result of calculation and deliberate choice by the retaliator; it is rather that the mechanism of natural selection mimics calculated, purposive, action. Spontaneous retaliation will thus develop because it is often beneficial, either immediately or in a longer term, but it will be spontaneous, not chosen by the retaliator for the sake of the benefit. Of course, we need not assume that retaliation is always beneficial, as it clearly is not, and we can well admit that what is thus biologically developed is likely to be a "mixed strategy," a combination of retaliatory tendencies with tendencies, say, to flight or, at least among members of the same species, to conciliation. All that we need is that there should be a retaliatory component in whatever mixed strategy is developed, and it is easy to see why this should be so. And the spontaneous repaying of benefit with benefit may be developed in a corresponding way.

The paradox of retribution ceases to be puzzling when . . . we make the Humean move
of saying that moral distinctions are founded on sentiment, not on reason.

Initially what is thus explained is retributive behavior, but in creatures that have the capacity for emotion this will naturally be accompanied by the development of retributive emotions directed towards the sources of injury or help. However, these are still only the nonmoral retributive emotions. In order to account for their moral counterparts we must, as Westermarck says, turn to society as the birthplace of the moral consciousness. Among animals that live in social groups, it is easy to explain cooperation in the resentment of injuries. The helping, in this as in other ways, of individuals closely related to an agent will be of direct genetic advantage, of a sort that results in selection in its favor, insofar as close relatives will tend to share the agent's genes. There can also be selective pressures in favor of reciprocal altruism, the tendency to help those who help the agent in return.[9] But what may be most important, especially among human beings, is that cooperative social practices or conventions can grow up by social interaction. A simple model will illustrate this possibility. If two agents will do better in some way if they cooperate, they may begin to do so gradually and tentatively, each making his further cooperative moves conditional upon a favorable response from the other. Such a tentative development of a cooperative practice is easy to describe in terms of a series of conscious choices; but it could equally well grow up more automatically, through agents coming habitually to adopt ways of behaving in relation to one another that tend to help each in whatever pursuits are already established as part of his behavior. Reciprocal sanctioning, the fact that each will be less cooperative if the other is less cooperative, can generate and maintain cooperative conventions even without any series of conscious choices.[10] Since cooperation in general is thus explicable, cooperation in resentment can be understood in social animals and particularly in human beings once resentment itself has been explained. And cooperation in resentment is more likely to be useful to those who develop it than cooperation in gratitude: the repelling of injuries will often require greater concentrations of force than are needed in order to make a worthwhile return for a benefit.

From cooperation in resentment to moral disapproval or indignation is a further step, but not an enormous one. It requires that certain *kinds* of behavior should be cooperatively resented and opposed and seen as generally harmful. For this will yield the "disinterestedness" and "apparent impartiality" that are characteristic of the moral sentiments. The fact that it is kinds of behavior that are resented is linked with what I call the first stage of universalization and with disinterestedness, while the notion

---

[9] For an account of these genetic mechanisms, see R. Dawkins, *The Selfish Gene* (Oxford: Oxford University Press, 1976). In my "The Law of the Jungle: Moral Alternatives and Principles of Evolution," *Philosophy* 53 (1978): 455–64, I have shown that although, in general, tendencies will not be favored by selection simply because they will benefit a group in whose members they occur, such "group selection" can take place in special circumstances, and the example used was one of reciprocal altruism.

[10] Hume, in the *Treatise of Human Nature*, Book III, Part ii, finds the origin of the "artificial virtues" in such "conventions" established and maintained by the indirect operation of self-love. I interpret and develop his account in my *Hume's Moral Theory* (London: Routledge and Kegan Paul, 1980).

that they are harmful generally, not just to this or that person or group, is linked with the second stage of universalization and with apparent impartiality.[11] But both these moves result from the need for a morality to be accepted by a society as a whole, to be strengthened by each person's influencing of others in its favor and to be passed on by collective teaching to later generations. All of this is only a further development of such conventions as those mentioned above and is supported in the same way by social interaction where there is a partial conflict of interests. Such a development presupposes fairly advanced intellectual powers associated with the retributive emotions and the socially maintained retributive behavior. Nevertheless, the essential drives, the directing forces which sustain the resulting patterns of action, still come from the emotions and the conventions, and are only further canalized by the recognition of kinds of behavior. And the judgment that a certain kind of behavior is harmful, even when it is true, may often follow rather than precede the cooperative resentment and opposition to it. For, as we have seen, there are both genetic and social mechanisms which can pick out what is harmful and develop hostile reactions to it, reactions that will themselves be beneficial, without the agents themselves having consciously realized that these reactions are beneficial or that what they are reacting against is harmful. The apparent purposiveness is explained throughout by procedures of natural selection and the growth of conventions.

Of course, this is only a sketch. Further explanations are needed for all the details of human moral attitudes and their objectivization into moral beliefs, and much of Westermarck's work was meant as a contribution to such explanations. But what was crucially required, and was not, I think, given by him with sufficient clarity, was an outline of the basic mechanisms and main steps by which recognizably moral thinking could arise in the first place.

We can, then, describe a possible course of evolution by which retributive behavior and emotions, cooperative resentment, and the disinterested moral sentiments could have developed in turn. It is an essential feature of this hypothetical account that at every stage it involves spontaneous, noncalculating, retributive tendencies, mainly hostile, though there is room for some kindly retribution too. In this lies the solution of our paradox of retribution. For what we have sketched is the development of a system of sentiments (which, through objectivization, yield beliefs) which from the point of view of those who have them are both originally and persistently retrospective. They are essentially retributive, essentially connected with previous harmful—or, occasionally, beneficial—actions. When we seek to rationalize our moral thinking, to turn it into a system of objective requirements, we cannot make sense of this retrospectivity. We either, with the utilitarians, attempt to deny it and eliminate it or to subordinate it to forward-looking purposes, or, with their retributivist opponents, try various desperate and incoherent devices, none of which, as we have seen, will really accommodate the principle of desert within any otherwise intelligible order of ideas. But if we recognize them simply as sentiments—though socially developed sentiments—we have

---

[11] I distinguish the various stages of universalization, and discuss their place in moral thinking, in Chapter 4 of *Ethics: Inventing Right and Wrong*.

no difficulty in understanding their obstinately retrospective character. Moreover, we can now elucidate Westermarck's otherwise obscure reference to "some connection between these ends [such as deterrence and reformation] and the retributive aim of moral resentment."[12] These utilitarian "ends" are the results for which moral resentment, and its non-moral forerunners, have been selected and encouraged by genetic and social evolutionary mechanisms. They are functions in terms of which we—as scientists, not as moralists—can explain the development of moral resentment: they are the apparent ends in evolution's imitation of purposiveness.

Since an objectivist moral view can neither avoid nor resolve the paradox of retribution, which pervades moral thinking insofar as the positive retributivist principle is involved in the central concept of a wrong action, whereas a sentimentalist or subjectivist view can resolve it, this whole problem constitutes a powerful support for the latter sort of view, and therefore for Westermarck's thesis that the moral concepts are ultimately based on emotions. Our resolution of the paradox also included a hypothetical account of how the moral emotions could have developed from their nonmoral counterparts by the addition of disinterestedness and apparent impartiality; and though this was only a hypothesis, it is confirmed by its success in helping to explain what otherwise resists explanation. Thus we have been able to supplement and round out Westermarck's theory, fitting his various theses into a more tightly argued and causally coherent account.

---

[12] Westermarck, *Ethical Relativity*, p. 80.

19

THE ROLE OF MORAL PHILOSOPHERS
IN THE COMPETITION BETWEEN
DEONTOLOGICAL AND EMPIRICAL
DESERT

*Paul H. Robinson**

INTRODUCTION

Desert has become increasingly attractive as a principle by which to distribute criminal liability and punishment. A number of modern sentencing guidelines have adopted it as their distributive principle.[1] Most recently, a committee of the American Law Institute proposed revising the Model Penal Code "purposes" section to adopt desert as the dominant distributive principle.[2]

---

* Colin S. Diver Distinguished Professor of Law, University of Pennsylvania. The author wishes to acknowledge the valuable research assistance of Desiree Liverseidge and the useful comments of Leo Katz, Stephen Morse, and participants of the Conference on Law and Morality, Institute of Bill of Rights Law, William & Mary School of Law, especially Claire Finkelstein and Michael Moore.

[1] *See, e.g.*, David Boerner & Roxanne Lieb, *Sentencing Reform in the Other Washington*, 28 CRIME & JUST. 71, 71–72 (2001) ("[Washington State's] Sentencing Reform Act of 1981 rejected many core tenets of indeterminate sentencing, putting into place a sentencing system based on principles of just desert and accountability."); Michele Cotton, *Back with a Vengeance: The Resilience of Retribution as an Articulated Purpose of Criminal Punishment*, 37 AM. CRIM. L. REV. 1313, 1358 (2000) ("California endorsed retribution as 'the' purpose for its punishment in 1977 and Pennsylvania identified it as the 'primary' purpose in 1982...." (footnote omitted)); Barry C. Feld, *The Juvenile Court Meets the Principle of Offense: Punishment, Treatment, and the Difference It Makes*, 68 B.U.L. REV. 821, 874 (1988) ("Minnesota's sentencing guidelines for adult offenders...[are] expressly designed to achieve 'just deserts'...."); *cf.* Michael Tonry, *U.S. Sentencing Systems Fragmenting, in* PENAL REFORM IN OVERCROWDED TIMES 21, 28 tbl.1.1 (Michael H. Tonry ed., 2001) (showing that desert is a highly expressed value in comprehensive structured sentencing jurisdictions such as Minnesota and Washington).

[2] According to the Model Penal Code,

The general purposes of the provisions governing sentencing and corrections, to be discharged by the many official actors within the sentencing and corrections system, are:

But these reforms, and the current debates, are unclear as to whether the conception of desert under consideration is a deontological or an empirical one.[3] The two can be quite different. A deontological conception of desert, based on reasoning from principles of right and good and aimed toward giving us a transcendent notion of justice,[4] would distribute criminal liability and punishment differently than would an empirical conception of desert, based upon empirical research into the shared intuitions of justice of the community that is to be governed by the code or practice being formulated. For example, moral philosophers disagree about the significance of resulting harm, and each side of the debate has plausible arguments to make.[5] In contrast, all available data suggest a nearly universal and deeply held view among the community that resulting harm does matter, that it increases an offender's deserved punishment.[6] This practical difference is only one of a host of issues on which a moral philosopher's conclusion might vary from the empirical data on lay persons' shared intuitions of justice.[7]

(a) in decisions affecting the sentencing and correction of individual offenders:

(i) to render punishment within a range of severity proportionate to the gravity of offenses, the harms done to crime victims, and the blameworthiness of offenders;

(ii) when possible with realistic prospect of success, to serve goals of offender rehabilitation, general deterrence, incapacitation of dangerous offenders, and restoration of crime victims and communities, provided that these goals are pursued within the boundaries of sentence severity permitted in subsection (a)(i); and

(iii) to render sentences no more severe than necessary to achieve the applicable purposes from subsections (a)(i) and (ii)....

Model Penal Code § 1.02(2) (Preliminary Draft No. 3, 2004) [hereinafter Model Penal Code].

[3] Although deontological desert traditionally has carried the desert banner in academic circles, today's law- and policymakers often give people's-sense-of-justice explanations for desert-based legislation. In other words, legislators make empirical claims, not philosophical arguments. *See, e.g.,* Model Penal Code, *supra* note 2, § 1.02(2) cmt. c (suggesting that because desert can be difficult to quantify at times, sentencing commissions should solicit a diverse range of community perspectives, and that doing so gives the commissions a "unique credibility").

[4] But, as the reader will see in the text following note 19, only some moral philosophers—moral realists—conceive of desert as having such transcendent nature.

[5] Those that have argued that resulting harm should matter include Leo Katz, *Why the Successful Assassin Is More Wicked than the Unsuccessful One,* 88 Cal. L. Rev. 791, 806 (2000) (arguing by hypothetical that principled moral analysis suggests harm should be considered when assessing blameworthiness); Ken Levy, *The Solution to the Problem of Outcome Luck: Why Harm Is Just As Punishable As the Wrongful Action that Causes It,* 24 Law & Phil. 263, 303 (2005); and Michael S. Moore, *The Independent Moral Significance of Wrongdoing,* 5 J. Contemp. Legal Issues 237, 267–71 (1994) (positing that because we resent successful wrongdoers more than we do those who unsuccessfully attempt harm, we feel more guilty about our own completed misdeeds than we do about attempts, and we are dissatisfied with reasonable moral choices that produce undesirable consequences, which suggests that "results matter" in the moral arena). Those that have argued that resulting harm should not matter include Larry Alexander, *Crime and Culpability,* 5 J. Contemp. Legal Issues 1, 8 (1994); Joel Feinberg, *Equal Punishment for Failed Attempts: Some Bad but Instructive Arguments Against It,* 37 Ariz. L. Rev. 117, 119 (1995); Sanford H. Kadish, *Foreword: The Criminal Law and the Luck of the Draw,* 84 J. Crim., L. & Criminology 679, 680 (1994); Stephen J. Morse, *The Moral Metaphysics of Causation and Results,* 88 Cal. L. Rev. 879, 881–82 (2000); Stephen J. Morse, *Reason, Results, and Criminal Responsibility,* 2004 U. Ill. L. Rev. 363, 409; Richard Parker, *Blame, Punishment, and the Role of Result,* 21 Am. Phil. Q. 269, 273 (1984) (advocating that resulting harm should not be relevant to punishment determinations, as "[f]ortune may make us healthy, wealthy, or wise, but it ought not determine whether we go to prison"); and Stephen J. Schulhofer, *Harm and Punishment: A Critique of Emphasis on the Results of Conduct in the Criminal Law,* 122 U. Pa. L. Rev. 1497, 1600–03 (1974).

[6] *See, e.g.,* Paul H. Robinson & John M. Darley, Justice, Liability, and Blame: Community Views and the Criminal Law 14–28, 181–97 (1995) (reporting empirical studies); John H. Mansfield, *Hart and Honoré, Causation in the Law—A Comment,* 17 Vand. L. Rev. 487, 494–95 (1964) (concluding that "[t]he notion that there should be a difference in punishment [between unsuccessful attempts and completed crimes] is deeply rooted in popular conscience, and to ignore it is to risk [jury] nullification").

[7] *See generally* Robinson & Darley, *supra* note 6 (comparing community views on a wide variety of criminal law issues to existing legal rules and discussing the points of disagreement). Finding wide and persistent disagreement among moral philosophers on many if not most significant issues is common. *See*

Should we prefer one conception of desert over the other for use as a distributive principle for criminal liability and punishment? Each of the two competing conceptions of desert offer distinct advantages and disadvantages.

I. DEONTOLOGICAL DESERT

Deontological desert can offer a unique and critically important value to the criminal justice law- or policymaker: it can provide a foundation for desert that transcends any particular case, community, or culture. That is, it can give us a means by which we can tell the truth of what is deserved, insulated from the vicissitudes of human irrationality and emotions. This deontological conception of desert gives us the ability to determine when our shared intuitions of justice may be wrong. Even though a liability or punishment rule may be popular, it nonetheless may be unfair or unjust, and the deontological conception of desert lets us spot these justice errors in people's intuitions.

The standard complaint against relying upon such a deontological conception of desert in distributing criminal liability and punishment is that it leads to disutility.[8] Those consequentialists who seek to minimize future crime, for example, will be quick to point out that deontological desert as a distributive principle will allow future crimes to occur that could have been avoided under a utilitarian distributive principle.[9] Traditionally, that fact has meant a utilitarian preference for distributing liability to optimize deterrence, rehabilitation, incapacitation, or some combination of them.[10]

II. EMPIRICAL DESERT

Reliance upon an empirical conception of desert in the distribution of criminal liability and punishment prompts its own set of complaints. One primary objection is that people's intuitions of justice are too vague and suffer too much disagreement to be effectively operationalized. But empirical studies show this common wisdom to be false. In fact, people's shared intuitions of justice are quite nuanced: small changes in facts

---

supra note 5. Indeed, it is likely that on any issue over which law- or policymakers themselves disagree—prompting them to look to other disciplines for guidance—philosophers almost certainly will disagree among themselves. Other disciplines may have disagreements, but because most have some objective test by which a writer ultimately may be proven right or wrong, over time some coalescence tends to emerge around an accepted view. A proposed theory ends up either explaining more of the available data, and is accepted; or does not, and is rejected. But without such a clear test mechanism, moral philosophy lacks a path to coalescence. Because philosophers will disagree on nearly any significant issue, an outsider often has difficulty gaining something useful, in part because, to make an informed judgment as to which view ought to be given deference, the outsider must herself know something about moral philosophy. In other words, the outsider must become a bit of an insider. Ultimately, the moral philosophy literature is not terribly accessible, and thus its informed use is commonly costly.

[8] *See* Aya Gruber, *Righting Victim Wrongs: Responding to Philosophical Criticisms of the Nonspecific Victim Liability Defense,* 52 BUFF. L. REV. 433, 450–52 (2004) (describing deontological theories of punishment); Eyal Zamir, *The Efficiency of Paternalism,* 84 VA. L. REV. 229, 233 (1998) (contrasting consequentialist and deontological theories).

[9] *See* ROBINSON & DARLEY, *supra* note 6, at 5–7.

[10] *See, e.g.,* MODEL PENAL CODE § 1.02(1) (1962) (listing the general purposes of the provisions).

produce large and predictable changes in the assessment of blameworthiness.[11] Further, an astounding level of agreement exists across cultures and demographics on the relative degree of blameworthiness. Although people and cultures disagree about the general level of punishment severity a criminal justice system should adopt, once the endpoint of a society's punishment continuum is set, there is significant agreement on the ordinal ranking of cases along that continuum, at least for the core wrongs of physical aggression, unconsented-to takings, and deception or dishonesty in exchanges.[12] Thus, empirical desert does not produce an indeterminate range of punishment, as some have suggested,[13] but rather a specific amount. It is not that a particular violation necessarily deserves a specific amount of punishment in some absolute sense; rather, each violation, once placed on a fixed continuum of punishment, deserves a particular amount of punishment because that amount is required to give that violation its proper ordinal ranking among the range of possible violations. One can easily imagine how the erroneous common wisdom about disagreement developed: disagreement over general punishment severity—the continuum endpoint—masked the agreement on the ordinal ranking of violations.

As noted, the broad consensus on ordinal ranking exists primarily for the core wrongs: injury to others, the taking of property, and deceit or dishonesty in dealings.[14] As the harm or wrong moves away from this core, disagreements appear across cultures and demographics, depending primarily upon the perceived strength of the analogy between the new conduct and the core wrongs. Ultimately, operationalizing empirical desert is quite feasible, more so than deontological desert, because of the higher level of agreement on the former than the latter.

Consequentialists might offer a second kind of objection to empirical desert as a distributive principle, similar to the disutility complaint they make against deontological desert: such a desert distribution of criminal liability and punishment allows future crime that could be avoided with a distribution that optimizes deterrence, rehabilitation, incapacitation, or other traditional utilitarian crime control mechanisms.[15] But, as I have suggested elsewhere, strong arguments suggest greater utility in a distribution based on shared intuitions of justice than in a distribution based upon optimizing deterrence, rehabilitation, or incapacitation.[16]

To briefly summarize those "utility of desert" arguments:[17] deviating from a community's intuitions of justice inspires resistance and subversion among participants—juries, judges, prosecutors, and offenders—when effective criminal justice depends upon acquiescence and cooperation.[18] Relatedly, some of the system's power to control conduct derives from its potential to stigmatize violators—with some persons this is

---

[11] *See* Paul H. Robinson & Robert Kurzban, Intuitions of Justice pt. I (Mar. 19, 2006) (unpublished manuscript, on file with author).

[12] *Id.* pt. II.

[13] *See, e.g.*, NORVAL MORRIS, THE FUTURE OF IMPRISONMENT 74 (1974).

[14] *See supra* note 12 and accompanying text.

[15] *See* Gruber, *supra* note 8, at 454–68 (discussing consequentialist theories of punishment, including deterrence, rehabilitation, and incapacitation).

[16] *See* Paul H. Robinson & John M. Darley, *The Utility of Desert*, 91 Nw. U. L. REV. 453, 456 (1997).

[17] *Id.*

[18] ROBINSON & DARLEY, *supra* note 6, at 202.

a more powerful, yet essentially cost-free, control mechanism compared to imprisonment.[19] Yet the system's ability to stigmatize depends upon it having moral credibility with the community; for a violation to trigger stigmatization, the law must have earned a reputation for accurately assessing what violations do and do not deserve moral condemnation.[20] Liability and punishment rules that deviate from a community's shared intuitions of justice undercut this reputation.[21]

Perhaps the greatest utility of desert comes through a more subtle but potentially more influential form.

The real power to gain compliance with society's rules of prescribed conduct lies not in the threat of official criminal sanction, but in the [influence] of the intertwined forces of social and individual moral control. The networks of interpersonal relationships in which people find themselves, the social norms and prohibitions shared among those relationships and transmitted through those social networks, and the internalized representations of those norms and moral precepts [control people's conduct].

...The law is not irrelevant to these social and personal forces. Criminal law, in particular, plays a central role in creating and maintaining the social consensus necessary for sustaining moral norms. In fact, in a society as diverse as ours, the criminal law may be the only society-wide mechanism that transcends cultural and ethnic differences. Thus, the criminal law's most important real-world effect may be its ability to assist in the building, shaping, and maintaining of these norms and moral principles. It can contribute to and harness the compliance-producing power of interpersonal relationships and personal morality.

The criminal law [also] can have...effect in gaining compliance with its commands [through another mechanism]. If it earns a reputation as a reliable statement of what the community...perceive[s] as condemnable, people are more likely to defer to its commands as morally authoritative and as appropriate to follow in those borderline cases in which the propriety of certain conduct is unsettled or ambiguous in the mind of the actor. The importance of this role should not be underestimated; in a society with the complex interdependencies characteristic of ours, an apparently harmless action can have destructive consequences. When the action is criminalized by the legal system, one would want the citizen to "respect the law" in such an instance even though he or she does not immediately intuit why that action is banned. Such deference will be facilitated if citizens are disposed to believe that the law is an accurate guide to appropriate prudential and moral behavior.

The extent of the criminal law's effectiveness in [all] these respects—in [avoiding resistance and subversion of an unjust system, in bringing the power

---

[19] *Id.* at 201.
[20] *Id.* at 201–02.
[21] *Id.* at 202.

of stigmatization to bear,] in facilitating[,] communicating[, and maintaining] societal consensus on what is and is not condemnable, and in gaining compliance in borderline cases through deference to its moral authority...is to a great extent dependent on the degree of moral credibility that the criminal law has [gained] in the minds of the citizens governed by it. Thus,...the criminal law's moral credibility is essential to effective crime control, and is enhanced if the distribution of criminal liability is perceived as "doing justice," that is, if it assigns liability and punishment in ways that the community perceives as consistent with [their shared intuitions of justice]. Conversely, the system's moral credibility, and therefore its crime control effectiveness, is undermined by a distribution of liability that deviates from community perceptions of just desert.[22]

The important point here is that distribution according to the moral philosophy conception of desert is not only unnecessary for these utilitarian crime control benefits, but indeed ineffective in gaining them. The beneficial consequences of a desert distribution, described above, flow not from following a deontological desert distribution, but only from following an empirical desert distribution—one that tracks the community's shared intuitions of justice. It is the community's *perception* that justice is being done that pays dividends, not the system's actual success as measured by a deontological conception of desert.[23]

On the other hand, empirical desert can be criticized on the ground that it is not a reliable source for determining what is truly deserved, as deontological desert can claim. In other words, generally tracking a community's shared intuitions of justice may well build some credibility within that population that the criminal justice system is doing justice, but it does not follow that in fact justice is being done. Shared intuitions might simply be wrong; they tell us only what lay persons *believe* is just. Only deontological desert can reliably tell us what is just.[24]

III. THE ROLE OF MORAL PHILOSOPHERS IN THE COMPETITION BETWEEN DEONTOLOGICAL AND EMPIRICAL DESERT

What role do moral philosophers play in this competition between deontological and empirical desert? We nonphilosophers might well assume that they stand on the side of deontological desert, reasoning out justice from principles of right and good, facing on the other side the social psychology researchers mapping people's shared intuitions of justice to determine empirical desert. In fact, the situation is somewhat more complex than this, in ways that reflect both well and badly on the usefulness of the current moral philosophy project.

[22] *Id.* at 587–88.
[23] *See id.* at 7.
[24] *Id.* at 6.

First, consider the special usefulness moral philosophy provides. Unfortunately, social psychologists are rather unsophisticated about what drives people's intuitions of justice. Most of the studies that they have done without the involvement of moral philosophers or criminal law theorists are nearly useless, because the investigators are testing concepts that muddle together what moral philosophers know to be distinct and importantly different issues. The moral philosophy literature is the richest and most sophisticated source about lay intuitions of justice that exists today, and it is the starting point that I recommend to any social psychologist doing research in the area.

The reason for this superiority is clear: the current methodology of moral philosophers relies heavily upon intuitions of justice, both informally and formally, as in Rawls's "reflective equilibrium."[25] A standard analytic form, if not *the* standard form, among moral philosophers today is to use hypotheticals and philosophers' own intuitions about the proper resolution of the hypothetical as a basis for building moral principles.[26] Their judgments about the intuitively proper resolution of each of a series of hypotheticals are used as data points, as it were, from which philosophers derive a moral principle, which can then be tested and refined by comparing the moral principle results to philosophers' intuitions on other hypotheticals.[27] The ultimate effect of this standard methodology is that philosophers have thought more carefully about intuitions of justice than any other group, and their literature reflects this sophistication.

But this methodology is problematic, for several reasons. First, presumably philosophers want to rely upon intuitions that accurately capture the shared intuitions of the community, not some idiosyncratic intuition that only philosophers share. The danger here is not only that philosophers as a group may be different from the rest of the community—some nonphilosophers would think this an obvious truth—but also that, even if philosophers are not idiosyncratic, their methods of testing their own intuitions violate many rules of reliable empirical testing. Presumably, in no situation would moral philosophers be happy to use inaccurate representations of intuitions of justice. But, as I have described elsewhere,[28] the methods by which moral philosophers think they are learning intuitions of justice are simply bad research techniques, giving good reason to believe that they produce unreliable results in assessing intuitions of justice.[29] If philosophers think intuitions of justice are useful to their enterprise, they

---

[25] *See* JOHN RAWLS, A THEORY OF JUSTICE 42–43 (rev. ed. 1999) (explaining that the best sense of justice is one that matches a person's judgments in reflective equilibrium—a state reached after consideration of various conceptions of justice).

[26] *See generally* Kadish, *supra* note 5 (employing numerous hypotheticals in an attempt to prove the harm doctrine unsupportable); Katz, *supra* note 5 (employing hypotheticals to counter Kadish's view of the harm doctrine); Paul H. Robinson, *Some Doubts About Argument by Hypothetical*, 88 CAL. L. REV. 813 (2000) (critically analyzing Professor Katz's use of the "argument-by-hypothetical" method).

[27] *See also* Leo Katz, *Incommensurable Choices and the Problem of Moral Ignorance*, 146 U. PA. L. REV. 1465, 1480, 1482–84 (1998) (providing an example of moral philosophers using intuitive analysis of case hypotheticals as a standard method by using a hypothetical, derived from the application of the necessity defense to situations where the actor has culpably created the justifying situation, to argue that at times persons can be blamed for making the wrong decision in a state "of unavoidable moral ignorance").

[28] *See* Robinson, *supra* note 26, at 823 ("[In some cases, t]he results we get…are probably not intuitive judgments of blameworthiness but more likely intellectualized answers generated by applying the professor's resident collection of theoretical positions—[for example,] whether resulting harm ought to be judged significant.").

[29] *Id.* at 825.

ought to at least get them right. They ought to look to a more reliable source, or adopt more reliable methods of social psychology research, and not "wing it" on their own.

A second, more problematic feature of moral philosophy's heavy reliance upon intuitions of justice is that it compromises philosophy's ability to reliably spot community intuitions of justice that are wrong, in the sense of conflicting with a notion of justice that transcends shared intuitions.[30] The methodological reliance of moral philosophy on intuitions of justice creates a bias in favor of moral principles consistent with intuitions. Thus, moral principles with principled, reasoned support might nonetheless fail to gain currency among philosophers, or might be discarded, simply because philosophers as a group think their results inconsistent with intuitions—a practical veto by philosophers' shared intuitions.

But providing this transcendent check on intuitions is how philosophers are most useful to law- and policymakers. It is for this check—to assure that a shared intuition of justice does not violate a transcendent principle of justice—that philosophy is given deference. Yet moral philosophers, by their heavy reliance upon intuitions of justice, have become unreliable in performing just this task.

Many nonphilosophers may be shocked to hear that many, if not most, of today's moral philosophers no longer see themselves as being in the business of trying to provide this transcendent check. The moral relativists have given up the enterprise entirely; only the moral realists continue to see it as an explicit and attainable goal. Everyone in between sees themselves as providing some kind of useful guidance to law- and policymakers, but guidance of a sort that is different from the transcendent check on people's intuitions of justice that law- and policymakers need.

The useful guidance they think they provide is, in a sense, to "rationalize" intuitions, as, for example, in translating a set of shared intuitions of justice on a set of cases into a general principle. But social psychologists do that when they interpret data from lay intuition studies to construct a principle that seems to explain how subjects are thinking about the test cases. Philosophers might argue that they also examine and resolve conflicts between competing intuitions, in part by taking account of the relative depth of our commitment to the intuitions in conflict. But, of course, that too is just an empirical question—to which intuition do people have greater allegiance when two conflict?—that social psychologists can more reliably investigate.

But one can imagine that moral philosophers might respond that they are doing something more here than just resolving conflicts between intuitions by testing the relative depth of commitment—the relative strength—of the conflicting intuitions. They might claim that their analysis here goes beyond the empirical to bring to bear some more fundamental, transcendent analysis, relying upon objective principles of right and good. And if they did this, they would have something useful to say to law- and policymakers. They would be providing that needed transcendent check on people's intuitions of justice. Unfortunately, most of today's moral philosophers do not do this, and do not claim to do this. Perhaps they do not because they think it impossible to do, which is fine, but then they ought to accept their limited usefulness to law- and policymakers, which many of them may do.

---

[30] Robinson & Darley, *supra* note 6, at 5–7.

A defense of the intuition-dependent methodology that many moral philosophers appear to make is found in a claim that intuitions of justice provide some validating effect in assessing true moral principles of justice:[31] that many people share an intuition means that a moral principle consistent with that intuition is thereby made stronger. Social psychologists would find this an odd claim, for one has good reason to believe that a person's intuitions of justice are simply behavioral phenomena. It is well documented that people hold strong intuitions of justice even though the reasons for their holding those intuitions are inaccessible to them.[32] When asked to explain an intuition, many people will have nothing to offer, other than perhaps "It's obvious." Others, perhaps those who prize their self-image as a rational being, will offer an explanation, yet different people offer different explanations even though their intuitions are identical.

In other words, the research suggests that the source of intuitions of justice is not rational reasoning but rather the effects of evolutionary and social forces.[33] And such a source of intuitions provides no reason to think that intuitions have any claim to validate a moral principle in any transcendent philosophical sense. What gave evolutionary advantage six million years ago on the savanna hardly justifies enshrining as a moral truth today. Monkeys and other primates have intuitions of a similar phenomenological sort, even intuitions about fairness.[34] Are we to assume that monkey "intuitions" about fairness contribute to the validation of moral principles for monkeys?

CONCLUSION

Do I think that moral philosophers should cease their reliance upon intuitions of justice as they construct what they offer as the deontological conception of desert? Not entirely, for I see great benefit from their work in the research to map shared intuitions of justice. But my guess is that moral philosophers themselves would want to contribute something more than what social psychologists already can do. If they are to provide a philosophical conception of desert that transcends our intuitions of justice, they must adopt a methodology that is more skeptical of reliance upon those intuitions.

---

[31] *See, e.g.,* RAWLS, *supra* note 25, at 42–43; JUDITH JARVIS THOMSON, THE REALM OF RIGHTS 20 (1990) ("We certainly act as if we thought of many of our moral beliefs as necessary truths.").

[32] *See, e.g.,* Jonathan Haidt, *The Emotional Dog and Its Rational Tail: A Social Intuitionist Approach to Moral Judgment,* 108 PSYCHOL. REV. 814, 814 (2001) (describing a situation in which subjects were asked for a reason to believe incest is wrong, and generally could not supply one, but simply asserted that the act is wrong even if they could not explain why); Jonathan Haidt & Matthew A. Hersh, *Sexual Morality: The Cultures and Emotions of Conservatives and Liberals,* 31 J. APPLIED SOC. PSYCHOL. 191, 217–18 (2001); Debra Lieberman et al., *Does Morality Have a Biological Basis? An Empirical Test of the Factors Governing Moral Sentiments Relating to Incest,* 270 PROC. ROYAL SOC'Y LONDON 819, 825–26 (2003).

[33] *See supra* note 32.

[34] *See, e.g.,* FRANS DE WAAL, CHIMPANZEE POLITICS: POWER AND SEX AMONG APES 38–39 (rev. ed. 1998) (reporting evidence that some nonhuman primates have capacities to think purposefully). In a recent experiment, brown capuchin monkeys (*Cebus apella*) refused to participate in an exchange if they observed another monkey receiving a better deal than they received. Some researchers suggest that this refusal implies not only understanding of exchange and unfairness, but a willingness to endure a cost in what can be interpreted as a kind of protest. Sarah F. Brosnan & Frans B.M. de Waal, *Monkeys Reject Unequal Pay,* 425 NATURE 297, 297–98 (2003). Indeed, Brosnan and de Waal mention cases of monkeys "[t]hrowing the token at the experimenter." *Id.* at 299. Similarly, some evidence from the field indicates that rhesus macaques (*Macaca mulatta*) are subject to harassment if they do not let others know when they have found food, an intriguing potential example of moralistic punishment. Marc D. Hauser & Peter Marler, *Food-Associated Calls in* Rhesus Macaques (Macaca mulatta): *II. Costs and Benefits of Call Production and Suppression,* 4 BEHAV. ECOLOGY 206, 211–12 (1993).

20

———

FOR THE LAW, NEUROSCIENCE CHANGES NOTHING AND EVERYTHING

Joshua Greene and Jonathan Cohen

The rapidly growing field of cognitive neuroscience holds the promise of explaining the opera-tions of the mind in terms of the physical operations of the brain. Some suggest that our emerging understanding of the physical causes of human (mis)behaviour will have a trans-formative effect on the law. Others argue that new neuroscience will provide only new details and that existing legal doctrine can accommodate whatever new information neuroscience will provide. We argue that neuroscience will probably have a transformative effect on the law, despite the fact that existing legal doctrine can, in principle, accommodate whatever neu-roscience will tell us. New neuroscience will change the law, not by undermining its current assumptions, but by transforming people's moral intuitions about free will and responsibility. This change in moral outlook will result not from the discovery of crucial new facts or clever new arguments, but from a new appreciation of old arguments, bolstered by vivid new illus-trations provided by cognitive neuroscience. We foresee, and recommend, a shift away from punishment aimed at retribution in favour of a more progressive, consequentialist approach to the criminal law.

Keywords: law; brain; morality; free will; punishment; retributivism

1. INTRODUCTION

The law takes a long-standing interest in the mind. In most criminal cases, a successful conviction requires the prosecution to establish not only that the defendant engaged in proscribed behaviour, but also that the misdeed in question was the product of *mens rea*, a 'guilty mind'. Narrowly interpreted, *mens rea* refers to the intention to commit a criminal act, but the term has a looser interpretation by which it refers to all mental states consistent with moral and/or legal blame. (A killing motivated by insane delusional beliefs may meet the requirements for *mens rea* in the first sense, but not the second.) (Goldstein *et al.* 2003) Thus, for centuries, many legal issues have turned on the question: 'what was he thinking?'.

To answer this question, the law has often turned to science. Today, the newest kid on this particular scientific block is cognitive neuroscience, the study of the mind through the brain, which has gained prominence in part as a result of the advent of functional neuroimaging as a widely used tool for psychological research. Given the law's aforementioned concern for mental states, along with its preference for 'hard' evidence, it is no surprise that interest in the potential legal implications of cognitive neuroscience abounds. But does our emerging understanding of the mind as brain really have any deep implications for the law? This theme issue is a testament to the thought that it might. Some have argued, however, that new neuroscience contributes nothing more than new details and that existing legal principles can handle anything that neuroscience will throw our way in the foreseeable future (Morse 2004).

In our view, both of these positions are, in their respective ways, correct. Existing legal principles make virtually no assumptions about the neural bases of criminal behaviour, and as a result they can comfortably assimilate new neuroscience without much in the way of conceptual upheaval: new details, new sources of evidence, but nothing for which the law is fundamentally unprepared. We maintain, however, that our operative legal principles exist because they more or less adequately capture an intuitive sense of justice. In our view, neuroscience will challenge and ultimately reshape our intuitive sense(s) of justice. New neuroscience will affect the way we view the law, not by furnishing us with new ideas or arguments about the nature of human action, but by breathing new life into old ones. Cognitive neuroscience, by identifying the specific mechanisms responsible for behaviour, will vividly illustrate what until now could only be appreciated through esoteric theorizing: that there is something fishy about our ordinary conceptions of human action and responsibility, and that, as a result, the legal principles we have devised to reflect these conceptions may be flawed.

Our argument runs as follows: first, we draw a familiar distinction between the consequentialist justification for state punishment, according to which punishment is merely an instrument for promoting future social welfare, and the retributivist justification for punishment, according to which the principal aim of punishment is to give people what they deserve based on their past actions. We observe that the common-sense approach to moral and legal responsibility has consequentialist elements, but is largely retributivist. Unlike the consequentialist justification for punishment, the retributivist justification relies, either explicitly or implicitly, on a demanding—and some say overly demanding—conception of free will. We therefore consider the standard responses to the philosophical problem of free will (Watson 1982). 'Libertarians' (no relation to the political philosophy) and 'hard determinists' agree on 'incompatibilism', the thesis that free will and determinism are incompatible, but they disagree about whether determinism is true, or near enough true to preclude free will. Libertarians believe that we have free will because determinism is false, and hard determinists believe that we lack free will because determinism is (approximately) true. 'Compatibilists', in contrast to libertarians and hard determinists, argue that free will and determinism are perfectly compatible.

We argue that current legal doctrine, although officially compatibilist, is ultimately grounded in intuitions that are incompatibilist and, more specifically, libertarian. In other words, the law *says* that it presupposes nothing more than a metaphysically modest notion of free will that is perfectly compatible with determinism. However, we argue that the law's intuitive support is ultimately grounded in a metaphysically overambitious, libertarian notion of free will that is threatened by determinism and, more pointedly, by forthcoming cognitive neuroscience. At present, the gap between what the law officially cares about and what people really care about is only revealed occasionally when vivid scientific information about the causes of criminal behaviour leads people to doubt certain individuals' capacity for moral and legal responsibility, despite the fact that this information is irrelevant according to the law's stated principles. We argue that new neuroscience will continue to highlight and widen this gap. That is, new neuroscience will undermine people's common sense, libertarian conception of free will and the retributivist thinking that depends on it, both of which have heretofore been shielded by the inaccessibility of sophisticated thinking about the mind and its neural basis.

The net effect of this influx of scientific information will be a rejection of free will as it is ordinarily conceived, with important ramifications for the law. As noted above, our criminal justice system is largely retributivist. We argue that retributivism, despite its unstable marriage to compatibilist philosophy in the letter of the law, ultimately depends on an intuitive, libertarian notion of free will that is undermined by science. Therefore, with the rejection of common-sense conceptions of free will comes the rejection of retributivism and an ensuing shift towards a consequentialist approach to punishment, i.e. one aimed at promoting future welfare rather than meting out just deserts. Because consequentialist approaches to punishment remain viable in the absence of common-sense free will, we need not give up on moral and legal responsibility. We argue further that the philosophical problem of free will arises out of a conflict between two cognitive subsystems that speak different 'languages': the 'folk psychology' system and the 'folk physics' system. Because we are inherently of two minds when it comes to the problem of free will, this problem will never find an intuitively satisfying solution. We can, however, recognize that free will, as conceptualized by the folk psychology system, is an illusion and structure our society accordingly by rejecting retributivist legal principles that derive their intuitive force from this illusion.

2. TWO THEORIES OF PUNISHMENT: CONSEQUENTIALISM AND RETRIBUTIVISIM

There are two standard justifications for legal punishment (Lacey 1988). According to the forward-looking, consequentialist theory, which emerges from the classical utilitarian tradition (Bentham 1982), punishment is justified by its future beneficial effects. Chief among them are the prevention of future crime through the deterrent effect of the law and the containment of dangerous individuals. Few would deny that the deterrence of future crime and the protection of the public are legitimate justifications for punishment. The controversy surrounding consequentialist theories concerns their serviceability as *complete* normative theories of punishment. Most theorists find them inadequate in this regard (e.g. Hart 1968), and many argue that consequentialism fundamentally mischaracterizes the primary justification for punishment, which, these critics argue, is retribution (Kant 2002). As a result, they claim, consequentialist theories justify intuitively unfair forms of punishment, if not in practice then in principle. One problem is that of Draconian penalties. It is possible, for example, that imposing the death penalty for parking violations would maximize aggregate welfare by reducing parking violations to near zero. But, retributivists claim, whether or not this is a good idea does not depend on the balance of costs and benefits. It is simply wrong to kill someone for double parking. A related problem is that of punishing the innocent. It is possible that, under certain circumstances, falsely convicting an innocent person would have a salutary deterrent effect, enough to justify that person's suffering, etc. Critics also note that, so far as deterrence is concerned, it is the *threat* of punishment that is justified and not the punishment itself. Thus, consequentialism might justify letting murderers and rapists off the hook so long as their punishment could be convincingly faked.

The standard consequentialist response to these charges is that such concerns have no place in the real world. They say, for example, that the idea of imposing the death penalty for parking violations to make society an overall happier place is absurd. People everywhere would live in mortal fear of bureaucratic errors, and so on. Likewise, a legal system that deliberately convicted innocent people and/or secretly refrained from punishing guilty ones would require a kind of systematic deception that would lead inevitably to corruption and that could never survive in a free society. At this point critics retort that consequentialist theories, at best, get the right answers for the wrong reasons. It is wrong to punish innocent people, etc. because it is fundamentally unfair, not because it leads to bad consequences in practice. Such critics are certainly correct to point out that consequentialist theories fail to capture something central to common-sense intuitions about legitimate punishment.

The backward-looking, retributivist account does a better job of capturing these intuitions. Its fundamental principle is simple: in the absence of mitigating circumstances, people who engage in criminal behaviour *deserve* to be punished, and that is why we punish them. Some would explicate this theory in terms of criminals' forfeiting rights, others in terms of the rights of the victimized, whereas others would appeal to the violation of a hypothetical social contract, and so on. Retributivist theories come in many flavours, but these distinctions need not concern us here. What is important for our purposes is that retributivism captures the intuitive idea that we legitimately punish to give people what they deserve based on their past actions—in proportion to their 'internal wickedness', to use Kant's (2002) phrase—and not, primarily, to promote social welfare in the future.

The retributivist perspective is widespread, both in the explicit views of legal theorists and implicitly in common sense. There are two primary motivations for questioning retributivist theory. The first, which will not concern us here, comes from a prior commitment to a broader consequentialist moral theory. The second comes from scepticism regarding the notion of desert, grounded in a broader scepticism about the possibility of free will in a deterministic or mechanistic world.

3. FREE WILL AND RETRIBUTIVISM

The problem of free will is old and has many formulations (Watson 1982). Here is one, drawing on a more detailed and exacting formulation by Peter Van Inwagen (1982): determinism is true if the world is such that its current state is completely determined by (i) the laws of physics and (ii) past states of the world. Intuitively, the idea is that a deterministic universe starts however it starts and then ticks along like clockwork from there. Given a set of prior conditions in the universe and a set of physical laws that completely govern the way the universe evolves, there is only one way that things can actually proceed.

Free will, it is often said, requires the ability do otherwise (an assumption that has been questioned; Frankfurt 1966). One cannot say, for example, that I have freely chosen soup over salad if forces beyond my control are sufficient to necessitate my choosing soup. But, the determinist argues, this is precisely what forces beyond your control do—always. You have no say whatsoever in the state of the universe before your birth; nor do you have any say about the laws of physics. However, if determinism is true, these two things together are sufficient to determine your choice of soup over salad. Thus, some say, if determinism is true, your sense of yourself and others as having free will is an illusion.

There are three standard responses to the problem of free will. The first, known as 'hard determinism', accepts the incompatibility of free will and determinism ('incompatibilism'), and asserts determinism, thus rejecting free will. The second response is libertarianism (again, no relation to the political philosophy), which accepts incompatibilism, but denies that determinism is true. This may seem like a promising approach. After all, has not modern physics shown us that the universe is *in*deterministic (Hughs 1992)? The problem here is that the sort of indeterminism afforded by modern physics is not the sort the libertarian needs or desires. If it turns out that your ordering soup is completely determined by the laws of physics, the state of the universe 10 000 years ago, *and* the outcomes of myriad subatomic coin flips, your appetizer is no more freely chosen than before. Indeed, it is *randomly* chosen, which is no help to the libertarian. What about some other kind of indeterminism? What if, somewhere deep in the brain, there are mysterious events that operate independently of the ordinary laws of physics and that are somehow tied to the will of the brain's owner? In light of the available evidence, this is highly unlikely. Say what you will about the 'hard problem' of consciousness (Shear 1999), there is not a shred of scientific evidence to support the existence of *causally effective* processes in the mind or brain that violate the laws of physics. In our opinion, any scientifically respectable discussion of free will requires the rejection of what Strawson (1962) famously called the 'panicky metaphysics' of libertarianism.[1]

Finally, we come to the dominant view among philosophers and legal theorists: compatibilism. Compatibilists concede that some notions of free will may require indefensible, panicky metaphysics, but maintain that the kinds of free will 'worth wanting', to use Dennett's (1984) phrase, are perfectly compatible with determinism. Compatibilist theories vary, but all compatibilists agree that free will is a perfectly natural, scientifically respectable phenomenon and part of the ordinary human condition. They also agree that free will can be undermined by various kinds of psychological deficit, e.g. mental illness or 'infancy'. Thus, according to this view, a freely willed action is one that is made using the right sort of psychology—rational, free of delusion, etc.

Compatibilists make some compelling arguments. After all, is it not obvious that we have free will? Could science plausibly deny the obvious fact that I am free to raise my hand *at will*? For many people, such simple observations make the reality of free will non-negotiable. But at the same time, many such people concede that determinism, or something like it, is a live possibility. And if free will is obviously real, but determinism is debatable, then the reality of free will must not hinge on the rejection of determinism. That is, free will and determinism must be compatible. Many compatibilists sceptically ask what would it mean to give up on free will. Were we to give it up, wouldn't we have to immediately reinvent it? Does not every decision involve an implicit commitment to the idea of free will? And how else would we distinguish between ordinary rational adults and other individuals, such as young children and the mentally ill, whose will—or whatever you want to call it—is clearly compromised? Free will, compatibilists argue, is here to stay, and the challenge for science is to figure out how exactly it works and not to peddle silly arguments that deny the undeniable (Dennett 2003).

The forward-looking-consequentialist approach to punishment works with all three responses to the problem of free will, including hard determinism. This is because consequentialists are not concerned with whether anyone is really innocent or guilty in some ultimate sense that might depend on people's having free will, but only with the likely effects of punishment. (Of course, one might wonder what it means for a hard determinist to justify any sort of choice. We will return to this issue in § 8.) The retributivist approach, by contrast, is plausibly regarded as requiring free will and the rejection of hard determinism. Retributivists want to know whether the defendant truly *deserves* to be punished. Assuming one can deserve to be punished only for actions that are freely willed, hard determinism implies that no one really deserves to be punished. Thus, hard determinism combined with retributivism requires the elimination of all punishment, which does not seem reasonable. This leaves retributivists with two

---

[1] Of course, scientific respectability is not everyone's first priority. However, the law in most Western states is a public institution designed to function in a society that respects a wide range of religious and otherwise metaphysical beliefs. The law cannot function in this way if it presupposes controversial and unverifiable metaphysical facts about the nature of human action, or anything else. Thus, the law must restrict itself to the class of intersubjectively verifiable facts, i.e. the facts recognized by science, broadly construed. This practice need not derive from a conviction that the scientifically verifiable facts are necessarily the only facts, but merely from a recognition that verifiable or scientific facts are the only facts upon which public institutions in a pluralistic society can effectively rely.

options: compatibilism and libertarianism. Libertarianism, for reasons given above, and despite its intuitive appeal, is scientifically suspect. At the very least, the law should not depend on it. It seems, then, that retributivism requires compatibilism. Accordingly, the standard legal account of punishment is compatibilist.

4. NEUROSCIENCE CHANGES NOTHING

The title of a recent paper by Stephen Morse (2004), 'New neuroscience, old problems', aptly summarizes many a seasoned legal thinker's response to the suggestion that brain research will revolutionize the law. The law has been dealing with issues of criminal responsibility for a long time, Morse argues that there is nothing on the neuroscientific horizon that it cannot handle.

The reason that the law is immune to such threats is that it makes no assumptions that neuroscience, or any science, is likely to challenge. The law assumes that people have a general capacity for rational choice. That is, people have beliefs and desires and are capable of producing behaviour that serves their desires in light of their beliefs. The law acknowledges that our capacity for rational choice is far from perfect (Kahneman & Tversky 2000), requiring only that the people it deems legally responsible have a *general* capacity for rational behaviour.

Thus, questions about who is or is not responsible in the eyes of the law have and will continue to turn on questions about rationality. This approach was first codified in the *M'Naghten* standard according to which a defence on the ground of insanity requires proof that the defendant laboured under 'a defect of reason, from disease of the mind' (Goldstein 1967). Not all standards developed and applied since *M'Naghten* explicitly mention the need to demonstrate the defendant's diminished rationality (e.g. the *Durham* standard; Goldstein 1967), but it is generally agreed that a legal excuse requires a demonstration that the defendant 'lacked a general capacity for rationality' (Goldstein *et al.* 2003). Thus, the argument goes, new science can help us figure out who was or was not rational at the scene of the crime, much as it has in the past, but new science will not justify any fundamental change in the law's approach to responsibility unless it shows that people in general fail to meet the law's very minimal requirements for rationality. Science shows no sign of doing this, and thus the basic precepts of legal responsibility stand firm. As for neuroscience more specifically, this discipline seems especially unlikely to undermine our faith in general minimal rationality. If any sciences have an outside chance of demonstrating that our behaviour is thoroughly irrational or arational it is the ones that study behaviour directly rather than its proximate physical causes in the brain. The law, this argument continues, does not care if people have 'free will' in any deep metaphysical sense that might be threatened by determinism. It only cares that people in general are minimally rational. So long as this appears to be the case, it can go on regarding people as free (compatibilism) and holding ordinary people responsible for their misdeeds while making exceptions for those who fail to meet the requirements of general rationality.

In light of this, one might wonder what all the fuss is about. If the law assumes nothing more than general minimal rationality, and neuroscience does nothing to undermine this assumption, then why would anyone even *think* that neuroscience poses some sort of threat to legal doctrines of criminal responsibility? It sounds like this is just a simple mistake, and that is precisely what Morse contends. He calls this mistake 'the fundamental psycholegal error' which is 'to believe that causation, especially abnormal causation, is *per se* an excusing condition' (Morse 2004, p. 180). In other words, if you think that neuroscientific information about the causes of human action, or some particular human's action, can, by itself, make for a legitimate legal excuse, you just do not understand the law. Every action is caused by brain events, and describing those events and affirming their causal efficacy is of no legal interest in and of itself. Morse continues, '[The psycholegal error] leads people to try to create a new excuse every time an allegedly valid new "syndrome" is discovered that is thought to play a role in behaviour. But syndromes and other causes do not have excusing force unless they sufficiently diminish rationality in the context in question' (Morse 2004, p. 180).

In our opinion, Morse and like-minded theorists are absolutely correct about the relationship between current legal doctrine and any forthcoming neuroscientific results. For the law, as written, neuroscience changes nothing. The law provides a coherent framework for the assessment of criminal responsibility that is not threatened by anything neuroscience is likely to throw at it. But, we maintain, the law nevertheless stands on shakier ground than the foregoing would suggest. The legitimacy of the law itself depends on its adequately reflecting the moral intuitions and commitments of society. If neuroscience can change those intuitions, then neuroscience can change the law.

As it happens, this is a possibility that Morse explicitly acknowledges. However, he believes that such developments would require radical new ideas that we can scarcely imagine at this time, e.g. a new solution to the mind-body problem. We disagree. The seeds of discontent are already sown in common-sense legal thought. In our opinion, the 'fundamental psycholegal error' is not so much an error as a reflection of the gap between what the law officially cares about and what people really care about. In modern criminal law, there has been a long tense marriage of convenience between compatibilist legal principles and libertarian moral intuitions. New neuroscience, we argue, will probably render this marriage unworkable.

5. What Really Matters for Responsibility? Materialist Theory, Dualist Intuitions and the 'Boys from Brazil' Problem

According to the law, the central question in a case of putative diminished responsibility is whether the accused was sufficiently rational at the time of the misdeed in question. We believe, however, that this is not what most people really care about, and that for them diminished rationality is just a presumed correlate of something deeper. It seems that what many people really want to know is: was it really *him*? This question usually comes in the form of a disjunction, depending on how the excuse is constructed: was it *him*, or was it his *upbringing?* Was it *him,* or was it his *genes?* Was it *him,* or was it his *circumstances?* Was it *him,* or was it his *brain?* But what most people do not understand, despite the fact that naturalistic philosophers and scientists have been saying it for centuries, is that there is no 'him' independent of these other things. (Or, to be a bit more accommodating to the supernaturally inclined, there is no 'him' independent of these things that shows any sign of affecting anything in the physical world, including his behaviour.)

Most people's view of the mind is implicitly *dualist* and *libertarian* and not *materialist* and *compatibilist.* Dualism, for our purposes, is the view that mind and brain are separate, interacting, entities.[2] Dualism fits naturally with libertarianism because a mind distinct from the body is precisely the sort of non-physical source of free will that libertarianism requires. Materialism, by contrast, is the view that all events, including the operations of the mind, are ultimately operations of matter that obeys the laws of physics. It is hard to imagine a belief in free will that is materialist but not compatibilist, given that ordinary matter does not seem capable of supplying the non-physical processes that libertarianism requires.

Many people, particularly those who are religious, are explicitly dualist libertarians (again, not in the political sense). However, in our estimation, even people who do or would readily endorse a thoroughly material account of human action and its causes have dualist, libertarian intuitions. This goes not only for educated people in general, but for experts in mental health and criminal behaviour. Consider, for example, the following remarks from Jonathan Pincus, an expert on criminal behaviour and the brain.

> When a composer conceives a symphony, the only way he or she can present it to the public is through an orchestra... If the performance is poor, the fault could lie with the composer's conception, or the orchestra, or both... Will is expressed by the brain. Violence can be the result of volition only, but if a brain is damaged, brain failure must be at least partly to blame. (Pincus 2001, p. 128)

To our untutored intuitions, this is a perfectly sensible analogy, but it is ultimately grounded in a kind of dualism that is scientifically untenable. It is not as if there is *you,* the composer, and then *your brain,* the orchestra. You *are* your brain, and your brain is the composer and the orchestra all rolled together. There is no little man, no 'homunculus', in the brain that is the real you behind the mass of neuronal instrumentation. Scientifically minded philosophers have been saying this *ad nauseum* (Dennett 1991), and we will not belabour the point. Moreover, we suspect that if you were to ask Dr Pincus whether he thinks there is a little conductor directing his brain's activity from within or

---

[2] There are some forms of dualism according to which the mind and body, although distinct, do not interact, making it impossible for the mind to have any observable effects on the brain or anything else in the physical world. These versions of dualism do not concern us here. For the purposes of this paper, we are happy to allow the metaphysical claim that souls or aspects of minds may exist independently of the physical body. Our concern is specifically with interactionist versions of dualism according to which non-physical mental entities have observable physical effects. We believe that science has rendered such views untenable and that the law, insofar as it is a public institution designed to serve a pluralistic society, must not rely on beliefs that are scientifically suspect (see previous endnote).

beyond he would adamantly deny that this is the case. At the same time, though, he is comfortable comparing a brain-damaged criminal to a healthy conductor saddled with an unhealthy orchestra. This sort of doublethink is not uncommon. As we will argue in § 7, when it comes to moral responsibility in a physical world, we are all of two minds.

A recent article by Laurence Steinberg and Elizabeth Scott (Steinberg & Scott 2003), experts respectively on adolescent developmental psychology and juvenile law, illustrates the same point. They argue that adolescents do not meet the law's general requirements for rationality and that therefore they should be considered less than fully responsible for their actions and, more specifically, unsuitable candidates for the death penalty. Their main argument is sound, but they cannot resist embellishing it with a bit of superfluous neuroscience.

> Most of the developmental research on cognitive and psychosocial functioning in adolescence measures behaviors, self-perceptions, or attitudes, but mounting evidence suggests that at least some of the differences between adults and adolescents have neuropsychological and neurobiological underpinnings. (Steinberg & Scott 2003, p. 5)

Some of the differences? Unless some form of dualism is correct, *every* mental difference and *every* difference in behavioural tendency is a function of some kind of difference in the brain. But here it is implicitly suggested that things like 'behaviours, self-perceptions, or attitudes' may be grounded in something other than the brain. In summing up their case, Steinberg and Scott look towards the future.

> Especially needed are studies that link developmental changes in decision making to changes in brain structure and function…In our view, however, there is sufficient indirect suggestive evidence of age differences in capacities that are relevant to criminal blameworthiness to support the position that youths who commit crimes should be punished more leniently then their adult counterparts. (Steinberg & Scott 2003, p. 9)

This gets the order of evidence backwards. If what the law ultimately cares about is whether adolescents can behave rationally, then it is evidence concerning adolescent behaviour that is *directly* relevant. Studying the adolescent brain is a highly *indirect* way of figuring out whether adolescents in general are rational. Indeed, the only way we neuroscientists can tell if a brain structure is important for rational judgement is to see if its activity or damage is correlated with (ir)rational *behaviour*.[3]

---

[3] It is conceivable that rationality could someday be redefined in neurocognitive rather than behavioural terms, much as water has been redefined in terms of its chemical composition. Were that to happen, neuroscientific evidence could then be construed as more direct than behavioural evidence. But Steinberg and Scott's argument appears to make use of a conventional, behavioural definition of rationality and not a neurocognitive redefinition.

If everyone agrees that what the law ultimately cares about is the capacity for rational behaviour, then why are Steinberg and Scott so optimistic about neuroscientific evidence that is only indirectly relevant? The reason, we suggest, is that they are appealing not to a legal argument, but to a moral intuition. So far as the law is concerned, information about the physical processes that give rise to bad behaviour is irrelevant. But to people who implicitly believe that real decision-making takes place in the mind, not in the brain, demonstrating that there is a brain basis for adolescents' misdeeds allows us to blame adolescents' brains instead of the adolescents themselves.

The fact that people are tempted to attach great moral or legal significance to neuroscientific information that, according to the letter of the law, should not matter, suggests that what the law cares about and what people care about do not necessarily coincide. To make this point in a more general way, we offer the following thought experiment, which we call '*The Boys from Brazil* problem'. It is an extension of an argument that has made the rounds in philosophical discussions of free will and responsibility (Rosen 2002).

In the film *The Boys from Brazil*, members of the Nazi old guard have regrouped in South America after the war. Their plan is to bring their beloved *führer* back to life by raising children genetically identical to Hitler (courtesy of some salvaged DNA) in environments that mimic that of Hitler's upbringing. For example, Hitler's father died while young Adolph was still a boy, and so each Hitler clone's surrogate father is killed at just the right time, and so on, and so forth.

This is obviously a fantasy, but the idea that one could, in principle, produce a person with a particular personality and behavioural profile through tight genetic and environmental control is plausible. Let us suppose, then, that a group of scientists has managed to create an individual—call him 'Mr Puppet'—who, by design, engages in some kind of criminal behaviour: say, a murder during a drug deal gone bad. The defence calls to the stand the project's lead scientist: 'Please tell us about your relationship to Mr Puppet...'

It is very simple, really. I designed him. I carefully selected every gene in his body and carefully scripted every significant event in his life so that he would become precisely what he is today. I selected his mother knowing that she would let him cry for hours and hours before picking him up. I carefully selected each of his relatives, teachers, friends, enemies, etc. and told them exactly what to say to him and how to treat him. Things generally went as planned, but not always. For example, the angry letters written to his dead father were not supposed to appear until he was fourteen, but by the end of his thirteenth year he had already written four of them. In retrospect I think this was because of a handful of substitutions I made to his eighth chromosome. At any rate, my plans for him succeeded, as they have for 95% of the people I've designed. I assure you that the accused deserves none of the credit.

What to do with Mr Puppet? Insofar as we believe this testimony, we are inclined to think that Mr Puppet cannot be held fully responsible for his crimes, if he can be held responsible for them at all. He is, perhaps, a man to be feared, and we would not want to return him to the streets. But given the fact that forces beyond his control played a dominant role in causing him to commit these crimes, it is hard to think of him as anything more than a pawn.

But what does the law say about Mr Puppet? The law asks whether or not he was rational at the time of his misdeeds, and as far as we know he was. For all we know, he is psychologically indistinguishable from the prototypical guilty criminal, and therefore fully responsible in the eyes of the law. But, intuitively, this is not fair.

Thus, it seems that the law's exclusive interest in rationality misses something intuitively important. In our opinion, rationality is just a presumed correlate of what most people really care about. What people really want to know is if the accused, as opposed to something else, is responsible for the crime, where that 'something else' could be the accused's brain, genes or environment. The question of someone's ultimate responsibility seems to turn, intuitively, on a question of internal versus external determination. Mr Puppet ought not be held responsible for his actions because forces beyond his control played a dominant role in the production of his behaviour. Of course, the scientists did not have complete control—after all, they had a 5% failure rate—but that does not seem to be enough to restore Mr Puppet's free will, at least not entirely. Yes, he is as rational as other criminals, and, yes, it was his desires and beliefs that produced his actions. But those beliefs and desires were rigged by external forces, and that is why, intuitively, he deserves our pity more than our moral condemnation.[4]

The story of Mr. Puppet raises an important question: what is the difference between Mr Puppet and anyone else accused of a crime? After all, we have little reason to doubt that (i) the state of the universe 10 000 years ago, (ii) the laws of physics, and (iii) the outcomes of random quantum mechanical events are together sufficient to determine everything that happens nowadays, including our own actions. These things are all clearly beyond our control. So what is the real difference between us and Mr Puppet? One obvious difference is that Mr Puppet is the victim of a diabolical plot whereas most people, we presume, are not. But does this matter? The thought that Mr Puppet is not fully responsible depends on the idea that his actions were externally determined. Forces beyond his control constrained his personality to the point that it was 'no surprise' that he would behave badly. But the fact that these forces are connected to the desires and intentions of evil scientists is really irrelevant, is it not? What matters is only that these forces are beyond Mr Puppet's control, that they're not really *his*. The fact that someone could deliberately harness these forces to reliably design criminals is an indication of the strength of these forces, but the fact that these forces are being guided by other minds rather than simply operating on their own seems irrelevant, so far as Mr Puppet's freedom and responsibility are concerned.

Thus, it seems that, in a very real sense, we are all puppets. The combined effects of genes and environment determine all of our actions. Mr Puppet is exceptional only in that the intentions of other humans lie behind his genes and environment. But, so

---

[4] This is not to say that we could not describe Mr Puppet in such a way that our intuitions about him would change. Our point is only that, when the details are laid bare, it is very hard to see him as morally responsible.

long as his genes and environment are intrinsically comparable to those of ordinary people, this does not really matter. We are no more free than he is.

What all of this illustrates is that the 'fundamental psycholegal error' is grounded in a powerful moral intuition that the law and allied compatibilist philosophies try to sweep under the rug. The foregoing suggests that people regard actions only as fully free when those actions are seen as robust against determination by external forces. But if determinism (or determinism plus quantum mechanics) is true, then no actions are truly free because forces beyond our control are always sufficient to determine behaviour. Thus, intuitive free will is libertarian, not compatibilist. That is, it requires the rejection of determinism and an implicit commitment to some kind of magical mental causation.[5]

Naturalistic philosophers and scientists have known for a long time that magical mental causation is a non-starter. But this realization is the result of philosophical reflection about the nature of the universe and its governance by physical law. Philosophical reflection, however, is not the only way to see the problems with libertarian accounts of free will. Indeed, we argue that neuroscience can help people appreciate the mechanical nature of human action in a way that bypasses complicated arguments.

6. NEUROSCIENCE AND THE TRANSPARENT BOTTLENECK

We have argued that, contrary to legal and philosophical orthodoxy, determinism really does threaten free will and responsibility as we intuitively understand them. It is just that most of us, including most philosophers and legal theorists, have yet to appreciate it. This controversial opinion amounts to an empirical prediction that may or may not hold: as more and more scientific facts come in, providing increasingly vivid illustrations of what the human mind is really like, more and more people will develop moral intuitions that are at odds with our current social practices (see Robert Wright (1994) for similar thoughts).

Neuroscience has a special role to play in this process for the following reason. As long as the mind remains a black box, there will always be a donkey on which to pin dualist and libertarian intuitions. For a long time, philosophical arguments have persuaded some people that human action has purely mechanical causes, but not everyone cares for philosophical arguments. Arguments are nice, but physical demonstrations are far more compelling. What neuroscience does, and will continue to

---

[5] Compatibilist philosophers such as Daniel Dennett (2003) might object that the story of Mr Puppet is nothing but a misleading 'intuition pump'. Indeed, this is what Dennett says about a similar case of Alfred Mele's (1995). We believe that our case is importantly different from Mele's. Dennett and Mele imagine two women who are psychologically identical: Ann is a typical, good person, whereas Beth has been brainwashed to be just like Ann. Dennett argues, against Mele, that if you take seriously the claim that these two are psychologically identical and properly imagine that Beth is as rational, openminded, etc. as Ann, you will come to see that the two are equally free. We agree with Dennett that Ann and Beth are comparable and that Mele's intuition falters when the details are fleshed out. But does the same hold for the intuition provoked by Mr Puppet's story? It seems to us that the more one knows about Mr Puppet and his life the less inclined one is to see him as truly responsible for his actions and our punishing him as a worthy end in itself. We can agree with Dennett that there is a sense in which Mr Puppet is free. Our point is merely that there is a legitimate sense in which he, like all of us, is not free and that this sense matters for the law.

do at an accelerated pace, is elucidate the 'when', 'where' and 'how' of the mechanical processes that cause behaviour. It is one thing to deny that human decision-making is purely mechanical when your opponent offers only a general, philosophical argument. It is quite another to hold your ground when your opponent can make detailed predictions about how these mechanical processes work, complete with images of the brain structures involved and equations that describe their function.[6]

Thus, neuroscience holds the promise of turning the black box of the mind into a *transparent bottleneck*. There are many causes that impinge on behaviour, but all of them—from the genes you inherited, to the pain in your lower back, to the advice your grandmother gave you when you were six—must exert their influence through the brain. Thus, your brain serves as a bottleneck for all the forces spread throughout the universe of your past that affect who you are and what you do. Moreover, this bottleneck contains the events that are, intuitively, most critical for moral and legal responsibility, and we may soon be able to observe them closely.

At some time in the future we may have extremely high-resolution scanners that can simultaneously track the neural activity and connectivity of every neuron in a human brain, along with computers and software that can analyse and organize these data. Imagine, for example, watching a film of your brain choosing between soup and salad. The analysis software highlights the neurons pushing for soup in red and the neurons pushing for salad in blue. You zoom in and slow down the film, allowing yourself to trace the cause-and-effect relationships between individual neurons—the mind's clockwork revealed in arbitrary detail. You find the tipping-point moment at which the blue neurons in your prefrontal cortex out-fire the red neurons, seizing control of your pre-motor cortex and causing you to say, 'I will have the salad, please'.

At some further point this sort of brainware may be very widespread, with a high-resolution brain scanner in every classroom. People may grow up completely used to the idea that every decision is a thoroughly mechanical process, the outcome of which is completely determined by the results of prior mechanical processes. What will such people think as they sit in their jury boxes? Suppose a man has killed his wife in a jealous rage. Will jurors of the future wonder whether the defendant acted in that moment *of his own free will*? Will they wonder if it was *really him* who killed his wife rather than his *uncontrollable anger*? Will they ask whether he *could have done otherwise*? Whether he really *deserves* to be punished, or if he is just a victim of unfortunate circumstances? We submit that these questions, which seem so important today, will lose their grip in an age when the mechanical nature of human decision-making is fully appreciated. The law will continue to punish misdeeds, as it must for practical reasons, but the idea of distinguishing the truly, deeply guilty from those who are merely victims of neuronal circumstances will, we submit, seem pointless.

---

[6] We do not wish to imply that neuroscience will inevitably put us in a position to predict any given action based on a neurological examination. Rather, our suggestion is simply that neuroscience will eventually advance to the point at which the mechanistic nature of human decision-making is sufficiently apparent to undermine the force of dualist/libertarian intuitions.

At least in our more reflective moments. Our intuitive sense of free will runs quite deep, and it is possible that we will never be able to fully talk ourselves out of it. Next we consider the psychological origins of the problem of free will.

7. FOLK PSYCHOLOGY AND FOLK PHYSICS COLLIDE: A COGNITIVE ACCOUNT OF THE PROBLEM OF ATTRIBUTIVE FREE WILL

Could the problem of free will just melt away? This question begs another: why do we have the problem of free will in the first place? Why does the idea of a deterministic universe seem to contradict something important in our conception of human action? A promising answer to this question is offered by Daniel Wegner in *The illusion of conscious will* (Wegner 2002). In short, Wegner argues, we feel as if we are uncaused causers, and therefore granted a degree of independence from the deterministic flow of the universe, because we are unaware of the deterministic processes that operate in our own heads. Our actions appear to be caused by our mental states, but not by physical states of our brains, and so we imagine that we are metaphysically special, that we are non-physical causes of physical events. This belief in our specialness is likely to meet the same fate as other similarly narcissistic beliefs that we have cherished in our past: that the Earth lies at the centre of the universe, that humans are unrelated to other species, that all of our behaviour is consciously determined, etc. Each of these beliefs has been replaced by a scientific and humbling understanding of our place in the physical universe, and there is no reason to believe that the case will be any different for our sense of free will. (For similar thoughts, see Wright (1994) on Darwin's clandestine views about free will and responsibility.)

We believe that Wegner's account of the problem of free will is essentially correct, although we disagree strongly with his conclusions concerning its (lack of) practical moral implications (see below). In this section we pick up on and extend one strand in Wegner's argument (Wegner 2002, pp. 15–28). Wegner's primary aim is to explain, in psychological terms, why we attribute free will to ourselves, why we feel free from the inside. Our aim in this section is to explain, in psychological terms, why we insist on attributing free will to *others*—and why scientifically minded philosophers, despite persistent efforts, have managed to talk almost no one out of this practice. The findings we review serve as examples of how psychological and neuroscientific data are beginning to characterize the mechanisms that underlie our sense of free will, how these mechanisms can lead us to assume free will is operating when it is not, and how a scientific understanding of these mechanisms can serve to dismantle our commitment to the idea of free will.

Looking out at the world, it appears to contain two fundamentally different kinds of entity. On the one hand, there are ordinary objects that appear to obey the ordinary laws of physics: things like rocks and puddles of water and blocks of wood. These things do not get up and move around on their own. They are, in a word, inanimate. On the other hand, there are things that seem to operate by some kind of magic. Humans and other animals, so long as they are alive, can move about at will, in apparent defiance of the physical laws that govern ordinary matter. Because things like rocks and puddles, on the one hand, and mice and humans, on the other, behave in such radically different ways, it makes sense, from an evolutionary perspective, that creatures would evolve separate cognitive systems for processing information about each of these classes of objects (Pinker 1997). There is a good deal of evidence to suggest that this is precisely how our minds work.

A line of research beginning with Fritz Heider illustrates this point. Heider and Simmel (Heider & Simmel 1944) created a film involving three simple geometric shapes that move about in various ways. For example, a big triangle chases a little circle around the screen, bumping into it. The little circle repeatedly moves away, and a little triangle repeatedly moves in between the circle and the big triangle. When normal people watch this movie they cannot help but view it in social terms (Heberlein & Adolphs 2004). They see the big triangle as *trying* to harm the little circle, and the little triangle as trying to *protect* the little circle; and they see the little circle as *afraid* and the big triangle as *frustrated*. Some people even spontaneously report that the big triangle is a *bully*. In other words, simple patterns of movement trigger in people's minds a cascade of complex social inferences. People not only see these shapes as 'alive'. They see beliefs, desires, intentions, emotions, personality traits and even moral blameworthiness. It appears that this kind of inference is automatic (Scholl & Tremoulet 2000). Of course, you, the observer, know that it is only a film, and a very simple one at that, but you nevertheless cannot help but see these events in social, even *moral*, terms.

That is, unless you have damage to your amygdala, a subcortical brain structure that is important for social cognition (Adolphs 1999). Andrea Heberlein tested a patient with rare bilateral amygdala damage using Heider's film and found that this patient, unlike normal people, described what she saw in completely asocial terms, despite that fact that her visual and verbal abilities are not compromised by her brain damage. Somehow, this patient is blind to the 'human' drama that normal people cannot help but see in these events (Heberlein & Adolphs 2004).

The sort of thinking that is engaged when normal people view the Heider–Simmel film is sometimes known as 'folk psychology' (Fodor 1987), 'the intentional stance' (Dennett 1987) or 'theory of mind', (Premack & Woodruff 1978). There is a fair amount of evidence (including the work described above) suggesting that humans have a set of cognitive subsystems that are specialized for processing information about intentional agents (Saxe *et al.* 2004). At the same time, there is evidence to suggest that humans and other animals also have subsystems specialized for 'folk physics', an intuitive sense of how ordinary matter behaves. One compelling piece of evidence for the claim that normal humans have subsystems specialized for folk physics comes from studies of people with autism spectrum disorder. These individuals are particularly bad at solving problems that require 'folk psychology', but they do very well with problems related to how physical objects (e.g. the parts of machine) behave, i.e. 'folk physics' (Baron Cohen 2000). Another piece of evidence for a 'folk physics' system comes from discrepancies between people's physical intuitions and the way the world actually works.

People say, for example, that a ball shot out of a curved tube resting on a flat surface will continue to follow a curved path outside the tube when in fact it will follow a straight path (McCloskey *et al.* 1980). The fact that people's physical intuitions are slightly, but systematically, out of step with reality suggests that the mind brings a fair amount of implicit theory to the perception of physical objects.

Thus, it is at least plausible that we possess distinguishable cognitive systems for making sense of the behaviour of objects in the world. These systems seem to have two fundamentally different 'ontologies'. The folk physics system deals with chunks of matter that move around without purposes of their own according to the laws of intuitive physics, whereas the folk psychology system deals with unseen features of minds: beliefs, desires, intentions, etc. But what, to our minds, is a mind? We suggest that a crucial feature, if not the defining feature, of a mind (intuitively understood) is that it is an uncaused causer (Scholl & Tremoulet 2000). Minds animate material bodies, allowing them to move without any apparent physical cause and in pursuit of goals. Moreover, we reserve certain social attitudes for things that have minds. For example, we do not resent the rain for ruining our picnic, but we would resent a person who hosed our picnic (Strawson 1962), and we resent picnic-hosers considerably more when we perceive that their actions are intentional. Thus, it seems that folk psychology is the gateway to moral evaluation. To see something as morally blameworthy or praiseworthy (even if it is just a moving square), one has to first see it as 'someone', that is, as having a mind.

With all of this in the background, one can see how the problem of attributive free will arises. To see something as a responsible moral agent, one must first see it as having a mind. But, intuitively, a mind is, among other things, an uncaused causer. Consequently, when something is seen as a mere physical entity operating in accordance with deterministic physical laws, it ceases to be seen, intuitively, as a mind. Consequently, it is seen as an object unworthy of moral praise or blame. (Note that we are not claiming that people automatically attribute moral agency to anything that appears to be an uncaused causer. Rather, our claim is that seeing something as an uncaused causer is a *necessary but not sufficient* condition for seeing something as a moral agent.)

After thousands of years of our thinking of one another as uncaused causers, science comes along and tells us that there is no such thing—that all causes, with the possible exception of the Big Bang, are caused causes (determinism). This creates a problem. When we look at people as physical systems, we cannot see them as any more blameworthy or praiseworthy than bricks. But when we perceive people using our intuitive, folk psychology we cannot avoid attributing moral blame and praise.

So, philosophers who would honour both our scientific knowledge and our social instincts try to reconcile these two competing outlooks, but the result is never completely satisfying, and the debate wears on. Philosophers who cannot let go of the idea of uncaused causes defend libertarianism, and thus opt for scientifically dubious, 'panicky metaphysics'. Hard determinists, by contrast, embrace the conclusions of modern science, and concede what others will not: that many of our dearly held social practices are based on an illusion. The remaining majority, the compatibilists, try to talk themselves into a compromise. But the compromise is fragile. When the physical details of human action are made vivid, folk psychology loses its grip, just as folk physics loses its grip when the morally significant details are emphasized. The problem of free will and determinism will never find an intuitively satisfying solution because it arises out of a conflict between two distinct cognitive subsystems that speak different cognitive 'languages' and that may ultimately be incapable of negotiation.

8. FREE WILL, RESPONSIBILITY AND CONSEQUENTIALISM

Even if there is no intuitively satisfying solution to the problem of free will, it does not follow that there is no correct view of the matter. Ours is as follows: when it comes to the issue of free will itself, hard determinism is mostly correct. Free will, as we ordinarily understand it, is an illusion. However, it does not follow from the fact that free will is an illusion that there is no legitimate place for responsibility. Recall from § 2 that there are two general justifications for holding people legally responsible for their actions. The retributive justification, by which the goal of punishment is to give people what they really deserve, does depend on this dubious notion of free will. However, the consequentialist approach does not require a belief in free will at all. As consequentialists, we can hold people responsible for crimes simply because doing so has, on balance, beneficial effects through deterrence, containment, etc. It is sometimes said that if we do not believe in free will then we cannot legitimately punish anyone and that society must dissolve into anarchy. In a less hysterical vein, Daniel Wegner argues that free will, while illusory, is a necessary fiction for the maintenance of our social structure (Wegner 2002, ch. 9). We disagree. There are perfectly good, forward-looking justifications for punishing criminals that do not depend on metaphysical fictions. (Wegner's observations may apply best to the personal sphere: see below.)

The vindication of responsibility in the absence of free will means that there is more than a grain of truth in compatibilism. The consequentialist approach to responsibility generates a derivative notion of free will that we can embrace (Smart 1961). In the name of producing better consequences, we will want to make several distinctions among various actions and agents. To begin, we will want to distinguish the various classes of people who cannot be deterred by the law from those who can. That is, we will recognize many of the 'diminished capacity' excuses that the law currently recognizes such as infancy and insanity. We will also recognize familiar justifications such those associated with crimes committed under duress (e.g. threat of death). If we like, then, we can say that the actions of rational people operating free from duress, etc. are free actions, and that such people are exercising their free will.

At this point, compatibilists such as Daniel Dennett may claim victory: 'what more could one want from free will?'. In a word: retributivism. We have argued that commonsense retributivism really does depend on a notion of free will that is scientifically suspect. Intuitively, we want to punish those people who truly deserve it, but whenever the causes of someone's bad behaviour are made sufficiently vivid, we no longer see that person as truly deserving of punishment. This insight is expressed by the old

French proverb: 'to know all is to forgive all'. It is also expressed in the teachings of religious figures, such as Jesus and Buddha, who preach a message of universal compassion. Neuroscience can make this message more compelling by vividly illustrating the mechanical nature of human action.

Our penal system is highly counter-productive from a consequentialist perspective, especially in the USA, and yet it remains in place because retributivist principles have a powerful moral and political appeal (Lacey 1988; Tonry 2004). It is possible, however, that neuroscience will change these moral intuitions by undermining the intuitive, libertarian conceptions of free will on which retributivism depends.

As advocates of consequentialist legal reform, it behoves us to briefly respond to the three standard criticisms levied against consequentialist theories of punishment. First, it is claimed that consequentialism would justify extreme overpunishing. As noted above, it is possible in principle that the goal of deterrence would justify punishing parking violations with the death penalty or framing innocent people to make examples of them. Here, the standard response is adequate. The idea that such practices could, in the real world, make society happier on balance is absurd. Second, it is claimed that consequentialism justifies extreme underpunishment. In response to some versions of this objection, our response is the same as above. Deceptive practices such as a policy of faking punishment cannot survive in a free society, and a free society is required for the pursuit of most consequentialist ends. In other cases consequentialism may advocate more lenient punishments for people who, intuitively, deserve worse. Here, we maintain that a deeper understanding of human action and human nature will lead people—more of them, at any rate—to abandon these retributivist intuitions. Our response is much the same to the third and most general criticism of consequentialist punishment, which is that even when consequentialism gets the punishment policy right, it does so for the wrong reasons. These supposedly right reasons are reasons that we reject, however intuitive and natural they may feel. They are, we maintain, grounded in a metaphysical view of human action that is scientifically dubious and therefore an unfit basis for public policy in a pluralistic society.

Finally, as defenders of hard determinism and a consequentialist approach to responsibility, we should briefly address some standard concerns about the rejection of free will and conceptions of responsibility that depend on it. First, does not the fact that you can raise your hand 'at will' prove that free will is real? Not in the sense that matters. As Daniel Wegner (2002) has argued, our first-person sense of ourselves as having free will may be a systematic illusion. And from a third-person perspective, we simply do not assume that anyone who exhibits voluntary control over his body is free in the relevant sense, as in the case of Mr Puppet.

A more serious challenge is the claim that our commitments to free will and retributivism are simply inescapable for all practical purposes. Regarding free will, one might wonder whether one can so much as make a decision without implicitly assuming that one is free to choose among one's apparent options. Regarding responsibility and punishment, one might wonder if it is humanly possible to deny our retributive impulses (Strawson 1962; Pettit 2002). This challenge is bolstered by recent work in the behavioural sciences suggesting that an intuitive sense of fairness runs deep in our primate lineage (Brosnan & De Waal 2003) and that an adaptive tendency towards retributive punishment may have been a crucial development in the biological and cultural evolution of human sociality (Fehr & Gachter 2002; Boyd *et al.* 2003; Bowles & Gintis 2004). Recent neuroscientific findings have added further support to this view, suggesting that the impulse to exact punishment may be driven by phylogentically old mechanisms in the brain (Sanfey *et al.* 2003). These mechanisms may be an efficient and perhaps essential, device for maintaining social stability. If retributivism runs that deep and is that useful, one might wonder whether we have any serious hope of, or reason for, getting rid of it. Have we any real choice but to see one another as free agents who deserve to be rewarded and punished for our past behaviours?

We offer the following analogy: modern physics tells us that space is curved. Nevertheless, it may be impossible for us to see the world as anything other than flatly Euclidean in our day-to-day lives. And there are, no doubt, deep evolutionary explanations for our Euclidean tendencies. Does it then follow that we are forever bound by our innate Euclidean psychology? The answer depends on the domain of life in question. In navigating the aisles of the grocery store, an intuitive, Euclidean representation of space is not only adequate, but probably inevitable. However, when we are, for example, planning the launch of a spacecraft, we can and should make use of relativistic physical principles that are less intuitive but more accurate. In other words, a Euclidean perspective is not necessary for *all* practical purposes, and the same may be true for our implicit commitment to free will and retributivism. For most day-to-day purposes it may be pointless or impossible to view ourselves or others in this detached sort of way. But—and this is the crucial point—it may not be pointless or impossible to adopt this perspective when one is deciding what the criminal law should be or whether a given defendant should be put to death for his crimes. These may be special situations, analogous to those routinely encountered by 'rocket scientists', in which the counter-intuitive truth that we legitimately ignore most of the time can and should be acknowledged.

Finally, there is the worry that to reject free will is to render all of life pointless: why would you bother with anything if it has all long since been determined? The answer is that you will bother because you are a human, and that is what humans do. Even if you decide, as part of a little intellectual exercise, that you are going to sit around and do nothing because you have concluded that you have no free will, you are eventually going to get up and make yourself a sandwich. And if you do not, you have got bigger problems than philosophy can fix.

9. Conclusion

Neuroscience is unlikely to tell us anything that will challenge the law's stated assumptions. However, we maintain that advances in neuroscience are likely to change the way people think about human action and criminal responsibility by vividly illustrating lessons that some people appreciated long ago. Free will as we ordinarily understand it is an illusion generated by our cognitive architecture. Retributivist notions of criminal responsibility ultimately depend on this illusion, and, if we are lucky, they will give way to consequentialist ones, thus radically transforming our approach to criminal justice. At this time, the law deals firmly but mercifully with individuals whose behaviour is obviously the product of forces that are ultimately beyond their control. Some day, the law may treat all convicted criminals this way. That is, humanely.

REFERENCES

Adolphs, R. 1999. Social cognition and the human brain. *Trends Cogn. Sci.* 3, 469–479.

Baron Cohen, S. 2000. Autism: deficits in folk psychology exist alongside superiority in folk physics. In *Understanding other minds: perspectives from autism and developmental cognitive neuroscience* (ed. S. Baron Cohen, H. Tager Flusberg & D. Cohen), pp. 78–82. New York: Oxford University Press.

Bentham, J. 1982. *An introduction to the principles of morals and legislation.* London: Methuen.

Bowles, S. & Gintis, H. 2004. The evolution of strong reciprocity: cooperation in heterogeneous populations. *Theor. Popul. Biol.* 65, 17–28.

Boyd, R., Gintis, H., Bowles, S. & Richerson, P. J. 2003. The evolution of altruistic punishment. *Proc. Natl Acad. Sci. USA* 100, 3531–3535.

Brosnan, S. F. & De Waal, F. B. 2003. Monkeys reject unequal pay. *Nature* 425, 297–299.

Dennett, D. C. 1984. *Elbow room: the varieties of free will worth wanting.* Cambridge, MA: MIT Press.

———. 1987. *The intentional stance.* Cambridge, MA: MIT Press.

———. 1991. *Consciousness explained.* Boston, MA: Little Brown.

———. 2003. *Freedom evolves.* New York: Viking.

Fehr, E. & Gachter, S. 2002. Altruistic punishment in humans. *Nature* 415, 137–140.

Fodor, J. A. 1987. *Psychosemantics: the problem of meaning in the philosophy of mind.* Cambridge, MA: MIT Press.

Frankfurt, H. 1966. Alternate possibilities and moral responsibility. *J. Philosophy* 66, 829–839.

Goldstein, A. M., Morse, S. J. & Shapiro, D. L. 2003. Evaluation of criminal responsibility. In *Forensic psychology.* vol. 11 (ed. A. M. Goldstein), pp. 381–406. New York: Wiley.

Goldstein, A. S. 1967. *The insanity defense.* New Haven, CT: Yale University Press.

Hart, H. L. A. 1968. *Punishment and responsibility.* Oxford University Press.

Heberlein, A. S. & Adolphs, R. 2004. Impaired spontaneous anthropomorphizing despite intact perception and social knowledge. *Proc. Natl Acad. Sci. USA* 101, 7487–7491.

Heider, F. & Simmel, M. 1944. An experimental study of apparent behavior. *Am. J. Psychol.* 57, 243–259.

Hughs, R. I. G. 1992. *The structure and interpretation of quantum mechanics.* Cambridge, MA: Havard University Press.

Kahneman, D. & Tversky, A. (eds) 2000. *Choices, values, and frames.* Cambridge University Press.

Kant, I. 2002. *The philosophy of law: an exposition of the fundamental principles of jurisprudence as the science of right.* Union, NJ: Lawbook Exchange.

Lacey, N. 1988. *State punishment: political principles and community values.* London and New York: Routledge & Kegan Paul.

McCloskey, M., Caramazza, A. & Green, B. 1980. Curvilinear motion in the absence of external forces: naive beliefs about the motion of objects. *Science* 210, 1139–1141.

Mele, A. 1995. *Autonomous agents: from self-control to autonomy.* Oxford University Press.

Morse, S. J. 2004. New neuroscience, old problems. In *Neuroscience and the law: brain, mind, and the scales of justice* (ed. B. Garland), pp. 157–198. New York: Dana Press.

Pettit, P. 2002. *The capacity to have done otherwise. Rules, reasons, and norms: selected essays.* Oxford University Press.

Pincus, J. H. 2001. *Base instincts: what makes killers kill?* New York: Norton.

Pinker, S. 1997. *How the mind works.* New York: Norton.

Premack, D. & Woodruff, G. 1978. Does the chimpanzee have a theory of mind? *Behav. Brain Sci.* 4, 515–526.

Rosen, G. 2002. The case for incompatibilism. *Philosophy Phenomenol. Res.* 64, 699–706.

Sanfey, A. G., Rilling, J. K., Aronson, J. A., Nystrom, L. E. & Cohen, J. D. 2003. The neural basis of economic decision-making in the ultimatum game. *Science* 300, 1755–1758.

Saxe, R., Carey, S. & Kanwisher, N. 2004. Understanding other minds: liking developmental psychology and functional neuroimaging. *A. Rev. Psychol.* 55, 87–124.

Scholl, B. J. & Tremoulet, P. D. 2000. Perceptual causality and animacy. *Trends Cogn. Sci.* 4, 299–309.

Shear, J. (ed.) 1999. *Explaining consciousness: the hard problem.* Cambridge, MA: MIT Press.

Smart, J. J. C. 1961. Free will, praise, and blame. *Mind* 70, 291–306.

Steinberg, L. & Scott, E. S. 2003. Less guilty by reason of adolescence: developmental immaturity, diminished responsibility, and the juvenile death penalty. *Am. Psychol.* 58, 1009–1018.

Strawson, P. F. 1962. Freedom and resentment. *Proc. Br. Acad.* xlviii, 1–25.

Tonry, M. 2004. *Thinking about crime: sense and sensibility in American penal culture.* New York: Oxford University Press.

Van Inwagen, P. 1982. The incompatibility of free will and determinism. In *Free will* (ed. G. Watson), pp. 46–58. New York: Oxford University Press.

Watson, G. (ed.) 1982. *Free will.* New York: Oxford University Press.

Wegner, D. M. 2002. *The illusion of conscious will.* Cambridge, MA: MIT Press.

Wright, R. 1994. *The moral animal: evolutionary psychology and everyday life.* New York: Pantheon.

V

RESTORATIVE THEORIES

Restorative justice is a potentially transformative set of ideas, potentially a competitive paradigm to prevailing conceptions of the criminal justice system, whose time seems never quite to come. It has generated a huge literature, including a serious jurisprudential literature.[1] It has catalyzed the initiation of countless new programs. For all that, it largely remains at the margins of the criminal justice system, dealing mostly with minor crimes and young offenders.

This stands in stark contrast to a competing set of new ideas—therapeutic jurisprudence (e.g., Wexler 2008a, 2008b)—that has generated a much smaller literature but penetrated more deeply into the criminal justice system. Drug and other problem-solving courts (mental health, domestic violence), expressly premised on therapeutic jurisprudence logic, have proliferated and number in the thousands. They deal with a wide range of crimes, including many serious ones, and are being integrated into criminal court systems across the country. The literature of therapeutic jurisprudence is, however, small, descriptive, and largely prosaic. Here, for example, are the titles of the major recent works of David Wexler and Bruce Winick, the movement's founders and preeminent theorists: *Rehabilitating Lawyers: Principles of Therapeutic Jurisprudence for Criminal Law Practice* (Wexler 2008a); *Civil Commitment: A Therapeutic Jurisprudence Model* (Winick 2005). Nuts and bolts.

The greater influence and lesser intellectual excitement generated by therapeutic jurisprudence may be because it emerged from a clinical law reform initiative, the "law

---

[1] The literature is so voluminous that competing restorative justice handbooks contain articles on many different specialist subjects (Johnstone and van Ness 2006; Dennis and Tifft 2008). There are numerous edited collections, countless journal articles, and many single-author monographs (e.g., Braithwaite 2001; Dorne 2007; Walgrave 2008), including some on highly specialized subjects (e.g., Ptacek 2009).

and mental health movement," is resolutely practical in its focus, and is almost on principle atheoretical. Its major claim is that much that the law does is anti-therapeutic, that is, much that the law does causes unnecessary harm to the mental health of individuals. The harmed individuals may be offenders, victims, lawyers, or judges. Its major proposal is that laws and legal processes and procedures should be assessed to determine when and why they have anti-therapeutic effects and whether and how they can be made less destructive or under the right circumstances therapeutic. Judges running drug courts need not buy into a complex theoretical literature. They need only decide that drug dependence is a chronic relapsing condition, that dealing effectively with it requires a therapeutic medical-model approach, and that courts and judges can provide a setting and structural conditions to facilitate that approach.

I discuss therapeutic jurisprudence only to point to its deeper penetration and contrast it with restorative justice. Restorative justice likewise is premised on the notion that conventional criminal justice processes are too rigid, often ineffective, and sometimes destructive. Restorative justice likewise is premised on ideas about individualization of treatment. Both effectively reject retributivist ideas about the importance of equal treatment of offenders convicted of comparable crimes with comparable criminal records.

Why the different experiences? One reason may be that therapeutic jurisprudence activists tend to be lawyers and practitioners rather than, as with restorative justice, people from outside the justice system. Another is that drug courts are seldom adversary: they become involved only after a prosecutor waives prosecution or a judge makes a referral, and an offender agrees to participate. A third is that victims seldom have strong interest in what happens in drug or similar courts and usually do not have interests contrary to the offender's.

Restorative justice initiatives, by contrast, typically occur at the dispositional stage and often involve conflicting interests of victims and offenders. Most importantly, however, they are actively resisted by many lawyers, law professors, and judges. Lawyers and judges involved with drug courts typically accept that individualization of treatment for a drug-dependent offender is necessary, and that this often will result in substantial differences in handling of otherwise comparable cases. Lawyers and judges working in felony courts typically are not as amenable to individualization resulting from restorative processes.

The articles in this part canvass the major issues. Walgrave (2004 [chapter 21 in this volume], 2008) lays out the underlying logic of restorative justice and sketches a taxonomy of challenges to be overcome before it moves, if ever, from the periphery to the mainstream. The logic is that offenses should be thought of as problems to be solved rather than as crimes to be punished; that defendants, victims, supporters of each, and others should be involved in deliberative processes aimed at finding solutions; that the overriding goal should be to build or restore relations among and between victims, offenders, and communities; and that solutions be unanimously agreed. If highly similar cases result in strikingly divergent outcomes, that is okay so long as everyone involved, including the offender, agrees. How can it be unjust if everyone directly involved believes it to be appropriate?

Braithwaite (2003 [chapter 22 in this volume]), the preeminent theoretician of restorative justice, discusses and proposes solutions to the major policy and normative issues it raises. Robinson (2003 [chapter 23 in this volume]) offers a standard critique from a person committed to *positive retributivist* ideas (offenders *must* rather than *may at most* be punished a certain amount): restorative justice is acceptable only if the dispositions it produces are consistent with those that would occur if the case were dealt with in court. Duff (2003 [chapter 24 in this volume]), by contrast, attempts to show that restorative and retributive ideas have more in common than is ordinarily recognized, and can be reconciled in ways that allow wider scope for the use of restorative justice programs than is widely recognized.

Nonetheless, the condition Robinson sets is demanding, it is plausible to many practitioners, and it largely explains why restorative justice programs remain at the periphery. Offenses involving juveniles and minor adult crimes are important, and it is a good thing if restorative processes produce better experiences for victims and offenders, and produce constructive outcomes. Thought of in that way, restorative justice is a device for improving processes for dealing with minor criminal events, and not something transformative. Its proponents sought and seek more. Proponents of therapeutic jurisprudence sought less and got more. Go figure.

References

Bibliographic details concerning works that are mentioned but are not reprinted in this volume can be found in the reference list to the introduction except for the following:

Braithwaite, John. 2001. *Restorative Justice and Responsive Regulation.* New York: Oxford University Press.

Dorne, Clifford K. 2007. *Restorative Justice in the United States.* Upper Saddle River, New Jersey: Prentice-Hall.

Johnstone, Gerry, and Daniel W. van Ness, eds. 2006. *Handbook of Restorative Justice.* Cullompton, Devon, UK: Willan.

Ptacek, James. 2009. *Restorative Justice and Violence Against Women.* New York, New York: Oxford University Press.

Sullivan, Dennis, and Larry Tifft, eds. 2008. *Handbook of Restorative Justice: A Global Perspective.* London: Routledge.

Walgrave, Lode. 2008. *Restorative Justice, Self-Interest and Responsible Citizenship.* Cullompton, Devon, UK: Willan.

Wexler, David B. 2008a. *Rehabilitating Lawyers: Principles of Therapeutic Jurisprudence for Criminal Law Practice.* Durham, North Carolina: Carolina Academic Press.

———. 2008b. "Two Decades of Therapeutic Jurisprudence." *Touro Law Review* 24:7–29.

Winick, Bruce J. 2005. *Civil Commitment: A Therapeutic Jurisprudence Model.* Durham, North Carolina: Carolina Academic Press.

21

Restoration in Youth Justice

Lode Walgrave

II. Restorative Justice

Restorative justice is deeply rooted in "human thought grounded in traditions of justice from the ancient Arab, Greek, and Roman civilizations...the restorative approach of the public assemblies of the Germanic peoples...Indian Hindus...and ancient Buddhist, Taoist, and Confucian traditions" (Braithwaite 2002, p. 3). The fall of the ancient versions of restorative justice coincided with the establishment of central power, transforming crime from a wrong done to another person in to a transgression of the king's law (Weitekamp 1999). The restorative response model reemerged during the 1980s and became an important factor in practice and policy in the 1990s.

It is difficult to delimit restorative justice because its impetus comes from multiple origins (Faget 1997; Van Ness and Strong 2002). The victims' movements claimed an expanded role and demanded outcomes that were more focused on reparation (Peters and Aertsen 1995; Young 1995). Feminist movements drew attention to feminine aspects of primary and secondary victimization (Harris 1990). Critical criminology emphasized the negative effects of the criminal justice system and its inability to assure peace in social life. Many adherents of restorative justice consider it an alternative to criminal justice as a whole (de Haan 1990; van Swaaningen 1997) or to juvenile justice more specifically (Walgrave 1995; Bazemore and Walgrave 1999). Communitarians advocate the revival of community as the organic resource of informal mutual support and control, seeing communities as means and ends for restorative justice. Part of communitarianism is rooted in indigenous emancipation movements (Corrado and Griffiths 1999) or in religion (Zehr 1990).

Given its diverse roots and current forms, it is not surprising that restorative justice appears somewhat confused. It is now a complex domain, covering a wide realm of practices. It is a challenging subject for legal and normative reflection and debate and a fruitful field for theorizing and empirical research. Restorative justice is also a social movement of believers. Adding to the confusion are apparently similar movements under banners like transformative justice, relational justice, community justice, peacemaking justice, and the like. All express a general tendency that I call here "restorative justice."[1]

Only recently have practitioners and researchers recognized a fundamental commonality underlying most versions of mediation, conferencing, and circles. Unsurprisingly, no generally accepted definition of restorative justice exists (McCold 1998). Based on an earlier definition by Bazemore and myself (1999, p. 48), by restorative justice I mean "an option on doing justice after the occurrence of a crime which gives priority to repairing the harm that has been caused by that crime."

This clearly is outcome-based. Most "restorativists" prefer a process-based definition (Zehr 1990; Boyes-Watson 2000; McCold 2000). Marshall's often-quoted definition is typical: "Restorative justice is a process whereby all the parties with a stake in a particular offense come together to resolve collectively how to deal with the aftermath of the offense and its implications for the future" (1996, p. 37). Marshall does not require that the outcome be restorative (and not purely punitive or rehabilitative, for example) and excludes initiatives that may lead to restorative outcomes without parties coming together (as in victim support). In my view, restoration is the goal, and voluntary processes are means only, though crucial ones. Process-based definitions confuse the means with the goal and limit the possible means to achieve (partial) restoration. Deliberative processes appear to hold the highest potentials for achieving restoration, but if voluntary agreements cannot be accomplished, coercive obligations in pursuit of (partial) reparation must be encompassed in the restorative justice model.

This section comments on three basic elements in the definition I offered: harm (Sec. IIA), restoration (Sec. IIB), and doing justice (Sec. IIC). It examines the socioethical foundations of restorative justice (Sec. IID) and draws conclusions on its practical feasibility (Sec. IIE).

A. HARM

A focus on repairing harm and not on what should be done to the offender is the key to understanding restorative justice and is what distinguishes it from punitive and rehabilitative justice approaches. That is why it is presented as another paradigm (Zehr 1990; Bazemore and Walgrave 1999; McCold 2000). It offers a distinctive "lens," in Zehr's term, for defining the problem caused by crime and for solving it. Crime is defined by the harm it causes and not by its transgression of a legal order. The primary

---

[1] The presentation of restorative justice in this essay thus cannot but be my personal view. In some respects, as I try to make clear, it deviates from "mainstream" restorative justice options.

function of responses to it should be neither to punish nor to rehabilitate the offender but to set the conditions for repairing as much as possible the harm caused. Restorative justice thus can go a long way without an offender involved. If the offender is not caught, while the harm caused is assessed, (partial) justice can be done by trying to repair or compensate the victim and by restoring public assurance that the crime is not acceptable. However, as we shall see, it remains important to involve the offender in formulating the aftermath of the offense.

1. *Limits to the Harm Considered.* Harm includes the material damage, psychological and relational suffering by the victim, social unrest and community indignation, uncertainty about legal order and about authorities' capacity to assure public safety, and the social damage the offender causes to himself.[2]

The only limitation is that the harm considered by the restorative process must be that caused by the particular offense. This positions restorative justice as a reactive option, "a way of responding to crimes which have been already committed" (Johnstone 2002, p. 19). Not all restorative justice adherents would accept this limitation. Some writers believe that restorative processes should address underlying causes of offending (Masters and Roberts 2000). Some conditions, like social exclusion or psychological problems of the offender, are not caused by the offense but may be among its causes. In my view, including offenders' broader needs in the restorative justice reaction is a dangerous option. It blurs the contrast with the rehabilitative approach and risks shifting from a harm-focused to an offender-focused program (Braithwaite 1999). It would also degrade the victim into being a tool in service of the offender's rehabilitation and not recognize the victim as a party on his own. Problems and needs of the offender are important elements in the search for reasonable restorative outcomes, but they are not the subject of the restoration itself.

The offender is not involved primarily because something must be done to him, but because this will serve the goal of restoration. Positive influences on the offender are a secondary objective only. The kind and amount of obligation is decided primarily by the needs of reasonable restoration, not by needs for adequate treatment or proportionate punishment.

2. *From Collective Harm to Intrusion upon Dominion.* Restorative justice addresses more than the harm to the individual victim. It is not limited to settling a tort according to civil law but deals with crimes, which are also public events, traditionally dealt with by criminal law. It is difficult to come to grips with this public aspect of crime-caused harm (Thorvaldson 1990; Van Ness 1990; Walgrave 1999). Distinctions between "communities of care" and the broader community (Braithwaite and Daly 1994), or among "affected communities," "local communities," and "society" (McCold 2000), do not resolve the problem.

What makes an offense a collective or public event? A burglary, for example, is a private and a public affair. Restitution of or compensation for the individual victim's losses could be private, to be arranged by civil law. But there is also a public side. We all

---

[2] The male form is used as the general form. This is done not to be politically incorrect, but as a practical solution to a practical problem.

are concerned that authorities intervene and try to make things right. The particular victim stands as an example of risks all citizens face. If the authorities do nothing, it hurts all citizens' trust in their right to privacy and property.

This leads to a crucial concept: "dominion," as introduced by Braithwaite and Pettit (1990) in their "republican theory of criminal justice." Dominion can be understood as the set of assured rights and freedoms. "Freedom as non-domination" (or dominion)[3] is the mental and social territory in which we freely move, guaranteed by the state and the social environment. The assurance of rights and freedoms is crucial.[4] "I know that I have rights, I know that the others know it, and I trust that they will respect it." I am assured only if I trust that my fellow citizens and the state will take my rights and freedoms seriously. Only then can I fully enjoy my mental and social territory.

That assurance provides the crucial distinction between the social concept of "freedom as non-domination" and the liberal concept of "freedom as non-interference." In the latter, the rights and freedoms of the individual citizen end where the rights and freedoms of the other citizen begin. Rights and freedoms are conceived as a stable given, which must be divided as justly as possible among citizens. Every other citizen is a possible interferer in my freedom and a rival in my struggle to expand my freedom. In the republican view, on the contrary, rights and freedoms are a collective good. "Dominion" is not a stable given but a value to be promoted and expanded by individual and collective action. The other citizen is an ally in trying to extend and mutually assure dominion as a collective good.

In this theory, crime is an intrusion upon dominion, and especially on the assurance of rights and freedoms. The burglary does not diminish the existing legal rights of privacy and property, but the extent to which the victim and his fellow citizens are assured that these rights are respected and taken seriously. Public intervention after a crime is primarily needed to enhance assurance by communicating the authorities' public disapproval of the norm transgression and by responding through their action in view of restoration. It makes clear that authorities take dominion seriously. The intervention reassures the victim, the public, and the offender of their set of rights and freedoms. Involving the offender in these actions, if possible, is important because it demonstrates the responsibilities and enhances the restorative impact of the action. Voluntary cooperation by the offender is more effective to restore assurance, but only if it is backed by public institutions. The assurance comes not primarily from the individual offender's repentance and apologies, but from the authorities' determination to take the assured set of rights and freedoms seriously.

---

[3] In later publications, "dominion" has been renamed as "freedom as non-domination." It may make it easier to oppose it to the liberal concept typified as "freedom as non-interference," but I see no other advantage in complicating the wording. I therefore use the "old" term, "dominion."

[4] See also what Putnam (1993) called "trust" in social capital. Social capital is defined as "features of social organization such as trust, norms and networks, that can improve the efficiency of society by facilitating coordinated actions" (1993, p. 167). Trust is crucial. Putnam does not limit trust to "thick trust" based on strong ties with family, friends, and close neighbors. The strongest social capital lies in the generalized trust based on weak ties with social organizations and the generalized other. It is this trust that constitutes our assurance of rights and freedoms.

B. WAYS OF RESTORATION

Different processes may lead to a restorative outcome, but not all processes are equally appropriate for it. The main distinction is between voluntary processes and coercive procedures.

   1. *Deliberative Restoration.* Most suitable are processes that consist of voluntary deliberation between the victim and the offender, the main stakeholders. Many deliberative processes are known today (McCold 2001; Morris and Maxwell 2001), including mediations between the individual victim and offender, most of which are face-to-face, but some intermediated by a go-between (Umbreit 1994; European Forum 2000); various forms of conferencing in which the victim and offender are supported by their communities of care, some of which also include participation by police or community representatives (Hudson et al. 1996; Masters and Roberts 2000; Daly 2001; Dignan and Marsh 2001); and sentencing circles, in which the local indigenous community as a whole is a part of the meeting on the occasion of a crime in its midst (Lilles 2001). Such sessions may happen once only or consist of a series of meetings.

Well-conducted restorative processes offer a powerful sequence of moral and social emotions and exchanges like shame, guilt, remorse, empathy, compassion, support, apology, and forgiveness in the offender, the victim, and other participants (Braithwaite 1989; Braithwaite and Mugford 1994; Maxwell and Morris 1999; Walgrave and Braithwaite 1999; Harris 2001). This "encounter" (Van Ness and Strong 2002) may lead to a common understanding of the harm and suffering caused and to an agreement on how to make amends. It may enhance the willingness of the offender to fulfill these agreements. It may lead to satisfaction of the victim, reintegration of the offender, and restored assurance of rights and freedoms in society. Such a sequence is of course the ideal, which is often far from being fully achieved. Even the claimed voluntariness to participate may be seriously reduced by social pressure or subtle threat (Boyes-Watson 2000).

Some identify restorative justice with such processes. Regardless of its outcome, they claim that the process itself has the most powerful restorative impact. However, this may push the difference between process and outcome too far. Why would such a process be more restorative? Because the expressions of remorse, compassion, apology, and forgiveness promote feelings of respect, peace, and satisfaction? These feelings are outcomes, even if they are not explicitly written down in the final agreement. Thus, it seems impossible to evaluate restorative processes without taking account of the restorative outcomes they explicitly or implicitly promote.

The agreement after such processes may include a wide range of actions like restitution, compensation, reparation, reconciliation, and apologies. They may be direct or indirect, concrete or symbolic. The degree of the offender's willingness to undertake such actions is crucial. It expresses his understanding of the wrong committed and his willingness to make up for it. For the victim, it means the restoration of his citizenship as a bearer of rights, and possibly also a partial material redress. For the larger community, it contributes to assurance that the offender takes rights and freedoms seriously and will respect them in the future. Even the offender's agreement to undergo a treatment has a restorative meaning that expresses his recognition of a problem that he wants to resolve in accordance with his social environment.

2. *Imposed Restoration.* There will always be cases in which voluntary processes cannot be achieved or are judged to be insufficient. Pressure or coercion on the offender must then be considered. According to the maximalist view of restorative justice, these coercive interventions also should serve restoration (Claassen 1995; Walgrave 2000a; Dignan 2002). In a constitutional democracy, coercion may only be exerted through a judicial procedure, but these procedures can be oriented to obligations or sanctions with a restorative significance. Examples are material restitution or compensation to the victim, paying a fine to the benefit of a victims' fund, or community service. Although these judicially imposed obligations can have an explicit restorative meaning (Wright 1996; Dignan 2002; Walgrave 2003), their restorative impact will be reduced. Restorative justice is not a black-and-white option. Between the fully restorative processes and the not-at-all-restorative reactions, degrees of restorativeness exist (McCold 2000; Dignan 2002; Van Ness 2002).

Enforced restorative sanctions, imposed according to judicial procedures and as a result of assessed accountability for the consequences of offending, seem to leave few or no differences between such sanctions and traditional punishments (Daly 2000; McCold 2000; Johnstone 2002). There are, however, essential differences (Walgrave 2000a, 2001, 2003).

First, punishment is a means in the eyes of law enforcement, and it is "morally neutral." It does not issue any message about the moral value of the enforced law itself. For example, in some political regimes, punishment is used to enforce very criticizable or even immoral laws. Restoration, on the contrary, is a goal, and different means can be chosen to achieve it. Moreover, the goal of restoration itself expresses an orientation toward the quality of peaceful social life, which is an intrinsic moral orientation. The a priori position that crime has to be punished is thus counterproductive as a means for achieving restoration.

Second, "punishing someone consists of visiting a deprivation (hard treatment) on him, because he supposedly has committed a wrong" (von Hirsch 1993, p. 9). The pain is intentionally inflicted. An obligation aimed at restoration may be painful but is not inflicted with the intention to cause suffering. It may be a secondary effect only (Wright 1996). Painfulness in punishment is the primary yardstick, while painfulness in restorative obligations is a secondary consideration only.

Third, intentional infliction of pain "involves actions that are generally considered to be morally wrong or evil were they not described and justified as punishments" (Keijser 2000, p. 7). Retributivist and instrumentalist justifications of criminal punishments (von Hirsch 1998) do not convincingly demonstrate the need for systemic punishment. The a priori position that crime must be punished is itself dubious from an ethical standpoint. Thorough exploration is thus needed regarding alternative ways to express blame, to favor repentance, and to promote social peace and order (Fati 1995).

Restorative justice proponents claim that their approach is more promising in that respect. Deliberative processes, if possible, or imposed obligations in view of restoration, if necessary, make more sense. Acts are criminalized because they cause victimization and disturb public life; the social reaction should thus primarily aim at redressing the victimization and the disturbance. Restorative justice is also socially more constructive: it does not respond to harm caused by the offense by inflicting further harm on the offender, which after all "only adds to the total amount of harm in the world" (Wright 1992, p. 525), but by aiming at repair of the harm caused. Finally, restorativists consider it ethically more acceptable to aim at (imposing) restoration than deliberately to inflict pain.

C. DOING JUSTICE

Restorative justice not only is about restoration, it is also about justice. The notion of "justice" has two meanings here. One is justice as the outcome of an ethical evaluation; the other is justice as respecting legal rights and freedoms.

1. *Ethical Justice.* "Justice" refers to a feeling of equity, of being dealt with fairly, according to a moral balance of rights and wrongs, benefits, and burdens. In retributive justice, this balance is achieved by imposing suffering on the offender that is commensurate to the social harm he caused by his crime. In restorative justice, the balance is restored by taking away or compensating the suffering and harm caused by the crime. Restorative justice then aims at achieving "procedural fairness" (Tyler 1990) and satisfaction (Van Ness and Schiff 2001) for all parties involved. Victims feel that their victimization has been taken seriously and that the compensation and support are reasonably in balance with their sufferings and losses. Offenders experience that their dignity has not unnecessarily been hurt and that they are given the opportunity to make up for their mistake in a constructive way. All participants, including the community, feel reassured that rights and freedoms are taken seriously by fellow citizens and the authorities.

The best way to guarantee that losses are well-understood and the methods of reparation are adequate is to leave the decision to those with a direct stake: victims, offenders,
and others directly affected. "Justice" is what those concerned experience as such. This
bottom-up approach is crucial in restorative justice and contrasts with the top-down
approach of the criminal justice system.

However, the state cannot withdraw completely. If it did, it would leave the parties
alone to find a solution. State authorities would not guarantee respect for rights and freedoms and, thus, would not assure dominion. To give assurance, the state must guarantee
that everything possible will be done to respect and restore the intruded-on dominion. In
a voluntary restorative deliberation, the state must be present at least in the background
to assure that the deliberation takes place and results in an acceptable outcome, to guarantee the power balance in the deliberation, and to provide an opportunity to the parties
to leave the deliberative process and turn to the traditional judicial response if one of
them feels that their interests are not adequately acknowledged in the deliberative process. That way, the state's rule of law percolates into restorative justice (Braithwaite and
Parker 1999). Authorities demonstrate that they take dominion seriously not only with
regard to the victim's rights and freedoms but also as a guarantor of the offender's rights
and as a safeguard for the collectively assured set of rights and freedoms.

> 2. *Legal Justice.* Justice also encompasses legality. Restorative justice means that
> the processes and their outcomes respect legal safeguards (Van Ness 1996,
> 2002, Trépanier 1998; Walgrave 2000b; Dignan 2002). Legal safeguards
> protect citizens not only against illegitimate intrusions by fellow citizens but
> also by the state. This is obvious in coerced interventions, but it applies also in
> voluntary settlements. Participation may not be imposed. Agreements must
> be accepted by the parties and be reasonable in relation to the seriousness
> of the harm and to the parties' accountability and capacities. How to make
> sure rights are observed is a matter of debate among restorative justice
> proponents. Some rely fully on the potentials of communities (Pranis 2001)
> and try to reduce state control over restorative processes to a strict minimum
> out of fear of the state's power to invade the process and undo its informal,
> humane, and healing potentials. Others try to find a balanced social and
> institutional context, which allows maximum space for genuine deliberative
> processes but also offers full opportunities for all parties to appeal to judicial
> agencies if they feel not respected in the process.

In a coercive procedure, all legal guarantees must be observed. In a traditional criminal
justice procedure, safeguards like legality, due process, and proportionality are evident.
The rights that they protect should be protected in coercive restorative interventions
as well (Ashworth 1993; Warner 1994). However, as these principles are meant for a
punishment-oriented system, it is not obvious that they should be applied unchanged
in a system premised on restoration (Walgrave 2000b). The main function is different,

the actors are partly different, and the social and judicial context is different. Contrary to the traditional top-down approach, a restorative system should allow ample space for a bottom-up approach. The role of the state must be limited to its core functions and be oriented to enhancing the opportunities for settling the aftermath of a crime constructively (Declaration of Leuven 1997). The rule of law must not only percolate down into restorative justice, as stated above, but restorative justice must also bubble up into the rule of law (Braithwaite and Parker 1999).

Thinking about a legal context that combines maximum space for deliberative conflict resolution with complete legal safeguards is only beginning (Walgrave 2002c; von Hirsch et al. 2003). Braithwaite speaks of "responsive regulation": "law enforcers should be responsive to how effectively citizens or corporations are regulating themselves before deciding whether to escalate intervention" (2002, p. 29). In Braithwaite's view, intervention after a crime should be planned according to a "regulatory pyramid," in which persuasion, or restorative processing, is the foundation, and incapacitation of "incompetent or irrational actors" is at the top. "What we want is a legal system where citizens learn that responsiveness is the way our legal institutions work. Once they see the legal system as a responsive regulatory system, they know there will be a chance to argue about unjust laws.... The forces of law are listening, fair and therefore legitimate, but also are seen as somewhat invincible" (Braithwaite 2002, p. 34).

Such an ideal presupposes responsible citizens in a society in which the state is at the service of the community or the communities. It is far from being achieved at the moment. That brings us to the next subsection.

D. SOCIAL ETHICS

Restorative justice is more than a technical model of how to respond to crime. It is an ideal of justice in an idealized society. Concern for the broader quality of social life is the inspiring source of restorative justice.

The community occupies a focal position in restorative rhetoric (Bazemore and Schiff 2001). The priority of restoring harms caused by crime necessarily draws attention to social unrest suffered by the community. Restorative interventions require a minimum of "community": the victim and the offender must feel a minimal common interest. However, community as a concept poses great problems (Crawford 1996; Crawford and Clear 2001; Pavlich 2001; Walgrave 2002a). First, the "community" concept suggests a difference between what community is and what it is not, as if it were an ontological territorial or mental "area." It is hard to find the limitations. Community is too vague a concept to characterize and delimit a part of social reality adequately. Second, building on communities for developing restorative responses to crime, as many restorativists do, presupposes its general availability, which is far from being evident. It is difficult, for example, to mobilize community in the settlement of a street robbery in the city where the victim and offender live miles from each other and belong to completely different social networks. Third, leaving community as the loose concept that it is now makes it vulnerable to misuses and excesses. Community may contain "the seeds of parochialism which can lead...to atrocious totalitarian exclusions" (Pavlich 2001, p. 58), as has recently been demonstrated by ethnic wars and purges.

Skepticism about the concept of community need not result in rejection of the ideals communitarians promote: social unity, harmonious living based on shared values and beliefs, and mutual commitment. Most communitarians promote social ethics and values, not areas, as suggested by the community notion. "Community" is a container for ethical and social values. They should be unpacked from their container. While rejecting community as the container, "communitarianism" may be a useful label for a socioethical movement. It refers to the pursuit of a utopian social life in which the distinction between society and community is meaningless, because the collectivity would be governed in view of individual and collective emancipation in which autonomy and solidarity are not seen as opposed but as mutually reinforcing. Collective life would draw its strength not from top-down rules enforced by threat, coercion, and fear, but from bottom-up motivation based on trust, participation, and support. Elsewhere I have tried to show that such a view promotes social-ethical "guidelines" like respect, solidarity, and active responsibility and that these guidelines are better achieved through restorative justice than through the traditional criminal justice approach (Walgrave 2002a, 2003).

The communitarian option goes far beyond regulatory models of criminal justice. It penetrates how people interact and try to settle conflicts in everyday life (Wachtel and McCold 2001). It is implemented in problems in school contexts (Ahmed 2001) and in neighborhood conflicts (Peper and Spierings 1999). Its deliberative philosophy also applies to world peacemaking (Braithwaite 2002).

In a communitarian ideal, the state must act responsively. The state must respond to the reality of social life in order to serve the quality of that social life. The same communitarian ideal also substantiates the concept of "dominion" as the set of assured rights and freedoms to be promoted by the state. Dominion can be considered a formalization of the communitarian ideal into a political theory. The communitarian utopia can be achieved only if the state acts responsively in view of assuring and expanding dominion. Inversely, the assurance of rights and freedoms is achieved only to the degree that citizens accept active responsibility for respect and solidarity.

E. Empirical Evaluation

Sometimes, brilliant ideas are unrealistic or evolve into being terrible practices. An increasing stream of empirical research explores the extent to which restorative aspirations are achieved in reality.

1. *Methodological Issues.* The evaluation of interventions is precarious. It is difficult to compose appropriate control groups, to isolate and measure adequate evaluation criteria, and to prove the link between programs and observed outcomes. Much restorative justice research suffers from serious methodological shortcomings. Many evaluated practices are limited in

scope or are carried out in exceptionally favorable circumstances. They seldom include process evaluations of the procedural quality of the practice. Despite these problems, several surveys of empirical evaluations suggest that restorative practices hold great promise. In general, projects for juveniles appear to achieve better results than those for adults.

2. *Results.* As there are many publications presenting empirical data, it is impossible to refer to all of them at every statement. I therefore draw on some of the available surveys (Braithwaite 1999; Schiff 1999; Umbreit 1999; Kurki 2003; McCold 2003) and concentrate on initiatives for juveniles.

Most programs find a majority of victims are willing to participate in mediation or in a conference. The variation in the proportion (between 90 percent and 32 percent, with an average of 60 percent; Umbreit 1999) depends, among other things, on the kind and seriousness of crime or on the way that the victims are invited to participate. The reasons for nonparticipation usually relate to its futility, like not wanting to spend another evening discussing the offense, not finding it worth investing more time, or last-minute cancellations. Maxwell and Morris (1996) found that only 4 percent of the refusals to participate in conferences were for principled or emotional reasons. Participation by juvenile offenders is very high, reaching a participation rate of between 87 percent and 92 percent (as in Hartmann and Stroezel 1996). Most surveys indicate agreement rates of over 80 percent, although some programs achieve much lower rates (as in Aertsen and Peters 1998).

Compliance with agreements is achieved in a great majority of cases, reaching more than nine out of ten, if partial compliance and compliance with difficulties are included (as in Hartmann and Stroezel 1996). The same figures apply for successful completion of community service for juveniles (Geudens 1996; Schiff 1999). Whereas the seriousness of the crime appears to be a complicating factor in all this, very serious crimes have been successfully dealt with through mediation or conferencing. New Zealand's experience, described by Allison Morris (in this volume), is illustrative. The first conclusion therefore must be that restorative responses are realistic, reaching more kinds of crimes and more serious crimes than originally expected.

All comparisons of victims' experiences find that victims who participated in a mediation or a conference had greater satisfaction than victims who were involved in traditional responses to crime. They say that they are better informed and supported, experienced more respect and equity, and appreciated the emotional opportunities (see, among others, Strang and Sherman 1997; McCold and Wachtel 1998; Strang 2002). The material restitution or compensation is considered important to them but is not as crucial as the emotional benefits. Even when the process does not lead to an agreement, the majority of victims still are more satisfied than those involved in a traditional judicial procedure. A small minority of victims feel worse after a restorative process. This minority always is smaller in the restorative process group than in the justice system group.

During and after restorative interventions, offenders better understand the reason for the intervention than they do after a traditional juvenile justice procedure. They express feelings of "procedural justice" (Tyler 1990), feeling more fairly treated and seeming better able to accept the outcome of the process. More than after a traditional court session, offenders express respect for police and for the law and say that they will stop further offending (as in Sherman and Strang 1997). Research on recorded reoffending mostly reveals less recidivism in the "restorative justice group," but the differences are not always statistically significant. There is no research pointing to more reoffending.

The effects of the intensive use of restorative interventions on local communities and public safety have not been systematically researched (Kurki 2003). This might be because, except for New Zealand, restorative justice practices have not been implemented so extensively that one might expect observable changes in the community at large, or because it is difficult to construct measures of the impact of restorative justice on public life. Communitarian rhetoric proposes that restorative justice should be beneficial to the community and public life in general, and no data available so far lead to opposite conclusions.

Samples of lay respondents in several countries have presented options for responding to several crimes. A majority prefer responses that promote or allow for reparation. Sessar concludes that "the conception of the public's strong punitive sentiments is a myth" (1999, p. 301). Professional respondents, on the contrary, are more comfortable with traditional criminal justice responses and, thus, stick to their own approach.

3. *Conclusions.* Available data do not indicate that the ambitions of restorative justice proponents are unfeasible or counterproductive. Victims, offenders, and their communities mostly do come together and do reach constructive agreements, which are carried out reasonably well. Involved parties generally express higher degrees of satisfaction than they do with traditional approaches, and reoffending risks are mostly lower, and certainly not higher. Variations in outcomes depend on several variables. The seriousness of the crime is one of them, but even the most serious crimes can be dealt with restoratively. Another is the technical quality of the methodology in monitoring the restorative process. There are no indications that social life and public security are adversely affected by restorative practices, and the public appears to support their implementation.

This optimistic summary must be accepted cautiously. The research results are provisional only and need expansion and improvement, strong methodologies for monitoring restorative interventions must be developed, and much theoretical and normative work is still to be done.

Even in the best possible circumstances, however, a purely restorative approach to all crimes will never be workable. Concerns for public safety, very recalcitrant offenders, and unreasonably vindictive victims may raise insuperable difficulties and oblige the use of other approaches, as set out in Braithwaite's "regulatory pyramid" (Braithwaite 2002; see also Dignan 2002; Walgrave 2002*b*). Indeed, the restorative justice option does not mean that all crimes, in all circumstances, must be dealt with restoratively. The restorative option should be the first to be considered, but it must sometimes be completed or replaced by other intervention models.

REFERENCES

Aertsen, Ivo, and Tony Peters. 1998. "Meditation and Restorative Justice in Belgium." *European Journal on Criminal Policy and Research* 6:507–25.

Ahmed, Eliza. 2001. "Shame Management: Regulating Bullying." In *Shame Management through Reintegration*, edited by Eliza Ahmed, Nathan Harris, John Braithwaite, and Valerie Braithwaite. Cambridge: Cambridge University Press.

Ashworth, Anthony. 1993. "Some Doubts about Restorative Justice." *Criminal Law Forum* 4:277–99.

Bazemore, Gordon, and Mara Schiff, eds. 2001. *Restorative Community Justice: Repairing Harm and Transforming Communities*. Cincinnati: Anderson.

Bazemore, Gordon, and Lode Walgrave. 1999. "Restorative Justice: In Search of Fundamentals and an Outline for Systemic Reform." In *Restorative Juvenile Justice: Repairing the Harm of Youth Crime*, edited by Gordon Bazemore and Lode Walgrave. Monsey, N.Y.: Criminal Justice.

Boyes-Watson, Carolyn. 2000. "Reflections on the Purist and the Maximalist Models of Restorative Justice." *Contemporary Justice Review* 3:441–50.

Braithwaite, John. 1989. *Crime, Shame, and Reintegration*. Cambridge: Cambridge University Press.

———. 1999. "Restorative Justice: Assessing Optimistic and Pessimistic Accounts." In *Crime and Justice: A Review of Research*, vol. 25, edited by Michael Tonry. Chicago: University of Chicago Press.

———. 2002. *Restorative Justice and Responsive Regulation*. Oxford: Oxford University Press.

——— and Kathleen Daly. 1994. "Masculinities, Violence, and Communitarian Control." In *Just Boys Doing Business? Men, Masculinities, and Crime*, edited by Tim Newburn and Elizabeth Stanko. London: Routledge.

——— and Stephen Mugford. 1994. "Conditions of Successful Reintegration Ceremonies: Dealing with Juvenile Offenders." *British Journal of Criminology* 34:139–71.

——— and Christine Parker. 1999. "Restorative Justice Is Republican Justice." In *Restorative Juvenile Justice: Repairing the Harm of Youth Crime*, edited by Gordon Bazemore and Lode Walgrave. Monsey, N.Y.: Criminal Justice.

——— and Philip Pettit. 1990. *Not Just Deserts: A Republican Theory of Criminal Justice*. Oxford: Oxford University Press.

Claassen, Ron. 1995. "Restorative Justice Principles and Evaluation Continuums." Paper presented at National Center for Peacemaking and Conflict Resolution, Fresno, Calif., May.

Corrado, Ray, and Curt Griffiths. 1999. "Implementing Restorative Youth Justice: A Case Study in Community Justice and the Dynamics of Reform." In *Restorative Juvenile Justice: Repairing the Harm of Youth Crime*, edited by Gordon Bazemore and Lode Walgrave. Monsey, N.Y.: Criminal Justice.

Crawford, Adam. 1996. "The Spirit of Community: Rights, Responsibilities and the Communitarian Agenda." *Journal of Law and Society* 2:247–62.

———and Todd Clear. 2001. "Community Justice: Transforming Communities through Restorative Justice?" In *Restorative Community Justice: Repairing Harm and Transforming Communities*, edited by Gordon Bazemore and Mara Schiff. Cincinnati: Anderson.

Daly, Kathleen. 2000. "Revisiting the Relationship between Retributive and Restorative Justice." In *Restorative Justice: Philosophy to Practice*, edited by Heather Strang and John Braithwaite. Aldershot: Ashgate.

———. 2001. "Conferencing in Australia and New Zealand: Variations, Research Findings and Prospects." In *Restorative Justice for Juveniles: Conferencing, Mediation and Circles*, edited by Allison Morris and Gabrielle Maxwell. Oxford: Hart.

Declaration of Leuven. 1997. "On the Advisability of Promoting the Restorative Approach to Juvenile Crime." Issued on the Occasion of the First International Conference on Restorative Justice for Juveniles, Louvain, Belgium, May.

de Haan, Willem. 1990. *The Politics of Redress: Crime, Punishment, and Penal Abolition*. London: Unwyn Hyman.

Dignan, James. 2002. "Restorative Justice and the Law: The Case for an Integrated, Systemic Approach." In *Restorative Justice and the Law*, edited by Lode Walgrave. Cullompton, U.K.: Willan.

———and Peter Marsh. 2001. "Restorative Justice and Family Group Conferences in England: Current State and Future Prospects." In *Restorative Justice for Juveniles: Conferencing, Mediation and Circles*, edited by Allison Morris and Gabrielle Maxwell. Oxford: Hart.

European Forum for Victim-Offender Mediation and Restorative Justice, ed. 2000. *Victim-Offender Mediation in Europe: Making Restorative Justice Work*. Louvain: Leuven University Press.

Faget, Jacques. 1997. *La médiation: Essai de politique pénale* (Mediation: An essay on penal policy). Ramonville Saint-Agne, France: Erès.

Fatić, Aleksandar. 1995. *Punishment and Restorative Crime-Handling: A Social Theory of Trust*. Aldershot: Avebury.

Geudens, Hilde. 1996. *De toepassing van de Gemenschapsdienst in bet kader van de Belgische Jeugdbescherming* (The implementation of community service in Belgian juvenile justice). Louvain: Katholieke Universiteit Leuven, Onderzoeksgroep Jeugdcriminologie.

Harris, M. 1990. "Moving into the New Millennium: Towards a Feminist Vision of Justice." In *Criminology as Peacemaking*, edited by Harold E. Pepinsky and Richard Quinney. Bloomington: Indiana University Press.

Harris, Nathan. 2001. "Shaming and Shame: Regulating Drink-Driving." In *Shame Management through Reintegration*, edited by Eliza Ahmed, Nathan Harris, John Braithwaite, and Valerie Braithwaite. Cambridge: Cambridge University Press.

Hartmann, Arthur, and Holger Stroezel. 1996. "Die Bundesweite TOA-Statistik" (Statistics on victim-offender mediation in Germany). In *Täter-Opfer-Ausgleich in Deutschland* (Victim-offender mediation in Germany), edited by Dieter Dölling, Dieter Banneberg, Arthur Hartmann, Elke Hassemer, Wolfgang Heinz, Susanne Henninger, Hans-Jürgen Kerner, Thomas Klaus, Dieter Rössner, Holger Stroezel, Petra Uhlmann, Michael Walter, Michael Wandrey and Elmar Weitekamp. Bonn: Bundesministerium der Justiz.

Hudson, Joe, Allison Morris, Gabrielle Maxwell, and Burt Galaway, eds. 1996. *Family Group Conferences: Perspectives on Policy and Practice*. Annandale, New South Wales: Federation; Monsey, N.Y.: Willow Tree.

Johnstone, Gerry. 2002. *Restorative Justice: Ideas, Values, Debates.* Cullompton, U.K.: Willan.

Keijser, Jan Willem de. 2000. *Punishment and Purpose: From Moral Theory to Punishment in Action.* Amsterdam: Thela Thesis.

Kurki, Leena. 2003. "Evaluating Restorative Practices." In *Restorative Justice and Criminal Justice: Competing or Reconcilable Paradigms?* edited by Andrew von Hirsch, Julian V. Roberts, Anthony E. Bottoms, Kent Roach, and Mara Schiff. Oxford: Hart.

Lilles, Heino. 2001 "Circle Sentencing: Part of the Restorative Justice Continuum." In *Restorative Justice for Juveniles: Conferencing, Mediation and Circles,* edited by Allison Morris and Gabrielle Maxwell. Oxford: Hart.

Marshall, Tony. 1996. "The Evolution of Restorative Justice in Britain." *European Journal of Criminal Policy and Research* 4:21–43.

Masters, Guy, and Ann Roberts. 2000. "Family Group Conferencing for Victims, Offenders and Communities." In *Mediation in Context,* edited by Marian Liebmann. London: Kingsley.

Maxwell, Gabrielle, and Allison Morris. 1996. "Research on Family Group Conferences with Young Offenders in New Zealand." In *Family Group Conferences: Perspectives on Policy and Practice,* edited by Joe Hudson, Allison Morris, Gabrielle Maxwell, and Burt Galaway. Annandale, New South Wales: Federation; Monsey, N.Y.: Willow Tree.

————1999. *Understanding Reoffending: Final Report.* Wellington: Victoria University, Institute of Criminology.

McCold, Paul. 1998. "Restorative Justice: Variation on a Theme." In *Restorative Justice for Juveniles: Potentialities, Risks and Problems for Research,* edited by Lode Walgrave. Louvain: Leuven University Press.

————. 2000. "Towards a Holistic Vision of Restorative Juvenile Justice: A Reply to the Maximalist Model." *Contemporary Justice Review* 3:357–414.

————. 2001. "Primary Restorative Practices." In *Restorative Justice for Juveniles: Conferencing, Mediation and Circles,* edited by Allison Morris and Gabrielle Maxwell. Oxford: Hart.

————. 2003. "A Survey of Assessment Research on Mediation and Conferencing." In *Positioning Restorative Justice,* edited by Lode Walgrave. Cullompton, U.K.: Willan (forthcoming).

————and Ted Wachtel. 1998. *Restorative Policing Experiment.* Pipersville, Pa.: Community Service Foundation.

Morris, Allison, and Gabrielle Maxwell, eds. 2001. *Restorative Justice for Juveniles: Conferencing, Mediation and Circles.* Oxford: Hart.

Pavlich, George. 2001. "The Force of Community." In *Restorative Justice and Civil Society,* edited by Heather Strang and John Braithwaite. Cambridge: Cambridge University Press.

Peper, Bram, and Frans Spierings. 1999. "Settling Disputes between Neighbours in the Lifeworld: An Evaluation of Experiments with Community Mediation." *European Journal on Criminal Policy and Research* 7:483–507.

Peters, Tony, and Ivo Aertsen. 1995. "Restorative Justice: In Search of New Avenues in Judicial Dealing with Crime." In *Crime and Insecurity in the City,* vol. 1, edited by Cyrille Fijnaut, Johan Goethals, Tony Peters, and Lode Walgrave. The Hague: Kluwer International.

Pranis, Kay. 2001. "Restorative Justice, Social Justice and the Empowerment of Marginalized Populations." In *Restorative Juvenile Justice: Repairing the Harm of Youth Crime,* edited by Gordon Bazemore and Lode Walgrave. Monsey, N.Y.: Criminal Justice.

Putnam, Robert D. 1993. *Making Democracy Work: Civic Traditions in Modern Italy.* Princeton, N.J.: Princeton University Press.

Schiff, Mara. 1999. "The Impact of Restorative Interventions on Juvenile Offenders." In *Restorative Juvenile Justice: Repairing the Harm of Youth Crime,* edited by Gordon Bazemore and Lode Walgrave. Monsey, N.Y.: Criminal Justice.

Sessar, Klaus. 1999. "Punitive Attitudes of the Public: Reality and Myth." In *Restorative Juvenile Justice: Repairing the Harm of Youth Crime,* edited by Gordon Bazemore and Lode Walgrave. Monsey, N.Y.: Criminal Justice.

Sherman, Lawrence W., and Heather Strang. 1997. "Restorative Justice and Deterring Crime." RISE (Restorative Justice in Australia) Working Papers no. 4. Canberra: Australian National University.

Strang, Heather. 2002. *Repair or Revenge: Victims and Restorative Justice.* Oxford: Oxford University Press.

———and Lawrence W. Sherman. 1997. "The Victim's Perspective." RISE (Restorative Justice in Australia) Working Papers no. 2. Canberra: Australian National University.

Thorvaldson, Sveinn. 1990. "Restitution and Victim Participation in Sentencing." In *Criminal Justice, Restitution and Reconciliation,* edited by Burt Galaway and Joe Hudson. Monsey, N.Y.: Criminal Justice.

Trépanier, Jean. 1998. "Restorative Justice: A Question of Legitimacy." In *Restorative Justice for Juveniles: Potentialities, Risks and Problems for Research,* edited by Lode Walgrave. Louvain: Leuven University Press.

Tyler, Tom R. 1990. *Why People Obey the Law.* New Haven, Conn.: Yale University Press.

Umbreit, Mark S. 1994. *Victim Meets Offender: The Impact of Restorative Justice and Mediation.* Monsey, N.Y.: Criminal Justice.

———. 1999. "Avoiding the 'McDonaldization' of Victim-Offender Mediation: A Case Study in Moving Toward the Mainstream." In *Restorative Juvenile Justice: Repairing the Harm of Youth Crime,* edited by Gordon Bazemore and Lode Walgrave. Monsey, N.Y.: Criminal Justice.

Van Ness, Daniel W. 1990. "Restorative Justice." In *Criminal Justice, Restitution and Reconciliation,* edited by Burt Galaway and Joe Hudson. Monsey, N.Y.: Criminal Justice.

———. 1996. "Restorative Justice and International Human Rights." In *Restorative Justice: International Perspectives,* edited by Burt Galaway and Joe Hudson. Monsey, N.Y.: Criminal Justice.

———. 2002. "The Shape of Things to Come: A Framework for Thinking about a Restorative Justice System." In *Restorative Justice: Theoretical Foundations,* edited by Elmar Weitekamp and Hans-Jürgen Kerner. Cullompton, U.K.: Willan.

———and Mara Schiff. 2001. "Satisfaction Guaranteed? The Meaning of Satisfaction in Restorative Justice." In *Restorative Juvenile Justice: Repairing the Harm of Youth Crime,* edited by Gordon Bazemore and Lode Walgrave. Monsey, N.Y.: Criminal Justice.

———and Karen Heetderks Strong. 2002. *Restoring Justice.* 2d ed. Cincinnati: Anderson.

van Swaaningen, René. 1997. *Critical Criminology: Visions from Europe.* London: Sage.

von Hirsch, Andrew. 1993. *Censure and Sanctions.* Oxford: Clarendon.

———. 1998. "Penal Theories." In *The Handbook of Crime and Punishment,* edited by Michael Tonry. New York: Oxford University Press.

———, Julian V. Roberts, Anthony E. Bottoms, Kent Roach, and Mara Schiff, eds. 2003. *Restorative Justice and Criminal Justice: Competing or Reconcilable Paradigms?* Oxford: Hart.

Wachtel, Ted, and Paul McCold. 2001. "Restorative Justice in Everyday Life: Beyond the Formal Ritual." In *Restorative Justice and Civil Society*, edited by Heather Strang and John Braithwaite. Cambridge: Cambridge University Press.

Walgrave, Lode. 1995. "Restorative Justice for Juveniles: Just a Technique or a Fully Fledged Alternative?" *Howard Journal* 34:228–49.

———. 1999. "Community Service as a Cornerstone of a Systemic Restorative Response to (Juvenile) Crime." In *Restorative Juvenile Justice: Repairing the Harm of Youth Crime*, edited by Gordon Bazemore and Lode Walgrave. Monsey, N.Y.: Criminal Justice.

———. 2000a. "How Pure Can a Maximalist Approach to Restorative Justice Remain? Or Can a Purist Model of Restorative Justice Become Maximalist?" *Contemporary Justice Review* 3:415–32.

———. 2000b. "Restorative Justice and the Republican Theory of Criminal Justice: An Exercise in Normative Theorizing on Restorative Justice." In *Restorative Justice: Philosophy to Practice*, edited by Heather Strang and John Braithwaite. Aldershot: Ashgate.

———. 2001. "On Restoration and Punishment: Favourable Similarities and Fortunate Differences." In *Restorative Justice for Juveniles: Conferencing, Mediation and Circles*, edited by Allison Morris and Gabrielle Maxwell. Oxford: Hart.

———. 2002a. "From Community to Dominion: In Search of Social Values for Restorative Justice." In *Restorative Justice: Theoretical Foundations*, edited by Elmar Weitekamp and Hans-Jürgen Kerner. Cullompton, U.K.: Willan.

———. 2002b. "Restorative Justice and the Law: Socio-Ethical and Juridical Foundations for a Systemic Approach." In *Restorative Justice and the Law*, edited by Lode Walgrave. Cullompton, U.K.: Willan.

———. 2003. "Imposing Restoration Instead of Inflicting Pain: Reflections on the Judicial Reaction to Crime." In *Restorative Justice and Criminal Justice: Competing or Reconcilable Paradigms?* edited by Andrew von Hirsch, Julian V. Roberts, Anthony E. Bottoms, Kent Roach, and Mara Schiff. Oxford: Hart.

Walgrave, Lode, ed. 2002c. *Restorative Justice and the Law*. Cullompton, U.K.: Willan.

——— and John Braithwaite. 1999. "Schaamte, Schuld en Herstel" (Shame, guilt and restoration). *Justitiële Verkenningen* 25:71–81.

Warner, K. 1994. "Family Group Conferences and the Rights of the Offender." In *Family Conferencing and Juvenile Justice: The Way Forward or Misplaced Optimism?* edited by Christine Alder and Joy Wundersitz. Canberra: Australian Institute of Criminology.

Weitekamp, Elmar. 1999. "History of Restorative Justice." In *Restorative Juvenile Justice: Repairing the Harm of Youth Crime*, edited by Gordon Bazemore and Lode Walgrave. Monsey, N.Y.: Criminal Justice.

Wright, Martin. 1992. "Victim-Offender Mediation as a Step toward a Restorative System of Justice." In *Restorative Justice on Trial*, edited by Heinz Messmer and Hans-Uwe Otto. Dordrecht: Kluwer Academic.

———. 1996. *Justice for Victims and Offenders: A Restorative Response to Crime*. 2d ed. Winchester: Waterside.

———. 1999. *Restoring Respect for Justice*. Winchester: Waterside.

Young, Marlene. 1995. *Restorative Community Justice: A Call to Action*. Washington, D.C.: National Organization for Victim Assistance.

Zehr, Howard. 1990. *Changing Lenses: A New Focus for Crime and Justice*. Scottdale, Pa.: Herald.

22

IN SEARCH OF RESTORATIVE JURISPRUDENCE

John Braithwaite

THE RESTORATIVE CONSENSUS ON LIMITS

It is of course far too early to articulate a jurisprudence of restorative justice. Innovation in restorative practices continues apace. The best programmes today are very different from best practice a decade ago. As usual, practice is ahead of theory. The newer the ideas, the less research and development (R&D) there has been around them.

Within the social movement for restorative justice, there is and always has been absolute consensus on one jurisprudential issue. This is that restorative justice processes should never exceed the upper limits on punishment enforced by the courts for the criminal offence under consideration. Retributive theorists often pretend in their writing that this is not the case, but when they do, they are unable to cite any scholarly writings, any restorative justice legislation or any training manuals of restorative justice practitioners to substantiate loose rhetoric about restorative justice being against upper limits or uncommitted to them. Moreover, the empirical experience of the courts intervening to overturn the decisions of restorative justice processes, which has now been considerable, particularly in New Zealand and Canada, has been overwhelmingly in the direction of the courts increasing the punitiveness of agreements reached between victims, offenders and other stakeholders. In New Zealand, for example, Maxwell and Morris (1993) report that while courts ratified conference decisions 81 per cent of the time, when they did change them, for every case where they reduced the punitiveness of the order there were eight where they increased it. Similar results have been obtained in the Restorative Resolutions project for adult offenders in Manitoba (83 per cent judicial ratification of plans, with five times as much modification by addition of requirements as modification by deletion) (Bonta *et al.* 1998: 16). While there were no cases where the restorative process recommended imprisonment and the court over-ruled this, there were many of the court overruling the process by adding prison time to the sentence.

Retributivist voices have been absent in condemnation of excesses of courts in overturning non-punitive restorative justice outcomes while persisting with rhetoric on the disrespect of restorative justice for upper limits. I suspect this is not a matter of bad faith on their part, but simply a result of their acceptance of a false assumption that the problem will turn out to be one of punitive populism as the driver of punitive excess.

Secondly, there is near universal consensus among restorative justice advocates that fundamental human rights ought to be respected in restorative justice processes. The argument is about what that list of rights ought to be. I have suggested that there could be consensus on respect for the fundamental human rights specified in the Universal Declaration of Human Rights, the International Covenant on Economic, Social and Cultural Rights, the International Covenant on Civil and Political Rights and its Second Optional Protocol, the United Nations Declaration on the Elimination of Violence Against Women and the Declaration of Basic Principles of Justice for Victims of Crime and Abuse of Power (Braithwaite 2002b). While restorative justice advocates would agree that it can never be right to send an offender to a prison where his fundamental human rights are not protected, in Australia there is never likely to be consensus on whether it can be right to allow traditional Aboriginal spearing as an indigenous response to the problem of Aboriginal deaths in custody. The dilemma here is that for some traditional Aboriginal people in outback Australia, imprisonment is a fundamental assault on their human rights because it deprives them of spiritual contact with their land, which is everything to their humanity. When they feel strongly that ritualized spearing is less cruel and more reintegrative than imprisonment, little wonder that here it is difficult for westerners to be sure about what is right.

Basically, however, the restorative justice consensus on limits and rights is very similar to the retributive consensus: there ought to be upper limits on punishment, while there is disagreement on what should be the quantum of those upper limits, and fundamental human rights should constrain what is permissible in justice processes, with disagreements about what some of those rights should be and how they should be framed.

FERMENT ON PROPORTIONALITY

Where there is both strong disagreement between restorativists and retributivists, and among restorativists themselves, is on proportionality. Some restorativists are attracted to calibrating the proportionality of restorative agreements in terms of whether the repair is proportional to the harm done. This cuts no ice with retributivists who see this as a tort-based form of proportionality. For retributivists, punishment must be proportional to culpability. The harm in need of repair is only one component of culpability. An attempted murder where no one is hit by the bullet is more culpable than injuring someone seriously as a result of unintentionally or slightly exceeding the speed limit. Such restorative proportionality is also unattractive to cultures who seek healing by allowing victims to give a gift to the offender (for examples, see Braithwaite 2002a: Box 3.3). The grace that comes from such gift-giving by victims can be helpful for their own healing and trigger remorse in offenders. It might be nurtured as a practice attractive to a number of cultural groups present in Western societies, not condemned as negative proportionality when what is required is positive proportionality.

For my part, I am not attracted to any conception of proportionality in restorative justice programmes. Limits are essential, but an upper constraint is quite a different matter from believing that the amount of punishment or repair ought in some way to be proportional to the seriousness of the crime. It may be that an underlying difference between retributivists and people like myself is that while retributivists tend to be deeply pessimistic that whatever the justice system does will make little difference to the safety of people. In contrast, my theoretical position is that poorly designed criminal justice interventions can make the community considerably less safe and well designed ones can help make it much safer. While it seems true that most attempts to reduce crime through restorative justice, rehabilitation, deterrence and incapacitation fail in the majority of cases where each is attempted, it is also true that all of these things succeed often enough for it to be true that there are cost-effective ways of reducing crime through best-practice restorative, rehabilitative, deterrence and incapacitative programmes. More importantly, I am an optimist that through programmes of rigorous research we can learn how to design a criminal justice system that has places for restorative justice, rehabilitation, deterrence and incapacitation that cover the weaknesses of one paradigm with the strengths of another. Through openness to innovation and evaluation, it should be quite possible for us to craft a criminal justice system that is both more decent in respecting rights and limits and more effective in creating community safety.

There is no evidence that upper limits inhibit this R&D aspiration. If they did, from my republican perspective we would have to scale back our aspirations (see Braithwaite and Pettit 1990). But there is no dilemma here. It is not true that if only we could execute murderers, or boil them in oil, we could reduce the homicide rate. There is no reason for thinking that we could reduce crime by locking up first-time juvenile shoplifters for five years. If it reduced shoplifting without generating subcultural defiance, it would only do so by shifting resources away from combating much more serious crimes.

Unlike upper limits, proportionality is an obstacle to crime prevention. In my corporate crime work, I believe I have shown persuasively that mercy for corporate criminals (disproportionate leniency) is often important for making the community safer (see Braithwaite 1984, 1985; Braithwaite and Pettit 1990). That is why corporate regulators have policies that they inelegantly call leniency policies. Regulators routinely face a choice between the out and out warfare of a criminal prosecution aimed at incarcerating the CEO and cutting a deal where the company agrees to increasing its investment in safety, internal discipline, staff retraining, in internal compliance systems and industry-wide compliance systems, and to compensation to victims in return for dropping criminal charges against top management. Or the individual penalties are reduced in a plea agreement that keeps top management out of prison. The reason this mercy works is that the power of major corporate criminals for ill is matched by their power for good. The consequentialist impulse is to harness that power for good. Once we have done that, we must be troubled by the fact that while power is the reason we let the white corporate criminal free, it is also the reason we lock up the black street criminal. The social movement for restorative justice here might set as its aspiration showing the path to progressively reduce the incarceration of the poor in a way that increases community safety. This is no less plausible a policy idea than largely dispensing with the incarceration of corporate criminals in a way that increases community safety.

Obviously, we can never hope to do either if we are morally constrained in both domains to inflict punishment proportional to the wrongdoing. Many retributivists are attracted to Hart's (1968) move of seeing consequentialist considerations as general justifying aims of having a criminal justice system, but proportionality as a principle that should guide the distribution of punishments. A justifying principle that is consequentialist; a distributive one that is retributive. This is the formulation that appeals to von Hirsch (1993), for example. But what if I am right that proportionality destroys our capacity to experiment with crime prevention programmes that sometimes grant mercy, sometimes not, depending on the responsiveness of offenders to reform and repair, or depending on the agreement of victims and other stakeholders in restorative processes that this responsiveness justifies mercy? If I am right that often it will prove to be in the interests of community safety to give offenders other than a proportionate punishment, the Hartian principle of distributing punishment will defeat the general justifying aim of having an institution of punishment. That is, if we honour the distributive principle of proportionality, we will increase crime. The effect of the distribution will be to defeat the aim of establishing the punitive institution. The Hartian move of separating justifying and distributive principles is incoherent. It is only rendered coherent by the empirical assumptions that punishment reduces crime, and that while excessive punishment might reduce crime even more, we must place proportionality constraints on the pursuit of that good.[1] That is, the general justifying aim is to reduce crime through punishment. While we might achieve that aim even more through disproportionately heavy punishment, we still achieve it by proportionate punishment. If, on the other hand, these empirical assumptions fall apart in the way I suggest, then the distributive principle actually defeats the justifying aim of reducing crime (instead of simply limiting it).

Proportionality is a hot issue with surveillance and policing, just as it is with 'sentencing'. Just as there is a liberal impulse for equal punishment for equal wrongs, there is also the compelling intuition that black people should not be subject to more police

---

[1] A restorative theory of deterrence (see Braithwaite 2002a: Chapter 4) suggests that the Hartian assumptions are wrong. Empirically, there is now a lot of evidence that increasing punishment produces both increasing deterrence and increasing defiance (or reactance) effects (Sherman 1993; Brehm and Brehm 1981). Where the defiance effect is stronger than the deterrance effect, higher penalties increase crime. In their meta-analysis of correctional studies, Cullen and Gendreau (2000) found that the punitive severity of sentences actually had a small positive coefficient—more punishment, more reoffending.

surveillance than white people. This is the dilemma in US cities where Compstat computer targeting of crime hotspots for special police surveillance both seems able to reduce serious crimes like gun homicides and disproportionately targets black people (Sherman 1998).

Here I think there are lessons for restorative justice jurisprudence in the contrast between the Boston and New York police targeting of recent years, both of which make some plausible claims for reducing crime through improved targeting (Berrien and Winship 2000). In early 1999, both law enforcement officials and community members became greatly concerned at the shocking number of violent incidents in Boston's Cape Verdean community. The police believed they knew who were the gangs behind the violence. They believed they 'had the right guys' each of whom they could take out with several charges for offences not necessarily having anything to do with the violence (Berrien and Winship 2000: 30). They also wanted to do an Immigration and Naturalization Service sweep, with the threat of deportation for certain youths, unless the gang violence threatening the community stopped. Such an aggressive targeted swoop on a non-white community was obviously controversial and open to the interpretation of being racist. But what the lead police officer did was consult with both city-wide leaders of colour who had been critical of the police in the past for racist enforcement and consulted with the local Cape Verdean community. The police would not go ahead with this aggressive targeting unless it would be well received by the affected community. In the event, locals did seem so fed up with the violence that they wanted decisive policing. The targeting was of course still controversial, but it occurred with considerable local buy-in and it did not come as a shock to the local community when these young people were targeted. As far as I understand the case, limits and fundamental human rights were not breached. People were charged with offences they had actually committed. What is controversial is that many in white communities might have been targeted for the same kinds of offences. There are two relevant differences: the race difference and the fact that such a swoop in some other community that did not have the level of violence of the Cape Verdean community would not have picked up guns, would not have given a signal that might end gang violence. Police paralysis in the face of the moral dilemma seems a bad option. But a New York style police pounce aimed at reducing gun violence is also an inferior option to the Boston path of targeting combined with community consultation. While 'New York has gained national attention for dramatic reductions in violence...Boston has found a way to achieve dramatic reductions in violent crime while making equally strong efforts to build partnerships with the community' (Berrien and Winship 2000: 32). A better option still than the Boston approach might involve consultation with the community followed by offering the targeted youths an option of a restorative community justice process as an alternative to incarceration (see Braithwaite 2002a: Chapter 2).

While I doubt there will ever be a settled restorative justice view on proportionality, my submission would be to abandon proportionality in favour of a commitment to limits and to honouring rights. Then under those constraints we might rely heavily on richly deliberated consent when the interventions that seem necessary to secure public safety involve selective enforcement against some but not others.

THE JURISPRUDENCE OF RESPONSIBILITY

Declan Roche and I have argued that restorative justice involves a shift towards an active conception of responsibility, while still finding a more limited place for passive responsibility than is standard in criminal jurisprudence (Braithwaite and Roche 2000). While passive responsibility means an offender being held responsible for a wrong he has committed in the past, active responsibility is a virtue, the virtue of taking responsibility for repairing the harm that has been done, the relationships that have been damaged. Restorative justice is about creating spaces where not only offenders, but other concerned citizens as well, will find it safe to take active responsibility for righting the wrong.

With respect to offenders, Roche and I found appeal in Fisse's (1983) concept of reactive fault. This means that even though an individual can reasonably be held passively responsible for a crime, if she takes active responsibility for righting the wrong, she can acquit that responsibility. She does not need to be punished for it; indeed in many contexts it would be wrong to do so.

In recent years, I have noticed on visits to women's prisons, not only in my own country, a new feminist consciousness that sees posters in public areas of the prison that point to the injustice of the revelation in research studies that a majority of the inmates of womens' prisons have been victims of sexual abuse in their past. When I read those posters their feminist polemic is always persuasive to me: 'Yes', I think, 'that is the most profound injustice about most of these women being in this place.' I particularly thought that recently when I met Yvonne Johnson (see Wiebe and Johnson 1998), a Cree woman raped as a child by a number of men, in prison for the brutal murder of a man she believed had sexually molested her children. Then I would quickly move to the thought that it would nevertheless be dangerous to excuse terrible crimes on these grounds.

Shadd Maruna's (2001) wonderful book, *Making Good: How Ex-Convicts Reform and Rebuild their Lives* is relevant here. It showed that serious Liverpool offenders who went straight had to find a new way of making sense of their lives. They had to restory their life histories. They defined a new ethical identity for themselves that meant that they were able to say, looking back at their former criminal selves, that they were 'not like that any more' (Maruna 2001: 7). His persistent reoffender sample, in contrast, were locked into 'condemnation scripts' whereby they saw themselves as irrevocably condemned to their criminal self-story.

This suggests a restorative justice that is about 'rebiographing', restorative storytelling that redefines an ethical conception of the self. Garfinkel (1956: 421–2) saw what was at issue in 'making good': 'the former identity stands as accidental; the new identity is the basic reality. What he is now is what, after all, he was all along.' So, Maruna found systematically that desisters from crime reverted to an unspoiled identity. Desisters had restoried themselves to believe that their formerly criminal self 'wasn't me'. The self that did it was in William James' terms, not the I (the self-as-subject, who acts) nor the Me (the self-as-object, that is acted upon), but what Petrunik and Shearing (1988) called the It, an alien source of action (Maruna 2001: 93). Restorative justice might learn from this research how to help wrongdoers write their It out of the story of their true ethical identity. Maruna (2001: 13) also concluded that 'redemption rituals' as communal processes were important in this sense-making because desisting offenders often narrated the way their deviance had been decertified by important others such as family members or judges – the parent or policeman who said Johnny was now his old self. Howard Zehr (2002: 10) makes the point that whether we have victimized or been victimized, we need social support in the journey 'to re-narrate our stories so that they are no longer just about shame and humiliation but ultimately about dignity and triumph.'

Maruna (2001: 148) commends to us the Jesse Jackson slogan: 'You are not responsible for being down, but you are responsible for getting up.' In the all-too-common cases of children in poverty who have been physically or sexually abused, they do frequently feel that they are not responsible, that their life circumstances have condemned them to regular encounters with the criminal justice system. While there is moral peril in allowing the law to accept poverty as an excuse, an attraction of restorative justice is that it creates a space where it can be accepted as just for such victimized offenders to believe: 'I am one of the victims in this room. While I am not responsible for the abused life that led me into a life of crime on the streets, I am responsible for getting out of it and I am also responsible for helping this victim who has been hurt by my act.' Maruna (2001) found empirically that desisters from crime moved from 'contamination scripts' to 'redemption scripts' through just this kind of refusal to take responsibility for being down while accepting responsibility for getting up. In short, by accepting a jurisprudence of active responsibility, it may be that we can respond more compassionately to the injustices offenders have suffered while increasing community safety, instead of threatening community safety in the way implied by our moral hazard intuitions against allowing poverty as an excuse. Hence, when a woman like Yvonne Johnson has good reason for thinking that she has been the most profound victim of injustice in the events swirling around her, yet has remorse for her crimes, wants to do the best she can to right the wrongs of her past, help others to avoid that path themselves, why not let her keep the interpretation that she was not really responsible for her terrible circumstances, so long as she takes responsibility for getting out of them and for doing what she can to heal those she has hurt? Why not say, 'because you have acquitted your fault reactively, because you are not a danger but a blessing to others, go in peace.' Because you have taken active responsibility for making good, you will no longer be held responsible for any debt to the community. This links to the core restorative intuition that because crime hurts, justice should heal. And punishments that obstruct healing by insisting on adding more hurt to the world are not justice.

CONTEXTUAL JUSTICE, NOT CONSISTENT JUSTICE

Restorative processes put the problem in the centre of the circle, not the person (Melton 1995). The right punishment of the person according to some retributive theory will almost always be the wrong solution to the problem. By wrong I mean less just. Both restorative justice and responsive regulation (Ayres and Braithwaite 1992) opt for contextual rather than consistent justice. With restorative justice, it is the collective wisdom of the stakeholders in the circle that decides what is the agreement that is just in all the circumstances, not perhaps the ideal agreement in the view of any one person in the circle, but one that all in the circle can sign off on as contextually just. That agreement that seems contextually just to all of them may or may not include punishment, compensation, apology, community work, rehabilitation or other measures to prevent recurrence. Because punishment, apology and measures to dissuade others from taking the same path are not commensurable in the terms of retributive theory, asking if the outcomes are consistent across a large number of cases makes little sense.

Similarly, responsive regulation is contextual justice. With responsive regulation, the regulator moves up a regulatory pyramid in the direction of progressively more onerous state interventions until there is a response to improve compliance with the law, compensate victims of wrongdoing, put better compliance systems in place, and so on (see the example of a responsive regulatory pyramid that integrates restorative justice with deterrence and incapacitation in Figure 8.1).[2] So restorative justice and responsive regulation share the notion that state response can become contextually more punitive if offenders are not responsive to appeals to take their obligations more seriously. Reactive fault again.

Retributive intuitions are that such contextual justice on both fronts is inferior to the consistent justice of equal punishment for equal wrongs. Rather restorative justice, as I have conceived it here, involves unequal punishment in response to unequal reactions (to unequal active responsibility). With restorative justice, a particular concern from the consistent punishment perspective is that whether you get a lighter or a harsher punishment will depend on how punitive or forgiving victims and others in the circle are. A rich victim might not need full compensation as desperately as a poor one. But that is part of the point for the restorativist. If the poor victim is in more desperate trouble then she has a greater need and it would be a greater injustice to fail to fully respond to it.[3] For most of the great philosophers of the past, and for contemporarily influential ones such as Dworkin (1986) as well, fundamental to genuine justice is equal concern and equal respect for the needs of all of those hurt by an injustice. It follows that privileging equal punishment for offenders narrows us to concern for only one type of justice affecting one type of actor. Philosophers who take the equal application of rules very seriously in a wide

---

[2] The pyramid implies a willingness to abandon restorative justice in favour of more determinedly punitive justice primarily oriented to either deterrence or incapacitation when restorative justice fails (Braithwaite, 2002a: Ch. 2). It assumes that restorative justice will often fail and fail again and in such cases the safety of the community requires escalation to more punitive approaches. Even when this means imprisonment, however, restorative justice values should be given as much space as possible within the punitive justice institution. More importantly, however, responsive regulation means contextually responsive de-escalation back down the pyramid to restorative justice whenever punishment has succeeded in getting the safety concerns under control.

[3] On the idea of a restorative justice philosophy based on responding to needs see Sullivan and Tifft (2001). See also the discussion in Braithwaite (2002a) of the compatibility between a concern with freedom as non-domination and the approach of Nussbaum (1995) of nurturing human capabilities.

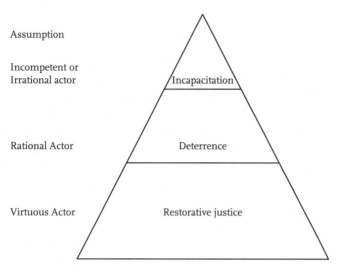

Assumption

Incompetent or
Irrational actor   Incapacitation

Rational Actor   Deterrence

Virtuous Actor   Restorative justice

FIGURE 22.1. Toward an integration of restorative, deterrent and incapacitative justice.

range of contexts – from Cass Sunstein to Fred Schauer – are also clear that if we could perfect equal concern for all affected by an injustice we would not do it by enforcement of simple rules like equal punishment for equal wrongs. As Sunstein puts it; 'If human frailties and institutional needs are put to one side, particularized judgments, based on the relevant features of the single case, represent the highest form of justice' (Sunstein 1996: 135). And indeed the presumptive positivist Schauer argues even more emphatically:

> When we entrench a generalization, therefore, we do not further the aim of treating like cases alike and unalike cases differently. On the contrary, it is particularism that recognizes relevant unlikeness, drawing all the distinctions some substantive justification indicates ought to be drawn. And it is particularistic rather than rule-based decision-making that recognizes all relevant similarities, thereby ensuring that substantively similar cases will in fact be treated similarly (Schauer 1991: 136–137).

Schauer's case for rules is arguments from reliance, efficiency, from stability and about enabling a proper allocation of power. The restorativist can argue that reliance that punishment will be prevented from exceeding upper limits that track the seriousness of an offence is quite enough reliance. Who wants the reliance of knowing that you are prevented from getting less than this, or much less? Reliance makes a good case for the existence of criminal law with upper limits, as opposed to open-textured evaluation of wrongdoing unconstrained by rules. But it does not make much of a case for lower limits or proportionality all the way down. I could work through a restorativist spin on all of Schauer's reasons for rules and why in criminal law they do not make a case for equal punishment for equal wrongs. But this would distract me from my core point, which is that equal punishment for equal wrongs is a travesty of equal justice.

Restorative justice has no easy escape from the horns of the dilemma that equal justice for victims is incompatible with equal justice for offenders. First, because it is a trilemma; restorativists are enjoined also to be concerned with justice for the community. So of course restorativists must reject a radical vision of victim empowerment that says that any result the victim wants she should get so long as it does not breach upper constraints on punishment. Restorativists must abandon both equal punishment for offenders and equal justice (compensation, empowerment, etc.) for victims as goals and seek to craft a superior fidelity to the goal of equal concern and respect for all those affected by the crime. The restorative justice circle is an imperfect vehicle for institutionalizing that aspiration. We can improve it without ever perfecting it. But I would argue that the aspiration is right.

The restorative circle heads down the path of the holistic consideration of all the injustices that matter in the particular case (Zehr 1995; Van Ness and Strong 1997; Luna 2002), as suggested in the quotation from Schauer (1991), but in a way constrained by limits on punishments, rights and rules that define what is a crime and what is not. We might be stumbling as we feel our way, but it does seem a better path than the narrow road of proportional punishment.

While we should not seek to guarantee offenders equal punishment for equal wrongs, the law can and should assure citizens that they will never be punished beyond upper limits. While victims cannot be guaranteed their wishes, the law should assure them of a right to put their views in their own voice. It should also guarantee a minimum level of victim support when they are physically or emotionally traumatized by a crime. This falls far short of an equal right of victims for full empowerment and full compensation. But the minimum guarantees I propose on the offender side and the victim side put some limits on how much inequality we can produce as we stumble down the path that pursues holistic justice. We are constrained that however we try to implement the ideal of equal concern and respect for all affected, we must assure that certain minimum guarantees are always delivered to certain key players. This puts limits on the inequality of the justice any one person can suffer, just as it enjoins us to eschew the error of single-minded pursuit of equality for the one that produces inequality for others.

The difficult choices were well illustrated by the Clotworthy case in New Zealand (see the Box below). Clotworthy is a paradigm case, albeit an extreme one, because, as we saw earlier, the evidence is that when courts overrule restorative justice conferences it is overwhelmingly to increase punishment, to trump the mercy victims have agreed to, and is rarely to reduce punitive excess demanded by victims. In my view, it was Justice Thorburn who decided the case correctly. But the more important point to emphasize is that the retributive presumption here tends to be empirically wrong. That presumption is that the problem is that victims will demand more punishment than the courts deem proportionate, whereas in fact the 'problem' is that they more often demand less than the courts deem proportionate. This is another instance of where the retributive philosophers have been led to unbalanced, decontextualized analyses by adopting a perspective which grows out of the less likely rather than the more likely empirically arising ethical dilemma.

CLOTWORTHY

Mr. Clotworthy inflicted six stab wounds, which collapsed a lung and diaphragm, upon an attempted robbery victim. Justice Thorburn of the Auckland District Court imposed a 2 year prison sentence, which was suspended, a compensation order of $15,000 to fund cosmetic surgery for an 'embarrassing scar' and 200 hours of community work. These had been agreed at a restorative conference organized by Justice Alternatives. The Judge found a basis for restorative justice in New Zealand law and placed weight on the wish of the victim for financial support for the cosmetic surgery and emotional support to end through forgiveness 'a festering agenda of vengeance or retribution in his heart against the prisoner'. The Court of Appeal allowed the victim to address it, whereupon the victim 'reiterated his previous stance, emphasising his wish to obtain funds for the necessary cosmetic surgery and his view that imprisonment would achieve nothing either for Mr. Clotworthy or for himself' (p.12). The victory for restorative justice was that 'substantial weight' was given by the court to the victim's belief that expiation had been agreed; their honours accepted that restorative justice had an important place in New Zealand sentencing law. The defeat was that greater weight was given to the empirical supposition that a custodial sentence would help 'deter others from such serious offending' (p.12). The suspending of the two year custodial sentence was quashed in favour of a sentence of four years and a $5,000 compensation order (which had already been lodged with the court); the community service and payment of the remaining compensation were also quashed. The victim got neither his act of grace nor the money for the cosmetic surgery. Subsequently, for reasons unknown, the victim committed suicide, The Queen v Patrick Dale Clotworthy, Auckland District Court T. 971545, Court of Appeal of New Zealand, CA.

Principles of restorative justice

How do we evaluate the adequacy of this elusive contextual justice? How do we assess how satisfactorily active the active responsibility has been? Are there ever circumstances where we should dishonour rights and limits on punishment? I have written on these questions elsewhere, so I will not traverse them here except to say that Philip Pettit and I have argued that freedom as non-domination or dominion, republican freedom, is an attractive ultimate yardstick of the justice of any criminal justice practice (Braithwaite and Pettit 1990). More recently, Walgrave (2002) has worked through, in a manner I find congenial, the way dominion can guide the day to day practice of restorative justice.

What comes with civic republicanism is an approach to institutionalizing plurally deliberative justice under a rule of law and a separation of powers that accepts that citizens will often, indeed mostly, argue from a non-republican perspective. This is a great strength compared to retributivism or utilitarianism, which are stuck with the problem that if some judges are retributivists and some are utilitarians, the theory of the second best outcome is of a disastrous outcome. The republican argues for republican institutions and procedures without expecting that most people will manifest republican values within them. Sadly, sometimes they will be retributivists. But republicans must support giving voice to retributivists, indeed influence to them in deciding matters in which they are stakeholders. They can join hands with retributivists in defending upper limits, respectful communication and fundamental human rights as the only limits restorativists would want to place on the sway of retributive arguments. So when a restorativist is deeply disturbed by the threat to dominion in the agreement proposed in a restorative justice conference, what she should do, and all she should do, after failing to persuade others that the agreement is unjust, is argue that there is no consensus on the agreement and, this being so, the matter should be sent to court.

For most restorative justice advocates, freedom as non-domination is rather too abstract a philosophical concept to offer detailed practical guidance. I am grateful to Lode Walgrave for saying in his comments on this chapter that restoring freedom as non-domination is not for him too abstract, 'but a very clarifying principle'. While it is my hope people will come to this conclusion, I hope the following discussion will help them to do so, and even if they come to reject it, they might find the longer derived list of values useful for guiding evaluation research. At this early stage of the debate around restorative jurisprudence we must be wary against being prematurely prescriptive about the precise values we wish to maximize. Elsewhere, I have combined a set of still rather abstract restorative justice values into three groups. I will not defend the values again here (Braithwaite 2002b). Yes, they are vague, but if we are to pursue contextual justice wisely, both considerable openness and revisability of our values would be well advised, especially when the values debate is still so immature. The first group of values I submit for consideration by restorative jurisprudence are the values that take priority when there is any serious sanction or other infringement of freedom at risk. These are the fundamental procedural safeguards. In the context of liberty being threatened in any significant way, if no other values are realized, these must be.

Priority list of values 1

- Non-domination.
- Empowerment.
- Honouring legally specific upper limits on sanctions.
- Respectful listening.
- Equal concern for all stakeholders.
- Accountability, appealability.
- Respect for the fundamental human rights specified in the Universal Declaration of Human Rights, the International Covenant on Economic, Social and Cultural Rights, the International Covenant on Civil and Political Rights and its Second Optional Protocol, the United Nations Declaration on the Elimination of Violence Against Women and the Declaration of Basic Principles of Justice for Victims of Crime and Abuse of Power.

The second group of restorative justice values are values participants are empowered to ignore. Their being ignored is not reason for abandoning a restorative justice process.

It might, however, be reason for asking the participants to agree to an adjournment so new participants might be brought in to give these values more chance of realization. While the second group are values that can be trumped by empowerment, they are values against which the success of restorative processes must be evaluated. Moreover they are values around which the restorativist is democratically active, seeking to persuade the community that these are decent values.

Priority list of values 2

- Restoration of human dignity.
- Restoration of property loss.
- Restoration of safety/injury.
- Restoration of damaged human relationships.
- Restoration of communities.
- Restoration of the environment.
- Emotional restoration.
- Restoration of freedom.
- Restoration of compassion or caring.
- Restoration of peace.
- Restoration of a sense of duty as a citizen.
- Provision of social support to develop human capabilities to the full.
- Prevention of future injustice.

The third list are values that restorativists do not actively encourage participants to manifest in restorative justice processes. To urge people to apologize or forgive is wrong and cruel. These are gifts that have no power as gifts when they are demanded. Being on the third list does not mean they are less important values. It means they are values we promote simply by creating spaces where it is easy for people to manifest them.

Priority list of values 3

- Remorse over injustice.
- Apology.
- Censure of the act.
- Forgiveness of the person.
- Mercy.

List 3 are emergent values, list 2 maximizing values, list 1 constraining values. What follows from the above is that the evaluation of restorative justice should occur along many dimensions. Narrowly evaluating restorative justice in terms of whether it reduces crime (the preeminent utilitarian concern) or honours limits (the preeminent retributive concern), important as they are, are only two of 25 dimensions of evaluation considered important here. If 25 is too many, we can think of restorativists as concerned about securing freedom as non-domination through repair, transformation, empowerment with others, and limits on the exercise of power over others. From a civic republican perspective, the 25-value version, the four-value version and the one-value version (freedom as non-domination) are mutually compatible.

CONCLUSION

The point of jurisprudence is to guide us in how we ought to evaluate the justice of disputing practices. That also implies an obligation to be empirically serious in measuring performance against these evaluation criteria. The restorative justice research community has a long way to go before it can marshall empirical evidence on all the outcomes discussed in this essay. Yet in a short time, a considerable portfolio of studies of variable quality has been assembled. The critics of restorative justice have not been as empirically serious. A contribution of this chapter has been to illustrate how this has rendered their analyses myopic. One illustration is that retributive critics launch their attacks from an assumption that the disturbing problem will be victims insisting on excessive punishment. Yet the empirical reality is of courts insisting on overruling restorative processes that include victims for not being excessive enough in their punishment. Hartian critics assume that punishment is justified because it reduces crime, and that this is still true of punishing proportionately. Yet empirically punishment often increases crime in a way that makes it plausible that we can reduce crime by abandoning proportionality (while maintaining upper limits). The possibility of this empirical conjuncture is a blank page of the leading jurisprudential texts.

I have conceived the fundamental principles of restorative jurisprudence here as the republican dominion of citizens secured through repair, transformation, empowerment with others, and limits on the exercise of power over others. Repair is a very different value to punishment as hard treatment; repair does not have to hurt, though of course it often does. While restorativists share with retributivists a concern to limit abuse of power over others, restorative justice is distinguished from retributive justice by its obverse commitment to empowerment with others. Finally, our discussion of responsibility has illustrated how restorative justice aspires to transform citizens through deliberation into being democratically active. The active responsibility ideal is a republican transformative ideal or a positive liberty ideal. Retributive passive responsibility is an ideal of negative liberalism, of non-interference beyond holding citizens to legal obligations. In action, of course, retributivism is not liberal at all, but is the stuff of law and order conservatism at best, totalitarianism at worst. In action, restorative justice is a bit better than this, though it too will forever suffer a wide gap between normative ideal and political practice.

REFERENCES

Ayres, I., and J. Braithwaite. 1992. *Responsive Regulation: Transcending the Deregulation Debate*. New York: Oxford University Press.

Berrien, J., and C. Winship. 2000. "Lesson's Learned from Boston's Police-Community Collaboration," *Federal Probation* 63:25–33.

Bonta, J., Rooney J., and S. Wallace-Capretta. 1998. *Restorative Justice: An Evaluation of the Restorative Resolutions Project*. Ottawa: Solicitor General Canada.

Braithwaite, J. 1984. *Corporate Crime in the Pharmaceutical Industry*. London and Boston: Routledge and Kegan Paul.

———. 1985. *To Punish or Persuade: Enforcement of Coal Mine Safety*. Albany, NY: State University of New York Press.

———and D. Roche. 2000. "Responsibility and Restorative Justice." In *Restorative Community Justice*, edited by M. Schiff and G. Bazemore. Cincinnati, OH: Anderson.

———. 2002a. *Restorative Justice and Responsive Regulation*. New York: Oxford University Press.

———. 2002b. "Setting Standards for Restorative Justice." *British Journal of Criminology* 42:563–77.

———and P. Pettit. 1990. *Not Just Deserts: A Republican Theory of Criminal Justice*. Oxford: Oxford University Press.

Brehm, S. S., and J. W. Brehm. 1981. *Psychological Reactance: A Theory of Freedom and Control*. New York: Academic Press.

Cullen, F. T., and P. Gendreau. 2000. "Assessing Correctional Rehabilitation: Policy, Practice, and Prospects." In *Changes in Decision Making and Discretion in the Criminal Justice System*, vol. 3, edited by J. Horney. Washington, D.C.: U.S. Department of Justice.

Dworkin, R. 1986. *Law's Empire*. Cambridge, MA: Harvard University Press.

Fisse, B. 1983. "Reconstructing Corporate Criminal Law: Deterrence, Retribution, Fault, and Sanctions." *Southern California Law Review* 56:1141–246.

Garfinkel, H. 1956. "Conditions for Successful Degradation Ceremonies." *American Journal of Sociology* 61:420–24.

Hart, H.L.A. 1968. "Prolegomenon to the Principles of Punishment." *Punishment and Responsibility*. Oxford: Oxford University Press.

Luna, E. 2002. "Punishment Theory and the Holistic Process." *University of Utah Law Review*.

Maruna, S. 2001. *Making Good: How Ex-Convicts Reform and Rebuild Their Lives*. Washington, D.C.: American Psychological Association.

Maxwell, G., and A. Morris. 1993. *Family, Victims and Culture: Youth Justice in New Zealand*. Wellington, New Zealand: Social Policy Agency and Institute of Criminology, Victoria University.

Melton, A. P. 1995. "Indigenous Justice Systems and Tribal Society." *Judicature* 79:126.

Nussbaum, M. 1995. "Human Capabilities: Female Human Beings." In *Women, Culture, and Development*, edited by M.C. Nussbaum and J. Glover. Oxford: Clarendon Press.

Petrunik, M. G, and C. Shearing. 1988. "The 'I,' the 'Me,' and the 'It': Moving beyond the Meadian conception of self." *Canadian Journal of Sociology* 13(4):435–48.

Schauer, F. 1991. *Playing by the Rules: A Philosophical Examination of Rule-Based Decision-Making in Law and in Life*. Oxford: Clarendon Press.

Sherman, L. W. 1993. "Defiance, Deterrence and Irrelevance: A Theory of the Criminal Sanction." *Journal of Research in Crime and Delinquency* 30:445–73.

Sherman, L. W. 2000. "American Policing." In *The Handbook of Crime and Punishment*. New York: Oxford University Press.

Sullivan, D., and L. Tifft. 2001. *Restorative Justice: Healing the Foundations of our Everyday Lives*. Monsey, NY: Willow Tree Press.

Sunstein, C.R. 1996. *Legal Reasoning and Political Conflict*. New York: Oxford University Press.

Van Ness, D. and K.H. Strong. 1997. *Restoring Justice*. Cincinnati, OH: Anderson.

von Hirsch, A. 1993. *Censure and Sanctions*. Oxford: Clarendon Press.

Walgrave, L. 2002. "Imposing Restoration Instead of Inflicting Pain: Reflections on the Judicial Reaction to Crime." In *Restorative Justice and Criminal Justice: Competing or Reconcilable Paradigms*. Oxford: Hart Publishing.

Wiebe, R., and Y. Johnson. 1998. *Stolen Life: The Journey of a Cree Woman*. Toronto: Alfred A. Knopf.

Zehr, H. 1995. "Justice Paradigm Shift? Values and Visions in the Reform Process." *Mediation Quarterly* 12:207–16.

———. 2002. Paper presented at the Fourth International Conference on Restorative Justice, Tubingen, October 2000. In *Restorative Justice: Theoretical Foundations* edited by E. Weitekamp and H. J. Kerner. Cullumpton: Willan.

23

THE VIRTUES OF RESTORATIVE PROCESSES, THE VICES OF "RESTORATIVE JUSTICE"

Paul H. Robinson

This Symposium is important for its ability to make better known the great benefits in the use of restorative processes. Below, I try to summarize some of the many promising achievements of those processes, by which I mean to include such practices as victim-offender mediation, sentencing circles, and family-group conferences to name just the most common. While many people refer to such processes by the name "restorative justice," that term and its originators, in fact, have a more ambitious agenda than simply encouraging their use. But that agenda is not one that the frontline practitioners of restorative processes necessarily share. It is primarily an anti-justice agenda, which prompts impassioned opposition. In this brief Article I try to explain why this is so and why it need not be so. I argue that restorative processes can and should be used more widely in ways entirely consistent with doing justice, and that the best thing for the restorative processes movement would be to publicly disavow the anti-justice agenda of the restorative justice movement.

I. THE VIRTUES OF RESTORATIVE PROCESSES

First, let me speak to the virtues of restorative processes. Frankly, it is hard to see why anyone would oppose such practices. They have the potential to change an offender's perspective—to make them fully appreciate the human side of the harm they have done—which can change their behavior when an opportunity for crime arises in the future. They also have the potential to deter offenders. That is, to the extent that there is some discomfort to having family and friends brought together to discuss one's wrongdoing, the social discomfort and the risk to social relations can stimulate offenders to avoid wrongdoing in the future. Restorative processes also provide an important mechanism of norm reinforcement. The concern of the people present makes clear to the offender—and to everyone present—the validity and importance of the norm violated. It is a unique opportunity for each person to see that *other* people share the norm, and it is that reinforcement that makes the norm stronger in the community. The power of such social influence on conduct ought not be underestimated. Social science studies increasingly suggest that it is the force of such social influence, more than the threat of official sanction by the criminal justice system, that induces law-abidingness. What could be better than a process that advances several crime control mechanisms at the same time: rehabilitation, deterrence, and norm reinforcement?

Finally, the restorative processes advance other valuable interests, beyond those normally held to be the charge of the criminal justice system: providing restitution to the victim (normally the charge of civil tort law); giving victims a direct involvement in the disposition process, thereby providing an emotional sense of restoration and justice done; and putting a human face on the offender, thereby reducing the victim's generalized fear of victimization and perhaps giving the victim some appreciation of how the circumstances may have brought the offender to commit the offense.

Other articles in this Symposium give us specific evidence and illustrations of the value of restorative processes. William Nugent reports a nine percent reduction in recidivism.[1] This is quite impressive when one considers how small the investment of resources is in restorative processes as compared to other programs that typically do little better. Barton Poulson finds that restorative processes do much more than reduce recidivism.[2] I note of particular importance its effect in making people feel better about the adjudication system—feeling that it is more fair and more likely to give an appropriate sanction[3]—because these effects can build the moral credibility and legitimacy of the system, which can produce its own significant crime control benefits.

As hinted above, social science data suggests the great power of social influence in gaining law-abidingness. Criminal law is not irrelevant to this influence: If law can earn a reputation of moral authority with the community, it can to some extent harness this power. John Darley and I suggest two kinds of mechanisms by which criminal law can have an effect.[4] First, it can help shape—build up or tear down—social norms. We have recently seen such norm shifting, as in the increasing opposition to domestic violence and drunk driving and decreasing opposition to same-sex intercourse. These changes did not come about *because* of changes in criminal law, but criminal law changes played an important role in reinforcing the change in norms. Second,

---

[1] *See* William Nugent et al., *Participation in Victim-Offender Mediation and the Prevalence and Severity of Subsequent Delinquent Behavior: A Meta-Analysis*, 2003 Utah L. Rev. 137, 163.

[2] *See* Barton Poulson, *A Third Voice: A Review of Empirical Research on the Psychological Outcomes of Restorative Justice*, 2003 Utah L. Rev. 167, *passim*.

[3] *See id.* at 192–93. Also recall Kathy Elton's moving accounts—such as her story about the Christmas presents stolen by a neighborhood youth, which frightened so many, but which, in the end, produced a positive good of greater understanding and closer relationships—of how restorative processes could work so effectively on so many levels. Kathy Elton & Michelle M. Roybal, *Restoration, A Component of Justice*, 2003 Utah L. Rev. 43, 53 n.57.

[4] *See* Paul H. Robinson & John M. Darley, *The Utility of Desert*, 91 Nw. U. L. Rev. 453, 471–77 (1997).

the criminal law can directly influence conduct in those instances in which the moral status of the conduct is ambiguous. Thus, it may not be initially obvious that insider trading or computer hacking are condemnable acts, but a criminal prohibition from a morally credible criminal justice system can signal that they are. Of course, neither of these mechanisms can work to give law power to alter conduct unless it has moral credibility with the community it seeks to influence. And it is for this reason that the criminal law gains in crime control effectiveness by heeding the community's shared intuitions of justice, for its dispositions will then reinforce its reputation as a moral authority rather than undercut it. Ultimately, then, the ability of restorative processes to build the criminal law's moral credibility and legitimacy can give the law a greater ability to gain compliance.

Finally, there seems to be little downside to the use of restorative processes. If in some cases there could be an increased danger to victims from an unrepentant offender learning more about the victim, organizers can screen out such cases. The only real risk, then, is that the restorative processes will not work—that they will not give the full payoff that is their potential. But that is no reason not to try them.

II. THE VICES OF RESTORATIVE JUSTICE

With this enthusiasm for *restorative processes*, how can I be opposed to restorative justice when such processes are its central feature? Answer: Because of what "restorative justice" adds to restorative processes.

It is clear that many advocates of restorative processes use the term "restorative justice" as if it were interchangeable with restorative processes. But the literature by the leaders of the restorative justice movement make clear that they conceive of restorative processes not simply as a potentially useful piece of, or complement to, the criminal justice system, but as a *substitute* for it.[5] Further, restorative justice ideally would ban all "punishment," by which is meant, apparently, banning all punishment based on just deserts. (The restorative justice advocates concede, as they must, that in practice participants in restorative sessions commonly bring to bear their own intuitions of justice in sorting out an acceptable disposition, but the restorative justice ideal is forgiveness and reintegration, not deserved punishment.) Bowing to what they see as the demands of reality, the restorative justice advocates reluctantly direct the use of deterrence mechanisms if restorative processes fail, and incapacitation mechanisms if deterrence fails.[6] But giving offenders the punishment they deserve—no more, no less—is rejected as never an appropriate goal.[7]

---

[5] *See, e.g.,* John Braithwaite, *A Future Where Punishment Is Marginalized: Realistic or Utopian?*, 46 UCLA L. REV. 1727, 1746 (1999) (classifying restorative justice as competing with punitive justice).

[6] *Id.* at 1742.

[7] Consider the 1998 New Zealand case of Patrick Clotworthy, who inflicted six stab wounds upon an attempted robbery victim, which collapsed a lung and diaphragm and left the victim badly disfigured. *See* John Braithwaite, *Restorative Justice: Assessing Optimistic and Pessimistic Accounts*, 25 CRIME & JUST. 1, 87–88 (1999) (discussing *Clotworthy*); *see also* The Queen v. Patrick Clotworthy [1998], *available at* http://www.restorativejustice.org.nz/Judgements%20Page.htm (providing texts of opinions and

The centrality of this anti-justice view is expressed in the movement's name: restorative justice. The point of the naming exercise is to present restorative processes as if they were a form of doing justice. But, of course, these kind of word games only work so far. Calling something "justice" does not make it so. The term "justice" has an independent meaning and common usage that cannot be so easily cast aside: "reward or penalty as deserved; just deserts."[8] The naming move can create confusion, and perhaps that is all the leaders of restorative justice want at this point: time to get a foothold in common practice before it becomes too obvious that their restorative *justice* program is in fact anti-justice. But such word-trickery is not likely to be sufficient for gaining longer-term or wider support. For that, they must face the anti-justice issue squarely and persuade people, if they can, that people ought no longer care about doing justice.

It is this anti-justice agenda that restorative justice adds to restorative processes and that I find objectionable, somewhat odd, and potentially dangerous. (In this Article, I use the term "restorative justice" to include the more ambitious, anti-justice agenda, and the term "restorative processes" to refer to just the processes themselves.)

III. Giving Restorative Justice Priority Over Deterrence and Incapacitation

Let me look separately at the two components of restorative justice's proposed program: (1) giving restorative justice priority over deterrence and incapacitation, and (2) barring punishment based on justice.

As to the first, I am highly skeptical of the effectiveness of deterrence as a distributive principle. No doubt having some kind of sanctioning system has some deterrent effect. But the notion that we can construct distributive rules that will optimize deterrence is, I suspect, unrealistic. Offenders simply are not likely to alter their conduct because the law formulates a liability rule one way or another.[9] In any case,

---

sentencing notes for case). At a restorative conference organized by Justice Alternatives, the victim agreed to a disposition of a suspended prison sentence, two hundred hours of community work, and a compensation order of $15,000 to fund his cosmetic surgery. *See* Braithwaite, *supra*, at 87–88. Justice Thorburn of the Auckland District Court entered the disposition agreed upon at the conference. *See id.* (also noting that Court of Appeal ultimately quashed disposition and entered sentence of four years in prison and $5,000 compensation).

Requiring the offender to pay the victim $15,000 for the needed surgery seems entirely appropriate, but such a sanction hardly reflects the extent of the punishment the offender deserves for so vicious an attack. Even if the offender were allowed to stay out of prison long enough to earn the $15,000, why would it not be appropriate for him to spend his weekends in jail, or to serve a term of imprisonment after the compensation had been earned? Restorative justice proponents like John Braithwaite support the disposition and decry the fact that it was later quashed, noting that the victim subsequently committed suicide for reasons unknown. The suicide is obviously tragic, but it does not alter the fact that the original disposition failed to do justice. Indeed, many would see the restorative conference as a second victimization—a desperate victim must agree to forgo justice in order to rid himself of the disfiguring scar the offender caused. It is a case of an offender benefitting from his own wrongdoing. That restorative justice proponents support such a disposition seems only to confirm their anti-justice orientation.

[8] Webster's New World Dictionary of the American Language 766 (2d ed. 1970).

[9] *See* Paul H. Robinson & John M. Darley, Does Criminal Law Deter? A Social Science Investigation 3 (forthcoming 2003); Paul H. Robinson & John M. Darley, *The Role of Deterrence in the Formulation of Criminal Law Rules: At Its Worst When Doing Its Best*, 91 Geo. L.J. (forthcoming 2003).

deterrence as a distributive principle often produces results that a just society ought not tolerate.

As for incapacitation as a principle for distributing liability and punishment, I concede that it does work. One can prevent offenders from committing most offenses by keeping them in prison. However, as I have argued elsewhere, using the criminal justice system for such preventive detention purposes is bad for both detainees and for society, for such a system is both unfair to detainees—detaining even when there is little preventive justification and confining under inappropriately punitive conditions—and is inefficient and ineffective in protecting society.[10]

So I am inclined to let these distributive programs fend for themselves in response to restorative justice claims for superiority. I am happy to have them replaced.

Before moving on, however, I should say I am not sure I understand the restorative justice arguments for why it should take priority over these distributive principles. The restorative justice perspective on deterrence is particularly confusing. The proposal is that restorative justice should be used first, and repeatedly, until it is clear that it cannot work, and only then should the system resort to deterrence. Of course, by turning first to restorative justice, repeatedly, deterrence has already been sacrificed. The signal to potential offenders is that they will be given repeated chances to escape the threatened deterrent sanction. That message cannot be undone when the system finally does "turn to deterrence," upon a failure of restorative justice.

I will let the deterrence advocates press these arguments. My real opposition to restorative justice is based on its conflict with just punishment.

IV. Restorative Justice vs. Just Punishment

First, let me define what I mean by distributing punishment according to justice—for the restorative justice proponents seem inclined to caricature notions of just desert. (I understand the appeal of the move: if one can make the alternative a monster, then restorative justice looks more attractive. But that kind of distortion only tends to signal weakness in one's own theory.) Here is what I mean by doing justice: Giving a wrongdoer punishment according to what he deserves—no more, no less—by taking account of all those factors that we, as a society, think are relevant in assessing personal blameworthiness.[11] Justice, then, requires that, in assessing an offender's blameworthiness, we must take account of not only the seriousness of the offense and its consequences but also the offender's own state of mind and mental and emotional capacities, as well as any circumstances of the offense that may suggest justification or excuse. Indeed, a rich desert theory would take account of many facets of what can happen during

---

[10] *See* Paul H. Robinson, *Punishing Dangerousness: Cloaking Preventive Detention as Criminal Justice*, 114 Harv. L. Rev. 1429, 1446–47 (2001) (arguing that using criminal justice system for preventive detention is ineffective and unfair).

[11] There are two sources of data for determining what is relevant to desert—moral philosophy and empirical studies of a community's shared intuitions of justice—but for present purposes I do not believe that the difference between them is significant. I have written elsewhere about these differences. *See* Paul H. Robinson & Michael T. Cahill, Law Without Justice (forthcoming 2004).

restorative processes. Genuine remorse, public acknowledgment of wrongdoing, and sincere apology can all, in my view, reduce an offender's blameworthiness—and, thereby, the amount of punishment deserved.[12]

It is a peculiar view of just desert to see it as "degrading to both its subject and its object,"[13] as the restorative justice proponents suggest. How many times have we seen on the television news the bereaved family of a victim—ordinary people with good hearts—express their often tearful relief that justice has finally been done. Frankly, I do not know of anyone (other than restorative justice proponents) who would think of the family members as degrading themselves by taking relief in justice being done. That certainly is not the way most societies judge the feeling.

Restorative processes can provide some wonderful benefits, but they can also create serious injustices and failures of justice if used in a way that systematically conflicts with doing justice—where offenders are given more punishment, or less punishment, than their wrongdoing deserves. That does not mean that we must avoid restorative processes. It only means that we must use them in a way that does not conflict with doing justice—something that I will suggest later *can be done* easily for a *full range of cases.*

Let me flesh out this relation between restorative justice and justice by addressing three questions:

A. Does restorative justice conflict with doing justice?
B. Why is such conflict objectionable?
C. Can restorative processes be used in a way that does not conflict with doing justice?

A. DOES RESTORATIVE JUSTICE CONFLICT WITH DOING JUSTICE?

It is more than obvious that restorative justice *can* conflict with doing justice. That does not need much discussion. I can imagine a devoted Jew finding it in her heart to "take the great opportunity for grace to inspire a transformative will"[14] to forgive Dr. Mengele for his ghastly concentration camp experiments on her and her family. But few would think justice was done if that meant Dr. Mengele was free to skip away to a happy life, even if he genuinely apologized to her.

Another obvious problem is the potential disparity in treatment of identical offenders committing identical offenses. Every "sentencing circle" will have a different cast of characters. Having the offender's punishment depend not on his personal blameworthiness but rather on the chance collection of persons at the circle is objectionable in itself, whatever the disposition in the case.

---

[12] I do not know that retributivists as a group would agree with this; I offer it only as my own view.
[13] *See* Braithwaite, *supra* note 5, at 1742.
[14] *See* Braithwaite, *supra* note 7, at 1–2.

The discussions in this Symposium by David Dolinko and Stephen Garvey provide persuasive illustrations of just how inconsistent restorative justice can be with doing justice.[15]

While it seems clear that restorative justice *can* seriously conflict with doing justice, I think I would be more cautious than most in predicting that the use of restorative processes necessarily will conflict. John Darley and I have researched lay intuitions of justice and found a surprising amount of agreement among laypersons, over a wide range of situations and cutting across most demographic variables.[16] Thus, when people in a restorative process session are sorting out what they think is an acceptable disposition, their intuitions are likely to track those of the larger community, especially as the sentencing circle is made larger. No doubt some members will tend to be more harsh in their demands and some more lenient, but typically there will be general agreement as to what factors affect the offender's blameworthiness and how they affect it, and the harsh and the lenient sentencers will average out across the group. Indeed, I might predict that a sentencing circle would be more likely to track the shared intuitions of justice of the community than would a single sentencing judge.

But I remain uneasy about a sentencing circle operating without articulated guidelines, for some of the reasons addressed by Robert Weisberg.[17] Even for the fair-minded person, it is easy to be distracted by the particular characteristics of the offender at hand and hard to stand back and put this case in the larger perspective of other cases. There is too much danger for participants left without articulated guidelines to be influenced, perhaps unconsciously, by things such as how similar or different this offender is from themselves. What would be better than pure ad hoc decision-making would be articulated guidelines that captured the larger community's shared intuitions of the principles of justice, to provide at least a benchmark that could inform the sentencing circle's discussions. (On the other hand, it is also my view, as many of you know from my dissent from the United States Sentencing Commission guidelines, that badly-drafted guidelines can do more harm than good.[18])

My ultimate conclusion, then, is that the use of restorative processes might or might not conflict with doing justice, depending upon how they are structured. That is, one could use restorative processes in a way that would *guarantee* failures of justice, and that is just what true restorative justice proponents appear to want: Specifically, to require disposition by restorative processes where the dispositional options available are inadequate to satisfy the demands of justice. In fact, from what I can tell from the restorative justice literature, it is this justice-frustrating effect of restorative processes that is thought of by its proponents as being one of its most important virtues.

---

[15] *See generally* David Dolinko, *Restorative Justice and the Justification of Punishment,* 2003 UTAH L. REV. 319, 331–34 (noting that restorative justice may give similar offenders disparate treatment); Stephen P. Garvey, *Restorative Justice, Punishment, and Atonement,* 2003 UTAH L. REV. 303, 306–08 (distinguishing harms from wrongs and arguing that restorative justice repairs harms but ignores wrongs).

[16] *See* PAUL H. ROBINSON & JOHN M. DARLEY, JUSTICE, LIABILITY, AND BLAME: COMMUNITY VIEWS AND THE CRIMINAL LAW *passim* (1995).

[17] Robert Weisberg, *Restorative Justice and the Danger of "Community,"* 2003 UTAH L. REV. 343, 370–71.

[18] *See* Sentencing Guidelines for United States Courts, Dissenting View of Commissioner Paul H. Robinson on the Promulgation of Sentencing Guidelines by the United States Sentencing Commission, 52 Fed. Reg. 18,046, 18,121 (May 13, 1987).

B. Why is the Conflict of Restorative Justice with Doing Justice Objectionable?

For those who believe that "doing justice" is a value in itself, the question is rhetorical. Neither the value of doing justice nor the harm of conflicting with justice needs further explanation or independent justification.

For crime control utilitarians, doing justice has traditionally been thought of as suboptimal in reducing crime, or at least as less effective than the mechanisms of deterrence and incapacitation. But crime control utilitarians *ought* to be interested in doing justice (in the sense of having the criminal justice system distribute liability and punishment according to the intuitive principles of justice shared by the community) because, as noted above, social science data suggests that the criminal law can harness the great power of social influence to gain lawabidingness if it can earn a reputation of moral authority and legitimacy with the community.[19] By distributing punishment that conflicts with the demands of doing justice, restorative justice ultimately undercuts the system's crime control effectiveness.

Let me also speak to those persons who care neither about doing justice for its own sake nor about crime control, but rather in something more ethereal such as promoting forgiveness for its own sake. I would advise the devoted Jew in her forgiveness of Dr. Mengele that, despite all the virtues of forgiveness that have been expressed by advocates for restorative processes, there is more at stake in how we deal with Dr. Mengele than just this victim's forgiveness.

First, the harm of most criminal offenses spreads to persons beyond the immediate "official victim." Many Jews not part of Dr. Mengele's experiments may nonetheless feel victimized by him. Indeed, criminal law is unique in embodying norms against violation of societal, rather than personal, interests. All crimes have society as their victim, not merely a single person. Further, not all victims may be as forgiving as the one at hand. Are the feelings of many to be overlooked because of the forgiveness of a few? Are the societal norms that protect us all to be undercut because of the forgiveness of the victim at hand?

Second, many people believe that forgiveness is appropriate only after a wrongdoer accepts full responsibility for his wrongdoing and fully atones for it. Being remorseful, by itself, is not full atonement. Atonement is not achieved simply by making restitution, but may require suffering beyond restitution, a suffering the acceptance of which will show the person's acceptance of the wrongfulness of his actions. Indeed, the offender who does not expect and accept his just punishment may be seen as one who does not understand or accept the wrongfulness of his conduct.[20]

---

[19] *See* Tom Tyler, Why People Obey the Law 108 (1990); Robinson & Darley, *supra* note 4, at 471–77. This represents a different kind of "hybrid" distributive principle from that which Erik Luna has discussed. *See* Erik Luna, *Punishment Theory, Holism, and the Procedural Conception of Restorative Justice*, 2003 Utah L. Rev. 205, 225–27. Here there are no trade-offs between utility and doing justice. Rather, the greatest utility is found in a justice distribution of liability and punishment, or at least in a distribution according to a community's shared intuitions of justice.

[20] In fact, genuinely remorseful offenders will think their just punishment is *less* than that actually deserved, for this reason: The offenders' genuine remorse reduces their blameworthiness for the offense, yet offenders cannot expect or insist that their remorse reduce their punishment, any more than they

Finally, it is not entirely clear to me that the *personal* virtue of forgiveness can be an effective operating principle for a society. One can admire and encourage forgiveness, and believe that it is a personal virtue that ought to guide people in their daily lives, yet also conclude that those who have the responsibility to build a better society—where victims as well as wrongdoers can live fruitful lives—must leave forgiveness to the realm of personal virtue.

C. CAN RESTORATIVE PROCESSES BE USED IN A WAY THAT DOES NOT CONFLICT WITH JUSTICE?

The short answer is yes. Where restorative processes are used to complement the criminal justice process rather than to replace it, such processes have little justice-distorting opportunity. There seems every reason to embrace their use.

Can restorative processes ever be used *as a substitute* for the traditional criminal justice adjudication in a way that is consistent with doing justice? In many kinds of cases it can. The most serious limiting factor is the restriction commonly placed on the kinds of dispositions restorative processes are authorized to make.

Given the present limitations, restorative processes seem consistent with doing justice in at least four kinds of cases:

1. *Crimes by juveniles.* Even for serious offenses, juvenile offenders are likely to have significantly reduced blameworthiness due to their limited maturity. That is, (a) they may not fully appreciate the consequences of the harm they cause, (b) they may not have had an opportunity to fully appreciate the societal norm they have violated, and (c) they may be too young for us to expect them to have developed the impulse control that we would expect of an adult in responding to difficult situations or temptations or provocative conduct.[21]

2. *Minor offenses by adults.* Minor offenses will call for deserved punishment levels sufficiently low that they may be satisfied by the dispositions that are typically within the authority of restorative processes.

3. *Serious offenses by adults for which there are significant mitigations.* If strong arguments for justification or excuse exist, the ultimate level of punishment deserved may be within the range of the sanctions available in restorative processes.

4. *Offenses by nonhuman legal entities.* Entities, such as corporations, are not moral beings for whom the notion of justice has meaning. (In fact, in my

---

can expect or insist on forgiveness. To insist on a mitigation for remorse is to undercut the sincerity of the remorse itself. Thus, the punishment discount for remorse will always be a pleasant surprise to the genuinely remorseful offender.

[21] *See* Kim Taylor-Thompson, States of Mind/States of Development 20–24 (Nov. 19, 2002) (unpublished manuscript, on file with author).

view, to use the criminal justice system to "convict" and "punish" such legal fictions risks obscuring the moral content of criminal liability. Better that such entities are dealt with through methods outside of the criminal justice process.[22])

What is most interesting about these four categories of cases in which restorative processes avoid conflict with justice is that, as far as I can tell, all of the dispositional authority that has been granted to restorative processes to date falls into one of these four categories. Examples of some well-known programs are as follows:

New South Wales and New Zealand: Restorative processes are used for disposition of juvenile offenders.[23]

Vermont: Restorative processes operate as a condition of probation, and therefore are subject to all of the limitations as to what offenses can be given a sentence of probation and are subject to screening by the sentencing judge.[24]

Delaware: Restorative processes are available only upon the prosecutor's approval, as with traditional pretrial diversion programs; presumably prosecutors screen cases according to whether a restorative process disposition can do justice.[25]

Minnesota: Restorative processes are used informally, running in parallel to the criminal justice process, rather than as a substitute for it.[26]

In these jurisdictions I found no instance in which the existing statutes limited either: (a) a prosecutor's traditional ability to charge and prosecute offenses to insure that justice is done, or (b) a court's traditional ability to impose a deserved sentence.

This is good news in judging the attractiveness and potential acceptability of current restorative processes. But it seems inconsistent with the claims of restorative justice proponents that their program is "a global social movement" with some good momentum.[27] If the primary contribution that restorative justice makes beyond the virtues of simple restorative processes is to discard concerns about doing justice, one would think that with all its "great success" one could find at least a few programs in which it was achieving its anti-justice mission.

This also means that the label "restorative justice" is misleading when used to describe our present practices. The current use of restorative processes appears to be deliberately limited to cases where the available sanctions are enough to do justice; that is, the current system is careful to preserve its ability to do justice. What exists today, then, is not the anti-justice "restorative justice" but rather the simple use of restorative processes.

---

[22] Paul H. Robinson, *The Criminal-Civil Distinction and the Utility of Desert*, 76 B.U.L. Rev. 201, 211 n.40 (1996) (noting that, unlike people, legal fictions neither feel nor deserve moral condemnation).

[23] *See* Leena Kurki, *Restorative and Community Justice in the United States*, 27 Crime & Just. 235, 240, 273–76 (2000) (discussing programs in New South Wales and New Zealand).

[24] *See* Susan M. Olson & Albert W. Dzur, *Reconstructing Professional Roles in Restorative Justice Programs*, 2003 Utah L. Rev. 57, 65–68 (discussing Vermont's reparative boards program).

[25] *See* Del. Code Ann. tit. 11, §§ 9501–9505 (2001) (setting forth Delaware's victim-offender mediation program).

[26] *See* Univ. of Minn., School of Social Work, Center for Restorative Justice & Peacemaking, *available at* http://ssw.che.umn.edu/rjp/ (last updated Feb. 7, 2003) (discussing various programs in Minnesota).

[27] Braithwaite, *supra* note 5, at 1728, 1743.

V. Can Present Restorative Processes Be Expanded to Include a Full Range of Cases While Remaining True to Justice?

Can the use of restorative processes be expanded to serious offenses and remain consistent with desert? This is a particularly important question because, according to the empirical results Heather Strang and Lawrence Sherman report, it may be that restorative processes have their greatest benefit in the most serious cases.[28]

I believe such expansion is possible in a way that is consistent with justice. How can this be done? First, as is obvious from the previous discussion, if the seriousness of the authorized dispositions by restorative processes are increased, the kinds of cases dealt with could be widened. Some people will be hesitant to give serious sentencing authority, such as imprisonment, to a restorative process body, no matter what an offender's veto power. But one can conceive of versions of restorative processes that include judicial participation and/or include guidelines that structure discretion.

A second point may be the most important for expanding restorative processes. Consider for a moment the demands of justice: justice cares about *amount, not method* of punishment. Thus, one could impose deserved punishment through any variety of alternative methods without undercutting justice—fine, community service, house arrest, curfew, regular reporting, diary keeping, and so on—as long as the total punitive "bite" (the "punishment units") of the disposition satisfies the total punishment the offender deserves, no more, no less.[29]

This characteristic of justice has two important implications for restorative processes. First, because all forms of sanction can give rise to "punishment credit," good-faith participation in restorative processes can count toward satisfying the required punishment, at least to the extent of the personal suffering that it produces. No doubt there is discomfort in attending a meeting where family and friends have gathered to discuss one's wrongdoing. Second, restorative processes may provide an effective means for sorting out just how the total punishment units called for are best "spent"—i.e., restorative processes may be a particularly effective means of fashioning a disposition from among the wide variety of available methods, that will best advance the interests of restoring the victim, the offender, and society.

Finally, as has been noted above, the problem of limitations on the dispositional authority of restorative processes is relevant only in instances where such restorative processes are used as the dispositional process—that is, where it is substituting for the criminal justice system or becoming the dispositional mechanism for that system. This is equally true when restorative processes are used for serious offenses. Where such processes are only complementary to the criminal justice system—where they operate parallel to criminal justice—there is no reason for any limitation on their use, for there is no

---

[28] *See* Heather Strang & Lawrence W. Sherman, *Repairing the Harm: Victims and Restorative Justice*, 2003 Utah L. Rev. 15, 40.

[29] I have written about such a proposal. Paul H. Robinson, *Desert, Crime Control, Disparity, and Units of Punishment, in* Penal Theory and Practice: Tradition and Innovation in Criminal Justice 93, 99–104 (Anthony Duff et al. eds., 1994).

danger that justice will be undercut. (One might worry that if restorative processes were an entirely complimentary rather than a substitute system, offenders might have little motivation to participate. But one could have the criminal justice system look to and take account of the restorative processes disposition in setting the criminal justice sentence.)

VI. Conclusion

Ultimately, my reaction to restorative justice—the theory of restorative justice, not the practice of restorative processes—is one of puzzlement, for this reason: What makes restorative processes work is the emotional need of the participants—a victim's or participant's sense of satisfaction or release in justice being done or, on occasion, an offender's sense of atonement from a just result. Yet it is this same emotional need—inherent in human nature—that restorative justice is so quick to reject outside of the restorative process.

Imagine the people who have attended a sentencing circle one day, who the next day read in their morning newspaper a story of a twenty-two year old who runs on foot from police when police spot him in a car he has failed to return to its owner. During the police chase, an officer on foot is killed by an officer driving a patrol car. The offender is convicted of murder under the felony-murder rule and sentenced to forty years imprisonment.[30] The readers are likely to be offended by this result; it violates their collective notions of what the offender deserves. (Empirical studies confirm that people typically see such cases of accidental killings in the course of a felony as tantamount to manslaughter at most, not murder.[31] Indeed, in this case it is not even clear that people would see the offender in such a case as having much, if any, causal accountability for the death.[32]) Yet this is apparently irrelevant to the restorative justice proponents. If the restorative process does not work—assume the dead police officer's family is of a very unforgiving sort—the restorative justice proponents would defer to deterrence, and the felony-murder rule makes good sense under a deterrence theory; deterrence is the primary basis on which it is justified. Why wouldn't the restorative justice proponents, sensitive as they are to the importance of people's feelings about justice, enthusiastically support attempts to track shared community intuitions of justice as the criminal justice system's distributive principle? How can the feelings of those at the sentencing circle be so legitimate and so central the day before, but now so irrelevant?

Or imagine that our sentencing circle members the next morning read the story of an unrepentant Nazi concentration camp officer who, it is decided, will not be prosecuted because he is now elderly and no longer a danger—classic incapacitation analysis. Our sentencing circle people are offended: They see a failure of justice in this disposition. Yesterday their collective views were central, but today their views are

---

[30] This is the *McCarty* case from South Chicago. *See* Paul H. Robinson, Criminal Law Case Studies 1–5 (2d ed. 2002); Paul H. Robinson, Teacher's Manual for Criminal Law Case Studies 13–14 (2d ed. 2002).

[31] *See* Robinson & Darley, *supra* note 16, at 169–81.

[32] *See id.* at 181–89.

irrelevant, something the criminal justice system should ignore? Restorative justice tells us to follow the principle of incapacitation, which lets the Nazi officer go free because there is no danger of future crime to be avoided by his incarceration, rather than to look to doing justice.

To summarize my proposal, it is this: Use restorative processes as much as possible, as either complementary to the criminal justice system or as a dispositional process within it. Where restorative processes are used as the dispositional process, the sanctioning options made available ought to be sufficiently serious to allow justice to be done. This can be done either by limiting the use of restorative processes to cases where deserved punishment is not great—as is typically done today—or by increasing the punishment available to restorative processes. In the latter case in particular, articulated guidelines are desirable, as would be a "punishment units" system that allows the restorative processes greater unfettered discretion in determining the method of punishment than in determining its amount.

24

RESTORATIVE PUNISHMENT AND PUNITIVE RESTORATION

R. A. Duff

INTRODUCTION

My thesis can be stated quite simply. Our responses to crime should aim for 'restoration', for 'restorative justice': but the kind of restoration that criminal wrongdoing makes necessary is properly achieved through a process of retributive punishment. To put it the other way round, offenders should suffer retribution, punishment, for their crimes: but the essential purpose of such punishment should be to achieve restoration. To put it yet more simply, my slogan is 'Restoration through retribution'. That thesis sets me in opposition to advocates of restorative justice, and to those critics of restorative justice who argue for a 'just deserts' retributivism.

Both sides to this controversy are right in important respects. Advocates of restorative justice are right to insist that in our responses to, and understanding of, crime we should seek restoration, and such related aims as reparation and reconciliation; that we should not punish offenders just for the sake of making them suffer, or to deter them and others; and that our existing criminal procedures – our criminal trials, the kinds of punishment typically imposed on offenders – are ill-suited to the restorative ends that we should be pursuing. Proponents of just deserts are right to insist that punishment is the proper response to criminal wrongdoing, and that what justifies punishment is that it is deserved for that wrongdoing: it is the state's proper responsibility, and our responsibility as citizens, to bring criminal wrongdoers to suffer the punishments that they deserve.

However, both 'restorative' and 'retributive' theorists are wrong insofar as they suppose, as they often do, that we must choose between restoration and retribution as our primary aim. Thus critics of the restorative justice movement often assume that we have to choose between the 'punishment paradigm' and the 'restorative paradigm' (Ashworth 1993) – and argue that we should choose the former, since the pursuit of restorative aims is incompatible with the demands of penal justice. Advocates of restorative justice often assume that we must choose between restorative and retributive justice – and argue that we must choose the former, since punitive retribution cannot serve the aim of restoration.[1] This shared assumption is, as I will argue, mistaken. Once we understand what restoration must involve in the context of criminal wrongdoing, and what retribution can mean in the context of criminal punishment, we will see that restoration is not only compatible with retribution and punishment, but requires it.

Restorative theorists will therefore accuse me of undermining the eirenic, reconciliatory aims of restorative justice by a desire to punish, to 'deliver pain' (see Christie 1981), which is utterly at odds with those aims; proponents of punishment as 'just deserts' will accuse me of abandoning the principles of penal justice in favour of ill-defined aspirations to 'restoration' which are utterly at odds with the central demands of proportionality and penal restraint. My argument will be, however, that restorative and retributive justice are not thus opposed.

My claim is not that existing 'restorative justice' programmes are punitive (though many do have a punitive dimension); nor that our existing penal practices are generally restorative (which would be absurd). There is an obvious incompatibility between existing restorative practices and existing penal practices, and between the conceptions of 'restoration' favoured by many restorative theorists and the conceptions of punishment held by many advocates of punitive or retributive justice. I will argue, however, that once we gain a better understanding of the concepts of restoration and of punishment, we will be able to dissolve the apparent conflict between them, and to see that criminal punishment should aim at restoration, whilst restorative justice programmes should aim to impose appropriate kinds of punishment.

To make out this argument, I begin, in the next section, with the question of what 'restoration' should mean in the context of wrongdoing – of what needs to be restored and how it can be restored; apology and moral reparation will be crucial here. In the third section I apply the results of the second to the case of crime, and offer an account of the proper aims of victim-offender mediation programmes – which are often portrayed as paradigms of restorative justice: such programmes, I will argue, should be understood not as alternatives to punishment, but as paradigms of punishment, and thus as models for the criminal justice system.

---

[1] For just a few examples see Christie 1981: 11 on 'alternatives to punishment' as opposed to 'alternative punishments'; Marshall 1988: 47–8 on 'reparative' as against 'retributive' justice; Zehr 1990: 178–81 on the alternative 'lenses' of retributive and restorative justice; Walgrave 1994: 57 on 'restorative justice' as against the 'retributive and rehabilitative justice systems'; Dignan 1999: 54, 60, on the 'restorative justice approach' as against the 'retributive approach'; Braithwaite 1999a: 60 on the need to strive for 'restorative justice' rather than 'retributive justice'. For further references and apt criticism, see Daly and Immarigeon 1998: 32–34.

RESTORATION AND WRONGDOING

Standard definitions of 'restorative justice' are, inevitably, rather vague. To say, for instance, that it is 'a process whereby parties with a stake in a specific offence collectively resolve how to deal with the aftermath of the offence and its implications for the future' (Marshall 1999: 5); or that its purpose 'is the restoration into safe communities of victims and offenders who have resolved their conflicts' (Van Ness 1993: 258): leaves open crucial questions about the significance of the 'offence' or 'conflict', and about what can count as successfully 'dealing with' the 'aftermath' or 'implications' of the offence, or 'resolving' the conflict. My main concern in this section is with the question of what kind of 'restoration' is made necessary by criminal wrongdoing: but it is worth pausing briefly to think about the implications of the basic idea of 'restoration'.

Many different kinds of thing can be 'restored'. Property which was lost or stolen can be restored, i.e. given back, to its owner; paintings which have been damaged can be restored to their pristine glory. Health which was undermined through illness can be restored – the sick can become well again. Reputations which were damaged by accusation or by slander can be restored, if the truth is established and published, which can also restore the person's standing in the community. Security – both the fact of being safe from danger and the awareness that one is thus safe[2] – can be restored after it has been undermined; the danger which threatened, or seemed to threaten, is removed, and we are re-assured of our safety. Trust which has been undermined can be restored; so too can relationships – of friendship, of love, of collegiality, of fellow citizenship – which have been damaged or weakened. What is common to all these cases is the retrieval of an original favourable condition. That original condition – of health, of security or trust, of good reputation, of friendship, for instance – is lost or removed, so that the good internal to it is lost. But that good is then regained: the condition is reinstated, the *status quo ante* is restored.

Restoration strictly speaking must thus be distinguished from such concepts as reparation and compensation. Restoration requires the reinstatement of the *status quo ante*. A harm was caused, a wrong was done, and its memory might remain: but when restoration is achieved, it is now (apart from the memory) as if the harm or wrong had never occurred. Reparation and compensation, by contrast, seek to make up for the loss of what cannot thus be restored. Thus when property is lost or stolen, it might be restored – the owner might get back the very thing she lost. But it might not be restorable: it might have been destroyed or sold on beyond recall, in which case all that is possible is reparation or compensation rather than restoration. If the silver I inherited from my mother is stolen and melted down, my property cannot be restored; the most I can gain is a replacement, or compensation that will to some degree 'make up for' my loss.[3] Similarly, when health is lost, it might be restorable: the patient might return

---

[2] Compare Braithwaite and Pettit 1990: 60–65, on 'dominion' as involving both an assured liberty and the knowledge of that assurance. The value of assured liberty and of security depends in crucial part on our knowing that we have such liberty or security.

[3] The position with property is complicated by the way in which property is often fully fungible – as far as the owner is concerned, what she owns is not so much a distinctive individual item, but a token of a

to as healthy a condition as she was in before illness struck. But it might not be thus restorable: she might be left permanently disabled or weakened; and the pain that she might have undergone during the illness cannot be 'restored', even if the illness is cured. This point raises a serious question about what we could even hope to restore in the context of crime or wrongdoing: we must ask what harm is done, what goods are lost or damaged, that we could even aspire to restore.

We might at first think of the material, physical or psychological effects that wrongdoing typically causes: property is lost or damaged; physical injuries are suffered; fear, anxiety and distress are caused, as may be other, more lasting kinds of psychological damage. But, first, even if some such harms do permit genuine restoration (if the victim's property or physical or psychological health can be restored), others do not: we cannot make it for the victim as if the wrong had never been done, since we cannot wipe out her suffering; we cannot make it as if she never suffered that fear, anxiety or distress. If we focus on these kinds of non-restorable harm, we must therefore think of reparation or compensation, not of restoration. (This is not to deny that reparation and compensation have an important role to play in an enterprise of restorative justice: it is simply to insist that they cannot in themselves constitute restoration – that their role should rather be seen as means to restoration.) Second, to focus on such harms as these is to ignore the fact that the victim was wronged. He did not simply lose his property, or suffer accidental damage to it – it was stolen, or maliciously destroyed or damaged; he did not simply suffer injury through natural causes or in an accident – he was attacked. Surely the harm he has suffered, what needs to be restored, must be understood in a way that includes its wrongful character.[4]

We might meet both these points by talking not (just) about the material or psychological effects of the wrongdoing on the victim, but about the relationships it damaged: between the wrongdoer and his direct victim (when there is one), between the wrongdoer and the wider communities to which he and the victim belong – communities which might be intimate and close, such as a family or a group of friends; or less intimate but still relatively local, such as a village or residential neighbourhood; or impersonally large, such as a political community whose bounds are coextensive with those of a particular legal system.[5] Those relationships were damaged by the wrongdoer's deed, and need now to be restored. However, if we are to understand what could

---

type, and any token of that type would do. This is most obviously true of money: it would be absurd to deny that the money which I lost had been restored simply on the grounds that I did not get back the individual coins or notes that I lost; what matters is that I lost £100 and got £100 back. It is also to some extent true of other kinds of property, especially purely functional kinds; and to the extent that it is true, property that has been irretrievably destroyed or lost *qua* individual token can still be fully restored, *qua* type.

[4] I am not suggesting that the wrong done to the victim is separate from the harm caused to him: whilst not all wrongdoings cause any identifiable harm, those that properly concern the criminal law do typically cause or threaten harm, and their character as wrongs is in part determined by that harm. My point is, rather, that we must understand the harm done by wrongdoing as *wrongful* harm, which gives it a normative character crucially distinct from that of naturally or accidentally caused harms: see further Duff 1996: 366–9.

[5] Much more needs to be said about the idea of community as it figures here, especially about the idea of a political community (and about the extent to which we now have or live in such communities). I cannot pursue this point here, but see Duff 2001: chs. 2, 5.

restore such relationships, what could even count as their restoration, we must get clear about the kind of damage they have suffered.

It might be tempting to try to describe that damage in purely factual or empirical terms: the victim, and others, are angry with the wrongdoer, or fearful or mistrustful of him, or are unwilling still to engage in their former common activities with him; the wrongdoer himself might feel ill at ease with or estranged from them. Now if we see the damage in such terms, we will naturally see 'restoration' in similarly empirical terms, as a matter of securing such changes in the attitudes and feelings of those concerned that they are no longer angry, fearful, untrusting or hostile; and we will look for techniques that might help to secure such changes. But such a perspective is quite inadequate, since it leaves out the crucial fact that the victim was wronged by the wrongdoer. We are not just dealing with an empirical breakdown in the relationship – a breakdown which, as thus described, leaves it open whether it was anyone's fault; we are dealing with a breach created in the relationship, or damage done to it, by one party's wrongdoing.[6] The wrongdoer denied or flouted the values – of mutual trust, concern and respect – by which their relationship as friends, neighbours, colleagues or fellow citizens was supposedly defined; in doing so, he damaged that relationship as a normative relationship which is partly constituted by those values.

The damage to the relationship must therefore be understood in normative, not merely in empirical, terms. There are three crucial features of this normative perspective.

First, we must understand, and appraise, the responses of those involved as responses to a wrong that was done – and as being reasonable or unreasonable, justified or unjustified, as responses to that wrong. The victim is not just angry, but indignant at the wrong he suffered; and we cannot then avoid asking whether his anger is justified. Perhaps it is excessive – the wrong was not that serious, the wrongdoer was not that culpable. Or perhaps it is too weak – he should be more indignant, more angry, than he is: for not to be angered by a wrong done to me can display a lack of self-respect (see Murphy 1988: 16–18), or a blindness to the moral quality of others' conduct. The reactions of others, and of the wrongdoer, are likewise subject to normative appraisal: we must ask not just what they in fact feel, but what they should feel; and our understanding of the damage done to their relationships is determined in crucial part by our understanding of their responses as reasonable or as unreasonable. If someone is so angry with me that he will have no more to do with me unless and until I offer him a profuse apology, our relationship has broken down: but our understanding of the character and the implications of that breach will depend on whether his anger is a justified response to some serious wrong that I did him, or an unjustified response to an imagined slight.

Second, we might sometimes want to say – and be justified in saying – that a relationship has been thus damaged even if those directly involved do not react as if

---

[6] Some restorative theorists are unhappy with such a focus on wrongdoing; they prefer to talk of 'conflicts' or 'troubles' rather than of 'crimes' or 'wrongdoings' (see e.g. Christie 1977, Hulsman 1986 – on which see Duff 2001: 60–64). Others, however, recognize the importance of the category of wrongdoing, and of the criminal law as defining the kinds of wrongdoing that properly concern the whole political community.

it has been damaged, or do not even realize that it has been damaged. Suppose that a friend – or someone I thought was a friend – seriously betrays my trust for his own profit. Perhaps, because I do not want to have to face up to the implications of this, I try to persuade myself that the breach of trust was not that serious; or perhaps I don't even know what he has done, and so sincerely believe that our friendship is intact.[7] Others might still properly say that the friendship has been seriously damaged by his betrayal, since that betrayal was utterly inconsistent with, a complete denial of, the bonds of mutual trust and concern by which friendship is defined. If the betrayal was serious enough, others might indeed think that the friendship has been destroyed, unless the friend and I together face up to its implications and try to deal with it: whatever relationship we might maintain, that is, can no longer count as a friendship.

Third, when we ask what can restore the relationship, or repair the damage done to it, we must ask not just what will in fact make the parties feel better, or quell their anger, mistrust or fear, but what would be normatively adequate to restore it – what would make it appropriate to desist from anger, to renew trust, to restore community? Since it was the wrongdoing that damaged the relationship, it is that that must be repaired: but how can that be done? Material damage that was caused might be repaired; property that was stolen might be given back or replaced; physical injuries might be healed: but what can repair the wrong that was done?

Different relationships admit of different kinds of repair: but the obvious, paradigmatic way of repairing the normative harm wrought by wrongdoing is apology; and whilst apology can take various different forms in different relationships and contexts, and can be implicit rather than explicit, we can make some general points about the character or meaning of apologies for wrongdoing.[8] These points can be summarized as the three 'R's of apology: recognition, repentance and reconciliation. Apology expresses the wrongdoer's recognition of the wrong he has done, his repentance, and his desire for reconciliation with those whom he wronged – for the restoration of the relationships he damaged. (I am speaking here of sincere apologies; I will comment later on the problem of insincerity.)

Recognition of the wrong as a wrong is clearly an indispensable first step. It is something that is owed to the victim by others in general (whose sympathetic response to him should be structured by the recognition that he has been not just harmed, but wronged), but especially by the wrongdoer; in recognizing the wrong done to him, we recognize his moral standing as a fellow human being who demands our concern and respect (see Gaita 1991: chs. 1–4). Such recognition on the part of the wrongdoer might of course be spontaneous: she comes, perhaps at once, to see for herself the wrong she has done, and to understand its implications. But it is a painfully familiar fact about

---

[7] My claim that a friendship can be damaged even by wrongdoing that has no empirical or felt impact on its victim, is related to the familiar – if controversial – claim that one can be harmed by wrongdoing even if it has no empirical impact on one's consciousness or material well-being: someone for whom well-being and happiness depend crucially on a faithful and loving marriage is harmed, and their marriage is destroyed, by their spouse's infidelity, even if that infidelity remains concealed and unknown.

[8] Apologies are not, of course, always for wrongdoing: I can apologize for some harm or inconvenience that I caused you through non-culpable inadvertence or accident; or for harm that I caused you intentionally but justifiably. But my focus here is on apologies for culpable wrongdoing.

human beings that we are for a host of reasons often very slow to recognize our own wrongdoings: we often need others to persuade us to face up to what we have done. This is an important role that such responses as blame, criticism and censure play, as well as the often forcible expression of such emotions as anger and indignation: to bring a wrongdoer to recognize what she has done – a recognition that her apology then expresses.

Recognition includes understanding: to recognize the wrong I have done involves not just realizing that I did wrong, but coming to grasp the character, seriousness and implications of that wrong. It also includes or leads to repentance: for sincerely to recognize what I did as a wrong is to recognize it as something that I should not have done – which is also to repent my having done it. One who says 'Yes, I recognize that I did wrong, but so what? I'd do it again tomorrow' has not, we should say, truly recognized the wrong as a wrong; at most, he sees it as something that others call 'wrong'.[9] To repent my past wrongdoing is both to own and to disown it: I own it as mine, as something for which I must accept responsibility (and blame); but I disown it as something that I now wish I had not done, and that I repudiate (and, since repentance also involves a commitment to self-reform, as something that I will try to avoid in future). What I owe to those I have wronged, and what others may try to persuade me to if I need persuasion, is such a repentant recognition of the wrong I have done – a repentance that apology can also express. We should note too that such repentance is of its nature painful: the repentant wrongdoer cares, or has come to care, for those whom she wronged, for the values she violated; she must therefore be pained by that wrong and that violation.

An apology which expresses my repentant recognition of the wrong I have done thereby also expresses my desire, my hope, for reconciliation with those whom I wronged. At least in the case of serious wrongs, I realize that I have by my wrongdoing damaged or threatened (if not destroyed) my relationship with them – our friendship, our marriage, our relationship as neighbours or as colleagues; if that relationship is to be restored, I must seek their forgiveness through my apology.[10] For reconciliation to be complete, the other must accept my apology: it might not be possible, psychologically or morally, literally to 'forgive and forget', but the forgiving acceptance of my apology does suffice, normatively, to restore the relationship and to heal the breach.

Now apologies are supposed to be sincere, and in many contexts they have value only if they are, and are known to be, sincere. It is worth noting, however, that there can sometimes be value even in apologies that are not or might not be sincere, in formal apologies that might be to some degree a matter of ritual. Just as – or so it is said – hypocrisy is a homage that vice pays to virtue, so insincere apology can be a homage that an unrepentant wrongdoer pays to social morality: if it is not merely

---

[9] If I know myself to be weak-willed, and prone to give in to temptation, I might predict that I will repeat the wrong in future, as I have so often in the past: but that prediction, if it is not to give the lie to my claim to have recognized the wrong, must be infused with pain and remorse.

[10] It might of course be questionable whether the relationship can be restored; or whether I can ask that it be restored. This is not an issue that I can pursue here, nor one that can be dealt with in the same way for all kinds of relationship. On the version of it which arises in the case of crime, see Duff 2001: ch. 4.4.2.

offered out of short-term prudence, it can express a concern to preserve the bonds of community. Furthermore, the demand that the wrongdoer apologize, even if we suspect that his apology will not be sincere, can communicate both to him and to the victim our recognition of the wrong that he did; and we can hope that the experience of apologizing might help to bring him to recognize for himself the wrong that he did.[11]

Sometimes, however, merely verbal apology might not be enough, at least for a relatively serious wrong: even a sincere verbal apology might not be adequate to the seriousness of the wrong done. It is a general, deep feature of our lives that we need to give more than merely verbal form and expression to things that matter to us, especially when that expression has a public significance. We express our gratitude for a great service done to us by a gift or, in the public realm, by a public reward or honour; we express our grief at a death through the rituals of a funeral. Such more-than-merely-verbal modes of expression have two related purposes: they make the expression more forceful to others than a merely verbal expression would have been, and they can help to focus the expresser's own attention on what needs to be expressed.

An apology can thus be strengthened, made more forceful, if it is given more than merely verbal form; and this can also help to focus the wrongdoer's attention (an attention which, as we all know from painful personal experience, is all too easily distracted) on the wrong that he did and the need to seek forgiveness and reconciliation for it. Mere words, and especially between strangers, can be too cheap – too easy to say, without any real depth of meaning; too easy to forget, without thinking about their meaning;[12] by giving apology some more material expression, we can both strengthen and express its sincerity.

If we then ask what this more than merely verbal form could be, the obvious answer is that it could consist in some kind of reparation. If the wrongdoing caused a material harm or loss that it is within the wrongdoer's power to make good, he can make reparation by making it good. If it caused no such harm, or if the wrongdoer cannot make the harm good, he must find some other way of 'making up' for what he did: some other way of making his repentant recognition of what he did forcefully clear both to the victim and to others. Depending on the context, on the nature of the wrong, and on the relationship it threatened, this might involve, for instance, undertaking some service for the victim, or for the wider community; or buying the victim a thoughtful gift; or contributing time or money to a suitable charity; or agreeing to seek appropriate help to avoid repeating the wrong (someone whose addiction has led him to steal from his friends might agree to embark on a treatment programme).

We must be clear about the meaning and point of these kinds of reparation, and how they differ from reparation or compensation that aims only to repair or make up for some

---

[11] I say only 'might', since it is obvious that undertaking such a required apology can have quite different effects, including a resentful anger at those who require the apology and at those to whom it is made. Much depends on the context, the tones and the spirit in which the apology is demanded.

[12] Though we should not forget how hard it can be for individuals, for governments, and for other corporate bodies to apologize even when a verbal apology is all that is sought: not just because apologies might open the door to claims for compensation, but because to apologize is to admit wrongdoing.

Suppose that some kind of mediation programme is available, and that both offender and victim (violent husband and battered wife; burglar and victim) agree to take part in it.[15] What should be the aims of the mediation?

It is important, I suggest, that the mediation focus not just on the harm that was caused, but on the wrong that was done. What matters is not just that the victim has suffered certain kinds of physical injury, or loss of property, or distressing psychological states; nor just that, since it was the offender who culpably caused those harms, the cost of repairing them or of providing compensation for them should fall on him: but that he committed a serious wrong against her. It is that wrong on which the criminal law focuses (by contrast, the civil law is concerned with harms or losses, and with who should pay for them); it is on that wrong that any adequate response to the offender's crime, and to the victim, must focus; and we must therefore ask what kind of 'restoration' that wrong makes necessary.

The answer that I suggest should be obvious from the previous section. What needs to be restored, and what can in principle be restored, is the offender's normative relationship with his victim as a fellow citizen, and with his fellow citizens more generally. For the criminal law is concerned not with our more local, intimate and optional relationships as friends, as lovers, as neighbours, as colleagues, but simply with our (somewhat more abstract, detached and non-optional) relationships as fellow citizens: it defines the values and constraints which make our common life as citizens possible. What matter to the criminal law is therefore the wrongs done by one citizen to other citizens, and the damage done by those wrongs to their relationships as citizens. The offender's crime damaged his relationships both with his victim, as a fellow citizen, and with his fellow citizens more generally, by denying those values – of mutual respect and concern – that are supposed to define their civic relations, and that make civic life possible; it is that damage that must be repaired, to restore those relationships.

When such a wrong has been committed, it should be recognized: this is something that is owed to the victim, and is anyway a simple implication of taking seriously the values that the offender has violated. It should be recognized by the victim's fellow citizens, who can manifest that recognition both in their direct responses to the victim (responses of sympathy, of assistance), and in their responses to the offender: in, most obviously, the way in which they condemn or criticize him for what he has done – a kind of condemnation and criticism that is given formal expression by a criminal trial and conviction.[16] It should be recognized by the offender: he owes it to his victim to recognize the wrong he has done to her, and to his fellow citizens to recognize the way in which he has violated the public values of the polity. It is then quite appropriate that one of the initial aims of the mediation process should be, as it is often said to be, to get the offender to recognize, to understand, what he has done (and to give him a chance to explain himself to the victim).

---

[15] There are important differences between different kinds of mediation programme, which I skate over here (see Marshall and Merry 1990; Daly and Immarigeon 1998; Braithwaite 1999a; Kurki 2000): but I hope that my general claims about the proper nature of criminal mediation can still stand.

[16] On the trial, as a procedure which calls a citizen to answer a charge of wrongdoing and condemns her if the charge is proved against her, see Duff 1986: ch. 4.

What he should recognize is that he has culpably committed this wrong. Thus the tones in which he is addressed by others in the process (by the victim, by the mediator, by his or the victim's supporters) should be not the neutral tones of bare description, but the normative tones of censure and criticism – of blame.[17] This is not to say that those tones must be hostile, or such as to humiliate him or exclude him: although it is all too easy for censure and blame to become exercises in oppression, humiliation or exclusion, we must try to censure in a way that displays our recognition of, and concern for, the offender as a fellow citizen. But since what we must try to persuade him to recognize, or join with him in recognizing, is the wrong that he committed, we cannot but be engaged in censuring him. And, if he comes to recognize for himself the wrong he has committed, he must censure himself: which is to say that, if he comes to recognize it as a wrong that he culpably committed and for which he is responsible, he must thereby come to a remorseful, repentant recognition of his guilt. A mediation process which is to take the wrongdoing seriously, and which aims to get the offender to recognize, to face up to, what he has done, must thus aim to induce remorse and repentance; it must aim to bring the offender to suffer the painful burden both of repentance, and of being censured by his fellow citizens.

What the offender also owes is, minimally, an apology: this is owed both to the victim and to his fellow citizens. If he has come to recognize and repent his wrong, he will want to offer such an apology: to find some way of expressing his repentant recognition and his new or renewed concern both for the victim and for his relationships with his fellow citizens. If he has not yet come to such a recognition, others can properly try to persuade him that he ought to apologize; they might indeed demand that he apologize, or – if that is within their power – require him to apologize. In making such a demand or requirement, they must of course hope that it will be, or will become, sincere: but the demand or requirement can be justified even if it is likely that the apology will not be sincere. For there can be, as I noted above, value even in ritual or formal apology; and we can hope that the experience of making even a demanded, non-voluntary apology might help bring the offender to a clearer grasp of the character and implications of what he has done. A mediation process that takes the wrongdoing seriously will thus properly aim to bring the offender to apologize to his victim, and to his fellows.

But a mere verbal apology might not, as we have seen, be enough: something more may be necessary to give manifest weight to the apology – and to help to focus the offender's own repentant attention on what he has done. That 'more' might take the form of direct reparation or compensation to the victim; or undertaking – in, as it were, the victim's name – some task or service for the wider community or for a charity; or just making a suitable donation to a charity; or perhaps agreeing to enter a programme that will address the motives and factors that led the offender to commit the wrong.[18] What is at stake here is not material reparation for material harm that was caused,

---

[17] Compare Christie 1977: 9, on giving the offender an 'opportunity to receive a type of blame that it would be very difficult to neutralize'.

[18] The CHANGE programme for domestically violent men is a good example: it focuses on getting them to accept responsibility both for their own violent behaviour and for finding ways to deal with it: see Scourfield and Dobash 1999.

but moral reparation for the wrong that was done (though the moral reparation might of course take the form of making material reparation). It must, therefore, be something that is burdensome for the offender – even if it is a burden that he welcomes, as enabling him to make reparation: for only if it is burdensome can it serve the role of giving more forceful expression to the apology that is owed.

Some restorative theorists, whilst agreeing that the making of reparations as a result of a mediation process might well in fact be burdensome, deny that they have to be burdensome: any pain or hardship that they cause is a side-effect, not part of their purpose (see Walgrave 2001a). Suppose, Lode Walgrave once asked me, that the victim would be content with the gift of a box of chocolates: should not that then suffice? Or suppose, John Braithwaite suggested, that victim and offender could be reconciled by a hug: why then insist that the offender must undertake or suffer some further burden?[19] There are two replies to such questions.

First, what matters is not simply whether the victim would be satisfied by, for instance, a box of chocolates: we must ask whether he should be so easily satisfied; and we might think that he should not – indeed, that to regard a box of chocolates as adequate moral reparation, as an adequate expression of the wrongdoer's apologetic repentance, would be to close one's eyes to the seriousness of the offence, or to denigrate oneself by implying that that is all one is worth. After all, the gift of a box of chocolates carries a familiar kind of meaning: it is the kind of thing one gives a hostess, or someone one does not know that well, or when one cannot make the effort to think of something more imaginative. It is a rather trivial gift, and to treat it as sufficient to make up for a serious wrong implies that the wrong was trivial. If we ask why that should matter, part of the answer is that we should try to dissuade the victim from thus denigrating himself; but the more forceful answer is that the offender owes an apology to his fellow citizens in general, and thus owes it to them to make a kind of reparation that will be proportionate to the seriousness of his offence.

Of course, boxes of chocolates can carry different meanings in different contexts, as can hugs; and I do not wish to claim *a priori* that neither a box of chocolates nor a hug could ever, in any context or any relationship, be an adequate expression of apology for a serious wrong. But, and this is my second reply, we are dealing here with public, not private, wrongs, and so with public, not private, reparation: we must therefore ask what could count as an adequately forceful expression of apology between citizens, and what public meaning different possible modes of reparation could have – how they could be understood by the rest of the polity. A box of chocolates or a hug, whatever private meanings they might have in particular contexts, do not, I suggest, have the right kind of public meaning.

The kind of mediation that is an appropriate response to crime (at least to serious crime) should therefore aim to bring the offender to recognize and repent the wrong she has done – which involves censuring her; and to make some suitable moral reparation for that wrong. Furthermore, whilst existing mediation programmes typically seek a reparation which is voluntary in the sense that the offender and victim both agree to

---

[19] They raised these questions in discussion: but see also Braithwaite 1999a: p. 20, fn. 6.

it, I would argue that it is fully consistent with the aims sketched above to require the offender to make reparation if he does not agree to something suitable – in the same way as we could appropriately require a wrongdoer to apologize.[20]

What we have, then, is a process which the offender undertakes or undergoes – a process of being confronted with his wrongdoing, of being censured, of making reparation – because he has committed a crime. That process is focused on, and justified by, his wrongdoing: he is censured for that wrongdoing, he is asked to recognize and repent it, and he must apologize and make reparation for it. The process is also intended to be painful or burdensome, as we have seen. The wrongdoer should be pained by the censure of his fellow citizens: if he is not pained, their censure has failed to achieve its intended result. He should be pained by the recognition of his wrongdoing, since that should be a repentant recognition, and repentance is necessarily painful. He should be burdened, and in that sense pained, by the reparation that he has to make, since it can have the appropriate apologetic meaning only if it is burdensome. These related kinds of pain or burden are not mere side-effects of the process which – if he is lucky – might not ensue; they are integral to the aims of the process as a process of seeking restoration after a crime.

That is to say, however, that the process of what we could call criminal mediation – the kind of mediation appropriate to crime – is a punitive process; it constitutes a punishment for the offender. For it is something that is imposed on or required of her, for the crime that she committed, and it is intended to be burdensome or painful – to make her suffer for that crime. It is indeed a retributive process: for if we ask why it is appropriate that she should be thus burdened, why she should be brought to suffer, the answer is, in effect, that this is what she deserves for her crime. She deserves to suffer the censure of others, and her own remorse: for that censure and that remorse are appropriate responses to her crime. She deserves to suffer the burden of making moral reparation for what she has done: since it was her wrong, as one that she culpably committed, it is just and proper that she should bear that burden. The central retributivist slogan is that the guilty should be punished as they deserve and because that is what they deserve – that punishment should bring them to suffer what they deserve to suffer; and criminal mediation, as I have described it, is precisely a way of trying to bring them thus to suffer what they deserve.[21]

This is not to say that we do or should aim to make offenders suffer just for its own sake. What has given retributivism such a bad reputation is the impression – sometimes admittedly conveyed by retributivists themselves (see e.g. Moore 1997: ch. 4) – that the sole purpose of retributive punishment is to inflict pain on offenders: but

---

[20] Compare Walgrave 2002b on 'coerced restorative sanctions'.

[21] It might seem that, in my enthusiasm to portray criminal mediation as punishment, I have skated over two defining features of punishment (see e.g. Hart 1968: 4–6; Scheid 1980) – that it is *imposed* on the offender (whereas in mediation programmes the offender must agree to enter mediation and to undertake reparation) *by an authority* (whereas mediation and reparation are matters of negotiation and agreement between the parties involved). I cannot deal with these points here, but would argue that mediation and reparation could properly be required of, and in that sense imposed on, the offender; and that the process should be conducted under the aegis and supervision of the criminal courts. See further Duff 2001: 96–7, 111, 158–63.

retributivism need not mean that. On the account I have sketched here, what matters is that the offender should come to suffer the appropriate kind of pain or burden – of being censured, of remorse, of making reparation; and that appropriate pain is in part at least, insofar as it involves the remorseful recognition of wrongdoing, to be self-imposed. Furthermore, if we ask why that matters, the answer is not to be simply that the offender must suffer, or be made to suffer: her suffering is meaningful, as being intrinsically related to a repentant recognition of wrongdoing (see Tudor 2001); and it is valuable, as the appropriate way both of coming to terms with the wrong she committed and of making reparation for that wrong.

My claim that we should see criminal mediation, and the kinds of reparation to which it leads, as punishment might seem to be nothing more than a merely verbal claim which lacks substantial significance or implications – or even a philosopher's verbal trick, which need not detain those engaged in the practical enterprise of promoting restorative justice. But it is more significant than that, for two reasons.

First, it is a claim about how we should portray the proper aims of 'restorative justice', and thus of mediation programmes which seek restorative justice. The claim is that the kind of restoration that crime, as a kind of public wrongdoing, makes necessary must involve the offender in being pained or burdened – burdened by criticism, by remorse, and by the need to make apologetic reparation. If that is right, restorative justice processes are not alternatives to punitive 'pain delivery': they are themselves ways of trying to induce the appropriate kind of pain.

Second, I would go on to argue – though I cannot do so here – that we should see such processes of mediation and reparation not merely as processes that can count, in an extended or etiolated sense, as punishment, but as paradigms of what punishment ought to be. Criminal punishment should aim to bring offenders to recognize, repent and make moral reparation for their crimes, through a process of moral communication with them – a communication which includes some appropriate kinds of penal 'hard treatment'. Once an offender's guilt has been determined by a criminal trial that calls him to answer the charge of wrongdoing, his sentence would ideally be negotiated in something like a mediation process – with his direct victim if there was one, or with an official (a probation officer, for instance) as representing the victim and the wider community; and that punishment would have the aims, and the meaning, of the moral reparation that I have argued should result from criminal mediation (but it might make more central a feature which is often less prominent in mediation and reparation programmes – the need to get the offender to attend to, to think about, the wrong that he committed). Such negotiated punishments would need to be approved by a criminal court – in part to ensure that the demands of negative proportionality are satisfied: but courts would impose punishments without any such negotiation only when negotiation proved impossible or futile.

Of course, much more needs to be said to explain, develop and defend this view:[22] but I hope that in this chapter I have at least rendered plausible one of the central claims on which it depends – that the kind of 'restoration' which crime makes necessary, and

---

[22] I offer such an explanation, development and defence in Duff 2001.

which mediation and reparation programmes should aim to achieve, is to be achieved precisely through the retributive punishment of the offender. This is not to offer a justification of our existing penal practices, which are for the most part obviously neither designed nor apt to serve the properly restorative ends that punishment should, on my account, serve: it is, rather, to argue that what we should aspire to create is a system which seeks neither restoration rather than retribution, nor retribution rather than restoration, but restoration through retribution.

VI

SOCIAL THEORIES

Life and punishment are more complicated than philosophers and legal theorists usually want to acknowledge. Social theorists try to describe the functions punishment performs and to explain why it takes the forms that it does, rather than to justify it in normative terms. Social institutions and practices exist for reasons, and they are not always obvious. The three most influential functionalist analyses relating to the criminal law and punishment are associated with the French writer Emile Durkheim, the German writer Karl Marx and some of his followers, and the French writer Michele Foucault.[1] Legislators or practitioners may believe themselves to be concerned with sanctioning and preventing crimes. A social theorist might observe that while that is what they think they are doing, they are actually doing other things—for example, reinforcing basic social norms (Durkheim), protecting the interests of the powerful (Marx), or tailoring individuals to fit the roles they must play in modern bureaucratic society (Foucault). Contemporary social theorists (e.g., Garland 2001; Simon 2007) make a different kind of argument when they suggest that criminal law and punishment often are used to achieve conscious goals other than to reduce crime, to increase public safety, or to impose deserved or otherwise appropriate punishments.

When social theorists write about punishment's functions, they seldom mean crime-preventive effects such as rehabilitation, deterrence, and incapacitation. Instead, they are interested in broader social processes. Work by the French sociologist Loïc

---

[1] Garland (1990) long has been and remains that best synthesis of writings by social theorists on punishment.

Wacquant (2002a [chapter 25 in this volume], 2002b) provides an illustration. Modern American punishment policies and practices, he argues, operate to maintain existing patterns of social, economic, and political domination of blacks by whites. Punishment, in his analysis, is the latest in a series of social and legal institutions that have maintained a racial hierarchy. The earlier ones were slavery, "Jim Crow" laws and social conventions that allowed explicit racial discrimination after the Civil War, and the urban ghettos of mid- and late-twentieth-century America. In our time, he argues, mass imprisonment and a wide array of criminal justice policies and practices perform that role. When one form of hierarchy maintenance becomes no longer possible or effective, another one takes its place. This is not because a self-perpetuating racist cabal makes it happen. It is just how things are.

Durkheim (1933 [1893], 1982 [chapter 27 in this volume]) argued that the criminal law is primarily a mechanism for declaring, reinforcing, and changing basic social norms about wrongful behaviors. The criminal law's ostensible functions of incapacitation, deterrence, and rehabilitation are not, he argued, very important (or especially effective). Criminal convictions and punishments serve instead to channel public dissatisfaction and indignation about wrongdoing and wrongdoers and through those processes to reaffirm behavioral norms. Criminal trials and punishments serve as morality plays that denounce bad behaviors and validate good ones. Practitioners and lawmakers may act and talk as if the criminal law affects behavior by changing or controlling peoples' behavior, Durkheim would say, but they are mistaken. What they are doing, even if it is not what they think they are doing, is important all the same.

Many Scandinavian judges and scholars subscribe to ideas akin to Durkheim's (e.g., Andenaes 1974; Lappi-Seppälä 2001 [chapter 15 in this volume]). They believe with Durkheim that incapacitation, deterrence, and rehabilitation have at best marginal influence on crime; except under extreme conditions, people do or do not commit crimes because they have or have not been socialized into values with which much criminality is incompatible. They also believe that law's role is collateral; families, schools, churches, neighborhoods, and other primary institutions do the heavy lifting in instilling and reinforcing social norms. But they believe it important that the law back up those norms. As a result, though criminal punishments in Scandinavia are not severe by international standards, punishments are more likely to be imposed than elsewhere (so that bad behavior has consequences) and are highly proportionate (so that norms about the comparative seriousness of different kinds of misconduct are not undermined). Scandinavians refer to law's "moral-educative" or "general-preventive" effects as its most important ones.

Karl Marx might be expected to have written about the criminal law as an institution for furthering the interests of the dominant economic classes, but he wrote little on the subject (e.g., Marx 1853). Others did, most influentially the German scholars Georg Rusche and Otto Kirschheimer (1968 [1939]; see also Rusche 1978 [chapter 26 in this volume]). They tried to show that the criminal law, and especially prisons and capital punishment, are best understood as mechanisms by which societies adapt to changing economic and labor market conditions. When economies are strong and labor is valuable and in demand, prison use and executions fall: able-bodied workers are too valuable to waste. When economies are weak and workers are idle and not economically valuable, prisons fill, prison conditions worsen, and executions rise ("life is cheap").

Michele Foucault (1979 [chapter 28 in this volume]) argued that punishment forms vary over time and serve different functions depending on historical circumstance. Before the Enlightenment, and the development of modern bureaucratized police, court, and prison systems, punishments though rare were sometimes extravagantly severe and served to emphasize and celebrate the power of the state. Beginning in the nineteenth century, however, the primary function of punishment (and of other mass institutions like schools, armies, industrial factories) became the socialization and reformation of people into conformity with the kinds of roles a mass and heavily bureaucratized society requires be played.

Contemporary social theorists analyze other ways the criminal law and punishment are used by politicians to achieve goals besides crime prevention or imposition of deserved or otherwise appropriate punishments. Garland (2001) focuses on punishment policies as primarily "expressive," meant more to acknowledge public anxieties and demonstrate that something is being done about crime than to affect crime rates or patterns. The aim sought—the expression—is accomplished when policies or decisions are announced, and it does not much matter whether they are effective. Simon (2007) focuses on ways that emotional and moralistic appeals related to crime and criminals are used by politicians to attract and retain general political support that then empowers them to do other things they care more about.

REFERENCES

Bibliographic details concerning works that are mentioned but are not reprinted in this volume can be found in the reference list to the introduction except for the following:

Andenaes, Johannes. 1974. *Punishment and Deterrence.* Ann Arbor: University of Michigan Press.

Durkheim, Emile. 1933 [1893]. *The Division of Labor in Society.* Trans. George Simpson. New York: Macmillan (orig. pub. 1893).

Garland, David. 1990. *Punishment and Modern Society.* Chicago: University of Chicago Press.

———. 2001. *The Culture of Complaint.* Chicago: University of Chicago Press.

Marx, Karl. 1853. "Capital Punishment—Mr. Cobden's Pamphlet's—Regulations of the Bank of England." *New York Tribune* (February 17), p. 3.

Rusche, Georg, and Otto Kirchheimer 1968. *Punishment and Social Structure.* New York: Russell & Russell. (Orig. pub. 1939). New York: Columbia University Press.

Simon, Jonathan. 2007. *Governing Through Crime: How the War on Crime Transformed American Democracy and Created a Culture of Fear.* New York: Oxford University Press.

Wacquant, Loïc. 2002a. "From Slavery to Mass Incarceration: Rethinking the 'Race Question' in the U.S." *New Left Review* 13 (January–February):41–60.

———. 2002b. "Deadly Symbiosis: Rethinking Race and Imprisonment in Twenty-First-Century America." *Boston Review* (April–May).

25

FROM SLAVERY TO MASS INCARCERATION

RETHINKING THE "RACE QUESTION" IN THE US
Loïc Wacquant

NOT ONE BUT SEVERAL 'peculiar institutions' have successively operated to define, confine, and control African-Americans in the history of the United States. The first is *chattel slavery* as the pivot of the plantation economy and inceptive matrix of racial division from the colonial era to the Civil War. The second is the *Jim Crow system* of legally enforced discrimination and segregation from cradle to grave that anchored the predominantly agrarian society of the South from the close of Reconstruction to the Civil Rights revolution which toppled it a full century after abolition. America's third special device for containing the descendants of slaves in the Northern industrial metropolis is the *ghetto*, corresponding to the conjoint urbanization and proletarianization of African-Americans from the Great Migration of 1914–30 to the 1960s, when it was rendered partially obsolete by the concurrent transformation of economy and state and by the mounting protest of blacks against continued caste exclusion, climaxing with the explosive urban riots chronicled in the Kerner Commission Report.[1]

The fourth, I contend here, is the novel institutional complex formed by the *remnants of the dark ghetto and the carceral apparatus* with which it has become joined by a linked relationship of structural symbiosis and functional surrogacy. This suggests that slavery and mass imprisonment are genealogically linked and that one cannot understand the latter—its timing, composition, and smooth onset as well as the quiet

---

[1] See, respectively: Kenneth Stampp, *The Peculiar Institution: Slavery in the Ante-Bellum South*, New York [1956] 1989; Ira Berlin, *Many Thousands Gone: The First Two Centuries of Slavery in North America*, Cambridge, MA 1998; C. Vann Woodward, *The Strange Career of Jim Crow*, Oxford [1957] 1989; Leon Litwack, *Trouble in Mind: Black Southerners in the Age of Jim Crow*, New York 1998; Allan Spear, *Black Chicago: The Making of a Negro Ghetto, 1890–1920*, Chicago 1968; Kerner Commission, 1968 *Report of the National Advisory Commission on Civil Disorders*, New York [1968] 1988.

Racial disproportionality in US imprisonment

Three brute facts stand out and give a measure of the grotesquely disproportionate impact of mass incarceration on African-Americans. First, the ethnic composition of the inmate population of the United States has been virtually inverted *in the last half-century, going from about 70% (Anglo) white at the mid-century point to less than 30% today. Contrary to common perception, the predominance of blacks behind bars is not a long-standing pattern but a novel and recent phenomenon, with 1988 as the turning point: it is the year when then- Vice-President George Bush ran his infamous 'Willie Horton' advertisement during the presidential campaign, featuring sinister images of the black rapist of a white woman as emblematic of the contemporary 'crime problem,' as well as the year after which African-American men supply a majority of prison admissions for the country as a whole.*[1]

Next, whereas the difference between arrest rates for whites and blacks has been stable, with the percentage of blacks oscillating between 29% and 33% of all arrestees for property crimes and between 44 and 47% for violent offences between 1976 and 1992,[2] *the white-black incarceration gap has grown rapidly in the past quarter-century, jumping from 1 for 5 in 1985 to about 1 for 8 today. This trend is all the more striking for occurring during a period when significant numbers of African-Americans have entered into and risen through the ranks of the police, the courts, and the corrections administration and when the more overt forms of racial discrimination that were commonplace in them into the seventies have been greatly reduced, if not stamped out.*[3]

Lastly, the lifelong cumulative probability of 'doing time' in a state or federal penitentiary based on the imprisonment rates of the early 90s is 4% for whites, 16% for Latinos and a staggering 29% for blacks.[4] *Given the class gradient of incarceration, this figure suggests that* a majority of African-Americans of (sub)proletarian status are facing a prison term of one or several years (and in many cases several terms) at some point in their adult life, with all the family, occupational and legal disruptions this entails, including the curtailment of social entitlements and civil rights and the temporary or permanent loss of the right to vote. As of 1997, nearly one black man in six nationwide was excluded from the ballot box due to a felony conviction and more than one fifth of them were prohibited from casting a vote in Alabama, Connecticut, Florida, Iowa, Mississippi, New Mexico, Texas, Washington, and Wyoming.[5] A short thirty-five years after the Civil Rights movement finally gained African-Americans effective access to the voting booth, a full century after Abolition, this right is being taken back by the penal system via legal dispositions that are of dubious constitutional validity and violate in many cases (notably lifetime disenfranchisement) international conventions on human rights ratified by the United States.

---

[1]   *David Anderson*, Crime and the Politics of Hysteria, *New York 1995.*
[2]   *Michael Tonry*, Malign Neglect, *Oxford 1995. p. 64.*
[3]   *Alfred Blumstein, 'Racial Disproportionality of US Prisons Revisited'.* University of Colorado Law Review, *vol. 64, 1993. pp. 743–60: but see the powerful counter-argument offered by David Cole, No Equal Justice. New York 1999.*
[4]   *Thomas Bonczar and Allen Beck, 'Lifetime Likelihood of Going to State or Federal Prison',* Bureau of Justice Statistics Special Report, *Washington, BJS, March 1997. p. 1; for a state-by-state analysis, see Marc Mauer, 'Racial Disparities in Prison Getting Worse in the 1990s',* Overcrowded Times, *vol. 8, no. 1, February 1997, pp. 9–13.*
[5]   *John Hagan and Ronit Dinowitzer, 'Collateral Consequences of Imprisonment for Children, Communities, and Prisoners', in Michael Tonry and Joan Petersilia, eds.,* Prisons, *Chicago 1999. pp. 121–62; and Jamie Fellner and Marc Mauer,* Losing the Vote: the Impact of Felony Disenfranchisement in the US, *Washington 1998.*

TABLE I. The Four "Peculiar Institutions" and Their Basis

Institution	Form of Labour	Core of Economy	Dominant Social Type
slavery (1619–1865)	unfree fixed labor	plantation	slave
Jim Crow (South, 1865–1965)	free fixed labour	agrarian and extractive	sharecropper
ghetto (North, 1915–68)	free mobile labour	segmented industrial manufacturing	menial worker
hyperghetto and prison (1968–)	fixed surplus labor	polarized postindustrial services	welfare recipient and criminal

ignorance or acceptance of its deleterious effects on those it affects—without returning to the former as historic starting point and functional analogue.

Viewed against the backdrop of the full historical trajectory of racial domination in the United States (summed up in Table 1), the glaring and growing 'disproportionality' in incarceration that has afflicted African-Americans over the past three decades can be understood as the result of the 'extra-penological' functions that the prison system has come to shoulder in the wake of the crisis of the ghetto and of the continuing stigma that afflicts the descendants of slaves by virtue of their membership in a group constitutively deprived of ethnic honour (Max Weber's *Massehre*).

Not crime, but the need to shore up an eroding caste cleavage, along with buttressing the emergent regime of desocialized wage labour to which most blacks are fated by virtue of their lack of marketable cultural capital, and which the most deprived among them resist by escaping into the illegal street economy, is the main impetus behind the stupendous expansion of America's penal state in the post-Keynesian age and its de facto policy of 'carceral affirmative action' towards African-Americans.[2]

LABOUR EXTRACTION AND CASTE DIVISION

America's first three 'peculiar institutions', slavery, Jim Crow, and the ghetto, have this in common: they were all instruments for the conjoint *extraction of labour* and *social ostracization* of an outcast group deemed unassimilable by virtue of the indelible threefold stigma it carries. African-Americans arrived under bondage in the land of freedom. They were accordingly deprived of the right to vote in the self-appointed cradle of democracy (until 1965 for residents of the Southern states). And, for lack of a recognizable national affiliation, they were shorn of ethnic honour, which implies that, rather than simply standing at the bottom of the rank ordering of group prestige in American society, they were barred from it *ab initio*.[3]

---

[2] See my 'Crime et châtiment en Amérique de Nixon à Clinton', *Archives de politique criminelle*, vol. 20, pp. 123–38; and *Les Prisons de la misère*, Paris 1999, pp. 71–94 (English trans. *Prisons of Poverty*, Minneapolis 2002).

[3] 'Among the groups commonly considered unassimilable, the Negro people is by far the largest. The Negroes do not, like the Japanese and the Chinese, have a politically organized nation and an accepted culture of their own outside of America to fall back upon. Unlike the Oriental, there attaches to the Negro an historical memory of slavery and inferiority. It is more difficult for them to answer prejudice with prejudice and, as the Orientals may do, to consider themselves and their history superior to the

1. *Slavery (1619–1865)*. Slavery is a highly malleable and versatile institution that can be harnessed to a variety of purposes, but in the Americas property-in-person was geared primarily to the provision and control of labour.[4] Its introduction in the Chesapeake, Middle Atlantic and Low Country regions of the United States in the 17th century served to recruit and regulate the unfree workforce forcibly imported from Africa and the West Indies to cater to their tobacco, rice and mixed-farming economy. (Indentured labourers from Europe and native Indians were not enslaved because of their greater capacity to resist and because their servitude would have impeded future immigration as well as rapidly exhausted a limited supply of labour.) By the close of the 18th century, slavery had become self-reproducing and expanded to the fertile crescent of the Southern interior, running from South Carolina to Louisiana, where it supplied a highly profitable organization of labour for cotton production and the basis for a plantation society distinctive for its feudal-like culture, politics, and psychology.[5]

An *unforeseen by-product* of the systematic enslavement and dehumanization of Africans and their descendants on North American soil was the creation of a racial caste line separating what would later become labelled 'blacks' and 'whites.' As Barbara Fields has shown, the American ideology of 'race', as putative biological division anchored by the inflexible application of the 'one-drop rule' together with the principle of hypodescent, crystallized to resolve the blatant contradiction between human bondage and democracy.[6] The religious and pseudo-scientific belief in racial difference reconciled the brute fact of unfree labor with the doctrine of liberty premised on natural rights by reducing the slave to live property—three-fifths of a man according the sacred scriptures of the Constitution.

2. *Jim Crow (South, 1865–1965)*. Racial division was a consequence, not a precondition, of US slavery, but once it was instituted it became detached from its initial function and acquired a social potency of its own. Emancipation thus created a double dilemma for Southern white society: how to secure anew the labour of former slaves, without whom the region's economy would collapse, and how to sustain the cardinal

---

white Americans and their recent cultural achievements. The Negroes do not have these fortifications of self-respect. They are more helplessly *imprisoned* as a subordinate caste, a caste of people deemed to be lacking a cultural past and assumed to be incapable of a cultural future.' Gunnar Myrdal, *An American Dilemma: The Negro Problem and Modern Democracy*. New York [1944] 1962, p. 54; emphasis added.

[4] Seymour Drescher and Stanley Engerman, *A Historical Guide to World Slavery*, Oxford 1998.

[5] Gavin Wright, *The Political Economy of the Cotton South*, New York 1978; Peter Kolchin, *American Slavery: 1619–1877*, New York 1993.

[6] 'Slavery, Race and Ideology in the United States of America', NLR 1/181, May–June 1990.

status distinction between whites and 'persons of colour,' i.e, the social and symbolic distance needed to prevent the odium of 'amalgamation' with a group considered inferior, rootless and vile. After a protracted interregnum lasting into the 1890s, during which early white hysteria gave way to partial if inconsistent relaxation of ethnoracial strictures, when blacks were allowed to vote, to hold public office, and even to mix with whites to a degree in keeping with the intergroup intimacy fostered by slavery, the solution came in the form of the 'Jim Crow' regime.[7] It consisted of an ensemble of social and legal codes that prescribed the complete separation of the 'races' and sharply circumscribed the life chances of African-Americans while binding them to whites in a relation of suffusive submission backed by legal coercion and terroristic violence.

Imported from the North where it had been experimented within cities, this regime stipulated that blacks travel in separate trains, streetcars and waiting rooms; that they reside in the 'darktown' slums and be educated in separate schools (if at all); that they patronize separate service establishments and use their own bathrooms and water fountains; that they pray in separate churches, entertain themselves in separate clubs and sit in separate 'nigger galleries' in theatres; that they receive medical care in separate hospitals and exclusively from 'coloured' staff; and that they be incarcerated in separate cells and buried in separate cemeteries. Most crucial of all, laws joined mores in condemning the 'unspeakable crime' of interracial marriage, cohabitation or mere sexual congress so as to uphold the 'supreme law of self-preservation' of the races and the myth of innate white superiority. Through continued white ownership of the land and the generalization of sharecropping and debt peonage, the plantation system remained virtually untouched as former slaves became a 'dependent, propertyless peasantry, nominally free, but ensnared by poverty, ignorance, and the new servitude of tenantry'.[8] While sharecropping tied African-American labour to the farm, a rigid etiquette ensured that whites and blacks never interacted on a plane of equality, not even on the running track or in a boxing ring—a Birmingham ordinance of 1930 made it unlawful for them to play at checkers and dominoes with one another.[9] Whenever the 'colour line' was breached or even brushed, a torrent of violence was unleashed in the form of periodic pogroms, Ku Klux Klan and vigilante raids, public floggings, mob killings and lynchings, this ritual caste murder designed to keep 'uppity niggers' in their appointed place. All this was made possible by the swift and near-complete disenfranchisement of blacks as well as by the enforcement of 'Negro law' by courts

---

[7] The term comes from a song-and-dance routine, 'Jumping Jim Crow', first performed in 1828 by Thomas Dartmouth Rice, a popular travelling actor considered the father of the 'black-and-white' minstrel show; see Woodward, *Strange Career of Jim Crow*.

[8] Neil McMillen, *Dark Journey: Black Mississippians in the Age of Jim Crow*, Urbana 1990.

[9] The Mississippi legislature went so far as to outlaw the advocacy of social equality between blacks and whites. A law of 1920 subjected to a fine of 500 dollars and 6 months' jail anyone 'found guilty of printing, publishing or circulating arguments in favour of social equality or intermarriage': McMillen, *Dark Journey*, pp. 8–9.

which granted the latter fewer effective legal safeguards than slaves had enjoyed earlier by dint of being both property and persons.

3. *Ghetto (North, 1915–68).* The sheer brutality of caste oppression in the South, the decline of cotton agriculture due to floods and the boll weevil, and the pressing shortage of labour in Northern factories caused by the outbreak of World War I created the impetus for African-Americans to emigrate en masse to the booming industrial centers of the Midwest and Northeast (over 1.5 million left in 1910–30, followed by another 3 million in 1940–60). But as migrants from Mississippi to the Carolinas flocked to the Northern metropolis, what they discovered there was not the 'promised land' of equality and full citizenship but another system of racial enclosure, the ghetto, which, though it was less rigid and fearsome than the one they had fled, was no less encompassing and constricting. To be sure, greater freedom to come and go in public places and to consume in regular commercial establishments, the disappearance of the humiliating signs pointing to 'Coloured' here and 'White' there, renewed access to the ballot box and protection from the courts, the possibility of limited economic advancement, release from personal subservience and from the dread of omnipresent white violence, all made life in the urban North incomparably preferable to continued peonage in the rural South: it was 'better to be a lamppost in Chicago than President of Dixie,' as migrants famously put it to Richard Wright. But restrictive covenants forced African-Americans to congregate in a 'Black Belt' which quickly became overcrowded, underserved and blighted by crime, disease, and dilapidation, while the 'job ceiling' restricted them to the most hazardous, menial, and underpaid occupations in both industry and personal services. As for 'social equality', understood as the possibility of 'becoming members of white cliques, churches and voluntary associations, or marrying into their families', it was firmly and definitively denied.[10]

Blacks had entered the Fordist industrial economy, to which they contributed a vital source of abundant and cheap labour willing to ride along its cycles of boom and bust. Yet they remained locked in a precarious position of structural economic marginality and consigned to a secluded and dependent microcosm, complete with its own internal division of labour, social stratification, and agencies of collective voice and symbolic representation: a 'city within the city' moored in a complexus of black churches and press, businesses and professional practices, fraternal lodges and

---

[10] St. Clair Drake and Horace Cayton, *Black Metropolis: A Study of Negro Life in a Northern City*, New York [1945] 1962, vol. 1, pp. 112–28.

communal associations that provided both a 'milieu for Negro Americans in which they [could] imbue their lives with meaning' and a bulwark 'to "protect" white America from "social contact" with Negroes'.[11] Continued caste hostility from without and renewed ethnic affinity from within converged to create the ghetto as the third vehicle to extract black labour while keeping black bodies at a safe distance, to the material and symbolic benefit of white society.

The era of the ghetto as paramount mechanism of ethnoracial domination had opened with the urban riots of 1917–19 (in East St. Louis, Chicago, Longview, Houston, etc.). It closed with a wave of clashes, looting and burning that rocked hundreds of American cities from coast to coast, from the Watts uprising of 1965 to the riots of rage and grief triggered by the assassination of Martin Luther King in the summer of 1968. Indeed, by the end of the sixties, the ghetto was well on its way to becoming functionally obsolete or, to be more precise, increasingly *unsuited* to accomplishing the twofold task historically entrusted to America's 'peculiar institutions.' On the side of *labour extraction*, the shift from an urban industrial economy to a suburban service economy and the accompanying dualization of the occupational structure, along with the upsurge of working-class immigration from Mexico, the Caribbean and Asia, meant that large segments of the workforce contained in the 'Black Belts' of the Northern metropolis were simply no longer needed. On the side of *ethnoracial closure*, the decades-long mobilization of African-Americans against caste rule finally succeeded, in the propitious political conjuncture of crisis stemming from the Vietnam war and assorted social unrest, in forcing the federal state to dismantle the legal machinery of caste exclusion. Having secured voting and civil rights, blacks were at long last full citizens who would no longer brook being shunted off into the separate and inferior world of the ghetto.[12]

But while whites begrudgingly accepted 'integration' in principle, in practice they strove to maintain an unbridgeable social and symbolic gulf with their compatriots of African descent. They abandoned public schools, shunned public space, and fled to the suburbs in their millions to avoid mixing and ward off the spectre of 'social equality' in the city. They then turned against the welfare state and those social programmes upon which the collective advancement of blacks was most dependent. *A contrario*, they extended enthusiastic support for the 'law-and-order' policies that vowed to firmly repress urban disorders connately perceived as racial threats.[13] Such policies pointed to yet another special institution capable of confining and controlling if not the entire

---

[11] *Black Metropolis*, vol. 2, p. xiv.

[12] This was the meaning of Martin Luther King's Freedom Campaign in the summer of 1966 in Chicago: it sought to apply to the ghetto the techniques of collective mobilization and civil disobedience successfully used in the attack on Jim Crow in the South, to reveal and protest against the life to which blacks were condemned in the Northern metropolis. The campaign to make Chicago an open city was swiftly crushed by formidable repression, spearheaded by 4,000 National Guards. Stephen Oakes, *Let the Trumpet Sound: A Life of Martin Luther King*, New York 1982.

[13] Thomas Byrne Edsall and Mary Edsall, *Chain Reaction: The Impact of Race, Rights and Taxes on American Politics*, New York 1991; Jill Quadagno, *The Colour of Welfare: How Racism Undermined the War on Poverty*, Oxford 1994; Katherine Beckett and Theodore Sasson, *The Politics of Injustice*, Thousand Oaks 2000, pp. 49–74.

African-American community, at least its most disruptive, disreputable and dangerous members: the prison.

The ghetto as prison, the prison as ghetto

To grasp the deep kinship between ghetto and prison, which helps explain how the structural decline and functional redundancy of the one led to the unexpected ascent and astonishing growth of the other during the last quarter-century, it is necessary first to characterize accurately the ghetto.[14] But here we come upon the troublesome fact that the social sciences have failed to develop a robust *analytic concept* of the ghetto; instead they have been content to borrow the *folk concept* current in political and popular discourse at each epoch. This has caused a good deal of confusion, as the ghetto has been successively conflated with—and mistaken for—a segregated district, an ethnic neighbourhood, a territory of intense poverty or housing blight and even, with the rise of the policy myth of the 'underclass' in the more recent period, a mere accumulation of urban pathologies and antisocial behaviours.[15]

A comparative and historical sociology of the reserved Jewish quarters in the cities of Renaissance Europe and of America's 'Bronzeville' in the Fordist metropolis of the twentieth century reveals that a ghetto is essentially a sociospatial device that enables a dominant status group in an urban setting simultaneously to ostracize and exploit a subordinate group endowed with negative symbolic capital, that is, an incarnate property perceived to make its contact degrading by virtue of what Max Weber calls 'negative social estimation of honour.' Put differently, it is a relation of ethnoracial control and closure built out of four elements: (i) stigma; (ii) constraint; (iii) territorial confinement; and (iv) institutional encasement. The resulting formation is a distinct *space*, containing an ethnically homogeneous *population*, which finds itself forced to develop within it a set of interlinked *institutions* that duplicates the organizational framework of the broader society from which that group is banished and supplies the scaffoldings for the construction of its specific 'style of life' and social strategies. This parallel institutional nexus affords the subordinate group a measure of protection, autonomy and dignity, but at the cost of locking it in a relationship of structural subordination and dependency.

The ghetto, in short, operates as an *ethnoracial prison*: it encages a dishonoured category and severely curtails the life chances of its members in support of the 'monopolization of ideal and material goods or opportunities' by the dominant status group dwelling on its outskirts.[16] Recall that the ghettos of early modern Europe were typically

---

[14] By 1975 the carceral population of the US had been steadily declining for nearly two decades to reach a low of 380,000 inmates. The leading analysts of the penal question, from David Rothman to Michel Foucault to Alfred Blumstein, were then unanimous in predicting the imminent marginalization of the prison as an institution of social control or, at worst, the stabilization of penal confinement at a historically moderate level. No one foresaw the runaway growth that has quadrupled that figure to over two million in 2000 even as crime levels remained stagnant.

[15] See my 'Gutting the Ghetto' for a historical recapitulation of the meanings of 'ghetto' in American society and social science, leading to a diagnosis of the curious expurgation of race from a concept expressly forged to denote a mechanism of ethnoracial domination, which ties it to the changing concerns of state elites over the nexus of poverty and ethnicity in the metropolis. In Malcolm Cross and Robert Moore, eds, *Globalization and the New City*, Basingstoke 2000.

[16] Max Weber, *Economy and Society*, Berkeley 1978, p. 935.

delimited by high walls with one or more gates which were locked at night and within which Jews had to return before sunset on pain of severe punishment, and that their perimeter was subjected to continuous monitoring by external authorities.[17] Note next the structural and functional homologies with the prison conceptualized as a *judicial ghetto*: a jail or penitentiary is in effect a reserved *space* which serves to forcibly confine a legally denigrated *population* and wherein this latter evolves its distinctive *institutions*, culture and sullied identity. It is thus formed of the same four fundamental constituents—stigma, coercion, physical enclosure and organizational parallelism and insulation—that make up a ghetto, and for similar purposes.

Much as the ghetto protects the city's residents from the pollution of intercourse with the tainted but necessary bodies of an outcast group in the manner of an 'urban condom,' as Richard Sennett vividly put it in his depiction of the 'fear of touching' in sixteenth-century Venice,[18] the prison cleanses the social body from the temporary blemish of those of its members who have committed crimes, that is, following Durkheim, individuals who have violated the sociomoral integrity of the collectivity by infringing on 'definite and strong states of the collective conscience.' Students of the 'inmate society' from Donald Clemmer and Gresham Sykes to James Jacobs and John Irwin have noted time and again how the incarcerated develop their own argot roles, exchange systems and normative standards, whether as an adaptive response to the 'pains of imprisonment' or through selective importation of criminal and lower-class values from the outside, much like residents of the ghetto have elaborated or intensified a 'separate sub-culture' to counter their sociosymbolic immurement.[19] As for the secondary aim of the ghetto, to facilitate exploitation of the interned category, it was central to the 'house of correction' which is the direct historical predecessor of the modern prison and it has periodically played a major role in the evolution and operation of the latter.[20] Finally, both prison and ghetto are authority structures saddled with inherently dubious or problematic legitimacy whose maintenance is ensured by intermittent recourse to external force.

By the end of the seventies, then, as the racial and class backlash against the democratic advances won by the social movements of the preceding decade got into full swing, the prison abruptly returned to the forefront of American society and offered itself as the universal and simplex solution to all manners of social problems. Chief among these problems was the 'breakdown' of social order in the 'inner city,' which is scholarly and policy euphemism for the patent incapacity of the dark ghetto to contain a dishonoured and supernumerary population henceforth viewed not only as deviant and devious but as downright dangerous in light of the violent urban upheavals of mid-sixties. As the walls of

---

[17] Louis Wirth, *The Ghetto*, Chicago 1928.

[18] *Flesh and Stone: The Body and the City in Western Civilization*, New York 1994.

[19] *Black Metropolis*, vol. 2, p. xiii.

[20] Describing London's Bridewell, the *Zuchthaus* of Amsterdam and the Paris *Hôpital général*, Georg Rusche and Otto Kirschheimer show that the main aim of the house of correction was 'to make the labour power of the unwilling people socially useful' by forcing them to work under close supervision in the hope that, once released, 'they would voluntarily swell the labour market'. *Punishment and Social Structure*, New York 1939, p. 42; for the modern prison, see Pieter Spierenburg, *The Prison Experience*, New Brunswick, NJ 1991.

the ghetto shook and threatened to crumble, the walls of the prison were correspondingly extended, enlarged and fortified, and 'confinement of differentiation', aimed at keeping a group apart (the etymological meaning of *segregare*), gained primacy over 'confinement of safety' and 'confinement of authority'—to use the distinction proposed by French sociologist Claude Faugeron.[21] Soon the black ghetto, converted into an instrument of naked exclusion by the concurrent retrenchment of wage labour and social protection, and further destabilized by the increasing penetration of the penal arm of the state, became bound to the jail and prison system by a triple relationship of functional equivalency, structural homology and cultural syncretism, such that they now constitute a single *carceral continuum* which entraps a redundant population of younger black men (and increasingly women) who circulate in closed circuit between its two poles in a self-perpetuating cycle of social and legal marginality with devastating personal and social consequences.[22]

Now, the carceral system had already functioned as an *ancillary* institution for caste preservation and labour control in America during one previous transition between regimes of racial domination, that between slavery and Jim Crow in the South. On the morrow of Emancipation, Southern prisons turned black overnight as 'thousands of ex-slaves were being arrested, tried, and convicted for acts that in the past had been dealt with by the master alone' and for refusing to behave as menials and follow the demeaning rules of racial etiquette. Soon thereafter, the former confederate states introduced 'convict leasing' as a response to the moral panic of 'Negro crime' that presented the double advantage of generating prodigious funds for the state coffers and furnishing abundant bound labour to till the fields, build the levees, lay down the railroads, clean the swamps, and dig the mines of the region under murderous conditions.[23] Indeed, penal labour, in the form of the convict-lease and its heir, the chain gang, played a major role in the economic advancement of the New South during the Progressive era, as it 'reconciled modernization with the continuation of racial domination'.[24]

What makes the racial intercession of the carceral system different today is that, unlike slavery, Jim Crow and the ghetto of mid-century, it does not carry out a positive economic mission of recruitment and disciplining of the workforce: it serves only to warehouse the precarious and deproletarianized fractions of the black working class, be it that they cannot find employment owing to a combination of skills deficit, employer discrimination and competition from immigrants, or that they refuse to submit to the indignity of substandard work in the peripheral sectors of the service economy—what ghetto residents commonly label 'slave jobs.' But there is presently

---

[21] 'La dérive pénale', *Esprit* 215, October 1995.

[22] A fuller discussion of this 'deadly symbiosis' between ghetto and prison in the post-Civil Rights era is provided in my 'Deadly Symbiosis', *Punishment and Society*, vol. 3, no. 1, pp. 95–134.

[23] This is not a figure of speech: the annual mortality rate for convicts reached 16 per cent in Mississippi in the 1880s, where 'not a single leased convict ever lived long enough to serve a sentence of ten years or more'. Hundreds of black children, many as young as six years old, were leased by the state for the benefit of planters, businessmen and financers, to toil in conditions that even some patrician Southerners found shameful and 'a stain upon our manhood'. See David Oshinsky, *Worse Than Slavery: Parchman Farm and the Ordeal of Jim Crow Justice*, New York 1996, p. 45.

[24] Alex Lichtenstein, *Twice the Work of Free Labour: The Political Economy of Convict Labour in the New South*, London and New York 1999, p. 195.

mounting financial and ideological pressure, as well as renewed political interest, to relax restrictions on penal labour so as to (re)introduce mass unskilled work in private enterprises inside American prisons: putting most inmates to work would help lower the country's 'carceral bill' as well as effectively extend to the inmate poor the work-fare requirements now imposed upon the free poor as a requirement of citizenship.[25] The next decade will tell whether the prison remains an appendage to the dark ghetto or supersedes it to go it alone and become America's fourth 'peculiar institution.'

RACE MAKING AND SOCIAL DEATH

Slavery, the Jim Crow system and the ghetto are 'race making' institutions, which is to say that they do not simply process an ethnoracial division that would somehow exist outside of and independently from them. Rather, each *produces* (or co-produces) this division (anew) out of inherited demarcations and disparities of group power and inscribes it at every epoch in a distinctive constellation of material and symbolic forms. And all have consistently racialized the arbitrary boundary setting African-Americans apart from all others in the United States by actively denying its cultural origin in history, ascribing it instead to the fictitious necessity of biology.

The highly particular conception of 'race' that America has invented, virtually unique in the world for its rigidity and consequentiality, is a direct outcome of the momentous collision between slavery and democracy as modes of organization of social life *after* bondage had been established as the major form of labour conscription and control in a underpopulated colony home to a precapitalist system of production. The Jim Crow regime reworked the racialized boundary between slave and free into a rigid caste separation between 'whites' and 'Negros'—comprising all persons of known African ancestry, no matter how minimal—that infected every crevice of the postbellum social system in the South. The ghetto, in turn, imprinted this dichotomy onto the spatial makeup and institutional schemas of the industrial metropolis. So much so that, in the wake of the 'urban riots' of the sixties, which in truth were uprisings against intersecting caste and class subordination, 'urban' and black became near-synonymous in policy making as well as everyday parlance. And the 'crisis' of the city came to stand for the enduring contradiction between the individualistic and competitive tenor of American life, on the one hand, and the continued seclusion of African-Americans from it, on the other.[26]

---

[25] See my *Les Prisons de la misère*, Paris 1999, pp. 71–94. Expert testimony presented to the House Committees on the Judiciary and Crime during discussion of the Prison Industries Reform Act of 1998 explicitly linked welfare reform to the need to expand private prison labour.

[26] Two indicators suffice to spotlight the enduring ostracization of African-Americans in US society. They are the only group to be 'hypersegregated', with spatial isolation shifting from the macro-level of state and county to the micro-level of municipality and neighbourhood so as to minimize contacts with whites throughout the century. See Douglas Massey and Nancy Denton, *American Apartheid*, Cambridge 1993; Douglas Massey and Zoltan Hajnal, 'The Changing Geographic Structure of Black–White Segregation in the United States', *Social Science Quarterly*, vol. 76, no. 3, September 1995, pp. 527–42. They remain barred from exogamy to a degree unknown to any other community, notwithstanding the recent growth of so-called multiracial families, with fewer than 3 per cent of black women marrying out compared to a majority of Hispanic and Asian women. Kim DaCosta, 'Remaking the Colour Line: Social Bases and Implications of the Multiracial Movement,' Berkeley, Ph.D Dissertation.

As a new century dawns, it is up to the fourth 'peculiar institution' born of the adjoining of the hyperghetto with the carceral system to remould the social meaning and significance of 'race' in accordance with the dictates of the deregulated economy and the post-Keynesian state. Now, the penal apparatus has long served as accessory to ethnoracial domination by helping to stabilize a regime under attack or bridge the hiatus between successive regimes: thus the 'Black Codes' of Reconstruction served to keep African-American labour in place following the demise of slavery while the criminalization of civil rights protests in the South in the 1950s aimed to retard the agony of Jim Crow. But the role of the carceral institution today is different in that, for the first time in US history, it has been elevated to the rank of main machine for 'race making.'

Among the manifold effects of the wedding of ghetto and prison into an extended carceral mesh, perhaps the most consequential is the practical revivification and *official solidification of the centuries-old association of blackness within criminality and devious violence*. Along with the return of Lombroso-style mythologies about criminal atavism and the wide diffusion of bestial metaphors in the journalistic and political field (where mentions of 'superpredators', 'wolf-packs', 'animals' and the like are commonplace), the massive over-incarceration of blacks has supplied a powerful common-sense warrant for 'using colour as a proxy for dangerousness'.[27] In recent years, the courts have consistently authorized the police to employ race as 'a negative signal of increased risk of criminality' and legal scholars have rushed to endorse it as 'a rational adaptation to the demographics of crime', made salient and verified, as it were, by the blackening of the prison population, even though such practice entails major inconsistencies from the standpoint of constitutional law. Throughout the urban criminal justice system, the formula 'Young + Black + Male' is now openly equated with 'probable cause' justifying the arrest, questioning, bodily search and detention of millions of African-American males every year.

In the era of racially targeted 'law-and-order' policies and their sociological pendant, racially skewed mass imprisonment, the reigning public image of the criminal is not just that of 'a *monstruum*—a being whose features are inherently different from ours', but that of a *black* monster, as young African-American men from the 'inner city' have come to personify the explosive mix of moral degeneracy and mayhem. The conflation of blackness and crime in collective representation and government policy (the other side of this equation being the conflation of blackness and welfare) thus re-activates 'race' by giving a legitimate outlet to the expression of anti-black animus in the form of the public vituperation of criminals and prisoners. As writer John Edgar Wideman points out:

> It's respectable to tar and feather criminals, to advocate locking them up and throwing away the key. It's not racist to be against crime, even though the archetypal criminal in the media and the public imagination almost always wears 'Willie' Horton's face. Gradually, 'urban' and 'ghetto' have become codewords for terrible places where only blacks reside. Prison is rapidly being re-lexified in the same segregated fashion.[28]

[27] Randall Kennedy, *Race, Crime and the Law*, New York 1997, pp. 136–67.
[28] John Edgar Wideman, 'Doing Time, Marking Race', *The Nation*, 30 October 1995.

Indeed, when 'to be a man of colour of a certain economic class and milieu is equivalent in the public eye to being a criminal', being processed by the penal system is tantamount to being made black, and 'doing time' behind bars is at the same time 'marking race'.[29]

By assuming a central role in the post-Keynesian government of race and poverty, at the crossroads of the deregulated low-wage labour market, a revamped 'welfare-workfare' apparatus designed to support casual employment, and the vestiges of the ghetto, the overgrown carceral system of the United States has become a major engine of symbolic production in its own right. It is not only the pre-eminent institution for signifying and enforcing blackness, much as slavery was during the first three centuries of US history. Just as bondage effected the 'social death' of imported African captives and their descendants on American soil, mass incarceration also induces the civic death of those it ensnares by extruding them from the social compact.[30] Today's inmates are thus the target of a threefold movement of exclusionary closure:

(i) Prisoners are denied access to valued *cultural capital*: just as university credentials are becoming a prerequisite for employment in the (semi) protected sector of the labour market, inmates have been expelled from higher education by being made ineligible for Pell Grants, starting with drug offenders in 1988, continuing with convicts sentenced to death or lifelong imprisonment without the possibility of parole in 1992, and ending with all remaining state and federal prisoners in 1994. This expulsion was voted by Congress for the sole purpose of accentuating the symbolic divide between criminals and 'law-abiding citizens' in spite of overwhelming evidence that prison educational programmes drastically cut recidivism as well as help to maintain carceral order.[31]

(ii) Prisoners are systematically excluded from *social redistribution* and public aid in an age when work insecurity makes access to such programmes more vital than ever for those dwelling in the lower regions of social space. Laws deny welfare payments, veterans' benefits and food stamps to anyone in detention for more than 60 days. The Work Opportunity and Personal Responsibility Act of 1996 further banishes most ex-convicts from Medicaid, public housing, Section 8 vouchers and related forms of assistance. In the spring of 1998, President Clinton denounced as intolerable 'fraud and abuse' perpetrated against 'working families' who 'play by the rules' the fact that some prisoners (or their households) continued to get public payments due to lax bureaucratic enforcement of these prohibitions. And he proudly launched 'unprecedented federal, state, and local cooperation as well as new, innovative incentive programs' using

---

[29] 'Doing Time, Marking Race'.
[30] Orlando Patterson, *Slavery as Social Death*, Cambridge, MA 1982.
[31] Josh Page, 'Eliminating the Enemy: A Cultural Analysis of the Exclusion of Prisoners from Higher Education', MA paper, Department of Sociology, University of California, Berkeley.

the latest 'high-tech tools to weed out any inmate' who still received benefits (see opposite), including the disbursement of bounties to counties who promptly turn in identifying information on their jail detainees to the Social Security administration.

(iii) Convicts are banned from *political participation* via 'criminal disenfranchisement' practised on a scale and with a vigour unimagined in any other country. All but four members of the Union deny the vote to mentally competent adults held in detention facilities; 39 states forbid convicts placed on probation from exercising their political rights and 32 states also interdict parolees. In 14 states, ex-felons are barred from voting even when they are no longer under criminal justice supervision—for life in ten of these states. The result is that nearly 4 million Americans have temporarily or permanently lost the ability to cast a ballot, including 1.47 million who are not behind bars and another 1.39 million who served their sentence in full.[32] A mere quarter of a century after acceding to full voting rights, one black man in seven nationwide is banned from the electoral booth through penal disenfranchisement and seven states permanently deny the vote to more than one fourth of their black male residents.

Through this *triple exclusion*, the prison and the criminal justice system more broadly contribute to the ongoing *reconstruction of the 'imagined community' of Americans* around the polar opposition between praiseworthy 'working families'—implicitly white, suburban, and deserving—and the despicable 'underclass' of criminals, loafers, and leeches, a two-headed antisocial hydra personified by the dissolute teenage 'welfare mother' on the female side and the dangerous street 'gang banger' on the male side—by definition dark-skinned, urban and undeserving. The former are exalted as the living incarnation of genuine American values, self-control, deferred gratification, subservience of life to labour; the latter is vituperated as the loathsome embodiment of their abject desecration, the 'dark side' of the 'American dream' of affluence and opportunity for all, believed to flow from morality anchored in conjugality and work. And the line that divides them is increasingly being drawn, materially and symbolically, by the prison.

On the other side of that line lies an institutional setting unlike any other. Building on his celebrated analyses of Ancient Greece, classical historian Moses Finley has introduced a fruitful distinction between 'societies with slaves' and 'genuine slave societies.'[33] In the former, slavery is but one of several modes of labour control and the division between slave and free is neither impermeable nor axial to the entire social order. In the latter, enslaved labour is epicentral to both economic production and class structure, and the slave-master relation provides the pattern after which all other social relations are built or distorted, such that no corner of culture, society and self is

[32] Jamie Fellner and Marc Mauer, *Losing the Vote.*
[33] 'Slavery', *International Encyclopaedia of the Social Sciences*, New York 1968.

Clinton proudly 'cracks down' on inmate 'fraud and abuse'

Good morning. This morning I'd like to talk to you about one way we are working to restore Americans' faith in our national government, in our efforts to shore up Social Security and other vital benefits by cracking down on fraud and abuse.

For 60 years, Social Security has meant more than just an ID number on a tax form, even more than a monthly check in the mail. It has reflected our deepest values, the duties we owe to our parents, to each other, to our children and grandchildren, to those who misfortune strikes, to those who deserve a decent old age, to our ideal of one America.

That's why I was so disturbed some time ago to discover that many prisoners who are, by law, barred from receiving most of these federal benefits, were actually collecting Social Security checks while locked up behind bars. Inmates were, in effect, under our law, getting away with fraud, primarily because it was so difficult to gather up-to-date information on criminals in our nation's more than 3,500 jails. But thanks to an unprecedented federal, state, and local cooperation, as well as new, innovative incentive programs, we're now finishing the job.

The Social Security Administration has produced a continually updated database that now covers more than 99 percent of all prisoners, the most comprehensive list of our inmate population in history. And more important, the Social Security Administration is using the list to great effect. By the end of last year we had suspended benefits to more than 70,000 prisoners. That means that over the next five years we will save taxpayers $2.5 billion—that's $2.5 billion—that will go toward serving our hard-working families.

Now we're going to build on the Social Security Administration's success in saving taxpayers from inmate fraud. In just a few moments I will sign an executive memorandum that directs the Departments of Labor, Veterans Affairs, Justice, Education and Agriculture to use the Security Administration's expertise and high-tech tools to enhance their own efforts to weed out any inmate who is receiving veteran's benefits, food stamps, or any other form of federal benefit denied by law.

We expect that these comprehensive sweeps by our agencies will save taxpayers millions upon millions of more dollars, in addition to the billions already saved from our crackdown on Social Security fraud. We will ensure that those who have committed crimes against society will not have an opportunity to commit crimes against taxpayers as well.

The American people have a right to expect that their national government is always on guard against every type of waste, fraud and abuse. It is our duty to use every power and every tool to eliminate that kind of fraud. We owe it to the American people to ensure that their Social Security contributions and other tax dollars are benefiting only those who worked hard, played by the rules, and are, by law, eligible to receive them. That's exactly what we're trying to do.

Thanks for listening.

President Clinton's Saturday Radio Address, 25 April 1998. Available on the White House website.

---

left untouched by it. The astronomical overrepresentation of blacks in houses of penal confinement and the increasingly tight meshing of the hyperghetto with the carceral system suggests that, owing to America's adoption of mass incarceration as a queer social policy designed to discipline the poor and contain the dishonoured, lower-class African-Americans now dwell, not in a society with prisons as their white compatriots do, but in the *first genuine prison society* in history.

26

LABOR MARKET AND PENAL SANCTION: THOUGHTS ON THE SOCIOLOGY OF CRIMINAL JUSTICE

Georg Rusche*

TRANSLATED BY GERDA DINWIDDIE

Editors' Introduction

The following English translation of Georg Rusche's "Arbeitsmarkt und Strafvollzug" (1933) appears in print for the first time. Orginally submitted as a research proposal to the Frankfurt Institute of Social Research in 1931, Rusche's article laid the foundation for the book, Punishment and Social Structure, *which he later co-authored with Otto Kirchheimer. First published in 1939 by Columbia University Press, the book was re-issued in 1968 by Russell and Russell Company.*

Punishment and Social Structure *continues to be neglected by American criminologists.* Barnes and Teeters (New Horizons in Criminology, *Prentice-Hall, 1943) and Edwin Sutherland* (Principles of Criminology, 4th Edition, 1947) *are the only two "older" textbooks that acknowledge its existence. While Sutherland merely listed the work as suggested reading, Barnes and Teeters at least recognized the importance of the book: "In a stimulating and provocative work on the subject, Rusche and Kirchheimer have given us a clear idea of how changing social and economic systems fundamentally altered the ways of thinking and acting in relation to crime and punishment."*

---

* Georg Rusche (1900-?) studied law, philosophy, economics and the social sciences in Paris, London and at several German universities, graduating from Cologne University in 1924. He pursued his studies at that same university and completed his thesis on economic theory in 1929, followed by the writing of "Arbeitsmarkt und Strafvollzug" in 1931 (published in 1933). After Hitler came to power, Rusche left Germany and experienced years of difficult exile from Paris to London, then to Palestine, and back to London. Interned in a camp in Great Britain, Rusche was later released and was on his way to Canada when his ship was torpedoed. He was returned to London where he remained, at least until March 1941. There is no further information on Georg Rusche.

The only American criminologist to employ the thesis developed in Punishment and Social Structure *was Thorsten Sellin in* Pioneering in Penology *(1944) and in his most recent work,* Slavery and the Penal System *(1976). (See the review essay of Sellin's writings by Greg Shank in this issue of the journal.) Sellin was also familiar with Rusche's "Arbeitsmarkt und Strafvollzug" (see Sellin's* Research Memorandum on Crime in the Depression, *Social Science Research Council, Bulletin 27, 1937).*

In a review essay of Punishment and Social Structure *in* Crime and Social Justice *9 (Spring-Summer 1978), Dario Melossi points out how Rusche's writings in Chapters II through VIII, which carefully follow the hypothesis laid down in "Arbeitsmarkt und Strafvollzug," were re-worked by Otto Kirchheimer. Rusche was less than enthusiastic about what had been done to his portion of the book. For this reason,* Crime and Social Justice *made the decision to print an English translation of how Rusche originally viewed his plan of research.*

This English translation is almost a faithful reproduction from the original German. We have, however, modernized the language and idioms without fundamentally altering the original meaning. It is apparent that Rusche was embarking on a radically new kind of analysis and, therefore, his vocabulary and categories of analysis are sometimes unclear and tentative.

I.

The study of crime and crime control is a fruitful field for sociological research. We are dealing with phenomena here which are determined to a large extent by social forces. Consequently, on the one hand, they practically compel an explanation derived from social relationships; on the other hand, they lend themselves especially well to an illumination of these relationships. The reason for this is that mystification and cover-up, which make the investigation of other social interconnections so very difficult, are to a great extent forced aside by the brutality of these phenomena and by conflicts which must necessarily be fought in the open.

Surprisingly, research has made only minimal use of the possibilities offered here. Sociological considerations have been included extensively in the examination of criminological problems. However, they have not been done justice in any way. For, even if the relationship between socioeconomic phenomena and the problems of crime and crime control are obvious to sociologists, there is still a long way to go from the naive recognition of this fact to making use of it in a systematic and scientific fashion.

This failure is explained by the fact that, in general, the researchers who devote themselves to criminological problems are not familiar with the fundamental principles of the social sciences, but approach them more from the outside. They are usually jurists or doctors. When they employ sociological categories in their work, they are derived from naive experience or, at best, if these categories are scientifically founded, they rely exclusively on social psychology.

Certainly the more recent criminology, partially stimulated by psychoanalysis, has produced valuable insights about the individual and social causes of crime and about the sociopsychological functions of punishment. But these studies lack a foundation in the basic principles of sociological knowledge. They are neither connected to economic theory, nor are they historically oriented. Rather, they imply a fixed social structure which does not exist in reality, and they unconsciously characterize the social system as eternal and unchanging rather than as a historical process.

The social function of crime and criminal justice can be clarified far beyond previous research, if simple axioms of economic theory are used and one does not presuppose a more or less static and ahistorical system of class relations. In this paper, some basic ideas for research along these lines will be proposed and discussed.

Although highly complex and somewhat independent circumstances influence the field of criminology, especially biological and psychological aspects, nevertheless economic theory and historical observation can clarify many questions. The dependency of crime and crime control on economic and historical conditions does not, however, provide a total explanation. These forces do not alone determine the object of our investigation and by themselves are limited and incomplete in several ways. For example, the penal system and the ritual of criminal procedure are shaped by various forces, including religious and sexual phenomena. Similarly, our method of investigation is not sufficient to explain the specific fate of a single individual who becomes a criminal and his particular punishment. But, within these limits, certain mechanisms can be discovered by economic-historical analysis with sufficient accuracy.

II.

It can be said without contradiction that crimes are acts which are forbidden in society. Debates about the meaning of punishment will not be addressed here. I shall not discuss whether the goal of punishment is retribution, deterrence or reform of the criminal. One thing, though, is certain: no society wants its penal system to incite the commission of crimes. In other words, punishment has to be constituted in such a way that those people who appear to be criminally inclined or inclined to commit acts that are undesirable to the society, are at least not encouraged to do so by the prospect of being discovered and punished. On the contrary, it is even hoped that the prospect of punishment will deter if not all members of this class, then at least a substantial part.

Indeed, the anticipation of future suffering and painful reprisal, which by far exceed the possible pleasurable gain, should be an effective counterbalance for any rational person. Now experience teaches us that most crimes are committed by members of those strata who are burdened by strong social pressures and who are relatively disadvantaged in satisfying their needs when compared to other classes. Therefore, a penal sanction, if it is not to be counter-productive, must be constituted in such a way that the classes which are most criminally inclined prefer to abstain from the forbidden acts than become victims of criminal punishment.

Perhaps, one could argue that such a proposition does not sufficiently consider the impact of the sense of honor and fear of disgrace associated with punishment. Indeed, the solidity of the social structure does in no way depend only on the strength of external measures of coercion which are supposed to guarantee the continuation of society. The great majority of people has to be psychically willing to accommodate to the existing society, to regard the state as their state, the law as their law. But, according to experience, there are classes for whom this adjustment and identification break down.

Criminality certainly occurs throughout all social classes. But disregarding persons for whom social inhibitions are without effect, or a few crimes which are not affected by social position, such as slander or political and related offenses or isolated cases of sensational trials, then it becomes clear that the criminal law and the daily work of the criminal courts are directed almost exclusively against those people whose class background, poverty, neglected education, or demoralization drove them to crime. It is rarely maintained anymore today that the individual alone is responsible for his crime. On the other hand, not everybody necessarily becomes a criminal even under the heaviest social pressure. Thus, the range of possibilities extends from law-abiding people in a wretched environment to confirmed criminals in a bourgeois milieu. Indeed, the power of resistance can be abnormally low or the inducement overly high in an individual case. At any rate, an extremely high capacity for resistance is expected of the lower strata, of whom large masses are regularly deprived of their livelihood by long, severe winters, inflation and crises, and the spiritually and physically weakest are thrown into the path of crime. If penal sanctions are supposed to deter these strata from crime in an effective manner, they must appear even worse than the strata's present living conditions. One can also formulate this proposition as follows: all efforts to reform the punishment of criminals are inevitably limited by the situation of the lowest socially significant proletarian class which society wants to deter from criminal acts. All reform efforts, however humanitarian and well-meaning, which attempt to go beyond this restriction are condemned to utopianism. If penal reforms should be demanded by public opinion and carried out, the reforms would have to be undermined by a more subtle deterioration of prison conditions. For, a genuine improvement in the conditions of imprisonment beyond this limit would no longer deter such large groups of people, and, as a consequence, the purpose of punishment would be destroyed. George Bernard Shaw once said:

> When we get down to the poorest and most oppressed of our population we find the conditions of their life so wretched that it would be impossible to conduct a prison humanely without making the lot of the criminal more eligible than that of many free citizens. If the prison does not underbid the slum in human misery, the slum will empty and the prison will fill.[1]

III.

The preceding analysis, though abstract and formal, has been stated often enough.[2] Naturally, it should not be assumed that this proposition will be exactly reproduced

---

[1] See the Forward to Sidney and Beatrice Webb, *English Prisons Under Local Government*, London, 1922, p. xi.

[2] The most concise example is found in Kriegsmann, *Einführung in die Gefängniskunde (Introduction to Penology)*, Heidelberg, 1912, p. 175: "The care must not go so far, that the prisoner is being spoiled, that the prison becomes el dorado of the poorest classes of the population."

in society in the manner in which it has been expressed here. It is only a principle of investigation, a guide to approach the subject matter. We will then find that there are very peculiar and unpredictable events, often strangely intertwined and quite different in conception and execution, which determine the course of real life.

If we want to make concrete the proposition that effective penal sanctions must deter the lower social classes which are the most criminally inclined, we must clarify what economic categories determine the fate of these classes. It is not at first easy to realize that these classes have no other goods at their disposal but their ability to sell their labor power and that, therefore, the labor market is the determining category. The situation of the working class is different in an economy in which a large reserve army of starving proletariat follows the employers and drives the wage for each job opportunity offered down to a minimum, than in an economy in which workers are scarce, as for example where free land is available and therefore nobody is forced to earn a living through dependent labor, and the employers compete for the few available workers and drive wages up.

Naturally, the scarcity or surplus of workers does not *unequivocally* determine the nature of the labor market. Political interventions can correct the fluctuation of supply and demand. When there is a lack of workers, for instance, the employers can try to compensate for the lack of economic incentives by introducing slavery or other forms of forced labor, or by setting maximum wages or taking similar measures pertaining to labor law. When there is a surplus of workers, the unions can protect wages from falling by withholding the supply of labor, or the state can do so through sociopolitical measures, particularly payment of aid to the unemployed. Depending on which of these situations prevails, the criminal justice apparatus will have to meet different tasks.

Unemployed masses, who tend to commit crimes of desperation because of hunger and deprivation, will only be stopped from doing so through cruel penalties. The most effective penal policy seems to be severe corporal punishment, if not ruthless extermination. In China, where there is a huge reserve army of wretched and starving proletariat which pours into the cities and is forced to sell its labor for any price (if it can find work at all), large gangs of mercenaries are always fighting one another. Under these conditions, the mere fact of being given food would make prison an enticement, not a deterrent. Prison sentences, therefore, only exist where European influence has asserted itself, and they are an indescribable cruelty. "Every socially thinking person who comes to China," writes Agnes Smedley in a report, "*Prisons in China*,"[3] "receives an extremely sad, depressing impression when he must see how lowly an ordinary human life weighs. This disregard becomes particularly clear when one realizes that criminals of any kind, who are caught here, are being shot, hanged or beheaded, and that these executions arouse hardly more than fleeting notice."

In a society in which workers are scarce, penal sanctions have a completely different function. They do not have to stop hungry masses from satisfying elementary needs. If everybody who wants to work can find work, if the lowest social class consists of unskilled workers and not of wretched unemployed workers, then punishment is

---

[3] *Frankfurter Zeitung*, September 15, 1930.

required to make the unwilling work, and to teach other criminals that they have to content themselves with the income of an honest worker. Even more: when workers are scarce, the wages will be high. But then it will be profitable to lock up criminals and let them work for food only, since the costs of guarding and enforcement will still be less than than the normal wage. Therefore, there is in all societies in which workers are scarce a tendency away from corporal punishment and the extermination of the criminal. Where the criminal's labor is valuable, exploitation is preferred to capital punishment, and forced labor is the corresponding mode of punishment.

IV.

This economic theory of punishment which has been developed here in a broad outline seems to me to be the key to understanding the criminal law. It would be quite wrong, however, to apply it to the present in exactly the same way as it has been presented here.

Important peculiarities in the contemporary criminal law cannot be explained without a historical framework. . . . That our criminal law exists in its present-day form is to a great extent comprehensible only through an appreciation of its origins and development. Its present form is, so to speak, a projection of the past. In spite of fluctuations in the political economy, the criminal law has not become insignificant and, though adjusted to a great extent to present-day tasks, it exerts far-reaching effects. This cannot be comprehended if one tries to understand the penal system only from the viewpoint of today. Without a historical overview, it is impossible to rationally explain an incomprehensible state of affairs. That means, however, that our economic theory has to be supplemented by a historical analysis without which the present system of crime control is incomprehensible. This work has not been done so far by legal historians. The history of law, as it is practiced at the moment, is far too much a brand of positivist jurisprudence to be capable of analyzing it socio-historically.

The history of the penal system is more than a history of the alleged independent development of legal "institutions." It is the history of the relations of the "two nations," as Disraeli called them, that constitute a people–the rich and the poor. The unproductive and conventional notions which legal historians usually hang onto hinder more often than help a truly scientific explanation. And when jurists rise above the juristic horizon, they often treat their object of interest in the manner of a meticulous collector of curiosities, without any criteria for the selection of the significant, because they do not question the legitimacy of traditional archives. But historians record things which appear important and remarkable to them, while we, however, are interested in day-to-day events. It is the same with reports about sensational legal cases which fill all the newspapers but tell us little about the actual criminality of the masses.

Often, legal historians are guided not by an unprejudiced analysis of social laws, but by an evolutionary conception of the development of legal institutions: from barbaric cruelty to the humanitarianism of the relatively perfect gal system which we supposedly enjoy today. They overlook that we are dealing with a very long, now halting, now regressive movement. Accordingly, they are often rather generous with praise for the eras which confirm their theory and at the same time scathing about those centuries which do not fit into it—a procedure which does not always promote the understanding of facts.

Therefore, the task has been to study the historical relationship between criminal law and economics, the history of class struggle, and to utilize these interrelationships to analyze the present prison system. At this point, only a short overview of the results of this research can be given, as much as is necessary to explain the logic of this essay....

V.

In the history of punishment, three epochs succeed one another. They are characterized by the prevalence of quite different methods of punishment: penance and monetary fines are practically the only form of punishment in the early Middle Ages; they are replaced in the late Middle Ages by a system of cruel corporal punishment and death sentences, which in turn make way for prison sentences in the 17th century. If one compares these phases in the history of penology with changes in social history, one finds surprising interconnections.

The early medieval system of fines and penance corresponded to the needs of a thinly populated, peasant economy. The possibility of settling on free land hindered any strong social pressure on the lower classes and led to a relatively even distribution of society's wealth. Thus, there were few crimes against property, for a farmer would hardly take things from his neighbor which he could produce himself at a much lesser cost in psychic expenditure. What led to crimes were rather the primitive stirrings of sexuality and hatred. A real deterrent at this time was the fear of private revenge by the injured party. In order to prevent this situation from degenerating into blood feuds and anarchy, society strove for accommodation. Crime was regarded as a form of war and the goal of legislators was the reconciliation of the enemies by recognized principles rather than crime control as we know it today.

In the later Middle Ages, the situation changed completely. If, until then, as Schmoller says, "people were more in demand than property,"[4] now there is a growth in population, the land is settled and a crowding of the available living space occurs. A separation of classes into rich and poor begins; propertyless workers drive down wages; and, for the first time, a quasi-capitalistic mode of production emerges; armies of beggars, social unrest and revolts, culminating in the peasant wars are the result. The nature of criminality is completely changed: a rapid increase in property crimes occurs and hordes of beggars, thieves and robbers flourish. As a result, the sphere of action of criminal justice had to be completely altered. If in the Middle Ages fines were preferred over corporal punishment, now the traditional system of monetary fines had outlived its usefulness because these criminals had no possessions with which they

---

[4] *Grundriss der Allgemeinen Volkswirtschaftslehre (Principles of General Economy)*, Volume II, Leipzig, 1901, p. 513.

could pay. Gradually, traditional punitive methods were replaced by whippings, mutilation and killing, at first still redeemable through money, later the universal means of punishment of and protection against the criminality of the gathering crowds of have-nots. The most gruesome imagination is hardly sufficient to visualize the justice of that time, which soon plunged vagabonds into destruction side by side with bandits and murderers and ended with the extermination of the jobless proletariat.

Around 1600, the conditions of the labor market again changed fundamentally. The supply of labor became scarcer as a result of the expansion of trade and new markets, the influx of precious metals from the New World, and wars and plagues, especially the Thirty Years' War and its decimation of the population. A period of noticeable shortage of workers occurred; workers' wages rose and the standard of living of the lowest class improved considerably. People became valuable and workers thought twice before putting their labor power at anybody's disposal. As the gains of the contractors receded and the "economy" declined, force replaced economic incentive. The whole social structure is determined by this effort and, as a consequence of it, the system of mercantilism emerges. From this perspective, it is easy to interpret the well-known fact that until then it had been easy to collect soldiers in sufficient numbers simply through the "propaganda drum," for jobless proletarians streamed together in crowds wherever they saw a possibility for continuing their existence. But now they had to be enlisted with force and trickery because they could find more favorable conditions outside the military. In this situation of constant scarcity of workers, where everybody's labor is valuable, it would be an economically "senseless" cruelty to keep destroying criminals. Confinement to prison takes over the role of corporal punishment and death sentences, "humanitarianism" replaces cruelty; wherever there used to be gallows, now prisons stand. This humanitarianism was absolutely profitable: "What good is a thief, who has been hanged because of 50 Gulden, either for himself or for the one he stole it from, when he can earn four times that amount in one year in a workhouse?" asks a distinguished labor economist of that time, J.J. Becher.[5]

This "humanitarian" system of punishment lost its utility when the Industrial Revolution, the replacement of the worker by the machine at the turn of the 18th century, removed the scarcity of workers, and the industrial reserve army came into existence. The lower classes sank into misery, underbid each other on the labor market, and compulsory measures lost their meaning. Prisons were no longer profitable. When wages were high, they had brought high gains; but when workers voluntarily offered their labor for a minimum existence, it was no longer worth it to come up with the cost for confinement and supervision. The proceeds of prisoners' labor were not even sufficient for the upkeep of the building and the maintenance of the guards and prisoners. The prison failed in two ways: again, as in the Middle Ages, the criminality of the pauperized masses rose and the penitentiary no longer terrorized them. Some advocated the return to medieval methods of punishment. Though it was demanded loud

---

[5] Johann Joachim Becher, *Politischer Discurs: Von den eigentlichen Ursachen dess Auff- und Abnehmens der Städt, Länder und Republicken (Political Discourse: Of the Actual Causes of the Rise and Fall of Cities, Countries and Republics)*, Frankfurt, 1688, p. 245.

enough, it did not materialize because hard-earned humanitarian ideals hindered it and political wisdom kept the ruling class from overstraining an already revolutionary situation with such open provocation. Penal punishment remained a leftover from a previous and quite different epoch, but adjusted by necessity to changing needs. Institutions of forced labor, penitentiaries became places of pure torture, suitable to deter even the most wretched. Prisoners were insufficiently clothed and were cramped together. Work, having become unprofitable, served as torture: loads of stone had to be lugged without purpose from one place to another by the prisoners; they had to work waterpumps which let the water flow back again, or treadmills which were not used for any purpose. The discipline of this routine was reenforced by the deterrent effect of beatings.

The introduction of solitary confinement was only an apparent reform. It too was a punitive device which could arouse fear even in the hungry and act as a deterrent for people who did not know how to stay alive. For there is hardly a greater torment than the feeling of total dependency and helplessness, being cut off from all stimulations and distractions, which is induced by solitary confinement. Only in form did the idea of deterrence differ from the corporal punishments of the Middle Ages, but the conscience of the reformers could be at peace. In solitary confinement they could see, not torture, but the reform of the penitentiaries.

In America, punishment developed differently than in Europe because there was a greater demand for workers than during mercantilism. The free land and industrial development created a vacuum in the labor market which immigration could not fill. Everybody who was the least bit useful could find work, wages were high, possibilities of upward mobility were not closed to any capable person. The lowest socially important class were the unskilled, recent immigrants or the native colored workers. Public assistance for the unemployed was not needed. For the sick and weak, and those unable to work, private philanthropy was enough. The number of crimes was low and the form of punishment could take this into account. As under mercantilism, prisons became very profitable places of production whose main task was to transform criminals through education into useful members of society, i.e., industrious workers. Conséquently, reformers were able to make surprising gains–education, learning of skills, hygiene, indeterminate sentencing, conditional pardon, probation, parole, separate treatment of juvenile delinquents and first offenders all had their starting point here. Also, scientific organizations investigated the individual and social causes of crime and methods of crime control through welfare and prevention.

Only when the situation improved somewhat in Europe, when the pressure of the unemployed which had weighed on the labor market since the Industrial Revolution slowly subsided, when unemployment as a permanent phenomenon disappeared, when social welfare lessened the misery of the helpless and, therefore, the rate of criminality went down considerably, was the American example slowly and hesitatingly followed, more perhaps in theory than in praxis. The development, for example, of effective aid for released prisoners in the period before the war was motivated by the scarcity of agricultural labor and employers' willingness to accept any labor force, provided that they contented themselves with sufficiently low wages. Thus, there was an urgent demand for vagabonds and criminals, as well as foreigners.

VI.

After the war, when there was chronic unemployment, a breakdown of the labor market in the countries which were most affected was avoided by unemployment assistance. Wages and the standard of living did not sink as low as they would have in an unregulated economy. Even those who dropped out of the production process were assured of satisfying their most immediate needs and, generally, they did not need to become criminals. Consequently, the penal system was saved from the task, which it had to perform several times in its history, of containing criminals for whom prison would not be intimidating, given the regular supply of food. Disregarding the short period of inflation, criminality did not rise above its prewar level; it even showed until recently a declining tendency. As a result, penal reforms which began even before the war did not at first have to be given up, but were partially continued, given the favorable political climate....

This effort, which was carried out in the last few years with considerable public participation, shall not be discussed at this point. As far as the results can be estimated, it is not necessary to abandon the simple heuristic maxim to which we evidently owe so many correct results.

In Germany, the class which is the most criminally endangered is the unemployed on relief, particularly young singles who keep house on their relief alone and at the moment receive about seven to eight Mark per week for all their living needs. Besides this class, there exists a group of people who do not receive assistance, for to a great extent the effectiveness of our very humane welfare laws is undermined by the apparatus created for their realization. A large part of the welfare law in Germany demands a high degree of a personal sense of responsibility from the officials. Given that the administration is cutting back personnel, establishing written records, and asking for the centralization of authority, the justification of aid in each case means a new burden for the functionaries, a burden which can be avoided by a simple denial of aid to the petitioner. Anyway, considering the extremely limited budget of public welfare, the officials are encouraged to make a negative decision and to refuse aid in case of doubt. Therefore, strong motives exist for an unfavorable decision in any case.

The class of the unaided supplies the beggars, vagabonds, peddlers, prostitutes, pimps and those who lower the wages for occasional work of any kind—guests of the hostels and asylums, when they have "sleeping money," otherwise without shelter, desperately awaiting the morning in waiting rooms and hallways.[6]

According to our heuristic maxim, we should assume that in the interest of deterring these classes, punishment must mean a hell which they would not voluntarily

---

[6] The released prisoners should not be driven into joining these classes, but are to receive welfare; but even then enough of them wind up among these groups: those who do not know their rights or do not know how to defend them in a suitable manner, those who cannot register with the police because of previously committed crimes, namely runaways from juvenile reformatories.

exchange for their living conditions. But until now, the satisfaction of the elementary needs of food and warmth does not seem to have been denied the prisoners too much. On the contrary, they receive "appropriate nourishment," which perhaps would even compare favorably with the nutrition of the unemployed (the price of food in the prisons is about .70 Reichsmark per day). The degradation, the meaninglessness of penal labor, the prison discipline with its enforced order, the exclusion of all normal sexual activity, as well as the hostility of the overworked guards—in short, the deprivation of freedom—appears to be effective enough so far. According to the scandalous trials of the last few years, a similar state of affairs must be assumed for education in juvenile reformatories. Naturally, the forces which bring about this state of affairs are anything else than conscious intent.

There is, however, an extraordinary confirmation of the proposition expressed here: the dramatic breakdown of "humane" punishment in America. In the United States today, the high level of unemployment is not absorbed by the welfare system. Consequently, there is an unimaginable rise in crime, an unimaginable brutality of repression, the breakdown of all humanitarian reforms, the overcrowding of the prisons, hunger, filth, joblessness, hopelessness and despair, leading to these penitentiary revolts, these outbreaks of madness, which for a time shocked world opinion.[7]

So far, the treatment of prisoners in Germany, though not as humane as some people assume, is nevertheless not as harsh as in America. But our humanitarianism is hardly effective enough to lift punishment out of the sphere of that fatal dependency on which we based our theoretical premise.

---

[7] Compare my essay, "Zuchthausrevolten oder Sozialpolitik" ("Penitentiary Revolts or Social Politics"), *Frankfurter Zeitung*, June 1, 1930, No. 403.

27

RULES FOR THE DISTINCTION OF THE NORMAL FROM THE PATHOLOGICAL

Emile Durkheim

If there is a fact whose pathological nature appears indisputable, it is crime. All criminologists agree on this score. Although they explain this pathology differently, they none the less unanimously acknowledge it. However, the problem needs to be treated less summarily.

Let us in fact apply the rules previously laid down. Crime is not only observed in most societies of a particular species, but in all societies of all types. There is not one in which criminality does not exist, although it changes in form and the actions which are termed criminal are not everywhere the same. Yet everywhere and always there have been men who have conducted themselves in such a way as to bring down punishment upon their heads. If at least, as societies pass from lower to higher types, the crime rate (the relationship between the annual crime figures and population figures) tended to fall, we might believe that, although still remaining a normal phenomenon, crime tended to lose that character of normality. Yet there is no single ground for believing such a regression to be real. Many facts would rather seem to point to the existence of a movement in the opposite direction. From the beginning of the century statistics provide us with a means of following the progression of criminality. It has everywhere increased, and in France the increase is of the order of 300 per cent. Thus there is no phenomenon which represents more incontrovertibly all the symptoms of normality, since it appears to be closely bound up with the conditions of all collective life. To make crime a social illness would be to concede that sickness is not something accidental, but on the contrary derives in certain cases from the fundamental constitution of the living creature. This would be to erase any distinction between the physiological and the pathological. It can certainly happen that crime itself has normal forms; this is what happens, for instance, when it reaches an excessively high level. There is no doubt that this excessiveness is pathological in nature. What is normal is simply that criminality exists, provided that for each social type it does not reach or go beyond a certain level which it is perhaps not impossible to fix in conformity with the previous rules.[10]

We are faced with a conclusion which is apparently somewhat paradoxical. Let us make no mistake: to classify crime among the phenomena of normal sociology is not merely to declare that it is an inevitable though regrettable phenomenon arising from the incorrigible wickedness of men; it is to assert that it is a factor in public health, an integrative element in any healthy society. At first sight this result is so surprising that it disconcerted even ourselves for a long time. However, once that first impression of surprise has been overcome it is not difficult to discover reasons to explain this normality and at the same time to confirm it.

In the first place, crime is normal because it is completely impossible for any society entirely free of it to exist.

Crime, as we have shown elsewhere, consists of an action which offends certain collective feelings which are especially strong and clear-cut. In any society, for actions regarded as criminal to cease, the feelings that they offend would need to be found in each individual consciousness without exception and in the degree of strength requisite to counteract the opposing feelings. Even supposing that this condition could effectively be fulfilled, crime would not thereby disappear; it would merely change in form, for the very cause which made the well-springs of criminality to dry up would immediately open up new ones.

Indeed, for the collective feelings, which the penal law of a people at a particular moment in its history protects, to penetrate individual consciousnesses that had hitherto remained closed to them, or to assume greater authority – whereas previously they had not possessed enough – they would have to acquire an intensity greater than they had had up to then. The community as a whole must feel them more keenly, for they cannot draw from any other source the additional force which enables them to bear down upon individuals who formerly were the most refractory. For murderers to disappear, the horror of bloodshed must increase in those strata of society from which murderers are recruited; but for this to happen the abhorrence must increase throughout society. Moreover, the very absence of crime would contribute directly to bringing about that result, for a sentiment appears much more respectable when it is always and uniformly respected. But we overlook the fact that these strong states of the common consciousness cannot be reinforced in this way without the weaker states, the violation of which previously gave rise to mere breaches of convention, being reinforced at the same time, for the weaker states are no more than the extension and attenuated form of the stronger ones. Thus, for example, theft and mere misappropriation of property offend the same altruistic sentiment, the respect for other people's possessions. However, this sentiment is offended less strongly by the latter action than the former. Moreover, since the average consciousness does not have sufficient intensity of

---

[10] From the fact that crime is a phenomenon of normal sociology it does not follow that the criminal is a person normally constituted from the biological and psychological viewpoints. The two questions are independent of each other. This independence will be better understood when we have shown later the difference which exists between psychical and sociological facts.

feeling to feel strongly about the lesser of these two offences, the latter is the object of greater tolerance. This is why the misappropriator is merely censured, while the thief is punished. But if this sentiment grows stronger, to such a degree that it extinguishes in the consciousness the tendency to theft that men possess, they will become more sensitive to these minor offences, which up to then had had only a marginal effect upon them. They will react with greater intensity against these lesser faults, which will become the object of severer condemnation, so that, from the mere moral errors that they were, some will pass into the category of crimes. For example, dishonest contracts or those fulfilled dishonestly, which only incur public censure or civil redress, will become crimes. Imagine a community of saints in an exemplary and perfect monastery. In it crime as such will be unknown, but faults that appear venial to the ordinary person will arouse the same scandal as does normal crime in ordinary consciences. If therefore that community has the power to judge and punish, it will term such acts criminal and deal with them as such. It is for the same reason that the completely honourable man judges his slightest moral failings with a severity that the mass of people reserves for acts that are truly criminal. In former times acts of violence against the person were more frequent than they are today because respect for individual dignity was weaker. As it has increased, such crimes have become less frequent, but many acts which offended against that sentiment have been incorporated into the penal code, which did not previously include them.[11]

In order to exhaust all the logically possible hypotheses, it will perhaps be asked why this unanimity should not cover all collective sentiments without exception, and why even the weakest sentiments should not evoke sufficient power to forestall any dissentient voice. The moral conscience of society would be found in its entirety in every individual, endowed with sufficient force to prevent the commission of any act offending against it, whether purely conventional failings or crimes. But such universal and absolute uniformity is utterly impossible, for the immediate physical environment in which each one of us is placed, our hereditary antecedents, the social influences upon which we depend, vary from one individual to another and consequently cause a diversity of consciences. It is impossible for everyone to be alike in this matter, by virtue of the fact that we each have our own organic constitution and occupy different areas in space. This is why, even among lower peoples where individual originality is very little developed, such originality does however exist. Thus, since there cannot be a society in which individuals do not diverge to some extent from the collective type, it is also inevitable that among these deviations some assume a criminal character. What confers upon them this character is not the intrinsic importance of the acts but the importance which the common consciousness ascribes to them. Thus if the latter is stronger and possesses sufficient authority to make these divergences very weak in absolute terms, it will also be more sensitive and exacting. By reacting against the slightest deviations with an energy which it elsewhere employs against those what are more weighty, it endues them with the same gravity and will brand them as criminal.

---

[11] Calumny, insults, slander, deception, etc.

Thus crime is necessary. It is linked to the basic conditions of social life, but on this very account is useful, for the conditions to which it is bound are themselves indispensable to the normal evolution of morality and law.

Indeed today we can no longer dispute the fact that not only do law and morality vary from one social type to another, but they even change within the same type if the conditions of collective existence are modified. Yet for these transformations to be made possible, the collective sentiments at the basis of morality should not prove unyielding to change, and consequently should be only moderately intense. If they were too strong, they would no longer be malleable. Any arrangement is indeed an obstacle to a new arrangement; this is even more the case the more deep-seated the original arrangement. The more strongly a structure is articulated, the more it resists modification; this is as true for functional as for anatomical patterns. If there were no crimes, this condition would not be fulfilled, for such a hypothesis presumes that collective sentiments would have attained a degree of intensity unparalleled in history. Nothing is good indefinitely and without limits. The authority which the moral consciousness enjoys must not be excessive, for otherwise no one would dare to attack it and it would petrify too easily into an immutable form. For it to evolve, individual originality must be allowed to manifest itself. But so that the originality of the idealist who dreams of transcending his era may display itself, that of the criminal, which falls short of the age, must also be possible. One does not go without the other.

Nor is this all. Beyond this indirect utility, crime itself may play a useful part in this evolution. Not only does it imply that the way to necessary changes remains open, but in certain cases it also directly prepares for these changes. Where crime exists, collective sentiments are not only in the state of plasticity necessary to assume a new form, but sometimes it even contributes to determining beforehand the shape they will take on. Indeed, how often is it only an anticipation of the morality to come, a progression towards what will be! According to Athenian law, Socrates was a criminal and his condemnation was entirely just. However, his crime – his independence of thought – was useful not only for humanity but for his country. It served to prepare a way for a new morality and a new faith, which the Athenians then needed because the traditions by which they had hitherto lived no longer corresponded to the conditions of their existence. Socrates's case is not an isloated one, for it recurs periodically in history. The freedom of thought that we at present enjoy could never have been asserted if the rules that forbade it had not been violated before they were solemnly abrogated. However, at the time the violation was a crime, since it was an offence against sentiments still keenly felt in the average consciousness. Yet this crime was useful since it was the prelude to changes which were daily becoming more necessary, Liberal philosophy has had as its precursors heretics of all kinds whom the secular arm rightly punished throught the Middle Ages and has continued to do so almost up to the present day.

From this viewpoint the fundamental facts of criminology appear to us in an entirely new light. Contrary to current ideas, the criminal no longer appears as an utterly unsociable creature, a sort of parasitic element, a foreign, unassimilable body introduced into the bosom of society.[12] He plays a normal role in social life. For its part, crime must no longer be conceived of as an evil which cannot be circumscribed closely enough. Far from there being cause for congratulation when it drops too noticeably below the normal level, this apparent progress assuredly coincides with and is linked to some social disturbance. Thus the number of crimes of assault never falls so low as it does in times of scarcity.[13] Consequently, at the same time, and as a reaction, the theory of punishment is revised, or rather should be revised. If in fact crime is a sickness, punishment is the cure for it and cannot be conceived of otherwise; thus all the discussion aroused revolves round knowing what punishment should be to fulfil its role as a remedy. But if crime is in no way pathological, the object of punishment cannot be to cure it and its true function must be sought elsewhere.

Thus the rules previously enunciated are far from having as their sole reason to satisfy a logical formalism which lacks any great utility. This is because, on the contrary, according to whether they are applied or not, the most essential social facts totally change their character. If the example quoted is particularly cogent – and this is why we thought we should dwell upon it – there are nevertheless many others which could usefully be cited. There is no society where it is not the rule that the punishment should fit the crime – and yet for the Italian school of thought this principle is a mere invention of legal theoreticians devoid of any solid basis.[14] For these criminologists the whole institution of punishment, as it has functioned up to the present among all known peoples, is a phenomenon which goes against nature. We have already seen that for Garofalo the criminality peculiar to the lower forms of society has nothing natural about it. For the socialists it is capitalist organisation, despite its widespread nature, which constitutes a deviation from the normal state and is an organisation brought about by violence and trickery. On the other hand for Spencer it is our administrative centralisation and the extension of governmental power which are the radical vices of our societies, in spite of the fact that both have developed entirely regularly and universally over the course of history. The belief is that one is never obliged systematically to decide on the normal or abnormal character of social facts according to their degree of generality. It is always by a great display of dialectic that these questions are resolved.

However, by laying this criterion on one side, not only is one exposed to confusion and partial errors like those just discussed, but science itself becomes impossible. Indeed its immediate object is the study of the normal type, but if the most general facts can be pathological, it may well be that the normal type has never really existed. Hence what use is it to study facts? They can only confirm our prejudices and root us more

[12] We have ourselves committed the error of speaking of the criminal in this way through not having applied our rule (cf. *Division du travail social*, pp.395, 396).

[13] But, although crime is a fact of normal sociology, it does not follow that we should not abhor it. Pain has likewise nothing desirable about it: the individual detests it just as society detests crime, and yet it is a normal physiological function. Not only does it necessarily derive from the very constitution of every living creature, but it plays a useful and irreplaceable role in life. Thus it would be a peculiar distortion to represent our thinking as an apologia for crime. We would not even have envisaged protesting against such an interpretation were we not aware of the strange accusations and misunderstandings to which one is exposed in undertaking to study moral facts objectively and to speak of them in language that is not commonly used.

[14] Cf. Garofalo, *Criminologie*, pp.299.

deeply in our errors, since they spring from them. If punishment and responsibility, as they exist in history, are merely a product of ignorance and barbarism, what use is it to strive to know them in order to determine their normal forms? Thus the mind is led to turn away from a reality which from then on lacks interest for us, turning in upon itself to seek the materials necessary to reconstruct that reality. For sociology to deal with facts as things, the sociologist must feel a need to learn from them. The principal purpose of any science of life, whether individual or social, is in the end to define and explain the normal state and distinguish it from the abnormal. If normality does not inhere in the things themselves, if on the contrary it is a characteristic which we impose upon them externally or, for whatever reason, refuse to do so, this salutary state of dependence on things is lost. The mind complacently faces a reality that has not much to teach it. It is no longer contained by the subject matter to which it applies itself, since in some respects it determines that subject matter. The different rules that we have established up to now are therefore closely linked. For sociology really to be a science of things, the generality of phenomena must be taken as the criterion of their normality.

Moreover, our method has the advantage of regulating action at the same time as thought. If what is deemed desirable is not the object of observation, but can and must be determined by some sort of mental calculus, no limit, in a manner of speaking, can be laid down to the free inventions of the imagination in their search for the best. For how can one assign to perfection bounds that it cannot exceed? By definition it escapes all limitations. The goal of humanity thus recedes to infinity, discouraging not a few by its very remoteness, arousing and exciting others, on the other hand, who, so as to draw a little nearer to it, hasten their steps and throw themselves into revolutionary activity. This practical dilemma is avoided if what is desirable is declared to be what is healthy, and if the state of health is something definite, inherent in things, for at the same time the extent of our effort is given and defined. There is no longer need to pursue desperately an end which recedes as we move forward; we need only to work steadily and persistently to maintain the normal state, to re-establish it if it is disturbed, and to rediscover the conditions of normality if they happen to change. The duty of the statesman is no longer to propel societies violently towards an ideal which appears attractive to him. His role is rather that of the doctor: he forestalls the outbreak of sickness by maintaining good hygiene, or when it does break out, seeks to cure it.[15]

---

[15] From the theory developed in this chapter it has sometimes been concluded that, in our view, the upward trend in criminality during the nineteenth century was a normal phenomenon. Nothing is farther from our thoughts. Several facts which we have pointed out in connexion with suicide (cf. *le Suicide*, p.420ff.) tend, on the contrary, to cause us to believe that this development has been, in general, pathological. However, it may be that a certain increase in certain forms of criminality would be normal, for every state of civilisation has its own criminality. But on this matter one can only hypothesise.

28

Discipline and Punish

The Birth of the Prison

Michel Foucault

The Carceral

Were I to fix the date of completion of the carceral system, I would choose not 1810 and the penal code, nor even 1844, when the law laying down the principle of cellular internment was passed; I might not even choose 1838, when books on prison reform by Charles Lucas, Moreau-Christophe and Faucher were published. The date I would choose would be 22 January 1840, the date of the official opening of Mettray. Or better still, perhaps, that glorious day, unremarked and unrecorded, when a child in Mettray remarked as he lay dying: 'What a pity I left the colony so soon' (Ducpétiaux, 1852, 383). This marked the death of the first penitentiary saint. Many of the blessed no doubt went to join him, if the former inmates of the penal colonies are to be believed when, in singing the praises of the new punitive policies of the body, they remarked: 'We preferred the blows, but the cell suits us better.'

Why Mettray? Because it is the disciplinary form at its most extreme, the model in which are concentrated all the coercive technologies of behaviour. In it were to be found 'cloister, prison, school, regiment'. The small, highly hierarchized groups, into which the inmates were divided, followed simultaneously five models: that of the family (each group was a 'family' composed of 'brothers' and two 'elder brothers'); that of the army (each family, commanded by a head, was divided into two sections, each of which had a second in command; each inmate had a number and was taught basic military exercises; there was a cleanliness inspection every day, an inspection of clothing every week; a roll-call was taken three times a day); that of the workshop, with supervisors and foremen, who were responsible for the regularity of the work and for the apprenticeship of the younger inmates; that of the school (an hour or an hour and a half of lessons every day; the teaching was given by the instructor and by the deputy-heads); lastly, the judicial model (each day 'justice' was meted out in the parlour: 'The least act of disobedience is punished and the best way of avoiding serious offences is to punish the most minor offences very severely: at Mettray, a useless word is punishable'; the principal punishment inflicted was confinement to one's cell; for 'isolation is the best means of acting on the moral nature of children; it is there above all that the voice of religion, even if it has never spoken to their hearts, recovers all its emotional power' – Ducpétiaux, 1852, 377); the entire parapenal institution, which is created in order not to be a prison, culminates in the cell, on the walls of which are written in black letters: 'God sees you.'

This superimposition of different models makes it possible to indicate, in its specific features, the function of 'training'. The chiefs and their deputies at Mettray had to be not exactly judges, or teachers, or foremen, or non-commissioned officers, or 'parents', but something of all these things in a quite specific mode of intervention. They were in a sense technicians of behaviour: engineers of conduct, orthopaedists of individuality. Their task was to produce bodies that were both docile and capable; they supervised the nine or ten working hours of every day (whether in a workshop or in the fields); they directed the orderly movements of groups of inmates, physical exercises, military exercises, rising in the morning, going to bed at night, walks to the accompaniment of bugle and whistle; they taught gymnastics;[1] they checked cleanliness, supervised bathing. Training was accompanied by permanent observation; a body of knowledge was being constantly built up from the everyday behaviour of the inmates; it was organized as an instrument of perpetual assessment: 'On entering the colony, the child is subjected to a sort of interrogation as to his origins, the position of his family, the offence for which he was brought before the courts and all the other offences that make up his short and often very sad existence. This information is written down on a board on which everything concerning each inmate is noted in turn, his stay at the colony and the place to which he is sent when he leaves' (Ducpétiaux, 1851, 61). The modelling of the body produces a knowledge of the individual, the apprenticeship of the techniques induces modes of behaviour and the acquisition of skills is inextricably linked with the establishment of power relations; strong, skilled agricultural workers are produced; in this very work, provided it is technically supervised, submissive subjects are produced and a dependable body of knowledge built up about them. This disciplinary technique exercised upon the body had a double effect: a 'soul' to be known and a subjection to be maintained. One result vindicated this work of training: in 1848, at a moment when 'the fever of revolution fired the imagination of all, when the schools at Angers, La Flèche, Alfort, even the boarding schools, rose up in rebellion, the inmates of Mettray were calmer than ever' (Ferrus).

Where Mettray was especially exemplary was in the specificity that it recognized in this operation of training. It was related to other forms of supervision, on which

---

[1] 'Anything that helps to tire the body helps to expel bad thoughts; so care is taken that games consist of violent exercise. At night, they fall asleep the moment they touch the pillow' (Ducpétiaux, 1854, 375–6).

it was based: medicine, general education, religious direction. But it cannot not be identified absolutely with them. Nor with administration in the strict sense. Heads or deputy-heads of 'families', monitors and foremen, had to live in close proximity to the inmates; their clothes were 'almost as humble' as those of the inmates themselves; they practically never left their side, observing them day and night; they constituted among them a network of permanent observation. And, in order to train them themselves, a specialized school had been organized in the colony. The essential element of its programme was to subject the future cadres to the same apprenticeships and to the same coercions as the inmates themselves: they were 'subjected as pupils to the discipline that, later, as instructors, they would themselves impose'. They were taught the art of power relations. It was the first training college in pure discipline: the 'penitentiary' was not simply a project that sought its justification in 'humanity' or its foundations in a 'science', but a technique that was learnt, transmitted and which obeyed general norms. The practice that normalized by compulsion the conduct of the undisciplined or dangerous could, in turn, by technical elaboration and rational reflection, be 'normalized'. The disciplinary technique became a 'discipline' which also had its school.

It so happens that historians of the human sciences date the birth of scientific psychology at this time: during these same years, it seems, Weber was manipulating his little compass for the measurement of sensations. What took place at Mettray (and in other European countries sooner or later) was obviously of a quite different order. It was the emergence or rather the institutional specification, the baptism as it were, of a new type of supervision – both knowledge and power – over individuals who resisted disciplinary normalization. And yet, in the formation and growth of psychology, the appearance of these professionals of discipline, normality and subjection surely marks the beginning of a new stage. It will be said that the quantitative assessment of sensorial responses could at least derive authority from the prestige of the emerging science of physiology and that for this alone it deserves to feature in the history of the sciences. But the supervision of normality was firmly encased in a medicine or a psychiatry that provided it with a sort of 'scientificity'; it was supported by a judicial apparatus which, directly or indirectly, gave it legal justification. Thus, in the shelter of these two considerable protectors, and, indeed, acting as a link between them, or a place of exchange, a carefully worked out technique for the supervision of norms has continued to develop right up to the present day. The specific, institutional supports of these methods have proliferated since the founding of the small school at Mettray; their apparatuses have increased in quantity and scope; their auxiliary services have increased, with hospitals, schools, public administrations and private enterprises; their agents have proliferated in number, in power, in technical qualification; the technicians of indiscipline have founded a family. In the normalization of the power of normalization, in the arrangement of a power-knowledge over individuals, Mettray and its school marked a new era.

But why choose this moment as the point of emergence of the formation of an art of punishing that is still more or less our own? Precisely because this choice is somewhat 'unjust'. Because it situates the 'end' of the process in the lower reaches of criminal law. Because Mettray was a prison, but not entirely; a prison in that it contained young delinquents condemned by the courts; and yet something else, too, because it also contained minors who had been charged, but acquitted under article 66 of the code, and boarders held, as in the eighteenth century, as an alternative to paternal correction. Mettray, a punitive model, is at the limit of strict penality. It was the most famous of a whole series of institutions which, well beyond the frontiers of criminal law, constituted what one might call the carceral archipelago.

Yet the general principles, the great codes and subsequent legislation were quite clear on the matter: no imprisonment 'outside the law', no detention that had not been decided by a qualified judicial institution, no more of those arbitrary and yet widespread confinements. Yet the very principle of extra-penal incarceration was in fact never abandoned. (A whole study remains to be done of the debates that took place during the Revolution concerning family courts, paternal correction and the right of parents to lock up their children.) And, if the apparatus of the great classical form of confinement was partly (and only partly) dismantled, it was very soon reactivated, rearranged, developed in certain directions. But what is still more important is that it was homogenized, through the mediation of the prison, on the one hand with legal punishments and, on the other, with disciplinary mechanisms. The frontiers between confinement, judicial punishment and institutions of discipline, which were already blurred in the classical age, tended to disappear and to constitute a great carceral continuum that diffused penitentiary techniques into the most innocent disciplines, transmitting disciplinary norms into the very heart of the penal system and placing over the slightest illegality, the smallest irregularity, deviation or anomaly, the threat of delinquency. A subtle, graduated carceral net, with compact institutions, but also separate and diffused methods, assumed responsibility for the arbitrary, widespread, badly integrated confinement of the classical age.

I shall not attempt here to reconstitute the whole network that formed first the immediate surroundings of the prison, then spread farther and farther outwards. However, a few references and dates should give some idea of the breadth and precocity of the phenomenon.

There were agricultural sections in the *maisons centrales* (the first example of which was Gaillon in 1824, followed later by Fontevrault, Les Douaires, Le Boulard); there were colonies for poor, abandoned vagrant children (Petit-Bourg in 1840, Ostwald in 1842); there were almshouses for young female offenders who 'recoiled before the idea of entering a life of disorder', for 'poor innocent girls whose mothers' immorality has exposed to precocious perversity', or for poor girls found on the doorsteps of hospitals and lodging houses. There were penal colonies envisaged by the law of 1850: minors, acquitted or condemned, were to be sent to these colonies and 'brought up in common, under strict discipline, and trained in agricultural work and in the principal industries related to it;' later, they were to be joined by minors sentenced to hard labour for life and 'vicious and insubordinate wards of the Public Assistance' (on all these institutions, cf. Gaillac, 99–107). And, moving still farther away from penality in the strict sense, the carceral circles widen and the form of the prison slowly diminishes and finally disappears altogether: the institutions for abandoned or indigent children, the orphanages (like Neuhof or Mesnil-Firmin), the establishments for apprentices (like the Bethléem de Reims or the Maison de Nancy); still farther away the factory-convents, such as La Sauvagère, Tarare and Jujurieu (where the girl workers entered about the age of thirteen, lived confined for years and were allowed out only under surveillance, received instead of wages pledged payment, which could be increased by bonuses for zeal and good behaviour, which they could use only on leaving). And then, still farther, there was a whole series of mechanisms that did not adopt the 'compact' prison model, but used some of the carceral methods: charitable societies, moral improvement associations, organizations that handed out assistance and also practised surveillance, workers' estates and lodging houses – the most primitive of which still bear the all too visible marks of the penitentiary system.[2] And, lastly, this great carceral network reaches all the disciplinary mechanisms that function throughout society.

We have seen that, in penal justice, the prison transformed the punitive procedure into a penitentiary technique; the carceral archipelago transported this technique from the penal institution to the entire social body. With several important results.

1. This vast mechanism established a slow, continuous, imperceptible gradation that made it possible to pass naturally from disorder to offence and back from a transgression of the law to a slight departure from a rule, an average, a demand, a norm. In the classical period, despite a certain common reference to offence in general,[3] the order of the crime, the order of sin and the order of bad conduct remained separate in so far as they related to separate criteria and authorities (court, penitence, confinement). Incarceration with its mechanisms of surveillance and punishment functioned, on the contrary, according to a principle of relative continuity. The continuity of the institutions themselves, which were linked to one another (public assistance with the orphanage, the reformitory, the penitentiary, the disciplinary battalion, the prison; the school with the charitable society, the workshop, the almshouse, the penitentiary convent; the workers' estate with the hospital and the prison). A continuity of the punitive criteria and mechanisms, which on the basis of a mere deviation gradually strengthened the rules and increased the punishment. A continuous gradation of the established, specialized and competent authorities (in the order of knowledge and in the order of power) which, without resort to arbitrariness, but strictly according to the regulations, by means of observation and assessment hierarchized, differentiated, judged, punished and moved gradually from the correction of irregularities to

   [2] Cf., for example, the following description of workers' accommodation built at Lille in the mid-nineteenth century: 'Cleanliness is the order of the day. It is the heart of the regulations. There are a number of severe provisions against noise, drunkenness, disorders of all kinds. A serious offence brings expulsion. Brought back to regular habits of order and economy, the workers no longer desert the workshops on Mondays...The children are better supervised and are no longer a cause of scandal...Prizes are given for the upkeep of the dwellings, for good behaviour, for signs of devotion and each year these prizes are competed for by a large number of competitors' (Houzé de l'Aulnay, 13–15).
   [3] Crime was explicitly defined by certain jurists such as Muyart de Vouglans, 1767, 108 and 1780, 3, or Rousseaud de la Combe, 1–2.

the punishment of crime. The 'carceral' with its many diffuse or compact forms, its institutions of supervision or constraint, of discreet surveillance and insistent coercion, assured the communication of punishments according to quality and quantity; it connected in series or disposed according to subtle divisions the minor and the serious penalties, the mild and the strict forms of treatment, bad marks and light sentences. You will end up in the convict-ship, the slightest indiscipline seems to say; and the harshest of prisons says to the prisoners condemned to life: I shall note the slightest irregularity in your conduct. The generality of the punitive function that the eighteenth century sought in the 'ideological' technique of representations and signs now had as its support the extension, the material framework, complex, dispersed, but coherent, of the various carceral mechanisms. As a result, a certain significant generality moved between the least irregularity and the greatest crime; it was no longer the offence, the attack on the common interest, it was the departure from the norm, the anomaly; it was this that haunted the school, the court, the asylum or the prison. It generalized in the sphere of meaning the function that the carceral generalized in the sphere of tactics. Replacing the adversary of the sovereign, the social enemy was transformed into a deviant, who brought with him the multiple danger of disorder, crime and madness. The carceral network linked, through innumerable relations, the two long, multiple series of the punitive and the abnormal.

2. The carceral, with its far-reaching networks, allows the recruitment of major 'delinquents'. It organizes what might be called 'disciplinary careers' in which, through various exclusions and rejections, a whole process is set in motion. In the classical period, there opened up in the confines or interstices of society the confused, tolerant and dangerous domain of the 'outlaw' or at least of that which eluded the direct hold of power: an uncertain space that was for criminality a training ground and a region of refuge; there poverty, unemployment, pursued innocence, cunning, the struggle against the powerful, the refusal of obligations and laws, and organized crime all came together as chance and fortune would dictate; it was the domain of adventure that Gil Blas, Sheppard or Mandrin, each in his own way, inhabited. Through the play of disciplinary differentiations and divisions, the nineteenth century constructed rigorous channels which, within the system, inculcated docility and produced delinquency by the same mechanisms. There was a sort of disciplinary 'training', continuous and compelling, that had something of the pedagogical curriculum and something of the professional network. Careers emerged from it, as secure, as predictable, as those of public life: assistance associations, residential apprenticeships, penal colonies, disciplinary battalions, prisons, hospitals, almshouses. These networks were already well mapped out at the beginning of the nineteenth century: 'Our benevolent establishments present an admirably coordinated whole

by means of which the indigent does not remain a moment without help
from the cradle to the grave. Follow the course of the unfortunate man:
you will see him born among foundlings; from there he passes to the
nursery, then to an orphanage; at the age of six he goes off to primary
school and later to adult schools. If he cannot work, he is placed on the
list of the charity offices of his district, and if he falls ill he may choose
between twelve hospitals... Lastly, when the poor Parisian reaches the end
of his career, seven almshouses await his age and often their salubrious
régime has prolonged his useless days well beyond those of the rich man'
(Moreau de Jonnès, quoted in Touquet).

The carceral network does not cast the unassimilable into a confused hell; there is no
outside. It takes back with one hand what it seems to exclude with the other. It saves
everything, including what it punishes. It is unwilling to waste even what it has decided
to disqualify. In this panoptic society of which incarceration is the omnipresent arma-
ture; the delinquent is not outside the law; he is, from the very outset, in the law, at the
very heart of the law, or at least in the midst of those mechanisms that transfer the individual imperceptibly from discipline to the law, from deviation to offence. Although it
is true that prison punishes delinquency, delinquency is for the most part produced in
and by an incarceration which, ultimately, prison perpetuates in its turn. The prison is
merely the natural consequence, no more than a higher degree, of that hierarchy laid
down step by step. The delinquent is an institutional product. It is no use being surprised, therefore, that in a considerable proportion of cases the biography of convicts
passes through all these mechanisms and establishments, whose purpose, it is widely
believed, is to lead away from prison. That one should find in them what one might call
the index of an irrepressibly delinquent 'character': the prisoner condemned to hard
labour was meticulously produced by a childhood spent in a reformatory, according to
the lines of force of the generalized carceral system. Conversely, the lyricism of marginality may find inspiration in the image of the 'outlaw', the great social nomad, who
prowls on the confines of a docile, frightened order. But it is not on the fringes of society and through successive exiles that criminality is born, but by means of ever more
closely placed insertions, under ever more insistent surveillance, by an accumulation
of disciplinary coercion. In short, the carceral archipelago assures, in the depths of the
social body, the formation of delinquency on the basis of subtle illegalities, the overlapping of the latter by the former and the establishment of a specified criminality.

3. But perhaps the most important effect of the carceral system and of its
   extension well beyond legal imprisonment is that it succeeds in making
   the power to punish natural and legitimate, in lowering at least the
   threshold of tolerance to penality. It tends to efface what may be exorbitant
   in the exercise of punishment. It does this by playing the two registers
   in which it is deployed – the legal register of justice and the extra-legal

register of discipline – against one another. In effect, the great continuity of the carceral system throughout the law and its sentences gives a sort of legal sanction to the disciplinary mechanisms, to the decisions and judgements that they enforce. Throughout this network, which comprises so many 'regional' institutions, relatively autonomous and independent, is transmitted, with the 'prison-form', the model of justice itself. The regulations of the disciplinary establishments may reproduce the law, the punishments imitate the verdicts and penalties, the surveillance repeat the police model; and, above all these multiple establishments, the prison, which in relation to them is a pure form, unadulterated and unmitigated, gives them a sort of official sanction. The carceral, with its long gradation stretching from the convictship or imprisonment with hard labour to diffuse, slight limitations, communicates a type of power that the law validates and that justice uses as its favourite weapon. How could the disciplines and the power that functions in them appear arbitrary, when they merely operate the mechanisms of justice itself, even with a view to mitigating their intensity? When, by generalizing its effects and transmitting it to every level, it makes it possible to avoid its full rigour? Carceral continuity and the fusion of the prison-form make it possible to legalize, or in any case to legitimate disciplinary power, which thus avoids any element of excess or abuse it may entail.

But, conversely, the carceral pyramid gives to the power to inflict legal punishment a context in which it appears to be free of all excess and all violence. In the subtle gradation of the apparatuses of discipline and of the successive 'embeddings' that they involve, the prison does not at all represent the unleashing of a different kind of power, but simply an additional degree in the intensity of a mechanism that has continued to operate since the earliest forms of legal punishment. Between the latest institution of 'rehabilitation', where one is taken in order to avoid prison, and the prison where one is sent after a definable offence, the difference is (and must be) scarcely perceptible. There is a strict economy that has the effect of rendering as discreet as possible the singular power to punish. There is nothing in it now that recalls the former excess of sovereign power when it revenged its authority on the tortured body of those about to be executed. Prison continues, on those who are entrusted to it, a work begun elsewhere, which the whole of society pursues on each individual through innumerable mechanisms of discipline. By means of a carceral continuum, the authority that sentences infiltrates all those other authorities that supervise, transform, correct, improve. It might even be said that nothing really distinguishes them any more except the singularly 'dangerous' character of the delinquents, the gravity of their departures from normal behaviour and the necessary solemnity of the ritual. But, in its function, the power to punish is not essentially different from that of curing or educating. It receives from them, and from their lesser, smaller task, a sanction from below; but one that is no less important for that, since it is the sanction of technique and rationality. The carceral 'naturalizes' the legal power to punish, as it 'legalizes' the technical power to discipline. In thus homogenizing them, effacing what may be violent in one and arbitrary in the other, attenuating the effects of revolt that they may both arouse, thus depriving excess in either of any purpose, circulating the same calculated, mechanical and discreet methods from one to the other, the carceral makes it possible to carry out that great 'economy' of power whose formula the eighteenth century had sought, when the problem of the accumulation and useful administration of men first emerged.

By operating at every level of the social body and by mingling ceaselessly the art of rectifying and the right to punish, the universality of the carceral lowers the level from which it becomes natural and acceptable to be punished. The question is often posed as to how, before and after the Revolution, a new foundation was given to the right to punish. And no doubt the answer is to be found in the theory of the contract. But it is perhaps more important to ask the reverse question: how were people made to accept the power to punish, or quite simply, when punished, tolerate being so. The theory of the contract can only answer this question by the fiction of a juridical subject giving to others the power to exercise over him the right that he himself possesses over them. It is highly probable that the great carceral continuum, which provides a communication between the power of discipline and the power of the law, and extends without interruption from the smallest coercions to the longest penal detention, constituted the technical and real, immediately material counterpart of that chimerical granting of the right to punish.

4. With this new economy of power, the carceral system, which is its basic instrument, permitted the emergence of a new form of 'law': a mixture of legality and nature, prescription and constitution, the norm. This had a whole series of effects: the internal dislocation of the judicial power or at least of its functioning; an increasing difficulty in judging, as if one were ashamed to pass sentence; a furious desire on the part of the judges to judge, assess, diagnose, recognize the normal and abnormal and claim the honour of curing or rehabilitating. In view of this, it is useless to believe in the good or bad consciences of judges, or even of their unconscious. Their immense 'appetite for medicine' which is constantly manifested – from their appeal to psychiatric experts, to their attention to the chatter of criminology – expresses the major fact that the power they exercise has been 'denatured'; that it is at a certain level governed by laws; that at another, more fundamental level it functions as a normative power; it is the economy of power that they exercise, and not that of their scruples or their humanism, that makes them pass 'therapeutic' sentences and recommend 'rehabilitating' periods of imprisonment. But, conversely, if the judges accept ever more reluctantly to condemn for the sake of condemning, the activity of judging has increased precisely to the extent that the normalizing power has spread. Borne along by the omnipresence of the mechanisms of discipline, basing itself on all

the carceral apparatuses, it has become one of the major functions of our society. The judges of normality are present everywhere. We are in the society of the teacher-judge, the doctor-judge, the educator-judge, the 'social worker'-judge; it is on them that the universal reign of the normative is based; and each individual, wherever he may find himself, subjects to it his body, his gestures, his behaviour, his aptitudes, his achievements. The carceral network, in its compact or disseminated forms, with its systems of insertion, distribution, surveillance, observation, has been the greatest support, in modern society, of the normalizing power.

5. The carceral texture of society assures both the real capture of the body and its perpetual observation; it is, by its very nature, the apparatus of punishment that conforms most completely to the new economy of power and the instrument for the formation of knowledge that this very economy needs. Its panoptic functioning enables it to play this double role. By virtue of its methods of fixing, dividing, recording, it has been one of the simplest, crudest, also most concrete, but perhaps most indispensable conditions for the development of this immense activity of examination that has objectified human behaviour. If, after the age of 'inquisitorial' justice, we have entered the age of 'examinatory' justice, if, in an even more general way, the method of examination has been able to spread so widely throughout society, and to give rise in part to the sciences of man, one of the great instruments for this has been the multiplicity and close overlapping of the various mechanisms of incarceration. I am not saying that the human sciences emerged from the prison. But, if they have been able to be formed and to produce so many profound changes in the episteme, it is because they have been conveyed by a specific and new modality of power: a certain policy of the body, a certain way of rendering the group of men docile and useful. This policy required the involvement of definite relations of knowledge in relations of power; it called for a technique of overlapping subjection and objectification; it brought with it new procedures of individualization. The carceral network constituted one of the armatures of this power-knowledge that has made the human sciences historically possible. Knowable man (soul, individuality, consciousness, conduct, whatever it is called) is the object-effect of this analytical investment, of this domination-observation.

6. This no doubt explains the extreme solidity of the prison, that slight invention that was nevertheless decried from the outset. If it had been no more than an instrument of rejection or repression in the service of a state apparatus, it would have been easier to alter its more overt forms or to find a more acceptable substitute for it. But, rooted as it was in mechanisms and strategies of power, it could meet any attempt to transform it with a great force of inertia. One fact is characteristic: when it is a question of altering the system of imprisonment, opposition

does not come from the judicial institutions alone; resistance is to be found not in the prison as penal sanction, but in the prison with all its determinations, links and extrajudicial results; in the prison as the relay in a general network of disciplines and surveillances; in the prison as it functions in a panoptic régime. This does not mean that it cannot be altered, nor that it is once and for all indispensable to our kind of society. One may, on the contrary, site the two processes which, in the very continuity of the processes that make the prison function, are capable of exercising considerable restraint on its use and of transforming its internal functioning. And no doubt these processes have already begun to a large degree. The first is that which reduces the utility (or increases its inconveniences) of a delinquency accommodated as a specific illegality, locked up and supervised; thus the growth of great national or international illegalities directly linked to the political and economic apparatuses (financial illegalities, information services, arms and drugs trafficking, property speculation) makes it clear that the somewhat rustic and conspicuous work force of delinquency is proving ineffective; or again, on a smaller scale, as soon as the economic levy on sexual pleasure is carried out more efficiently by the sale of contraceptives, or obliquely through publications, films or shows, the archaic hierarchy of prostitution loses much of its former usefulness. The second process is the growth of the disciplinary networks, the multiplication of their exchanges with the penal apparatus, the ever more important powers that are given them, the ever more massive transference to them of judicial functions; now, as medicine, psychology, education, public assistance, 'social work' assume an ever greater share of the powers of supervision and assessment, the penal apparatus will be able, in turn, to become medicalized, psychologized, educationalized; and by the same token that turning-point represented by the prison becomes less useful when, through the gap between its penitentiary discourse and its effect of consolidating delinquency, it articulates the penal power and the disciplinary power. In the midst of all these mechanisms of normalization, which are becoming ever more rigorous in their application, the specificity of the prison and its role as link are losing something of their purpose.

If there is an overall political issue around the prison, it is not therefore whether it is to be corrective or not; whether the judges, the psychiatrists or the sociologists are to exercise more power in it than the administrators or supervisors; it is not even whether we should have prison or something other than prison. At present, the problem lies rather in the steep rise in the use of these mechanisms of normalization and the wide-ranging powers which, through the proliferation of new disciplines, they bring with them.

In 1836, a correspondent wrote to *La Phalange*: 'Moralists, philosophers, legislators, flatterers of civilization, this is the plan of your Paris, neatly ordered and arranged, here is the improved plan in which all like things are gathered together. At the centre, and within a first enclosure: hospitals for all diseases, almshouses for all types of poverty, madhouses, prisons, convict-prisons for men, women and children. Around the first enclosure, barracks, courtrooms, police stations, houses for prison warders, scaffolds, houses for the executioner and his assistants. At the four corners, the Chamber of Deputies, the Chamber of Peers, the Institute and the Royal Palace. Outside, there are the various services that supply the central enclosure, commerce, with its swindlers and its bankruptcies; industry and its furious struggles; the press, with its sophisms; the gambling dens; prostitution, the people dying of hunger or wallowing in debauchery, always ready to lend an ear to the voice of the Genius of Revolutions; the heartless rich... Lastly the ruthless war of all against all' (*La Phalange*, 10 August 1836).

I shall stop with this anonymous text. We are now far away from the country of tortures, dotted with wheels, gibbets, gallows, pillories; we are far, too, from that dream of the reformers, less than fifty years before: the city of punishments in which a thousand small theatres would have provided an endless multicoloured representation of justice in which the punishments, meticulously produced on decorative scaffolds, would have constituted the permanent festival of the penal code. The carceral city, with its imaginary 'geo-politics', is governed by quite different principles. The extract from *La Phalange* reminds us of some of the more important ones: that at the centre of this city, and as if to hold it in place, there is, not the 'centre of power', not a network of forces, but a multiple network of diverse elements – walls, space, institution, rules, discourse; that the model of the carceral city is not, therefore, the body of the king, with the powers that emanate from it, nor the contractual meeting of wills from which a body that was both individual and collective was born, but a strategic distribution of elements of different natures and levels. That the prison is not the daughter of laws, codes or the judicial apparatus; that it is not subordinated to the court and the docile or clumsy instrument of the sentences that it hands out and of the results that it would like to achieve; that it is the court that is external and subordinate to the prison. That in the central position that it occupies, it is not alone, but linked to a whole series of 'carceral' mechanisms which seem distinct enough – since they are intended to alleviate pain, to cure, to comfort – but which all tend, like the prison, to exercise a power of normalization. That these mechanisms are applied not to transgressions against a 'central' law, but to the apparatus of production – 'commerce' and 'industry' – to a whole multiplicity of illegalities, in all their diversity of nature and origin, their specific role in profit and the different ways in which they are dealt with by the punitive mechanisms. And that ultimately what presides over all these mechanisms is not the unitary functioning of an apparatus or an institution, but the necessity of combat and the rules of strategy. That, consequently, the notions of institutions of repression, rejection, exclusion, marginalization, are not adequate to describe, at the very centre of the carceral city, the formation of the insidious leniencies, unavowable petty cruelties, small acts of cunning, calculated methods, techniques, 'sciences' that permit the fabrication of the disciplinary individual. In this central and centralized humanity, the effect and instrument of complex power relations, bodies and forces subjected by multiple mechanisms of 'incarceration', objects for discourses that are in themselves elements for this strategy, we must hear the distant roar of battle.

At this point I end a book that must serve as a historical background to various studies of the power of normalization and the formation of knowledge in modern society.

REFERENCES

Ducpétiaux, E., *Des colonies agricoles*, 1851.

———. *De law condition physique et morale des jeunes ouvriers*, II, 1854.

Ferrus, G., *Des prisonniers*, 1850.

Gaillac, H., *Les Maisons de correction*, 1971.

Houzé de l'Aulnay, A., *Des logements ouvriers à Besançon*, 1907.

Muyart de Vouglans, P. F., *Réfutation du Traité des délits et des peines*, 1767.

———. P. F., *Les lois criminelles en France*, 1780.

Phalange, La, 10 August 1836.

Rousseaud de law Combe, G., *Traité des matières criminelles*, 1741.

Touquet, H. du, *De law condition des classes pauvres*, 1846.